▼ FILM STUDIES:
THE ESSENTIAL RESOURCE

Film Studies: The Essential Resource is a collection of resource material for all those studying film at university and pre-university level. *The Resource* brings together a wide variety of material ranging from academic articles; advertisements; websites; interviews with directors and actors; magazines and newspapers. With each extract introduced and contextualized by the editors, and suggestions for further activities and further reading included, *Film Studies: The Essential Resource* is the perfect resource to kick-start student autonomy.

Individual sections address:

- **codes** – examines the language of film; production; narrative and canon
- **concepts** – considers genre; the auteur; stars and realism
- **contexts** – cover themes of textual analysis; theoretical perspectives; industry and audience
- **cinemas** – investigates Hollywood; British cinema; national cinemas and alternative takes.

Peter Bennett is Senior Lecturer in Post-compulsory Education at the University of Wolverhampton. He is former Head of Communications and Film at Rowley Regis College, Chief Examiner for Communication Studies at A Level, co-editor of *Communication Studies: The Essential Resource* (2003) and co-author of *AS Communication Studies: The Essential Introduction* (2004), *A2 Media Studies: The Essential Introduction* (2005) and *Framework Media: Channels* (2003). **Andrew Hickman** is Head of Film and Media Studies at Matthew Boulton College and a freelance video editor. **Peter Wall** is Chair of Examiners for Media and Communication Studies at A Level, Chief Examiner for GCSE Media Studies and GNVQ Media, co-editor of *Media Studies: The Essential Resource* (2004) and co-author of *AS Media Studies: The Essential Introduction* (2004), *A2 Media Studies: The Essential Introduction* (2005) and *Framework Media: Channels* (2003) and author of *Media Studies for GCSE* (2002).

D0522487

The *Essentials* Series
Series Editor: Peter Wall

AS *Communication Studies: The Essential Introduction*
Andrew Beck, Peter Bennett and Peter Wall

Communication Studies: The Essential Resource
Andrew Beck, Peter Bennett and Peter Wall

AS Film Studies: The Essential Introduction
Sarah Casey Benyahia, Freddie Gaffney and John White

A2 Film Studies: The Essential Introduction
Sarah Casey Benyahia, Freddie Gaffney and John White

Film Studies: The Essential Resource
Peter Bennett, Andrew Hickman and Peter Wall

AS Media Studies: The Essential Introduction
Philip Rayner, Peter Wall and Stephen Kruger

A2 Media Studies: The Essential Introduction
Peter Bennett, Jerry Slater and Peter Wall

AS Media Studies: The Essential Revision Guide for AQA
Jo Barker and Peter Wall

A2 Media Studies: The Essential Revision Guide for AQA
Jo Barker and Peter Wall

Media Studies: The Essential Resource
Philip Rayner, Peter Wall and Stephen Kruger

FILM STUDIES:
THE ESSENTIAL RESOURCE

Peter Bennett, Andrew Hickman and Peter Wall

Routledge
Taylor & Francis Group

LONDON AND NEW YORK

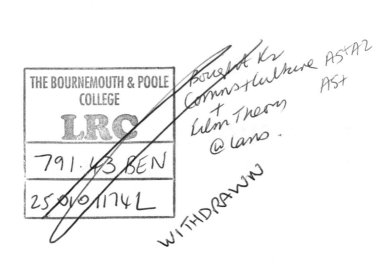
First published 2007
by Routledge
2 Park Square, Milton Park, Abingdon, Oxon OX14 4RN

Simultaneously published in the USA and Canada
by Routledge
270 Madison Ave, New York, NY 10016

Routledge is an imprint of the Taylor & Francis Group, an informa business

Selection and Editorial Matter © 2007 Peter Bennett, Andrew Hickman
and Peter Wall

Typeset in Bell Gothic Standard by Fakenham Photosetting Ltd
Printed and bound in Great Britain by
The Cromwell Press, Trowbridge, Wiltshire

British Library Cataloguing in Publication Data
A catalogue record for this book is available from the British Library

Library of Congress Cataloging in Publication Data
Bennett, Peter, 1961–
Film studies : the essential resource / Peter Bennett, Andrew Hickman, and
Peter Wall.
p. cm.
Includes bibliographical references and index.
1. Motion pictures.   2. Film criticism. I. Hickman, Andrew. II. Wall, Peter.
III. Title.

PN1994.B424 2006
791.43—dc22   2006017728

ISBN10: 0-415-36567-8 (hbk)
ISBN10: 0-415-36568-6 (pbk)

ISBN13: 978-0-415-36567-3 (hbk)
ISBN13: 978-0-415-36568-0 (pbk)

▼ CONTENTS

▼ ACKNOWLEDGEMENTS

The following were reproduced with kind permission. While every effort has been made to trace copyright holders and obtain permission, this has not been possible in all cases. Any omissions brought to our attention will be remedied in future editions.

1 Williams, R. 'British Film History: New Perspectives' in Curran and Porter (ed.) *British Cinema History*, 1983, Weidenfeld and Nicolson, an imprint of The Orion Publishing Group. Reproduced with permission.

2 Wenders, W. (1988) 'Why do you make films?' in *The Logic of Images*, Faber and Faber Ltd. Reproduced with permission of the publisher.

3 Coe, J. (1995) pp. 280–3 from *What a carve up!* Viking 1994. Copyright © Jonathan Coe, 1994. Reproduced by permission of Penguin Books Ltd.
From THE WINSHAW LEGACY: OR WHAT A CARVE UP! By Jonathan Coe, copyright © 1994 by Jonathan Coe. Used by permission of Alfred A. Knopf, a division of Random House, Inc.

4 Excerpt from 'On Style' from *Against Interpretation* by Susan Sontag. Copyright © 1964, 1966, renewed 1994 by Susan Sontag. Reprinted by permission of Farrar, Straus and Giroux, LLC.

5 Monaco, James (2000) *How to Read a Film: the art, technology, language, history, and theory of film and media*, pp. 64–5. Reproduced by permission of Oxford University Press.

6 Monaco, James (2000) *How to Read a Film: the art, technology, language, history, and theory of film and media*, pp. 175–9. Reproduced by permission of Oxford University Press.

7 Bresson, R. *Notes on Sound* (translated by Jonathon Griffin) from *Film Sound: Theory and Practice*, by Weis, E. and Belton, J. (eds). Copyright © 1985 Columbia University Press. Reprinted with permission of the publisher.

8 Wharton, D. and Grant, J. (2005) *Teaching Analysis of Film Language.* Published by the BFI. Reproduced with permission.

9 Crittenden, R. (1991) *Manual of Film Editing*, chapter 5. Published by Thames and Hudson. Reproduced with kind permission of the author.

10   Kolker, R. (2001) *Film Form and Culture*. Published by McGraw Hill Education. Reproduced with the permission of The McGraw-Hill Companies.

11   Kael, P. (1994) 'Trash, Art and the Movies' in Kael, P. *I Lost it at the Movies*, pp. 87–9 (originally from *Going Steady*). Reproduced with kind permission of Gina James and Marion Boyars Publishers.

12   Swallow, J. (2003) *Dark Eye: The Films of David Fincher*. Published by Reynolds and Hearn. Reproduced with permission of Reynolds and Hearn Ltd.

13   Uhl, J. *Fight Club*, Screenplay, pp. 5–7.

14   'Where do you put the camera?' from *On Directing Film* by David Mamet. Copyright © 1992 by David Mamet. Used by permission of Viking Penguin, a division of Penguin Group (USA) Inc. and the Wylie Agency.

15   Bordwell, D. and Thompson, K. (1990) *Film Art: An Introduction*, pp. 218–20. Published by McGraw Hill. Reproduced with the permission of The McGraw-Hill Companies.

16   Sergi, G. 'A Cry in the Dark' in *Contemporary Hollywood Cinema*, Neale, Steve and Smith, Murray (eds), copyright © 1999, Routledge. Reproduced by permission of Taylor & Francis Books UK.

17   Sammon, P. M. *Future Noir: The Making of Blade Runner*, 1996, pp. 349–52. Reproduced by permission of The Orion Publishing Group.

18   Excerpt from 'Introduction to the Structural Analysis of Narratives', from Image/ Music/Text by Roland Barthes, translated by Stephen Heath. English translation copyright © 1977 Stephen Heath. Reprinted by permission of Hill and Wang, a division of Farrar, Straus and Giroux, LLC.

19   Branigan, E. *Narrative, Comprehension and Film*. Copyright © 1992, Routledge. Reproduced by permission of Taylor and Francis Books UK.

20   Bordwell, D. and Thompson, K. (1990) *Film Art: An Introduction*, pp. 73–5. Published by McGraw Hill. Reproduced with the permission of The McGraw-Hill Companies.

21. Murphy, R. *Realism and Tinsel*. Copyright © 1989, Routledge. Reproduced by permission of Taylor and Francis Books UK.

22   Wenders, W. (1988) 'Why do you make films?' in *The Logic of Images*, Faber and Faber Ltd. Reproduced with permission of the publisher.

23   Roberts, Graham and Wallis, Heather *Key Film Texts*, Arnold, 2002. Copyright © 2002 Graham Roberts and Heather Wallis. Reproduced by permission of Edward Arnold.

24   *Sight and Sound* ten-yearly polls 1952–2002. Published by the BFI. Reproduced with permission.

25   Callow, Simon 'Millennium Masterworks: Citizen Kane', *Sunday Times* 1999.

Copyright © 1999 Simon Callow. Reproduced by kind permission of Margaret Hanbury on behalf of Simon Callow.

26 'What will be the ultimate film?' (http://www.channel4.com/film/newsfeatures/microsites/U/ultimate_film/index/html). Reproduced by kind permission of North One Television Ltd.

27 Wollen, Peter 'Why do some films survive and others disappear?' *Sight and Sound* (3)5. Published by the BFI. Reproduced with permission.

28 Raynor, P., Wall, P. and Kruger, S. *Media Studies: The Essential Introduction.* Copyright © 2003, Routledge. Reproduced by permission of Taylor and Francis Books UK.

29 Ryall, T. 'The Notion of Genre', *Screen* Vol. 11, number 2, pp. 23–4. Reproduced by kind permission of the author and *Screen*.

30 Neale, Steve *Genre and Hollywood*. Copyright © 2000, Routledge. Reproduced by permission of Taylor and Francis Books UK.

32 'D.I.Y. Generic Analysis' from Daniel Chandler's website: http://www.aber.ac.uk/media/Documents/intgenre/intgenre5.htlml. Reproduced by kind permission of the author.

33 Dyer, R. 'Entertainment and Utopia', from *Only Entertainment*. Copyright © 2002 Routledge. Reproduced by permission of the author and Taylor and Francis Books UK.

34 Walker, M. 'Film Noir Introduction', pp. 8–13, in Cameron (ed.) *The Movie Book of Film Noir*. Copyright © 1994, Cameron Books.

35 Schrader, P. 'Notes on Film Noir', from FILM COMMENT, Spring, 1972. Copyright © 1972 by Film Comment Publishing corporation. Reprinted by permission of The Film Society of Lincoln Center. All rights reserved.

36 Modleski, T. 'The Terror of Pleasure: The Contemporary Horror Film and Postmodern Theory' in *Studies in Entertainment: Critical Approaches to Mass Culture*, 1986, Indiana University Press. Reproduced by permission of the publisher.

37 Sontag, Susan *Against Interpretation*, (Picador 2001) pp. 32–33. Copyright © 1969 by Susan Sontag, permission of The Wylie Agency.

38 This article is licensed under the [GNU Free Documentation License] (http://www.gnu.org/copyleft/fdl.html). It uses material from the 'Auteur theory' http://en.wikipedia.org/wiki/Auteur_theory.

39 Philips, Patrick P. 'The Auteur Theory' in Nelmes, J. (ed.) *An Introduction to Film Studies*, 3rd edition, Nelmes J. (ed.). Copyright © 2003, Routledge. Reproduced by permission of Taylor and Francis Books UK.

40 Wollen, Peter *Signs and meaning in the Cinema*, 1997. Published by the BFI. Reproduced with permission.

41 Kawin, Bruce *How Movies Work* (MacMillan 1987, California University Press 1992) pp. 292–4. Reproduced by kind permission of the author.

42 Perkins, Victor 'Direction and authorship' in *Film as Film: Understanding and Judging Movies* (Penguin Books 1972), pp. 158–61 (Chapter 8). Copyright © Victor Perkins. Reproduced by permission of Penguin Books Ltd.

43 Ellis, J. 'Stars as Cinematic Phenomenon' in Mast, Cohen and Brandy (eds) *Film Theory and Criticism*, (1992). Reproduced with permission.

44 MacDonald, P. 'Star Studies' from *Approaches to Popular Film*, by Jancovich, M. and Hollows, J. (eds), 2006, Manchester University Press, Manchester UK. Reproduced with permission.

45 Dyer, R. (1979) *Stars*. Published by the BFI. Reproduced with permission.

46 Tasker, Y. 'Muscle culture; the bodybuilder as hero and star' from *Spectacular Bodies*, Tasker, Y. Copyright © 1993, Routledge. Reproduced by permission of Taylor and Francis Books UK.

47 de Vany, A. *Hollywood Economics: How Extreme Uncertainty Shapes the Film Industry*. Copyright © 2004, Routledge. Reproduced by permission of Taylor and Francis Books UK.

48 Anger, Kenneth 'The Trouble with Jimmy' from HOLLYWOOD BABYLON II. Copyright © 1984, Kenneth Anger. Used by permission of Dutton, a division of Penguin Group USA, Inc. From Hollywood Babylon II by Kenneth Anger, published in the UK by Arrow. Reprinted by permission of The Random House Group Ltd.

49 Hayward, Susan *Key Concepts in Cinema Studies*. Copyright © 1996, Routledge. Reproduced by permission of Taylor and Francis Books UK.

50 Bazin, Andre 'An Aesthetic of Reality: Neorealism' in *What is Cinema*, Vol. 2, pp. 26–7, UC Press.

51 Stam, Robert 'The Question of Realism' in Stam and Miller *Film Theory: An anthology*, Blackwell Publishing. Reproduced with permission.

52 Williams, C. *Realism and the Cinema*. Copyright © 1980. Reproduced by permission of Taylor and Francis Books UK.

53 Minha-ha, Trinh T. 'The totalising quest for meaning' in Renov, M. (ed.) *Theorizing documentary*, Routledge, 1993. Copyright © 1991 in *When The Moon Waxes Red* by Trinh T. Minh-ha. Reproduced by permission of Routledge/Taylor and Francis Group, LLC and the author.

54 Hallam, J. and Marshment, M. *Realism and Popular Cinema (Inside Popular Film)*, 2000, Manchester University Press, Manchester UK. Reproduced with permission.

55 Branston, G. *Cinema and Cultural Modernity*, pp. 164–5, Copyright © 2000,

Open University Press. Reproduced by permission of the Open University Press Publishing Company.

56 McBride, J. and Wilmington, M. *The Films of John Ford*. Published by the BFI. Reproduced with permission.

57 Müller, Jürgen and Hetebrügge, Jörn 'The Sceptical Eye' in Jürgen Müller (ed.) *Movies of the 70s*, Cologne, London, Los Angeles, Madrid, Paris, Tokyo: Taschen 2003, pp. 4–19. Reproduced with permission.

58 Buckland, Warren 'Notes on narrative aspects of the New Hollywood blockbuster' in Neale, Steve and Smith, Murray *Contemporary Hollywood Cinema*. Copyright © 1995, Routledge. Reproduced by permission of Taylor and Francis Books UK.

59 Ebert, R. *City of God* review, accessed at www.rogerebert.com. Reproduced by kind permission of the author.

60 Kermode, M. '*Exorcist*: "The Beginning review"' *Sight and Sound* (December 2004). Published by the BFI. Reproduced with permission.

61 Brunette, Peter, 'Adolescence Both Savage and Innocent; Ken Loach's "Sweet Sixteen"', accessed at www.indiewire.com. Reproduced with permission.

62 Weddle, David '*Lights, Camera, Action: Marxism, Semiotics, Narratology*', article in *Los Angeles Times* magazine July 13 2003. Reproduced by kind permission of the author.

63 Strinati, D. *Introduction to Theories of Popular Culture*. Copyright © 2004, Routledge. Reproduced by permission of Taylor and Francis Books UK.

64 Allinson, M. *A Spanish Labyrinth: The Films of Pedro Almodóvar*, 2000, I.B. Tauris Publishers. Reproduced by permission of the publisher.

65 Henry, Matthew, 'The Eyes of Laura Mulvey: Subjects, Objects and Cinematic Pleasures', accessed at http://www.rlc.dcccd.edu/annex/comm/english/mah8420/EyesofLauraMulvey.htm. Reproduced by kind permission of the author.

66 Barlet, Olivier, 'Postcolonialism and cinema: from difference to relationships', accessed at http://www.africultures.com/anglais/articles_anglais/postcol_cine.htm. Reproduced by kind permission of the author.

67 Henderson, Brian, 'Towards a non-bourgeois camera style' in Mast and Cohen (eds), *Film Theory: A reader* (originally from *A Critique of Film Theory*, New York: E. P. Dutton, 1980). Reproduced by kind permission of the author.

68 Schatz, Thomas (1998) *The Genius of the System*, Faber and Faber Ltd. Reproduced with permission of the publisher and author.

69 Adorno, T. and Horkheimer, M. 'Dialectic of Enlightenment' in *The Culture Industry: Enlightenment as Mass Deception*, translated by John Cumming, Verso Editions 1979. Reproduced with permission.

70   Turner, G. *Film As Social Practice*. Copyright © 1999, Routledge. Reproduced by permission of Taylor and Francis Books UK.

71   Meehan, E. 'Holy commodity Fetish Batman! the political economy of a commercial intertext'. Copyright © 1991 in Pearson, Roberta E. and Uricchio, William (eds) *The Many Lives of the Batman*. Reproduced by permission of Routledge/Taylor & Francis Group, LLC and the author.

72   Wyatt, Justin *High Concept: Movies and Marketing in Hollywood*. Copyright © 1994. By permission of University of Texas Press.

73   Chanan, M. *The Chronic Crisis of British Cinema*, inaugural lecture as professor of Cultural Studies, 8 April 2003, pp. 16–19. Reproduced by kind permission of the author.

74   All time highest grossing movies worldwide (accessible at http://www.the-numbers.com/movies/records/worldwide.html). Source: Nash Information Services, LLC – The Numbers (www.the-numbers.com).

75   Cherry, B. 'Screaming for release: femininity and horror film fandom in Britain' in Chibnall and Petley (eds) *British Horror Reader*. Copyright © 2002, Routledge. Reproduced by permission of Taylor and Francis Books UK, Brigid Cherry and Steve Chibnall.

76   Turner, G. *Film As Social Practice*. Copyright © 1999, Routledge. Reproduced by permission of Taylor and Francis Books UK.

77   Jancovich, M. and Faire, L. 'The best place to see a film' in Stringer, J. (ed.) *Movie Blockbusters*. Copyright © 2003, Routledge. Reproduced by permission of Taylor and Francis Books UK and the authors and volume editor.

78   Hoskins, C., McFadyen, S. and Finn, A. *Global Television and Film: An Introduction to the Economics of the Business*, pp. 51–9 (OUP 1997). By permission of Oxford University Press.

79   Maltby, R. *Hollywood Cinema*, 2nd edition, Blackwell Publishing, 1995. Reproduced with permission of the publisher.

80   King, G. 'Narrative and The Spectacular Hollywood Blockbuster' in Stringer, J. (ed.) *Movie Blockbusters*. Copyright © 2003, Routledge. Reproduced by permission of the author, volume editor and Taylor and Francis Books UK.

81   From BBC News 20 October 2005 at http://news.bbc.co.uk/1/hi/entertainment/arts/4360496.stm). Reproduced with permission.

82   James, Nick 'Nul Britannia' *Sight and Sound* 38. Published by the BFI. Reproduced with permission.

83   Hill, J. (1986) *Sex, Class and Realism*. Published by the BFI. Reproduced with permission.

84   Collins, Alex 'Grim Realities', 11/3/97 *Guardian*. Copyright Guardian Newspapers Limited 1997. Reproduced with permission.

85   Higson, A. 'Representing the National Past: Nostalgia and Pastiche in the Heritage Film', in Lester Friedman (ed.) (2006) *Fires Were Started: British Cinema and Thatcherism* (2nd edition), London: Wallflower Press.

86   Monk. C. 'From Underworld to Underclass in Chibnall, Steve and Murphy, Robert *British Crime Cinema*. Copyright © 1999. Reproduced by permission of Taylor and Francis Books UK.

87   Issues 'tartanry' (previously available at http://www.hatii.arts.gla.ac.uk/MultimediaStudent projects/00-01/9704793m/mmcourse/project/html/Issues.htm). Reproduced by kind permission of David Morgan.

88   Higson, Andrew (1989) 'The Concept of National Cinema' *Screen*, pp. 36–8. Reproduced by permission of the author and *Screen*.

89   Jordan and Morgan-Tamosunas *Contemporary Scottish Cinema*, pp. 9–10, Manchester University Press, 1998.

90   Elsaesser, Thomas *Weimar Cinema And After: Germany's historical imaginary*. Copyright © 2000, Routledge. Reproduced by permission of Taylor and Francis Books UK.

91   Eisenstein, S. 'The Montage of Film Attractions' in *S.M. Eisenstein: Selected works, volume 1*. Published by the BFI. Reproduced with permission.

92   Cardullo, Bert (1991) *What is Neorealism? A Critical English-Language bibliography of Italian Cinematic Neorealism*, University Press of America. Reproduced with permission of the publisher.

93   Thompson, David 'That Breathless Moment' *Sight and Sound 7*. Published by the BFI. Reproduced with permission.

94   Teo, S. (1997) *Hong Kong Cinema the Extra Dimensions*. Published by the BFI. Reproduced with permission.

95   Anderson, Joseph *The Japanese Film*. © 1982 Princeton University Press. Reprinted by permission of Princeton University Press.

96   Godard interviewed by Henri Behar *On Film Technique and Video*, www.filmscouts.com/scripts/interview.cfm?File=2800, accessed on 9 December 2005.

97   Penning, Lars 'Jean-Luc Godard: Every Man For Himself / Slow Motion'. In Müller, Jürgen (ed.) *Movies of the 70s*. Cologne, London, Los Angeles, Madrid, Paris, Tokyo: TASCHEN 2003, pp. 670–7. Reproduced with permission.

98   Peake, Tony *Derek Jarman*, pp. 325–6, Little, Brown 1999. Reproduced by permission of Time Warner Book Group.

99   Buñuel, Louis *My Last Breath* published by Jonathan Cape. Reprinted by permission of The Random House Group Ltd.
     From *My last sigh* by Luis Buñuel, translated by Abigail Israel, copyright © 1983 by Alfred A. Knopf. Used by permission of Alfred A. Knopf, a division of Random House, Inc, and Editions Robert Laffont.

100 From *Un chien andalou: original shooting script*, Faber and Faber Ltd. Reproduced with permission of the publisher.

101 Edward, Gwynne (1991) *The Discreet Art of Luis Bunuel*. Reproduced by permission of Marion Boyars Publishers.

102 Finkelstein, Haim 'Dali and un chien andalou: The nature of a Collaboration' in Kuernzl, Rudolf (ed.) *Dada and Surrealist Film*, 1996, the MIT Press. Reproduced with permission of the publisher.

103 Buñuel, Juan Luis 'Foreword' in Evans and Santaolalla (eds) *New Readings*, pp. xi, BFI, 2004.

▼ INTRODUCTION

I am always coming back to the question that has tormented me for thirty years now: 'is cinema more important than life?'

Francois Truffaut

Cinema is the most beautiful fraud in the world.

Jean-Luc Godard

Any book about film should begin with an apology to the reader. The time you spend reading this book might well have been more profitably spent watching a film or more probably several films. So how can another book added to the many weighty tomes that litter the shelves of the library and bookshop possibly be justified? Let us turn for help to one of the great wise men of film scholarship. Christian Metz said simply that: 'A film is difficult to explain because it is easy to understand.'

There in a nutshell you have the essence of film theory. Film is, in general, a popular cultural form produced for mass consumption. By its very nature then it is accessible to interpretation by a wide range of audiences at many different levels of sophistication and from different cultural and social backgrounds. Yet film has probably attracted more academic and critical attention than any other popular cultural form in the past 100 years. Film at one level appears to be simple and yet as the welter of accumulated film theory suggests it is in fact a complex cultural form that is open to the application of a range of analytical approaches, each offering a different take on that which seemed straightforward.

One function of this book is to help try to reconcile these opposites. Good criticism should always seek to enhance our appreciation of the text. Poor criticism is likely to obscure the text. So the extracts we have chosen for you to consider are designed to enhance your appreciation of film. They do this in at least two ways. First, by adding to your understanding and enjoyment of film by revealing to us some of the complexity that our own viewing of a film may have missed. Despite its essentially transcendent nature, however, film fulfils important cultural and social functions that are very much the domain of the film theorist. Film acts as an important social and cultural barometer, measuring for us the prevailing issues and concerns at any given point in our history. In consequence film itself provides an important historical document offering insight into the preoccupations of bygone ages. Second, of all popular cultural forms, film is perhaps the one that aspires most directly to be art. Certainly it would be hard to argue that there are not a dozen or so films which have the aesthetic worth one might expect and that they will be considered of artistic interest a couple of centuries from now.

For cultural theorist Raymond Williams, film is 'the central art form of the twentieth century'. His essay in *British Cinema History* (Curran and Porter) deserves our attention:

Film was to become the central art form of the twentieth century, but it took a long time – longer in some nations and in some classes than in others – for this centrality to be recognized in relation to already established culture. From its marginal beginnings, within both the content and the institutions of popular culture, it made its way to a qualitatively different position: not only or even primarily because of its individual qualities as art, but mainly because of the radical change in the means of artistic production employed.

In the early decades most cinema industries tried to move towards respectability within the terms of the established culture. The earliest settled sites of distribution were modelled on theatres, and often went on being called theatres. The process of the luxurious refurbishing of theatre interiors, which had been such a feature of theatre building and adaptation from the 1860s, was extensively contained in the period of the 'picture palaces', with a future continuity of characteristically aristocratic or exotic names. Most of the films shown in them were derived from various forms of the popular culture, especially the commercial popular culture. But there were also many attempts to draw on the more prestigious theatre (both in the enlistment of stage actors and in the adaptation of plays), on musical comedy and light opera, on novels in the established literary tradition and on other literary forms such as biography. As late as 1940 the quality of film was often evidenced from these borrowings and adaptations – a thin blue line above the assumed typical 'vulgarity' of the cinematic popular culture. Yet what went into film from these sources formed, of course, a real contribution to the medium. Dismissal of such work as merely 'theatrical' or 'literary' can only emanate from an arbitrary idealization of film. In one cultural area after another, film, as it became (before television) the dominant form, was in effect a common carrier of many different kinds of art, and cinemas were the central institutions of this wide range of drama and entertainment.

Yet alongside these adaptive and incorporating processes something more fundamental was happening – something consequent on the nature of the new means of distribution. The prestige of the established cultures was very closely linked with the predominance of the old metropolitan centres. London and Paris, Berlin and New York were the places where high art, especially in drama, music and painting, was produced or exhibited. This situation corresponded with a phase of political and cultural centralization and with the general dominance of orthodox metropolitan criteria. What happened beyond the metropolis – in what, during this whole phase, from the eighteenth century onwards, could be defined as 'the provinces' – submitted itself, for the most part, to these allegedly superior and fashionable centres. In fact however in some of the relevant arts, and especially in drama, this became an inherently false situation, particularly in Britain. During the period from 1870, when European drama was moving into a new great period, it was not from the fashionable metropolitan centres and the dominant national cultures that creativity was flowing. It was from what were regarded in most countries of Western Europe as marginal or distant cultures: Scandinavia, Russia, Ireland. In Britain the established theatre was locked into social fashion rather than into anything which could be even momentarily mistaken for high art. Indeed, the persistence of this enclosed and self-reflecting 'West End' is at least a contributory reason for some of the failures of British cinema, if only because its exceptionally class-marked enclosure raised, in its shadow, what was often a reductive and self-impoverishing 'provincial' and popular culture.

One major factor shifted the old kind of metropolitan dominance, and eventually, and ironically, produced a quite new form of dominance. The central material characteristic of film was that its productions and performances could be fixed, and could then be distributed in standard multiple forms. Thus, quite apart from its new technical capacity to enhance and extend older forms, there could be a simultaneous high investment of both talent and resources in any single production, and, when such a production was achieved, very widespread and indefinite reproduction. Obviously this matching of potentialities made sense in financial terms also. Thus the dominant centres of production became, first, less dependent on the established metropolitan centres, and, in all later phases, in effect dominant of them. In the theatre the old kinds of prestige persisted, in remarkably reproductive ways, but whereas they had previously dominated all relevant activity elsewhere, they were now in a less important position, with major new institutions and forms surpassing them – nationally, and, even more crucially, internationally – in the eyes of newly enlarged, regular audiences.

The results have been complex. In relation to the established culture – a very different matter from traditional culture – film and cinema have been in general quite remarkably liberating. Yet, quite apart from the effects of new kinds of centralized dominance, which must be separately examined, there has remained a certain parasitism on established forms and styles, often most noticeable when the 'industry' has taken itself most seriously and produced 'serious' films. It is clear that in much mainstream cinema there have been nothing like the cultural breaks that might have been predicted from the new possibilities of the technology and from its new and potentially new social relations. There has been some evidence, from time to time, that this situation may be changing, but the continued prestige of 'theatre', as opposed to 'film', is remarkable after a half-century in which it is quite clear that film has

CONTINUED

produced much more important new work. Moreover, deference towards the forms and styles of the established culture seems continually to re-establish itself within cinema, for predominantly social rather than artistic reasons.

(Williams 1983: 17–19)

A certain part of the fascination of film is that it straddles the cultural divide by both capturing the popular imagination while at least in some cases aspiring to the condition of high art. Of course, criticism and academic scholarship are not without their downside. Quite fairly the accusation is levelled at critics and scholars that what they do is unproductive. In fact it is sometimes suggested that people turn critic because they are incapable of actually making anything themselves. Perhaps these comments are a little harsh, but it is worth bearing in mind that what a film-maker says about his or her craft is probably much more worthy of our attention than the offerings of a host of critics. In consequence we have tried wherever possible to make space for film-makers themselves to talk about their craft. Here, for example, is Wim Wenders responding to the question: Why do you make films?

WHY DO YOU MAKE FILMS?
Reply to a questionnaire

Ever since this terrible question was put to me, I've done nothing but think of how to answer it. I have one answer in the morning and one at night, one at the editing-table, one when I'm looking at stills of earlier films of mine, another when I'm speaking to my accountant, and yet another when I think of the team I've been working with for years now. Every one of these different answers, these reasons for making films, is sincere and genuine, but I keep saying to myself there must be something 'more fundamental', some 'commitment', or even a 'compulsion'.

I was twelve yeas old when I made my very first film, with an 8 mm camera. I stood by a window and filmed the street below, the cars and pedestrians. My father saw me and asked: 'What are you doing with your camera?' And I said: 'Can't you see? I'm filming the street.' 'What for?' he asked. I had no answer. Ten or twelve years later, I was making my first short film in 16 mm. A reel of film lasted three minutes. I filmed a crossroads from the sixth floor, without moving the camera until the reel was finished. It didn't occur to me to pull away or stop shooting any earlier. With hindsight, I suppose it would have seemed like sacrilege to me.

Why sacrilege?

I'm no great theorist. I tend not to remember things I've read in books. So I can't give you Béla Balázs's exact words, but they affected me profoundly all the same. He talks about the ability (and the responsibility) of cinema 'to show things as they are'. And he says cinema can 'rescue the existence of things'.

That's precisely it.

I have another quote, from Cézanne, where he says: 'things are disappearing. If you want to see anything, you have to hurry.'

So back to the awful question: why do I make films? Well, because … Something happens, you see it happening, you film it as it happens, the camera sees it and records it, and you can look at it again, afterwards. The thing itself may no longer be there, but you can still see it, the fact of its existence hasn't been lost. The act of filming is a heroic act (not always, not often, but sometimes). For a moment, the gradual destruction of the world of appearances is held up. The camera is a weapon against the tragedy of things, against their disappearing. Why make films? Bloody stupid question!

(April 1987)
(Wenders 1988: 1–2)

Our book has been organised, we hope, in such a way as to help you get the best from it. There are four major parts, each divided into individual chapters. Few readers are likely to benefit from reading the book from cover to cover. This is a book for dipping into at your leisure as well as a source of information and reference. You should navigate your way through the book using the contents list and the index to point you in the direction of those chapters that are going to be of greatest interest and most use to you.

A word of caution is appropriate at this point. This book pretends to offer you no more than a starting point. Most of the texts we have included are extracts from much larger works. We have generally chosen them for their accessibility. Our intention is that they should act as a sort of trailer to tease you to see a forthcoming feature. Of course some of these forthcoming features will be more to your taste than others. We would, however, urge you to persevere when you come across a text that you are not too keen on, perhaps because you find it hard going. The more you are prepared to immerse yourself in the study of film, the easier it will become and the greater will be the rewards.

We have resisted the temptation to offer you a long and clever list of films you should see, books you should read, or websites you should visit. Such a resource would say rather more about what we enjoy than it would offer you a genuine map into the further study of film. If you have got so far that you have absorbed what this book has to offer, then it is time to stand on your own two feet and be confident in your judgement about these things. If you are really stuck, look back at some of the extracts that you have found most stimulating and seek out more of the same.

Perhaps an interesting way to conclude this introduction is to consider the intertextual nature of film. Many fictional works have inspired films. Some estimates suggest that as many as 75 per cent of films find their narrative inspiration in books, mostly fictional. Some of these films are good, some mediocre and some downright awful. It is perhaps unusual to find a novel that has been inspired by a film. Jonathan Coe's novel *What a Carve Up!* takes its title from a British comedy starring Sid James, Shirley Eaton and Kenneth Connor that leaves an indelible impression on a young boy's mind. In this extract from the novel, the young boy, now grown up, is invited to watch a film made as an end-of-year assignment by a Sheffield film student:

It was a less painful experience than I had anticipated. Graham's film was only about ten minutes long, and proved to be an efficient if unsubtle piece of polemic about the Falklands conflict, called 'Mrs Thatcher's War'. The title was double-edged, because he had somehow managed to find a pensioner called Mrs Thatcher who lived in Sheffield, and shots of warships steaming into battle and extracts from the Prime Minister's speeches were juxtaposed with scenes from the life of her less eminent namesake: making trips to the shops, preparing frugal meals, watching news bulletins on the television and so on. In a disjointed voice-over commentary, the old woman spoke of the difficulties of getting by on her pension and wondered what had become of all the money she had paid in taxes throughout her working life: this was usually the cue for a rapid cut to some brutal and expensive-looking piece of military hardware. The film ended with the Prime Minister's famous speech to the Scottish Conservative Party, in which she described the war as a battle between good and evil and declared that 'It must be finished', followed by a lingering shot of the other Mrs Thatcher carrying a heavy bag of groceries up a steep, forbidding street. Then the screen faded to black and two captions appeared: 'Mrs Emily Thatcher supports herself on a weekly income of £43.37'; 'The cost of the Falklands War has already been estimated at £700,000,000.'

Graham turned off the tape.

'So – what did you think? Come on, your honest opinion.'

'I liked it. It was good.'

'Look, just try to forget that Southern middle-class politeness kick for a minute. Give it to me straight.'

'I told you, it was good. Powerful, and direct, and ... truthful. It tells the truth about something.'

'Ah, but does it, though? You see, film's such a tightly structured medium, that even in a short piece of work like this, all sorts of decisions have to be made. How long a shot's going to last, how a shot's going to be framed, which shots are going to come before it, which ones are going to come after. Now doesn't that whole process become suspect when you're dealing with something that advertises itself explicitly as a political film? Doesn't it make the role of the film-maker himself intensely problematic, prompting the question – not "Is this the truth?" but "Whose truth is it anyway?"'

'You're absolutely right, of course. Do you think you could show me how this freeze frame business works?'

'Sure.' Graham picked up the remote control, rewound the tape a few minutes and then pressed Play. 'So my point is that the whole thing is deeply manipulative, not just of the audience, but of its subject. Mrs Thatcher invaded the Falklands and I invaded this woman's life – both of us on the same pretext, that we had their best interests at heart.' He pressed Pause and the old woman froze into jittery stillness, in the act of opening a can of soup. 'In a way the only really honest thing for me to do would be to expose the mechanics of my involvement: to have the camera pan round and suddenly rest on me, the director, sitting in the room with her. Perhaps that's what Godard would have done.'

'Can't you get rid of those lines across the screen?' I asked.

'Sometimes you can. You just have to keep pressing the button and eventually they go away.'

He pressed the pause button some more times.

'It's a bit blurred, isn't it?'

'The technology'll improve. Anyway, would it have been anything more than an empty self-referential gesture, that's what I have to ask myself. Because I know exactly what you're going to say next: you're going to say that any attempt to foreground issues of authorship would just be a throwback to formalism, a futile strategy to shift emphasis from the signified to the signifier which can't do anything to alter the basic fact that, at the end of the day, all truth is ideological.'

'Do all the machines have this feature,' I asked, 'or do you have to go to the more expensive end of the market?'

'They've all got them,' he said. 'It's their main selling point. Quite a radical development, when you think about it: for the first time in history, control over cinematic time is being given to the audience and taken out of the film-maker's hands. You could argue that it's the first real move towards the democratisation of the viewing process. Though of course' – he switched off the tape and stood up to draw the curtains – 'it'd be naïve to suggest that that's why people were buying them. At college we call it the WP button.'

'WP?'

'Wankers' paradise. All your favourite movie stars in the buff, you see. No more of those tantalizing scenes when some gorgeous actress drops them for a couple of seconds and then disappears out of the frame: now you can stare at her for as long as you like for an eternity, in theory. Or at least until the tape wears out.'

I looked past him, gazing sightlessly at the window. 'That would certainly ... have its uses,' I said.

(Coe 1995: 281–283)

PART 1: CODES

▼   1 FILM LANGUAGE

> If you want to tell the untold stories, if you want to give voice to the voiceless, you've got to find a language. Which goes for film as well as prose, for documentary as well as autobiography. Use the wrong language, and you're dumb and blind.
>
> Salman Rushdie

Long before anyone thought of films as suitable things for study, let alone imagined creating the academic discipline of Film Studies, films were inviting, if not inventing, their own critical vocabulary. How we 'talk' about films naturally owes something to a critical discourse which derives from more traditional objects of study such as literature, art and music. However, as films asserted themselves, claiming to be the most significant twentieth-century art form/form of entertainment it was inevitable that a new vocabulary would be needed, which would in turn seep back into the critical mainstream. As a result we are now used to terms such as 'close-up', 'point of view' and even 'cinematic' being used across a range of creative contexts, from computer games to novels.

What this process has been about, apart from consolidating film's position at the very centre of contemporary culture, is trying to find a critical vocabulary to meet the particular creative challenge of films. These questions have been asked, for example, of literature, and by the early twentieth century there was a substantial 'database' of answers (or at least responses). Some of these were heavily leant upon by early film criticism which often used this critical heritage to cover up its lack of knowledge of the mechanics of the new medium, of its specific techniques. In this way films based on classic literary texts attracted particular attention since it seemed to some that they could be 'read' as degraded books. What was often missing was the understanding that film has/is a language, or at least a specific set of codes, and that without an understanding of its language (its syntax, its grammar, its vocabulary) no criticism would be adequate.

If we can only read films as if they are disguised literary texts, we are failing to address their specific qualities. The game that film plays may include elements from other and older media (James Monaco borrows the literary term 'tropes', suggesting 'turns' or 'routines') but it is the particular ways in which these are employed in a new 'whole' that must be our focus. In his preface to the second edition of his highly influential and pertinent book *How to Read a Film*, Monaco addresses this ground specifically:

Is it necessary, really, to learn how to read a film? Obviously, anyone of *minimal* intelligence over the age of four can – more or less – grasp the basic content of a film, record, radio, or television program without any special training. Yet precisely because the media so very closely mimic reality, we apprehend them much more easily than we comprehend them. Film and the electronic media have drastically changed the way we perceive the world – and ourselves – during the past eighty years, yet we all too naturally accept the vast amounts of information they convey to us in massive doses without questioning how they tell us what they tell us. *How To Read a Film* is an essay in understanding that crucial process – on several levels.

The key for us is that half a line, 'questioning how they tell us what they tell us' which is the project of film criticism in a nutshell. We are more interested always in the 'how' than the 'what'. In Sontag's major critical manifesto, film has a special and crucial role:

> Ideally, it is possible to elude the interpreters in another way, by making works of art whose surface is so unified and clean, whose momentum is so rapid, whose address is so direct that the work can be ... just what it is. Is this possible now? It does happen in films, I believe. This is why cinema is the most alive, the most exciting, the most important of all art forms right now. Perhaps the way one tells how alive a particular art form is, is by the latitude it gives for making mistakes in it, and still being good. For example, a few of the films of Bergman – though crammed with lame messages about the modern spirit, thereby inviting interpretations – still triumph over the pretentious intentions of their director. In *Winter Light* and *The Silence*, the beauty and visual sophistication of the images subvert before our eyes the callow pseudo-intellectuality of the story and some of the dialogue. (The most remarkable instance of this sort of discrepancy is the work of D. W. Griffith.) In good films, there is always a directness that entirely frees us from the itch to interpret. Many old Hollywood films, like those of Cukor, Walsh, Hawks, and countless other directors, have this liberating anti-symbolic quality, no less than the best work of the new European directors, like Truffaut's *Shoot the Piano Player* and *Jules and Jim*, Godard's *Breathless* and *Vivre Sa Vie*, Antonioni's *L'Avventura*, and Olmi's *The Fiancés*.
>
> The fact that films have not been overrun by interpreters is in part due simply to the newness of cinema as an art. It also owes to the happy accident that films for such a long time were just movies; in other words, that they were understood to be part of mass, as opposed to high, culture, and were left alone by most people with minds. Then, too, there is always something other than content in the cinema to grab hold of, for those who want to analyze. For the cinema, unlike the novel, possesses a vocabulary of forms – the explicit, complex, and discussable technology of camera movements, cutting, and composition of the frame that goes into the making of a film.
>
> (Sontag 2001: 11–12)

Armed with that 'vocabulary of forms', which you may derive in part from Parts 1 and 2 of this 'resource', you will be ready to find 'something to grab hold of'. As Sontag suggests, cinema offers plenty of encouragement for addressing the real issues in the form of a set of useful and effective technical terms and tools. Identifying technique immediately addresses the artificiality of the medium and prompts evaluation rather than acceptance. This in turn encourages the use of a set of critical tools (such as those proposed by semiotics or structuralism) to push the analysis further and in so doing to demystify the illusion. The key is to see a film for what it is: the result of a complex set of collaborative decisions, a matrix of competing and conflicting codes. So much of Monaco's approach is useful here, particularly his common sense.

Film may not have grammar, but it does have systems of 'codes.' It does not, strictly speaking, have a vocabulary, but it does have a system of signs. It also uses the systems of signs and codes of a number of other communication systems. Any musical code, for instance, can be represented in the music of film. Most painterly codes, and most narrative codes, can also be represented in film. Much of the preceding discussion of the relationship between film and other arts could be quantified by describing the codes that exist in those other arts that can be translated into film as opposed to those that cannot. Remember Frost: 'Poetry is what gets lost in translation.' So the genius of an art may be just those codes that don't work well in any other art.

Yet while the code system of semiotics goes a long way toward making possible a more precise description of how film does what it does, it is limited in that it more or less insists that we reduce film, like language, to basic discrete units that can be quantified. Like linguistics, semiotics is not especially well adapted to describing the complete, metaphysical effect of its subject. It describes the language, or system of communication of film very well. But it does not easily describe the artistic activity of film. A term borrowed from literary criticism may be useful in this respect: 'trope.'

Generally, in literary criticism the term 'trope' is used to mean 'figure of speech': that is, a 'turn' of phrase in which language is bent so that it reveals more than literal meanings. The concepts of code and sign describe the elements of the 'language' of an art; the concept of trope is necessary to describe the often very unusual and illogical way those codes and signs are used to produce new, unexpected meanings. We are concerned now with the active aspect of art. 'Trope,' from the Greek *tropos* (via Latin *tropus*) originally meant 'turn,' 'way,' or 'manner,' so even etymologically the word suggests an activity rather than a static definition.

Rhythm, melody, and harmony, for example, are essential codes of music. Within each of these codes there are elaborate sets of subcodes. A syncopated beat, such as that essential to the idiom of jazz, can be considered as a subcode. But the exciting, idiosyncratic syncopations of Thelonious Monk's music are tropes. There is no way to quantify them scientifically; and that, precisely, is the genius of Thelonious Monk.

Likewise, in painting, form, color, and line are generally regarded as the basic codes. Hard edge and soft edges are subcodes. But the precise, exquisite lines of a painting by Ingres, or the subtle soft edges of a study by Auguste Renoir, are idiosyncratic tropes.

In stage drama, gesture is central to the art, one of its basic codes. The offering of a ringed hand for the kiss of devotion is a specific subcode. But the way Laurence Olivier performs this gesture in Richard III is very peculiarly his own: a trope.

The system of an art can generally be described in semiotic terms as a collection of codes. The unique activity of an art, however, lies in its tropes. Film can be used to record most of the other arts. It can also translate nearly all the codes and tropes common to narrative, environmental, pictorial, musical, and dramatic arts. Finally, it has a system of codes and tropes all its own, unique to the recording arts.

Poetry is what you can't translate. Art is what you can't define. Film is what you can't explain. But we're going to try, anyway.

(Monaco 2000: 64–65)

Again the direction is clear: 'the genius of an art may be just those codes that don't work well in any other art'. Monaco also demonstrates our next 'trope': 'say what you mean'. He is forceful but he does not care to overstate, returning us to the initial point about the importance of the critic (in this case himself) and thus of the imperfect and glorious humanity of the whole process. He concludes with this call to arms (pens/ critical tools):

Poetry is what you can't translate. Art is what you can't define. Film is what you can't explain. But we're going to try, anyway.

Monaco is a man who practises what he preaches. His writing on 'Codes' in the section 'The language of film', complete with an illustrative reading of the most famous shower scene in cinema, is perhaps the best (most useful) two pages'-worth of writing on film anywhere:

CODES

The structure of cinema is defined by the codes in which it operates and the codes that operate within it. Codes are critical constructions – systems of logical relationship – derived after the fact of film. They are not preexisting laws that the filmmaker consciously observes. A great variety of codes combine to form the medium in which film expresses meaning. There are culturally derived codes – those that exist outside film and that filmmakers simply reproduce (the way people eat, for example). There are a number of codes that cinema shares with the other arts (for instance, gesture, which is a code of theatre as well as film). And there are those codes that are unique to cinema. (Montage is the prime example.)

The culturally derived codes and the shared artistic codes are vital to cinema, naturally, but it is the unique codes, those that form the specific syntax of film, that most concern us here. Perhaps 'unique' is not a completely accurate adjective. Not even the most specifically cinematic codes, those of montage, are truly unique to cinema. Certainly, cinema emphasizes them and utilizes them more than other arts do, yet something like montage has always existed in the novel. Any storyteller is capable of switching scenes in midstream. 'Meanwhile, back at the ranch,' is clearly not an invention of cinema. More important, for nearly a century film art has had its own strong influence on the older arts. Not only did something like montage exist prior to 1900 in prose narrative, but also since that time, novelists, increasingly influenced by film, have learned gradually to make their narratives even more like cinema.

• • •

The point is, simply, that codes are a critical convenience – nothing more – and it would be wrong to give them so much weight that we were more concerned with the precise definition of the code than with the perception of the film.

Taking the shower scene in *Psycho* once again as an example, let's derive the codes operating there. It is a simple scene (only two characters – one of whom is barely seen – and two actions – taking a shower and murdering) and it is of short duration, yet all three types of codes are evident. The culturally derived codes have to do with taking showers and murdering people. The shower is, in Western culture, an activity that has elements of privacy, sexuality, purgation, relaxation, openness, and regeneration. In other words, Hitchcock could not have chosen a more ironic place to emphasize the elements of violation and sexuality in the assault. Murder, on the other hand, fascinates us because of motives. Yet the dimly perceived murderer of *Psycho* has no discernible motive. The act seems gratuitous, almost absurd – which makes it even more striking. Historically, Jack the Ripper may come to mind, and this redoubles our sense of the sexual foundation of the murder.

Since this particular scene is so highly cinematic and so short, shared codes are relatively minor here. Acting codes hardly play a part, for instance, since the shots are so brief there isn't time to act in them, only to mime a simple expression. The diagonals that are so important in establishing the sense of disorientation and dynamism are shared with the other pictorial arts. The harsh contrasts and back-lighting that obscure the murderer are shared with photography. The musical code of Bernard Herrmann's accompaniment also exists outside film, of course.

(Monaco 2000: 175–178)

The idea that the codes of film constitute the syntax of film is an interesting and useful one. Monaco assumes that film is/has a language: *syntax* is the term used to describe the unwritten rules which govern how words combine to produce meaning. What follows across this chapter and the next is a partly interchangeable set of explications and explorations of Monaco's argument in various kinds of practical and theoretical ways. In this chapter the emphasis is on the creative palette, the principles and rules that might govern artistic selection. This is followed by a chapter that gets rather more involved in the rather less idealistic, because human and collective, process of putting this theory into practice.

While it may be a commonplace to emphasise that film is a visual medium, that 'talks' in pictures, it has, at least since 1927, been significantly audio-visual. Arguably the most common revelation for the new Film Studies students is just that: the enormous significance of film sound. Put simply, sound most often provides anchorage, the process through which meaning is applied to otherwise open signs. How often is the status and function of a character simply indicated by the soundtrack theme that introduces him, or more crudely by how or what he says (i.e. by what we hear)? Connections between sound and vision are vital to a film's coherence and effectiveness.

ACTIVITY

➤ Choose three films from your video/DVD collection and watch a random scene with no sound. What is the major 'problem'? Now do the same thing but choose a music track to accompany each sequence. Why does this improve matters? Try to select tracks that are appropriate to particular sequences.

To this end the distinguished French director Robert Bresson provided this almost poetic checklist:

NOTES ON SOUND

Sight and Hearing

To know thoroughly what business that sound (or that image) has there.

☐

What is for the eye must not duplicate what is for the ear.

☐

If the eye is entirely won, give nothing or almost nothing to the ear.*
One cannot be at the same time all eye and all ear.

☐

When a sound can replace an image, cut the image or neutralize it.
The ear goes more toward the within, the eye toward the outer.

☐

> A sound must never come to the help of an image, nor an image to the help of a sound.
>
> ☐
>
> If a sound is the obligatory complement of an image, give preponderance either to the sound or to the image. If equal, they damage or kill each other, as we say of colors.
>
> ☐
>
> Image and sound must not support each other, but must work each in turn through a *sort of relay*.
>
> ☐
>
> The eye solicited alone makes the ear impatient, the ear solicited alone makes the eye impatient. *Use these impatiences*. Power of the cinematographer who appeals to the two senses in a governable way.
>
> *Against the tactics of speed, of noise, set tactics of slowness, of silence.*
>
> (Translated by Jonathan Griffin)
>
> * And *vice versa*, if the ear is entirely won, give nothing to the eye.
>
> (Bresson 1985: 149)

If sound and image 'must work each in turn through a sort of relay', then it is as well to be well versed in the mechanics of image-making. Some of the more emotive and philosophical writing about cinematography seems to suggest almost an absence of technique, as if in this way a purer relationship between representation and reality can be achieved. Astruc makes this case when he writes:

> The camera fixes; it does not transcend, It looks. One has to be naïve to imagine that the systematic use of an 18.5 lens will make things any different from what they are. In exchange it never lies.

However, a much better starting point is the kind of technical glossary provided by a book like *Teaching Analysis of Film Language*, which was compiled for the BFI by David Wharton and Jeremy Grant. Here technique is efficiently presented for what it is: a series of possibilities. Monaco might call them 'tropes' or 'turns'.

ASPECT RATIOS

The most basic element of framing is the shape of the screen onto which the film is projected. The business of aspect ratios is much more clearly understood by audiences these days, since the development of widescreen television and DVD; and audiences in general are far more aware of the need to respect the director's original intentions. Nevertheless, there are still confusions and misapprehensions, which we will try to clarify here. Obviously,

when analysing film language, the first stage is to show the film in its correct ratio, and to understand why it was chosen.

There is a very wide variety of original aspect ratios. The four we identify below are the commonest. See **Student notes** on **Common aspect ratios** for activities to encourage students to consider the effects of changing frame ratios at www.bfi.co.uk/tfms. (Enter user name: **filmlang@bfi.org.uk** and password: **te1306fl**.)

- Academy (4:3)

  This is the aspect ratio used in almost every film made before the 1950s. Until relatively recently it was also the shape of every television set and computer screen in the world. If you have an electronic whiteboard in your classroom, it will probably be this shape too.

  All film frames are around 4:3, no matter what aspect ratio the film is shot on. The different ratios are created either by use of mattes (which block off the top and bottom of the frame) or by anamorphic lenses (which squeeze a wider image into a narrower space).

- European widescreen (1.66:1)

  This ratio has been used for a large number of European movies, as well as several Disney films and much of Stanley Kubrick's output.

- American widescreen (16:9 or 1.85:1)

  This is now the commonest ratio for American films. It is also the shape of 'widescreen' TVs. The 1.85:1 ratio can fit a 16:9 TV screen (which is closer to 1.78:1) with minimal compromises.

- Scope anamorphic (2.35:1 and others)

  These very wide ratios have been made by a variety of processes, and include aspects ranging between 2.66:1 and 2.20:1. They tend to be used for large-scale, epic productions such as *The Fellowship of the Ring* (Peter Jackson, New Zealand/USA, 2001) or *Lawrence of Arabia* (David Lean, UK, 1962).

ASPECT RATIO AS AN ELEMENT OF FILM LANGUAGE

Usually, your interest in the aspect ratio should end with getting it correct for showing and analysing the film. There are, however, some instances in which the ratio becomes a distinctive element of the film's language.

The very wide scope ratios emphasise the horizontal plane, and tend to support compositions involving large numbers of characters and/or highly dramatic exterior locations. Thus, these ratios have become part of the accepted language of the epic, used to communicate the scale of the narrative, the isolation of the hero and so on. It is usually chosen to frame stories that are massive and heroic, rather than intimate and personal.

An exception to this general principle is *American Beauty*, a domestic style which was shot using Super 35 to produce a cinematic version in a ratio of 2.35:1. *American Beauty* exploits the tendency of wide ratios to seem very static. Mendes and his cinematographer Conrad Hall created symmetrical frames and avoided movement. Much of the film is composed of long takes, often combined with minimal camera and character movement. In this way, Mendes emphasised the movie's key themes of stillness and beauty.

FOCUS AND DEPTH-OF-FIELD

Cameras can be equipped with lenses of various focal lengths, and this gives the filmmaker control over what is or is not in focus at any time.

- Deep focus is used when the detail of an entire scene needs to be shown. It means that everything that is visible, near to and far from the camera, is in focus.
- Selective focus simplifies the image. It reduces the importance of certain elements within the frame by showing them blurred.
- Pulling focus, or racking focus, changes the subject of selective focus. See, for example, the killing of the guard and Felix in *Die Hard* 3 (**Worksheet 16**).

CAMERA MOVEMENT

The main purposes for moving a camera while filming are:

1. To reframe the scene;
2. To reveal new aspects of *mise en scène*;
3. To create kinetic energy;
4. To follow a character or object in motion;
5. To show the perspective of a character or object in motion.

We can categorise camera movements into five types:

1. Axis
2. Dolly
3. Vehicle
4. Aerial
5. Handheld

1. Axis movements
- Pans (rotation L-R or R-L on a vertical axis)

   These create the perspective of a static observer. For example, showing a cattle stampede, or a motor race, a panning camera movement would place the spectator in the position of someone being passed by. In establishing shots, a pan can be used to create the impression that we are taking a leisurely look around the landscape.

■ Tilts (up and down or down and up on a horizontal left-right axis)

These can serve various purposes. One is to reveal how tall something is. The camera is pointed at the ground floor of a building and then tilted up to show its full height. Another common tilt is the search up. We see a character's feet, then the camera tilts to reveal the rest of the character.

Focus film: The Die Hard 3 extract contains a less usual technique: a search down to show the military boots a character is wearing.

■ Rolls (rotation on a horizontal front-back axis).

These are the least common of the axis movements. Their classic use is to show the point of view of someone drunk, drugged, falling over in a daze or waking up.

2. Dolly shots

The camera is mounted on a 'dolly' or mobile support. Traditionally, dollies run on specially laid tracks for smoothness and precision, hence the term 'tracking shot'. A crab dolly, which does not require tracks, can be steered in any direction to give more flexibility. Mostly this has been superseded by steadicam. The third type is a crane dolly, used to create high-angle shots and massive, dramatic sweeping motions.

Focus film: In the Die Hard 3 robbery sequence, a crane shot moves from overhead to ground level as Simon (Jeremy Irons) and his gang enter the bank. (See **Worksheet 12.2**.)

[To access worksheets and other online materials go to **www.bfi.org.uk/tfms** and enter User name: **filmlang@bfi.org.uk** *and* **Password**: **te1306fl**.]

Dollies are used for a massive variety of purposes. However, all of their movements are formed from combinations of:

■ Track – moving along a horizontal plane;
■ Crane – up/down;
■ Push-in/pull-out – moving nearer to or further away from a subject.

It is a common mistake in analysis to say that the camera 'zooms in' or 'zooms out' during a sequence. In fact, zoom – increasing the size of the subject using the lens – is relatively rare in professional filmmaking. Actual movement of the camera towards or away from the subject creates a different psychological effect. Pushing in feels as if we are moving nearer to the subject; zooming in feels more like it is being pulled towards us. Zoom draws attention to the fact that we are looking through a lens, while pushing in or pulling out seems far more natural.

Filmmakers are always looking for interesting ways to move the camera, and as soon as technology allowed, were experimenting with combinations of motion. Track and pan, pull back and tilt up, crane up and roll are fairly basic combinations. Using computer-controlled dollies, it is now possible to choreograph extremely sophisticated mixtures of camera movements. The large-scale action set-pieces that characterise high concept Hollywood cinema frequently utilise these new possibilities.

3. Vehicle-mounted shots

Placing the camera on board a moving car or van enables the filmmaker to show point of view from inside a moving vehicle, or to create a travelling shot from outside a moving vehicle. A genre that makes much use of these types of shot is the road movie. In *Thelma and Louise* many shots looking at the front of Louise's Thunderbird car in motion were created by towing the car from a van, on which a camera was mounted. Once the spectator is aware that this is how the shot was achieved, the illusion that Susan Sarandon is driving quickly vanishes. Films like *The Fast and the Furious* (Rob Cohen, USA/Germany, 2001) use vehicle-mounted shots to create excitement, putting the spectator into car chase sequences.

4. Aerial shots

The camera is mounted on a helicopter or aeroplane. This technique is sometimes used to film other airborne objects, such as planes; sometimes to shoot tall, dramatic objects, such as high cliffs and mountains, or cityscapes filled with skyscrapers. Michael Mann is particularly fond of this technique, and uses it repeatedly in *Collateral* (USA, 2004) to create a sense of the massive scale of modern Los Angeles.

5. Handheld shots

Handheld cameras give extra freedom of movement, and are sometimes used in action sequences. The disadvantage of the handheld camera is its unsteadiness. This is answered by the steadicam, which uses a gyroscope system to keep the shot more stable while the camera operator can be very mobile. The earliest use of steadicam in a Hollywood film was by Steven Spielberg for the boat sequences in *Jaws* (USA, 1975). Steadicam is also useful when the approach to filmmaking is more improvisational, and can create a

lot of energy. Handheld work, whether using steadicam or not, is also good for creating a *cinema verité* or documentary feel. This is a technique used extensively in *The Bourne Supremacy* (Paul Greengrass, USA/Germany, 2004). The slight shakiness, even of steadicam work, has led to the industry slang term 'wobble shot' to describe this type of filming.

Focus film: The entry to the lower part of the bank as the lorries unload, in our *Die Hard 3* sequence, uses some very wobbly handheld work, to generate a sense of urgency and place the audience closely within the scene. This can be contrasted with the very smooth tracking work used on Simon and his men on the ground floor of the bank to create a feeling of tension.

TECHNOLOGICAL DEVELOPMENTS AND CAMERA MOVEMENT

With the development of CGI (computer-generated images), it has become increasingly difficult to be certain just how much of what we see has been created with a camera, and how much is generated inside a computer, although sometimes DVD extras can be very revealing. There are times when it is more important than others to consider this issue. If we cannot easily tell, for example, whether a helicopter shot is 'real' or was created in a computer, then it makes most sense to consider it in terms of the effect on the audience. However, it was constructed, we experience it as a helicopter shot.

On the other hand, a film like *The Matrix* (Andy and Larry Wachowski, USA, 1999) combines complex tracking shots with CGI effects to create sequences that would very obviously have been impossible to achieve in reality. Explicitly drawing the audience's attention to its own artificiality is a key element of the style and language of *The Matrix*, and so would be an important point for discussion of that film. Subsequently, many action movies have been influenced by the style of *The Matrix*. You can see such techniques in use in the James Bond film *Die Another Day* (Lee Tamahori, UK/USA, 2002) or the opening sequence of *Swordfish* (Dominic Sena, USA, 2001).

In *The Matrix*, artificial techniques were used to alter the language of film. This is different from the way George Lucas has operated in his *Star Wars* franchise. There, although much of the world he presents is created through special effects (using models in the first three films, CGI in the prequels), the style of camerawork is completely traditional.

(Wharton and Grant 2005: 50–55)

Our third film menu is provided by Roger Crittenden's excellent *Manual of Film Editing*. Jean-Luc Godard once wrote tellingly that 'If direction is a look, montage is a heartbeat', suggesting not only that editing provides a rhythm to a set of images but also by implication, a pulse, a sign of life. He went on to suggest that 'to foresee is the characteristic of both, but what one seeks to foresee in space the other seeks in time'. Crittenden begins the chapter appropriately entitled 'The language of editing: giving your material form and refining its meaning' by quoting Kevin Brownlow's claim that 'Editing is directing the film for a second time.'

THE LANGUAGE OF EDITING: GIVING YOUR MATERIAL FORM AND REFINING ITS MEANING

In *The Parade's Gone By* Brownlow wrote: 'Editing is directing the film for the second time. To gauge the psychological moment – to know exactly where to cut – requires the same intuitive skill as that needed by a director.' Every film presents the editor with an imprecise agenda. Without experience it is natural to conclude that a well-cut film only requires the editor to put the pieces together in the right order. In fact, no editor believes that his task is simply to find the one perfect conjunction that is just waiting to be discovered. If this were so cutting would be analogous to jigsaw solving.

The difference between editing a film and assembling a jigsaw is that with a film nothing is completely predetermined. The film-maker may claim that the film already exists in his head, and that it is also on paper in the script, but the film that emerges from the cutting room has never existed before, neither in someone's head nor on paper. It is only through the editing process that the material is translated into the form that can communicate its narrative and meaning to the audience.

To understand the language of editing requires us to define in what ways it involves 'directing the film for the second time'. In that way we can unearth what Brownlow calls 'the hidden power' of the editor.

Selection

The way films are conceived and shot assumes the function of editing. This is especially true in the selection of what is to be shot, a process that leaves levels of decision-making to be refined in the cutting. In dramatic films this provides the editor with different kinds of choices. The first is the choice between several attempts at the same shot. Every time two or more takes are shot on the same slate selection in the editing is being allowed for. This implies both the desire to obtain the most effective version of the action for a particular shot and the realization that the choice of take may depend on which one dovetails best into other shots which cover the same segment of the script. Secondly, it is normal to shoot the same action in more than one set-up: the resulting changes of angle and sizes of shot allow a further level of selection in the cutting. Thirdly, this kind of shooting leaves open the question of when to cut and what to cut to.

Structuring

To be able to understand the way in which editing selects, you must first understand the structuring of a scene and also the placing of each scene in the overall film. To be able to structure a scene effectively you must understand its function. It is the misunderstanding of function that leads to the most superficial use of editing technique. If the writing and/or shooting of a film is meant to convey more than just the words and actions of its characters then the cutting must be used to serve those aspects of the drama that lie beneath the surface. If you edit merely to ensure that the dialogue is heard and the actions seen then your structuring will be only something mechanical.

Helen van Dongen arrived at her own list of factors affecting the structuring of material through her experience as Flaherty's editor: the subject-matter of the scene; spatial movements in each image; the tonal value of each shot (atmosphere); the emotional content. This can be taken to represent the specific agenda for documentaries, although in general terms it overlaps in its application to dramatic material.

Balance and emphasis

The real contribution of editing is to provide support to the inherent drama through balance and emphasis. The balance in a scene is a delicate matter which must be retained with every cut, and if we use emphasis correctly it will help this balance. For instance, each time you cut to a closer shot it is imperative that the shift in visual emphasis supports the dramatic balance at that point.

The dynamic axis

Already in the way a scene is staged – in the way character and camera movement are controlled – the director is seeking to use physical space to support the emotional content of the scene by balance and emphasis. Editing should respect and reinforce these intentions. As each scene evolves the editor must be aware of changes in the dominant line of dramatic tension, or what I like to call the dynamic axis. This is not simply a matter of analysing the flow of a scene and deciding who is 'centre stage' at any point; any such obvious dominance must be taken in conjunction with the point of the scene and its purpose in the overall drama. To take a simple example, if a fight occurs between two characters it may be that the effect on a third party not directly involved in the fight is more important in the film than the actual conflict. The reactions of this third party could be the element that the cutting needs to emphasize. Even here, you have to be careful not to over-emphasize by cutting: for instance, the director may have carefully staged the action to focus on reactions of the third party while still including the other two characters in the shot. Understanding this dynamic axis in a scene will always give the editor the right clues in deciding what to cut to and when.

Motivation

All cuts should be motivated. Again it must be emphasized that this is not something mechanical. Just because there is movement that could be followed or emphasized by a cut is not necessarily enough reason for the cut. The dramatic focus of a scene and the point of view that has been established are often far more important than the details of the action. Staying wide can sometimes serve the tension far better than cutting in close, and the cut to a close-up may provide undue emphasis on the insignificant.

Point of focus

The editor must be aware that at each moment in a shot the audience's attention is focused on a particular area of the frame. Often a cut that is sufficiently motivated is prevented from working properly by the switch of attention on the cut. If the eye has to adjust its focus in an unexpected way the moment of the cut will be a dead spot and will dislocate the flow of the scene.

Sequencing

We must also be aware of the way in which cuts work at the junctions between scenes. Much will depend upon the way the director has ensured that the shots that are meant to open and close each adjacent scene can be matched in the cutting. The success of sequencing will be affected by the composition and, of course, by the control of pace and rhythm.

Parallel action

Scenes that are meant to be cut in parallel are often conceived without due attention being given to the pacing and balance. Such intercutting will seldom work unless the material has been preconceived for that purpose, especially since the normal function of parallel action is to lead to a denouement which brings together the separate dramatic threads.

Rhythm and pacing

As we construct a scene the aim must be to provide the right pacing and to establish or emphasize the inherent rhythm. In both dramatic and documentary films the events being shown have a natural rhythm. It is important to be able to use this rhythm to motivate the cutting. Of all the elements which must be considered for effective use of the editing process, the use of and control of rhythm and pace are finally what will determine the contribution that cutting makes to your film.

(Crittenden 1981: 74–76)

Having established the rules, Crittenden goes on to offer practical advice to would-be film-makers. What follows is part of his 'Reasons for cutting' section: in this case, here are the 'positive reasons':

The most important thing is that your decision to cut should be based on positive reasons. An awareness of the general factors just discussed – structuring, balance and emphasis, the dynamic axis, rhythm and pacing, etc. – is the essential starting point. But it is only by then analysing the elements of dramatic development in the scene under consideration that you will be able to arrive at the correct *particular* solutions.

In attempting to respect dramatic development in cutting you should be aware of the following elements:

1 Is the audience to *identify* with a particular character or are we merely observers?
2 Does a particular character *dominate*; does that dominance shift during the scene?
3 Does the dialogue function as narrative or is it merely embroidery, i.e. aside from the real drama of the scene?
4 Is there a necessary eloquence in the silences?
5 How does the movement of camera and/or characters contribute to the scene?
6 Should the scene be carried wide or are close shots essential?
7 If we cut in close will it preclude cutting wide again?
8 Are there significant details that must be seen?
9 Doe a reaction need to be explained?
10 Does a moment in the scene demand a shock cut to point up the drama?
11 Does the scene have a natural climax?
12 What elements apart from the characters are important to the scene?

FILM STUDIES: THE ESSENTIAL RESOURCE

13 Do other sounds have significance apart from the dialogue?
    and of course:
14 What is the function of the scene?
15 How does the scene fit into the overall film?

(Crittenden 1981: 77)

Classical cutting, in which editing is directed by the dramatic and emotional needs of the content, is still the dominant force in mainstream Hollywood film. Warren Buckland's 'reading' of Steven Spielberg's *Raiders of the Lost Ark* in Chapter 9 begins by specifically addressing this aspect of mainstream film editing. He references a fight scene in which a sequence lasting two minutes and forty-four seconds has ninety shots and concludes: 'This makes for an average shot length (or a cut every) 1.8 seconds.' The effect of this is often that the film does a lot of work on behalf of the spectator, which is partly what Luis Buñuel meant when he indelicately suggested that 'Sometimes, watching a movie is a bit like being raped' (see Chapter 16: the paragraph less controversially begins 'Movies have an hypnotic power ...'). The manipulation of images through montage may be an attempt by the director to ensure his intentions are clear, that we do recognise the important elements of a sequence as important: the look the hero gives the girl or vice versa, the heavy bulge in the henchman's pocket, the clear blue sky which tells us that everything will be alright.

By contrast films which privilege *mise-en-scène*, which is involved in the composition of shots, by operating in and on space, often ask much more of us. In this way the director defines an area of 'furnished' space for us to explore on a number of levels. This defining of space is the director's unique contribution, our inhabiting of it is our particular role. Astruc said he saw *mise-en-scène* as 'a means of making the spectacle ones own', where what is seen is less important than the desire to show and see in a particular way. In this version *mise-en-scène* is a record of the director's engagement with his material and the world rather than a studied attempt to control the audience's mode of reception. Robert Kolker is a little more descriptive in his clarification of this significant filmic language, which he defines as 'the articulation of cinematic space'. He also makes clear the relationship between *mise-en-scène* and editing.

MISE-EN-SCÈNE

Mise-en-scène is a French term and originates in the theatre. It means, literally, 'put in the scene.' For film, it has a broader meaning, and refers to almost everything that goes into the composition of the shot, including the composition itself: framing, movement of the camera and characters, lighting, set design and general visual environment, even sound as it helps elaborate the composition. *Mise-en-scène* can be defined as the articulation of cinematic space, and it is precisely space that it is about. Cutting is about time; the shot is about what

occurs in a defined area of space, bordered by the frame of the movie screen and determined by what the camera has been made to record. That space, the mise-en-scène, can be unique, closed off by the frame, or open, providing the illusion of more space around it. In *Travelling Players* (1975), a film by the Greek director Theo Angelopoulos, a group of people move into the past by taking a long walk down a street in one shot; time moves backward as they walk. There is a sequence in the film *Grand Illusion* (1937) by the director (and son of the Impressionist painter) Jean Renoir in which a group of World War I POWs receive a carton of gifts. Among the gifts is, unaccountably, some women's clothing. One of the soldiers puts the clothing on, and the rest stare at him in stunned silence. Renoir creates their response by gently, slowly, panning to the men staring. The movement yields up the space the men inhabit, suggests that it extends beyond the frame, and delicately emphasizes their confused sexual response to this sudden appearance of a man in woman's clothes. Had Renoir cut from face to face, the effect would have been quite different, suggesting the isolation of one man and his emotional response from the next person in the group. If he had offered only a wide shot of all the men together, their individual expressions would have been lost. The pan joins individual to group, making the revelation of space not only physical but emotional and communal, and the response more generally and genuinely human. It allows us to understand the response and not lose our perspective. Closeness and comfortable distance remain.

Editing is a way to form a narrative temporally, both in the making and the viewing of a film. Editing speeds up the shooting process in ways outlined earlier: it speeds up the viewing process by creating a rhythm of forward action. Even the over-the-shoulder cutting of a dialogue sequence, which creates an event that takes place in one space over a short period of time, is moved along by the rapid shifts of point of view between the participants. *Mise-en-scène* filmmaking directs our attention to the space of the shot itself. It slows down production, i.e., where care must be taken in performance lighting, and composition. If a long take is involved, careful planning is required to make sure that actors and camera move synchronously. In a long take actors must act. There's no chance to save a performance by cutting away to someone or something else in the scene. If a mistake is made, the entire shot has to be made again. The economics of Hollywood production frown on such methods. For the viewer, a film that depends upon *mise-en-scène* and long shots makes special demands. Without editing to analyze what's important in a scene but cutting to a closeup of a face or an object, the viewer is required to do the looking around in the shot, to be sensitive to changes in spatial relationships and the movements of camera and actor. Even a film that uses a lot of shots and cutting may still depend on the *mise-en-scène* to articulate meaning as each cut reveals a different spatial relationship. Perhaps a general rule is that films made in the classical continuity style point of view usher the viewer through the progress of the narrative. Films that depend on *mise-en-scène* ask true viewers to pause and examine the compositional spaces of the narrative. The classical continuity style is directive the *mise-en-scène* style contemplative.

(Kolker 2001: http://research.umbc.edu/~landon/Local_Information_Files/
Mise-en-scene.htm)

Cartoon: *Private Eye*

> I did take a one semester course at NYU in production, but that was the only real film school experience I had.
>
> Brian De Palma

Chapter 1 gave us the language of film and a sense of the technical and creative possibilities: it spoke of cinematic codes, of *mise-en-scène* and montage. Chapter 2 will attempt to root this potential in the complex and at times confused processes of film production, in the real contexts in which films are made and displayed. In doing so it sketches a map of the many and various highways that lead from ideas to images on the screen. It is a road map on which most of the roads are finally dead-ends, where not getting there is far more common than arriving. Terry Gilliam's *Lost in La Mancha* (2004) is partly a homage to this 'failure', creating a new sub-genre of films which are 'films about films that didn't get made'.

Gilliam's career, like many, is a catalogue of projects, less than half of which became films. Unlike other art forms it is hard to argue that we get the 'best' films largely due to the complexity of the process of production. Which scripts are eventually filmed depends on such a range of factors as well as the involvement of many people. It is a context where even the idea of 'a script' is a flexible one and where 'concepts' are often more significant 'counters'.

Of course no film resource can ignore the industrial nature of film-making, particularly in the context of Hollywood. This fact will be embedded within this book. Here the intention is to tease open the process of negotiation that must go on if ideas are ever to become films. The fact that every film has a substantial army of contributors immediately causes problems for those theories that see film as merely the latest art form. A film, of course, is not only a massive act of co-operation but also a compilation of elements, some of which include:

- Concept
- Specification
- Script
- Personnel
- Direction
- Technical skills
- Editing
- Soundtrack
- Packaging

And it doesn't stop there, for marketing and exhibition then take over. If 'art' gets made it is perhaps a miracle, and we should be grateful if we at least get some entertainment.

Film critic Pauline Kael is a great deal more realistic in her book *Trash, Art and the Movies* (the title says it all) when she sums up our love affair with this 'tawdry corrupt art for a tawdry corrupt world'.

Like those cynical heroes who were idealists before they discovered that the world was more rotten than they had been led to expect, we're just about all of us displaced persons, 'a long way from home.' When we feel defeated, when we imagine we could now perhaps settle for home and what it represents, that home no longer exists. But there are movie houses. In whatever city we find ourselves we can duck into a theatre and see on the screen our familiars – our old 'ideas' aging as we are and no longer looking so ideal. Where could we better stoke the fires of our masochism than at rotten movies in gaudy seedy picture palaces in cities that run together, movies and anonymity a common denominator. Movies – a tawdry corrupt art for a tawdry corrupt world – fit the way we feel. The world doesn't work the way the schoolbooks said it did and we are different from what our parents and teachers expected us to be. Movies are our cheap and easy expression, the sullen art of displaced persons. Because we feel low we sink in the boredom, relax in the irresponsibility and maybe grin for a minute when the gunman lines up three men and kills them with a single bullet, which is no more 'real' to us than the nursery-school story of the brave little tailor.

We don't have to be told those are photographs of actors impersonating characters. We know, and we often know much more about both the actors and the characters they're impersonating and about how and why the movie has been made than is consistent with theatrical illusion. Hitchcock teased us by killing off the one marquee-name star early in 'Psycho,' a gambit which startled us not just because of the suddenness of the murder or how it was

CONTINUED

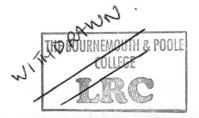

committed but because it broke a box-office convention and so it was a joke played on what audiences have learned to expect. He broke the rules of the movie game and our response demonstrated how aware we are of commercial considerations. When movies are bad (and in the bad parts of good movies) our awareness of the mechanics and our cynicism about the aims and values is peculiarly alienating. The audience talks right back to the phony 'outspoken' condescending 'The Detective'; there are groans of dejection at 'The Legend of Lylah Clare,' with, now and then, a desperate little titter. How well we all know that cheap depression that settles on us when our hopes and expectations are disappointed *again*. Alienation is the most common state of the knowledgeable movie audience, and though it has the peculiar rewards of low connoisseurship, a miser's delight in small favor, we long to be surprised out of it – not to suspension of disbelief nor to a Brechtian kind of alienation but to pleasure, something a man can call good without self-disgust.

A good movie can take you out of your dull funk and the hopelessness that so often goes with slipping into a theatre; a good movie can make you feel alive again, in contact, not just lost in another city. Good movies make you care, make you believe in possibilities again. If somewhere in the Hollywood-entertainment world someone has managed to break through with something that speaks to you, then it isn't *all* corruption. The movie doesn't have to be great; it can be stupid and empty and you can still have the joy of a good performance, or the joy in just a good line. An actor's scowl, a small subversive gesture, a dirty remark that someone tosses off with a mock-innocent face, and the world makes a little bit of sense. Sitting there alone or painfully alone because those with you do not react as you do, you know there must be others perhaps in this very theatre or in this city, surely in other theatres in other cities, now, in the past or future, who react as you do. And because movies are the most total and encompassing art form we have, these reactions can seem the most personal and, maybe the most important, imaginable. The romance of movies is not just in those stories and those people on the screen but in the adolescent dream of meeting others who feel as you do about what you've seen. You do meet them, of course, and you know each other at once because you talk less about good movies than about what you love in bad movies.

There is so much talk now about the art of the film that we may be in danger of forgetting that most of the movies we enjoy are not works of art.

(Kael 1994: 87–89)

In the face of the primer in film-making which we provided in Chapter 1, Kael injects a weary but constructive realism. She takes the arguments about personal expression and clarity of communication, even artistic integrity, and places them in the context of production. Here she argues that the supplanting intention is 'the intention to make money':

III

Let's clear away a few misconceptions. Movies make hash of the schoolmarm's approach of how well the artist fulfilled his intentions. Whatever the original intention of the writers and director, it is usually supplanted, as the production gets under way, by the intention to make money – and the industry judges the film by how well it fulfills that intention. But if you could see the 'artist's intentions' you'd probably wish you couldn't anyway. Nothing is so deathly to enjoyment as the relentless march of a movie to fulfill its obvious purpose. This is, indeed, almost a defining characteristic of the hack director, as distinguished from an artist.

The intention to make money is generally all too obvious. One of the excruciating comedies of our time is attending the new classes in cinema at the high schools where the students may quite shrewdly and accurately interpret the plot developments in a mediocre movie in terms of manipulation for a desired response while the teacher tries to explain everything in terms of the creative artist working out his theme – as if the conditions under which a movie is made and the market for which it is designed were irrelevant, as if the latest product from Warners or Universal should be analyzed like a lyric poem.

People who are just getting 'seriously interested' in film always ask a critic, 'Why don't you talk about technique and "the visuals" more?' The answer is that American movie technique is generally more like technology and it usually isn't very interesting. Hollywood movies often have the look of the studio that produced them – they have a studio style. Many current Warner films are noisy and have a bright look of cheerful ugliness, Universal films the cheap blur of money-saving processes, and so forth. Sometimes there is even a *spirit* that seems to belong to the studio. We can speak of the Paramount comedies of the Thirties or the Twentieth-Century Fox family entertainment of the Forties and CinemaScope comedies of the Fifties or the old MGM gloss, pretty much as we speak of Chevvies or Studebakers. These movies look alike, they move the same way, they have just about the same engines because of the studio policies and the *kind* of material the studio heads bought, the ideas they imposed, the way they had the films written, directed, photographed, and the labs where the prints were processed, and, of course, because of the presence of the studio stable of stars for whom the material was often purchased and shaped and who dominated the output of the studio. In some cases, as at Paramount in the thirties, studio style was plain and rather tacky and the output – those comedies with Mary Boland and Mae West and Alison Skipworth and W. C. Fields – looks the better for it now. Those economical comedies weren't slowed down by a lot of fancy lighting or the adornments of 'production values.' Simply to be enjoyable, movies don't need a very high level of craftsmanship: wit, imagination, fresh subject matter, skillful performers, a good idea – either alone or in any combination – can more than compensate for lack of technical knowledge or a big budget.

(Kael 1994: 92–94)

All of the elements that Kael addresses at the end of this extract are tied up in the intricate process of negotiation that constitutes 'Production'. When all the competing interests have had their say a film will 'occur' and we will have 'showtime'! This is about roles, about personalities, about egos, but it is also about creative functions: conceiving, developing, writing, directing, editing, creating sound. A film is, in every sense, a major project to which many will make fundamental contributions. As they enter and ultimately leave the project so it gathers momentum. It might start with a concept which becomes a pitch, a treatment. Sometimes the process starts with a star actor or actors and the project builds around them. The whole focus of the ultimately celebrated *American Beauty* was significantly changed by the arrival on board of Kevin Spacey.

A very common point of origin is an existing book or a narrative from another medium. Most successful paperback fiction attracts interest from the film industry, eager to fuel the need for stories to tell (see Chapter 3). This was the case with the highly acclaimed and commercially successful *Fight Club* (Fincher 1999) which was adapted from Chuck Palahniuk's novel. James Swallow in his book *Dark Eye*, which is a study of Fincher's films, offers a telling case study of the process of adaptation. The extract below is headed 'Development' and reveals much about the decision-making involved.

DEVELOPMENT

Fight Club followed a steep arc into feature film production. Even before its publication, the original novel by Chuck Palahniuk had found its way, still in galley form, into the hands of Laura Ziskin and Kevin McCormick at Fox 2000 Pictures. A common occurrence in an industry hungry for fresh ideas, the book had been quietly slipped by its publisher into the sights of Fox's creative fire-watchers.

But from the beginning, it had been the dream of another production executive, Raymond Bongiovanni, to get *Fight Club* made into a feature. The movie ends with a dedication to Bongiovanni, who died before production began, and it was his initial interest in Palahniuk's book that set the ball rolling. 'God bless Raymond,' noted the novelist, remembering their first phone conversation about the project in 1995, when Bongiovanni called 'just to see if I wasn't insane.' Around the same time, the producer had been introduced to a script called *Hard Hearts* by Jim Uhls, who was subsequently chosen to adapt the book. The script Uhls would create was a remix version of Palahniuk's slim 1996 novel, shifting key scenes and dialogue passages into a narrative better suited to the big screen.

When Bongiovanni died, his obituary in *Variety* ended by affirming his last wish – to get *Fight Club* filmed – and Palahniuk describes how his agent telephoned him after the producer's funeral. 'He said, "Your name was mentioned eight times during the eulogy. You can't buy better press than that."' Although he would never see it Bongiovanni would posthumously get what he wanted. Ziskin recalled that, within 36 hours of hearing about the novel, I was sitting on the edge of my bed in the middle of the night, reading passages to my husband.' In turn, McCormick recruited partners Joshua Donen and Ross Grayson Bell to be *Fight Club*'s 'cheerleaders' at Fox. 'The studio's internal coverage condemned the material as being exceedingly disturbing,' said Bell. "I read the manuscript and all the reasons the studio reader cited for *not* making the book into a movie were exactly the reasons to make the movie.'

In turn, Donen and Bell passed the novel to David Fincher and began to woo him for the directing job. At the time, Fincher was contemplating an unproduced script called *The Sky is Falling*, about two priests who discover proof of the non-existence of God and go on a commandment-busting crime spree.

McCormick was certain that Fincher was the best choice to helm *Fight Club*. 'I got chills,' he said. 'David is one of the only directors who can tell you two years before he's shot a scene exactly what you'll get when he's through.' Donen was instrumental in getting Fincher on board, performing the 'Human Sacrifice' scene down the telephone when the director initially resisted reading the book. At the time, Fincher was busy working 12-hour days as he completed his cut of *The Game*.

'Josh Donen, who is my agent now, was the lead producer on *Fight Club*,' Fincher recalls. 'He called me and he said, "I have this book, and you have to read it tonight," and I said, "Ah, Josh, I'm not going to read a book tonight." "You gotta read this. It's really fast." "I can't, I've got a dub tomorrow …" "Look, take three hours and finish this book, just sit down and read it." "Well, give me one reason why." "Okay, there's this scene where there's this guy called Raymond K Hessel …" and he goes into the Raymond K Hessel scene and explains all this to me. I said, "Okay. I have to read this book, all right, you've got to send it over. I have to read this." So I read it that night and I flipped out. I was laughing so hard that I just said to myself, I've got to be involved in this. If anyone should make this movie, I should at least give it my best shot.'

Fincher had acted quickly but, it seemed, not quickly enough – he called Donen the next day only to learn that Fox had already bought the feature rights. The director was wary of working with 20th Century Fox again after his experiences with them during the production of *Alien 3*. 'I was not happy. I said, "Well, there goes that idea." But Josh said, "No, no. Joe Roth is not there any more, Tom Jacobsen's not there …" The one good thing about these multinational corporations is that once you decide you loathe the people that are there, they're usually gone so quickly that it doesn't really matter.'

With monumental understatement, the director told *Digital Bits*: 'I didn't have a very good time with Fox the first time – but Josh called and told me to just go in and talk with Laura Ziskin, and tell her that I wanted to make it.' He continues: 'I read the book and know that you couldn't make this movie in 2003, this movie had to be 1999, you had to make it before the next millennium, because a lot of things the book talked about in such a startling way would be silly today, they wouldn't have the same sort of visceral impact.'

Fincher was energised by the material, citing features of the story in which he identified with the narrator Jack. 'At some points in my life, I've said, "I could get that sofa and then I'll have the sofa problem handled." As I was reading Chuck's book, I was blushing and feeling horrible. How did this guy know what everybody was thinking?'

He adds: 'It seemed kind of a coming of age story for people who are coming of age in their thirties instead of in their late teens or early twenties. In our society, kids are much more sophisticated at an earlier age and much less emotionally capable at a later age. Those two things are sort of moving against each other. There's an idea that on the path to enlightenment you have to kill you parents, your god, and your teacher. So the story begins at the moment when the Edward Norton character is 29 years old. He's tried to do everything he was taught to do, tried to fit into the world by becoming the thing that he isn't. He's been told, "If you do this, get an education, get a good job, be responsible, present yourself in a certain way, your furniture and your car and your clothes, you'll find happiness." And he hasn't.

'And so the movie introduces him at the point when he's killed off his parents and he realises that they're wrong. But he's still caught up, trapped in this world he's created for himself. And then he meets Tyler Durden, and they fly in the face of God – they do all these things that they're not supposed to do, all the things that you do in your twenties when you're no longer being watched over by your parents, and end up being, in hindsight, very dangerous. And then finally, he has to kill off this teacher, Tyler Durden. So the movie is really about that process of maturing. It is talking about very simple concepts. We're designed to be hunters and we're in a society of gatherers. There's nothing to kill any more, there's nothing to fight, nothing to overcome, nothing to explore. In that societal emasculation, this everyman is created.'

With its story of a protagonist placed before conflicting life paths, Fincher compared the movie to *The Graduate*. 'It was talking about that moment in time when you have this world of possibilities, all these expectations, and you don't know who it is you're supposed to be. And you choose this one path – Mrs Robinson – and it turns out to be bleak, but it's part of your initiation, your trial by fire. And then, by choosing the wrong path, you find your way onto the right path, but you've created this mess. *Fight Club* is the nineties inverse of that, a guy who does not have a world of possibilities in front of him, he had no possibilities, he literally cannot imagine a way to change his life.' Edward Norton agreed: 'My grandfather was very uncomfortable with *The Graduate*. He thought it was negative and inappropriate. But my father loved it, thought it was a great metaphoric black comedy that dealt with his generation's feeling of disjointedness, and that's exactly what *Fight Club* is. My character is sort of like Benjamin, and Brad's character is like a postmodern Mrs Robinson.'

Fincher reflects on one of *Fight Club*'s simple truths. 'There's something about getting hit in the face that gives you an adrenalised vision of life that's very profound, it's like nothing else you experience.' It was just that experience that inspired Palahniuk to write the novel. After getting into a fist-fight that left his face bruised and discoloured for weeks, the author realised that people around him were afraid to ask him how he'd got that way. 'It was like, if you looked bad enough, no one would dare ask you what you did with your free time.'

Given *Fight Club*'s edgy material, it would have been easy for Fox to take the route of least resistance, casting unknowns and avoiding the pitfalls a big budget would create; but the director wanted to go full tilt to do the book justice. 'I told [Ziskin]; "Here's the movie I'm interested in making and I'm not interested in watering any of this shit down. I have no interest in making this anything other than what this book is, which is a kind of sharp stick in the eye." She was very cool with it. We could have made it a $3 million *Trainspotting* version, or we could do the balls-out version where planes explode and it's just a dream and buildings explode and it's for real, which is the version I preferred to do – and she backed it. The real act of sedition is not to do the $3 million version, it's to do the big version.'

Fincher demanded – and got – the autonomy that he needed to do the film right, telling the producers, 'When I come back to you, I'm coming back with a script and it's going to be the script I want to shoot. Instead of coming back and saying, "What do you think? Oh, yeah, I can change that," I'm coming back with a script I'm willing to kill for. But I'm also coming back with a budget and I'm coming back with a schedule and a cast.' With the fierce content of *Fight Club*, part of the wonder if it is just how Fox agreed to make it in the first place. 'Movies don't get made at major studios because people say, "Well, this is a major political topic and we should jump all over this." They look at it and go, "Will kids like it? Can we get the 18-to-24 demographic?"' 'I didn't have any kind of mission,' says Fincher, 'I just knew that I liked the story, I liked the journey and I thought it was incredibly cinematic.'

Producer Art Linson told AICN: 'It's very simple. You've got Brad Pitt and David Fincher together for the first time since *Seven*. You've got me as a producer. The last time those guys worked together, the movie did $300 million worldwide. They're looking at the cost of this thing and thinking, "We're not going to get killed on this thing, no matter what.' They're not thinking, "We have to put this on screen. I was born to make this movie." No executive thinks like that. They're looking at Fincher and Brad and thinking, "Maybe it will be *Seven* in another costume." Of course, it can't be. And if we'd told them, "Brad's going to play it with a shaved head and part of his teeth knocked out," they might not have been as receptive to it. It was courage on the part of Fincher and courage on the part of Brad. They had more to lose.'

The director felt that Fox knew what they were letting themselves in for. 'There's nothing about any of our pasts that would lead them to believe we were gonna go off and make *Runaway Bride*. I think there was always a worry that it was going to be sinister and seditious. And we always said, "No, it's gonna be funny and seditious." The sinister element is the context for the understanding. The things we talk about in the film are dark fantasies or stewing rages that come out in unexpected ways. We always wanted to temper it with humour.'

The evolution of themes from *The Game* was clear to him early on. He called the films 'cousins'. '*The Game* is a *Twilight Zone* episode. That's all it's supposed to be. In *Fight Club* it's even worse, having to contend with somebody who is powerful and you look up to them and his ideas become all too questionable, but then to find out that they are indeed your ideas, that this is your mess, that you are the leader.'

Pitt was on board almost from the beginning, while Sean Penn had passed after being briefly considered for the roles of both the dour Jack and the charismatic Tyler. 'I sent Brad the book and he turned up on my doorstep the next day,' Fincher jokes. 'And I live in a gated community. I don't know how he got past security.' Pitt's desire for the part raised eyebrows in the Hollywood community. 'People who don't know Brad think he's a strange choice for the role, but people who do know him, who know the Brad Pitt who hangs out at his house with his five dogs, who chain-smokes, who lives under an inch of dust, they think he's perfect.'

Fincher had been instrumental in getting the actor on board, to the extent of flying to Pitt's home in New York City while the actor was working on *Meet Joe Black* and waiting for hours on his doorstep until he returned in the morning. At the time, Pitt wasn't interested in looking at new projects, so Fincher took him out for a pizza and convinced him to read *Fight Club* on the strength of his excitement about the project.

In *Fight Club*, Pitt shook off any pretence at the pretty-boy mantle he'd gathered from *Legends of the Fall* and *Seven Years in Tibet*, amping up the trend-bucking courage he'd shown in *Seven* to maximum. 'His work in *Fight Club* was stellar,' said Linson. 'He never showed any evidence of an actor who was out there trying to protect his 'Brad Pitt-ness'. Without a shred of false vanity or the use of old tricks to win over an audience, Pitt proved to be a formidable actor of enormous talent. Can anyone imagine 30 years ago, Robert Redford or Warren Beatty shaving his head or working without caps on his teeth or exposing himself so raw and ruthless as Brad had done and just let the chips fall?'

Pitt himself saw the risk as a logical one. 'It didn't seem gutsy to me at all. It seemed like it would be foolish not to do it.' The actor was effusive about

Fincher and the movie. 'It's a pummelling of information. It's Mr Fincher's Opus. It's provocative, but thank God it's provocative. People are hungry for films like this, films that make them think.' And from the start, Pitt saw the explosive nature of *Fight Club* before it hit. 'Fincher is piloting the *Enola Gay* on this one. He's got the A-bomb.'

Then it was on to Edward Norton, taking the role of the film's narrator, named as Jack in the script, although he's never actually called that in the dialogue. But this was not without a delay courtesy of Norton's previous employers at Paramount Pictures. In 1995, Norton had made his feature debut in Paramount's *Primal Fear* on a contract that locked him in to making two more films for the studio; the role got him an Oscar nomination and a Golden Globe award, followed by parts in three other features at three other studios. Norton considered by 1997 that Paramount's option on him had lapsed, but as he went into contractual negotiations for *Fight Club*, Paramount demanded he fulfil his obligation with a part in an unmade feature, *Twenty Billion*, which would prevent him appearing in Fincher's movie.

Fox refused to go head-to-head with Paramount and left Norton to sort out the situation, which he did by extending the option. However, the revised deal would have ramifications for the actor when Paramount exercised their rights in 2002 and cast him in their remake of *The Italian Job*. Norton had offered to take roles in a handful of other Paramount projects, including *Mission: Impossible 3* (which at the time Fincher was set to direct), but the studio had reportedly refused.

Norton called *Fight Club* a film that was 'off the charts'. 'It's not a photograph, it's an El Greco, lurid and crazy. For me it's always about, have I seen this before? And I'd definitely never seen this before. Nobody's ever seen this before. Fincher sent me the novel, and I read it in one sitting. It's obviously a surreal piece that operates at an almost allegorical level within someone's madness, and I felt immediately that it was on the pulse of a zeitgeist I recognised. It speaks to my generation's conflict with the American material values system at its worst. I guess I've felt for a long time that a lot of the films that were aimed at my generation were some baby-boomer perception of what Gen-X was about. They seemed to be tailored to a kind of reductive image of us as slackers and to have a banal, glib, low-energy, angst-ridden realism none of which I or anyone I know relates to. They didn't speak to the deeper and darker underlying sense of despair and paralysis and numbness in the face of the overwhelming onslaught of media information that we've received from the cradle.'

Norton's everyman appeal and dour, measured ennui as the film's narrator brings a realistic feel to his performance in *Fight Club*, instantly selling the concept of a man adrift in his own life. 'His contribution is that he's exactly that guy,' Fincher told the Guardian. 'You can believe that he's over-thinking the whole situation and creating this whole problem for himself.'

The *Fight Club* triumvirate was now almost complete, with only the role of Goth queen Marla Singer to be cast. An early contender was singer-actress Courtney Love, co-star with former boyfriend Norton in *The People Vs Larry Flynt* (1996). But the part went to British actress Helena Bonham Carter in April 1998, a casting choice that blew holes in her earlier Merchant Ivory-type profile. Initially, the actress had reservations about the script, but she was wooed to the part after discussing *Fight Club* with Pitt at a post-Oscar party. One week later, she met with Fincher and agreed to join the production.

Bonham Carter's first impression of the script had been a strong one. 'I thought, "In the wrong hands, this could be abominable." I was the last one on board. I wanted to meet Fincher just to ascertain that he wasn't a complete misogynist. The script was awfully dark … it could have been immature or possibly even irresponsible. But after meeting him, I could tell that it wasn't going to be a concern. He's not just an all-out testosterone package. He's got a healthy feminist streak.'

The director's initial meeting with her involved showing the actress a rough outline of the 'brain ride' title sequence. '[It was] a glimpse inside the mind of Fincher,' she noted. 'Then I sort of knew that I could trust him, that I was in good hands. He has such a specific vision that I knew he'd be doing half the work for me.' *Fight Club*'s author Chuck Palahniuk later spoke of her performance in the film as a perfect 'Audrey Hepburn on heroin', and Fincher has nothing but praise for a woman he called 'a very gifted, very specific actress', commenting on her ability to play against type as Marla and handle the blackly comic character. 'She just cracks me up, she was very caustic and funny.'

For her part, Bonham Carter admitted she modelled the character partly on Fincher: 'He thinks he's Marla,' she noted. On set, the character was nicknamed Judy, after costume designer Michael Kaplan had described her as 'Judy Garland close to the end.' 'Helena would listen to her records while she was in her trailer,' said Kaplan.

The evolution of *Fight Club*'s script saw Jim Uhls and Fincher working together closely from the earliest drafts. After the scriptwriter and director combed through an initial outline with Ross Bell, Uhls created a new draft that formed the basis for their collaboration. Art Linson joined the development process as the writer shifted the pitch and movement of the novel to make it more cinematic. 'The challenges of the adaptation were finding a structure for the film in terms of cause and effect and building momentum, and exploring the characters deeper and further in dialogue and behaviour,' the writer noted. In addition, Fincher's writer on *Seven*, Andrew Kevin Walker, took a pass over the script in a series of uncredited rewrites. As a nod to his hidden work, the three police detectives who attempt to cut off Jack's scrotum near the end of the film were named Detective Andrew, Detective Kevin and Detective Walker.

One of the earlier drafts cut the narration completely, but the look of the story without Jack's dry stream-of-consciousness ramblings made the script suffer. '[Jim] had written a version that eliminated the voiceover because Ross Bell told him it was a crutch,' Fincher noted. 'It was like taking the voice out of Dashiell Hammett. The interior monologue is what gives you some sort of context, some sort of humour. Without the narration the story is just sad and pathetic.' Uhls agreed that the film should always have had a narration attached.

After five drafts over eight months – many of which Uhls wrote for free – Fincher and Linson took the Fox executives to dinner and presented them with the finished, ready-to-shoot script. 'We dropped this huge pile of stuff,' says Fincher. 'They came in and we gave them something like three bibles' worth, a huge package. I said, "This is the movie. $67 million, here's the cast, we have this many days of shooting, this is why, these are the stages we want at Fox. We're going to start inside Edward Norton's brain and pull out. We're going to blow up a plane. We don't know who's going to play Marla, but we think it's going to be this person. Give us your answer tomorrow." They called back and said, "Okay."'

For the writers, one of the more difficult scenes to craft was the bar-room conversation between Tyler and Jack that serves to introduce the viewer to Durden's anarchist worldview. Fincher, a director known for his tendency to shoot and shoot, set up two cameras for the scene and filmed nearly 40 takes, a weighty 40,000 feet of film, to get things right. In the end, the scene was allowed to evolve organically through Norton and Pitt's half-scripted, half-improvised dialogue. 'It was a collective effort,' notes Norton, and the director added that making the scene work involved a lot of time spent 'playing Nerf basketball.' Both Uhls and Palahniuk were more than happy with the director's translation of their storyline to the screen: '[I felt] a combination of being blown away by the finished product,' said the scriptwriter, 'and at the same time it matched [my] expectations in the sense that it looked exactly right to me – this is the way I saw it.' The novelist concurs: 'There is not one shot in this movie that is not a beauty shot.'

(Swallow 2003: 118–125)

What Chuck Palahniuk's slim novel became was Jim Uhl's muscular screenplay aided by a series of credited and uncredited co-writers, which David Fincher himself described as 'three bibles' worth'. What Uhls had achieved with help was a film, but one that had a very long way to travel before it could ever be shown. This is partly why there is more than a little astonishment in the writer's voice when he realises the finished film 'looked exactly right to me'. For those of us who know the opening sequence of the film *Fight Club*, the evidence of the screenplay is remarkable.

> ➤ Read the following extract aloud as if it were a playscript. Now watch the corresponding sequence from the film. Consider the differences between these experiences.

SCREEN BLACK

JACK (V.O.): People were always asking me, did I know Tyler Durden.

FADE IN

INT. SOCIAL ROOM — TOP FLOOR OF HIGH RISE

Tyler has one arm around Jack's shoulder; the other hand holds a handgun with the barrel lodged in Jack's mouth. Tyler is sitting in Jack's lap. They are both sweating and dishevelled, both around 30; Tyler is blond, handsome, and Jack, brunette, is appealing in a dry sort of way. Tyler looks at his watch.

TYLER: One minute. (*looking out the window*) This is the beginning. We're at ground zero. Maybe you should say a few words, to mark the occasion.

JACK: ... i... ann... iinn... ff... nnyin...

JACK (V.O.): With a gun barrel between your teeth, you only speak in vowels.

Jack tongues the barrel to the side of his mouth.

JACK: (*still distorted*) I can't think of anything.

JACK (V.O.): With my tongue, I can feel the rifling in the barrel. For a second, I totally forgot about Tyler's whole controlled demolition thing and I wondered how clean this gun is.

Tyler checks his watch.

TYLER: It's getting exciting now.

JACK (V.O.): That old saying, how you always hurt the one you love, well, it works both ways.

Jack turns so that he can see down – 31 stories.

JACK (V.O.): We have front-row seats for this Theater of Mass Destruction. The Demolitions Committee of Project Mayhem wrapped the foundation columns of ten buildings with blasting gelatin. In two minutes, primary charges will blow base charges, and those buildings will be reduced to smoldering rubble. I know this because Tyler knows this.

TYLER: Look what we've accomplished. (*checks watch*) 30 seconds.

JACK (V.O.): Somehow, I realize all of this – the gun, the bombs, the revolution – is really about Marla Singer.

Pull back from Jack's face. It's pressed against two large breasts that belong to ... Bob, 45, a moose of a man. Jack is engulfed by Bob in an intense embrace. Bob weeps openly.

JACK (V.O.): Bob had bitch tits.

Pull back to wide on. . .

INT. CHURCH MEETING ROOM — NIGHT

Men are paired off, hugging, talking in emotional tones. Near the door, a sign on a stand:
'REMAINING MEN TOGETHER.'

JACK (V.O.): This was a support group for men with testicular cancer. The big moosie slobbering all over me was Bob.

BOB: We're still men.

JACK: Yes. We're men. Men is what we are.

JACK (V.O.): Six months ago, Bob's testicles were removed. Then hormone therapy. He developed bitch tits because his testosterone was too high and his body upped the estrogen. That was where my head fit – into his huge, sweating tits that hung enormous, the way we think of God's as big.

BOB: They're gonna have to open my pec's again to drain the fluid.

Bob hugs tighter; then looks with empathy into Jack's eyes.

BOB: Okay. You cry now.

Jack looks at Bob.

JACK (V.O.): Wait. Back up. Let me start earlier.

INT. JACK'S BEDROOM — NIGHT

Jack lies in bed, staring at the ceiling.

JACK (V.O.): For six months, I could not sleep.

INT. COPY ROOM — DAY

Jack, sleepy, stands over a copy machine. His Starbucks cup sits on the lid, moving back and forth as the machine copies.

JACK (V.O.): With insomnia, nothing is real. Everything is far away. Everything is a copy of a copy of a copy.

Other people make copies, all with Starbucks cups, sipping. Jack picks up his cup and his copies and leaves.

INT. JACK'S OFFICE — SAME

Jack, sipping, stares blankly at a Starbucks bag on the floor, full of newspapers and fast-food garbage.

JACK (V.O.): When deep-space exploration ramps up, it will be corporations that name everything. The IBM Stellar Sphere. The Philip Morris Galaxy. Planet Starbucks.

Jack looks up as a pudgy man, Jack's boss, enters, Starbucks cup in hand, and slides a stack of reports on Jack's desk.

BOSS: I'm going to need you out of town a little more this week. We've got some 'red flags' to cover.

JACK (V.O.): It must've been Tuesday. He was wearing his 'cornflower bluc' tie.

JACK: (*listless management speak*) You want me to de-prioritize my current reports until you advise of a status upgrade?

BOSS: You need to make these your primary 'action items.'

JACK (V.O.): He was full of pep. Must've had his grande latte enema.

BOSS: Here are your flight coupons. Call me from the road if there are any snags. Your itinerary...

Jack hides a yawn, pretends to listen.

INT. BATHROOM — JACK'S CONDO — NIGHT

Jack sits on the toilet, cordless phone to his ear, flips through an IKEA catalog. There's a stack of old Playboy *magazines and other catalogs nearby.*

JACK (V.O.): Like everyone else, I had become a slave to the IKEA nesting instinct.

JACK: (*into phone*) Yes. I'd like to order the Erika Pekkari slip covers.

Jack drops the open catalog on the floor.

MOVE IN ON CATALOG — ON PHOTO OF COFFEE TABLE SET

JACK (V.O.): If I saw something like clever coffee tables in the shape of a yin and yang, I had to have it.

(Uhl 1999: 5–7)

What makes us surprised about the clarity of the transition from page to screen is our understanding of the real distance on a number of levels between them. Production is not a single process but rather a series of processes through which the film's central idea must pass. In doing so it is amended, sometimes improved, challenged, clarified (and sometimes complicated), celebrated and sometimes lost altogether. All we have time for here is to identify some issues, some key elements of this landscape. They appear below in abstract form and thereafter in the extracts that follow as essentially pragmatic.

Film production in the end is an expensive labour-intensive activity which produces collaborative work at a generally high technical standard for which only a few people get most of the credit. Central to the process is the director whose job it is to see the process through, either as 'artist' (*auteur*: see Chapter 9) or chief technician. Writing of David Fincher, James Swallow invokes the verb *to helm* to emphasise the 'captain of the ship' analogy: 'Fincher was the best choice to helm *Fight Club*.' To some extent the director is always caught between the often intimate aesthetic role of working with actors to create memorable moments and the logistical task of making hundreds of hired hands work in the same 'direction'. It is a division of energies which all too often leads to problems.

With the director at the helm the voyage can begin. Directing is about preparation and vision but it is most importantly about making decisions. The realisation of how many decisions there are to make in a film on a shot-by-shot basis is emphasised below. Here is the screenwriter and director David Mamet engaged in a master class with film students from the University of Columbia Film School: the workshop is entitled simply

'Where do I put the camera?' Mamet strips down the process by which the director first identifies the decisions he has to make. He is keen at all times to emphasise what the job of director really entails:

> You tell the story. Don't let the protagonist (the main character) tell the story. You tell the story; you direct it. We don't have to follow the protagonist around. We don't have to establish his 'character'. We don't need to have anybody's 'back story'.

What Mamet also proves in the process is how many decisions need to be made in even the simplest film sequence: not big decisions but crucial little ones.

'WHERE DO YOU PUT THE CAMERA?'

CONSTRUCTING A FILM
(A collaboration with students in the Columbia University Film School)

MAMET: Let's make a movie out of the situation we're in now. A bunch of people are coming to a class. What's an interesting way to film this?

STUDENT: From above.

MAMET: Now, why is that interesting?

STUDENT: It's interesting because it's a novel angle and it gives a bird's-eye view of everybody coming in, sort of accentuating the numbers. If there are a number of people coming in, you may want to suggest that that's significant.

MAMET: How can you tell if this is a good way to film the scene? There are any number of ways to film it. Why is 'from above' better than any other angle? How are you going to decide what's the best way to shoot it?

STUDENT: It depends what the scene is. You could say the scene is about a really tempestuous meeting and have people pacing around a lot. That would dictate a different scene than one in which the tension is underlying.

MAMET: That's exactly correct. You have to ask, 'what is this scene about?' So let's put aside the 'follow the hero around' way of making movies and ask what the scene is about. We have to say our task is *not* to follow the protagonist around. Why? Because there are an infinite number of ways to film a bunch of people in a room. So the scene is not simply about a bunch of people in a room; it's about something else. Let us suggest what the scene might be about. We know nothing about the scene other than it's a first meeting. So you're going to have to make an election as to what this scene is about. And it is this election, this choosing not 'an interesting way' to film a scene (which is an election based on novelty and basically a desire to be well-liked) but rather saying, 'I would like to make a statement based on the meaning of the scene, not the appearance of the scene,' which is the choice of the artist. So let's suggest what the scene might be about. I'll give you a hint: 'what does the protagonist want?' Because the scene ends when the protagonist gets it. What does the protagonist want? It's this journey that is going to move the story forward. What does the protagonist want? What does he or she do to get it – that's what keeps the audience in their seats. If you don't have that, you have to trick the audience into paying attention. Let's go back to the 'class' idea. Let's say it's the first meeting of a series of people. A person, in the first meeting, might be trying to get respect. How are we going to address this subject cinematically? In this scene the subject wants *to earn the instructor's respect*. Let's tell the story in pictures. Now, if you have trouble addressing this thing, and your mind draws a blank, just listen to yourself telling the story to a guy next to you in a bar. How would you tell that story?

STUDENT: 'So this guy comes into the class and the first thing he does is sit right next to the professor and he started to look at him very carefully and ... and listen very carefully to what he's saying and when the professor dropped his prosthetic arm, he reached down and grabbed it and gave it to the professor.'

MAMET: Well, yes. This is what the writers do today, the writer and directors. But we, on the other hand, want to keep everything that's 'interesting' out of the way. If the character is not *made* to be interesting, then the character can only be interesting or uninteresting as it serves the story. It's impossible to make a character 'interesting in general.' If the story is about a man who wants to earn the respect of the instructor, it's not important that the instructor have a prosthetic arm. It's not our task to make the story interesting. The story can only be interesting because we find the progress of the protagonist interesting. It is the *objective of the protagonist* that keeps us in our seats. 'Two small children went into a dark wood ...' Okay; somebody else? You're writing the film. The objective is *to earn the respect of the instructor*.

STUDENT: 'A guy in film class, who arrived twenty minutes early, sat at one end of the table. Then the class came in with the

	instructor, and he picked up his chair and moved it, trying to sit near the instructor, and the instructor sat on the other side of the room.'
MAMET:	Good. Now we've got some ideas. Let's work with them a little bit. A fellow arrived twenty minutes early. Why? *To earn the respect of his instructor.* He sat at one end of the table. Now, how can we reduce this to shots?
STUDENT:	Shot of him coming in, shot of the classroom, shot of him sitting, shot of the rest of the class coming in.
MAMET:	Good. Anybody else?
STUDENT:	A shot of a clock, a shot of the moment when he comes in, hold on this until he decides where he's going to sit, a shot of him waiting alone in the empty room, a shot of the clock, and a shot of many people coming in.
MAMET:	Do you need a shot of the clock? The smallest unit with which you most want to concern yourself is the shot. The larger concept of the scene is to win the respect of the instructor. This is what the protagonist wants – it's the superobjective. Now, how can we figure out the first beat of the scene? What do we do first?
STUDENT:	Establish the character.
MAMET:	The truth is, you never have to establish the character. In the first place, there is no such thing as character other than the habitual action, as Mr. Aristotle told us two thousand years ago. It just doesn't exist. Here or in Hollywood or otherwise. They always talk about the character out there in Hollywood, and the fact is there is no such thing. It doesn't exist. The character is just habitual action. 'Character' is exactly what the person literally does in pursuit of the superobjective, the objective of the scene. The rest doesn't count.

An example: a fellow goes to a whorehouse and comes up to the madam and says, 'what can I get for five bucks?' She says, ' you should have been here yesterday, because ...' Well, you, as members of the audience, want to know why he should have been there yesterday. That's what you want to know. Here, however, we tell the story, full of characterization.

A fellow, trim, fit, obviously enamored of the good things of life but not without a certain somberness, which might speak of a disposition to contemplation, goes to a gingerbread gothic whorehouse situated on a quiet residential street, somewhere in a once-elegant part of town. While walking up the flagstone steps ...

CONTINUED

This is one of those American movies we make. The script and the film are always 'establishing' something.

Now, don't *you* go 'establishing' things. Make the audience wonder what's going on *by putting them in the same position as the protagonist*.

As long as the protagonist wants something, the audience will want something. As long as the protagonist is clearly going out and attempting to get that something, the audience will wonder whether or not he's going to succeed. The moment the protagonist, or the *auteur* of the movie, stops trying to *get* something and starts trying to *influence* someone, the audience will go to sleep. The movie is not about establishing a character or a place, the way television does it.

Look at the story about the whorehouse: isn't that how most television shows are formed? A shot of 'air,' tilt down to frame a building. Pan down the building to a sign that says, 'Elmville General Hospital.' The point is not where does the story take place?' but 'what's it about?' That's what makes one movie different from another.

Let's go back to our movie. Now, what's the first concept? What is going to be a *building block that is necessary to 'achieve the respect of the instructor'*?

STUDENT: ... The guy arrives early?

MAMET: Exactly so. The guy arrives early. Now, the way you understand whether the concept is essential or not is to attempt to tell the story without it. Take it away and see if you need it or not. If it's not essential, you throw it out. Whether it's a scene or a shot, if it's not essential throw it out. 'The guy says to the madam ...' Well, obviously you can't start the whorehouse scene like that. You need something before that. 'A guy goes to a whorehouse and the madam says ...' In this example the first building block is 'a guy goes to a whorehouse.'

Here's another example: you have to walk to the elevator in order to get downstairs. In order to get down, you have to go to the elevator and get in there. That's essential to get downstairs. And if your objective is *to get to the subway* and you begin in an elevated floor of the building, the first step will be 'to get downstairs.'

To win the respect of the instructor is the superobjective. What steps are essential?

STUDENT: First, *show up early*.

MAMET: Good. Yes. How are we going to create this idea of earliness? We don't have to worry about *respect* now. *Respect* is the overall

	goal. All we have to worry about now is earliness; that's the first thing. So let's create the idea of earliness by juxtaposing uninflected images.
STUDENT:	He starts to sweat.
MAMET:	Okay, what are the images?
STUDENT:	The man sitting by himself, in a suit and tie, starting to sweat. You could watch his behavior.
MAMET:	How does this give us the idea of earliness?
STUDENT:	It would suggest that there's something he's anticipating.
MAMET:	No, we don't have to worry about anticipating. All we have to know in this beat is that he's early. Also, we don't have to watch behavior.
STUDENT:	An empty room.
MAMET:	Well, there we go, that's one image.
STUDENT:	A shot of a man by himself in an empty room juxtaposed with a shot of a group of people coming in from outside.
MAMET:	Okay, but this doesn't give us the idea of earliness, does it? Think about it.
STUDENT:	They could all be late.
MAMET:	Let's express this in absolutely pristine, uninflected images requiring no additional gloss. What are the two images that are going to give us the idea of *earliness*?
STUDENT:	A guy is walking down the street and the sun is rising and the street cleaners are going by and it's dawn and there's not a lot of activity on the street. And then maybe a couple of shots of some people waking up and then you see the guy, the first man, come into a room and other people are in there finishing up a job that they were doing, maybe finishing the ceiling or something like that.
MAMET:	Now, this scenario gives the idea of early morning, but we've got to take a little bit of an overview. We have to let our little alarm go off once in a while, if we stray too far off the track; the alarm that says, 'Yes – it's *interesting*, but does it fulfill the objective?' We want the idea of *earliness* so that we can use it as a building block to *winning respect*. We do not absolutely require the idea *early in the morning*.
STUDENT:	Outside the door you could have a sign saying 'Professor Such-and-such's class' and giving the time. Then you could have a shot of our guy obviously sitting by himself with the clock behind him.
MAMET:	Okay. Does anybody feel that it might be a good idea to stay away from a clock? Why might we feel that?
STUDENT:	Cliché.

CONTINUED

MAMET: Yeah, it's a little bit of a cliché. Not that it's necessarily bad. As Stanislavsky told us, we shouldn't shy away from things just because they are clichés. On the other hand, maybe we can do better. Maybe the clock ain't bad, but let's put it aside for a moment just because our mind, that lazy dastard, jumped to it first and, perhaps, it is trying to betray us.

(Mamet 1991: 9–17)

In film production it is not just clichés we must look out for. Mamet depicts the intellectual and creative cut and thrust very effectively and attractively. However, films are not made by bright, co-operative graduate students but by a legion of specialist technicians with their own conventions and agendas. Without knowledge of these technical codes directing a feature film would be next to impossible both practically and psychologically, not least because you the director need to be able to convince your 'crew' that you know what you are doing. The idea of film having a grammar of technique has its own implications: a grammar is after all a set of rules. For example, the classical continuity style of editing so favoured by mainstream Hollywood is supported by a certain regulation of shot composition and creation, by what Bordwell and Thompson call 'specific strategies of cinematography and mise-en-scene'. This is the 180-degree rule which, 'even today, a director or editor in narrative filmmaking is expected to be thoroughly familiar with'.

CONTINUITY EDITING

Editing might appear to present a dilemma to the filmmaker. On one hand, the physical break between one shot and another may seem to have a disturbing effect, interrupting the viewer's flow of attention. But on the other hand, editing is undeniably a primary means for constructing a film. How can one use editing and yet control its potentially disruptive force? This problem (though not stated in these terms) first confronted filmmakers around 1900–10. The solution eventually adopted was to plan the cinematography and mise-en-scene with a view to editing the shots according to a specific system. The purpose of the system was *to tell a story* coherently and clearly, to map out the chain of characters' actions in an undistracting way. Thus editing, supported by specific strategies of cinematography and mise-en-scene, was used to ensure *narrative continuity*. So powerful is this style that, even today, a director or editor in narrative filmmaking is expected to be thoroughly familiar with it. How does this stylistic system work?

The basic purpose of the continuity system is to control the potentially disunifying force of editing by establishing a smooth flow from shot to shot. All of the possibilities of editing we have already examined are bent to this

FILM STUDIES: THE ESSENTIAL RESOURCE

end. First, graphics are kept roughly similar from shot to shot. The figures are balanced and symmetrically deployed in the frame; the overall lighting tonality remains constant, the action occupies the central zone of the screen. Second, the rhythm of the cutting is usually made dependent on the camera distance of the shot: long shots are left on the screen longer than medium shots, and medium shots are left on longer than close-ups. (Sometimes, in scenes of physical action like the fire in *The Birds*, markedly accelerated editing rhythms may be present, regardless of the shot scale.) Since the continuity style seeks to present a narrative action, however, it is chiefly through the handling of space and time that editing furthers narrative continuity.

Spatial Continuity: the 180° system

In the continuity style the space of a scene is constructed along what is called variously the '**axis of action**,' the 'center line,' or the '180° line.' The scene's action – a person walking, two people conversing, a car racing along a road – is assumed to project along a discernible, predictable line. Consequently, the filmmaker will plan, film, and edit the shots to establish this center line as clearly as possible. The camera work and mise-en-scene in each shot will be manipulated to establish and reiterate the 180° space. A bird's-eye view [Figure 1] will clarify the system.

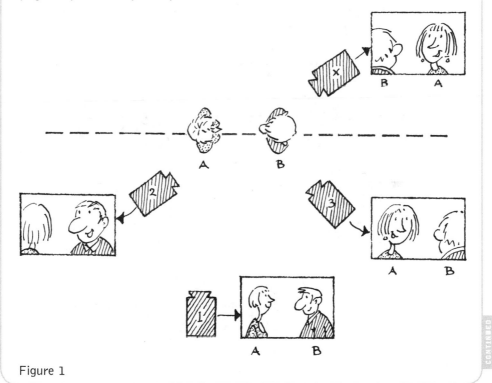

Figure 1

This bird's-eye view shows A and B conversing. The axis of action is that imaginary line connecting the two people. Under the continuity system, the director would arrange the mise-en-scene and camera placement so as to establish and sustain this line. The camera can be put at any point as long as it stays on the same *side* of the line (hence the 180° term). A typical series of shots would be: (1) a medium shot of A and B; (2) a shot over A's shoulder, 'favoring' B; (3) a shot over B's shoulder, favoring A. But to cut to a shot from camera position 'X' would be considered a violation of the system because it *crosses* the axis of action Indeed, one handbook on film directing calls shot X flatly 'wrong.' To see why, we need to examine what this 180° system does.

It ensures some common space from shot to shot. As long as the axis of action is not crossed, portions of the space will tally from shot to shot. In our example, assume that there is a wall with pictures and shelves behind A and B. If we follow shot 1 with shot 2, not only will one side of B reappear as a common factor but so will at least part of the wall, the pictures and shelves. We are thus oriented to the space presented in shot 2: it is simply part of the space of shot 1, observed from a new position. But if we follow shot 1 with shot X, we see both a new side of B and an entirely different background (another wall, a door, or whatever). A defender of traditional continuity would claim that this

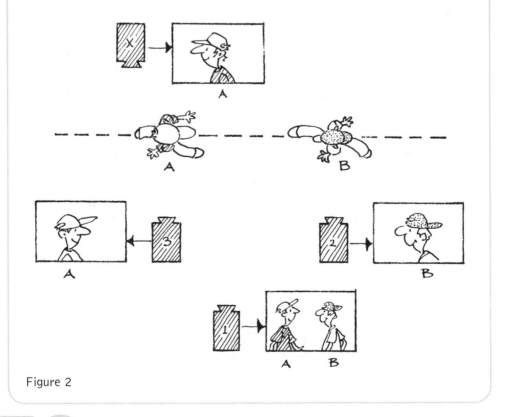

Figure 2

disorients us; has B moved to another locale? Thus the 180° rule generates a common area from shot to shot, which stabilizes space and orients the viewer within the scene.

It ensures constant screen direction. Assume now that A is walking left to right; A's path constitutes the axis of action. As long as our shots do not cross this axis, cutting them together will keep the screen direction of A's movement constant, from left to right. But if we *cross* the axis and film a shot from the other side, not only will the background change but also A will now appear on the screen as moving from *right to left*. Such a cut could be disorienting.

Consider a similar situation to that in Figure 1, a standard scene of two cowboys meeting for a shootout on a town street [Figure 2]. A and B again form the 180° line, but here A is walking from left to right and B is approaching from right to left, both seen in the shot taken from camera position one. A closer view, from camera position two, shows B still moving from right to left. A third shot, from camera position three, shows A walking, as he had been in the first shot, from left to right. But imagine that this third shot was instead taken from position X, on the opposite side of the line. He is now seen as moving from right to left. Has he taken fright and turned around while the second shot, of B, was on the screen? The filmmakers may intend that we understand that he is still walking toward his adversary, but it could be difficult for us to figure this out. Such breaks in continuity can be confusing Even more disorienting would be crossing the line while establishing the same shootout situation. If the first shot shows A walking from left to right and the second shot shows B (from the other side of the line) also walking left to right, we would probably not be able to tell whether they were walking toward each other. The two cowboys would seem to us to be walking in the same direction at different points on the street, as if one were following the other. We would very likely be startled if they suddenly came face to face within the same shot. Though we shall examine some stratagems for getting 'across the line,' it is enough for now to see that adhering to the 180° system ensures consistent screen direction from shot to shot.

(Bordwell and Thompson 1990: 218–220)

Other pressures also beset the would-be director. As we have suggested, sound is playing an increasingly important part in the way films have impact and make meaning. Massive technological improvements have transformed the ways in which film-makers have viewed sound. As Gianluca Sergi suggests, 'As a result contemporary film-makers have shown an increasing awareness of the "physical" three-dimensional qualities of sound and audiences are encouraged not just to listen to sounds but to "feel" them.' For Sergi, 'contemporary film sound … is significant not just in terms of its literal meaning, but also in terms of its weight, it power, its detail and its direction'. This 'upgrading' of the soundtrack 'as a site of interest and experiment in its own right' must have implications and not just in an increase in sound personnel. Here is a major slice of film production which may be devised and developed elsewhere and will function as an important component of the film. This may mean that the demands of sound designers are becoming increasingly relevant and separated from the central process in which the director oversees a film's production. In the extract below Sergi explores the changing meaning of sound and particularly 'soundtrack'.

The word 'sound' has always had several positive meanings. Indeed, expressions such as *sound* thinking, a *sound* person, and *sound* judgements belong to our everyday vocabulary. However, all this stops when we reach the realm of Film Studies. Here, sound seems like an obstacle in the way of the essence of cinema: the image. This bias against sound, generated mainly by early film scholars, was partly supported by the limitations that characterized Hollywood film production and reception prior to the mid-1970s, as we shall see. However, since then, a series of technological developments and changes in production and reception have ensued, and these have modified the ways in which film sound has been constructed, and the relationship between sound and image, audience and film. It is this period, which we may define as the 'Dolby era', upon which I wish to focus here. In exploring its characteristics I shall follow two distinct 'tracks', an aesthetic one and an economic one. It is in the interaction between them that one can perhaps begin to identify the parameters of what might be called 'post-classical' film sound.

THE SOUNDTRACK: A MISLEADING NOTION?

Before launching into any discussion of the role – or roles – of film sound, we need to confront a major problem: the lack of a proper vocabulary with which to articulate the complexity of the subject. Although this is true of other areas of film (production design and art direction come to mind), this particular lack is an acute one. There are several reasons for it. Film sound shares the same physical medium as music, that is, sound waves, and this has often helped to reinforce the use of musical terms in discussions of sound. This is particularly evident in the insistent use of terms like pitch, tone and timbre. These terms are relevant but insufficient. They are simply not flexible enough to articulate the complexities of contemporary soundtracks (for example, musical vocabularies are concerned with sound *per se*, while film sound works in symbiosis with the image). This problem is intensified by the disparity in critical attention given to popular music as compared to the cinema. Whereas in the UK at least there are a number of TV shows which set out to discuss or to analyse films (such as *Film 98* and *Moviewatch*), equivalent programmes on pop music simply present the product or performer without ever discussing their qualities or the ways in which they work (consider, for example, *Top of the Pops* and *The Chart Show*). In short, we have an inadequate vocabulary which is in any case rarely used in popular critical contexts. Perhaps we should attempt to side-step some of these problems by turning our attention to the soundtrack itself.

Rather than being conceived as a complex combination of different elements, the term 'soundtrack' has come principally to signify the music track of a film, dialogue being confined to another – 'superior' – realm, that of the screenwriter. This is a rather convenient way of arranging perception and appreciation. First, by singling out specific portions of a soundtrack, critics can praise the contributions of individual practitioners rather than focus on the much more complicated issue of what actually becomes of these contributions once they are recorded, mixed and reproduced not as independent elements, but as elements in a complex structure. Second, this type of approach betrays a certain attitude towards the more apparently 'ordinary' elements of the soundtrack, its everyday sounds: noise and silence. Critics seem to find it easier – and worthier – to focus on the art of the spoken word or the composed note than on the unsettling noise or the 'empty' silence. Yet it is precisely the relationship between all four elements – effects, music, dialogue and silence – that require investigation, and that mark the nature of the soundtrack itself. A soundtrack is like a cake. Each ingredient has its own distinctive flavour and makes its own individual contribution. However, once blended together they cannot and should not be separated one from another. Their contribution to the final product can only be considered by referring to the other ingredients and to the cake itself as a whole.

(Sergi 1998: 156–157)

Add to this the equally escalating importance of visual effects and film-making becomes a very different prospect to that modelled by David Mamet and his students. At best the director is engaging across the broadest range of techniques to maintain a genuine control or direction: Peter Jackson would be an example in his almost obsessive pursuit of a viable version of Tolkien's *The Lord of the Rings*. Otherwise there is a real need to understand that this complex business must, of necessity, confound the desire of anyone to have anything like control.

Even that most prized 'gift' of the *auteur* director, The Director's Cut, is subject to the confusions of this complex industrial context. Take Ridley Scott's controversial masterpiece *Blade Runner* whose Director's Cut was not only ten years in the making but even then was not necessarily the 'cut' the director wanted.

Even in its diluted form *Blade Runner* was a recognizable masterpiece – amusing to note the many critics who originally vilified it pretending they didn't in the light of it clearly being one of the most directional movies of the eighties. Now [with the release of the Director's Cut] it's even more of a masterwork than ever before. ...

– 'Preview: *Blade Runner*: The Director's Cut' by Alan Jones
Starburst Magazine
Issue # 172, September 1992

BUILDING A BETTER DIRECTOR'S CUT

As already noted in chapter XVI, by late September of 1991 the BR Workprint was selling out at its NuArt Theater engagement. Yet Ridley Scott, back in London and now casting for his upcoming 1492: *Conquest of Paradise*, hadn't been notified that this version of *Blade Runner* was even in circulation. World of the NuArt screenings finally did reach the director, however, while the engagement was still in progress. At this point Scott temporarily put his 1492 labors on hold to fly to Los Angeles and discuss the situation with Warner Brothers.

'Ridley had a number of concerns with this Workprint,' recalls Michael Arick. 'First, he didn't seem to appreciate the fact that the Workprint was being advertised as a Director's Cut, when it wasn't. Also, he felt very strongly that the Workprint itself wasn't up to the technical standards required for a broad theatrical release.[1] Ridley still felt there was an opportunity for him to restructure the film as a Director's Cut, particularly in the sense of being able to reinsert his unicorn footage.'

Therefore, in early October 1991, Arick, Scott, and Mimi Polk (Scott's then-producer) held a meeting with both Barry Reardon (President of Domestic Distribution at Warner Brothers) and Peter Gardiner (Vice President of Operations and Corporate Film Video Services) to discuss the situation. According to Scott and Arick, the meeting was cordial but divided. The Warners contingent pushed for the release of the Workprint as a Director's Cut, especially since the studio had already invested so much time and effort in making duplicate prints of the WP; Scott, on the other hand, stressed that he could not support the Workprint as a Director's Cut, because he was not satisfied with either its content or appearance. Warners countered by noting that the Workprint was doing such good business that it seemed more sensible just to let the issue ride.

---

[1]Hampton Fancher rejects the Workprint on more aesthetic grounds. 'Of all the versions, I prefer the Director's Cut,' the screenwriter said. 'After I finally saw the Workprint, I felt it was self-indulgent – too slow, too much music, too many extended scenes where nothing was really happening. The Workprint didn't have enough punch for me.'

'Ridley said this wasn't an issue of business,' adds Arick. 'It was art. His final film had been visually polished, and he'd done a lot of work to make it that way. But what was being shown at the NuArt was only an unrefined version of that final product. He didn't have a problem with letting people know that what they were seeing was a rough draft of *Blade Runner*, but calling it a restored Director's Cut was another thing.'

Scott then proposed using the Workprint as a blueprint to help construct an all-new *Blade Runner*, one that would be assembled from the best available negatives of the original shoot. Reardon, who had always been a fan of the film, agreed. Now a new deal was struck – the Workprint would be allowed to play out its runs at the NuArt and Castro, but not at the fourteen other theaters into which the WP had been booked to appear following its Castro engagement. Instead, the original theatrical version of the film would be shipped to these other sites, while Scott worked on a new BR Director's Cut (hereafter occasionally referred to as the BRDC).

As for who would be in charge of the BRDC project, the overall restoration itself would, on Warner's side, be supervised by Peter Gardiner. Arick was put in charge of Scott's end of the operation by Mimi Polk, who felt that the preservationist had both a firm grasp of the film and an insider's knowledge of Warner's workings, since Arick had recently been a employee of that studio. The final detail of this arrangement stated that no further distribution of the Workprint would take place until March 1992, at which date Scott was bound to deliver his newly restored cut.

Speaking to this author by telephone in 1993, Scott summed up his feelings and experiences regarding the origins of the Director's Cut this way·

'I came to Los Angeles to meet with Michael Arick and to see the 70mm print screened at the Fairfax. It had been some years, frankly, since I'd given thought to the film, and I wanted to refresh my memory. And after I saw it, I notified Arick and Warners that this was not the final cut of my film, pointing out the lack of my unicorn scene and the fact that the final fight between Deckard and Batty was using a temporary music track. Warners then agreed to pay for a sort of post-postproduction process where we could go back to the editing room and put the picture into the shape I'd originally wanted it.'

'Following our meeting at Warners, I flew to London to attend a film festival,' continues Michael Arick. 'I then stayed on in England after that event – at my own expense – throughout November and December of 1991, in an attempt to catalog a written outline of the version of *Blade Runner* that Ridley had always wanted.'

Arick was assisted in this task by Les Healey, who had worked on the original film under Terry Rawlings as BR's first assistant editor. But what version of

Blade Runner did Ridley Scott have in mind for his Director's Cut? After all, the Workprint had featured over seventy differences between it and the theatrical print, and there were also those additional shots seen in the San Diego sneak. What would stay, and what would be cut out?

The first decision was to completely remove any voice-over from the film. 'But that wasn't a situation where Ridley had had ten years to think about it and then decided to strip out the narration,' says Michael Deeley. 'He'd actually expressed reservations about releasing the film with a voice-over right after the Dallas and Denver previews. I'd had even stronger objections. In fact, in March of 1982, I wrote an open memo to Warners, Tandem, and The Ladd Company stating a number of reasons why I felt *Blade Runner* shouldn't go out with a narration. I'd mentioned how I'd thought we'd cleared up some of the storyline confusion through recutting after the Texas and Colorado sneaks, for example. I'd also noted that a voice-over would seriously interfere with both the flow of the story and Deckard's character. But my reservations weren't acted upon, obviously.'

Besides releasing the Director's Cut *sans* narration, Scott passed on a number of other suggestions to Arick which he felt would help improve his BRDC. These included: inserting the extra fifteen seconds of violence seen in the International Cut; removing the tacked-on happy ending; climaxing the film with the elevator doors closing on Rachael/Deckard; putting back in the two close-ups of the giant eye which had been missing from the Workprint; reinserting the scene showing Deckard visiting Holden in hospital; and clearing up various audio flubs. These last proposed improvements (which included eliminating the lip-flap seen between Deckard and Abdul Ben-Hassan at Animoid Row, and making sure that the snake scale ID number the Cambodian saleslady speaks aloud matched the number seen under her electron microscope), would be accomplished by assembling certain key actors and having them reloop their dialogue.

Scott also very much wanted to reinstate his beloved 'unicorn shot.' This (soon to be controversial) scene was filmed during post-production in 1982 and had been originally intended to take place while Deckard was in his apartment playing his piano – suddenly, Deckard daydreams about a horned horse. Scott intended this reverie to have chilling relevance at film's end, with Gaff leaving behind a tin-foil origami unicorn to signify his knowledge of Deckard's innermost thoughts.

'Interestingly enough,' Arick adds, 'we weren't going to do anything to change Bryant's line about only one replicant being killed breaking into the Tyrell Corporation. I asked Ridley if he wanted to have me change that and substitute the Workprint's line about two replicants being killed. He said, "Leave it alone,"'

One of the first originally trimmed sequences which Arick now attempted to track down for the BRDC was the Holden in the hospital scene. Twenty separate dailies of this sequence were subsequently unearthed but, according to Arick, 'there was no soundtrack available. It hadn't been preserved, so what we essentially had was a silent sequence. We could have looped in some dialogue later on. But we never had the chance to do that.'

(Sammon 1996: 349–352)

▼ 3 NARRATIVE

GRIFFIN (Tim Robbins): (The story) lacked certain elements that we need to market a film successfully.
JUNE (Greta Scacchi): What elements?
GRIFFIN: Suspense, laughter, violence, hope, heart, nudity, sex, happy endings. Mainly happy endings.

The Player (1992) – quoted by Richard Maltby in 'Nobody knows everything'

Stories give people the feeling that there is a meaning, that there is ultimately an order lurking behind the incredible confusion of appearances and phenomena that surrounds them.

Wim Wenders

No discussion of narrative can be complete without considering the contribution of Roland Barthes. Barthes' major influence on the disciplines of film and cultural studies has been through his work on structuralism. This approach to cultural theory is based around the assumption that there are common underlying structures which offer unity to diverse human cultural activities. Narrative, for Barthes, is just one of many structures that transcend cultural divides:

All classes, all human groups, have their narratives, enjoyment of which is very often shared by men with different, often opposing, cultural backgrounds. Caring nothing for the division between good and bad literature, narrative is international, transhistorical, transcultural: it is simply there, like life itself.

(Barthes 1982: 103)

Perhaps it is because narrative is 'simply there' that it is easy to take it for granted. Yet narrative is an important component in any film, both for controlling the flow of information and determining how an audience will respond to the text.

Barthes' essay, 'Introduction to the structural analysis of narratives', is a complex and demanding piece which focuses on such cultural issues as linguistics. However, the opening of the essay provides a broad overview of the cultural significance of narrative. Read it carefully and consider how it might be applied more specifically to Film Studies.

The narratives of the world are numberless. Narrative is first and foremost a prodigious variety of genres, themselves distributed amongst different substances – as though any material were fit to receive man's stories. Able to be carried by articulated language, spoken or written, fixed or moving images, gestures, and the ordered mixture of all these substances; narrative is present in myth, legend, fable, tale, novella, epic, history, tragedy, drama, comedy, mime, painting (think of Carpaccio's *Saint Ursula*), stained glass windows, cinema, comics, news items, conversation. Moreover, under this almost infinite diversity of forms, narrative is present in every age, in every place, in every society; it begins with the very history of mankind and there nowhere is nor has been a people without narrative. All classes, all human groups, have their narratives, enjoyment of which is very often shared by men with different, even opposing cultural backgrounds. Caring nothing for the division between good and bad literature, narrative is international, transhistorical, transcultural: it is simply there, like life itself.

Must we conclude from this universality that narrative is insignificant? Is it so general that we can have nothing to say about it except for the modest description of a few highly individualized varieties, something literary history occasionally undertakes? But then how are we to master even these varieties, how are we to justify our right to differentiate and identify them? How is novel to be set against novella, tale against myth, drama against tragedy (as has been done a thousand times) without reference to a common model? Such a model is implied by every proposition relating to the most individual, the most historical, of narrative forms. It is thus legitimate that, far from the abandoning of any idea of dealing with narrative on the grounds of its universality, there should have been (from Aristotle on) a periodic interest in narrative form and it is normal that the newly developing structuralism should make this form one of its first concerns – is not structuralism's constant aim to master the infinity of utterances [*paroles*] by describing the 'language' ['*langue*'] of which they are the products and from which they can be generated. Faced with the infinity of narratives, the multiplicity of standpoints – historical, psychological, sociological, ethnological, aesthetic, etc. – from which they can be studied, the analyst finds himself in more or less the same situation as Saussure confronted by the heterogeneity of language [*langage*] and seeking to extract a principle of classification and a central focus for description from the apparent confusion of the individual messages. Keeping simply to modern times, the Russian Formalists,* Propp and Lévi-Strauss have taught us to recognize the following dilemma: either a narrative is merely a rambling collection of events, in which case nothing can be said about it other than by referring back to the storyteller's (the author's) art, talent or genius – all mythical forms of chance – or else it shares with other narratives a common structure which is open to analysis, no matter how much patience its formulation requires. . . .

Where then are we to look for the structures of narrative? Doubtless, in narratives themselves. *Each and every* narrative? Many commentators who accept the idea of a narrative structure are nevertheless unable to resign themselves to dissociating literary analysis from the example of the experimental sciences;

nothing daunted, they ask that a purely inductive method be applied to narrative and that one start by studying all the narratives within a genre, a period, a society. This commonsense view is utopian. Linguistics itself, with only some three thousand languages to embrace, cannot manage such a programme and has wisely turned deductive, a step which in fact marked its veritable constitution as a science and the beginning of its spectacular progress, it even succeeding in anticipating facts prior to their discovery. So what of narrative analysis, faced as it is with millions of narratives? Of necessity, it is condemned to a deductive procedure, obliged first to devise a hypothetical model of description (which American linguists call a 'theory') and then gradually to work down from this model towards the different narrative species which at once conform to and depart from the model. It is only at the level of these conformities and departures that analysis will be able to come back to, but now equipped with a single descriptive tool, the plurality of narratives, to their historical, geographical and cultural diversity.

* A group of literary theorists, active in immediately post-revolutionary Russia, often regarded as the progenitors of structuralism.

(Barthes 1981: 165–166)

The concept of narrative then provides a useful tool with which to explore film texts. Narrative at its simplest level is story-telling and clearly one of the chief reasons for the popularity of film as a media is its ability to tell us stories. At the cinema we welcome the opportunity to suspend our disbelief and engage in the narrative that unfolds on the screen in front of us.

Narrative, however, does more than simply tell us stories. Narrative plays an important role in our wider responses to a film. One of its key impacts is upon the way in which we are positioned to respond to the action that takes place. Again at a very simple level most narratives involve some type of conflict. Typically this conflict is about the battle between good and evil. Generally these opposing forces are represented by characters within the film: the hero or heroine representing good and the villain, the forces of evil. Narrative, therefore, fulfils the important function of positioning us alongside the hero/heroine so that we are invited to see the action through their eyes. There are a number of specifically cinematic devices that can be used to achieve this narrative effect. These include the point-of-view shot where the camera shows us the action from the viewpoint of the hero and the use of voice-over where we are made privy to the thoughts of the main character when we hear them spoken on the soundtrack. In both of these ways the film privileges the hero by allowing him to tell/show the story.

Narrative performs an important ideological function in this way by helping anchor the meaning of the film by directing the audience to specific meanings contained within it. Given this key role, it is hardly surprising that there has been significant discussion about the role and nature of narrative in the cinema. Nor is it surprising that when the surrealist (see Chapter 16) film-maker Luis Buñuel set about attacking the conventions of mainstream film, chief among his targets was narrative. As the critic Michael Wood points out, 'Luis Buñuel's films can be seen as an act of war on the conventional story' and 'The work of Luis Buñuel is among other things a form of war on stories, cycles and meaning.'

So what is the nature of narrative? In the extract that follows, 'Narrative schema', Edward Branigan considers an important aspect of narrative in terms of causal relationships. Narrative structures can be defined by the fact that they are concerned with cause-and-effect relationships. A cause in one part of the narrative will have an effect in another.

ACTIVITY

> ➤ Before you read the extract consider how the idea of cause and effect might be applied to film narratives with which you are familiar. Make a list of examples of causes and effects within these narratives.

In this extract Branigan considers the work of the Bulgarian structuralist Tzvetan Todorov, who argued that narrative structures could be reduced to a basic form in which there was a transformation effected through five stages: equilibrium – disequilibrium – recognition – repair – reinstatement of equilibrium.

Again you might like to consider how some films with which you are familiar can have their narratives reduced to this basic structure.

In a narrative, some person, object, or situation undergoes a particular type of change and this change is measured by a sequence of attributions which apply to the thing at different times. Narrative is a way of experiencing a group of sentences or pictures (or gestures or dance movements, etc.) which together attribute a beginning, middle, and end to something. The beginning, middle, and end are not contained in the discrete elements, say, the individual sentences of a novel but signified in the overall relationships established among the totality of the elements, or sentences. For example, the first sentence of a novel is not itself 'the beginning.' It acquires that status in relationship to certain other sentences. Although being 'physically' first in some particular way may be necessary for a 'beginning,' it is not sufficient since a beginning must also be judged to be a proper part of an ordered sequence or pattern of *other* elements; the elements themselves are *not* the pattern. Narrative is thus a global interpretation of changing data measured through sets of relationships. We must now consider the nature of this overall pattern of relationships.

Tzvetan Todorov argues that narrative in its most basic form is a causal 'transformation' of a situation through five stages:

1 a state of equilibrium at the outset;
2 a disruption of the equilibrium by some action;
3 a recognition that there has been a disruption;
4 an attempt to repair the disruption;
5 a reinstatement of the initial equilibrium.

These changes of state are not random but are produced according to principles of cause and effect (e.g., principles which describe possibility, probability, impossibility, and necessity among the actions that occur). This suggests that there are two fundamental kinds of predication in narrative: *existents*, which assert the existence of something (in the mode of the verb 'to be'), and *processes*, which stipulate a change or process under a causal formula (in the mode of such verbs as 'to go, to do, to happen'). Typical existents are characters and settings while typical processes are actions of persons and forces of nature. But there is more: the changes of state create an *overall pattern* or 'transformation' whereby Todorov's third stage is seen as the 'inverse' of the first and fifth stages, and the fourth stage the 'inverse' of the second (since it attempts to reverse the effects of the disruption). The five stages may be symbolized as follows: A, B, −A, −B, A. This amounts to a large-scale pattern (repetition, antithesis, symmetry, gradation) among the causal relationships and is temporal in a new way; in fact, some theorists refer to such patterns as a 'spatial' form of narrative. This emergent form, or transformation, is a necessary feature of narrative because, as Christian Metz observes, 'A narrative is not a sequence of closed events but a closed sequence of events.'

Consider as an example the following limerick:

> There was a young lady of Niger
> Who smiled as she rode on a tiger.
> They returned from the ride
> With the lady inside
> And the smile on the face of the tiger.

Analyzing the limerick as a narrative using Todorov's transformations, results in the following global structure:

There was [once upon a time]:

A	smile
B	ride
−A	[swallowed: a horrible pleasure?]
−B	return
A	smile

[which goes to show that ...]

The limerick illustrates several important points about Todorov's transformations. First, the structure does not represent directly the actual processing of the narrative by a perceiver but only its conceptual or logical form after it has been interpreted. The reader discovers that the narrative did not begin with 'lady,' or 'youth,' or the place of 'Niger,' as its initial term ('A') because none of those beginnings will yield a macro-description of the required kind. Taking 'smile' as an initial term, however, produces a sequence of transformations that will embrace the limerick as a whole (A, B, −A, −B, A). Nevertheless, this does not yet explain why a reader may smile at the limerick. The humor of the limerick resides in the sudden realization of what must have happened, of what was *omitted* from its proper sequence *in the telling*. The absence of the woman at the end answers to a gap in the chronological structure of the telling of the event. Todorov's middle stage – a 'recognition' of the disruption – already hints that the *actual process* of moving from ignorance to knowledge will be of central importance to our experience of narrative. Not only characters and narrators, but readers are caught up in ways of perceiving and knowing.

Second, Todorov's structure does not represent the entirety of our comprehension of the narrative aspects of the limerick. The reader must supply an epilogue or moral to the story which justifies its being told (which goes to show that …). This involves a rereading and a reassignment of some of the meanings – a process facilitated in the first line by assuming that reference will be partially indeterminate in the manner of a fiction (once there was *a* time …). Eventually the reader must rationalize how he or she might know such an exotic world within his or her preconceptions of an ordinary world.

Finally, although this narrative is arranged to focus attention on what Todorov calls the inversion of the initial equilibrium (the middle cause which is the opposite of smiling, i.e., being swallowed, −A), the logical structure cannot account for all of the inferences that the reader must draw in discovering the nature of the 'inversion' which turns out to have an unexpected literal dimension (ingestion) as well as a number of metaphorical dimensions. What qualifies the inversion *as* an inversion? The reader must make inferences in spite of (and also because of) being misled by the verse. Consider, for instance, the deception of the phrase 'they returned' in line 3; and the fact that the lady's ride is enlarged by the word 'returned' to mean that she had departed on a *trip*, even if only a short trip; and the semantic play with the preposition 'on' and with the definite article of 'the smile': at the end only her smile 'rides on' the tiger and the smile is not hers but a smile of the tiger. The implications of the use of causation and metaphor in the narrative extend at least to the reader's knowledge and beliefs about female sexuality, pleasure, oral gratification, desire, risk and trust; and perhaps also to the consequences of being 'away from the home.' It is far from clear how the logical form of the limerick is able to summon these forms of knowledge. Would a reader, for example, be able to list all possible 'inversions' of a given initial state? Or is there instead a sense in which an inversion must be *discovered* to be appropriate through the operation of processes which are not all 'logical' in the same ways?

Before expanding our idea of narrative form, it may be useful to contrast the above limerick with a poem which is nonnarrative:

> Roses are red
> Violets are blue
> Sugar is sweet
> And so are you.

For reasons to be made clear shortly, I will refer to the structure of this poem as a *catalogue*, not a narrative. For now it is enough to notice that the verb 'to be' has been used four times in an attributive and atemporal sense (as in the extreme case of identity, a 'rose is a rose'). The reader does not interpret the poem as implying one or more temporal adverbial complements, such as, 'Roses are red at noon, violets are blue at two.' No temporal logic connects the redness of roses with the blueness of violets and the sweetness of sugar and 'you.' Instead the reader constructs a pair of categories which have no 'tense': one which contains two flowers, and another which contains both sugar and the reader himself or herself ('you'). The 'causation' at work in the poem – producing the conclusion signaled by 'and so' – is asserted to be as logical, natural, and timeless as grouping roses and violets together as flowers (or, perhaps, as objects having color). The rhyme (blue – you) brings together the two categories and implies that the logic of forming the flower category is as certain as the logic of grouping sugar and 'you.' Thus although both the poem and the limerick compare a person's desirable qualities to something which may be tasted or eaten, the poem is not a narrative because its conceptual structure does not depend on a definite temporal progression which ultimately reveals a global pattern (e.g., A, B, –A, –B, A). Instead the poem is based on forming simple pairs of things with the final intimation – an epilogue of sorts – that 'you,' the reader, and an implicit 'I,' the author, should also form a pair.

I would now like to imagine for a moment something incredible. Suppose that the limerick that tells the story of the woman riding on the tiger contains an interlude where the tiger sings for the woman the poem, 'Roses are red.' In one sense, the narrative has been interrupted by a nonnarrative, catalogue sequence. In another sense, however, there has been no real interruption, for both the narrative limerick and the nonnarrative poem develop a connection between taste and beauty in which the sexual drive is represented as an appetite that devours. Is the limerick-poem then a hybrid? Does the narrative dominate the catalogue, or is the narrative merely an excuse for a clever song? I believe that there is no definitive answer to what it really is. Rather, the answer will depend upon the purpose in asking the question: within what context must an answer be framed, how narrowly must the text be construed, which meanings are most important, and so forth. Recognizing the complexity and dynamism of a text is usually more important than assigning a final, decisive label to it.

Rick Altman has drawn attention to the importance of certain catalogue systems within narrative texts. He speaks of narrative as possessing a 'dual focus' where one focus is composed of a chronological and causal progression (the 'syntagmatic') while the other is composed of a multitude of binary oppositions among elements that are 'static' and that exist outside the time of the causal progression (the 'paradigmatic'). A textual element (shot, scene, aspect of style, character attribute, theme, etc.) that is functioning paradigmatically makes a pair not by calling forth its 'effect' in a linear fashion, but by suggesting a *parallel* with something else, a similarity or contrast. Paradigmatic pairing (or, what I have described as a 'catalogue') creates collections of objects organized according to 'conceptual' principles. Altman finds that in the genre of the American musical film, a special kind of paradigmatic focus, described to show that opposed sets of categories are not mutually exclusive, overwhelms the causal, frame story.

For present purposes, I am less interested in reaching a definitive judgment about the precise nature of a text than in describing the different types of organization that underlie a reader's experience moment by moment. Accordingly, I will construe Altman's notions of 'duality' and 'focus' more narrowly and shift them to a new realm. I will also introduce new terms that divide up the field of study in a somewhat different way, allowing for finer distinctions. As we shall see, the reason for such a shift in terminology is correlated with a change in the object of study: an attempt to specify the formal logic of narrative gives way to an examination of the interaction of narrative with a perceiver – a pragmatics of comprehension.

(Branigan 1992: 4–8)

In their book, *Film Art: An Introduction* (1990), David Bordwell and Kristin Thompson argue that 'we need to take a close look at how films may embody **narrative form**' (p. 54). They point out that we often approach a film with definite expectations about its narrative in terms of character, action and 'a series of incidents that will be connected in some way' (p. 55).

Although the range of possible narratives is limitless, they argue that cinema has been dominated by a single mode of narrative form which they call 'classical Hollywood cinema'. The idea behind this narrative form is 'the assumption that the action will spring primarily from *individual characters as causal agents*' (p. 70). Central to the narrative is conflict. Characters will attempt to realise the goals they seek but will encounter opposition from other characters who may seek to prevent them from doing so.

You may like to make a list of films and their genres in which characters set out with a goal or goals and are thwarted by other characters.

Another quality that Bordwell and Thompson identify as typical of classical Hollywood narrative is a strong sense of closure at the end: 'We learn the fate of each character, the answer to each mystery, and the outcome of each conflict' (p. 71).

Bordwell and Thompson offer an interesting approach to analysing narrative in films. They suggest 'segmenting' it into sequences. These sequences are usually the same as scenes in a film in terms of 'distinct phases of the action'. By undertaking such a segmentation, it allows the film student to see 'how the plot organizes story causality and time' (p. 73).

Here is how they approach the segmenting of Citizen Kane:

CITIZEN KANE'S CAUSALITY

In *Citizen Kane*, two distinct sets of characters cause events to occur. On the one hand, a group of reporters seeks information about Kane; on the other hand, Kane and the characters who know him provide the subject of the reporters' investigations. The initial causal connection between the two groups is Kane's death, which leads the reporters to make a newsreel summing up his career But the newsreel is already finished when the plot introduces the reporters; the boss, Rawlston, supplies the cause that initiates the investigation of Kane's life. Thompson's newsreel fails to satisfy him; Rawlston's desire for 'an angle' for the newsreel gets the search for 'Rosebud' under way. Thompson thus gains a goal, which sets him delving into Kane's past. His investigation constitutes one main line of the plot.

But another line of action, Kane's life, has already taken place in the past. There too a group of characters has caused actions to occur. Many years before, a poverty-stricken boarder at Kane's mother's boardinghouse has paid her with a deed to a silver mine. The wealth provided by this mine causes Mrs. Kane to appoint Thatcher as young Charles's guardian; Thatcher's guardianship results (in somewhat unspecified ways) in Kane's growing up into a spoiled, rebellious young man.

Citizen Kane is an unusual film in that the object of the investigator's search is a set of character traits. Thompson seeks to know what traits in Kane's personality led him to say 'Rosebud' on his deathbed; this 'mystery' motivates Thompson's detectivelike investigation. Kane, a very complex character, has many traits that influence the other character's actions. As we shall see, however, *Citizen Kane's* narrative does not ultimately define all of Kane' character traits.

CITIZEN KANE: PLOT SEGMENTATION

C. Credit title

1. Xanadu: Kane dies

2. Projection room:
   - a. 'News on the March'
   - b. Reporters discuss 'Rosebud'

3. El Rancho nightclub: Thompson tries to interview Susan

4. Thatcher Library;

First flashback
- a. Thompson enters and reads Thatcher's manuscript
- b. Kane's mother sends the boy off with Thatcher
- c. Kane grows up and buys the *Inquirer*
- d. Kane launches the *Inquirer*'s attack on big business
- e. The Depression: Kane sells Thatcher his newspaper chain
- f. Thompson leaves library

5. Bernstein's office:

Second flashback
- a. Thompson visits Bernstein
- b. Kane takes over the *Inquirer*
- c. Montage: the *Inquirer*'s growth
- d. Party: the *Inquirer* celebrates getting the *Chronicle* staff
- e. Leland and Bernstein discuss Kane's trip abroad
- f. Kane returns with his fiancée Emily
- g. Bernstein concludes his reminiscence

6. Nursing home:

Third flashback
- a. Thompson talks with Leland
- b. Breakfast table montage: Kane's marriage deteriorates

Third flashback (cont.)
- c. Leland continues his recollections
- d. Kane meets Susan and goes to her room
- e. Kane's political campaign culminates in his speech
- f. Kane confronts Gettys, Emily, and Susan
- g. Kane loses election and Leland asks to be transferred
- h. Kane marries Susan
- i. Susan's opera premiere
- j. Because Leland is drunk, Kane finishes Leland's review
- k. Leland concludes his reminiscence

7. El Rancho nightclub:

Fourth flashback
- a. Thompson talks with Susan
- b. Susan rehearses her singing
- c. Susan's opera premiere
- d. Kane insists that Susan go on singing
- e. Montage: Susan's opera career

  f. Susan attempts suicide and Kane promises she can quit singing

Fourth flashback (cont.)

  g. Xanadu: Susan bored
  h. Montage: Susan plays with jigsaw puzzles
  i. Xanadu: Kane proposes a picnic
  j. Picnic. Kane slaps Susan
  k. Xanadu: Susan leaves Kane
  l. Susan concludes her reminiscence

8. Xanadu:

  a. Thompson talks with Raymond
  b. Kane destroys Susan's room and picks up paperweight, murmuring 'Rosebud'

Fifth flashback

  c. Raymond concludes his reminiscence; Thompson talks with the other reporters; all leave
  d. Survey of Kane's possessions leads to a revelation of Rosebud; exterior of gate and of castle; the end

E. End Credits

Kane himself has a goal; he too seems to be searching for something related to 'Rosebud.' At several points characters speculate that Rosebud was something that Kane lost or never was able to get. Again, the fact that Kane's goal remains so vague makes this an unusual narrative.

Other characters in Kane's life provide causal material for the narrative. The presence of several characters who knew Kane well makes Thompson's investigation possible, even though Kane himself has died. Significantly, the characters provide a range of information that spans Kane's entire life. This is important if we are to be able to reconstruct the progression of story events in the film. Thatcher knew Kane as a child; Bernstein, his manager, knew his business dealings; his best friend, Leland, knew of his personal life (his first marriage in particular); Susan Alexander, his second wife, knew him in middle age; and the butler, Raymond, managed Kane's affairs during his last years. Each of these characters has a causal role in Kane's life, as well as in Thompson's investigation. Note that Kane's wife, Emily, does not tell a story, since Emily's story would simply duplicate Leland's and would contribute no additional information to the 'present-day' part of the narrative, the investigation; hence the plot simply eliminates her (via a car accident).

(Bordwell and Thompson 1990: 73–75)

Narrative in film is very often character driven. As you will have seen earlier in this section, characters have an important causal function in driving forward a narrative. Characters in films do, however, often conform to specific types. For example, we associate certain character types with specific genres and sub-genres. This grouping of similar characters is called *character typology* and it provides an interesting dimension to any discussion of narrative not least because so much of the narrative that we encounter in film is driven by character.

In the extract that follows, Robert Murphy looks at a character common in British cinema of the 1950s, The Spiv.

The Spiv was a product of the post-war economy in Britain. The Second World War had led to a world shortage of food and raw materials, and rationing was introduced to try to share out fairly what was available. In this climate, the spivs thrived as they were able to get hold of scarce items, such as nylon stockings, and sell them on the black market.

THE RISE OF THE SPIV

The idea of using a working-class setting which included members of the underworld, introduced in *The Bells Go Down*, was more fully developed in *Waterloo Road*. It was originally intended as a portmanteau film with six stories set in the Waterloo area, but Gilliat decided to concentrate on the one which interested him most, that of a soldier, Jim Colter (John Mills), who goes AWOL to check on his wife's fidelity. It was a common enough problem, with barely consummated marriages having to withstand the strain of prolonged separation and the temptations of new relationships. The threat to the Colter marriage comes not from a glamorous GI or an amorous factory foreman but from a small-time gangster, Ted Purvis (Stewart Granger). He is undoubtedly a no-good wastrel but he is able to offer Tilly Colter (Joy Shelton) a good time. As a cynical ex-girlfriend tells the vengeful husband:

> 'Okay, now let's see. Ted might have taken her to the dogs, only there's no dogs today, he might be at the pictures picking up a few 'ints from Victor Mature, or he might be at the Alcazar, jitterbugging. I think that about covers his war effort.'

The reviewers call him 'the local pin table king, racketeer and bully', 'an amorous artful dodger', 'the local bad lot', but with his flash suit, his loud tie, his easy money, and his dangerous charm he is easily recognized as the screen's first spiv.

David Hughes does his best to provide a definition of this peculiar forties phenomenon:

> A spiv, it was agreed, was a relentless opportunist who earned his living by not working, preferably within the law. In fact they were not averse to a touch of crime, provided it looked (and perhaps felt) like something

else, just as they didn't mind driving lorries as long as their clothing vividly proclaimed that they weren't lorry-drivers. They never planned their opportunities, as criminals did; they merely took them, snatched and improvised, inventing as they went along.

In its original sense of a 'contact man', the spiv was as much a specialist as a peterman (safebreaker) or a buyer (receiver), but during the war the spiv became a sort of popular generic term for someone who dressed flashily and had underworld connections. Thus it was used to describe anyone from a barrow-boy to a gang-leader. The style of dress came from the more fashion-conscious of the racing gangsters of the thirties – a sizeable contingent of whom were Jewish or Italian with friends or relations in the rag trade.

The pre-war underworld was almost a separate caste: they spoke a language so riddled with argot and rhyming slang that it was virtually impossible for an outsider to comprehend. Spivs were generally tactful, unobtrusive characters who through judicious lounging, gossiping, and gambling acquired a comprehensive knowledge of who was who and what was what, and operated as intermediaries between various members of the underworld. The war caused something of a dilution of this criminal subculture as large numbers of amateurs – deserters and petty racketeers – swelled the ranks of the underworld. More important, the black market transformed the links between the public and the criminal world and required a different sort of contact man – a recognizable type who could be approached in the same way that a prostitute was approached – with a certain confidence that illicit requests would not be rejected.

The wartime black market was much bigger than was officially admitted, but it was a secretive, disreputable affair. When the war ended people expected conditions to improve, an end to shortages and restrictions, the beginning of the good life for which they had fought. Austerity meant more rather than less restrictions and shortages, and for many members of the respectable classes this was too much to take. The spiv, as the representative of the black market, became something of a popular hero, celebrated in the music-hall sketches of Arthur English and Sid Field, in the cartoons of Osbert Lancaster, in the gossip column of Arthur Helliwell in the *People*, and in a cycle of feature films.

David Hughes sees the spiv as a manifestation of working-class spontaneity:

> They were, more than trade union leaders, more than the politicians, the voice of the working class – busy undermining (oh, the irony) the future of their own people. The spivs, flashily displaying all the suppressed energies of the back streets, were an unconscious, dramatic protest, a form of civil disobedience that millions of English people found endearing.

The seeming moderation of the post-war Labour government and its defeat in the 1951 Election has tended to obscure its quite remarkable achievements in steering the country away from economic disaster and, despite vociferous media hostility, retaining a high level of popular support. Richard Acland, the founder of the Common Wealth party, standing as a Labour candidate in a marginal by-election in Gravesend in 1947, won decisively with a slogan 'Tough Times: So What?'; and the 1951 Elections were very closely fought.

It is easy to glamorize the black market – to see it as a healthy protest against bureaucratic strangulation – but there was a very seedy side to it. Arthur Helliwell, whose close contact with the underworld brought progressive disillusion, declared that Britain had become 'the land of the well-greased palm':

> We've developed into a nation of bribers. Everyone is on the game, from the big shot who buys the motor dealer's wife a fur coat and gets delivery of a new car in a week, to the housewife who slips the fishmonger a packet of cigarettes after the queue has gone. The butcher runs a car, but he can't get much petrol – slip him a couple of coupons and get an extra steak for yourself. The coal merchant can't get eggs – send him a couple of dozen and there's a ton of coal in your cellar. A page of clothing coupons to your tobacconist – and there'll always be a pack of twenty under the counter for you.

The pre-war underworld had been concerned either with semi-legal activities such as gambling, drugs, and prostitution, or with the traditional criminal pursuit of robbing the rich. It was not until the war years, with the growth of commodity crime and the black market, that the underworld became parasitic on the community at large. Except for a small minority of working-class people who participated in its profits, the black market inevitably benefited the rich more than the poor by subverting a rationing system designed to ensure equal shares for all. It is in this context that one has to understand the hostility of film critics – who like most intellectuals of the period were vaguely left-of-centre – to the cycle of spiv movies which flourished between 1945 and 1950.

(Murphy 1989: 145–147)

In the introduction we suggested that a film-maker's own words are often of much more value than several volumes of academic writing. We conclude this chapter with the words of Wim Wenders, director of such films as *Paris, Texas*, on narrative technique:

Where French and German each have a single word for it, English has only a two-part phrase: 'to tell stories'. That hints at my difficulty: the man you've invited to talk to you about telling stories is a man who over the years has had nothing but problems with stories.

Let me go back to the very beginning. Once I was a painter. What interested me was space; I painted cityscapes and landscapes. I became a film-maker when I realized that I wasn't getting anywhere as a painter. Painting lacked something, as did my individual paintings. It would have been too easy to say that they lacked life; I thought that what was missing was an understanding of time. So when I began filming, I thought of myself as a painter of space engaged on a quest for time. It never occurred to me that this search should be called 'storytelling'. I must have been very naïve. I thought filming was simple. I thought you only had to see something to be able to depict it, and I also thought a storyteller (and of course I wasn't one) had to listen first and speak afterwards. Making a film to me meant connecting all these things. That was a misconception, but before I straighten it out, there is something else I must talk about.

My stories all begin from pictures. When I started making my first film, I wanted to make 'landscape portraits'. My very first film, *Silver City*, contained ten shots of three minutes each; that was the length of a reel of 16 mm film. Each shot was of a cityscape. I didn't move the camera; nothing happened. The shots were like the paintings and watercolours I'd done previously, only in a different medium. However, there was one shot that was different: it was of an empty landscape with railway tracks; the camera was placed very close to these. I knew the train schedule. I began filming two minutes before one was due, and everything seemed to be exactly as it had been in all the other shots: a deserted scene. Except that two minutes later someone ran into shot from the right, jumped over the tracks just a couple of yards in front of the camera, and ran out of the left edge of the frame. The moment he disappeared, even more surprisingly, the train thundered into the picture, also from the right. (It couldn't be heard approaching, because there was no sync. sound, only music.) This tiny 'action' – man crosses tracks ahead of train – signals the beginning of a 'story'. What is wrong with the man? Is he being followed? Does he want to kill himself? Why is he in such a hurry? Etc., etc. I think it was from that moment that I became a storyteller. And from that moment all my difficulties began too, because it was the first time that something had happened in a scene I had set up.

After that, the problems came thick and fast. When I was cutting together the ten shots, I realized that after the shot where the man crosses the tracks hell for leather there would be the expectation that every subsequent shot would contain some action. So for the first time I had to consider the order of the shots, some kind of dramaturgy. My original idea, simply to run a series of fixed-frame shots, one after another, 'unconnected' and in no special order, became impossible. The assembling of scenes and their arrangement in an order was, it seemed already, a first step towards narrative. People would see entirely fanciful connections between scenes and interpret them as having narrative intentions. But that wasn't what I wanted. I was only combining time and space; but from that moment on, I was pressed into telling stories. From then on and until the present moment, I have felt an opposition between images and stories. A mutual incompatibility, a mutual undermining. I have always been more interested in pictures, and the fact that – as soon as you assemble them – they seem to want to tell a story, is still a problem for me today.

My stories start with places, cities, landscapes and roads. A map is like a screenplay to me. When I look at a road, for example, I begin to ask myself what kind of thing might happen on it; similarly with a building, like my own hotel room here in Livorno: I look out of the window, it's raining hard and a car stops in front of the hotel. A man gets out of it and looks around. Then he starts walking down the road, without an umbrella, in spite of the rain. My head starts working on a story right away, because I want to know where he's going, what kind of street he might be turning into.

Of course stories can also begin in other ways. Recently the following happened to me: I'm sitting alone in a hotel lobby, waiting to be collected by someone I don't know. A woman comes in, looking for someone *she* doesn't know. She comes up to me and asks: 'Excuse me, are you Mr So-and-so?' And I very nearly say 'Yes!' Just because I'm fascinated by the thought of experiencing the beginning of a story or a film. So it's possible that a story can be sparked off by a moment of drama, but usually it begins in contemplation, when I'm looking at landscapes, houses, roads and pictures.

For a writer, a story seems to be the logical end-product: words want to form sentences, and the sentences want to stand in some continuous discourse; a writer doesn't have to force the words into a sentence or the sentences into a story. There seems to be a kind of inevitability in the way stories come to be told. In films – or at least in my films, because of course there are other ways of going about it – in films the images don't necessarily lead to anything else; they stand on their own. I think a picture stands on its own more readily, whereas a word tends to seek the context of a story. For me, images don't automatically lend themselves to be part of a story. If they're to function in the way that words and sentences do, they have to be 'forced' – that is, I have to manipulate them.

My thesis is that for me as a film-maker, narrative involves forcing the images in some way. Sometimes this manipulation becomes narrative art, but not necessarily. Often enough, the result is only abused pictures.

I dislike the manipulation that's necessary to press all the images of a film into one story; it's very harmful for the images because it tends to drain them of their 'life'. In the relationship between story and image, I see the story as a kind of vampire, trying to suck all the blood from an image. Images are acutely sensitive; like snails they shrink back when you touch their horns. They don't have it in them to be carthorses: carrying and transporting messages or significance or intention or a moral. But that's precisely what a story wants from them.

So far everything seems to have spoken out against story, as though it were the enemy. But of course stories are very exciting; they are powerful and important for mankind. They give people what they want, on a very profound level – more than merely amusement or entertainment or suspense. People's primary requirement is that some kind of coherence be provided. Stories give people the feeling that there is meaning, that there is ultimately an order lurking behind the incredible confusion of appearances and phenomena that surrounds them. This order is what people require more than anything else; yes, I would almost say that the notion of order or story is connected with the godhead. Stories are substitutes for God. Or maybe the other way round.

For myself – and hence my problems with story – I incline to believe in chaos, in the inexplicable complexity of the events around me. Basically, I think that individual situations are unrelated to each other, and my experience seems to consist entirely of individual situations; I've never yet been involved in a story with a beginning, middle and end. For someone who tells stories this is positively sinful, but I must confess that I have yet to experience a story. I think stories are actually lies. But they are incredibly important to our survival. Their artificial structure helps us to overcome our worst fears: that there is no God; that we are nothing but tiny fluctuating particles with perception and consciousness, but lost in a universe that remains altogether beyond our conception. By producing coherence, stories make life bearable and combat fears. That's why children like to hear stories at bedtime. That's why the Bible is one long storybook, and why stories should always end happily.

Of course the stories in my films also work as a means of ordering the images. Without stories, the images that interest me would threaten to lose themselves and seem purely arbitrary.

For this reason, film-stories are like routes. A map is the most exciting thing in the world for me; when I see a map, I immediately feel restless, especially when it's of a country or city where I've never been. I look at all the names and I want to know the things they refer to, the cities of a country, the streets of a city. When I look at a map, it turns into an allegory for the whole of life. The only thing that makes it bearable is to try to mark out a route, and follow it through the city or country. Stories do just that: they become your roads in a strange land, where but for them, you might go to thousands of places without ever arriving anywhere.

What are the stories that are told in my films? There are two sorts; I draw a sharp distinction between them, because they exist in two completely separate systems or traditions. Furthermore, there is a continual alternation between the two categories of film, with a single exception, *The Scarlet Letter*, and that was a mistake.

In the first group (A) all the films are in black and white, except for *Nick's Film*, which belongs to neither tradition. (I'm not even sure that it counts as a film at all, so let's leave that one out.) In the other group (B) all the films are in colour, and they are all based on published novels. The films in group A, on the other hand, are based without exception on ideas of mine – the word 'idea' is used loosely to refer to dreams, daydreams and experiences of all kinds. All the A-films were more or less unscripted, whereas the others followed scripts very closely. The A-films are loosely structured, whereas the B-films are all tightly structured. The A-films were all shot in chronological sequence, beginning from an initial situation that was often the only known point in them; the B-films were shot in the traditional hopping-around way, and with an eye to the exigencies of a production team. With group A films, I never knew how they would finish; I knew the endings of B-films before I started.

Basically all the group A films operate in a very open system, the B-films in a very closed one. Both represent not only systems but also attitudes: openness on the one hand, discipline on the other. The themes of the A-films were identified only during shooting. The themes of the B-films were known; it was just a matter of deciding which bits should go in. The A-films were made from the inside, working out; the B-films the opposite. For the A-films a story had to be found; for the B-films the story had to be lost sight of.

The fact that – with the exception of the already-mentioned mistake – there has been a constant pendulum swing between A- and B-films shows that each film is a reaction to its predecessor, which is exactly my dilemma.

I made each of my A-films because the film before had had too many rules, hadn't been sufficiently spontaneous, and I'd got bored with the characters; also I felt that I had to 'expose' myself and the crew and the actors to a new situation. With the B-films it was exactly the other way round: I made them because I was unhappy that the film before had been so 'subjective', and because I needed to work within a firm structure, using the framework of a story. Actors in the B-films played parts 'other' than themselves, represented fictional characters; in the A-films they interpreted and depicted themselves, they *were* themselves. In these films I saw my task as bringing in as much as possible of what (already) existed. For the B-films, things had to be invented. It because ever clearer that one group could be called 'subjective' and the other 'search for objectivity'. Though, of course, it wasn't quite so simple.

In what follows I will talk about how the A-films began, and the role that story played in them. My first film was called *Summer in the City*; it's about a man who's spent a couple of years in prison. The first frame shows him emerging from prison and suddenly confronting life again. He tries to see his old friends and get into his old relationships, but he quickly realizes that nothing can be the way it was before. In the end he takes off and emigrates to America. The second film in the A-group, *Alice in the Cities*, is about a man who's supposed to be writing a feature about America. He can't do it, and the film begins with his decision to return to Europe. He happens to meet a little girl, Alice, and her mother, and promises to take her back to her grandmother in Europe. Only he doesn't know where she lives; all he has is a photograph of the house. The remainder of the film is taken up by the search for the house.

A man tries to kill himself – that's how *Kings of the Road* starts. By chance, there's another man watching, so he gives up his kamikaze behaviour. The other man is a truck-driver. They decide to travel together – pure chance, again. The film is about their journey and whether the two have anything to say to each other or not.

The last of the A-films, *The State of Things*, is about a film crew who have to stop working because the money's run out and the producer's vanished. The crew don't know whether they'll be able to finish the shoot or not. The film is about a group of people who've lost their way, particularly the director, who in the end goes to Hollywood to look for the producer.

All these films are about people who encounter unfamiliar situations on the road; all of them are to do with seeing and perception, about people who suddenly have to take a different view of things.

To be as specific about this as I can, I'd like to go back to *Kings of the Road*. How did that come about? One answer would be: because I'd just finished *False Movement* – it was a reaction to that previous work. I felt that I had to devise a story in which I could investigate myself and my country – Germany (the subject of my previous film too, though treated in a different way). This time it was to be a trip to an unknown country, to an unknown country in myself, and in the middle of Germany. I knew what I wanted but I didn't know how to begin. Then everything was set off by an image.

I was overtaking a truck on the Autobahn; it was very hot and it was an old lorry without air-conditioning. There were two men in the cab, and the driver had opened the door and was dangling his leg out in order to cool off. This image, seen from the corner of my eye when driving past, impressed me. I happened to stop at a motorway cafe where the lorry also stopped. I went up to the bar where the two men from the lorry were standing. Not a word passed between them; it was as though they had absolutely nothing in common. You got the impression they were strangers. I asked myself what do these two men see, how do they see, as they drive across Germany?

At that time I was doing quite a lot of travelling around Germany with my previous film, *False Movement*. During my travels I became aware of the situation of the rural cinema. The halls, the projection booths and the projectionists all fascinated me. Then I looked at a map of Germany and I realized there was one route down through it that I barely knew. It ran along the border between the GDR and the FRG; not only down the middle of Germany, but also along the very edge. And I suddenly realized that I had everything I needed for my new film: a route and the story of two men who don't know each other. I was interested to see what might happen to them, and between them. One of them would have a job that was something to do with the cinema, and I knew where the cinemas were to be found: along the border.

Of course that's not enough to make a story. All the films in the A-group started off with a few situations that I hoped might develop into a story. To assist that development, I followed the method of 'daydreaming'. Story always assumes control, it knows its course, it knows what matters, it knows where it begins and ends. Daydream is quite different; it doesn't have that 'dramaturgical' control. What it has is a kind of subconscious guide who wants to get on, no matter where; every dream is going somewhere, but who can say where that is? Something in the subconscious knows, but you can only discover it if you let it take its course, and that's what I attempted in all these films. The English word 'drifting' expresses it very well. Not the shortest line between two points, but a zigzag. Perhaps a better word would be 'meander', because that has the idea of distance in it as well.

A journey is an adventure in space and time. Adventure, space and time – all three are involved. Stories and journeys have them in common. A journey is always accompanied by curiosity about the unknown; it creates expectation and intensity of perception: you see things on the road that you never would at home. To get back to *Kings of the Road*: after ten weeks' filming we were still only halfway through, though I'd aimed to finish the film in that time. There was no money to go on filming, and we were still a long way short of an ending. The problem was: how should the journey end? Or: how might it be converted into a story? At first I thought of an accident. If it had been shot in America, it would certainly have finished with an accident. But thank God we weren't in America; we were free to do otherwise and get to the 'truth of our story'. So we broke off the filming and I tried to raise money for another five weeks' shooting. Of course a film of that type can be literally neverending, and that's a danger. The solution, finally, turned out to be that the men would have to realize they couldn't go on like that; a break had to come and they would have to change their lives.

But before that I had another idea, another 'bend' in the meander: the two protagonists look for their parents. I thought that might lead them to break off their relationship. So we filmed a long story about the first of them, how he visits his father, and then another long story about the second returning to the place where he grew up with his mother. Unfortunately, though, that only improved their relationship and left us even further from an ending than we were before. Suddenly, and for the first time, the two were able to speak to each other. We broke off the filming a second time. I thought the film might end with them both questioning what they had done before their relationship, and reconsidering their aims in life. The one travelling from cinema to cinema wonders whether there was any sense in keeping these places going, and the other goes back to his work as a paediatrician and speech therapist. In the end, that was how we shot. It.

The State of Things is also about stories. Of course the director figure represents my own dilemma, to a certain extent; at one stage he actually says: 'Life and stories are mutually incompatible.' That's his theory as a director. Later on, though, when he goes back to Hollywood, he himself becomes embroiled in a story, in one of those stories he never believed in, and in the end it kills him. Paradoxical, of course. And that's really the only thing I have to say about stories: they are one huge, impossible paradox! I totally reject stories, because for me they only bring out lies, nothing but lies, and the biggest lie is that they show coherence where there is none. Then again, our need for these lies is so consuming that it's completely pointless to fight them and to put together a sequence of images without a story – without the lie of a story. Stories are impossible, but it's impossible to live without them.

That's the mess I'm in.

(Wenders 1988: 51–59)

▼ 4 CANON

Art is not the application of a canon of beauty but what the instinct and the brain can conceive beyond any canon. When we love a woman we don't start measuring her.

Pablo Picasso

Have you noticed the size of *Haliwell's Film and Video Guide* recently? As more and more films are produced, it is becoming increasingly unwieldy and is fast outgrowing the regular-sized bookshelf space it used to occupy. In fact, for the 2001 edition, editor John Walker (2000: vi) began omitting titles, which was 'inevitable, since the guide cannot get any bigger'. Despite this pruning, the guide still carries in excess of an incredible 23,000 film reviews, which – when you consider the guide's obvious bias towards Western features with theatrical release – is just a fraction of the tremendous number of films our planet has produced in the 111 years since its first: *Sortie d'Usine* (Lumiere 1895).

No person could possibly watch all these films in a lifetime, and nor would they want to; the vast majority are derivative, dull and dated. This is partly why we must have a system that preserves titles in the public and academic consciousness; a loosely agreed-upon set of films that highlights the great and creates reference points enabling both consensus and a continuing debate. This list of films is known as the 'canon'. It should not be seen as official however; the canon does not exist in a tangible concrete form. The canon is malleable, ever-changing and updated as films drift in and out of relevance and popularity. The canon's boundaries expand and contract as it adjusts its catchment for the task required; a handful of core films are consistently rewarded with inclusion; others are more open to dispute.

In compiling the constituents of their *Key Film Texts* (2002), Graham Roberts and Heather Wallis consult the canon as a starting point, and at the same time feed and augment the list with the films they personally decide to include, many of which will be familiar to you in name at least:

1 *Intolerance*
2 *Nosferatu: A Symphony of Horror*
3 *Battleship Potemkin*
4 *The Gold Rush*
5 *Metropolis*
6 *The Man with the Movie Camera*
7 *Olympia*
8 *Bringing up Baby*
9 *Stagecoach*
10 *Citizen Kane*

Before attempting readings of each title, Roberts and Wallis further detail the notion of a canon and explain how they arrived at their own.

KEYS AND CANONS

When we first put together the idea for writing this book we were confronted with the tricky 'canon' question. Were we in fact – in a rather unfashionable non-postmodern way – trying to produce a canon?

Well ... yes!

'The canon' was a term originally used to describe a list of books accepted by the Catholic Church. Later it came to mean a list of recognised, genuine works by a particular author. More recently, it has become a vaguely defined but frequently cited list of works that 'everyone' agrees that everyone else should know – e.g. the literary canon.

How does a canon of films emerge?

Functionally, it is often really useful to have an agreed group of films that everyone else will 'take as read', a common reference point. If you are discussing popular music, it is reasonable to assume that everyone has heard – or ought to have heard – of the Beatles. You cannot start from scratch every time.

But, the canon is self-perpetuating. Good films get left out and bad films are kept in. We study a film because it is a film we study (and because it influenced other films we study).

Pragmatically, we need to impose order on a disparate field of study. You cannot study every film. You can sort them into sets, even 'Milestones and Monuments' (as Ernst Gombrich put it when discussing the visual arts).

The big questions remain. Who decides what goes into the canon? How does a text become canonical? What else can we do? If the idea of the canon is flawed, do we give up and stop studying cinema? If we cannot make perfect choices, do we make none at all?

Between 1915 and 1960 in excess of 20000 feature films were produced in the USA alone. Some of these films are frequently chosen for discussion and analysis; most others are ignored. Some films are frequently cited as examples. Some films are held to be influential, historical or even just spectacularly typical – whilst most are forgotten. It is not just academics and critics: film-makers themselves help form the canon by remaking 'classic' films, by alluding to them, even parodying them. You cannot parody a film that the audience has never heard of. By parodying it you in fact reinforce a film's importance.

The final reason for canonical activity is evaluative (and therefore selective). Someone decides which is best. What are the criteria? What values do we use to decide? Who gets to make the decisions? The reader is entitled to ask how *we* chose the films for this book.

CONTINUED

We have chosen films that everyone who claims to know anything about the history and the theory of cinema will be expected to know (by other people who *do* know something about the history and theory of cinema). It is not a perfect selection, but we all have to start somewhere. Even people who oppose the canon will still expect you to have the basic film knowledge that includes these films. It is a grounding, a common pool of references in which we can base our investigations into cinema. Secondly, it is important to know the films that have been influential – films that have clearly influenced the films that contemporary film-makers are making today.

We have tried to keep this volume focused on its introductory remit and make it reasonably representative – for example, only one or two films per director, apart from Hitchcock, and at least the beginnings of an attempt at a geographical spread.

On a practical level, we have tried to discuss only films that are readily available on video/DVD. Thus there are only a couple of women directors represented but plenty of stars. There are few non-Western films, although we have tried to illustrate the influence of international cinema even on the Hollywood hegemony.

For justifiable yet deeply regretted omissions we send our heartfelt apologies to: the Lumière Brothers and George Méliès along with many other notable omissions including Rainer Werner Fassbinder, Abel Gance, King Vidor, William Hanna and Joseph Barbera.

The films discussed in this volume are also very good films. They were made to be enjoyed (not always as pure entertainment but certainly to engage the viewer). We who 'study' film sometimes forget to enjoy. Don't let that happen to you!

(Roberts and Wallis 2002: 1–2)

Popular canons are somewhat different to the academic, and some of your relatives may be surprised to discover that your 'study' of film has little time for populist 'classics' such as *The Great Escape, Paint Your Wagon, The Italian Job, The Usual Suspects* and so on. *Sight and Sound*'s ten-yearly 'greatest' poll is a far better indicator of the specific films you will probably encounter. The following are the results of every poll since 1952.

SIGHT AND SOUND TOP 10 POLLS

1952
Bicycle Thieves
City Lights
The Gold Rush
Battleship Potemkin
Intolerance
Louisiana Story
Greed
Le Jour se lève
The Passion of Joan of Arc
Brief Encounter
Le Million
La Règle du jeu

1962
Citizen Kane
L'avventura
La Règle du jeu
Greed
Ugetsu Monogatari
Battleship Potemkin
Bicycle Thieves
Ivan the Terrible
La terra trema
L'Atalante

1972
Citizen Kane
La Règle du jeu
Battleship Potemkin
8½
L'avventura
Persona
The Passion of Joan of Arc
The General
The Magnificent Ambersons
Ugetsu Monogatari
Wild Strawberries

1982
Citizen Kane
La Règle du jeu
Seven Samurai
Singin' in the Rain
8½
Battleship Potemkin
L'avventura
The Magnificent Ambersons
Vertigo
The General
The Searchers

1992
Citizen Kane
La Règle du jeu
Tokyo Story
Vertigo
The Searchers
L'Atalante
The Passion of Joan of Arc
Pather Panchali
Battleship Potemkin
2001: A Space Odyssey

1992 (directors' choice)
Citizen Kane
Raging Bull
8½
La strada
L'Atalante
Modern Times
The Godfather
Vertigo
Seven Samurai
The Passion of Joan of Arc
The Godfather Part II
Rashomon

SIGHT AND SOUND DIRECTORS' TOP TEN POLL 2002

1 Citizen Kane (Welles)

Dazzlingly inventive, technically breathtaking, Citizen Kane reinvented the way stories could be told in the cinema, and set a standard generations of film-makers have since aspired to. An absorbing account of a newspaper tycoon's rise to power, Orson Welles' debut film feels as fresh as tomorrow's headlines. And he was only 26 when he made it. **Who voted for Citizen Kane?**

2 The Godfather and **The Godfather part II** (Coppola)

Few films have portrayed the US immigrant experience quite so vividly as Coppola's Godfather films, or exposed the contradictions of the American Dream quite so ruthlessly. And what a cast, formidable talent firing all cylinders: Brando, De Niro, Pacino, Keaton, Duvall, Caan. Now that is an offer you can't refuse. **Who voted for The Godfather?**

3 8½ (Fellini)

Wonderfully freefloating, gleefully confusing reality and fantasy, 8½ provides a ringside seat into the ever active imaginative life of its director protagonist Guido, played by Fellini's on-screen alter-ego Marcello Mastroianni. The definitive film about film-making – as much about the agonies of the creative process as the ecstasies – it's no wonder the movie is so popular with directors. **Who voted for 8½?**

4 Lawrence of Arabia (Lean)

Filmed in the desert in lavish widescreen and rich colours, Lawrence of Arabia is David Lean at his most epic and expansive. You can almost feel the waves of heat glowing from the cinema screen. **Who voted for Lawrence of Arabia?**

5 Dr. Strangelove (Kubrick)

A black comedy about impending nuclear annihilation that was made at the height of the cold war, Dr. Strangelove is perhaps Kubrick's most audacious movie and certainly his funniest. Peter Sellers has never been better, and provides good value playing three roles. **Who voted for Dr Strangelove?**

6 Bicycle Thieves (De Sica)

Mixing melodrama, documentary and social commentary, De Sica follows an impoverished father and son treading the streets of post-war Rome, desperately seeking their stolen bicycle. Deeply compassionate, this poignant film is one of the outstanding examples of Italian neorealism. **Who voted for Bicycle Thieves?**

6 Raging Bull (Scorsese)

An unblinkingly honest biopic of Jake La Motta – a great prizefighter but a deeply flawed human being – this catches Scorsese in fighting fit form. The boxing sequences are both brutal and beautiful, and De Niro, who famously put on weight to play the middle-aged La Motta, gives one of *the* performances of modern cinema. **Who voted for Raging Bull?**

6 Vertigo (Hitchcock)

A gripping detective story or a delirious investigation into desire, grief and jealousy? Hitchcock had a genius for transforming genre pieces into vehicles for his own dark obsessions, and this 1958 masterpiece shows the director at his mesmerising best. And for James Stewart fans, it also boasts the star's most compelling performance. **Who voted for Vertigo?**

9 Rashomon (Kurosawa)

Offering four different accounts of a rape and murder, all told in flashbacks, Kurosawa's 1951 film is a complex meditation on the distortive nature of memory and a gripping study of human behaviour at its most base. Mifune Toshiro is magnetic as the bandit Tajomaru. **Who voted for Rashomon?**

9 La Règle du jeu (Renoir)

Tragedy and comedy effortlessly combine in Renoir's country house ensemble drama. A group of aristocrats gather for some rural relaxation, a shooting party is arranged, downstairs the servants bicker about a new employee, while all the time husbands, wives, mistresses and lovers sweetly deceive one another and swap declarations of love like name cards at a dinner party. **Who voted for La Règle du jeu?**

9 Seven Samurai (Kurosawa)

The blueprint for The Magnificent Seven was Kurosawa's magnificent swordplay epic of self-sacrifice about a band of hired samurai who come together to protect a helpless village from a rapacious gang of 40 thieves who descend every year to steal the harvest and kidnap the women. The final sequence of the fight in the mud and rain has never been bettered. **Who voted for Seven Samurai?**

SIGHT AND SOUND CRITICS' TOP TEN POLL 2002

1 Citizen Kane (Welles)

Dazzlingly inventive, technically breathtaking, Citizen Kane reinvented the way stories could be told in the cinema, and set a standard generations of film-makers have since aspired to. An absorbing account of a newspaper tycoon's rise to power, Orson Welles' debut film feels as fresh as tomorrow's headlines. And he was only 26 when he made it. **Who voted for Citizen Kane?**

2 Vertigo (Hitchcock)

A gripping detective story or a delirious investigation into desire, grief and jealousy? Hitchcock had a genius for transforming genre pieces into vehicles for his own dark obsessions, and this 1958 masterpiece shows the director at his mesmerising best. And for James Stewart fans, it also boasts the star's most compelling performance. **Who voted for Vertigo?**

3 La Règle du jeu (Renoir)

Tragedy and comedy effortlessly combine in Renoir's country house ensemble drama. A group of aristocrats gather for some rural relaxation, a shooting party is arranged, downstairs the servants bicker about a new employee, while all the time husbands, wives, mistresses and lovers sweetly deceive one another and swap declarations of love like name cards at a dinner party. **Who voted for La Règle du jeu?**

4 The Godfather and **The Godfather part II** (Coppola)

Few films have portrayed the US immigrant experience quite so vividly as Coppola's Godfather films, or exposed the contradictions of the American Dream quite so ruthlessly. And what a cast, formidable talent firing all cylinders: Brando, De Niro, Pacino, Keaton, Duvall, Caan. Now that is an offer you can't refuse. **Who voted for The Godfather?**

5 Tokyo Story (Ozu)

A poignant story of family relations and loss, Ozu's subtle mood piece portrays the trip an elderly couple make to Tokyo to visit their grown-up children. The shooting style is elegantly minimal and formally reticent, and the film's devastating emotional impact is drawn as much from what is unsaid and unshown as from what is revealed. **Who voted for Tokyo Story?**

6 2001: A Space Odyssey (Kubrick)

One of the most ambitious Hollywood movies ever made, 2001 crams into its two-hour plus running time a story that spans the prehistoric age to the beginning of the third millennium, and features some of the most hypnotically beautiful special effects work ever committed to film. After seeing this, you can never listen to Strauss' Blue Danube without thinking space crafts waltzing against starry backdrops. **Who voted for 2001?**

7 Battleship Potemkin (Eisenstein)

Eisenstein's recreation of a mutiny by sailors of the battleship Potemkin in 1905 works as daring formal experiment – which pushed the expressive potential of film editing to its limit – and rousing propaganda for the masses. The Odessa Steps sequence remains one of the most memorable set-pieces in cinema. **Who voted for Battleship Potemkin?**

7 Sunrise (Murnau) More about Sunrise

Having left his native Germany for the US, F.W. Murnau had all the resources of a major Hollywood studio at his disposal for this, his American debut. What he produced was a visually stunning film romance that ranks as one of the last hurrahs of the silent period. **Who voted for Sunrise?**

9 8½ (Fellini)

Wonderfully freefloating, gleefully confusing reality and fantasy, 8½ provides a ringside seat into the ever active imaginative life of its director protagonist Guido, played by Fellini's on-screen alter-ego Marcello Mastroianni. The definitive film about film-making – as much about the agonies of the creative process as the ecstasies – it's no wonder the movie is so popular with directors. **Who voted for 8½?**

10 Singin' In the Rain (Kelly, Donen)

Impossible to watch without a smile on your face, this affectionate tribute to the glory days of Hollywood in the 1920s is pleasure distilled into 102 minutes. With Gene Kelly dance sequences that take your breath away and a great score by Brown and Freed, this is the film musical at its best. **Who voted for Singin' In the Rain?**

(Sight and Sound Top Ten Polls 2002)

If we think about these titles, we can consider the qualities that constitute 'greatness' in the eyes of the critics. They might include:

- **Formal excellence** (e.g. editing, camerawork, performance, set design)
- **Emotional depth/energy/intensity**
- **Innovation** (how many 'firsts' does it have? Does it advance film form?)
- **Complexity/ambiguity** (does the text invite varied readings?)
- **Insight/truth**
- **Longevity** (has it stood the test of time? Rarely do films enter the poll within a decade of their release)
- **Influence** (again, a period time of time is needed before a film's influence can be assessed)
- **Individual expression/ 'genius'**
- **Universality** (does it have a basic human message relevant to all, irrespective of generation or culture?)

Of course, these are largely subjective terms. Yet critics behind the *Sight and Sound* poll – for that matter, critics across the world – are in general agreement on one film's embodiment of these qualities. *Citizen Kane* is commonly considered to be 'The Greatest Film of All Time'. Here Simon Callow reflects on its excellence and critical history:

CITIZEN KANE

When *Citizen Kane* finally appeared in 1941, despite the brouhaha that attended its release – delayed because of distributors' fears of the harm William Randolph Hearst, its alleged subject, might do to them – and largely ecstatic reviews, it was not a commercial success and effectively disappeared. It was television that brought it back, slowly, to public consciousness in America, in the mid-1950s. The film, voted 34th in this reader survey, was shown in Britain shortly after its first release, but continental Europe caught up with the film only after the war, when it was immediately acclaimed as a masterpiece. It was nevertheless something of a surprise when a poll of readers in the British film magazine *Sight & Sound* in 1962 pronounced the film the most admired of all time.

Citizen Kane is perhaps the film, above all others, that has inspired people to become film-makers. This is the more astonishing since it was Orson Welles's first film (he had neither acted in a film, nor written one, much less edited or shot one). In fact, it is his very innocence, the fearlessness and the youthful audacity, that accounts for its influence.

Welles always maintained that its success arose from his having no idea of what he was or wasn't allowed to do: he just went ahead and did it. That does beg the question of why a 25-year-old celluloid virgin should have been given access to the resources of a major studio, but it also ignores the extraordinary team that he had at his disposal, above all, three key figures: the cameraman

CONTINUED

Gregg Toland, the screenwriter Herman J Mankiewicz, and the special-effects wizard Linwood Dunn. When he and Mankiewicz hit on the explosive notion of portraying a newspaper magnate who both was and wasn't Hearst, he realised that he had found a perfect vehicle for himself as director and as actor, and seized his chance with the energy of a whirlwind.

He had the good excuse to encourage his collaborators to contribute as much as they could. Dunn used every optical innovation available, and then invented more. Toland had been surreptitiously exploring certain techniques with other directors, but Welles urged him to go as far as he knew how. He had already encouraged Mankiewicz to risk all sorts of structural innovations and came up with one himself: the famous scene at breakfast during which we witness the whole life cycle of Kane's first marriage in three or four elegant minutes, an idea he acknowledged he had borrowed from the playwright Thornton Wilder.

Welles's experience in the theatre, and perhaps more significantly his uniquely effective work in radio drama – which produced *The War of the Worlds* – gave him the confidence to stage the film with almost reckless flair and exceptional fluidity. His actors functioned as a high-spirited theatre ensemble; there is a level of adrenaline in their performances that is quite uncommon on the screen.

The film celebrates, more than any other, the act of film-making; seeing it, one almost feels that one is present in the studio watching it being made. Small wonder that so many directors cite *Kane* as their greatest influence, not in any particular shot – curiously enough, the tracking shot that opens Welles's 1956 *Touch of Evil* has been more imitated than anything in *Kane* – but in its celebration of the medium. 'The best train set,' Welles said at the time, 'a boy ever had.'

(Callow 1999)

But who are the critics that celebrate *Citizen Kane* and similar landmarks of the critical canon? How are they qualified to tell us, the potential viewer, what is valuable and what is not? The problem with the critical canon is that it is self-perpetuating; critics' and scholars' notion of excellence is informed by their predecessors and in turn passed on to the next generation of writers and academics. A film like *Kane* is held up as a benchmark of perfection against which all other films are measured. In this way, it is virtually impossible for newer films to topple older examples. It is a cyclical process, hard to break; some texts seem monolithic, consistently escaping revaluation. Like Ouroboros, the critics behind the *Sight and Sound* canon – educated with heavy reference to the existing canon – further strengthen and fix that very canon in their voting.

There is much resistance to critical opinion, where it seems critics have been 'taught' to appreciate what is good. Many would argue that a critic's chief role is to select the great from the average and poor in order to inform the general public. However, countless consumers are left disappointed after being drawn to *Citizen Kane* by its 'greatest' tag. In fact, Callow's article highlights the discrepancy between public (*Sunday Times* ' readers' at least) and critical opinion – with *Citizen Kane* a mere thirty-fourth in the reader survey.

A Marxist (see also p. 268) might argue that this is a way of forging and preserving cultural capital. The fact that we might need educating in order to know how to enjoy *Citizen Kane* creates a boundary between high and low culture, thus helping to delineate and separate the classes. You can see how this works and you yourself may have inherited assumptions about the kind of person who enjoys the work of, say, Michael Powell and the kind of person who enjoys the work of Michael Bay.

We should also take into account that, because the critical approach is so entwined with academia, texts are sometimes canonised for their academic richness alone. Films with a plentiful supply of handy resources for the teaching of film form consistently appear on syllabuses and therefore acquire the status of 'classic' when their achievement and significance is really not that great. We should be cautious with this critical approach as it creates a revisionist history. Indeed, Callow notes that even *Citizen Kane* 'was not a commercial success and effectively disappeared'. The 1970s are another case in point. We look to the canonical titles of the decade: *Annie Hall, Taxi Driver, Cabaret* and so on, and consider it a time of artistic freedom and cinematic intelligence, the last gasp of the *auteur* – forgetting the huge popularity of staid and formulaic movies like *Towering Inferno* and *Smokey and the Bandit*.

For all these reasons, the canon constantly runs the risk of losing relevance and sight of its intended purpose. Academia has borrowed the word from Catholicism; it should leave behind the unquestionable reverence too often afforded the church. Otherwise the canon is a bitter old man, eager to officiously reel off a well-rehearsed list of favourites (infinitely superior in his day) even though he hasn't seen those, or indeed many other films for quite some time.

So if even the critics are self-critical – their notions of excellence flawed, at best counter-productive – to whom should we turn for the construction of a canon? Since 1992, *Sight and Sound,* sensing the value of the artist's opinion, has run a concurrent Directors' 'greatest poll'.

One does sense that the panel comprises names 'available at the time' and directors that *Sight and Sound* themselves canonise. And it still pools from the same crop of titles (*Vertigo, L'Atalante, The Passion of Joan of Arc, 8½, La Règle du jeu*, feature in each), *Kane* is still top (1992 *and* 2002). But is does appear to take the first steps along a bridge towards a more populist canon with *Raging Bull* and both *Godfathers* earning very respectable placing.

RESULTS

1992	2002
Citizen Kane	Citizen Kane
Raging Bull	The Godfather and The Godfather Part II
8½	8½
La strada	Lawrence of Arabia
L'Atalante	Dr Strangelove
Modern Times	Bicycle Thieves
The Godfather	Raging Bull
Vertigo	Vertigo
Seven Samurai	Rashomon
The Passion of Joan of Arc	La Règle du jeu
The Godfather Part II	Seven Samurai
Rashomon	

Yet how relevant and useful is a director's opinion? Structuralism has taught us to ignore the artist's will and focus on the multiple readings arrived at by various audiences. Film Studies is not about deciphering a director's intended meaning, hidden among the subtle camera movements and various clues within the *mise-en-scène*. Indeed, many directors would probably guffaw were they to read the often elaborate, sometimes pretentious readings that characterise much of the literature on film. Sometimes a low angle is just an innocent low angle, a gun just a gun. Yet don't be deterred from cultivating your own unique interpretations in exams and coursework. As long as you explain how you arrive at these opinions, with detailed reference to the way the text has created these meanings, then your reading is just as valid as Hitchcock's, or Spielberg's.

The directors' poll is further problematic because it contains films that, naturally, appeal to film-makers and not necessarily to the general cinema-goer (*8½* is a film *about* film-making). Just as a Joe Satriani concert brims with other guitarists appreciative of the fret board virtuosity that fails to move the rest of the world, the titles here, it could be argued, indicate an over-affection for the technical craft of film-making. And, whereas it may take a craftsman to truly assess the value of the craft, one need not be an artisan to appreciate the art.

Art is supposedly for all. If true, then why do we need any kind of critic to tell us, the consumers, what to preserve and exalt? If we are the ones who watch the films, can we the people not construct our own popular canon?

ACTIVITY

➤ In Chapter 12, 'Audience' you will find a list of the 'All-time Worldwide Box Office': those films which have literally made the most money. Compare this, in one sense definitive, list of 'popular' films with the more academic versions of the canon from this chapter. What comments would you like to make about these lists?

Yet financial success is rarely a reliable indicator of popularity. This list only accounts for money taken, which, in the context of the entire history of film and its worldwide audience, is not directly proportional to the amount of people who have even seen the films. Hatched in 1993, the oldest film in the top ten, *Jurassic Park*, is a mere baby compared to the real dinosaurs of the *Sight and Sound* canon. Forgetting their stuffy critics and the idea that longevity is a necessary constituent of greatness for the moment, we can find other reasons behind the relative youthfulness of the box-office chart. IMDB's list does not account for expanding world populations and increased access to cinemas; there are many more people around to see *Shrek* now than *Stagecoach* in its heyday. Neither does the chart make allowances for inflation. Modern films are bound to have made more money; a cinema ticket costs a lot more these days.

Even if this list did gauge 'bums on seats', it is still an inadequate indicator of popularity. First, some of these 'bums' sit through repeat screenings. The fanatical audiences that attend new releases in the *Star Wars* saga give films such as *The Phantom Menace* an inflated presence in such charts. A quick Google presents a host of phrases such as these:

'I saw *The Phantom Menace* in the theater 19 times. Largly[*sic*] due to other things that were going on in my life at the time, but I digress.'

(walkenaround.blogspot.com/ 2005_04_01_walkenaround_archive.html – 101k)

'I saw *The Phantom Menace* 11 times in the theater and the 11th was the best.'

(blogs.starwars.com/detentionblockaa23/49)

'I saw the Phantom Menace 50 times in theaters, and have 49 of the ticket stubs (My dad threw one away, ARG!)'.

(liningup.net/mb/viewtopic.php?t=1571&
sid=ea1afba22628befab9dbad9da034ac0d)
(Accessed 3 October 2005)

In 2004 Channel 4 teamed up with the British Film Institute in order to compile a list which eliminates many failings of gross takings polls like that of the IMDB. With 'The Ultimate Film', they claim to have an accurate record of actual cinema receipts in Britain. Here is the top ten:

> **Channel 4 and Stella Artois' The Ultimate Film counts down, for the first time ever, the most successful 100 films to show in UK cinemas since the dawn of film, based on actual bums on seats.**
>
> Using classic film clips, behind-the-scenes footage, new and contemporary interviews with stars, directors, producers, experts and critics, this celebration of cinema is a fascinating history of changing times, tastes and technology.
>
> This really is the definitive movie chart. Hollywood star and comedy legend John Cleese is our host through this epic, two-night, feature presentation. What will be The Ultimate Film?

10 *The Seventh Veil* (1945) – estimated admissions 17.9m

This Oscar-winning classic follows a psychologist's attempt at treating a pianist with an inability to play in public. James Mason's performance as the raging shrink made him a star and helped the film become a smash hit in the UK. *The Seventh Veil* was typical of British fascination with psychotherapy and Freudian psychology during the 1940s. Basically, we liked it because it was a closet S&M film.

9 *The Wicked Lady* (1946) – estimated admissions 18.4m

Heaving bosoms, cross-dressing and outdoor loving made this unusually racy costume melodrama from the 1940s a smash hit. Margaret Lockwood steals her best friend's betrothed and takes to the highway for kicks. *The Wicked Lady* was hated by critics of the time and Lockwood's considerable talent caused a sensation – it became the first British film to be cut by Hollywood censors due to cleavage. As a result, the public all loved it and Lockwood became one of the decade's biggest stars.

8 *Titanic* (1998) – estimated admissions 18.91m

Near, far, wherever you are . . . *Titanic* is the ultimate event movie. The central romance between Leonardo DiCaprio's poor artist and Kate Winslet's society girl might not work, but who cares when you have a huge ship and a killer iceberg. Director James Cameron pulls out every visual trick; the Titanic's sinking, and the results, are so powerful that even the most hardened cynic is drawn in. Luckily, the shrieking tones of Celine Dion are there at the end credits to bring you back down to earth.

7 *The Jungle Book* (1968) – estimated admissions 19.8m

Disney's animated adventure has show-stopping tunes and hilarious characterisations of Mowgli the Man Cub, Baloo the Bear and, of course, King Louie – king of the swingers, that is. Abandoned in an Indian jungle as a baby and raised by wolves, Mowgli tries to live a slacker's life with his good friend Baloo, but unfortunately, Shere Khan the Tiger has other ideas for him. *The Jungle Book* was the last Disney film overseen by Walt Disney himself, as he died in December 1966.

6 *The Best Years Of Our Lives* (1947) – estimated admissions 20.4m

William Wyler's classic emotional rollercoaster focuses on three Second World War vets who return home from the conflict to find things irrevocably changed. Not only are they physically disabled as a result of the war, but the families they left behind have also been marked and altered by events. By concentrating on the trio's inner conflict rather than their combat glories, Wyler paints a deeply moving picture of ordinary people struggling to repair their lives.

5 *Spring In Park Lane* (1948) – estimated admissions 20.5m

A wealthy merchant's daughter falls in love with a servant who is in fact a down-on-his-luck nobleman. Romantic comedy starring Anna Neagle and Michael Wilding and produced and directed by Herbert Wilcox. While in America they had Bogart and Bacall and Tracy and Hepburn, in Britain we had to make do with Anna Neagle and Michael Wilding. Between 1946 and 1952, this jolly pair co-starred in six movies, each of which enjoyed considerable success at the British box-office.

4 *Star Wars Episode* IV: *A New Hope* (1978) – estimated admissions 20.76m
George Lucas serves up his own homage to the Saturday morning adventure serials he loved as a child, in the process creating one of the most revered and successful films ever. The distributors were so sure his space opera was going to be a disaster that they signed over the merchandising rights to what would go on to become a $5 billion dollar franchise. The Force, Darth Vader and Obi-Wan Kenobi have achieved mythic status in Western culture in probably the most popular series of all time.

3 *Snow White And The Seven Dwarfs* (1938) – estimated admissions 28m
One of the all-time great Disney animations, and an unexpectedly resonant story, with oh-so-demure Snow White brilliantly counterpoised by the Wicked Queen and those great character 'actors' – the Dwarfs. The film's high position on the list may have something to do with the fact that Disney have re-released it every seven years since its debut, raking it in every time.

2 *The Sound Of Music* (1965) – estimated admissions 30m
How do you solve a problem like the Nazis? By becoming the von Trapp Family Singers and hoodwinking the SS with your floral costume and patriotic songs, of course. Julie Andrews made the hills come alive with the power of her voice in one of the most popular musicals of all time. The secret of the film's success lies in its brilliant songs; every one of them is a toe-tapping classic which will buzz around your head for days.

1 *Gone with The Wind* (1940) – estimated admissions 35m
The definitive technicolor romantic epic. Rhett, Scarlett, burning sets and a whole slew of nostalgic and/or reactionary values, this is creator-producer David O. Selznick's finest hour and a cornerstone of the Hollywood monolith. Selznick spent two years searching for the right actress, but boy was the wait for Vivien Leigh worth it as Ten Oscars and a huge amount of box-office followed.

Again this is a totally different list from those we have seen so far and again its claim to be 'definitive' is problematic. More than half the films listed here were released before Queen Elizabeth II's coronation in 1953, an event commonly cited as the reason for the enormous increase in television sales in Britain that year. Television's inevitable ubiquity caused a dramatic decrease in cinema attendance, and thus relatively little-known films such as *Spring in Park Lane* and *The Wicked Lady* occupy an unfair position in the list because cinema-going was a far more common pursuit at the time of their release.

Introducing television to the equation further complicates matters. The above list only accounts for theatre screenings, when films, of course, exist on television, DVD and VHS. Home video sales now constitute over 60 per cent of Hollywood profits. A film such as *The Shawshank Redemption*, absent from this top 100, enjoyed only a very modest theatrical run but benefited from a massive afterlife on DVD and VHS and is now one of the world's most loved and seen movies.

Ultimately however, aside from the debatable influence of word of mouth and the reviews of popular newspapers, the fact that neither the Channel Four nor IMDB lists actually gauge audience response is far more significant than the minor gripes already mentioned. These lists tell us how many people saw a film, not how many of them actually liked It. *The Phantom Menace* is again a case in point:

> 'I saw *The Phantom Menace* more times than I care to admit, even though it was an inherently disappointing movie.'

(www.maggiemasetti.com/me.html)

Anticipation fostered the giant turn-out for this film, a large percentage of whom were left disappointed. The IMDB runs a feature that allows users to rate each film they have seen out of ten. *The Phantom Menace,* which appears at number 4 in the box office list (28 for Channel Four) achieves a very *average* average score of 6.4 (5 November 2005). Its three *preceding sequels* all gain scores of 8 and above: *Star Wars* and *The Empire Strikes Back* have ratings impressive enough to permit their entry into the website's top ten user ranked films:

1	9.0	*The Godfather* (1972)	139,385
2	9.0	*The Shawshank Redemption* (1994)	168,708
3	8.9	*The Lord of the Rings: The Return of the King* (2003)	122,853
4	8.9	*The Godfather: Part II* (1974)	80,184
5	8.8	*Schindler's List* (1993)	107,434
6	8.8	*Shichinin no samurai* (1954)	36,956
7	8.7	*Casablanca* (1942)	72,521
8	8.7	*Star Wars* (1977)	150,521
9	8.7	*Star Wars Episode V: The Empire Strikes Back* (1980)	117,209
10	8.7	*Buono, il brutto, il cattivo, II* (1966)	36,003

Is this a definitive and trustworthy list? The answer again is probably not. Although we cannot dispute the fact that people like these movies, we can ask who these people are, and why they have seen these films. The majority of the American and British cinema-going public actually watch only a very narrow range of films.

They are unaware that the choice offered at the multiplexes is limited, a result of block booking and vertical integration. Popular polls therefore suffer a 'blanding' as the public, naturally, vote for films given heavy promotion and wide distribution. We need the critics to negate the marketing machine and seek out lesser known gems at the festivals, press screenings and on the art house circuit. But then we are back where we started.

The real truth is that there has always been an elitist resistance to popular taste. The famously pessimistic Schopenhauer wrote that the public 'are like sheep following the bell-wether wherever he leads them. They would sooner die than think...the universality of an opinion is no proof. In fact, it is not even a probability that the opinion is right'. Although we live in a democracy and allow the public to choose our political leader, the everyman canon is of dubious value. There is an assumption that the public are somehow lacking in intelligence and therefore feed an addiction for generic high-spectacle good-versus-evil narratives with watertight closure by way of a saccharine ending. There is a perception (and the polls support this) that popular equals recent; that the public are too lazy to discover films made outside their lifetime. Thus it is less likely to find older films in a popular canon, defeating one of its key functions: to preserve the great. Popular taste is transient, at the behest of fashion. This is symptomatic of all the arts: bands with critical acclaim and little commercial success such as The Velvet Underground of the 1960s, are now of much greater worth than relatively recent chart toppers such as Whigfield.

'The Popular', ultimately, is of more use in a sociological rather than aesthetic sense. Films are an index of the values, fashions, attitudes and lifestyle of the era in which they were produced. In this way we can construct a canon of titles notable for their very 'averageness'. While the critical canon preserves what it perceives to be extraordinary, a *typical canon* targets the ordinary as a document of the time.

Canons of typicality are a lifeless and moribund affair though, and with their wilfully esoteric and impenetrable masterpieces, so are the critical canons we opened with. The canon should be functional, the key to a box of delights, the map of a great adventure, not a list of names in a dusty history book. Canons have to compromise; otherwise they dim and flicker out like all the movies they choose to ignore.

FILMS

WHY DO SOME SURVIVE AND OTHERS DISAPPEAR?

Now, perhaps, we can begin to ask what the future might hold. The most recent film on the pivotal 1962 *Sight and Sound* list was Antonioni's *L'avventura*, released in 1960, only two years earlier. In 1972, it was Bergman's *Persona*, first shown five years before. In 1982 came Fellini's 8½, first shown 19 years earlier, even before *Persona*. And in the critics' 1992 poll, Kubrick's *2001*, released 24 years earlier, scraped in at number ten. The most recent European film in the 1992 poll is *La Règle du jeu* (just preceding *Citizen Kane*, the first American one). The canon has indeed begun to freeze.

GOODBYE TO THE 60S

The time certainly seems ripe for a new revolution in taste, taking us beyond the upheaval of the 60s. The auteurism of those years was more than a theory of 'authorship' in the cinema; it involved championing a specific set of film-makers, both in the past and immediate present. These were the new auteurs celebrated in critical articles and named, in hierarchical order, in the *Cahiers* annual top ten lists, in *Movie* magazine's histogram of British and American directors, and in Andrew Sarris' pantheon (two versions, with promotions and demotions which I studied carefully). Lists may seem trivial, but in fact they are crucial indices of underlying struggles over taste, evaluation and the construction of a canon.

And changes in the canon are crucially linked to changes in film-making. As the *Cahiers* critics saw it, the overthrow of the existing regime of taste was a precondition for the triumph of new film-makers with new films, demanding to be judged on a different scale of values. Like the Surrealists or the Leavisites, they mobilised the old to support the new. Today, if the current canon is to be unfrozen, the impetus must come from a challenge, not simply to the New Hollywood, but also to the festival regime first established at the time of the New Wave film-makers. Surely there are no more New Waves to be discovered at festivals around the world. Indeed, the current search for a New Wave inside America itself, now that Latin America, Africa and Asia have been exhaustively examined for New Waves to discover, simply shows the decadence of the whole concept.

A new cinema will create a new film history with it, perhaps deliberately, perhaps by accident. And we can be sure that, in its absence, the canon will continue to petrify. The art form of the twentieth century will dwindle and die, as stained glass and tapestry died before it. Only a new revolution of taste can rescue cinema from the jaws of death.

(Wollen 1997: 5)

PART 2: CONCEPTS

▼   5 GENRE

> Genre knowledge orientates competent readers of the genre towards appropriate attitudes, assumptions and expectations about a text which are useful in making sense of it.
>
> Daniel Chandler, Communication and Media Studies website

It would be difficult to underestimate the significance of genre as a core concept in the study of film. Much of the academic research and writing that informs our understanding of film as an academic discipline is centred on the concept of genre. Much of the work on genre emerges from academic discussion produced in the 1970s in the UK. As with any attempt to conceptualise an important aspect of study, there is inevitably a lot of debate around not only the value of genre as an analytical tool but also the significance of the term itself.

Before you get caught up in this debate, it may be useful to explore briefly some basic issues in relation to the concept of genre. The following is a no-frills introduction to genre which explains both the nature of genre and its function in relation to both audiences and producers:

THE FUNCTION OF GENRE

The concept of genre is useful in looking at the ways in which media texts are organised, categorised and consumed. It is applied to television, print and radio texts as well as to film. The concept of Genre suggests that there are certain types of media material, often story-types, which are recognised through common elements, such as style, narrative and structure, that are used again and again to make up that particular type of media genre.

KEY TERM
GENRE The term used for the classification of media texts into groups with similar characteristics.

An important element in identifying a genre is the look or iconography of the text. Iconography constitutes a pattern of visual imagery which remains common to a genre over a period of time.

KEY TERM

ICONOGRAPHY Those particular signs that we associated with particular genres, such as physical attributes and dress of the actors, the settings and the 'tools of the trade' (cars, guns, etc.).

Look at a selection of films that are currently being shown in your area and try to categorise them into different genres.

- What types of stories do the films tell?
- Where are the films set?
- What type of characters appear in the films?
- What particular actors and/or directors are associated with the films? Have they been involved with similar types of films before?
- What is the 'look' or iconography of the film?
- What music is used?

Genre is a formula which, if successful, is often repeated again and again and can be used over a long period of time. For instance in a gangster film (*Goodfellas*, 1990), we expect to see some, or all, of the following elements that will also probably have been in a gangster film from the 1930s:

Car chases	Urban settings
Guns	Mafia
Heroes	Corrupt police/politicians
Villains	Beautiful women
Violence	Italians

There are also certain actors that we may associate with this genre of films (James Cagney in the 1930s, Robert de Niro in the 1980s or currently Vinnie Jones) as well as certain directors (Martin Scorsese and Guy Ritchie).

Take two examples of films of the same genre from different eras that interest you, for instance *War of the Worlds* (1953) and *Independence Day* (1996), and identify their similarities and differences. Suggest reasons for these similarities and differences.

GENRE AND AUDIENCES

Audiences are said to like the concept of genre (although we may not identify it by that name) because of its reassuring and familiar promise of patterns of repetition and variation.

The concept of genre is important in arousing the expectations of an audience and how they judge and select texts. Placing a text within a specific genre plays an important role in signalling to an audience the type of text that they are being invited to consume. Audiences become familiar with the codes and conventions of specific genres. Familiarity through repetition is therefore one of the key elements in the way audiences understand and relate to media texts.

Audiences not only come to expect certain common codes and conventions but these can also provide a short cut which saves the audience (and the producers) time in developing a new set of conventions each time they consume a new text in that particular genre. This can be seen where two existing genres have been brought together to create a new one. For example, TV docu-soaps, which combine elements of documentary and soap opera. These rely on an audience's understanding and ability to read each specific genre – they understand how documentaries work and they understand how soap operas work. Therefore docu-soaps are able to satisfy their expectations of both.

Look at the promotional material that is used to market either a new radio, TV or cinema product.

- Identify those elements that are recognisable as belonging to a particular genre by the audience.
- Are there any elements that distinguish it from other established products of the same genre?

Often the promotion and marketing for new texts invite the audience to identify similarities between a text and predecessors in the same genre. The audience can then take comfort in the fact that what they are being offered is something that they have previously enjoyed and the producers hope that they will enjoy it again.

It has been suggested that proficiency in reading texts within a genre can also lead to the audience's pleasure being heightened as they recognise particular character types or storylines.

Select a magazine or newspaper that you read regularly and consider how you consume it.

- Make a list of the features that you most look forward to reading. In which order do you read them? Why?
- Do you read a range of magazines or newspapers from the same genre? If so, what are the similarities/differences between them?
- Do similar stores/features appear in similar places in different publications? If so, why?
- Are similar products advertised in these magazines or newspapers? If so, why?

Genre and producers

Producers are said to like the concept of genre because they can exploit a winning formula and minimise taking risks. The concept of genre also helps institutions budget and plan their finances more accurately and helps them to promote new products.

One of the main functions of most of the mainstream media is to make a profit. Just as a high-street retailer has to sell goods that the customers will want to buy, so a media producer has to create texts that audiences will want to consume.

One way to do this is to find what audiences already enjoy and offer something similar. Genre is an easy way of doing this. Where a formula has been proved popular with audiences it makes sense for the producer to use that formula again and to create a new product that contains similar recognisable features which it is hoped will have an immediate appeal to an established audience.

(Raynor *et al.* 2003: 56–59)

You may have spotted from this basic take on the nature of genre some of the issues, or even problems, the concept carries with it. Through genre we are exploring the relationship between producer/text and audience. Clearly this is a complex relationship and one where it is dangerous to make too many assumptions. However, an assumption that can be made is that in categorising a film in terms of a particular genre, we are in some way limiting the range of meanings the film will make available to its audiences. Peter Hutchings in his essay 'Genre Theory and Criticism' (Hollow and Janovich 1995: 65) quotes Tom Ryall:

When we suggest that a certain film is a Western we are really positing that a particular range of meanings will be available in the film, and not others. We are defining the limits of its significance. The master image for genre criticism is a triangle composed of artists/film/audience. Genres may be defined as patterns/forms/styles/structures which transcend individual films, and which supervise both their construction by the film maker, and their reading by an audience.

So genre potentially determines both the construction and consumption of films. Given this important function, we should move quickly to seeking out a definition.

INFOBOX

One of the interesting tensions in film studies is the extent to which film as an aesthetic form can aspire to the condition of art. In the section on auteur, you will read theory which is very much a counter-argument to genre theory, where some films form part of the canon not least because their directors have imbued them with a personal signature which transcends their categorising as genre products.

Genre study is often associated with popular texts created for mass consumption. In film as well as in other media, these are the products of an industrial process, such as the Hollywood Film Factory. Rather than dealing with them as individual texts, as we do auteur films, we lump them together into genres so that we can consider them collectively.

For Tom Ryall in his seminal essay 'The Notion of Genre', a concern for 'emphasizing the personality and pre-occupations of particular directors' has meant that an attempt to define the term *genre* had been overlooked. In the extract that follows from this essay he explores some of the key issues surrounding an attempt to define the term:

The term has frequently been used as a synonym for 'type'. Thus film genres include not only Western and gangster films, but also, musicals, social dramas, women's pictures, historical epics, horror films and so on. It does seem appropriate to sort Hollywood's output into a variety of categories or types, indeed the particular commercial structure of the American cinema makes the repetition of a proven success a major front-office consideration. But we can use the word 'type' or 'category' to assist us in the description of those features of the American cinema and we need not use the word 'genre' at all. My argument will be that we should reserve the title, 'genre', for certain types of films and deny it to others. The Western and gangster types of films certainly constitute genres, while social dramas do not. To refer to social dramas as a genre does no more than collect a number of disparate though loosely related films under a suitable heading, while to say that Westerns constitute a genre implies a number of internal relationships between the various constituents of the genre (the individual films), and a controlling relationship between the film-maker, the genre and the audience.

One notion of genre which has the merit of precision states that 'Genre criticism ... presupposes an ideal form for the genre' (Sarris). This approach is unsatisfactory, however, because once the ideal film is constructed in the mind of the critic, the tendency will be to evaluate examples of the genre against the artificial standard of the abstracted film. This approach implies that a director strives to make the archetypal Western or gangster film, or at least that when they deviate from the supposed ideal they are failing in some way. An example of this approach, which preceded Sarris's statement, is contained in André Bazin's article 'The Evolution of the Western' (*Cahiers du Cinéma*, Dec. 1955). Bazin's contention is that with *Stagecoach* (1939 – John Ford) the Western reached a position of classical maturity. Having stated this,

Bazin goes on to use the film (and others made in the same period which also display 'classical' qualities) as an index of subsequent productions. Post-war Westerns were to be evaluated according to their relationship to the classical model as exemplified by *Stagecoach*: thus *High Noon* (1952) and *Shane* (1953) are referred to as mutations of the genre, while *The Naked Spur* (1953) is praised for 'rediscovering (at an imaginative level) the essence of Westerns as it was contained, on a mythological level, in the Triangle films of long ago, and which has since proved elusive'. Bazin's argument is less crude than Sarris's dictum but it is no more than a refinement and both critical stances lead to an unduly prescriptive form of criticism. There is a danger of such criticism distorting a film by relating it to a standard which only reflects a particular aesthetic preference.

To take an example, a critic could construct an ideal gangster film along the following lines, paying attention only to thematic features: the model theme would involve the rise of a juvenile delinquent from the obscurity of the slums to the leadership of a large bootlegger syndicate, his subsequent decline and death (probably at the hands of his former colleagues). Many gangster films do, in fact, conform to this crude thematic abstract (*Little Caesar*, *Public Enemy*, *Portrait of a Mobster*) but there are numerous films which must be called 'gangster', but which have a very tenuous relationship with the abstract, if any. (*The Big Heat*, *Bonnie and Clyde*, *Underworld* U.S.A.) Confronted with this thematic diversity the critic would be driven into erecting a number of ideal forms to account for the variety of themes which the gangster film has confronted. Such a multiplication of forms would itself contradict the notion of an ideal form for the genre and hopes for critical precision in this approach would be frustrated. Moreover, this example does not take into account other important features of genre cinema such as iconography. The difficulties involved in integrating the variety of iconographical material into an ideal form would reproduce the problems of the thematic model.

Between the looseness of no specific definition (synonymity with 'type') and the rigidity of the Sarrisian position, an acceptable working definition may be arrived at. (Sarris's account of genre forms a minor part of an article putting forward a theory of film history; in no way does he explore the concept of genre in any detail, his commitment being to the notion of '*auteur*'.)

A crucial notion in any definition of genre, must be that the genre film is one which exhibits a relationship with other examples of the genre. This also implies a consciousness of this relationship on the part of the man who makes the film, and on the part of the audience who go to see it. If we consider the Western, the relationship will be in terms of a *complex* of basic material or subject matter, of thematic preoccupations and of iconographical continuity. This complex provides the director of genre films with a basic 'given' to work upon and it also provides an audience with a set of expectations which they will carry to the film. The tripartite division of the complex seems to be the most fruitful way of describing the Western genre, of breaking it into its basic elements.

(Ryall 2001: 23–26)

The influential genre critic, Steve Neale, takes this definition by Tom Ryall as his starting point and explores the nature of genre in his work *Genre and Hollywood* (Steve Neale 2000).

What follows is a lengthy and demanding extract. It does, however, offer an invaluable overview of the nature and value of genre criticism:

DEFINITIONS OF GENRE

.... However, at this point it is worth stressing the extent to which Ryall is critical of some of the writing on genre that immediately preceded his own. 'By and large', he writes, 'genre criticism has confined itself to producing taxonomies on the basis of "family resemblances", allocating films to their position within the generic constellation, stopping short of what are the interesting and informative questions about generic groupings'. (1975/6: 27). To a degree these remarks are well-founded. Some of the writing that preceded (and followed) Ryall's article was indeed taxonomic, devoted to the discovery and analysis of the components of individual genres rather than to the pursuit of theoretical questions about the nature of genre as such. However, while writing of this kind has its limitations, it also has its uses, provided as it does an initial means of 'collating the range of cultural knowledge ... genres assumed' (Gledhill 1985a: 61).

Moreover, not all the writing on genre in the late 1960s and early 1970s was taxonomic in kind. Both Buscombe (1970) and McArthur (1972), for instance, were concerned, among other things, to demonstrate the active role played by genre conventions in shaping the form and the meaning of individual Hollywood films. Here, for example, is Buscombe on *Guns in the Afternoon* (a.k.a. *Ride the High Country*) (1962), a western:

Knowing the period and location, we expect at the beginning to find a familiar western town. In fact, the first few minutes of the film brilliantly disturb expectations. As the camera moves around the town, we discover a policeman in uniform, a car, a camel, and Randolph Scott, dressed up as Buffalo Bill. Each of these images performs a function. The figure of the policeman conveys that the law has become institutionalised; the rough and ready frontier days are over. The car suggests ... that the

CONTINUED

west is no longer isolated from modern technology and its implications. Significantly, the camel is racing against a horse; such a grotesque juxtaposition is painful. A horse in a western is not just an animal but a symbol of dignity, grace and power. These qualities are mocked by it competing with a camel; and to add insult to injury, the camel wins.

(Buscombe 1970: 44)

He later continues:

the essential theme of *Guns in the Afternoon* is one that, while it could be put into other forms is ideally suited to the one chosen. The film describes the situation of men who have outlived their time ...

The cluster of images and conventions that we call the western genre is used by Peckinpah [the film's director] to define and embody this situation, in such a way that we know what the West was and what it has become. The first is communicated through images that are familiar, the second through those that are strange. And together they condition his subject matter. Most obviously, because the film is a western, the theme is worked out in terms of violent action. If it were a musical, the theme might be similar in some way, but because the conventions would be different, it would probably not involve violence ... And if it were a gangster picture, it seems unlikely that the effect of the film's ending, its beautifully elegiac background of autumn leaves, would be reproduced, suggesting as it does that the dead Judd is at one with nature, the nature which seems at the beginning of the film to have been overtaken by 'civilization'.

(Buscombe 1970: 44–5)

In this particular essay, Buscombe attempts also to advance a general theory about the aesthetic characteristics of popular genres. He borrows the concepts of 'inner' and outer' form from Warren and Welleck, who argued that 'Genres should be conceived as a grouping of literary works based, theoretically, upon both outer form (specific metre or structure) and also upon inner form (attitude, tone, purpose – more crudely, subject and audience)' (1956: 260). These particular concepts were not taken up by subsequent writers. But in illustrating the idea of 'outer form', Buscombe talked about 'visual conventions'. His work here thus drew on and fed into a concept that was to become much more influential – the concept of iconography.

ICONOGRAPHY

Along with its twin, 'iconology', the term 'iconography' derives from art history, and in particular from the work of Erwin Panofsky. Panofsky himself discussed the application of these terms to popular cinema ([1934] 1974), but it was Lawrence Alloway who sought to apply them in a systematic way to the analysis of genres and cycles (1963).

In 'Iconography and Iconology: An Introduction to the Study of Renaissance Art', first published in 1938 and reprinted in his *Meaning in the Visual Arts*, Panofsky distinguishes between three possible levels of states in the analysis of Renaissance paintings, corresponding to three possible 'strata' of meaning (1970: 51–81). The first involves the identification and description of what he calls 'motifs' (essentially, the objects and events depicted through lines, colours and volumes). The second involves the identification and description of what he calls 'images' (the 'secondary or conventional' meanings conveyed by these motifs, as determined in particular by reference to the Bible and to other written sources. This for Panofsky is the realm of iconography). And the third involves the interpretation of these images. (This for Panofsky is the realm of iconology.)

In arguing for the application of the concept of iconography to the cinema, Alloway writes that

> The meaning of a single movie is inseparable from the larger pattern of content-analysis of other movies. And the point is, that this knowledge, of concepts and themes, is the common property of the regular audience of the movies. It comes from 1) exposure to runs of related movies (soap, opera, westerns) and from the fact that 2) the movies connect with other topical interests and activities of the audience. Such themes as kitchen technology and domestic leisure in soap opera and male outdoor leisure clothes, as well as attitudes towards violence in westerns, exist outside the movies, but aid identification with the movies once you are inside the cinema.

> (Alloway 1963: 5)

He precedes this passage with another example, and with another facet of this argument:

> iconography is not to be isolated from other aspects of film making. For instance, *The Thousand Eyes of Dr Mabuse* and *Rear Window* can be related to a persistent theme of American movies since World War II. There were the F.B.I. movies in which the Department of Justice kept spies under observation with a battery of voyeuristic electronic devices. Since *The Glass Web* television monitor devices of every kind have been brilliantly handled in urban films: for instance, a telephone wired with a bomb, as in *The Case Against Brooklyn* or the difficulties of telephone tapping in the '30s in *The Scarface Mob*.

> (Alloway 1963: 4–5)

It should be noted that 'iconography' here tends to mean the objects, events and figures in films, as well as their identification and description. It should also be noted that Alloway tends to avoid interpretation. Partly for this reason, iconology does not even figure as a term. (It tends to disappear altogether in subsequent writing on genre. Only McArthur, in an unpublished paper written in 1973, briefly resurrects both the term and the conceptual distinction Panofsky originally designed it to make.) Finally, it should be pointed out that although Alloway discusses and exemplifies iconography in relation to genres and cycles, he also discusses its application to stars and to star personae.

The concept of iconography was widely used by genre theorists and critics during the course of the next decade. There were two main reasons for this. One was the extent to which, in Alloway's formulation at least, it dovetailed with a sympathetic interest in popular films. The other was the extent to which it could be used to stress the visual aspects of popular films (in keeping with the stress placed on style and *mise-en-scène* by auteurism, and in contrast to the emphasis placed on character, plot and theme by more literary-minded theorists and critics). Hence Buscombe's synonym for iconography – 'visual conventions'. Hence his insistence on the argument that 'Since we are dealing with a visual medium we ought surely to look for our defining criteria on the screen' (1970: 36). And hence the stress placed on 'visual conventions' as well as on the 'relationship between genre and audience' in the chapter on the iconography of the 'gangster film/thriller' in McArthur's *Underworld* USA:

> In *Little Caesar* (1930) a police lieutenant and two of his men visit a night-club run by gangsters. All three wear large hats and heavy coats, are grim and sardonic and stand in triangular formation, the lieutenant in front, his two men flanking him in the rear. The audience knows immediately what to expect of them by their physical attributes, their dress and deportment. It knows, too, by the disposition of the figures, which is dominant, which subordinate. In *The Harder They Fall* (1956) a racketeer and two of his men go to a rendezvous in downtown New York. As they wait for the door of the building to be opened they take up the same formation as the figures in the earlier film, giving the same information to the audience by the same means ... In *On the Waterfront* (1954) and *Tony Rome* (1967) there are carefully mounted scenes in which the central figure is walking down a dark and deserted street. In each case an automobile drives swiftly towards him; and the audience, drawing on accumulated experience of the genre, realises that it will be used as a murder weapon against the hero. Both these examples indicate the continuity over several decades of patterns of visual imagery, of recurrent objects and figures in dynamic relationship. These repeated patterns might be called the iconography of the genre.
>
> (McArthur 1972: 23)

McArthur goes on to categorize the genre's iconography, subdividing the patterns of its imagery into three basic types: 'those surrounding the physical presence, attributes and dress of the actors and the characters they play; those emanating from the milieux within which the characters operate; and those connected with the technology at the character's disposal' (ibid.: 24). However, it is unclear as to whether this taxonomy is meant to be applicable to other genres as well. It is also unclear as to whether iconography is to be thought of as one of the defining features of a genre.

There are certainly traces of such a position in McArthur's book. He says at one point, for instance, that the iconographic patterns of a genre 'set it off visually from other types of film and are the means by which primary definitions are made' (1972: 24). However, he himself does not elaborate, and it is Buscombe who comes closest to arguing a position of this kind. Although stressing that not all generic conventions are visual in kind, he argues nevertheless that 'the major defining characteristics of a genre will be visual: guns, cars, clothes in the gangster film; clothing and dancing in musical (apart from the music, of course!); castles, coffins and teeth in horror movies' (1970: 41). This argument occurs during the course of a much more detailed discussion of the western. Nevertheless, the paucity of these examples (together with the taxonomic tendencies both of genre criticism in general and of iconographic analysis in particular) is strikingly apparent. One of the major reasons for this is that the possible connections between the items (or icons) listed is unclear. Another, more important, reason is that it is actually very difficult to list the defining visual characteristics of more than a handful of genres, for the simple reason that many genres – among them the social problem film, the biopic, romantic drama and the psychological horror film – lack a specific iconography.

It is no accident, therefore, that the genres discussed at some length by Buscombe and McArthur are the western and the gangster film, two of the genres which (along with the gothic horror film and the biblical epic) the concept of generic iconography seems to fit rather well. The failure to apply the concept productively to other genres suggests on the one hand that the defining features of Hollywood's genres may be heterogeneous in kind (some visual, others not). It suggests on the other that a number of fundamental questions – to do with definition, to do with identification, and to do with the nature and role of genre theory – still needed to be asked. They began to be asked first by Tudor (1974a: 131–52, 1974b: 180–220) and then by Ryall. They were displaced during the decade that followed as attention was turned to structuralism, to semiotics and to psychoanalysis – to general theories of method and meaning (Stam, Burgoyne and Flitterman-Lewis 1992). Structuralism, in particular, placed a part in work on individual genres like the western (notably by Kitses 1969 and Wright 1975). However, although some or all of these theories were to have an impact on writing on genre in the 1980s, notably by Neale (1980) and Altman ([1984] 1986, 1987), and although feminist inflections and reworkings of these approaches were to find an important place in writing on hitherto neglected genres like the woman's film (see Doane 1987), issues and theories of genre as such were largely put to one side. Hence some of these questions remained unanswered and had to be re-raised, firstly by Alan Williams (1984), and then by Neale (1990a).

THEORETICAL QUESTIONS

The questions raised by Ryall derive from a distinction he draws between two types of analytical activity:

> The key to understanding the theoretical foundations of the concept of genre lies in pushing beyond ... classificatory exercises and confronting the crucial distinction between, on the one hand suggesting that a film is a Western; and, on the other, suggesting that a film is a genre film. The former simply involves observing similarities between films, while the latter urges us towards a more generalised theoretical activity in which our conclusions would not merely link one film with another under some category such as 'Western'; but rather, would link the established genres (Western, gangster films, musicals, etc) under the more general concepts of 'convention' and 'expectation', and would explore the variety of questions associated with the area of 'reading' film.
>
> (Ryall 1975/6: 27)

Ryall goes on to note the multi-dimensional aspects of genre, insisting on the importance of audience knowledge and audience expectation on the one hand, and of the industry and film reviewers on the other. It is clear, therefore, that for Ryall genres are not simply groups of films linked by common characteristics. He argues in addition that the problem of defining genre as a term is exacerbated by its pervasiveness: 'its widespread usage by film distributors, by reviewers and critics, and by popular audiences, poses problems for criticism insofar as ordinary usage carries with it the implication that the concept of genre is clear and well-defined, non-problematic' (1975/6: 27).

Similar points are made by Tudor (1974a), who tends both to pursue them further and to raise other issues as well. He begins by raising questions about genre identification and genre recognition:

> most writers tend to assume that there is some body of films we can safely call the western and then move on to the real work – the analysis of the crucial characteristics of the already recognized *genre* ... These writers, and almost all writers using the term *genre*, are caught in a dilemma. They are defining a western on the basis of analyzing a body

of films that cannot possibly be said to be westerns until after the analysis ... To take a *genre* such as the western, analyze it, and list its principal characteristics is to beg the question that we must first isolate the body of films that are westerns. But they can only be isolated on the basis of the 'principal characteristics', which can only be discovered from the films themselves after they have been isolated. That is, we are caught in a circle that first requires that the films be isolated, for which purpose a criterion is necessary, but the criterion is, in turn, meant to emerge from the empirically established common characteristics of the films. This 'empiricist dilemma' has two solutions. One is to classify films according to a priori criteria depending on the critical purpose. This leads back to the earlier position in which the special *genre* term is redundant. The second is to lean on a common cultural consensus as to what constitutes a western and then go on to analyze it in detail.

(Tudor 1974a: 135–8)

This is a fundamental point. It raises questions about the nature and purpose of genre criticism. And, implicitly at least, it raises questions as to how 'a common cultural consensus' is established. What agencies and institutions are involved? What is the role of the film industry? What is the role of film critics, film reviewers and the like? On the one hand it helps underline Ryall's point about the importance of distributors, reviewers and critics. On the other it helps stress the culturally relative, and therefore the culturally contingent, nature of genres themselves:

In short to talk about the western is (arbitrary definitions apart) to appeal to a common set of meanings in our culture. From a very early age most of us have built up a picture of the western. We feel that we know a western when we see one, though the edges may be rather blurred. Thus in calling a film a western a critic is implying more than the simple statement 'This film is a member of a class of films (westerns) having in common x, y, and z.' The critic is also suggesting that such a film would be universally recognized as such in our culture. In other words, the crucial factors that distinguish a *genre* are not only characteristics inherent in the films themselves; they also depend on the particular culture with which we are operating. And unless there is a world consensus on the subject (which is an empirical question), there is no basis for assuming that a western will be received in the same way in every culture. The way in which the *genre* term is applied can quite conceivably vary from case to case. *Genre* notions – except in the case of arbitrary definition – are not critics' classifications made for special purposes; they are sets of cultural conventions. *Genre* is what we collectively believe it to be.

(Tudor 1974a: 139)

The stress here on culture and cultures, rather than just on films, leads Tudor, like Ryall, to stress the role and the importance of audiences too. And this leads him in turn (and for the first time in work on genre and genres in the cinema) not just outside the realm of Hollywood but outside the realms of mainstream cinema altogether:

> the genre concept is indispensable in more strictly social and psychological terms as a way of formulating the interplay between culture, audience, films and filmmakers. For example, there is a class of films thought by a relatively highly educated middle-class group of filmgoers as 'art movies' [Tudor goes on to cite *The Seventh Seal* (1956), *L'Avventura* (1960) and *La Dolce Vita* (1959) as examples]. Now for the present purposes *genre* is a conception existing in the culture of any particular group or society; it is not a way in which a critic classifies films for methodological purposes, but the much looser way in which an audience classifies its films. According to this meaning of the term, 'art movies' is a *genre*.
>
> (Tudor 1974a: 145)

Thus, to reiterate, 'there does not seem to me to be any crucial difference between the most commonly applied *genre* term – the western – and the art-movie that I have been discussing. They are both conceptions held by certain groups about certain films' (ibid.: 147).

It is here, in including art films under the rubric of genre, and in defining genres as 'conceptions', that Tudor departs most radically from most of the ideas and definitions of genre in the cinema advanced hitherto. The questions he asks are radical ones. They challenge conventional notions as to the cinematic and cultural site of genre and genres. They open up the issue of groupings and classification. And they place spectatorial and audience activity and the cultural and institutional contexts within which that activity takes place firmly at the centre of theoretical debate. To that extent they are echoed not just by Williams and Neale, but also by a number of linguists, philosophers and literary theorists who have written on genre in recent years.

LITERATURE, LINGUISTICS AND GENRE

On a number of occasions in the 1960s and 1970s, writers on genre in the cinema referred to definitions and theories of genre in literature. Some, like Cawelti (1976), made use of particular literary theories (in Cawelti's case, those of Frye 1957). However, while the existence of literary theory was explicitly acknowledged, it was in practice usually ignored. One of the reasons for this, as Ryall points out, was the apparent discrepancy between generic terms and 'divisions' in literature, and the terms and divisions familiar to critics and theorists of the cinema:

As well as the widespread usage within film, the critic also has to contend with the term as it occurs in the discussion of other arts, notably literature where genre divisions have been made on the basis of formal distinctions (the novel, drama, poetry) compared with the subject or content divisions more usual in film criticism. The term, therefore, while having an apparent stability within the discussion of film becomes somewhat confusing in the context of, for example, genre definitions in literature.

(Ryall 1975/6: 27)

Hence while Buscombe, for instance, referred in passing to the divisions in Aristotle's *Poetics* between 'tragedy, epic, lyric, and so forth' (1970: 33), they were effectively forgotten by the time he turned to the gangster film, the western and the musical.

It was not until 1984 that this discrepancy was re-raised and discussed as an issue, during the course of Williams's review of Schatz's *Hollywood Genres* (1981):

Perhaps the biggest problem with genre or genre criticism in the field of the cinema is the word *genre*. Borrowed, as a critical tool, from literary studies (or at least having resonances from that area – the word does have a life of its own in the film industry) the applicability of 'genre' as a concept in film studies raises some fairly tough questions. Sample genres are held to be Westerns, Science Fiction Films, more recently Disaster Films, and so on. What do these loose groupings of works – that seem to come and go, for the most part, in ten- and twenty-year cycles – have to do with familiar genres such as tragedy, comedy romance, or (to mix the pot up a bit) the epistolary novel or the prose poem?

(A. Williams 1984: 121)

Williams continues:

For the phrase 'genre films', referring to a general category, we can frequently, though not always, substitute 'film narrative'. Perhaps *that* is the real genre. Certainly there is much more difference between *Prelude to Dog Star Man* and *Star Wars* than there is between the latter and *Body Heat*. It's mainly a question of terminology, of course, but I wonder if we ought to consider the principal film genres as being the narrative film, experimental/avant-garde film, and documentary. Surely these are the categories in film studies that have among themselves the sorts of significant differences that one can find between, say, epic and lyric poetry.

(A. Williams 1984: 121)

The first point to make in response to this is to highlight the extent to which genres and genre categories in literature are by no means always as systematically coherent or long-lived as Williams – or Ryall – seem to suggest. Comedy, romance and tragedy are long-lived as terms, but the criteria that define them, along with the types of work they encompass, have in each case changed over time (see Beer 1970 on romance, and Koelb 1975 on tragedy). Moreover, comedy and romance, at least, are familiar as terms and as genres to critics and theorists of film. In addition, the criteria that define, say, the epistolary novel and epic poetry on the one hand and comedy and romance on the other are very different in kind, varying from the purely formal (in the case of the epistolary novel), to a mix of criteria involving form, content and tone (in the case of most of the others). And to switch the focus of the argument, the western and science fiction are both literary genres as well as cinematic ones. Even the disaster film of the late 1960s and early 1970s has its analogue – indeed its origins – in contemporary novels written by Arthur Hailey, Paul Gallico, Richard Martin Stern, and others.

This leads me to a second point, a point that is crucial for understanding why genre and genres have so often been identified with Hollywood (rather than, say, the art film), and hence why some of the contradictions and discrepancies to which Williams points have arisen. Within a great deal of modern writing on literature, the kind of fiction exemplified by disaster novels and science fiction is often the only kind labelled as generic. The rest is 'literary fiction' or simply 'literature' proper. The latter is the province of 'genuine' literary art and 'authentic' authorial expression. The former, by contrast, is usually considered formulaic, stereotypical, artistically anonymous, and therefore artistically worthless. Hence the following, from Sutherland's *Fiction and the Fiction Industry*:

> Another feature of the increasing 'packaged' nature of all fiction – including the quality novel – is the advance of 'genre' or the categorised product. By 'genre' is meant such forms as Science Fiction, the detective novel, Gothic, etc. . . .
>
> Genre incorporates a high ration of familiar to strange elements. Habitually it eliminates the bewilderment associated with avant garde and experimentalism. It specialises in books without shock. If, as Ezra Pound says, the modernist's motto is 'make it new' then the genre author's motto is 'make it the same' . . . Genre fiction is, characteristically, convention-governed . . . There is a soothing quality to much genre fiction; a high incidence of what Q.D. Leavis calls 'living at the novelist's expense' . . . generally the material is bland, despite its claims to unbearable excitement. Similarly genre may have a superficially impressive specialised knowledge . . . But in the end there will be nothing to task the reader's capacities.
>
> (Sutherland 1978: 192–4. For a very different view, see Bloom 1996.)

It will be readily apparent that those writing on Hollywood's genres in the 1960s and 1970s decisively rejected – indeed often symmetrically inverted – the values and judgement evident in a passage like this. McArthur, for instance, argues that genre conventions can play a positive role in curbing authorial 'excess and self-indulgence' (1972: 94). However, the point to emphasize here is that they share its definitions and its terms, and that these definitions and terms, along with the values and judgements of someone like Sutherland, have a distinct and particular history. As Kress and Threadgold have pointed out:

> *Genre* is valorised very differently in different contexts. From the Romantics through modernism to postmodernism, *genre* is a devalued term in the dominant literary/aesthetic discourse. To be 'generic' is to be predictable and clichéd; within that ideology, literature and art generally has to be free, creative, individual … hence literature cannot be generic …
>
> In classical periods, for example the English Neo-classical period in the late seventeenth and early eighteenth centuries, or even before then in the Renaissance, the reverse was the case. Literature had to be generic to be considered literature (consider Dryden's famous essay on Dramatic Poesy), and notions of genre were so intimately tied up with what was to be literature that they overtly and in very conscious ways affected both the reading and writing of literary texts.

> (Kress and Threadgold 1988: 219–20)

Threadgold reiterates these points elsewhere, stressing the role of conceptions of genre within and across the cultural divisions in artistic practice, in particular those between 'high' and 'low', 'popular' and 'elite':

> Before Romanticism what was Generic was Literature. The rest, the 'popular culture' of political pamphlets, ballads, romances, chapbooks, was only *not* generic; it escaped the law of genre, was excluded by that law, suffering a kind of rhetorical exclusion by inclusion in the classical distinction between high, middle, and low styles. It was seen as a kind of anarchic, free area, unconstrained by the rules of polite society and decorum, by *genre* in fact.

> (Threadgold 1989: 121–2)

Thus genre has undergone 'a fundamental shift of positioning' (ibid.: 120). And this shift runs parallel with shifts both in cultural and aesthetic production and consumption, and in the history of the term 'genre' itself. As Cohen has pointed out, the use of the term in English to refer to aesthetic practices and products is a nineteenth-century phenomenon (1986: 203). Thus although the concept is clearly much older, the term itself emerges with industrialization, mass production, new technologies, new capital, new means of distribution (notably postal systems and the railways), the formation of a relatively

GENRE

CONTINUED

large literate (or semi-literate) population – and hence a potential market – at a point of profound transformation in the conditions governing cultural production and the discourses and debates with which it was accompanied. Now it is the new popular culture, the new mass culture that is marked – with a new term – as 'generic'. Repetitive patterns, ingredients and formulae are now perceived by many cultural commentators not as the law of Culture, but as the law of the market. It s therefore hardly surprising that genre was – and still is – principally associated with an industrial, commercial and mechanically based art like the cinema, and with its most obviously industrial, commercial and popular sectors like Hollywood in particular. And it is thus particularly important to consider ideas, definitions and theories of genre which challenge conventional conceptions.

One source of and for such ideas is the literary critic E. D. Hirsch (a surprising source, perhaps, given his commitment to traditional literary values). Hirsch insists on the fundamental role played by genre – not just in the framing and interpretation of works of art but also in the framing and interpretation of any kind of utterance. He also insists on the fact that genres centrally include – even consist of – a set of expectations. A reader's or interlocutor's 'preliminary generic conception', he writes, 'is constitutive of everything that he subsequently understands, ... and this [always] remains the case unless and until that generic conception is altered' (1967: 74). In elaborating this view at greater length, Hirsch makes clear that genre in this sense is as much a phenomenon of everyday discourse as it is of literary texts:

> quite apart from the speaker's choice of words, and, even more remarkably, quite aside from the context in which the utterance occurs, the details of meaning that an interpreter understands are powerfully determined and constituted by his meaning expectation. And these expectations arise from the interpreter's conception of the type of meaning that is being expressed.
>
> By 'type of meaning' I do not, of course, intend to imply merely a type of message or theme or anything so simple as content. The interpreter's expectations embrace far more than that. They include a number of elements that may not even be explicitly given in the utterance or its context, such as the relationship assumed to exist between the speaker and the interpreter, the type of vocabulary and syntax that is used, the type of attitude adopted by the speaker, and the type of inexplicit meanings that go with explicit ones. Such expectations are always necessary to understanding, because only by virtue of them can the interpreter make sense of the words he experiences along the way. He entertains the notion that 'this is a certain type of meaning,' and his notion of the meaning as a whole grounds and helps determine his understanding of details. This fact reveals itself whenever a misunderstanding is suddenly recognized. After all, how could it have been recognized unless the interpreter's

expectations had been thwarted? How could anything surprising or puzzling occur to force a revision of his past understanding unless the interpreter had expectations that could be surprised or thwarted? Furthermore, these expectations could have arisen only from the genre idea: 'In this type of utterance, we expect these types of traits.'

(Hirsch 1967: 72–3)

During the course of his discussion of genre, Hirsch draws in particular on the structural linguistics of Saussure ([1959] 1974). Issues of genre and parallels with Hirsch's position have been more apparent, however, in speech-act theory and pragmatics. Speech-act theory and pragmatics are branches of linguistics and of analytical philosophy, respectively. They are both concerned with language in use, and in particular with the rules and conventions that govern the production, reception and comprehension of specific kinds of linguistic utterance in specific kinds of context. Mary Louise Pratt (1977), for instance, has written a pioneering book on speech-act theory and literature stressing the generic aspects of all forms of discourse, indeed of 'literature' as such. More recently, in an essay on the short story, she highlights the role, importance and ubiquity of genre in literary and in non-literary discourse alike. 'Genre is not solely a literary matter', she writes. 'The concept of genres applies to all verbal behavior, in all realms of discourse. Genre conventions are in play in any speech situation, and any discourse belongs to a genre, unless it is a discourse explicitly designed to flaunt the genre system' (1981: 176).

Speech-act-oriented theories of genre have recently been drawn on (and sometimes modified, extended or criticized, though always from within a recognizable similar ambit of concerns) by Derrida (1992), Freadman (1988), Hunter (1989), Reid (1989) and Ryan (1981). Derrida criticizes speech-act theories of genre on the grounds that texts can always exceed specific expectations, contexts and labels. He would therefore contest Pratt's notion that texts 'belong' to genres. He would also deny, though, that any text or instance of discourse could ever escape being generic. A text or an instance of discourse might be able to 'flaunt' a particular 'genre system', but they could never flaunt the 'law of genre' as such, for the simple reason that all texts, all utterances, all instances of discourse are always encountered in some kind of context, and are therefore always confronted with expectations, with systems of comprehension, and in all probability with labels and names. Freadman gives a good example of this:

When the title 'Untitled' started appearing beneath paintings, it corresponded to the claim of abstract painting to be non-representational: to be 'painting', simply ... It is a title that represents the non-representational. Now, since the titles of paintings – place-names, personal names, the names of historical or legendary events, or kinds of subjects – designate not only their represented subjects but also, through the naming conventions themselves, their genres, the title 'Untitled' claims above all to transcend genre. Reflect on this. For 'untitled' paintings are themselves a genre; and the title 'Untitled' points to genre in the very act of its denial.

(Freadman 1988: 67)

A less spectacular example from the cinema would be a film like *Un Chien Andalou* (1928), which certainly flaunted the genre system predominant in Europe at the time it was made. It also flaunted the genre 'narrative feature film', and the genres of the contemporary European art film. One of its makers, Luis Buñuel, claimed it was not even an instance of avant-garde film-making, but rather 'a desperate appeal to murder' (Aranda 1975: 63). However, it is precisely for all these reasons that it is usually now understood, and now usually labelled generically, as an exemplary instance of Surrealism. Hence, to return to Derrida, 'Every text participates in one or several genres, there is no genreless text.' Although 'participation never amounts to belonging', 'there is always a genre or genres' (1992: 230).

Derrida's use of the phrase 'one or several genres', his stress on the possible plurality of generic participation, may not resolve the discrepancies between some of the genre terms used in literary studies and the terms that tend to dominate the study of the cinema. (Such discrepancies are historical in origin, and are thus not entirely susceptible to logical or conceptual resolution.) But it does point to a way of resolving Williams' dilemma about 'real' genres, and the validity of categories like the western and science fiction on the one hand, and 'narrative film, experimental/avant-garde film, or documentary' on the other. For from a Derridean perspective, this dilemma is ultimately false. Any film (like any text, utterance or instance of representation) can participate in several genres at once. In fact, it is more common than not for a film to do so. Thus, without trying to be too exhaustive (and leaving aside for the moment the issue of overt generic hybrids), both *Star Wars* (1977) and *Body Heat* (1981), to use two of Williams' (1984) examples, participate in the genres 'film', 'fiction film', 'Hollywood film' and 'narrative feature film'. The former also participates in the genre 'science fiction', and the latter in the genre 'thriller' (and possibly also 'neo-*noir*'). *Prelude to Dog Star Man* (1965), meanwhile, participates in the genres 'film' and 'avant-garde/experimental film' – and also, for some of its viewers at least, the genres 'mythopoeic' and/or 'visionary film', categories first suggested by the influential critic and historian of American avant-garde film, P. Adams Sitney (1979).

While challenging traditional definitions of genre, it is worth noting that there remains a degree of common ground between speech-act-oriented theorists like Pratt, Hirsch and Derrida and theorists like Tudor and Ryall. All agree that genre is a multi-dimensional phenomenon and that its dimensions centrally include systems of expectation, categories, labels and names, discourses, texts and corpuses of texts, and the conventions that govern them all. Some stress the primacy of expectations, others the primacy of texts, still others the primacy of categories, corpuses, the norms they encompass, the traditions they embody and the formulae that mark them. What seems clear is that all these dimensions need to be taken into account. What also seems clear is that they need to be distinguished one from another.

However, the argument that genre is ubiquitous, a phenomenon common to all instances of discourse, ignores or collapses the distinction between those instances which are relatively formulaic, relatively predictable, relatively conventional, and those which are not, between those produced in accordance with the conventions of a pre-signalled genre or genre system and those designed to flaunt them. It also ignores or collapses the boundaries between different ways of categorizing texts and of grouping expectations. The expectations triggered by the name of a star or director are as generic as those triggered by terms like 'western', 'thriller' or 'horror film'. One would normally want, though, to distinguish between the two.

These boundaries and distinctions underlie a great deal of traditional thinking about genres. They have often been tied, as we have seen, to issues of evaluation. They have often been linked to the establishment of aesthetic and cultural hierarchies. And they have often inhibited the development of genre theory. However, while it is important to question traditional thinking and to expand the definition, the meaning and the field of application of genre as a term, it is also important to recognize the differences these boundaries and distinctions serve to mark.

GENRE AND THE GENRE FILM

One way of acknowledging some of these differences without falling into the usual conceptual or cultural traps is to note that they apply to high art as well as to low: a sonnet is formulaic in a way that free verse is not; a Restoration comedy is conventional in a way that a modernist novel is not; and so on. In addition, it should be noted that when Warshow talked about the pleasures and characteristics of aesthetic 'types', he was referring to Restoration comedy and Elizabethan tragedy as well as to westerns and gangster films: 'For a type to be successful', he wrote

> its conventions have imposed themselves upon the general consciousness and become the vehicle of a particular set of attitudes and a particular aesthetic effect. One goes to any individual example of the type with very definite expectations, and originality is to be welcomed only in the degree that it intensifies the expected experience without fundamentally altering it.

> (Warshow [1948] 1975a: 129–30)

Within the realms of cinema, numerous movements or trends in art cinema and in avant-garde film-making are or become as predictable (and as typically pleasurable) as any Hollywood western. However, and conversely, there is a difference between academic or programmatic aesthetic formulae and formulae which arise as a result of commercial conditions. And there is a difference between films which are designed to conform, however broadly, to pre-existing categories, expectations and models, and those, like *Un Chien Andalou*, which are not. The latter may encounter expectations and those expectations may be based on previous films or on the tenets of a movement or a group. They may conform to labels or descriptions circulated in advance by critics, distributors, reviewers, perhaps even film-makers themselves. And they may all establish their own internal norms and hence become more familiar – and more predictable – as they unfold. But many of these norms are often unique to the films themselves. Thus the films are less predictable in advance, and at more or less every level. That does not necessarily make them better. But it does make them different.

Altman makes a further distinction. He points out that

> not all films engage spectators' generic knowledge in the same way and to the same extent. While some films simply borrow devices from established genres, others foreground their generic characteristics to the point where the genre concept itself plays a major role in the film.

> (Altman 1996a: 279)

Parodies are an obvious instance of the latter, as Altman goes on to indicate. So too are films like *Silverado* (1985), *Chinatown* (1974), *Scarface* (1983) and *Back to the Future* III (1990), films which pastiche, rework or in other ways foreground particular generic traditions, norms and conventions. Altman, following Schatz (1981: 16–18), goes on to propose two different terms, 'film genre' and 'genre film,' in order to mark this particular distinction:

> By definition, all films belong to some genre(s) ... but only certain films are self-consciously produced and consumed according to (or against) a specific generic model. When the notion of genre is limited to descriptive uses, as it commonly is when serving ... classification purposes, we speak of 'film genre'. However, when the notion of genre takes on a more active role in the production and consumption process, we appropriately speak instead of 'genre film', thus recognizing the extent to which generic identification becomes a formative component of film viewing.

> (Altman 1996a: 277)

While these terms and definitions are useful, Altman here tends to conflate genre as a category and genre as a corpus of films: *Stagecoach* (1939) is both a singular instance of the category 'western' and part of an expanding corpus that includes films like *Hell's Hinges* (1916), *Riders of the Range* (1923), *Bend of the River* (1952), *El Dorado* (1967) and *Tombstone* (1993). The two are distinct. He also tends, through the term 'self-conscious', to conflate routine generic production and routine generic consumption, both of which entail specific generic models and in both of which such models are 'active', with special and particular instances like parody and pastiche. In addition, he tends to imply that the activation of a generic model necessarily entails conformity or participation. But a model may be invoked in order to be reworked or rejected altogether, as is arguably the case with some of the 'revisionist' films of the late 1960s and early 1970s – films like *Chinatown*, *The Long Goodbye* (1973) and *Buffalo Bill and the Indians* (1976) – which rework or reject existing models of the detective film and the western, and as is certainly the case with *Un Chien Andalou*, which both invokes and decisively rejects the model of the contemporary narrative film. For all these reasons, the proposed term 'genre film' tends to evoke traditional definitions, thereby potentially reducing the multiplicity and scope of the phenomenon of genre itself. In order to avoid some of these problems, and in order to take some account of speech-act-oriented thinking, terms like 'generically marked film' and 'generically modelled film' might be preferable. The former would indicate films which rely on generic identification by an audience – and hence specific forms of audience knowledge – in order to make sense. (This would include parody, pastiche and other forms of self-consciousness. But it would also include less specialized instances as well.) The latter would indicate films which draw on and conform to existing generic traditions, conventions and formulae. In practice, of course, the two often overlap. But the former refers more to the moment of reception, and may include instances of generic reworking and generic rejection as well as instances of generic conformity. The latter refers to the moment of production, and by definition excludes generic rejection. Both remain distinct from genre as a category, and genre as a group or corpus of films.

What emerges from this overview is that genre as a term has been used in different ways in different fields, and that many of its uses have been governed by the history of the term within these fields – and by the cultural factors at play within them – rather than by logic or conceptual consistency. The questions raised by Ryall, Tudor and Williams are important ones, as are the questions raised by speech-act theory and pragmatics. The answers to these questions require thinking of genres as ubiquitous, multifaceted phenomena rather than as one-dimensional entities to be found only within the realms of Hollywood cinema or of commercial popular culture. Only then can some of the pitfalls identified by Ryall, by Tudor, by Williams and by others be avoided. And only then can the nature, the functions, and the general topic of genre in Hollywood itself be examined in more detail.

(Neale 2000: 12–28)

Of course one clear issue that genre critics need to address is what categories of films can be called *genres*. What, for example, is the difference between a genre and a style of film? How do we deal with films that have the characteristics of more than one genre?

A useful and reasonably comprehensive starting point is provided by Tim Dirks on the Filmsite genre web pages:

Main Film Genres (Iconic symbols represent the different genres of films)	Descriptions of Main Film Genres
Action Films **WOW!**	Action films usually include high energy, big-budget physical stunts and chases, possibly with rescues, battles, fights, escapes, destructive crises (floods, explosions, natural disasters, fires, etc.), non-stop motion, spectacular rhythm and pacing, and adventurous, often two-dimensional 'good-guy' heroes (or recently, heroines), battling 'bad guys' – all designed for pure audience escapism. Includes the James Bond 'fantasy' spy/espionage series, martial arts films, and so-called 'blaxploitation' films. A major sub-genre is the *disaster film*. See also *Greatest Disaster and Crowd Film Scenes* and *Greatest Classic Chase Scenes in Films*.
Adventure Films	Adventure films are usually exciting stories, with new experiences or exotic locales, very similar to or often paired with the *action* film genre. They can include traditional swashbucklers, *serialized films*, and historical spectacles (similar to the *epics* film genre), searches or expeditions for lost continents, 'jungle' and 'desert' epics, treasure hunts, disaster films, or searches for the unknown.
Comedy Films	Comedies are light-hearted plots consistently and deliberately designed to amuse and provoke laughter (with one-liners, jokes, etc.) by exaggerating the situation, the language, action, relationships and characters. This section describes various forms of comedy through cinematic history, including *slapstick*, *screwball*, *spoofs* and *parodies*, *romantic comedies*, *black comedy* (dark satirical comedy), and more. See this site's *Funniest Film Moments and Scenes* collection – illustrated.

Crime & Gangster Films	Crime (gangster) films are developed around the sinister actions of criminals or mobsters, particularly bankrobbers, underworld figures, or ruthless hoodlums who operate outside the law, stealing and murdering their way through life. Criminal and gangster films are often categorized as *film noir* or *detective-mystery* films – because of underlying similarities between these cinematic forms. This category includes a description of various 'serial killer' films.
Drama Films	Dramas are serious, plot-driven presentations, portraying realistic characters, settings, life situations, and stories involving intense character development and interaction. Usually, they are not focused on special-effects, comedy, or action. Dramatic films are probably the largest film genre, with many subsets. See also the *melodramas*, *epics* (*historical dramas*), or *romantic* genres. Dramatic *biographical films* (or '*biopics*') are a major sub-genre, as are 'adult' films (with mature subject content).
Epics/Historical Films	Epics include costume dramas, historical *dramas*, *war* films, medieval romps, or 'period pictures' that often cover a large expanse of time set against a vast, panoramic backdrop. Epics often share elements of the elaborate *adventure* films genre. Epics take an historical or imagined event, mythic, legendary, or heroic figure, and add an extravagant setting and lavish costumes, accompanied by grandeur and spectacle, dramatic scope, high production values, and a sweeping musical score. Epics are often a more spectacular, lavish version of a *biopic film*. Some 'sword and sandal' films (Biblical epics or films occurring during antiquity) qualify as a sub-genre.
Horror Films	Horror films are designed to frighten and to invoke our hidden worst fears, often in a terrifying, shocking finale, while captivating and entertaining us at the same time in a cathartic experience. Horror films feature a wide range of styles, from the earliest silent Nosferatu classic, to today's CGI monsters and deranged humans. They are often combined with *science fiction* when the menace or monster is related to a corruption of technology, or when Earth is threatened by aliens. The *fantasy* and *supernatural* film genres are not usually synonymous with the horror genre. There are many sub-genres of horror: slasher, teen terror, serial killers, satanic, Dracula, Frankenstein, etc. See this site's *Scariest Film Moments and Scenes* collection – illustrated.

Main Film Genres (Iconic symbols represent the different genres of films)	Descriptions of Main Film Genres
Musicals (Dance) Films	Musical/dance films are cinematic forms that emphasize full-scale scores or song and dance routines in a significant way (usually with a musical or dance performance integrated as part of the film narrative), or they are films that are centered on combinations of music, dance, song or choreography. Major subgenres include the *musical comedy* or the concert film.
Science Fiction Films	Sci-fi films are often quasi-scientific, visionary and imaginative – complete with heroes, aliens, distant planets, impossible quests, improbable settings, fantastic places, great dark and shadowy villains, futuristic technology, unknown and unknowable forces, and extraordinary monsters ('things or creatures from space'), either created by mad scientists or by nuclear havoc. They are sometimes an offshoot of *fantasy* films, or they share some similarities with *action/adventure* films. Science fiction often expresses the potential of technology to destroy humankind and easily overlaps with *horror* films, particularly when technology or alien life forms become malevolent, as in the 'Atomic Age' of sci-fi films in the 1950s.
War (Anti-War) Films	War films acknowledge the horror and heartbreak of war, letting the actual combat fighting (against nations or humankind) on land, sea, or in the air provide the primary plot or background for the action of the film. War films are often paired with other genres, such as *action*, *adventure*, *drama*, *romance*, *comedy* (black), *suspense*, and even *epics* and *westerns*, and they often take a denunciatory approach toward warfare. They may include POW tales, stories of military operations, and training.
Westerns	Westerns are the major defining genre of the American film industry – a eulogy to the early days of the expansive American frontier. They are one of the oldest, most enduring genres with very recognizable plots, elements, and characters (six-guns, horses, dusty towns and trails, cowboys, Indians, etc.). Over time, westerns have been re-defined, re-invented and expanded, dismissed, re-discovered, and spoofed.

➤ How useful do you find this categorising of films? Are there any genres you would want to add? Are there any you would take out?

Before proceeding to look at some examples of genre criticism you may like to have a go at some yourself. Here is a useful list of questions produced by Daniel Chandler on the Communication and Media Studies website that you can use for your own investigation.

D.I.Y. GENERIC ANALYSIS

The following questions are offered as basic guidelines for my own students in analysing an individual text in relation to genre. Note that an analysis of a text which is framed *exclusively* in terms of genre may be of limited usefulness. Generic analysis can also, of course, involve studying the genre more broadly: in examining the genre one may fruitfully consider such issues as how the conventions of the genre have changed over time.

General -

■ Why did you choose the text you are analysing?
■ In what context did you encounter it?
■ What influence do you think this context might have had on your interpretation of the text?
■ To what genre did you initially assign the text?
■ What is your experience of this genre?
■ What subject matter and basic themes is the text concerned with?
■ How typical of the genre is this text in terms of content?
■ What expectations do you have about texts in this genre?
■ Have you found any formal generic labels for this particular text (where)?
■ What generic labels have others given the same text?
■ Which conventions of the genre do you recognize in the text?
■ To what extent does this text stretch the conventions of its genre?
■ Where and why does the text depart from the conventions of the genre?
■ Which conventions seem more like those of a different genre (and which genre(s))?
■ What familiar motifs or images are used?
■ Which of the formal/stylistic techniques employed are typical/untypical of the genre?
■ What institutional constraints are reflected in the form of the text?
■ What relationship to 'reality' does the text lay claim to?
■ Whose realities does it reflect?
■ What purposes does the genre serve?
■ In what ways are these purposes embodied in the text?

- To what extent did your purposes match these when you engaged with the text?
- What ideological assumptions and values seem to be embedded in the text?
- What pleasures does this genre offer to you personally?
- What pleasures does the text appeal to (and how typical of the genre is this)?
- Did you feel 'critical or accepting, resisting or validating, casual or concentrated, apathetic or motivated' (and why)?
- Which elements of the text seemed salient because of your knowledge of the genre?
- What predictions about events did your generic identification of the text lead to (and to what extent did these prove accurate)?
- What inferences about people and their motivations did your genre identification give rise to (and how far were these confirmed)?
- How and why did your interpretation of the text differ from the interpretation of the same text by other people?

MODE OF ADDRESS

- What sort of audience did you feel that the text was aimed at (and how typical was this of the genre)?
- How does the text address you?
- What sort of person does it assume you are?
- What assumptions seem to be made about your class, age, gender and ethnicity?
- What interests does it assume you have?
- What relevance does the text actually have for you?
- What knowledge does it take for granted?
- To what extent do you resemble the 'ideal reader' that the text seeks to position you as?
- Are there any notable shifts in the text's mode of address (and if so, what do they involve)?
- What responses does the text seem to expect from you?
- How open to negotiation is your response (are you invited, instructed or coerced to respond in particular ways)?
- Is there any penalty for not responding in the expected ways?
- To what extent do you find yourself 'reading against the grain' of the text and the genre?
- Which attempts to position you in this text do you accept, reject or seek to negotiate (and why)?
- How closely aligned is the way in which the *text* addresses you with the way in which the *genre* positions you?

RELATIONSHIP TO OTHER TEXTS
- What intertextual references are there in the text you are analysing (and to what other texts)?
- Generically, which other texts does the text you are analysing resemble most closely?
- What key features are shared by these texts?
- What major differences do you notice between them?

(http://www.aber.ac.uk/media/Documents/intgenre/intgenre5.html)

An interesting example of a film genre is the musical, not least because despite its moving in and out of favour with audiences, it can claim a good degree of longevity as a genre. Musicals have been traditionally popular at times of economic depression, largely because they represent a potential escape from the grim realities of people's daily lives. Richard Dyer calls this quality of escapism *Utopianism*, a world of 'something better' to which the audience can find an escape. In the following extract, Dyer develops the argument by way of genre analysis of three musicals, *Golddiggers* (Mervyn Le Roy 1933), *Funny Face* (Stanley Donen 1957) and *On the Town* (Gene Kelly 1949).

Two of the taken-for-granted descriptions of entertainment, as 'escape' and as 'wish-fulfilment,' point to its central thrust, namely, utopianism. Entertainment offers the image of 'something better' to escape into, or something we want deeply that our day-to-day lives don't provide. Alternatives, hopes, wishes – these are the stuff of utopia, the sense that things could be better, that something other than what is can be imagined and maybe realised.

Entertainment does not, however, present models of utopian worlds, as in the classic utopias of Sir Thomas More, William Morris, *et al.* Rather the utopianism is contained in the feelings it embodies. It presents, head-on as it were, what utopia would feel like rather than how it would be organised. It thus works at the level of sensibility, by which I mean an effective code that is characteristic of, and largely specific to, a given mode of cultural production.

This code uses both representational and, importantly, non-representational signs. There is a tendency to concentrate on the former, and clearly it would be wrong to overlook them – stars are nicer than we are, characters more straightforward than people we know, situations more soluble than those we encounter. All this we recognise through representational signs. But we also recognise qualities in non-representational signs – colour, texture, movement, rhythm, melody, camerawork – although we are much less used to talking about them. The nature of non-representational signs is not however so different from that of representational. Both are, in C. S. Peirce's terminology, largely iconic; but whereas the relationship between signifier and signified in

125

GENRE

a representational icon is one of resemblance between their appearance, their look, the relationship in the case of the non-representational icon is one of resemblance at the level of basic structuration.

This concept has been developed (among other places) in the work of Suzanne K. Langer, particularly in relation to music. We feel music (arguably more than any other performance medium), yet it has the least obvious reference to 'reality' – the intensity of our response to music can only be accounted for by the way music, abstract, formal though it is, still embodies feeling. Langer puts it thus in *Feeling and Form*:

> The tonal structures we call 'music' bear a close logical similarity to the forms of human feeling – forms of growth and attenuation, flowing and slowing, conflict and resolution, speed, arrest, terrific excitement, calm or subtle activation or dreamy lapses – not joy and sorrow perhaps, but the poignancy of both – the greatness and brevity and eternal passing of everything vitally felt. Such is the pattern, or logical form, of sentience; and the pattern of music is that same form worked out in pure measures, sound and silence. Music is a tonal analogue of emotive life.
>
> Such formal analogy, or congruence of logical structures, is the prime requisite for the relation between a symbol and whatever it is to mean. The symbol and the object symbolized must have some common logical form.

Langer realises that recognition of a common logical form between a performance sign and what it signifies is not always easy or natural: 'The congruence of two given perceptible forms is not always evident upon simple inspection. The common *logical* form they both exhibit may become apparent only when you know the principle whereby to relate them.' This implies that responding to a performance is not spontaneous – you have to learn what emotion is embodied before you can respond to it. A problem with this as Langer develops it is the implication that the emotion itself is not coded, is simply 'human feeling'. I would be inclined, however, to see almost as much coding in the emotions as in the signs for them. Thus, just as writers such as E. H. Gombrich and Umberto Eco stress that different modes of representation (in history and culture) correspond to different modes of perception, so it is important to grasp that modes of experiential art and entertainment correspond to different culturally and historically determined sensibilities.

This becomes clear when one examines how entertainment forms come to have the emotional signification they do: that is, by acquiring their signification in relation to the complex of meanings in the social-cultural situation in which they are produced. Take the extremely complex history of tap dance – in black culture, tap dance has had an improvisatory, self-expressive function similar to that in jazz; in minstrelsy, it took on an aspect of jolly mindlessness, inane good humour, in accord with minstrelsy's image of the Negro; in vaudeville, elements of mechanical skill, tap dance as a feat, were stressed as part of vaudeville's celebration of the machine and the brilliant performer. Clearly there are connections between these different significations, and there are residues of all of them in tap as used in films, television and contemporary theatre shows. This has little to do however with the intrinsic meanings of hard, short, percussive, syncopated sounds arranged in patterns and produced by the movement of feet, and everything to do with the significance such sounds acquire from their place within the network of signs in a given culture at a given point of time. Nevertheless, the signification is essentially apprehended through the coded non-representational form (although the representational elements usually present in a performance sign – a dancer is always 'a person dancing' – may help to anchor the necessarily more fluid signification of the non-representational elements; for example, a black man, a white man in blackface, a troupe, or a white woman tap-dancing may suggest different ways of reading the taps, because each relates to a slightly different moment in the evolution of the non-representational form, tap dance).

I have laboured this point at greater length than may seem warranted, partly with polemic intent. Firstly, it seems to me that the reading of non-representational signs in the cinema is particularly undeveloped. On the one hand, the *mise-en-scène* approach (at least as classically developed in *Movie*) tends to treat the non-representational as a function of the representational, simply a way of bringing out, emphasising, aspects of plot, character, situation, without signification in their own right. On the other hand, semiotics has been concerned with the codification of the representational. Secondly, I feel that film analysis remains notoriously non-historical, except in rather lumbering, simplistic ways. My adaptation of Langer seeks to emphasise not the connection between signs and historical events, personages or forces, but rather the history of signs themselves as they are produced in culture and history. Nowhere here has it been possible to reproduce the detail of any sign's history (and I admit to speculation in some instances), but most of the assertions are based on more thorough research, and even where they are not, they should be.

The categories of entertainment's utopian sensibility are sketched in the accompanying table together with examples of them. The three films used will be discussed below; the examples from Westerns and television news are just to suggest how the categories may have wider application; the sources referred to are the cultural, historical situation of the code's production.

The categories are, I hope, clear enough, but a little more needs to be said about 'intensity'. It is hard to find a word that quite gets what I mean. What I have in mind is the capacity of entertainment to present either complex or unpleasant feelings (e.g., involvement in personal or political events, jealousy, loss of love, defeat) in a way that makes them seem uncomplicated, direct and vivid, not 'qualified' or 'ambiguous' as day-to-day life makes them, and without those intimations of self-deception and pretence. (Both intensity and transparency can be related to wider themes in the culture, as 'authenticity' and 'sincerity' respectively; see Lionel Trilling's *Sincerity and Authenticity*.)

The obvious problem raised by this breakdown of the utopian sensibility is where these categories come from. One answer, at a very broad level, might be that they are a continuation of the utopian tradition in Western thought. George Kateb, in his survey of utopian thought, *Utopia and Its Enemies*, describes what he takes to be the dominant motifs in this tradition, and they do broadly overlap with those outlined above. Thus:

> ... when a man [sic] thinks of perfection ... he thinks of a world permanently without strife, poverty, constraint, stultifying labour, irrational authority, sensual deprivation ... peace, abundance, leisure, equality, consonance of men and their environment.

We may agree that notions in this broad conceptual area are common throughout Western thought, giving it, and its history, its characteristic dynamic, its sense of moving beyond what is to what ought to be or what we want to be. However, the very broadness, and looseness, of this common ground does not get us very far – we need to examine the specificity of entertainment's utopia.

One way of doing so is to see the categories of the sensibility as temporary answers to the inadequacies of the society which is being escaped from through entertainment. This is proposed by Hans Magnus Enzensberger in his article, 'Constituents of a Theory of the Media' (in *Sociology of Mass Communication*, edited by Dennis McQuail). Enzensberger takes issue with the traditional left-wing use of concepts of 'manipulation' and 'false needs' in relation to the mass media:

> The electronic media do not owe their irresistible power to any sleight-of-hand but to the elemental power of deep social needs which come through even in the present depraved form of these media. ...
>
> Consumption as spectacle contains the promise that want will disappear. The deceptive, brutal and obscene features of this festival derive from the fact that there can be no question of a real fulfilment of its promise. But so long as scarcity holds sway, use-value remains a decisive category which can only be abolished by trickery. Yet trickery on such a scale is only conceivable if it is based on mass need. This need – it is a utopian one – is there. It is the desire for a new ecology, for a breaking-down of environmental barriers, for an aesthetic which is not limited to the sphere of the 'artistic'. These desires are not – or are not primarily – internalized rules of the games as played by the capitalist

system. They have physiological roots and can no longer be suppressed. Consumption as spectacle is – in parody form – the anticipation of a utopian situation.

This does, I think, express well the complexity of the situation. However Enzensberger's appeal to 'elemental' and 'physiological' demands, although we do not need to be too frightened by them, is lacking in both historical and anthropological perspectives. I would rather suggest, a little over-schematically, that the categories of the utopian sensibility are related to specific inadequacies in society as follows:

Social Tension/Inadequacy/Absence	*Utopian Solution*
Scarcity (actual poverty in the society; poverty observable in the surrounding societies, e.g., Third World); unequal distribution of wealth	Abundance (elimination of poverty for self and others; equal distribution of wealth)
Exhaustion (work as a grind, alienated labour, pressures of urban life)	Energy (work and play synonymous), city dominated (*On the Town*) or pastoral return (*The Sound of Music*)
Dreariness (monotony, predictability, instrumentality of the daily round)	Intensity (excitement, drama, affectivity of living)
Manipulation (advertising, bourgeois democracy, sex roles)	Transparency (open, spontaneous, honest communications and relationships)
Fragmentation (job mobility, rehousing and development, high-rise flats, legislation against collective action)	Community (all together in one place, communal interests, collective activity)

The advantage of this analysis is that it does offer some explanation of why entertainment *works*. It is not just left-overs from history, it is not *just* what show business, or 'they', force on the rest of us, it is not simply the expression of eternal needs – it responds to real needs *created by society*. The weakness of the analysis (and this holds true for Enzensberger too) is in the give-away absences from the left-hand column – no mention of class, race or patriarchy. That is, while entertainment is responding to needs that are real, at the same time it is also defining and delimiting what constitutes the legitimate needs of people in this society.

I am not trying to recoup here the false needs argument – we are talking about real needs created by real inadequacies, but they are not the only needs and inadequacies of the society. Yet entertainment, by so orienting itself to them, effectively denies the legitimacy of other needs and inadequacies, and

CONTINUED

especially of class, patriarchal and sexual struggles. (Though once again we have to admit the complexity and contradictions of the situation – that, for instance, entertainment is not the only agency which defines legitimate needs, and that the actual role of women, gay men and blacks in the creation of show business leaves its mark in such central oppositional icons as, respectively, the strong woman type, e.g., Ethel Merman, Judy Garland, Elsie Tanner, camp humour and sensuous taste in dress and decor, and almost all aspects of dance and music. Class, it will be noted, is still nowhere.)

Class, race and sexual caste are denied validity as problems by the dominant (bourgeois, white, male) ideology of society. We should not expect show business to be markedly different. However, there is one further turn of the screw, and that is that, with the exception perhaps of community (the most directly working class in source), the ideals of entertainment imply wants that capitalism itself promises to meet. Thus abundance becomes consumerism, energy and intensity personal freedom and individualism, and transparency freedom of speech. In other (Marcuse's) words, it is a partially 'one-dimensional' situation. The categories of the sensibility point to gaps or inadequacies in capitalism, but only those gaps or inadequacies that capitalism proposes itself to deal with. At our worse sense of it, entertainment provides alternatives *to* capitalism which will be provided *by* capitalism.

However, this one-dimensionality is seldom so hermetic, because of the deeply contradictory nature of entertainment forms. In variety, the essential contradiction is between comedy and music turns; in musicals, it is between the narrative and the numbers. Both these contradictions can be rendered as one between the heavily representational and verisimilitudinous (pointing to the way the world is, drawing on the audience's concrete experience of the world) and the heavily non-representational and 'unreal' (pointing to how things could be better). In musicals, contradiction is also to be found at two other levels – within numbers, between the representational and the non-representational, and within the non-representational, owing to the differing sources of production inscribed in the signs.

To be effective, the utopian sensibility has to take off from the real experiences of the audience. Yet to do this, to draw attention to the gap between what is and what could be, is, ideologically speaking, playing with fire. What musicals have to do, then (not through any conspiratorial intent, but because it is always easier to take the line of least resistance, i.e., to fit in with prevailing norms), is to work through these contradictions at all levels in such a way as to 'manage' them, to make them seem to disappear. They don't always succeed.

I have chosen three musicals which seem to me to illustrate the three broad tendencies of musicals – those that keep narrative and number clearly separated (most typically, the backstage musical); those that retain the division between narrative as problems and numbers as escape, but try to 'integrate' the numbers by a whole set of papering-over-the-cracks devices (e.g., the well-known 'cue for a song'); and musicals which try to dissolve the distinction between narrative and numbers, thus implying that the world of the narrative is also (already) utopian.

The clear separation of numbers and narrative in *Golddiggers of* 1933 is broadly in line with a 'realist' aesthetic: the numbers occur in the film in the same way as they occur in life, that is, on stages and in cabarets. This 'realism' is of course reinforced by the social-realist orientation of the narrative, settings and characterisation, with their emphasis on the Depression, poverty, the quest for capital, 'gold-digging' (and prostitution). However, the numbers are not wholly contained by this realist aesthetic – the way in which they are opened out, in scale and in cinematic treatment (overhead shots, etc.), represents a quite marked shift from the real to the non-real, and from the largely representational to the largely nonrepresentational (sometimes to the point of almost complete abstraction). The thrust of the narrative is towards seeing the show as a 'solution' to the personal, Depression-induced problems of the characters; yet the non-realist presentation of the numbers makes it very hard to take this solution seriously. It is 'just' escape, 'merely' utopian.

If the numbers embody (capitalist) palliatives to the problems of the narrative – chiefly, abundance (spectacle) in place of poverty, and (non-efficacious) energy (chorines in self-enclosed patterns) in place of dispiritedness – then the actual mode of presentation undercuts this by denying it the validity of 'realism'.

However, if one then looks at the contradiction between the representational and non-representational within the numbers, this becomes less clear-cut. Here much of the representational level reprises the lessons of the narrative – above all, that women's only capital is their bodies as objects. The abundant scale of the numbers is an abundance of piles of women; the sensuous materialism is the texture of femaleness; the energy of the dancing (when it occurs) is the energy of the choreographic imagination, to which the dangers are subservient. Thus, while the non-representational certainly suggests an alternative to the narrative, the representational merely reinforces the narrative (women as sexual coinage, women – and men – as expressions of the male producer).

Finally, if one then looks at the non-representational alone, contradictions once again become apparent – e.g., spectacle as materialism and metaphysics (that is, on the one hand, the sets, costumes, etc. are tactile, sensuous, physically exhilarating, but on the other hand, are associated with fairy-land, magic, the by-definition immaterial), dance as human creative energy and sub-human mindlessness.

In *Funny Face*, the central contradiction is between art and entertainment, and this is further worked through in the antagonism between the central couple, Audrey Hepburn (art) and Fred Astaire (entertainment). The numbers are escapes from the problems, and discomforts, of the contradiction – either by asserting the unanswerably more pleasurable qualities of entertainment (e.g., 'Clap Yo' Hands' following the dirge-like Juliette Greco-type song in the 'empathicalist', i.e., existentialist, *soirée*), or in the transparency of love in the Hepburn–Astaire numbers.

But it is not always that neat. In the empathicalist cellar club, Hepburn escapes Astaire in a number with some of the other beats in the club. This reverses the escape direction of the rest of the film (i.e., it is an escape from entertainment/Astaire into art). Yet within the number, the contradiction repeats itself. Before Hepburn joins the group, they are dancing in a style deriving from Modern Dance, angular, oppositional shapes redolent in musical convention of neurosis and pretentiousness (*cf.* Danny Kaye's number, 'Choreography', in *White Christmas*). As the number proceeds, however, more show biz elements are introduced – use of syncopated clapping, forming in a vaudeville line-up, and American Theatre Ballet shapes. Here an 'art' form is taken over and infused with the values of entertainment. This is a contradiction between the representational (the dreary night club) and the non-representational (the oomph of music and movement) but also, within the non-representational, between different dance forms. The contradiction between art and entertainment is thus repeated at each level.

In the love numbers, too, contradictions appear, partly by the continuation in them of troubling representational elements. In *Funny Face*, photographs of Hepburn as seen by Astaire, the fashion photographer, are projected on the wall as background to his wooing her and her giving in. Again, their final dance of reconciliation to ''S Wonderful' takes place on the grounds of a chateau, beneath the trees, with doves fluttering around them. Earlier, this setting was used as the finish for their fashion photography sequence. In other words, in both cases, she is reconciled to him only by capitulating to his definition of her. In itself, there is nothing contradictory in this – it is what Ginger Rogers always had to do. But here the mode of reconciliation is transparency and yet we can see the strings of the number being pulled. Thus the representational elements, which bespeak manipulation of romance, contradict the non-representational, which bespeaks its transparency.

The two tendencies just discussed are far more common than the third, which has to suggest that utopia is implicit in the world of the narrative as well as in the world of the numbers.

The commonest procedure for doing this is removal of the whole film in time and space – to turn-of-the-century America (*Meet Me in St. Louis*, *Hello Dolly!*),

Europe (*The Merry Widow, Gigi, Song of Norway*), cockney London (*My Fair Lady, Oliver!, Scrooge*), black communities (*Hallelujah!, Cabin in the Sky, Porgy and Bess*), etc. – to places, that is, where it can be believed (by white urban Americans) that song and dance are 'in the air', built into the peasant/black culture and blood, or part of a more free-and-easy stage in American development. In these films, the introduction of any real narrative concerns is usually considerably delayed and comes chiefly as a temporary threat to utopia – thus reversing the other two patterns, where the narrative predominates and numbers function as temporary escapes from it. Not much happens, plot-wise, in *Meet Me in St. Louis* until we have had 'Meet Me in St. Louis', 'The Boy Next Door', 'The Trolley Song' and 'Skip to My Lou' – only then does father come along with this proposal to dismantle this utopia by his job mobility.

Most of the contradictions developed in these films are over-ridingly bought off by the nostalgia or primitivism which provides them with the point of departure. Far from pointing forwards, they point back, to a golden age – a reversal of utopianism that is only marginally offset by the narrative motive of recovery of utopia. What makes *On the Town* interesting is that its utopia is a well-known modern city. The film starts as an escape – from the confines of Navy life into the freedom of New York, and also from the weariness of work, embodied in the docker's refrain, 'I feel like I'm not out of bed yet', into the energy of leisure, as the sailors leap into the city for their day off. This energy runs through the whole film, *including the narrative*. In most musicals, the narrative represents things as they are, to be escaped from. But most of the narrative of *On the Town* is about the transformation of New York into utopia. The sailors release the *social* frustrations of the women – a tired taxi driver just coming off shift, a hard-up dancer reduced to belly-dancing to pay for ballet lessons, a woman with a sexual appetite that is deemed improper – not so much through love and sex as through energy. This sense of the sailors as a transforming energy is heightened by the sense of pressure on the narrative movement suggested by the device of a time-check flashed on the screen intermittently.

This gives a historical dimension to a musical, that is, it shows people making utopia rather than just showing them from time to time finding themselves in it. But the people are men – it is still men making history, not men and women together. (And the Lucy Schmeeler role is unforgivably male chauvinist.) In this context, the 'Prehistoric Man' number is particularly interesting. It centres on Ann Miller, and she leads the others in the take-over of the museum. For a moment, then, a woman 'makes history'. But the whole number is riddled with contradictions, which revolve around the very problem of having an image of a women acting historically. If we take the number and her part in it to pieces, we can see that it plays on an opposition between self-willed and mindless modes of being; and this

CONTINUED

play is between representational (R) and non-representational (NR) at all aesthetic levels.

Self-willed	*Mindless*
Miller as star (R)	Miller's image ('magnificent animal') (R)
Miller character – decision-maker in narrative (R)	Number set in anthropology museum – associations with primitivism (R)
Tap as self-expressive form (NR) Improvisatory routine (R/NR)	Tap as mindless repetitions (NR)

The idea of a historical utopianism in narrativity derives from the work of Ernest Bloch. According to Frederic Jameson in *Marxism and Form*, Bloch 'has essentially two different languages or terminological systems at his disposition to describe the formal nature of Utopian fulfilment: the movement of the world in time towards the future's ultimate moment, and the more spatial notion of that adequation of object to subject which must characterise that moment's content, … [these] correspond to dramatic and lyrical modes of the presentation of not-yet-being.'

Musicals (and variety) represent an extraordinary mix of these two modes – the historicity of narrative and the lyricism of numbers. They have not often taken advantage of it, but the point is that they could, and that this possibility is always latent in them. They are a form we still need to look at if films are, in Brecht's words on the theatre, to 'organise the enjoyment of changing reality'.

[An earlier version of this article was used at a SEFT weekend school and at the BFI Summer School, where it greatly benefitted from comments and criticism offered.]

(Dyer 1979: 222–232)

Another example of genre criticism is Michael Walker's introduction to that well-known and much fêted genre film noir. 'Noir' films were the product of 1940s and 1950s Hollywood and provoked a great deal of critical attention not least from French film-makers and critics. In the following extract Walker identifies some of the generic features that makes 'noir' such an engaging genre:

- A distinctive and exciting visual style
- An unusual narrative complexity
- A more critical and subversive view of American ideology than normal.

He adds other features to this list such as:

- A lack of sentimentality

- A willingness to probe the darker areas of sexuality
- Richly suggestive texts
- The emotional force of the downbeat.

ACTIVITY

> ➤ Before you read Walker's account watch at least one 'noir' film, such as *The Maltese Falcon* (John Huston 1941) or *The Big Sleep* (Howard Hawks 1946), using the bullet points above as features to look out for.

The cycle of 'forties and 'fifties Hollywood films that retrospectively became known as *films noirs* seems at first sight to be rather too diverse a group to be constituted with any precision as a generic category. Nevertheless, various critics have sought different unifying features: motif and tone (Durgnat, 1970), social background and artistic/cultural influences (Schrader, 1971), iconography, mood and characterisation (McArthur, 1972), visual style (Place & Peterson, 1974), the 'hard-boiled' tradition (Gregory, 1976), narrative and iconography (Dyer, 1977), representation and ideology (Kaplan, 1978), a master plot paradigm (Damico, 1978), conditions of production (Kerr, 1979), paranoia (Buchsbaum, 1986, reprinted in this book) and patterns of narration (Telotte, 1989). Each of these approaches is productive, and one could construct a pretty good overview of the cycle by judiciously combining them – which is essentially Edgardo Cozarinsky's approach (1980) and Foster Hirsch's in his 1981 book. Finally, Frank Krutnik's 1991 book (published after this introduction was drafted) suggests another approach, combining psychoanalysis with a concern with ideology and representation, and complementing Kaplan by focusing primarily on the 'crisis in masculinity' found in *film noir*. In the interests of conciseness, I will not discuss these earlier expositions of the *noir* form (for such an exercise, *see* Jane Root's entry on *Film Noir* in Pam Cook, ed., *The Cinema Book*, British Film Institute, 1985), but will incorporate and summarise as seems appropriate.

The 'forties/'fifties *noir* cycle has traditionally been seen as stretching from *The Maltese Falcon* (John Huston, 1941), to *Touch of Evil* (Orson Welles, 1958), peaking between 1946 and 1950. The dates are somewhat fluid: a hitherto obscure B movie, *Stranger on the Third Floor* (Boris Ingster, 1940) is now generally taken to be the first film of the cycle, and there were few significant contributions after 1956. First labelled *films noirs* at the end of the war by French critics – who linked the films with the series of crime novels (including American novels in translation) known as *Série Noire* – the films mark a distinct break with the generic groupings of the 'thirties. Although almost always concerned with crime, they differ from earlier crime films in the hero's entanglement in the passions of the criminal world. Although usually located in an urban milieu, they differ from the gangster movies in the types of criminal activity involved and their focus on a lone, often introverted hero. And, although featuring heroes who are frequently victims of a hostile world, they differ from the social problem films in their shift from a political to a personal perspective, a perspective that is often informed by popular psychology. Characteristically, the mood of the films is downbeat and pessimistic.

However, *film noir* is not simply a certain type of crime movie, but also a generic field: a set of elements and features which may be found in a range of different sorts of film. The generic labelling of films adopted by the Hollywood studios for their own purposes (casting, production, marketing, etc.) does not do justice to the complex interaction of determinants – including generic elements – in any given film. *Pursued* (Raoul Walsh, 1947), for example, is primarily a western, but it is also part *film noir* and part psychological melodrama, and all three generic fields are crucial to its meaning. Undoubtedly there are problematical areas: the question of the transmission of generic influence, the complex synthesis of multiple influence, the complex synthesis of multiple determinants in a given film, the elusiveness of the concept of genre itself. But, as Cozarinsky cogently points out, 'the notion of genre is a theoretical tool, not a "natural" fact: to consider any group of works as a genre is to choose some traits as pertinent, others as irrelevant' (Cozarinsky, 1980, p. 58). As a generic field, *film noir* combines a number of elements in a way which makes it peculiarly complex and interesting: a distinctive and exciting visual style, an unusual narrative complexity, a generally more critical and subversive view of American ideology than the norm. For these and other reasons – the films' lack of sentimentality, their willingness to probe the darker areas of sexuality, their richly suggestive subtexts, the emotional force of the downbeat – *film noir* as a phenomenon continues to fascinate. The other essays in this volume address specific issues around the *noir* phenomenon and the particular pleasures of certain texts. What follows here is a summary of, on the one hand, the set of influences, determinants and factors which produced this particular cycle of films and, on the other, what seem to me to be its key features. Apart from certain exceptions which will become apparent, I have broadly followed the consensus listings of *films noirs* as included, for example, in Silver and Ward (1980) and Telotte (1989). Further discussion of the extent to which individual works possess *noir* elements may be found in the other essays in this book.

NARRATIVE AND CHARACTER TYPES

To a large extent, the typical *film noir* character types and narrative can be traced back to literary crime fiction of the 'thirties and 'forties. There seem to be three main strands of influence: Dashiell Hammett/Raymond Chandler, James M. Cain and Cornell Woolrich, although, inevitably, some films combine material from more than one.

Dashiell Hammett and Raymond Chandler: the 'hard-boiled' private eye.

Both Hammett and Chandler began by writing short stories for *Black Mask* magazine: Hammett in the 'twenties, Chandler in the 'thirties. John Cawelti (in *Adventure, Mystery and Romance*, University of Chicago Press, 1976) has discussed how Hammett's stories, and his subsequent novels – the latter published between 1929 and 1934 – introduced a new formula into the detective story, focusing on 'the hard-boiled hero', with his 'mixture of toughness and sentimentality, of cynical understatement and eloquence' (p. 163). He summarises the story's differences from the 'classical detective story' as 'the subordination of the drama of solution to the detective's quest for … justice; and the substitution of a pattern of intimidation and temptation of the hero for … what Northrop Frye calls "the wavering finger of suspicion" passing across a series of potential suspects' (p. 142). He also notes 'a greater personal involvement on the part of the hard-boiled detective. Since he becomes emotionally and morally committed to some of the persons involved, or because the crime poses some basic crisis in his image of himself, the hard-boiled detective remains unfulfilled until he has taken a personal moral stance towards the criminal' (p. 143). Of the nature of the world the detective investigates, Cawelti writes, 'As the … action develops, the rich, the powerful, and the beautiful attempt to draw the detective into their world and use him for their own corrupt purposes. He in turn finds that the process of solving the crime involves him in the violence, deceit and corruption that lies beneath the surface of the respectable world' (p. 145). Above all, the hard-boiled detective novel placed the emphasis on a tough detective in an urban milieu, moving firmly away from the classical 'whodunnit' tradition (Edgar Allan Poe, Arthur Conan Doyle, Agatha Christie, Dorothy Sayers, S.S. Van Dine *et al.*) of a refine, ratiocinative detective in a frequently upper middle-class milieu.

Although there was an early version of *The Maltese Falcon* (Roy Del Ruth, 1930) which was relatively faithful to the 1930 novel, it did not set a trend. Hollywood detective films of the 'thirties – particularly after 1934, when the Production Code was rigorously enforced – tended to be 'comedy-thrillers'. When Hammett went to Hollywood as a screenwriter, it was the success of his *The Thin Man* (W.S. Van Dyke, 1934), flip and light-hearted, which dictated the tone of most of his work there, including follow-up *Thin Man* screen stories. Such films are very different from *films noirs*, which depict a far darker view of the underworld of American crime and in which – apart from the occasional cynical/defensive/ barbed wisecrack – humour fits uneasily. When *The Maltese Falcon* was remade as *Satan Met a Lady* (William Dieterle, 1936), it moved much further from the original story, becoming not just light-hearted, but positively camp.

Nevertheless, Hammett is crucial to *film noir* as an influence. It was Huston's 1941 version of *The Maltese Falcon*, which stuck very closely to the novel, that effectively launched the private-eye *film noir*, to be developed – in its first phase – over the next fifteen years or so. *The Glass Key* (novel, 1931/film, Stuart Heisler, 1942), the only other Hammett novel to be made into a *film noir*, includes a murder investigation, but is more concerned with the violence and corruption of local politics. Nevertheless, the novel and film introduced what was to become a recurrent *noir* situation: the bloody beating-up of the hero by a sadistic thug.

Hammett ceased publishing in book form in the early 'thirties; his mantle was taken up by Raymond Chandler. Chandler's work was first published in *Black Mask* in 1933; then, in a series of novels beginning with *The Big Sleep* in 1939, he created Philip Marlowe, soon to become *film noir*'s most enduring private eye. However, the first two films adaptations of Marlowe novels – *The Falcon Takes Over* (Irving Reis, 1942) from *Farewell, My Lovely* (1940) and *Time to Kill* (Herbert I. Leeds, 1942) from *The High Window* (1942) – both reprocessed the stories to fit into already established B movie series with already established detectives: George Sanders's Falcon and Lloyd Nolan's Michael Shayne. Despite *The Maltese Falcon*, the detective movie still had to emerge from the low-budget series format, popularised in the 'thirties by the likes of Charlie Chan, Mr Moto and Bulldog Drummond.

In 1943, Chandler was employed as a screenwriter by Paramount. His first project was to assist Billy Wilder (who was also to direct the film) in adapting James M. Cain's *Double Indemnity*, which had been serialised in *Liberty* magazine in 1936. The success of the film of *Double Indemnity* (1944) was followed by film adaptations of the first four Marlowe novels which kept Marlowe as the hero. However, each of the novels was bought by a different studio, resulting in four very different films with four very different Marlowes: RKO's *Murder My Sweet* (Edward Dmytryk, 1944), with Dick Powell (from *Farewell My Lovely*; the original title was retained in the UK); Warners' *The Big Sleep* (Howard Hawks, 1946), with Humphrey Bogart; MGM's *The Lady in the Lake* (novel 1943/film 1946), the notorious subjective camera film, in which Robert Montgomery both directs and 'plays' Marlowe; and Twentieth Century-Fox's *The Brasher Doubloon* (John Brahm, 1947), with George Montgomery (from *The High Window*). (Later novels were filmed in the second *noir* cycle; *see* Edward Gallafent, 'Film Noir in the 'Seventies'.) Although the quality of these films seems to me to vary enormously, the two obvious successes, *Murder My Sweet* and *The Big Sleep*, developed the formula established by *The Maltese Falcon* and set the tone for subsequent private-eye *films noirs*.

In effect, Hammett and Chandler established the format of the first type of *noir* story. The novels and the films made from them influenced a range of subsequent films with an investigative structure, whether private-eye or not, e.g. *Phantom Lady* (Robert Siodmak, 1944), with its investigative heroine, *Deadline at Dawn* (Harold Clurman, 1946), *Somewhere in the Night* (Joseph L.

Mankiewicz, 1946), *The Killers* (Siodmak, 1946), *Dead Reckoning* (John Cromwell, 1946) – much of which is modelled on *The Big Sleep* – *Calcutta* (John Farrow, 1947), *Out of the Past/Build My Gallows High* (Jacques Tourneur, 1947), *The Big Heat* (Fritz Lang, 1953), *Kiss Me, Deadly* (Robert Aldrich, 1955), *The Big Combo* (Joseph H. Lewis, 1955). By contrast, *Laura* (Otto Preminger, 1944) still possesses much of the structure of the classical whodunnit detective story.

These may be termed seeker-hero *films noirs*: a major *noir* category. In these films, the hero's investigation takes the form of a quest into a dangerous and threatening world, the *noir* world. This *noir* world has two facets. On the one hand, it is an underworld of crime, vice and murder; on the other, it frequently lies behind what Cawelti calls the 'respectable world', the world of bourgeois order and propriety. It is a world of duplicity and dissimulation: the hero doesn't know who to trust and is confused about what's going on. The characters he encounters are indeed rarely trustworthy, but tend to be variously corrupt, perverse, threatening or violent. His quest may even assume mythical overtones: a descent into an underworld where, *à la Propp* (V. Propp, *Morphology of the Folktale*, University of Texas Press, 1968, pp. 39–42), he is repeatedly 'tested, interrogated, attacked, etc.,' not so much to prepare him for the receipt of a magical agent or helper as to test his wits, perseverance and integrity. As he unravels the often labyrinthine plot and uncovers the layers of deception, it is as much his incorruptibility as his intelligence which enables him, finally, to emerge safely.

The seeker hero is protected further by a generally cynical view of people's motivations and a frequently misogynistic attitude towards women. A particular danger is the *femme fatale* using her sexuality to get what *she* wants as well as being implicated in murder: *The Maltese Falcon*, *Murder My Sweet*, *The Killers*, *Dead Reckoning*, *Calcutta*, *Out of The Past*. Christine Gledhill has argued that the films may indeed displace 'solution of the crime as the object of the plot' to concentrate rather on investigation of the woman (Gledhill, 1978). The seeker hero strives to bring order to the *noir* world, an order which is often linked to the control of transgressive female sexuality.

Other character types in these films include those populating the criminal and night worlds of the city: small-time crooks, grifters, blackmailers, hoods, gamblers, and the women who try to survive in the same worlds: nightclub singers, showgirls, taxi-dancers, bar-girls, mistresses, prostitutes. There are also figures from the opposite end of the social scale: the decadent rich, who live in huge mansions and spawn wayward offspring; powerful, corrupt politicians and nightclub/casino owners. The films' representations of law officers vary. Where the hero is himself a cop, he is typically a loner, pursuing his obsessive quest against the orders of the department (*The Big Heat*; *The Big Combo*). Other cops vary from nuisances who get in the hero's way (the usual situation in Hammett and Chandler) to figures who offer useful assistance, which, untypically of Siodmak, they do in *Phantom Lady* and *The Killers*. Usually, however, the *noir* hero stands at an oblique angle to authority, and his relationship with the cops is frequently a crucial indicator of this. A film may even contrive an otherwise redundant scene in which the hero and cops are in conflict: late in *Dead Reckoning*, Lieutenant Kincaid (Charles Cane) blunders into the apartment of Coral (Lizabeth Scott) simply so that Rip (Humphrey Bogart) can tie him up and lock him in a cupboard. Finally, and especially associated with *film noir*, there are the figures who represent a marked deviance from the norms of society: grotesques such as Moose Malloy (Mike Mazurki) in *Murder My Sweet*; sadists such as Jeff (William Bendix) in *The Glass Key*, Canino (Bob Steele) in *The Big Sleep* and Krause (Marvin Miller) in *Dead Reckoning*; sexual 'deviants' such as Gutman (Sydney Greenstreet) and Cairo (Peter Lorre) in *The Maltese Falcon*.

It is the nature of the *noir* world and the hero's interaction with it which seems to me the essence of the seeker-hero *films noirs*. The moral certainties of the classical detective story are absent: even though the *noir* seeker hero solves the case, there is usually the sense at the end that little good will come of this or that the cost has been absurdly high (a regular feature of these narratives is the number of dead bodies the hero encounters during his investigation). It is this that distinguishes him from the complacent and invincible series detectives, who are not scarred by their investigations in the same way. Nevertheless, in the seeker-hero films, the hero tends to survive the dangers of the *noir* world. In other types of *film noir*, his survival is much more at risk.

James M. Cain: The femme fatale as destroyer.

Unlike Hammett and Chandler, Cain was employed as a screenwriter before he wrote the novels that made him famous: he joined Paramount in 1931 and subsequently went to Columbia. And, although his screenwriting credits are negligible, three of the novels he went on to write were made into particularly famous *films noirs*: *Double Indemnity*, *The Postman Always Rings Twice* (novel 1934/ film Tay Garnett, 1945), and *Mildred Pierce* (1941/Michael Curtiz, 1945). (A later film from a Cain novel, *Slightly Scarlet*, Allan Dwan, 1956 – from *Love's Lovely Counterfeit*, 1942 – is a rare example of a colour film which is nevertheless accepted as part of the first *noir* cycle.) No less hard-boiled than Hammett and Chandler, and arguably even more cynical and misogynistic, Cain introduced a very different type of story. In *The Postman Always Rings Twice* and *Double Indemnity*, the hero becomes so obsessed sexually by a woman that he is persuaded to murder her husband, and the *noir* world which he enters is psychological rather than physical, characterised above all by corrosive guilt and the fear of discovery. The importance of Cain's contribution to the cycle may be seen in the way in which Damico's master plot for *film noir* (quoted in Root and in Krutnik, 1991) is clearly based on the Cain story.

I would like to take the Cain story as a paradigm in a slightly different way from Damico, concentrating on the way i) the *femme fatale* becomes the key figure who lures/tempts/seduces the hero into the *noir* world and ii) the hero becomes a 'victim' of his own desires. As in the Russian fairytales analysed by Propp, these victim heroes are structurally quite distinct from seeker heroes. Apart from the paradigm movies – *Double Indemnity* and *The Postman Always Rings Twice* – examples would include *The Woman in the Window* (Lang, 1944), *Scarlet Street* (Lang, 1945), *The Locket* (Brahm, 1946), *The Lady from Shanghai* (Welles, 1947), *Pitfall* (Andre de Toth, 1948), *Criss Cross* (Siodmak, 1949), *The File on Thelma Jordon* (Siodmak, 1949), *The Woman on Pier* 13 (Robert Stevenson, 1949), *Where Danger Lives* (Farrow, 1950), *Sunset Boulevard* (Wilder, 1951), *Angel Face* (Preminger, 1952) and *Human Desire* (Lang, 1954). In addition, there are films which contain both sorts of hero: in *The Killers*, Reardon (Edmond O'Brien) is a seeker hero, the Swede (Burt Lancaster) a victim hero; in *Out of the Past*, the seeker hero becomes a victim hero when he is seduced by the *femme fatale*. The deadliness of the *femme fatale* varies, from Barbara Stanwyck's Phyllis Dietrichson in *Double Indemnity*, who is a ruthless killer, to an essentially sympathetic figure such as Lizabeth Scott's Mona in *Pitfall*. But her role is dramatically crucial: like the villain in 19th century melodrama, she gets the plot moving. Apart from the Cain movies, it is only occasionally in these films that the hero is driven to murder, but the power of the *femme fatale* is such that he has only about even chances of surviving the film. And, when he does, he often ends as a broken man: *Scarlet Street, Pitfall, The File on Thelma Jordon*. Related films – in which the central female figure is not a *femme fatale*, but in which the hero, desiring her, commits murder – include *Conflict* (Curtis Bernhardt, 1945), *The Suspect* (Siodmak, 1945), *711 Ocean Drive* (Joseph M Newman, 1950) and *The Prowler* (Joseph Losey, 1951).

A third feature of these films – that the *femme fatale* is already in the possession of another man – is more complicated. First, there is the question of the relationship between the *femme fatale* and this male figure. He may be a wealthy husband, in which case it is usually implied that she has used him to seek money and security, as in the Cain movies, *The Lady from Shanghai* and others. However, the crucial point is that he possesses some sort of proprietorial claim on the *femme fatale*. Accordingly, his presence is blatantly ideological: an entirely independent, sexually dangerous woman being rather more than Hollywood could countenance. This can be seen in the films where the male figure is seemingly absent or weak. In *The Woman on Pier* 13, the figure has been replaced by the Communist Party which, through the agency of master-villain Vanning (Thomas Gomez), explicitly attempts to control the *femme fatale*'s sexuality. Max (Erich von Stroheim) in *Sunset Boulevard* seems to be only the butler, but Joe (William Holden) subsequently discovers not only that he is the ex-husband of Norma (Gloria Swanson), but also that he actually writes her fan mail, keeping alive her fantasy that she is still a star.

GENRE

CONTINUED

In other words, he exercises considerable control over her. *Nightmare Alley* (Edmund Goulding, 1947) provides a complementary instance. Helen Walker's 'consulting psychologist' is indeed independent, but while she joins forces with the hero and then betrays him, her power over him is not sexual, i.e. she is not a *femme fatale* in the usual sense of the term.

Second, the representation of this proprietorial male figure relates strongly to the type of hero involved. Where the latter is single, and (also usually) relatively young and virile, the figure is typically older and economically more powerful, i.e. the films possess an implicit Oedipal structure. (This can occur, too, when the heroine is not a *femme fatale*: *711 Ocean Drive* and *The Prowler*.) By contrast, where the hero is married, and also usually middle-aged and non-virile, the male figure, if not always younger, is usually more potent: *The Woman in the Window, Scarlet Street, Pitfall, The File on Thelma Jordon*. These films tend to deal centrally with the hero as a 'castrated' figure: only in *Pitfall* does the film's coding imply that the hero actually manages to have sex with the *femme fatale*.

Clearly, some of these victim heroes are victims of their own villainy. But they, too, enter a *noir* world. And, because it is desire that has motivated them to step outside the normal, 'safe' world, this *noir* world differs from that of the seeker heroes in being more associated with a dissolution of the self, with a surrender to dangerous and disturbing passions. As a corollary of this, a victim hero is more likely to suffer the fear of discovery and punishment, not just in the films in which he is driven to murder, but when he has knowingly desired and possessed another man's woman, as in *The Killers, Out of the Past, Pitfall* and *Criss Cross*. Like the seeker hero, the victim hero also enters a network of relationships of which the true nature is masked, and which are frequently highly dangerous in their deceptiveness. He, too, struggles towards understanding which, in his case, is usually achieved too late. The most famous example of the impenetrability of the *noir* world in these films is probably *The Lady from Shanghai*, but all of them have elements of the impenetrability which may extend to the enigma of the *femme fatale*: what does she want? Again, the dangers of the *noir* world function in part as a 'test': is the hero capable of surviving them or not? But he has less control – particularly over the potentially threatening women – than the seeker hero: far from bringing order to the *noir* world, he is more likely to be engulfed by it.

A character type more frequent in these movies than in the seeker-hero examples is the domestic woman: a wife or girlfriend who is in opposition to the *femme fatale*, associated with the home and offering the hero love, understanding and nurturing (the two types are discussed at length by Place, 1978). Just as the heroine in the woman's film is regularly pulled between the lover figure and the husband figure, so the hero in these films is equally often pulled between these two similarly ideologically determined character types, and suffers equally disastrous consequences if the lure of the sexual figure proves too strong. In both generic triangles, one can see the persistence of puritanical nineteenth-century thought: sex is dangerous and destructive, and the figures who are defined as sexual, however alluring and exciting, are ultimately discredited. The same principle applies with the many female figures who are not *femmes fatales* but are, nevertheless, defined as 'sexual' as opposed to 'domestic': e.g. Gloria Grahame's taxi-dancer in *Crossfire* (Dmytryk, 1947) and her gangster's moll in *The Big Heat*; Rita Johnson's mistress in *The Big Clock* (Farrow, 1947); Hazel Brooks's good-time girl in *Body and Soul* (Robert Rossen, 1947); Shelley Winters's waitress in *A Double Life* (George Cukor, 1947). For want of a better collective term, I will refer to such figures as 'sexual women'. The *femme fatale* represents a particular elaboration of the sexual woman, one in which she is dominant in the (sexual) relationship and is seeking to get from it what she wants, whereas these figures are less deadly in their impact on the hero. Of course, no clear dividing line can be drawn between the two – is it fair to call Alice in *The Woman in the Window* or Mona in *Pitfall* a *femme fatale* at all? – but it is important to establish that, even in *film noir*, not all sexual women are necessarily *femmes fatales*, as can be seen in *The Big Sleep*.

Cain also introduced the *noir* 'confessional mode': the sense of the protagonist narrating his story out of an inner need to confess. The films take this further: in the novel of *The Postman Always Rings Twice*, Frank writes his story down for a priest to read, but in the film he actually narrates it – and it is only at the end that we discover he's been talking to a priest. Cain has said in an interview (with Peter Brunette and Gerald Peary, reprinted in Pat McGilligan, ed., *Backstory*, University of California Press, 1986, p. 125) that, if he'd thought of it, he would himself have used Wilder's solution to the problem of the first person narrative of *Double Indemnity*: Walter narrating into a Dictaphone as a 'confession' to his father-figure Keyes.

In their book on the effects of the Production Code, Leonard J. Leff and Jerold L. Simmons argue that it was Joseph Breen's sanctioning of a treatment of *Double Indemnity* in September 1943 that led to the Hays Office being 'flooded with murder and eros' (*The Dame in the Kimono*, Weidenfeld & Nicolson, London, 1990). In other words, it was Wilder and Chandler's skills at adaptation and Breen's more relaxed attitude to subjects he had hitherto considered unfilmable that enabled the *noir* cycle to develop into something substantial: *The Big Sleep*, *Mildred Pierce* and *The Postman Always Rings Twice* (this last vetoed for ten years) all received Breen's approval in the wake of the *Double Indemnity* decision. At the same time, the 'lurid and sensational' material in the novels still had to be appropriately 'toned down' to be acceptable to Breen. In particular screenwriters sought to find ways within the restrictions of the

CONTINUED

GENRE

Production Code of dealing with non-romantic sexuality; in which desire rather than affection is at stake. Again, *Double Indemnity* is the benchmark film: it is patently sex, not love, that attracts Walter to Phyllis, and it is after *Double Indemnity* that the twin *noir* concerns of murder and desire become focused as in the film adaptation of *Mildred Pierce*. Cain's novel (his least typical) has no murder, but the film begins with the murder of Monte (Zachary Scott), and an important thread to its narrative is the question of whodunnit. And when the murderer is finally identified, the film may readily be recast as – in part – another *femme fatale film noir*, in which Monte becomes the victim of his passion for Veda (Ann Blyth), the *femme fatale*.

(Walker 1992: 8–14)

You may like to contrast the account of film noir offered by Michael Walker with that of screenwriter Paul Schrader. Schrader is particularly interested in the style of film noir. He argues that noir was long neglected because it relies heavily on visual style. He suggests that American critics have always been 'slow on the uptake when it comes to visual style'.

In 1946 French critics, seeing the American films they had missed during the war, noticed the new mood of cynicism, pessimism, and darkness that had crept into the American cinema. The darkening stain was most evident in routine crime thrillers, but was also apparent in prestigious melodramas. The French cineastes soon realized they had seen only the tip of the iceberg: as the years went by, Hollywood lighting grew darker, characters more corrupt, themes more fatalistic, and the tone more hopeless. By 1949 American movies were in the throes of their deepest and most creative funk. Never before had films dared to take such a harsh uncomplimentary look at American life, and they would not dare to do so again for twenty years.

Hollywood's film noir has recently become the subject of renewed interest among moviegoers and critics. The fascination that film noir holds for today's young filmgoers and film students reflects recent trends in American cinema: American movies are again taking a look at the underside of the American character, but compared to such relentlessly cynical examples of film noir as *Kiss Me Deadly* (Robert Aldrich, 1955) or *Kiss Tomorrow Goodbye* (Gordon Douglas, 1959), the newer self-hate cinema of *Easy Rider* (Dennis Hopper, 1969) and *Medium Cool* (Haskell Wexler, 1969) seems naive and romantic. As the current political mood hardens, filmgoers and filmmakers will find the film noir of the late forties increasingly attractive. The forties may be to the seventies what the thirties were to the sixties.

Film noir is equally interesting to critics. It offers writers a cache of excellent, little-known films (film noir is oddly both one of Hollywood's best periods and least known) and gives auteur-weary critics an opportunity to apply themselves to the new questions of classification and transdirectorial style. After all, what is a film noir?

Film noir is not a genre, as Raymond Durgnat has helpfully pointed out over the objections of Higham and Greenberg's *Hollywood in the Forties*.[1] It is not defined, as are the western and gangster genre, by conventions of setting and conflict but rather by the more subtle qualities of tone and mood. It is a film 'noir,' as opposed to the possible variants of film 'gray' or film 'off-white.' Film noir is also a specific period of film history, like German expressionism or the French New Wave. In general, film noir refers to those Hollywood films of the forties and early fifties that portrayed the world of dark, slick city streets, crime and corruption.

Film noir is an extremely unwieldy period. It harks back to many previous periods: Warner's thirties gangster films, the French 'poetic realism' of Carné and Duvivier, Sternbergian melodrama, and ultimately German Expressionist crime films (Lang's Mabuse cycle). Film noir can stretch at its outer limits from *The Maltese Falcon* (John Huston, 1941) to *Touch of Evil* (Orson Welles, 1958), and most every dramatic Hollywood film from 1941 to 1953 contains some noir elements. There are also foreign offshoots of film noir, such as *The Third Man* (Carol Reed, 1949), *Breathless* (Jean-Luc Godard, 1959), and *Le Doulos* (Jean-Pierre Melville, 1963).

Almost every critic has his or her own definition of film noir, along with a personal list of film title and dates to back it up. Personal and descriptive definitions, however, can get a bit sticky. A film of urban nightlife is not necessarily a film noir, and a film noir need not necessarily concern crime and corruption. Since film noir is defined by tone rather than genre, it is almost impossible to argue one critic's descriptive definition against another's. How many noir elements does it take to make a film noir? Rather than haggle about definitions, I would rather attempt to reduce film noir to its primary colors (all shades of black), those cultural and stylistic elements to which any definition must return.

INFLUENCES

At the risk of sounding like Arthur Knight, I would suggest that there were four influences in Hollywood in the forties that brought about the film noir. (The danger of Knight's *Liveliest Art* method is that it makes film history less a matter of structural analysis and more a case of artistic and social forces magically interacting and coalescing.) Each of the following four catalytic elements, however, can define the film noir; the distinctly noir tonality draws from each of these elements.

War and postwar disillusionment

The acute downer that hit the United States after the Second World War was, in fact, a delayed reaction to the thirties. All through the Depression, movies were needed to keep people's spirits up, and, for the most part, they did. The crime films of this period were Horatio Algerish and socially conscious. Toward the end of the thirties a darker crime film began to appear (*You Only Live Once*, Fritz Lang, 1937; *The Roaring Twenties*, Raoul Walsh, 1939), and, were it not for the war, film noir would have been at full steam by the early forties.

The need to produce Allied propaganda abroad and promote patriotism at home blunted the fledgling moves toward a dark cinema, and the film noir thrashed about in the studio system, not quite able to come into full prominence. During the war the first uniquely film noir appeared in *The Maltese Falcon*, *The Glass Key* (Stuart Heisler, 1942), *This Gun for Hire* (Frank Tuttle, 1942), and *Laura* (Otto Preminger, 1944), but these films lacked the distinctly noir bite the end of the war would bring.

As soon as the war was over, however, American films became markedly more sardonic – and there was a boom in the crime film. For fifteen years the pressures against America's amelioristic cinema had been building up, and, given the freedom, audiences and artists were now eager to take a less optimistic view of things. The disillusionment that many soldiers, small businessmen, and housewife/factory employees felt in returning to a peacetime economy was directly mirrored in the sordidness of the urban crime film.

This immediate postwar disillusionment was directly demonstrated in films like *Cornered* (Edward Dmytryk, 1945), *The Blue Dahlia* (George Marshall, 1946), *Dead Reckoning* (John Cromwell, 1947), and *Ride the Pink Horse* (Robert Montgomery, 1947), in which a serviceman returns from the war to find his sweetheart unfaithful or dead, or his business partner cheating him, or the whole society something less than worth fighting for. The war continues, but now the antagonism turns with a new viciousness toward American society itself.

Postwar realism

Shortly after the war, every film-producing country had a resurgence of realism. In America it first took the form of films by such producers as Louis de Rochemont (*House on 92nd Street*, Henry Hathaway, 1945; *Call Northside 777*, Hathaway, 1948) and Mark Hellinger (*The Killers*, Robert Siodmak, 1946; *Brute Force*, Jules Dassin, 1947) and directors like Hathaway and Dassin. 'Every scene was filmed on the actual location depicted,' the publicity for the 1947 de Rochemont-Hathaway *Kiss of Death* proudly proclaimed. Even after de Rochemont's particular 'March of Time' authenticity fell from vogue, realistic exteriors remained a permanent fixture of film noir.

The realistic movement also suited America's postwar mood; the public's desire for a more honest and harsh view of America would not be satisfied by the same studio streets they had been watching for a dozen years. The postwar realistic trend succeeded in breaking film noir away from the domain of the high-class melodrama, placing it where it more properly belonged, in the streets with everyday people. In retrospect, the pre-de Rochemont film noir looks definitely tamer than the postwar realistic films. The studio look of films like *The Big Sleep* (Howard Hawks, 1946) and *The Mask of Dimitrios* (Jean Negulesco, 1944) blunts their sting, making them seem polite and conventional in contrast to their later, more realistic counterparts.

The German expatriates

Hollywood played host to an influx of German expatriates in the twenties and thirties, and these filmmakers and technicians had, for the most part, integrated themselves into the American film establishment. Hollywood never experienced the 'Germanization' some civic-minded natives feared, and there is a danger of overemphasizing the German influence in Hollywood.

But when, in the late forties, Hollywood decided to paint it black, there were no greater masters of chiaroscuro than the Germans. The influence of expressionist lighting has always been just beneath the surface of Hollywood films, and it is not surprising, in film noir, to find it bursting out into full bloom. Neither is it surprising to find a larger number of Germans and East Europeans working in film noir: Fritz Lang, Robert Siodmak, Billy Wilder, Franz Waxman, Otto Preminger, John Brahm, Anatole Litvak, Karl Freund, Max Ophuls, John Alton, Douglas Sirk, Fred Zinnemann, William Dieterle, Max Steiner, Edgar G. Ulmer, Curtis Bernhardt, Rudolph Maté.

On the surface the German expressionist influence, with its reliance on artificial studio lighting, seems incompatible with postwar realism, with its harsh unadorned exteriors; but it is the unique quality of film noir that it was able to weld seemingly contradictory elements into a uniform style. The best noir technicians simply made all the world a sound stage, directing unnatural and expressionistic lighting onto realistic settings. In films like *Union Station* (Maté, 1950), *They Live by Night* (Nicholas, Ray, 1948), and *The Killers*, there is an uneasy, exhilarating combination of realism and expressionism.

Perhaps the greatest master of noir was Hungarian-born John Alton, an expressionist cinematographer who could relight Times Square at noon if necessary. No cinematographer better adapted the old expressionist techniques to the new desire for realism, and his black-and-white photography in such gritty examples of film noir as *T-Men* (Anthony Mann, 1948), *Raw Deal* (Mann,

1948), I, *the Jury* (Harry Essex, 1953), and *The Big Combo* (Joseph H. Lewis, 1955) equals that of such German expressionist masters as Fritz Wagner and Karl Freund.

The hard-boiled tradition

Another stylistic influence waiting in the wings was the 'hard-boiled' school of writers. In the thirties, authors such as Ernest Hemingway, Dashiell Hammett, Raymond Chandler, James M. Cain, Horace McCoy, and John O'Hara created the 'tough,' a cynical way of acting the thinking that separated one from the world of everyday emotions – romanticism with a protective shell. The hard-boiled writers had their roots in pulp fiction or journalism, and their protagonists lived out a narcissistic, defeatist code. The hard-boiled hero was, in reality, a soft egg compared to his existential counterpart (Camus is said to have based *The Stranger* on McCoy), but he was a good deal tougher than anything American fiction had seen.

When the movies of the forties turned to the American 'tough' moral understrata, the hard-boiled school was waiting with preset conventions of heroes, minor characters, plots, dialogue, and themes. Like the German expatriates, the hard-boiled writers had a style made to order for film noir; and, in turn, they influenced noir screenwriting as much as the Germans influenced noir cinematography.

The most hard-boiled of Hollywood's writers was Raymond Chandler himself, whose script of *Double Indemnity* (from a James M. Cain story) was the best written and most characteristically noir of the period. *Double Indemnity* (Billy Wilder, 1944) was the first film that played film noir for what it essentially was: small-time, unredeemed, unheroic; it made a break from the romantic noir cinema of *Mildred Pierce* (Michael Curtiz, 1945) and *The Big Sleep*. In its final stages, however, film noir adapted and then bypassed the hard-boiled school. Manic, neurotic post-1948 films such as *Kiss Tomorrow Goodbye*, D.O.A. (Maté, 1950), *Where the Sidewalk Ends* (Preminger, 1950), *White Heat* (Raoul Walsh, 1949), and *The Big Heat* (Fritz Lang, 1953) are all post-hard-boiled: the air in these regions was even too thin for old-time cynics like Chandler.

STYLISTICS

There is not yet a study of the stylistics of film noir, and the task is certainly too large to be attempted here. Like all film movements, film noir drew upon a reservoir of film techniques, and given the time one could correlate its techniques, themes, and casual elements into a stylistic schema. For the present, however, I'd like to point out some of film noir's recurring techniques.

1. The majority of scenes are lit for night. Gangsters sit in offices at midday with the shades pulled and the lights off. Ceiling lights are hung low and floor lamps are seldom more than five feet high. One always has the suspicion that if the lights were all suddenly flipped on, the characters would shriek and shrink from the scene like Count Dracula at sunrise.

2. As in German expressionism, oblique and vertical lines are preferred to horizontal. Obliquity adheres to the choreography of the city, and is in direct opposition to the horizontal American tradition of Griffith and Ford. Oblique lines tend to splinter a screen, making it restless and unstable. Light enters the dingy rooms of film noir in such odd shapes – jagged trapezoids, obtuse triangles, vertical slits – that one suspects the windows were cut out with a penknife. No character can speak authoritatively from a space that is being continually cut into ribbons of light. Anthony Mann and John Alton's T-Men is the most dramatic example, but far from the only one, of oblique noir choreography.

3. The actors and setting are often given equal lighting emphasis. An actor is often hidden in the realistic tableau of the city at night, and, more obviously, his face is often blacked out by shadow as he speaks. These shadow effects are unlike the famous Warner Brothers lighting of the thirties in which the central character was accentuated by a heavy shadow; in film noir, the central character is likely to be standing *in* the shadow. When the environment is given an equal or greater weight than the actor, it, of course, creates a fatalistic, hopeless mood. There is nothing the protagonists can do; the city will outlast and negate even their best efforts.

4. Compositional tension is preferred to physical action. A typical film noir would rather move the scene cinematographically around the actor than have the actor control the scene by physical action. The beating of Robert Ryan in *The Set-Up* (Robert Wise, 1949), the gunning down of Farley Granger in *They Live by Night*, the execution of the taxi driver in *The Enforcer* (Bretaigne Windust, 1951) and of Brian Donlevy in *The Big Combo* are all marked by measured pacing, restrained anger, and oppressive compositions, and seem much closer to the film noir spirit than the rat-tat-tat and screeching tires of *Scarface* (Howard Hawks, 1932) twenty years before or the violent, expressive actions of *Underworld* U.S.A. (Samuel Fuller, 1960) ten years later.

5. There seems to be an almost Freudian attachment to water. The empty noir streets are almost always glistening with fresh evening rain (even in Los Angeles), and the rainfall tends to increase in direct proportion to the drama. Docks and piers are second only to alleyways as the most popular rendezvous points.

6. There is a love of romantic narration. In such films as *The Postman Always Rings Twice* (Tay Garnett, 1946), *Laura, Double Indemnity, The Lady from Shanghai* (Orson Welles, 1949), *Out of the Past* (Jacques Tourneur, 1947), and *Sunset*

CONTINUED

Boulevard (Billy Wilder, 1950), the narration creates a mood of *temps perdu*: an irretrievable past, a predetermined fate, and an all-enveloping hopelessness. In *Out of the Past* Robert Mitchum relates his history with such pathetic relish that it is obvious there is no hope for any future: one can only take pleasure in reliving a doomed past.

7. A complex chronological order is frequently used to reinforce the feelings of hopelessness and lost time. Such films as *The Enforcer*, *The Killers*, *Mildred Pierce*, *The Dark Past* (Maté, 1948), *Chicago Deadline* (Lewis Allen, 1949), *Out of the Past*, and *The Killing* (Stanley Kubrick, 1956) use a convoluted time sequence to immerse the viewer in a time-disoriented but highly stylized world. The manipulation of time, whether slight or complex, is often used to reinforce a noir principle: the *how* is always more important than the *what*.

THEMES

Raymond Durgnat has delineated the themes of film noir in an excellent article in the British *Cinema* magazine[2] and it would be foolish for me to attempt to redo his thorough work in this short space. Durgnat divides film noir into eleven thematic categories, and although one might criticize some of his specific groupings, he covers the whole gamut of noir production, thematically categorizing over 300 films. In each of Durgnat's noir themes (whether Black Widow, killers-on-the-run, *doppelgangers*), one finds that the upwardly mobile forces of the thirties have halted; frontierism has turned to paranoia and claustrophobia. The small-time gangster has now made it big and sits in the mayor's chair, the private eye has quit the police force in disgust, and the young heroine, sick of going along for the ride, is taking others for a ride.

Durgnat, however, does not touch upon what is perhaps the overriding noir theme: a passion for the past and present, but also a fear of the future. Noir heroes dread to look ahead, but instead try to survive by the day, and if unsuccessful at that, they retreat to the past. Thus film noir's techniques emphasize loss, nostalgia, lack of clear priorities, and insecurity, then submerge these self-doubts in mannerism and style. In such a world style becomes paramount; it is all that separates one from meaninglessness. Chandler described this fundamental noir theme when he described his own fictional world: 'It is not a very fragrant world, but it is the world you live in, and certain writers with tough minds and a cool spirit of detachment can make very interesting patterns out of it.'[3]

PHASES

Film noir can be subdivided into three broad phases. The first, the wartime period (1941 – 1946 approximately), was the phase of the private eye and the lone wolf, of Chandler, Hammett, and Greene, of Bogart and Bacall, Ladd and Lake, classy directors like Curtiz and Garnett, studio sets, and, in general, more talk than action. The studio look of this period was reflected in such pictures as *The Maltese Falcon*, *Casablanca* (Michael Curtiz, 1942), *Gaslight* (George Cukor, 1944), *This Gun for Hire*, *The Lodger* (Brahm, 1944), *The Woman in the Window* (Lang, 1945), *Mildred Pierce*, *Spellbound* (Alfred Hitchcock, 1945), *The Big Sleep*, *Laura*, *The Lost Weekend* (Wilder, 1945), *The Strange Love of Martha Ivers* (Lewis Milestone, 1946), *To Have and Have Not* (Howard Hawks, 1944), *Fallen Angel* (Preminger, 1946), *Gilda* (Charles Vidor, 1946), *Murder My Sweet* (Dmytryk, 1944), *The Postman Always Rings Twice*, *Dark Waters* (Andre de Toth, 1944), *Scarlet Street* (Fritz Lang, 1945), *So Dark the Night* (Joseph H. Lewis, 1946), *The Glass Key*, *The Mask of Dimitrios*, and *The Dark Mirror* (Siodmak, 1946).

The Wilder/Chandler *Double Indemnity* provided a bridge to the postwar phase of film noir. The unflinching noir vision of *Double Indemnity* came as a shock in 1944, and the film was almost blocked by the combined efforts of Paramount, the Hays Office, and star Fred MacMurray. Three years later, however, *Double Indemnitys* were dropping off the studio assembly lines.

The second phase was the postwar realistic period from 1945 to 1949 (the dates overlap and so do the films; these are all approximate phases for which there are exceptions). These films tended more toward the problems of crime in the streets, political corruption, and police routine. Less romantic heroes like Richard Conte, Burt Lancaster, and Charles McGraw were more suited to this period, as were proletarian directors like Hathaway, Dassin, and Kazan. The realistic urban look of this phase is seen in such films as *The House on 92nd Street*, *The Killers*, *Raw Deal*, *Act of Violence* (Zinnemann, 1949), *Union Station*, *Kiss of Death*, *Johnny O'Clock* (Robert Rossen, 1947), *Force of Evil* (Abraham Polonsky, 1948), *Dead Reckoning*, *Ride the Pink Horse*, *Dark Passage* (Delmer Daves, 1947), *Cry of the City* (Siodmak, 1948), *The Set-Up*, *T-Men*, *Call Northside 777*, *Brute Force*, *The Big Clock* (John Farrow, 1948), *Thieves' Highway* (Dassin, 1949), *Ruthless* (Ulmer, 1948), *The Pitfall* (de Toth, 1948), *Boomerang!* (Elia Kazan, 1947), and *The Naked City* (Dassin, 1948).

The third and final phase of film noir, from 1949 to 1953, was the period of psychotic action and suicidal impulse. The noir hero, seemingly under the weight of ten years of despair, started to go bananas. The psychotic killer, who had in the first period been a subject worthy of study (Olivia de Havilland in *The Dark Mirror*), and in the second a fringe threat (Richard Widmark in *Kiss of Death*), now became the active protagonist (James Cagney in *Kiss Tomorrow Goodbye*). There were no excuses given for the psychopathy in *Gun Crazy* (Joseph H. Lewis, 1949) – it was just 'crazy.' James Cagney made a neurotic comeback, and his instability was matched by that of younger actors like Robert Ryan and Lee Marvin. This was the phase of the B noir film and of psychoanalytically inclined directors like Ray and Walsh. The forces of personal disintegration are

CONTINUED

reflected in such films as *White Heat*, *Gun Crazy*, *D.O.A.*, *Caught* (Max Ophuls, 1949), *They Live by Night*, *Where the Sidewalk Ends*, *Kiss Tomorrow Goodbye*, *Detective Story* (William Wyler, 1951), *In a Lonely Place* (Ray, 1950), *I, the Jury*, *Ace in the Hole* (Wilder, 1951), *Panic in the Streets* (Kazan, 1950), *The Big Heat*, *On Dangerous Ground* (Ray, 1952), and *Sunset Boulevard*.

This third phase is the cream of the film noir period. Some critics may prefer the early 'gray' melodramas, others the postwar 'street' films, but film noir's final phase was the most aesthetically and sociologically piercing. After ten years of steadily shedding romantic conventions, the later noir films finally got down to the root causes of the period: the loss of public honor, heroic conventions, personal integrity, and, finally, psychic stability. The third-phase films were painfully self-aware; they seemed to know they stood at the end of a long tradition based on despair and disintegration and did not shy away from that fact. The best and most characteristically noir films – *Gun Crazy*, *White Heat*, *Out of the Past*, *Kiss Tomorrow Goodbye*, *D.O.A.*, *They Live by Night*, and *The Big Heat* – stand at the end of the period and are the results of self-awareness. The third phase is rife with end-of-the-line noir heroes: *The Big Heat* and *Where the Sidewalk Ends* are the last stops for the urban cop, *Ace in the Hole* for the newspaper man, the Victor Saville-produced Spillane series *I, the Jury*, *The Long Wait* (Victor Saville, 1954), and *Kiss Me Deadly* for the private eye, *Sunset Boulevard* for the Black Widow, *White Heat* and *Kiss Tomorrow Goodbye* for the gangster, *D.O.A.* for the John Doe American.

Appropriately, the masterpiece of film noir was a straggler, *Kiss Me Deadly*, produced in 1955. Its time delay gives it a sense of detachment and thoroughgoing seediness – it stands at the end of a long sleazy tradition. The private-eye hero, Mike Hammer, undergoes the final stages of degradation. He is a small-time 'bedroom dick,' and has no qualms about it because the world around him isn't much better. Ralph Meeker, in his best performance, plays Hammer, a midget among dwarfs. Robert Aldrich's teasing direction carries noir to its sleaziest and most perversely erotic. Hammer overturns the underworld in search of the 'great whatsit,' and when he finally finds it, it turns out to be – joke of jokes – an exploding atomic bomb. The inhumanity and meaninglessness of the hero are small matters in a world in which the Bomb has the final say.

By the middle fifties film noir had ground to a halt. There were a few notable stragglers – *Kiss Me Deadly*, the Lewis/Alton *The Big Combo*, and film noir's epitaph, *Touch of Evil* – but for the most part a new style of crime film had become popular.

As the rise of McCarthy and Eisenhower demonstrated, Americans were eager to see a more bourgeois view of themselves. Crime had to move to the suburbs. The criminal put on a grey flannel suit, and the footsore cop was replaced by the 'mobile unit' careening down the expressway. Any attempt at social criticism had to be cloaked in ludicrous affirmations of the American way of life. Technically, television, with its demand for full lighting and close-ups, gradually undercut the German influence, and color cinematography was, of course, the final blow to the noir look.

New directors like Seigel, Fleischer, Karlson, and Fuller, and TV shows like *Dragnet*, M-*Squad*, *Lineup*, and *Highway Patrol* stepped in to create the new crime drama. This transition can be seen in Samuel Fuller's 1953 *Pickup on South Street*, a film that blends the black look with the red scare. The waterfront scenes with Richard Widmark and Jean Peters are in the best noir tradition, but a later, dynamic fight in the subway marks Fuller as a director who would be better suited to the crime school of the middle and late fifties.

Film noir was an immensely creative period – probably the most creative in Hollywood's history – at least, if this creativity is measured not by its peaks but by its median level of artistry. Picked at random, a film noir is likely to be a better made film than a randomly selected silent comedy, musical, western, and so on. (A Joseph H. Lewis B film noir is better than a Lewis B western, for example.) Taken as a whole period, film noir achieved an unusually high level of artistry. Film noir seemed to bring out the best in everyone: directors, cameramen, screenwriters, actors. Again and again, a film noir will make the high point on an artist's career graph. Some directors, for example, did their best work in film noir (Stuart Heisler, Robert Siodmak, Gordon Douglas, Edward Dmytryk, John Brahm, John Cromwell, Raoul Walsh, Henry Hathaway); other directors began in film noir and, it seems to me, never regained their original heights (Otto Preminger, Rudolph Maté, Nicholas Ray, Robert Wise, Jules Dassin, Richard Fleischer, John Huston, André de Toth, and Robert Aldrich); and other directors who made great films in other molds also made great film noir (Orson Welles, Max Ophuls, Fritz Lang, Elia Kazan, Howard Hawks, Robert Rossen, Anthony Mann, Joseph Losey, Alfred Hitchcock, and Stanley Kubrick). Whether or not one agrees with this particular schema, its message is irrefutable: film noir was good for practically every director's career. (Two interesting exceptions to prove the case are King Vidor and Jean Renoir.) Film noir seems to have been a creative release for everyone involved. It gave artists a chance to work with previously forbidden themes, yet had conventions strong enough to protect the mediocre. Cinematographers were allowed to become highly mannered, and actors were sheltered by the cinematographers. It was not until years later that critics were able to distinguish between great directors and great noir directors.

Film noir's remarkable creativity makes its long-time neglect the more baffling. The French, of course, have been students of the period for some time (Borde and Chaumeton's *Panorama du film noir* was published in 1955), but American critics until recently have preferred the western, the musical, or the gangster film to the film noir.

Some of the reasons for this neglect are superficial; others strike to the heart of the noir style. For a long time film noir, with its emphasis on corruption and despair, was considered an aberration of the American character. The western, with its moral primitivism, and the gangster film, with its Horatio Alger values, were considered more American than the film noir.

This prejudice was reinforced by the fact that film noir was ideally suited to the low-budget B film, and many of the best noir films were B films. This odd sort of economic snobbery still lingers on in some critical circles: high-budget trash is considered more worthy of attention than low-budget trash, and to praise a B film is somehow to slight (often intentionally) an A film.

The fundamental reason for film noir's neglect, however, is the fact that it depends more on choreography than sociology, and American critics have always been slow on the uptake when it comes to visual style. Like its protagonists, film noir is more interested in style than theme, whereas American critics have been traditionally more interested in theme than style. American film critics have always been sociologists first and scientists second: film is important as it relates to large masses, and if a film goes awry, it is often because the theme has been somehow 'violated' by the style. Film noir operates on opposite principles: the theme is hidden in the style, and bogus themes are often flaunted ('middle-class values are best') that contradict the style. Although, I believe, style determines the theme in every film, it was easier for sociological critics to discuss the themes of the western and gangster film apart from stylistic analysis than it was to do for film noir.

Not surprisingly, it was the gangster film, not the film noir, which was canonized in *The Partisan Review* in 1948 by Robert Warshow's famous essay, 'The Gangster as Tragic Hero.' Although Warshow could be an aesthetic as well as a sociological critic, in this case he was interested in the western and gangster film as 'popular' art rather than as style. This sociological orientation blinded Warshow, as it has many subsequent critics, to an aesthetically more important development in the gangster film – film noir.

The irony of this neglect is that in retrospect the gangster films Warshow wrote about are inferior to film noir. The thirties gangster was primarily a reflection of what was happening in the country, and Warshow analyzed this. The film noir, although it was also a sociological reflection, went further than the gangster film. Toward the end film noir was engaged in a life-and-death struggle with the materials it reflected; it tried to make America accept a moral vision of life based on style. That very contradiction – promoting style in a culture that valued themes – forced film noir into artistically invigorating twists and turns. Film noir attacked and interpreted its sociological conditions and, by the close of the noir period, created a new artistic world that went beyond a simple sociological reflection, a nightmarish world of American mannerism that was by far more a creation than a reflection.

Because film noir was first of all a style, because it worked out its conflicts visually rather than thematically, because it was aware of its own identity, it was able to create artistic solutions to sociological problems. And for these reasons films like *Kiss Me Deadly*, *Kiss Tomorrow Goodbye*, and *Gun Crazy* can be works of art in a way that gangster films like *Scarface*, *The Public Enemy*, and *Little Caesar* can never be.

NOTES

1, Raymond Durgnat, 'Paint It Black: The Family Tree of Film Noir,' *Cinema* (U.K.), nos. 6–7 (August 1970): 49–56.

2. Ibid.

3. Raymond Chandler, 'The Simple Art of Murder,' in *Detective Fiction: Crime and Compromise*, edited by Dick Allen and David Chacko (New York: Harcourt Brace Jovanovich, 1974), p. 398.

(Schrader 1986: 169–182)

As you can see, genre criticism is a useful tool for exploring the nature of film, especially in relation to the artists/film/audience triangle proposed by Ryall. An interesting way to complete this section is by looking at the application of genre as a critical tool in relation to a postmodern theory. In the extract that follows Tanya Modleski considers the contemporary horror film in relation to postmodern theory. As you will be aware, one aspect of postmodernism is the breakdown of the distinction between 'high art' and popular art here represented by the horror movie.

While Barthes' *The Pleasure of the Text* has become one of the canonical works of postmodernism, in this respect it remains caught up in older modernist ideas about art. In an essay entitled 'The Fate of Pleasure,' written in 1963, the modernist critic Lionel Trilling speculated that high art had dedicated itself to an attack on pleasure in part because pleasure was the province of mass art: 'we are repelled by the idea of an art that is consumer-oriented and comfortable, let alone luxurious' (Trilling: 1963, 178). He went on to argue that, for the modernist, pleasure is associated with the 'specious good' – with bourgeois habits, manners, and morals – and he noted, 'the destruction of what is considered to be specious good is surely one of the chief literary enterprises of our age' (ibid., 182). Hence, Trilling has famously declared, aesthetic modernity is primarily adversarial in impulse.

The 'specious good,' or 'bourgeois taste,' remains an important target of contemporary thinkers, and postmodernism continues to be theorized as its adversary. Indeed, it might be argued that postmodernism is valued by many of its proponents insofar as it is considered *more* adversarial than modernism, and is seen to wage war on a greatly expanded category of the 'specious good,' which presently includes meaning (Barthes speaks of the 'regime of meaning') and even form (Barthes: 1977, 167). For example, in an essay entitled 'Answering the Question: What is Postmodernism?' Jean-François Lyotard explicitly contrasts postmodernism to modernism in terms of their relation to 'pleasure.' For Lyotard, modernism's preoccupation with form meant that it was still capable of affording the reader or viewer 'matter for solace and pleasure, [whereas the postmodern is] that which denies itself the solace of good forms, the consensus of a taste which would make it possible to share collectively the nostalgia for the unattainable' (Lyotard: 1983, 340). It is important to recognize the extent to which Lyotard shares the same animus as the Frankfurt School, although his concern is not merely to denounce *spurious* harmony, but to attack *all* harmony – consensus, collectivity – as spurious, that is, on the side of 'cultural policy,' the aim of which is to offer the public 'well-made' and 'comforting' works of art (ibid., 335).

Although Lyotard has elsewhere informed us that 'thinking by means of oppositions does not correspond to the liveliest modes of postmodern knowledge,' he does not seem to have extricated himself entirely from this mode (Lyotard: 1979, 29). Pleasure (or 'comfort' or 'solace') remains the enemy for the postmodernist thinker because it is judged to be the means by which the consumer is reconciled to the prevailing cultural policy, or the 'dominant ideology.' While this view may well provide the critic with 'matter for solace and pleasure,' it is at least debatable that mass culture today is on the side of the specious good, that it offers, in the words of Matei Calinescu, 'an ideologically manipulated illusion of taste,' that it lures its audience to a false complacency with the promise of equally false and insipid pleasures (Calinescu: 1977, 240). Indeed, the contemporary horror film – the so-called exploitation film or slasher film – provides an interesting counter-example to such theses. Many of these films are engaged in an unprecedented assault on all that bourgeois culture is supposed to cherish – like the ideological apparatuses of the family and the school. Consider Leonard Maltin's capsule summary of an exemplary film in the genre, *The Brood* (1979), directed by David Cronenberg and starring Samantha Eggar: 'Eggar eats her own afterbirth while midget clones beat grandparents and lovely young school teachers to death with mallets' (Maltin: 1981–2, 95). A few of the films, like *The Texas Chainsaw Massacre* (1974), have actually been celebrated for their adversarial relation to contemporary culture and society. In this film, a family of men, driven out of the slaughterhouse business by advanced technology, turns to cannibalism. The film deals with the slaughter of a group of young people travelling in a van and dwells at great length on the pursuit of the last survivor of the group, Sally, by the man named Leatherface, who hacks his victims to death with a chainsaw. Robin Wood has analyzed the film as embodying a critique of capitalism, since the film shows the horror both of people quite literally living off other people, and of the institution of the family, since it implies that the monster is the family (Wood *et al.*: 1979, 20–22).

In some of the films the attack on contemporary life strikingly recapitulates the very terms adopted by many culture critics. In George Romero's *Dawn of the Dead* (1979), the plot involves zombies taking over a shopping center, a scenario depicting the worst fears of the culture critics who have long envisioned the will-less, soul-less masses as zombie-like beings possessed by the alienating imperative to consume. And in David Cronenberg's *Videodrome* (1982), video itself becomes the monster. The film concerns a plot, emanating from Pittsburgh, to subject human beings to massive doses of a video signal which renders its victims incapable of distinguishing hallucination from reality. One of the effects of this signal on the film's hero is to cause a gaping, vagina-like wound to open in the middle of his stomach, so that the villains can program him by inserting a video cassette into his body. The hero's situation becomes that of the new schizophrenic described by Jean Baudrillard in his discussion of the effects of mass communication:

> No more hysteria, no more projective paranoia, properly speaking, but this state of terror proper to the schizophrenic: too great a proximity of everything, the unclean promiscuity of everything which touches, invests, and penetrates without resistance, with no halo of private protection, not even his own body, to protect him anymore. ... The schizo is bereft of every scene, open to everything in spite of himself, living in the greatest confusion.
>
> (Baudrillard: 1983, 132–3)

'You must open yourself completely to us,' says one of *Videodrome*'s villains, as he plunges the cassette into the gaping wound. It would seem that we are here very far from the realm of what is traditionally called 'pleasure' and much nearer to so-called *jouissance*, discussions of which privilege terms like 'gaps,' 'wounds,' 'fissures,' 'splits,' 'cleavages,' and so forth.

Moreover, if the text is 'an anagram for our body,' as Roland Barthes maintains (Barthes: 1975, 17), the contemporary text of horror could aptly be considered an anagram for the schizophrenic's body, which is so vividly imaged in Cronenberg's film. It is a ruptured body, lacking the kind of integrity commonly attributed to popular narrative cinema. For just as Baudrillard makes us aware that terms like 'paranoia' and 'hysteria,' which film critics have used to analyze both film characters and textual mechanisms, are no longer as applicable in mass culture today as they once were, so the much more global term 'narrative pleasure' is similarly becoming outmoded.

What is always at stake in discussions of 'narrative pleasure' is what many think of as the ultimate 'spurious harmony,' the supreme ideological construct – the 'bourgeois ego.' Contemporary film theorists insist that pleasure is 'ego-reinforcing' and that narrative is the primary means by which mass culture supplies and regulates this pleasure. For Stephen Heath, Hollywood narratives are versions of the nineteenth-century 'novelistic,' or 'family romance,' and their function is to 'remember the history of the individual subject' through processes of identification, through narrative continuity, and through the mechanism of closure (Heath: 1981, 157). Julia Kristeva condemns popular cinema in similar terms in her essay on terror in film, 'Ellipsis on Dread and the Specular Seduction':

> [The] terror/seduction node ... becomes, through cinematic commerce, a kind of cut-rate seduction. One quickly pulls the veil over the terror, and only the cathartic relief remains; in mediocre potboilers, for example, in order to remain within the range of petty bourgeois taste, film plays up to narcissistic identification, and the viewer is satisfied with 'three-buck seduction.'

(Kristeva: 1979, 46)

But just as the individual and the family are *dis*-membered in the most gruesomely literal way in many of these films, so the novelistic as family romance is also in the process of being dismantled.

First, not only do the films tend to be increasingly open-ended in order to allow for the possibility of countless sequels, but they also often delight in thwarting the audiences' expectations of closure. The most famous examples of this tendency are the surprise codas of Brian De Palma's films – for instance, the hand reaching out from the grave in *Carrie* (1976). And in *The Evil Dead*, *Halloween*, and *Friday and 13th*, the monsters and slashers rise and attempt to kill over and over again each time they are presumed dead. At the end of *The Evil Dead* (1983), the monsters, after defying myriad attempts to destroy them, appear finally to be annihilated as they are burned to death in an amazing lengthy sequence. But in the last shot of the film, when the hero steps outside into the light of day, the camera rushes toward him, and he turns and faces it with an expression of horror. In the final sequence of *Halloween* (1978), the babysitter looks at the spot where the killer was apparently slain and, finding it vacant, says, 'It really was the bogey man.'

Secondly – and this is the aspect most commonly discussed and deplored by popular journalists – these films tend to dispense with or drastically minimize the plot and character development that is thought to be essential to the construction of the novelistic. In Cronenberg's *Rabid* (1977), the porn star Marilyn Chambers plays a woman who receives a skin transplant and begins to infect everyone around her with a kind of rabies. The symptom of her disease is a vagina-like wound in her armpit out of which a phallic-shaped weapon springs to slash and mutilate its victims. While the film does have some semblance of a plot, most of it comprises disparate scenes showing Marilyn, or her victims, or her victims' victims, on the attack. Interestingly, although metonymy has been considered to be the principle by which narrative is constructed, metonymy in this film (the contagion signified by the title) becomes the means by which narrative is *disordered*, revealing a view of a world in which the center no longer holds. Films like *Maniac* and *Friday the 13th* and its sequels go even further in the reduction of plot and character. In *Friday the 13th* (1980), a group of young people are brought together to staff a summer camp and are randomly murdered whenever they go off to make love. The people in the film are practically interchangeable, since we learn nothing about them as individuals, and there is virtually no building of a climax – only variations on the theme of slashing, creating a pattern that is more or less reversible.

Finally, it should scarcely need pointing out that when villains and victims are such shadowy, undeveloped characters and are portrayed equally unsympathetically, narcissistic identification on the part of the audience becomes increasingly difficult. Indeed, it could be said that some of the films elicit a kind of *anti*-narcissistic identification, which the audience delights in indulging just as it delights in having its expectations of closure frustrated. Of *The Texas Chainsaw Massacre*, Robin Wood writes, 'Watching it recently with a large, half-stoned youth audience who cheered and applauded every one of Leatherface's outrages against their representatives on the screen was a terrifying experience' (Wood *et al.*: 1979, 22). The same might be said of films like *Halloween* and *Friday the 13th*, which adopt the point of view of the slasher, placing the spectator in the position of an unseen nameless presence which, to the audiences' great glee, annihilates one by one their screen surrogates. This kind of joyful self-destructiveness on the part of the masses has been discussed by Jean Baudrillard in another context – in his analysis of the Georges Pompidou Center in Paris to which tourists flock by the millions, ostensibly to consume culture, but also to hasten the collapse of the structurally flawed building (Baudrillard: 1977, 23–5). There is a similar paradox in the fact that *Dawn of the Dead* (1979), the film about zombies taking over a shopping center, has become a midnight favorite at shopping malls all over the United States. In both cases the masses are revelling in the demise of the very culture they appear most enthusiastically to support. Here, it would seem, we have another variant of the split, 'perverse' response favored by Roland Barthes.

(Modleski 2000: 287–290)

▼ 6 AUTEUR

Authors communicate with the world in some special and particular capacity.

Michel de Montaigne

There are no works, there are only authors.

Giradoux

> **Auteur:** An individual, inevitably the director, whose contribution to a film's style and theme is considered so significant that he or she can be considered the 'author' of the film despite the fact that a film's production is dependent on a large number of people with specific skills and talents working collaboratively. An auteur establishes his or her identity across a body of films which can be seen to bear a distinctive 'signature' (compare with **metteur-en-scène**).
>
> **metteur-en-scène:** a director often admired for the competence of his or her work, who lacks the recurring and distinctive 'signature' that would grant the status of **auteur**.
>
> (Nelmes 1996)

One of the most influential and problematic ideas to have entered the discourse of film study, auteur, has become one of film criticism's principal codes. Despite its origins in the somewhat closed world of the French 'nouvelle vague', the implications of auteurism are everywhere and evident. In fact in the wake of the explosion of DVD as a home movie format, 'auteur' has become the most accessible critical approach, with 'auteur' directors being signalled by serious documentary extras and celebratory packaging, offering, for example, the Stanley Kubrick 'Collection'.

To make sense of auteur it is useful to take a step back to the question that the 'policy of authors' was trying to address: who makes a film? One of the central problems for film is the absence or at least obscuring of the artist. Whereas it was obviously possible to create an aesthetic of film, a theory of film 'beauty', there remained the issue of defining the source of the stylistic decisions.

'Style' is a useful starting point for this debate. As the critic Susan Sontag points out, 'what is inevitable in a work of art is the style'. If films have style then the leading question must be: 'who dictates or decides this style?' In the following passage, taken from her essay 'On Style', Sontag marks out some general critical ground as well as raising a number of issues particularly pertinent to film criticism. The first line is crucial and quotable: 'Style is the principle of decision in a work of art, the signature of the artist's will.' We will return to artists' signatures later in the chapter (which are often prefigured by legends such as 'un film de …'), for now let us allow Sontag to set a more abstract agenda:

> Style is the principle of decision in a work of art, the signature of the artist's will. And as the human will is capable of an indefinite number of stances, there are an indefinite number of possible styles for works of art.
>
> Seen from the outside, that is, historically, stylistic decisions can always be correlated with some historical development – like the invention of writing or of movable type, the invention or transformation of musical instruments, the availability of new materials to the sculptor or architect. But this approach, however sound and valuable, of necessity sees matters grossly; it treats of 'periods' and 'traditions' and 'schools.'
>
> Seen from the inside, that is, when one examines an individual work of art and tries to account for its value and effect, every stylistic decision contains an element of arbitrariness, however much it may seem justifiable *propter hoc*. If art is the supreme game which the will plays with itself, 'style' consists of the set of rules by which this game is played. And the rules are always, finally, an artificial and arbitrary limit, whether they are rules of form (like *terza rima* or the twelve-tone row or frontality) or the presence of a certain 'content.' The role of the arbitrary and unjustifiable in art has never been sufficiently acknowledged. Ever since the enterprise of criticism began with Aristotle's *Poetics*, critics have been beguiled into emphasizing the necessary in art. (When Aristotle said that poetry was more philosophical than history, he was justified insofar as he wanted to rescue poetry, that is, the arts, from being conceived as a type of factual, particular, descriptive statement. But what he said was misleading insofar as it suggests that art supplies something like what philosophy gives us: an argument. The metaphor of the work of art as an 'argument,' with premises and entailments, has informed most criticism since.) Usually critics who want to praise a work of art feel compelled to demonstrate that each part is justified, that it could not be other than it is. And every artist, when it comes to his own work, remembering the role of change, fatigue, external distractions, knows what the critic says to be a lie, knows that it could well have been otherwise. The sense of inevitability that a great work of art projects is not made up of the inevitability or necessity of its parts, but of the whole.
>
> (Sontag 2001: 32–33)

Sontag raises many points; responding to these 'issues' will be the essence of this chapter. In simple terms Sontag's points are as follows:

■ Style is the human element in a work of art, 'capable of an indefinite number of stances';

- Style may be approached 'from the outside' in terms of historical movements (periods, traditions, schools) and technological advances ('like the invention of movable type');
- Style may be approached 'from the inside' in terms of an arbitrary set of decisions which owe as much to 'chance, fatigue, external distractions' as they do to an inevitable controlling artistic vision: 'that each part is justified, that it will not be other than it is'.

These translate very easily into a set of challenges for Film Studies to which this chapter (and section) will make response, though each response serves to maintain the fact that these challenges are ongoing. If we follow the bullets above we get something resembling the following:

- Who is the guiding human element in a film? Who provides 'the human will'?
- To what extent is the history of film 'styles' merely the history of film technology? Is it possible that film is after all a technology rather than an art form?
- If the 'sense of inevitability' that a great work of art projects is an inevitability of the whole, why cannot the work of art be a collaboration rather than an individual's sole responsibility? Are there perhaps other ideological reasons why the collective effort is downplayed in favour of the significant and talented individual?

How we respond to these questions will depend on who we are and what kind of cinema we see and want to see. The 'auteur' approach or theory offers one set of answers which derive from a particular set of circumstances and needs.

Martin Scorsese confirmed such an approach in an acceptance speech he made when receiving the John Huston Award for Artists' Rights in 1996. Here a significant American 'auteur' (author) is making the case for authorship, past, present and future. He is very definite in his opinions:

- 'you still need an author'
- 'cinema is not just technology'
- 'The "author" is not an abstract corporation'
- 'Film is not factory made ...'
- 'Let's keep the "human" in the creative process'
- 'The reality is that cinema is an art'.

It is interesting that Scorsese then goes on to use Hitchcock as his example, dismissing doubts about his 'validity' with 'some felt his films were just "thrillers", or clever storytelling'. The original 'Politique des auteurs' ('Policy' of the authors) itself was largely motivated by a desire to see Hitchcock's work taken seriously.

The 'history' of auteur studies is easily explicated and dated. The following entry from Wikipedia gives you all you need to know:

The **Auteur Theory** is a way of reading and appraising films through the imprint of an auteur, usually meant to be the director.

In the 1954 essay *Une certaine tendence du cinéma français* François Truffaut coined the phrase 'la politique des auteurs', and asserted that the worst of Jean Renoir's movies would always be more interesting than the best of Jean Delannoy's. 'Politique' might very well be translated as 'policy'; it involves a conscious decision to look at movies in a certain way and to value them in a certain way. Truffaut provocatively said, 'There are no good and bad movies, only good and bad directors.'

Truffaut and his colleagues at the magazine *Cahiers du cinéma* recognized that moviemaking was an industrial process. However, they proposed an ideal to strive for: using the commercial apparatus just the way a writer uses a pen. While recognizing that not all directors reached this ideal, they valued the work of those who neared it.

This theory espouses that all good directors (and many bad ones) have such a distinctive style that their fingerprints end up on the film. You cannot see a film by that director without recognizing their influence. The strength of their theory (and the logical penchant for directors to support it) has been blamed for the irrational lack of attention some early directors received during the heyday of film theory. Howard Hawks was argued to be a hack because he had too many movies across too many genres. Allan Dwan still has not received much critical recognition both because too few of his films are in circulation and he made too many without contemporary attention.

The auteurist critics – Truffaut, Godard, Chabrol, Rohmer – wrote mostly about directors, although they also produced some shrewd appreciations of actors. Later writers of the same general school have emphasized the contributions of star personalities like Mae West. However, the stress was on directors, and when Andrew Sarris exported the theory to the United States, screenwriters, producers and others reacted with a good deal of hostility. Writer William Goldman has said that, on first hearing the auteur theory, his first reaction was, 'What's the punchline?'

The auteur theory significantly influenced the *nouvelle vague* movement of French cinema in the 1960s.

(Wikipedia Internet Encyclopedia)

The real point to understand is that 'auteur' was a principle of film-makers which became a tool for critics and academics. The 'policy' was essentially a manifesto, 'a conscious decision to look at movies in a certain way and value them in a certain way', which became the benchmark for the evaluation of film-makers. It is then simply a matter of setting the criteria and deciding how extensive the definition might be, extending to stars, producers, even studios.

In its formulation of director as artist/author it also reached back to an influential essay from the late 1940s: Alexandre Astruc's 'The Birth of a New Avant-garde: La camera-stylo': 'Direction is no longer a means of illustrating, of presenting a scene, but a true act of writing. This film-maker/writer writes with his camera as a writer writes with his pen.' Astruc sees the 'camera as pen' transformation as key to the liberation of film and film-makers:

> By turning the camera into a pen, we will ... break free from the tyranny of what is visual, from the image for its own sake, from the immediate and concrete demands of the narrative, to become a means of writing just as flexible and subtle as written language ... more or less literal 'inscriptions' on images as essays.

It is this visual style, this personal signature, that the auteur approach seeks to identify and authenticate. The directors who are merely 'illustrating' or 'presenting the scene' are *metteurs-en-scène* (organisers/arrangers/positioners), craftsmen rather than artists. Only those who leave the mark of their personalities or a coherent body of signifiers (themes, style, motifs) are admitted to the 'brotherhood' (and very occasionally 'sisterhood') of auteurs.

In his work on 'auteur' in *An Introduction to Film Studies* (a collaborative effort edited by Jill Nelmes) Patrick Phillips underlines the simplicity of the approach, while at the same time implying some of its limitations:

AUTEUR

The auteur contrast

The director in modern Hollywood can function much like a star in offering an *insurance value* to the industry and a *trademark value* to an audience. Increasingly films are bought and sold on the basis of a director's name, which takes on the function of a sign. This sign will carry much information of significance concerning the popular and critical 'credit' of the director based on his previous work and the kind of promise offered by a new film bearing his name. The auteur sign, by contrast, is much more precise and specific. It will signify a set of stylistic and thematic features which, it is anticipated, will be identifiable in the text of a film bearing the auteur name. In other words, an auteur possesses a *sign(ature)* marking out his own individuality which is legible in a film over which he has enjoyed sufficient creative control for that sign(ature) to permeate the film. In practice the auteur sign, like the star sign, can be approached as a structure made up of a set of paradigms working in distinctive rules of combination.

Issues of definition and classification which are encountered in studying genre and stars are at least as problematic in Hollywood auteur study. Since the late 1950s, following the work of critics in France, it has been considered both possible and necessary in film studies to distinguish **the auteur** in Hollywood cinema from what they called the **metteur-en-scène**, that is to distinguish a director who brings to a film the signs of his own individuality as the dominant creative force in the film's production from the director who 'merely' brings competence to the particular specialist role of directing. It is difficult to determine in many instances where on a continuum the qualities of a metteur-en-scène become those of an auteur, and this is especially so as the Hollywood industry markets films increasingly in terms of a name, in the process collapsing distinctions students and critics may want to make.

This last point is particularly significant. In previous sections it has been apparent that genre and star are phenomena of importance to audiences; a genre or a star signifies myths and desires which circulate at the heart of popular culture. By contrast, the presence of an auteur structure is neither so easily 'felt' nor, as a consequence, so direct a focus for response. If genre and star study can be said, in broad terms, to have been developed out of the lived experience of Hollywood cinema, auteur study is a construct of criticism. As such its centrality within film studies has long been a cause of dispute. This is compounded not only by problems of definition touched upon above, but by fundamental questions surrounding the very idea of 'authorship'.

(Phillips 1996: 150–151)

ACTIVITY

➤ Which directors for you have a 'signature'? What does this 'signature' consist of? Across how many films will this need to be shown?

Patrick Phillips' exploration of Scorsese's authorship can perhaps take our discussion a little further. He provides what he calls an 'auteur structure' as a context for a discussion of the Scorsese musical *New York, New York*. This in turn is given a useful context when he identifies another issue/problematic: the biographical element, the part of the auteur 'persona' that becomes 'personal' (or threatens to). Phillips is convinced that auteur study has made a significant contribution to Film Studies. He suggests that not only did it encourage a serious study of mainstream Hollywood cinema but it also made technique, particularly in relation to *mise-en-scène*, a significant point of analysis. This gave close film reading a dual purpose:

■ the exploration of the key signifiers in the work of obvious auteurs (like Scorsese);
■ An evaluation of the cases of authorship of other directors with an eye to seeing them 'elevated' to the ranks of 'The auteurs'.

Contemporary work on Scorsese is very likely to concentrate on those features that define his 'authorship' since the body of work bearing his signature is indisputable. The next step is obviously the work, the films themselves. Here is a significant strength of the approach since films are what Film Studies is all about, and are both relatively accessible and relatively challenging. Critics may retreat from a single text in the direction of others by the same 'author' but they cannot avoid the fact that the revelation of the 'unifying signifiers' can be nowhere else but in the texts themselves.

> These paradigms, these features observable within the films can be amplified by reference to biographical information concerning Martin Scorsese. So, for example, his close identification with Little Italy in New York City, with its distinctive social formation, may be cited. More specifically, his Catholic background provides useful corroborating evidence, and some (overly neat?) personal statements such as that in which he says that as a boy he wished to be either a priest or a gangster. His immersion from a very early age in film culture helps to explain something of the rich repertoire of styles and images he is able to bring to the screen. His interest in the films of Powell and Pressburger, as well as the more obvious homage to the MGM classic musical, may, for example, advance our appreciation of *New York, New York.*

> (Phillips 1996: 158)

On the other hand some auteur readings are too often led by a host of biographical facts from unhappy childhoods to a fascination with clowns. Much of the work on the Italian film-maker Federico Fellini, for example, constructs an auteur structure around, among other things, his experiences with the circus, his former career as a cartoonist and his Catholic upbringing. Frank Burke's book on Fellini's films *From Postwar to Postmodern* is typical:

> Within the larger context of Western and American ideology, Fellini fashioned his own brand of individualism as an anti-authoritarian response to his Fascist and Catholic upbringing. ...
>
> Though Fellini abhorred Catholic dogmatism, this did not prevent him from fusing individualism in his early work with a secularized form of Christian humanism: a belief in the 'salvation' of the individual via psychological individuation. The road to salvation was not the Way of the Cross, but the evolution of consciousness from the unconscious and the integration of all the fragmented and repressed aspects of the individual psyche.

The danger here is that the life leads the art, that the man and the work are not allowed to be properly separate. Patrick Phillips chooses to excavate the work before the biographical material manages to 'amplify' it. He offers two sets of discovered evidence. The first is headed, 'we discover the following principal thematic preoccupations in two or more of Scorsese's "auteur" films':

- a strong focus on masculinity: on male friendship, on male sexuality and on the ways in which these are threatened or experienced as areas of personal crisis;
- more specifically, the male attitude to women as 'other', as unknowable, definable as 'whores' or 'virgins', as the source of the threat to masculinity, as the cause of male paranoia, and consequently as objects of abuse within relationships where the male seeks to assert dominance;
- explicitly or implicitly the male character is placed within a framework of guilt, sin, retribution, redemption;
- the male existing within a closed world, either a community (New York Italian) or a mental state of alienation and reality distortion;

- this reality distortion is sometimes linked to wider forms of reality distortion within American culture (*Taxi Driver* and *King of Comedy*);
- generally the resolution of internal conflict by means of external violence;
- as an extension to this, the dominance of the physical over the verbal – male characters are characteristically inarticulate but physically expressive;
- a representation of blacks which reflects either the overt or implicit racism of the protagonists.

However, thematic concerns are not the only way in which directors exhibit their individual influence on films. Scorsese may make films which are about similar issues, but he also makes films in a particular way or style. Thus Philips offers a second list, headed, 'we also note the following features of form and style recurring in two or more of the above named films':

- documentary-style realism in 'method' performances and locations;
- the expressive use of mobile camera, lighting, editing and sound which works against the documentary realism, placing it within a stylised artificiality;
- thus point of view is a complex interaction of the spectator's observations of an 'objective' world and the character's 'subjective' perception of that world;
- the primary role assigned to soundtrack in the creation of meaning;
- the adoption (and subsequent problematising) of generic forms and, in particular, the ambiguity and perplexity of the films' closures.

It is this division of issues of authorship into types (or schools), together with the development of the idea of 'auteur structure' rather than 'personality' that Phillips acknowledges are 'particularly associated with the work of Peter Wollen in the late 1960s'. In his 'influential and ground-breaking work' *Signs and Meaning in the Cinema* Wollen explicates the auteur approach and demonstrates its complexity and value with a celebrated comparison of the films of Howard Hawkes and John Ford. His approach is essentially structuralist, interested in the patterns that emerge from close reading. 'The auteur theory does not limit itself to acclaiming the director as the main author of a film,' he claims; 'it implies an operation of decipherment: it reveals authors where none had appeared before.' For Wollen, this 'decipherment' works in two basic 'languages', or as he describes them, 'schools of auteur critics'. These are the schools that Phillips has straddled in his two-part 'decipherment' of Scorsese. Wollen labels them 'thematic' and 'stylistic' schools.

INFOBOX

STRUCTURALISM

Structuralism is a philosophy or system of analysis which looks at the relationship between the units of a system (for example, the letters/sounds of a language) and the rules that make that system work (for example, the rules of grammar). In doing so it tries to identify the deep-rooted structures which it may be argued typify all systems: in different languages the grammar rules are different, as are the words, but the structure is still the same in all languages: words are put together within a grammatical system to make meaning.

JOHN FORD

John Ford is one of the most celebrated film-makers in history, the director of American Westerns such as *Stagecoach* (1939), *She Wore a Yellow Ribbon* (1949) and *The Searchers* (1956). *The Man Who Shot Liberty Valence (1962)* was one of the last of more than 140 films he directed.

HOWARD HAWKES

A friend and contemporary of Ford, Howard Hawkes was beaten by Ford on the only occasion when he was nominated for a Best Director Oscar (in 1941). The IMDb describes him as 'the most versatile of all American directors' and 'a first-rate craftsman and consummate Hollywood professional'.

Of course, some individual directors have always been recognised as outstanding: Charles Chaplin, John Ford, Orson Welles. The auteur theory does not limit itself to acclaiming the director as the main author of a film. It implies an operation of decipherment; it reveals authors where none had been seen before. For years, the model of an author in the cinema was that of the European director, with open artistic aspirations and full control over his films. This model still lingers on; it lies behind the existential distinction between art films and popular films. Directors who built their reputations in Europe were dismissed after they crossed the Atlantic, reduced to anonymity. American Hitchcock was contrasted unfavourably with English Hitchcock, American Renoir with French Renoir, American Fritz Lang with German Fritz Lang. The auteur theory has led to the revaluation of the second, Hollywood careers of these and other European directors; without it, masterpieces such as *Scarlet Street* or *Vertigo* would never have been perceived. Conversely, the auteur theory has been sceptical when offered an American director whose salvation has been exile to Europe. It is difficult now to argue that *Brute Force* has ever been excelled by Jules Dassin or that Joseph Losey's later work is markedly superior to, say, *The Prowler*.

In time, owing to the diffuseness of the original theory, two main schools of auteur critics grew up: those who insisted on revealing a core of meanings, of thematic motifs, and those who stressed style and *mise en scène*. There is an important distinction here, which I shall return to later. The work of the auteur has a semantic dimension, it is not purely formal; the work of the *metteur en scène*, on the other hand, does not go beyond the realm of performance, of transposing into the special complex of cinematic codes and channels a pre-existing text: a scenario, a book or a play. As we shall see, the meaning of the films of an auteur is constructed *a posteriori*; the meaning – semantic, rather than stylistic or expressive – of the films of a *metteur en scène* exists *a priori*. In concrete cases, of course, this distinction is not always clear-cut. There is controversy over whether some directors should be seen as auteurs or *metteurs en scène*. For example, though it is possible to make intuitive ascriptions there have been no really persuasive accounts as yet of Raoul Walsh or William Wyler as auteurs, to take two very different directors. Opinions might differ abut Don Siegel or George Cukor. Because of the difficulty of fixing the distinction in these concrete cases, it has often become blurred; indeed, some French critics have tended to value the *metteur en scène* above the auteur. MacMahonism sprang up, with its cult of Walsh, Lang, Losey and Preminger, its fascination with violence and its notorious text: 'Charlton Heston is an axiom of the cinema.' What André Bazin called 'aesthetic cults of personality' began to be formed. Minor directors were acclaimed before they had, in any real sense, been identified and defined.

Yet the auteur theory has survived despite all the hallucinating critical extravaganzas which it has fathered. It has survived because it is indispensable. Geoffrey Nowell-Smith has summed up the auteur theory as it is normally presented today:

> One essential corollary of the theory as it has been developed is the discovery that the defining characteristics of an author's work are not necessarily those which are most readily apparent. The purpose of criticism thus becomes to uncover behind the superficial contrasts of subject and treatment a hard core of basic and often recondite motifs. The pattern formed by these motifs … is what gives an author's work its particular structure, both defining it internally and distinguishing one body of work from another.

It is this 'structural approach', as Nowell-Smith calls it, which is indispensable for the critic.

The test case for the auteur theory is provided by the work of Howard Hawks. Why Hawks, rather than, say, Frank Borzage or King Vidor? Firstly, Hawks is a director who has worked for years within the Hollywood system. His first film, *Road to Glory*, was made in 1926. Yet throughout his long career he has only once received general critical acclaim, for his wartime film, *Sergeant York*, which closer inspection reveals to be eccentric and atypical of the main *corpus* of Hawks's films. Secondly, Hawks has worked in almost every genre. He has made Westerns (*Rio Bravo*), gangsters (*Scarface*), war films (*Air Force*), thrillers (*The Big Sleep*), science fiction (*The Thing from Another World*), musicals (*Gentlemen Prefer Blondes*), comedies (*Bringing up Baby*), even a Biblical epic (*Land of the Pharaohs*). Yet all these films (except perhaps *Land of the Pharaohs*, which he himself was not happy about) exhibit the same thematic preoccupations, the same recurring motifs and incidents, the same visual style and tempo. In the same way that Roland Barthes constructed a species

CONTINUED

of *homo racinianus*, the critic can construct a *homo hawksianus*, the protagonist of Hawksian values in the problematic Hawksian world.

(Wollen 1997: 51–53)

Wollen is very clear about the purpose and responsibilities of film criticism: 'to uncover … a hard core of basic and often recondite motifs' ('recondite' here suggests well hidden and difficult to extract). His exposition on Hawkes and Ford demonstrates his hypothesis with great style and skill. Here critical reading is the key to revealing the deep structure which is essentially for Wollen what 'auteur' is: a 'meaning structure' operating across the body of a film (in the same way that narrative, genre, even star, operate). A couple of paragraphs on John Ford will demonstrate the flavour of Wollen's approach. Like all good/great critical writing it requires no particular prior knowledge to appreciate it and makes the reader immediately wish to see the cited films for themselves.

It is instructive, for example, to consider three films of John Ford and compare their heroes: Wyatt Earp in *My Darling Clementine*, Ethan Edwards in *The Searchers* and Tom Doniphon in *The Man Who Shot Liberty Valance*. They all act within the recognisable Ford world, governed by a set of oppositions, but their *loci* within that world are very different. The relevant pairs of opposites overlap; different pairs are foregrounded in different movies. The most relevant are garden versus wilderness, ploughshare versus sabre, settler versus nomad, European versus Indian, civilised versus savage, book versus gun, married versus unmarried, East versus West. These antinomies can often be broken down further. The East, for instance, can be defined either as Boston or Washington and, in *The Last Hurrah*, Boston itself is broken down into the antipodes of Irish immigrants versus Plymouth Club, themselves bundles of such differential elements as Celtic versus Anglo-Saxon, poor versus rich, Catholic versus Protestant, Democrat versus Republican, and so on. At first sight, it might seem that the oppositions listed above overlap to the extent that they become practically synonymous, but this is by no means the case. As we shall see, part of the development of Ford's career has been the shift from an identity between civilised versus savage and European versus Indian to their separation and final reversal, so that in *Cheyenne Autumn* it is the Europeans who are savage, the victims who are heroes.

The master antinomy in Ford's films is that between the wilderness and the garden. As Henry Nash Smith has demonstrated, in his magisterial book *Virgin Land*, the contrast between the image of America as a desert and as a garden is one which has dominated American thought and literature, recurring in countless novels, tracts, political speeches and magazine stories.

In Ford's films it is crystallised in a number of striking images. *The Man Who Shot Liberty Valance*, for instance, contains the image of the cactus rose, which encapsulates the antinomy between desert and garden which pervades the whole film. Compare with this the famous scene in *My Darling Clementine*, after Wyatt Earp has gone to the barber (who civilises the unkempt), where the scent of honeysuckle is twice remarked upon: an artificial perfume, cultural rather than natural. This moment marks the turning-point in Wyatt Earp's transition from wandering cowboy, nomadic, savage, bent on personal revenge, unmarried, to married man, settled, civilised, the sheriff who administers the law.

(Wollen 1997: 66)

Wollen offers an extreme version of the auteur theory which is at once abstract and intellectual. The auteur as film artist is embodied/enacted in and by the film texts themselves, in the synthesis of the general and the particular (the work as a whole and the individual films). In this way the power is with the critic, since it is only the critic who is able to confer the title 'auteur' by being able to decrypt the 'recondite motifs', and therefore to have even more need of sharp critical support.

Perhaps it would be true to say that it is the lesser auteurs who can be defined, as Nowell-Smith put it, by a core of basic motifs which remain constant, without variation. The great directors must be defined in terms of shifting relations, in their singularity as well as their uniformity. Renoir once remarked that a director spends his whole life making one film; this film, which it is the task of the critic to construct, consists not only of the typical features of its variants, which are merely its redundancies, but of the principle of variation which governs it, that is its esoteric structure, which can only manifest itself or 'seep to the surface', in Lévi-Strauss's phrase, 'through the repetition process'. Thus Renoir's 'film' is in reality a 'kind of permutation group, the two variants placed at the far ends being in a symmetrical, though inverted, relationship to each other'. In practice, we will not find perfect symmetry, though as we have seen, in the case of Ford, some antinomies are completely reversed. Instead, there will be a kind of torsion within the permutation group, within the matrix, a kind of exploration of certain possibilities, in which some antinomies are foregrounded, discarded or even inverted, whereas others remain stable and constant. The important thing to stress, however, is that it is only the analysis of the whole *corpus* which permits the moment of synthesis when the critic returns to the individual film.

Of course, the director does not have full control over his work; this explains why the auteur theory involves a kind of decipherment, decryptment. A great many feature of the films analysed have to be dismissed as indecipherable because of 'noise' from the producer, the cameraman or even the actors. This concept of 'noise' needs further elaboration. It is often said that film is the result of a multiplicity of factors, the sum total of a number of different contributions. The contribution of the director – the 'directorial factor', as it were – is only one of these, though perhaps the one which carries the most weight. I do not need to emphasise that this view is quite the contrary of the auteur theory and has nothing in common with it at all. What the auteur theory does is to take a group of films – the work of one director – and analyse their structure. Everything irrelevant to this, everything non-pertinent, is considered logically secondary, contingent, to be discarded. Of course, it is possible to approach films by studying some other feature; by an effort of critical ascesis we could see films, as Sternberg sometimes urged, as abstract light-show or as histrionic feasts. Sometimes these separate texts – those of the cameraman or the actors – may force themselves into prominence so that the film becomes an indecipherable palimpsest. This does not mean, of course, that it ceases to exist or to sway us or please us or intrigue us; it simply means that it is inaccessible to criticism. We can merely record our momentary and subjective impressions.

(Wollen 1997: 66)

Wollen addresses the thorny issue of collaboration by simply dismissing the contributions of significant others as 'indecipherable' noise, interference. Wollen is unequivocal: those approaches which see film as 'the result of a multiplicity of factors, the sum total of a number of contributions' are offering a view 'quite the contrary of the auteur theory'. All producers, cameramen, even actors can contribute is to make the film text 'inaccessible to criticism'. He uses the term 'indecipherable palimpsest' to describe these films: a palimpsest is a reused manuscript, where one document is overwritten by another until nothing is legible.

A more balanced view is provided by Bruce Kawin in *How Movies Work*. Kawin addresses 'the Auteur Theory' in the context of a general examination of film authorship and as part of an attempt to answer the problematic 'Who makes a film?' in a section headed 'The Film Artist and the Movie Business'. Immediately before the extract quoted below, Kawin has used director John Huston's film *The Maltese Falcon* as an authorship case study. In doing so he introduces an interesting analogy. He has just informed us that 'John Huston wrote the screenplay and directed the movie so the final product became his as much as Hammett's (the writer of the original novel)' but feels the anomaly is that 'Huston did not "play an instrument".' His answer to his own question adds much to our discussion about authorship:

The resolution to this quandary is to realize that the instrument that a conductor plays is, in fact, the orchestra. The orchestra members depend on the conductor to keep time and let them know when and what emphasis to play. The conductor organizes the performance and it is therefore up to her or him how the composition will be realized.

What Kawin is implicitly acknowledging is 'the distinction between composition and performance', which Peter Wollen claims 'is vital to aesthetics'. Wollen presents the distinction clearly, though without teasing out a film's particular problematic. For Wollen, 'the score, or text, is constant and durable; the performance is occasional and transient'. While this may be useful when discussing the two film versions of Robert Bloch's novel *Psycho*, it is a distinction which applies more readily to a theatrical or musical text and performance. The extra problem with film is that, by this description, there are two obvious texts which can be acknowledged as 'constant and durable' (not withstanding the instability of nitrate film stock). A film like *Apocalypse Now Redux* can be legitimately called a 'performance' of a text conceived by John Milius and Francis Ford Coppola and performed in an earlier version as *Apocalypse Now,* but it is hardly 'occasional' or 'transient'. Moreover it has arguably become just as 'durable' as the literary text that inspired it: Joseph Conrad's existential novella *Heart of Darkness*. 'Performance' then as an idea in Film Studies is much more usefully applied to the infinite number of individual decisions and actions that constitute the recorded text. This is the stuff that Kawin is into in his second paragraph when he creates for us 'the moment when Queen Christina removes her crown':

THE AUTEUR THEORY

Sole authorship is a matter of conceiving, designing, executing, and owning a work. Hammett planned *The Maltese Falcon*, wrote it, and had the sole right to sell it to a publisher. In the majority of films, design, realization, and ownership are necessarily split among many people and companies, and 'authorship' becomes problematic.

Recall the moment when Queen Christina removes her crown. The physical movement was executed by Greta Garbo. The position of the camera, with its background view of a crown that cannot be removed, was chosen by the director, Rouben Mamoulian, and by the cinematographer, William Daniels. The action was designed in the first place by a team of screenwriters, based loosely on a historical event. The editor juxtaposed that shot with others that would enhance its impact. And the director, of course, coached Garbo on how to act the scene. But could Mamoulian have *told* Garbo every nuance of that gesture? Who took off that crown? Who should get credit for the brilliant, slow tenderness of Garbo's motions and the exquisite complexity of her face, in that light, at that moment? Who is the author of the total effect, of this scene, of this movie?

In this example there is no sole author. But there may have been a conductor – an artist with ultimate responsibility for approving the work of others – and it may well have been Mamoulian. The director is usually involved – or at least has a say – in all the major creative decisions from development through post-production, notably script approval, casting, production and costume design, the details of performance, and editing. That puts him or her in a position

CONTINUED

to unify the project and coach the team. But in the absence of reliable information about who did what while a picture was being made, there is little or no justification for assuming that the director has, in fact, performed this unifying function, let alone originated the themes, tropes, and gestures that have proved most distinctive and valuable in the finished work. It is difficult to make sense of the while body of cinema, or even of any individual movie, until some critical method, informed by a careful understanding of real filmmaking practices, make it possible to give credit where credit is due. Critical interpretations, especially of creative intentions and decisions, can be more reliable and sophisticated when one knows who the author is; otherwise, intentions are ascribed to a generalized vacuum.

First proposed by François Truffaut in the 1950s and further developed by Andrew Sarris in the 1960s, the **auteur theory** set out to provide just such a critical tool. It begins by acknowledging (or perhaps simply gives lip service to the idea) that film is a collaborative art, then goes on to argue that when a film reveals a thematic and stylistic coherence, that coherence can usually be attributed to the guiding vision of a single artist who was expressing his or her personal convictions and tastes. In order to have such power, the artist must almost invariably have been the director, though it is even better if the director has also written the screenplay. To distinguish this artist from a sole author, he or she is referred to as an 'auteur' (French for 'author,' but used in English to connote this more ambiguous position of control).

The problem with the auteur theory is that it *may* allow the critic to ignore creative collaboration and leap straight to the director. The special merit of the auteur theory is that it is *capable* of acknowledging the collaborative structure of the cinematic enterprise *and* the evidence of patterns of coherence that have the integrity of authorship. These may be stylistic patterns, characteristic approaches to recurring subject matter, or attitudes and strategies that have developed in the course of a career. Hitchcock's work, for example, is characterized by recurring content – notably the problematic relations between guilt and innocence – and a visual style that no one has been able to imitate with authority. This observation does not imply that an artist always says the same thing in the same way; rather, it allows for development and maturation within a structure whose consistency is that of the artist.

In the role of director, then, which touches nearly every aspect of the filmmaking process and may let an artist dominate a work without actually taking center stage, the auteurists found a site for these patterns of coherence. It is quite plain to them that Renoir films are Renoir films, that von Sternberg films could not have been made by Lumet, and that Welles was the auteur of *Citizen Kane*. This makes it simple to talk about a movie as a direct expression of one person's creative intentions. But auteurism has often been applied carelessly. It is by no means true that every film has an auteur. There are auteurs who are not directors, and directors who are not auteurs. Many auteurists have not taken the trouble to check these matters out, nor have they even begun to applaud the concertmaster.

Auteurism has had critical implications that are far-reaching and sometimes off-target. It appears, for one thing, to have been the only academic debate ever to affect the film industry. In its later critical manifestations it has become a cult of personal style, so that a director is considered interesting – or an author at all – only when he or she has exhibited a consistent style and a matrix of recurring interests. Directors in whose work such patterns cannot be discerned have often been dismissed by critics as 'hacks.' The industry itself has become 'director-conscious,' while many non-directors have become anti-auteurists. Under the influence of auteurism, many fledgling film artists have gathered that directing is the only important job and that they have to make *their* mark. But there is more to good directing than self-expression, and there are distinctly creative aspects to other film jobs. The public view now appears to be simply that films are made and signed by directors.

Critically, the conventional test of an auteur is that a pattern emerges when all of his or her pictures are viewed together or are considered in relation to each other. But the real value of auteurism – once it is extended beyond directors and as it may be critically applied to a single picture – is that it offers a reasonable explanation for a fact about cinema: that an often personal coherence *can* emerge from a collaborative project.

Even when a film does have an auteur – a Bergman or a Hitchcock, for example – the critical methodology is sometimes applied irresponsibly. Many auteurists want to find a single author and let it go at that. Although they may understand that actress Bibi Andersson and cinematographer Sven Nykvist are independent beings, they prefer to analyze every image and instant of *Persona* as if it proceeded directly from Ingmar Bergman's consciousness. Bergman himself has always been generous in acknowledging the contributions of the group he has worked with and would never endorse such a critical position.

(Kawin 1987: 292–294)

'Kawin finds a place for auteurism which does not disallow the notion of collaboration.' Other critics have been less accommodating (or forgiving). Faced with Andrew Sarris' 'Three Premises of the Auteur Theory' (1962) which became a blueprint for the wholesale adoption of auteur theory in America, Pauline Kael launched a systematic attack premise by premise. In the midst of her barely concealed contempt/disdain she concedes, 'I am angry, but am I unjust?'

SARRIS AND KAEL: PREMISE AND COUNTER-PREMISE

As Kawin points out above, Andrew Sarris does deserve credit for developing what he was first to dub 'the auteur theory' and popularising it in America. A summary of his premises and Kael's objections might read like this: Kael presents them somewhat sarcastically as 'circles' of enlightenment:

THE OUTER CIRCLE: *The first premise of the auteur theory is the technical competence of a director as a criterion of value*: Kael describes this as 'a shaky premise' for as she points out, 'sometimes the greatest artists in a medium bypass or violate the simple technical competence that is so necessary for hacks'.

THE MIDDLE CIRCLE: *The second premise of the auteur theory is the distinguishable personality of the director as a criterion of value*: Kael simply does not accept that the 'distinguishability' of personality can be important in judging the quality of work. The analogy she uses is a bitter one: 'the smell of a skunk is more distinguishable than the perfume of a rose; does that make it better?'

THE INNER CIRCLE: *The third and ultimate premise of the auteur theory is concerned with interior meaning, the ultimate glory of cinema as an art:* Here Kael is at her most scathing ('the bull's eye turns out to be an empty socket'). Kael is objecting to what Wollen referred earlier to as the 'operation of decipherment', which 'reveals authors where none had been seen before'. For Kael this is anathema ('the pits'): '"Interior meaning" seems to be what those in the know know. It's a mystique and a mistake.'
(Kael 1963)

Victor Perkins, in his influential book *Film as Film*, is much less polemical but his careful common sense does nevertheless punch massive holes in the auteur approach. In a chapter entitled 'Direction and Authorship' Perkins begins his gentle attack by suggesting that auteurism 'must be approached with at least some caution': he then addresses the theory obliquely by explicating the practice:

> In the factory-like conditions of film-making the notion of the director as a sole creator, uniquely responsible for a picture's qualities, defects, impact and meaning, must be approached with at least some caution. Because it is a collective enterprise, film-making involves many separate personalities, distinct and sometimes conflicting intentions, varying abilities and imperfect control. A movie cannot be fully and uniquely one man's creation.
>
> In *Limelight* Chaplin combined the functions of writer, director, leading actor and composer. We may assume, for argument's sake, that the editing, photography, set and costume design were carried out precisely according to Chaplin's

specifications. He would thus have had the greatest control which could be obtained by anyone setting out to tell a story on film. There is no question, in theory or in fact, that *Limelight* is dominated by Chaplin's personality. But it is not the work of Chaplin alone, nor are its qualities entirely derived from Chaplin's dominating presence. There are always the other actors. No complete assessment of *Limelight* could omit to consider the contributions of Claire Bloom and Buster Keaton, the distinct, if integrated, impact of their personalities and performances. However much and however well Chaplin has used them for his own purpose, these remain individual contributions which help to determine the ultimate effect. Simple distinctions between material and composition, conception and realization, group effort and personal control, become quite inapplicable. They ignore and obscure the complexity of a process in which there is no single material and no single treatment, but a series of materials organized in a series of treatments.

To the movie writer a story is material which must be shaped for screen presentation. The actor's material is a film-script with dialogue and action prescribed for a character. But the character can only be given life through the interaction of the writer's conception with the actor's other material: appearance, voice, gesture, intonation, emphasis. Already we have a complex situation in which a character is moulded by two mechanisms, each certainly controlling and probably modifying the other. However, the character as written and the actor employed become material again in the hands of a director. At this stage the image we see and the sounds we hear in the cinema will be established. The work of writers, actors and designers will again be modified in a treatment determined by the director and his photographer. The actor will be placed in a new relationship not only to the story but also to the décor, the camera and the other actors. Even if the director were to exercise no influence over the actor's work, the choice of lighting, composition, colour and camera position – angle, distance, movement – would certainly affect, and could transform, the impact of all the other contributions. The 'finished' performance, scripted, acted and recorded, is material once more when it reaches the cutting rooms. The editor, through his choice and arrangement of images and sounds, will create new, though not necessarily unforeseen patterns, rhythms and emphases. Thereafter the musical score is added and another series of modifications takes place.

The above account represents nothing more than a schematic, for-demonstration-only, plan of the film-making process. The various functions can be distributed or combined in a wide variety of ways. The plan serves its purpose if it makes it clear that so far from offering a simple material organized in a linear process, a film consists of many materials combined, interpreted and transformed through a chain of decisions, treatments and adjustments which continues from the moment the film is first conceived to the time when the spectator leaves the cinema. In this chain each decision limits the subsequent ones, but is also modified by them: for example, a given passage of dialogue limits the actor, but the effect of the dialogue will depend on the way it is delivered.

On film, as in any impure medium, we do not find one coherent material given stable form. Rather, we are offered a variety of materials, disparate in kind and function, brought into relationships which we can hope to find pleasant, beautiful, amusing, surprising, significant and so on. The film-maker's control is over these relationships rather than over the separate elements from which they are constructed. Hence our criteria depend more on an achieved balance than on an inherent purity.

A film may have its own unity, with its relationships coherent and its balance precise. But that the ultimate unity can be entirely foreseen is a dubious proposition: the distance between conception and delivery is so great, and the path between them so tortuous and unpredictable. In this connection there are few assertions so misleading, indeed so unlikely, as Lindgren's that 'when the script-writer gives himself up to thought, visualizing the white screen before him, he is in precisely the same position as Cézanne before his canvas'. A film (other, perhaps, than a cartoon which might be a one-man product) cannot be made in the mind and then transferred to celluloid precisely as conceived. One of the prime requirements for a film-maker is flexibility to improvise, and to adjust his conceptions to the ideas and abilities of his co-workers, to the pressures of circumstance, and the concrete nature of the objects photographed.

Yet the belief persists that a good film is necessarily a precise realization of one man's precisely imagined vision. Rotha maintains that 'theoretically, the only possible writer of the film manuscript is the director, who alone is capable of transferring to paper the preconception of the film he is about to make'.

But movies can seldom if ever be the unique expression of a creative spirit so dear to the heart and imagination of the orthodox theorist. The director may work in many ways – as creator, craftsman, interpreter, organizer, communicator, propagandist, technician. But whatever the function he performs and the privileges he enjoys, his status must under normal circumstances be that of an employee. The cost of movie production is so high that only a millionaire could afford to make pictures (other than home movies) simply for his own pleasure. Having done so, he would not long retain his wealth without persuading a huge number of people to share (and pay for sharing) his enjoyment. Even the distinction between 'popular' cinema and the 'minority' movie is dubious. The most popular film reaches only a minority of the public; the specialized picture requires a very large audience. Even a film society is a commercial venture which needs the steady support of a large audience in order to cover its costs. The difference between the popular and the specialized audiences

> is the difference between a huge minority and a large one. In order to remain active, the director must be the servant of a great mass of people. There is, however, the difference between service and servility.
>
> (Perkins 1993: 158–161

Interestingly, auteur theory often finds least support among the very people it is trying to 'validate' and celebrate: film-makers. British director Alan Parker, for example, has been a consistent, caustic and outspoken critic. The documentary film he made for British Film Year, *A Turnip Head's Guide to the Cinema* (1986), was described as 'a polemic against film critics, auteur theorists, and the British Film Institute'.

However, in spite of this professional concern (and sometimes contempt), auteur theory has very much survived. Like genre and star it has become a means of negotiating the practicalities of the film industry: of financing, making, distributing and marketing films. It seems these days that every other film has an 'auteurist' tag, announcing 'a film by X' where X may in fact be offering her first feature. Unfortunately in the process, a radical critical tool has been abandoned in favour of a general Romantic view: that films are an expression of the director's inner vision. This is where this chapter began with an influential, simple yet complex concept that can be represented in a number of conflicting ways. Put another way, Peter Wollen was probably right when he remarked that 'the auteur theory leaves us, as every theory does, with possibilities and questions'.

ACTIVITY

> ➤ Now look at the table on page 198 which lists the thirty most successful film directors. How many of these do you recognise as auteurs? You may need to do some research/wider reading (the IMDb is a useful tool at IMDb.com).

▼ 7 STAR

Garbo offered to one's gaze a sort of Platonic Idea of the human creature.

Roland Barthes

People who are both ordinary and extraordinary.

John Ellis

In the popular imagination stars are often synonymous with cinema. We associate stars not only with the films in which they appear but also with the glitz and glamour of the industry itself. This is of course most true of Hollywood, but it is also an important phenomenon in the film industries of countries throughout the world.

In the academic study of film, stars are also seen as important as a way of understanding the appeal of cinema to audiences.

ACTIVITY

> Before you read further into this chapter, try writing down some of the ways in which you think the study of stars can add to our understanding of cinema. An obvious starting point is their roles in films themselves, but you need to go beyond this to look at such issues as celebrity and fandom.

Star studies makes the assumption that the appeal of a star is something more than a function of their personality. Stars, although individual human beings, are constructed in such a way as to have ideological meanings. Central to this idea is the work of Richard Dyer whose book *Stars* (1979) signalled the idea that stars can be studied themselves as texts in the same way as can the films in which they appear.

Just as a film is constructed from a series of signs that constitute its meaning, so stars themselves are signs which signify to us certain meanings. Many of these meanings are created outside the sphere of film-making, for example, in the private lives and promotional activities of stars. You might like to think of the way in which many male stars create for themselves images of promiscuity and debauchery through their supposed off-screen adventures and how these images become part of the 'reading' audiences make in relation to that star.

ACTIVITY

> Are the readings made available through the 'private' lives of stars gendered? If so, how?

FILM STUDIES: THE ESSENTIAL RESOURCE

Let us start by considering how the image of a star works. What functions does the star's image perform? Here is a short extract from John Ellis' book *Visible Fictions* (1992). In the essay 'Stars as a Cinematic Phenomenon' he considers the nature of star 'image':

There is always a temptation to think of a 'star image' as some kind of fixed repertory of fixed meanings (Joan Crawford = tough, independent, ruthless, threateningly sexy, etc.). However, this seems to simplify the process, and to misstate the role of the star in producing meanings in films and beyond films. Star images are paradoxical. They are composed of elements which do not cohere, of contradictory tendencies. They are composed of clues rather than complete meanings, of representations that are less complete, less stunning, than those offered by cinema. The star image is an *incoherent* image. It shows the star both as an ordinary person and as an extraordinary person. It is also an *incomplete* image. It offers only the face, only the voice, only the still photo, where cinema offers the synthesis of voice, body, and motion. The star image is paradoxical and incomplete so that it functions as an invitation to cinema, like the narrative image. It proposes cinema as the completion of its lacks, the synthesis of its separate fragments.

The relationship is not, however, only that of star-image = incomplete: film performance = completion. It is also one where the process of the star image echoes, repeats and develops a fundamental aspect of cinema itself. The star image rests on the paradox that the star is ordinary and extraordinary at the same time. The cinematic image (and the film performance) rests on the photo effect, the paradox that the photograph presents an absence that is present. In this sense, the star image is not completed by the film performance, because they both rest on the same paradox. Instead the star image promises cinema. It restates the terms of the photo effect, renews the desire to experience this very particular sense of present-absence. So the star image is incomplete and paradoxical. It has a double relationship to the film performance: it proposes that the film performance will be more complete than the star image; and it echoes and promotes the photo effect which is fundamental to cinema as a regime of representation.

(Ellis 1992: 615–616)

In his essay 'Star Studies', Paul McDonald identifies four main approaches to star studies. These are: semiotics, intertextuality, psychoanalysis and audience studies. The first two approaches consider the star as text while the latter two focus on ways in which audiences relate to stars. In this extract from his essay, McDonald begins by considering the significance of Dyer's book *Stars* and the idea of studying stars as texts:

STARS IN CONTEXT

The study of stars as texts should not, and indeed cannot, be limited to the analysis of specific films or star performances. Star images are the product of intertextuality in which the non-filmic texts of promotion, publicity and criticism interact with the film text. Although the star's name and body anchor the image to one person, the process of intertextual associations is so complex that the meaning of a star's image is never limited, stable or total. The star's image is not one thing, but many things. As a result, this intertextuality is not simply an extension of the star's meaning, but is the only meaning that the star ever has. In other words, the star's image cannot exist or be known outside this shifting series of texts.

Dyer's later work on stars, *Heavenly Bodies*, examines this intertextuality and extends it beyond those texts which directly refer to the star. Instead, he studies the star's meaning within the context of a broader network of other texts which were in circulation during the same period. These other texts are used to construct the historical context in which a star's image became intelligible. For example, in extended studies of Marilyn Monroe and Paul Robeson, Dyer seeks to historicize the meaning of each star's image by examining them in relation to the complex of intertextual discourses on the respective issues of sexuality and ethnicity.

The aim of each study is to analyse how each star's image sought to produce a sense of individual identity within the context of modern capitalist society:

> Stars articulate what it is to be a human being in contemporary society; that is, they express the particular notion we hold of the person, of the 'individual' ... they articulate both the promise and the difficulty that the notion of individuality presents for all of us who live by it.

One of the ways in which star images achieve this is by continually juxtaposing the public image of on-screen appearances (the performer) with the publicized private image of the star's off-screen life (the 'real person'). Either the two seamlessly correspond to one another, or antagonistically conflict. In Western societies, the separation of public and private spheres which developed with the rise of capitalism, has resulted in a massive preoccupation with identifying the truth of ourselves, a truth which is supposedly hidden behind appearances. In this history it is possible to understand that stars fascinate because their performances make the private self into a public spectacle, as they seem to reveal the truths of their selves within a public forum.

This notion of a 'true' self which is hidden or repressed by social life has been criticized by the French philosopher Michel Foucault. In his work on the history of sexuality, Foucault suggests that we commonly think of sexuality as something which we possess, but which is repressed or distorted by society.

He refers particularly to psychoanalysis as an example of this way of thinking. This position, which he refers to as 'the repressive hypothesis', he sees as misunderstanding the workings of power within society. For Foucault, the interesting thing about the periods which were supposed to be particularly repressive of sexuality was that they witnessed a massive proliferation of texts which took sexuality as their central concern. This mass of texts, he suggests, rather than simply acting to repress sexuality, combined to form a discourse of sexuality which produced the very object which it sought to study. Prior to this period, there was no real concept of sexuality. People may have engaged in sexual acts, but there was no sense that they had a particular sexual identity, a sexuality. As a result, Foucault argues that power does not work in relation to sexuality through its repression, but through active and creative processes in which the concept of sexuality is produced and acts to regulate and define specific constructions of subjectivity. In this way, sexuality and subjectivity are intimately bound together in relations of power which produce them both simultaneously. In the contemporary world, a sense of self is intimately connected to a sense of one's own, private sexuality, a thing which is seen as natural rather than social; innate rather than constructed.

In his study of Marilyn Monroe, Dyer examines the ways in which Monroe's star image served to redefine female sexuality in 1950s America. Dyer reads across a series of texts from the period in order to establish the discourse of sexuality and femininity which was circulating in the period. With references to *Playboy* and *Reader's Digest*, among other texts, a context was reconstructed in which women were encouraged to attain the quality of 'desirability', a quality which it was suggested would make both men and women happy. In this context, Monroe's public and private image 'conforms to, and is part of the construction of, what constitutes desirability in women'. Monroe's blondeness and vulnerability offered a construction of female sexuality which is unthreatening and willing.

At the same time, in a context where the popularization of psychoanalysis in America had made sex a hot public issue, and in which the Kinsey report on women had addressed the question of whether American women had satisfying sex lives, Monroe's image coincided with a discourse on the psychosexual constitution of the female orgasm. To summarize Dyer's argument, the vaginal orgasm was discussed at the time as the peak of female sexual satisfaction. In this context, Monroe presented a quivering, wriggling, submissive sexuality which appeared as the visual analogue of the vaginal orgasm. She represented what was mysterious and enigmatic and made it seem visible and concrete. As Dyer points out, while women in the 1950s were encouraged to be sexually desirable, there were also more general fears concerning the emergence of a female sexuality which might exist independently from male sexuality. In this context, the vaginal orgasm was prized over the clitoral orgasm because the former defined female sexuality in terms of male sexuality in so far as it made women's pleasure dependent on penetration. This indicates the difficulty with Monroe figuring as a positive image of female sexual freedom.

The intertextual reconstruction of history faces the problem recognized by Fredric Jameson, that 'history is *not* a text' but 'is inaccessible to us except in textual form, or in other words, … it can be approached only by way of prior (re)textualization'. Texts return history in a tangible form, yet there is a need to recognize that the history which is so constructed can never be exhaustive or final. The intertextual construction of history omits the non-textual ephemera of everyday practices, which can only be imagined with reference to the textual record. Second, in constructing a context out of texts, historical analysis is faced with a basic problem. How do we tell which texts are significant and which are not, and how many texts do we need to reconstruct a context convincingly? History does not become unknowable, but it only becomes knowable in certain ways.

However, the intertextual approach is valuable in that it enables us to reconstruct the meanings which specific stars acquire at specific historical moments. Even an analysis of the present requires a work of reconstruction. Yet there is a need always to see such reconstructions as partial and provisional. In reconstructing these readings and readers, it must always be remembered that these are *hypothetical* readings and readers. The networking of texts is an endless task, and the results can only provide the possible conditions within which a star's image may have been intelligible. There may have been other ways in which a star was read. None the less, such tentative conclusions may be the best we can hope for.

OBJECTS OF DESIRE

Both the semiotic and intertextual approaches to star images clearly imply a spectator or audience for whom these images become meaningful. However, these approaches concentrate on the meanings of texts, rather than the effect of such meanings upon the subjectivity of the audience. As a result, Dyer's work on stars has been criticized for neglecting the ways in which human subjectivity is constructed through meaning and language, and the ways in which stars figure in this process.

Like Dyer, John Ellis regards stars as intertextual constructions, but he also distinguishes between the primacy of the film performance and the subsidiary texts of journalism and gossip. For the spectator, the star image emerges from the fragments of subsidiary texts, but it does so as a 'incomplete image' which is only completed in the film performance. As a result, Ellis argues that audiences are motivated to go to see stars by the desire to complete the puzzle of the star's image.

In his work, Ellis is drawing on psychoanalytic theories of subjectivity in order to explain why spectators are fascinated by stars and wish to identify with them. Psychoanalytic film criticism relates the cinema to a theory of desire. Christian Metz, for example, argues that the cinema was an institution for the commodification of desire. The industrial economy of film production, it is argued, is reproduced by the psychic economy of the spectator's pleasure. In other words, films make their money so long as they provide pleasure, and in this process, stars play a crucial role in attracting audiences to regular cinema-going.

For Ellis, the spectator's desire to see the star image completed in performance is the result of a problem within subjectivity – its necessary incompleteness. For psychoanalytic film theory, the formation of the subject creates division and lack, and this motivates its desire. Desire is seen as the pursuit of that which will fill the lack, and so make the subject whole and complete. For Lacan, from whom much of this theory is derived, the formation of desire is also centrally bound up with the act of looking, and gives rise to what Metz calls the 'perceptual passions' of narcissism, voyeurism and fetishism. As a result, psychoanalytic criticism regards the act of viewing film as fundamentally bound up with issues of desire which are related to the figure of the star.

The film text is organized around three types of looks: the spectator who looks at the screen; the camera which 'looks' at the action; and the characters within the film who look at one another. These looks create the conditions within which the spectator relates to stars, particularly through a process of identification. According to Lacan, infants go through the 'mirror stage' between the ages of six and eighteen months. During this stage of their development, they anticipate a sense of autonomy by identifying with an image of self-independence which is perceived as though through a mirror. In contrast to the powerlessness of the child's actual body, which Lacan refers to as the 'body-in-pieces', this 'mirror-image' appears complete and masterful. It is an object of narcissistic identification which presents an ego-ideal (or ideal self) which is believed to be the self. Cinema, it is argued, echoes this moment of the child's development, but substitutes the screen for the mirror. It replays the narcissistic process of identification. The audience identifies with stars who appear to them as complete in their idealized construction; stars become ideal selves for the audience.

The spectator also derives a sadistic pleasure in relation to stars. The star is presented as an object for the spectator who views him or her voyeuristically. The star has an exhibitionist aspect, and the spectator's sadistic sense of pleasure is derived from a position of control over the star who is presented as a spectacle which is presented for the spectator's pleasure. This voyeurism also takes on an 'illicit' quality. Unlike the theatre, where the spectator and performer are in the same room, cinema separates the spectator and the star in both time and space. The star is absent, though the cinematic image gives an impression of presence. As a result, the star's image exists for the spectator's pleasure and cannot respond to the spectator who surveys it. As Ellis puts it, the 'film photograph constructs the possibility of a voyeuristic effect of catching the star unawares', as if one is spying on someone who is unaware of being watched. For this reason, it also acquires the qualities of a 'revelation' because the star's performance appears to provide the spectator with a glimpse of what the star is really like and so gives the appearance of completeness.

Fetishism also figures in the spectator's relationship to the star. For psychoanalysis, fetishism originates in the child's Oedipal anxieties when it perceives the sign of sexual difference as the mother's symbolic castration. This situation is supposed to result in a 'splitting of belief'; the child unconsciously knows that the mother lacks the phallus, but fetishizes other objects so that they will compensate for that lack. These objects acquire 'magical' qualities for the child who is then able to disavow the mother's castrated state.

The cinematic image and the image of the star are also seen to work through a similar process of fetishistic disavowal. In both cases, the spectator chooses to believe that what is absent is in fact present. The spectators may know that they are simply watching a series of light patterns upon a screen, but they choose to believe that they are actually watching real people in real locations. They may know that the star is just another person, but they choose to believe that he or she is somehow magical and special.

These concepts have particular relevance in feminist film theory. Laura Mulvey argues that in cinema pleasure is also related to issues of sexual difference and sexual politics. The spectator's look, and that of the camera, are both mediated by the ways in which male characters look at female characters. It is the male star who acts as the spectator's ideal self. He is a point of identification rather than an object of desire. The female star, on the other hand, is defined as the object of his gaze. She is defined as a passive sexual spectacle. The subject of the look is defined as male, and woman is defined as the object of that look. In this way, cinema centres pleasure in male heterosexual desire, and defines the female as the passive object of male desire.

However, the viewer is held in a state of tension between fetishism and voyeurism. While looking at the woman's body involves a pleasure of voyeuristic control, the sight of that body always threatens to reawaken castration anxieties. As a result, popular cinema is said to fetishize the female body in order to avoid the threat of castration anxiety. Parts of the female body are invested with 'magical' qualities which disavow castration. The most often used examples of this process are Marilyn Monroe's breasts, Rita Hayworth's shoulders and Betty Grable's legs, although one might also include Julia Roberts's hair. All of these bodily parts are invested with power and significance. They become full of meaning as they operate to deny or disavow that which is absent. Heath uses the term 'intensities' to suggest the significance of these fetishised bits of bodies:

> The body in films is … moments, intensities, outside a simple constant unity of the body as a whole, the property of a some *one*; films are full of fragments, bits of bodies, gestures, desirable traces, fetish points – if we take fetishism here as investment in a bit, a fragment, of its own sake, as the end of the accomplishment of a desire.

This is also true of the gestures and movements which are part of a performer's performance.

However, while Ellis sees the star's performance as completing the star image, this completion is never as total as it at first appears. The apparent completion only provides more fragments and thereby reproduces the spectator's desire to return to the cinema in the expectation of finally, once and for all, completing the star image.

Many critics have criticized Mulvey's tendency to neglect the pleasures of female spectatorship. As should be clear, she suggests that spectators are addressed as though they were male, and that, as a consequence, women are only in a position either to assume an identification with the male protagonist or else identify with the position of passive sexual object.

As a result, some psychoanalytic film critics have turned to Joan Rivière's theory of 'womanliness as masquerade' as a way out of the problem. For example, Mary Ann Doane proposes that women can find pleasure in popular cinema through their recognition of, and identification with, the artificiality of femininity. Gender power, like all ideological constructions, is supposed to claim legitimacy by presenting gendered differences as though they were natural and unchanging, rather than socially constructed and historically specific. However, the masquerade reveals femininity as a performance; as something which is socially constructed rather than natural and inherent. In contrast to the taken-for-granted naturalness of the fetishized female image, Doane suggests that the masquerade, 'in flaunting femininity, holds it at a distance … resistance to patriarchal positioning would therefore lie in its denial of the production of femininity as closeness, as presence-to-itself, as, precisely, imagistic'. In a similar way, as Barbara Creed suggests, the hypermasculine bodies of Schwarzenegger and Stallone flaunt a performative masculinity and so reveal masculinity to be a sign, not an innate property of being male. Rather than being a celebration of male power, the masculine masquerade implied 'the ultimate threat … that under the mask there is *nothing*'.

This application of the masquerade to cinema brings together star performances and gender performances, and implies that both are social constructions. It also indicates another problem with Mulvey's hypothesis on male spectatorship. First, it illustrates that popular cinema continually defines men, and not just women, as the object of the look. If the body of the male action hero does progress the narrative and provide a point of identification, it is also clearly presented as a body to be looked at. As Paul Willeman and Steve Neale have suggested, looks between male characters are often sadistically motivated in order to displace the homoerotic implications of such looks. Even so, popular films still include moments where there is a direct, and for that reason eroticized, contemplation of the male body. The fetishistic fragmentation of Schwarzenegger's body in the title sequence of *Commando* (US, 1985) is not justified by any sense of narrative agency and stands as a moment of pure contemplation. Likewise, the display of male torsos in the volleyball sequence of *Top Gun* (US, 1986) is prolonged without narrative purpose. It exists to display the male body. The forms and pleasures of bodily display are in fact far more various that Mulvey's account even begins to suggest.

Second, as Ian Green has suggested, cinema offers the possibility of cross-gender identification for male spectators as can be seen in the many films which feature female protagonists, unsympathetic male characters or de-eroticized female characters. Spectatorship is far more complex than the easy association of male or female spectators with 'masculine' or 'feminine' positions. In the terminator films, for example, is the terminator (Arnold Schwarzenegger) really the only object of male identification? Is there really no identification with the character of Sarah Conner (Linda Hamilton)?

As a result, recent psychoanalytic film theory has seen a move away from the assumption that the spectator only identifies with a single narrative figure, and towards the claim that he or she engages in a more complex identification with the overall narrative. It has developed a theory of fantasy which suggests that any narrative provides the spectator with multiple and shifting points of identification. In this theory of fantasy, star identifications can either be of less significance than in previous forms of psychoanalysis – because the individual star is no longer seen as the defining point of the spectator's pleasure – or of more significance – because identifications are established with more than one star. Desire, then, is played through the progression of the narrative, with the spectator seemingly within the scene, occupying many and various associations with the stars.

(MacDonald 1995: 83–90)

It is easy to forget that stars, especially Hollywood stars, are also actors as well as celebrities and icons. Film-acting is in itself a specific skill often quite far removed from stage performance. The ability of the camera to get in much closer to the actor than any theatre audience can calls for a very different set of skills in portraying character, for example. Patrick Phillips makes much of the difference between **impersonation** and **personification** as approaches to film-acting. 'Impersonation,' he argues, 'involves an actor creating a role from the range of skills and imagination she possesses.' Ultimately this involves 'disappearing into the role'. By contrast, 'personification' is often the default for Hollywood star-acting. Personification, according to Phillips, 'involves the actor stepping into a role by virtue of her physical appearance'. Tellingly, the actor as personifier is 'evaluated in terms of what s/he is – rather than what s/he can do'.

If you make a list of the stars who you consider also to be great movie actors, you may well start with such names as Brando, Streep and Hoffman. An important aspect of the approach of these actors is their use of 'the method'. Method-acting is an approach to film-acting in which the actor seemingly becomes the person he or she is performing. Put another way, actors come to 'live the part' they are playing in order to give a convincing performance. An example of this approach is Robert de Niro's role as boxer Jake La Motta in *Raging Bull* (Scorsese 1980), in which he deliberately gained 50 pounds in weight to portray La Motta's decline from lithe boxer to corpulent stand-up comedian. A famous story tells of Dustin Hoffman working on the film *Marathon Man* with the great English stage actor (Lord) Lawrence Olivier. Hoffman was due to play a scene in which his character had been deprived of sleep for 48 hours. When he arrived to shoot the scene it was clear that he too had spent the previous couple of days without sleep (in the Method style), much to the disbelief of Olivier who was heard to remark, 'Dear boy, why don't you just act it?'

In the extract that follows, Richard Dyer explains the significance of the method-acting approach:

THE 'METHOD'

'Method acting' was the name given to the approach to performance taught by the Actors' Studio in New York, which was founded in 1947. It was an adaptation of the teaching of Konstantin Stanislavsky, and involved the performer feeling her/his way into a role from the inside, temporarily identifying with a character or, in a widespread distortion of the approach, actually becoming the character while playing him/her.

Like melodrama, Method acting privileges emotional meaning over all other aspects of character (such as social behaviour and 'intellectual physiognomy'), but where melodrama returns emotions to moral categories, the Method roots them in broadly understood psychoanalytic categories. The Method constructs a character in terms of her/his unconscious and/or inescapable psychological make-up. Although in principle the Method could be used to express any psychological state, in practice it was used especially to express disturbance, repression, anguish etc., partly in line with a belief that such feelings, vaguely conceptualisable as the Id and its repression, are more 'authentic' than stability and open expression. (I suspect that analysis would also show a sexist bias whereby disturbance and anguish were reserved for men and repression for women – men as the Id, women as its repression ...) In this perspective, character itself becomes more important than plot or structure, and as a result much of the performance is 'redundant' in these terms. Scott's description of Brando in A *Streetcar Named Desire* indicates these elements: the reduction of performance to a given 'basic' psychology, the accumulation of redundant performance signs, the emphasis on raw and violent emotion which is further validated as 'authentic' in this case by its opposition to the falsity of Blanche (both as played by the British repertory actor Vivien Leigh and as the dénouement 'proves' her to be):

> In *Streetcar* Brando evidently built the part around his sense of Stanley Kowalski's animal aggressiveness. Sometimes this is innocently canine, as when his incessant scratching of back and belly remind us of a dog going after fleas. But the Kowalski character is also destructive, as we are told in Brando's use of the mouth: he chews fruit with loud crunching noises, munches up potato chips with the same relentless jaw muscles, washes beer around in his mouth and then swallows it with physically noticeable gulps. These two Brando-generated metaphors come together in the scene where Kowalski rummages through Blanche's trunk, his clawlike hands burrowing furiously and throwing velveteen dresses and fake fox fur back over his shoulders with fierce determination. These apparently insubstantial bits of stage business prepare us for the climatic scene in which Kowalski, having worked havoc upon Blanche's wardrobe, at last destroys the woman herself, devouring her futile illusions of Southern gentility. (*Film – the Medium and the Maker*, p. 249)

Scott maintains that the Method is equally adaptable to performers (such as, he suggests, Brando) who are essentially the same in every film (for, despite 'fabricating an astonishing array of ethnic accents' he is always 'the surly proletarian who suspects every smell of middle-class decorum' (ibid.)), and to performers (Rod Steiger is Scott's example) who 'put aside [their] own personality to think [their] way into an alien psyche' (p. 251). In either case, the fact that many people did and do believe that the Method performer 'got inside the character' or 'became' him/her gave such performances a mark of authenticity that made other styles seem correspondingly artificial or stilted.

As has already been mentioned, a star will have a particular performance style that through its familiarity will inform the performance s/he gives in any particular film. The specific repertoire of gestures, intonations, etc. that a star establishes over a number of films carries the meaning of her or his image just as much as the 'inert' element of appearance, the particular sound of her/his voice or dress style. An example is provided by G. Hill who quotes ('John Wayne', p. 7) from a reviewer of *The War Wagon*: 'It is worth seeing to watch John Wayne wrap his horse's reins round a hitch post!' It is not only that it happens to be Wayne doing it or that the action is always redolent of meaning, but that the particular way Wayne habitually does it sums up a particular aspect of his image. (The relish with which men tell me of this example suggests that what it sums up above all is Wayne's easy and confident masculinity.)

Part of the business of studying stars is to establish what these recurrent features of performance are and what they signify in terms of the star's image. They will usually only sum up an aspect of that image. The example just given does not remind us of everything about Wayne – in particular its joyous appeal operates because he is in the saddle in the West, not in Vietnam, not with a woman.

(Dyer 1979: 141–143)

Yvonne Tasker has written extensively about issues relating to the male and female stars of films. In her seminal book, *Spectacular Bodies*, she focuses on action cinema as a somewhat neglected genre in terms of film criticism. Stars may be read as more perfect representations of ourselves. They have qualities that members of the audience aspire to possessing themselves. We the audience seek to be imbued with the same desirability as that of the stars themselves. In the extract that follows, Tasker considers the male body in action films, most specifically the bodies of male body-builders who have worked on and modified their bodies 'ultimately for display on the public stage'.

ACTIVITY

➤ Before you read this article, write down what you think might be the appeal of muscular action heroes as portrayed by the likes of Schwarzenegger, Stallone and Vin Deisel.

MUSCLE CULTURE: THE BODYBUILDER AS HERO AND STAR

The hero of the action narrative is often case as a figure who lacks a place within the community for which he fights, a paradox familiar from the Western genre. In the recent action cinema, problems of location and position are increasingly articulated through the body of the male hero. In this sense, the figure of the bodybuilder as star has a special significance, raising here a more general set of issues to do with activity and passivity and their relation to masculinity and femininity in film. These issues centre on the problematic aspects of the construction of the male body as spectacle, an issue that has generated much commentary and criticism. The male pin-up is certainly of a different order to the female pin-up, shot through with a different set of anxieties, difficulties and pleasures. Richard Dyer links these uncertainties to the problematic processes through which male power is maintained in western culture, processes that involve the disavowal of the very fact that the man is being looked at, and the use of an insistent imagery which stresses hardness, partly through muscularity, a quality traditionally associated with masculinity. Dyer's analysis draws attention to the way in which any display of the male body needs to be compensated for by the suggestion of action. Thus sports pin-ups and the portrayal of the feats of near-naked action heroes both offer the body as to-be-looked-at whilst refusing the 'femininity' implied by that quite passive position (Dyer 1982). This work provides a useful framework for analysis, and may tell us something about the choice of the *action* movie as one of the privileged spaces for the display of the male body.

An analysis of the figure of the male bodybuilder as a movie star, needs also to acknowledge that as the muscular hero is caught by the camera, he is both posed and in motion at the same time. The medium serves to emphasise the contradictions that Dyer finds in the male pin-up. The combination of passivity and activity in the figure of the bodybuilder as action star, is central to the articulation of gendered identity in the films in which they appear. It also represents one of the distinctive qualities of these films. This combination allows us to problematise any clear set of critical distinctions between passivity, femininity and women on the one hand and activity, masculinity and men on the other. The figure of the muscleman hero dramatises the instability of these categories and equations, combining qualities associated with masculinity and femininity, qualities which gender theory maintains in a polarised binary. Bodybuilding as a sport is defined by pleasurable display, but is also criticised as clumsy or ugly, as precisely lacking in the classical grace to which it aspires. It is sometimes seen as positively pathological. An article in the *Sunday Times* in 1988, speculating on a link between the 'Rambo cult and sex crimes', points to the cases of various murderers and rapists, seen by the writer as 'social misfits who spent hours in front of a mirror, flexing muscles or posing in combat gear'. Bodybuilding is here taken to signal a disturbing narcissism, a narcissism which is inappropriate to familiar definitions of manhood. In other words the bodybuilder, obsessed with his appearance as he is, is not a real man. This pathologising discourse is quite familiar, and in part sets the context for the uncertain tone of George Butler's film *Pumping Iron* (1977) in which the heterosexuality of the bodybuilders interviewed and portrayed is repeatedly reaffirmed. Heterosexuality here operates as a more general sign of 'normality', denying the supposed perversity of a man's interest in male flesh.

In some senses the bodybuilder is precisely unnatural, being as he is so clearly marked as *manufactured*. Bodybuilding offers the possibility of self-creation, in which the intimate space of the body is produced as a raw material to be worked on and worked over, ultimately for display on a public stage. Thus critics have seen stars like Stallone and Schwarzenegger as 'performing the masculine', drawing attention to masculinity and the male body by acting out an excessive caricature of cultural expectations. Barbara Creed, for example, speculates on these figures as 'simulacra of an exaggerated masculinity, the original completely lost to sight, a casualty of the failure of the paternal signifier and the current crisis in master narratives' (Creed 1987: 65). The 'current crisis in master narratives' is not seen by Creed as the inability to tell a good story, but in terms of the failing of the key terms around which stories are constructed, terms which include a coherent white male heterosexuality, along with the rationality and binary structures it is often taken to propose. For Creed it is the sheer physical excess of the muscular stars that indicates the performative status of the masculinity they enact. If bodybuilding draws attention to different ways of being a man, to definitions of manhood, it has also been characterised, along with any male concern with the body and appearance, as feminised and rather ridiculous. As I discuss in Chapter 7, women's involvement in the sport is conversely seen to *masculinise* them. For both men and women, the activity has been characterised as perverse in that bodybuilding, as a practice and in its results, transgresses supposedly 'normal' gendered behaviour.

The ridicule directed at bodybuilding stems in part from the ambiguous status of the musculature in question – what is it all for? As one critic commented, these 'baroque muscles' are, after all, 'largely, non-functional decoration' (Louvre and Walsh 1988: 96). They do not relate to the active function that the hero is called on to perform, indeed can be seen as positively disabling. Rather muscles serve as just one component of the excessive visual display that characterises the action cinema. Producer Mario Kassar is reported to have jokingly said of the search for a location for *Rambo* III (a search which eventually led to 'Afghanistan') that 'It's got to be hot so Stallone can show off his body'. If this comment functions partly at the level of a joke, it is also telling in other ways. Stallone has been insistently framed and marketed in

STAR

terms of the body. One of the publicity images for *Rambo* III self-consciously punned on the phrase 'Stallone's Back' heralding both his return as Rambo and the stylised visual image of his body. It is this emphasis on the body which distinguishes a muscular cinema from other action films, though other features may be held in common. Stallone functions quite clearly as an object of spectacle both as a movie star and within muscle culture. *Muscle and Fitness* magazine lovingly describes his workout with a feature in which he is set up as an example of the 'Great Body', getting the cover story and a pin-up centrefold. The text on the cover invites, or challenges, the reader to consider 'How Masculine Are You?', promising also to reveal the star's secrets – 'Stallone: How He Gets Muscular' (June 1989). Body culture, as manifest in magazines like this, represents a vast, and expanding, industry selling a variety of products to aspirant bodybuilders.

The industry surrounding bodybuilding plays on male insecurities in a form that could be seen as analogous to the ways in which women are addressed by beauty culture. Male readers are asked to judge themselves against the bodies portrayed in the pages of muscle magazines. The presentation of the male body as commodity represents, then, the creation of new market for a consumer culture. The commodification of the male body that is involved in this process, could be read as 'contained' within the framing narrative images of male activity, the activity of 'working out'. Alternatively, the two, contradictory, processes can be seen as working together in the images generated by body culture. This kind of commodification also intersects with, and draws upon, a long history of representation in which the terms of class and race are mapped over the male body, with sports, for example, traditionally providing an arena for working-class men and for black men to succeed when other routes are denied them. Within these terms, we might note that the kinds of male body – black and white working class – that have traditionally been displayed within western culture are those that are *already sexualised*, perceived through an accumulated history of sexual myths and stereotypes. The body is constituted through such myths, written through the terms of sex, class and race. Within the action cinema, these male bodies also tell powerful stories of subjection and resistance, so that muscles function both to give the action hero the power to resist, at the same time as they confirm him in a position that defines him almost exclusively through the body. As with the figure of the showgirl that Laura Mulvey refers to in classic Hollywood films, contemporary American action movies work hard, and often at the expense of narrative development, to contrive situations for the display of the hero's body. If the performance of a show functioned to produce the showgirl as spectacle, then the equivalent sites of the action movie are the gym, a space for rehearsal, and the arena for a fight, whether that be the boxing ring or a more expansive 'natural' setting. The other key site which has repeatedly been used to provide a narrative excuse for the hero's nakedness is not the bedroom but the prison.

The prison is also, crucially, a site of punishment, a place designed to separate off those elements perceived as socially undesirable or dangerous. All these sites involve a mapping of themes of punishment and triumphant resistance onto the male body.

In both academic and journalistic commentaries, the built body, both male and female, has often been the object of disgust and humour rather than admiration. There is, for example, a marked hostility towards the physical display involved in the films of muscular stars. A feature in the *Guardian* on *Rambo* suggests that 'Stallone's only preoccupation in the film is exposing his preposterous body', while his 'enormous breasts loom over the screen like Jane Russell in *The Outlaw*' and the 'acting is performed mostly by his biceps'. Here both the body, and the desire to display it, are seen as comical. This critic's reference to Stallone's 'enormous breasts' operates to define his masculinity as ridiculous, questioning the status of his maleness through the suggestion that when the male body is displayed it is revealed as womanly. Taking this further, Jeffrey Walsh cites a *Times* review which playfully describes the camera lingering over Stallone's muscles 'with an abandon not seen on the screen since Joseph von Sternberg made movies with Marlene Dietrich' (Louvre and Walsh 1988: 56). The Sternberg/Dietrich partnership, referred to here, has formed a central point of reference for a feminist film criticism concerned to explore the work of voyeurism and the sexualised performance constructed around the female star within Hollywood film. If, for some, the figure of the bodybuilder signals an assertion of male dominance, an eroticising of the powerful male body, for other critics it seems to signal an hysterical and unstable image of manhood. The muscular body of the action star seems to provide a powerful symbol of both desire and lack. The body is offered for display as both a static object of contemplation and, in the acting out of the hero's achievements, as both subjected and triumphant. In this sense there are no easy links to be made between the action hero, the muscleman and some unproblematic endorsement of a nationalistic macho. With critics caught between breasts and biceps, it is clear that both active and passive, both feminine and masculine terms, inform the imagery of the male body in the action cinema.

(Tasker 1993: 77–80)

Being a star is one thing but the ultimate recognition to be bestowed upon any Hollywood actor is to achieve the status of superstar. In case you thought that the nomenclature of 'superstar' was simply a superlative to describe stars who had made it big, then you will probably be surprised to read that stars in fact do need specific credentials to achieve this status. At least that is the argument put forward by Arthur de Vany in the next extract. For de Vany the precise definition of superstar status is 'those who made a movie that grossed $100 million or more'. Such a definition differentiates superstars from stars who have merely made movies grossing over $50 million.

Before you read de Vany's article you may find it useful to see if you can come up with your own list of superstars and match it to the table of top grossing actors. It is worth noting in the extract that de Vany makes use of some complex statistics to support his arguments. If you do choose to read the rest of the book, be warned that there is some pretty heavy-duty maths to negotiate.

I am going to focus on the superstars, those who made a movie that grossed $100 million or more. This moves us up the ladder of stardom to the top 30 actors and directors. The rule for super stardom is to make a movie that grosses $100 million or more; mere stardom (top 100 status) can be achieved with a single film grossing $50 million or more.

Tables 1 and 2 rank the top 30 directors and actors by the accumulated North American theatrical gross revenues of their movies from 1982 through 2001. The tables list by artist the number of movies (n), the cumulative sum of their movie revenues (sbo), the largest grossing film (mbo) and the average box-office revenues of their films (abo).

Both lists contain the familiar names. The qualification shared by every one on it is that they made a movie that grossed at least $100 million. The top 30 artists are busy, each made no fewer than 6 movies as an actor or 4 as a director. George Lucus is an exception because his two Star Wars movies grossed enough to put him among the top grossing directors.

In keeping with the dominance of extreme events in the movies, cumulative grosses depend heavily on a single movie. This is more true of directors than actors. *Forrest Gump*, one of the 23 movies Tom Hanks made, accounts for 14 percent of his cumulative gross. The same movie is one of 10 directed by Robert Zemeckis and it accounts for 22 percent of his cumulative gross. *Titanic* earned 53 percent of the gross revenues earned by James Cameron's 7 movies and 80 percent of Leonardo DiCaprio's cumulative gross from 6 movies. For actors, the portion of cumulative gross that is due to one film averages 22 percent and is no less than 10 percent; its high value is 80 percent. For directors, the average portion of their cumulative gross that is due to one film is 32 percent and this varies from a low of 16 percent to a high of 75 percent.

The lesson is clear. If you want to be a superstar direct or act in a movie that is a monster hit. There are no exceptions to this rule. Every director or actor who is in the top 30 had a movie that earned at least $100 million. This point, be lucky enough to make a hit, holds as one goes lower in the rankings too.

Here is another pattern: nearly everybody starts out small, with minor films that earn modest revenues. All the superstar actors and directors experience a turning point in their career when they make a $50 million movie. From then on, projects just seem to flow and they tend to become busy and get opportunities to make many more movies. Since it is hard to direct more than a movie per year or act in more than three per year, the superstars tend to have long careers. If you don't make a hit, you can still have a career, but it is less lucrative and more uncertain. There is such a thing as a big break in Hollywood – no one can become a top star without a break-out movie that makes at least $100 million.

Table 1 Top grossing actors

	cst 1	*n*	*sbo*	*mbo*	*abo*
1	Hanks, Tom	23	2.44e+09	3.30e+08	1.06e+08
2	Gibson, Mel	23	1.70e+09	1.83e+08	7.37e+07
3	Murphy, Eddie	19	1.66e+09	2.35e+08	8.75e+07
4	Ford, Harrison	19	1.62e+09	1.97e+08	8.54e+07
5	Cruise, Tom	16	1.58e+09	2.15e+08	9.84e+07
6	Williams, Robin	23	1.55e+09	2.19e+08	6.74e+07
7	Schwarzenegger, Arnold	20	1.42e+09	2.05e+08	7.12e+07
8	Willis, Bruce	21	1.40e+09	2.94e+08	6.67e+07
9	Travolta, John	23	1.21e+09	1.40e+08	5.26e+07
10	Carrey, Jim	10	1.18e+09	2.60e+08	1.18e+08
11	Stallone, Sylvester	22	1.16e+09	1.50e+08	5.27e+07
12	Douglas, Michael	19	1.13e+09	1.57e+08	5.93e+07
13	Costner, Kevin	19	1.12e+09	1.84e+08	5.92e+07
14	Roberts, Julia	10	9.05e+08	1.52e+08	9.05e+07
15	Martin, Steve	21	8.38e+08	1.00e+08	3.99e+07
16	Eastwood, Clint	17	7.96e+08	1.02e+08	4.68e+07
17	Neeson, Liam	14	7.89e+08	4.31e+08	5.63e+07
18	Fox, Michael J.	15	7.77e+08	2.08e+08	5.18e+07
19	DiCaprio, Leonardo	6	7.46e+08	6.01e+08	1.24e+08
20	Keaton, Michael	16	7.42e+08	2.51e+08	4.64e+07
21	Myers, Mike	6	7.04e+08	2.64e+08	1.17e+08
22	Connery, Sean	15	6.99e+08	1.34e+08	4.66e+07
23	Washington, Denzel	17	6.58e+08	1.16e+08	3.87e+07
24	Hoffman, Dustin	10	6.53e+08	1.77e+08	6.53e+07
25	Gere, Richard	18	6.41e+08	1.78e+08	3.56e+07
26	De Niro, Robert	24	6.31e+08	1.66e+08	2.63e+07
27	Cage, Nicolas	18	6.25e+08	1.02e+08	6.07e+07
28	Bullock, Sandra	10	6.07e+08	1.09e+08	6.07e+07
29	Reeves, Keanu	14	6.05e+08	1.71e+08	4.32e+07
30	Murray, Bill	9	5.90e+08	2.39e+08	6.55e+07

n, number of movies; *sbo*, cumulative sum of movie revenues; *mbo*, largest grossing film; *abo*, average box-office revenue.

CONTINUED

You can identify the real superstars in Hollywood if you raise the bar to three or more movies that gross at least $100 million. Only 16 stars have accomplished this feat in the past two decades. If you raise the standard to six hits, you are left with just nine actors: Jim Carrey (6), Tom Cruise (7), Harrison Ford (6), Mel Gibson (8), Tom Hanks (11), Eddie Murphy (7), Julia Roberts (6), Arnold Schwarzenegger (6) and Robin Williams (6).

It is easier to remain a star than it is to become one. When you become a star you gain access to more opportunities. You are offered the best roles in better movies with higher production and advertising budgets. And your movies open on more screens. So, the problem is easy; find that great role in a movie

Table 2 Top grossing directors

	dir	n	sbo	mbo	abo
1	Spielberg, Steven	13	2.08e+09	4.00e+08	1.60e+08
2	Zemeckis, Robert	10	1.52e+109	3.30e+108	1.52e+108
3	Cameron, James	7	1.13e+109	6.01e+108	1.61e+108
4	Howard, Ron	13	1.13e+109	2.60e+108	8.67e+107
5	Columbus, Chris	9	9.59e+108	2.86e+108	1.07e+108
6	Donner, Richard	12	8.87e+108	1.47e+108	7.39e+107
7	Reitman, Ivan	10	8.46e+108	2.39e+108	8.46e+107
8	Schumacher, Joel	14	7.78e+108	1.84e+108	5.56e+107
9	Burton, Tim	8	7.29e+108	2.51e+108	9.12e+107
10	Scott, Tony	10	7.28e+108	1.77e+108	7.28e+107
11	Levinson, Barry	16	7.16e+108	1.73e+108	4.48e+107
12	Emmerich, Roland	6	6.64e+108	3.06e+108	1.11e+108
13	Eastwood, Clint	15	6.15e+108	1.01e+108	4.10e+107
14	Sonnenfeld, Barry	6	6.10e+108	2.51e+108	1.02e+108
15	Lasseter, John	3	6.00e+108	2.46e+108	2.00e+108
16	Bay, Michael	4	5.99e+108	2.02e+108	1.50e+108
17	Petersen, Wolfgang	9	5.76e+108	1.83e+108	6.40e+107
18	Lucas, George	2	5.69e+108	4.31e+108	2.85e+108
19	Scott, Ridley	11	5.67e+08	1.88e+08	5.16e+07
20	Marshall, Garry	11	5.66e+08	1.78e+08	5.14e+07
21	McTiernan, John	9	5.63e+08	1.21e+08	6.26e+07
22	De Palma, Brian	11	5.28e+08	1.81e+08	4.80e+07
23	Shadyac, Tom	4	5.17e+08	1.81e+08	1.29e+08
24	Pollack, Sydney	6	5.17e+08	1.77e+08	8.62e+07
25	Stone, Oliver	12	5.14e+08	1.38e+08	4.28e+07
26	Reiner, Rob	12	5.09e+108	1.41e+108	4.24e+107
27	De Bont, Jan	4	5.03e+108	2.42e+108	1.26e+108
28	Nichols, Mike	11	4.85e+108	1.24e+108	4.41e+107
29	Musker, John	5	4.52e+108	2.17e+108	9.03e+107
30	Craven, Wes	11	4.41e+08	1.03e+08	4.01e+07

that will gross more than $100 million. Then make careful choices in selecting your new projects and you are a superstar.

But, how do you get that first big role in a hit? It is the movie that makes someone a star. Yet, no one knows how much a movie is going to make. You just have to be lucky. Only about 3 percent of movies are big hits; just 196 movies out of 6,289 movies released in North America during the two decades from 1982 through 2001 grossed at least $100 million. So, at the most, there is just a 3 percent chance of becoming a star. Just about half of the hits were first time break-out movies for actors and about half of the roles in hits were to stars who already had a big movie under their belt. There are about 200 hit movies per two decades, according to the sample data. About 100 of these roles will go to established stars and 100 to new ones. This leaves room for about 50 actors per decade to break out in a $100 grossing movie.

According to the model, Sylvester Stallone broke out in 1982, Harrison and Ford and Eddie Murphy in 1984, Tom Cruise in 1986, Robin Williams in 1987, Tom Hanks and Arnold Schwarzenegger in 1988, Mel Gibson in 1989. Sean Connery and Bruce Willis broke out in 1990 and Julia Roberts in 1991. Brad Pitt hit in 1995. Nicolas Cage, Matt Damon and Leonardo DiCaprio all broke into the $100 million plus ranks in 1997. They remain top stars today if we measure by the number of roles they get or what they are paid. It is a bit surprising how recently these actors came on the scene, so familiar are their names. Only Stallone has been around for 20 years. The average length of time on the list (at this date, they may stay longer) is 12.33 years. The differences among them are not that large; the average deviation from the mean is 3.9 and the median deviation is just 3.

(de Vany 2004: 232–235)

One of the commodities the star system is best known for is the gossip that surrounds the private lives of stars. In an age fixated with celebrity, it is perhaps inevitable that a whole media industry is kept busy providing us with information about how the stars conduct themselves. It is, of course, difficult to separate the reality from the fiction. Much gossip is part of an elaborate public relations system to ensure that stars are kept in the public eye.

ACTIVITY

➤ It is often said that there is no such thing as bad publicity by which it is meant that as long as stars are featured in the media it does not matter what the reason for this exposure is. Choose a couple of stars who interest you and research the type of publicity they have received in the recent past.

Of course, appearance and reality are often at odds with one another. Stars whose appeal is their attractiveness to the opposite sex have been revealed to enjoy gay lifestyles, often not until they are dead and buried.

An interesting writer on the 'truth' behind the lives of Hollywood's finest is Kenneth Anger. His books, *Hollywood Babylon* and *Hollywood Babylon II*, both of which were made into films, focus on the lives, or more precisely the scandals, of Hollywood stars. In the following extract Anger reveals details of the private life of James Dean, who prior to his death in a car crash in 1955 was one of the greatest male stars of his generation.

THE TROUBLE WITH JIMMY

During production of *Rebel Without a Cause*, James Dean was host to a thriving colony of crabs. He acquired the critters from a binge of sleeping around. Natalie Wood, Sal Mineo and Nick Adams had all observed their grungy co-star indulging in off-camera crotch-polishing; they thought he was imitating the scratch-'n-itch mannerisms of his slobbish hero, Marlon Brando. Director Nicholas Ray, amazed at his star's unconversance in such manners, dragged Dean off to a Burbank drugstore and treated him to a bottle of pungent crabocide.

Dean had taken to hanging out at the Club, an East Hollywood leather bar. The predatory night prowler, who dug anonymous sex, had recently discovered the magic world of S and M. He had gotten into beating, boots, belts, and bondage scenes. Regulars at the Club tagged him with a singular moniker: the Human Ashtray. When stoned, he would bare his chest and beg for his masters to stub out their butts on it. After his fatal car crash, the coroner made note of the 'constellation of keratoid scars' on Jimmy's torso.

Dean had avoided service in Korea by leveling with his draft board – he informed the Fairmount Selective Service Unit that he was gay. When Hedda Hopper asked him how he had managed to stay out of the Army, he replied: 'I kissed the medic.'

Shortly after arriving in Hollywood, Dean had adopted the route taken by many other broke, aspiring actors – he moved in with an older man. His host was TV director Rogers Brackett, who lived on posh Sunset Plaza Drive. The fan magazines spoke of their father–son relationship. If so, it was touched by incest.

During the period just before his death, Dean should have been sitting on top of the world. *East of Eden* had been released and was a hit. Dean was twenty-four. *Rebel Without a Cause* and the ambitious *Giant* had been completed; neither was yet released, but it was evident from the preview of *Rebel* that the movie would be big. A great career lay ahead.

Or did it? Dean was withdrawn, compulsively promiscuous, but friendless, suspicious, moody, uncooperative, boorish and rude. He could, on occasion, be charming; on most occasions he was annoyingly nuts. He betrayed a psychopathic personality, with fits of despondency that alternated with fits of wild jubilation. A classic manic-depressive. Mr. Nice Guy he wasn't – but his tormented screen persona hit a nerve with men, women, the young and the not-so-young.

Although his stage and screen experience was limited, he nonetheless felt himself competent to order camera and script changes. He blew his top when his suggestions were not taken. Directors humored him; behind his back they cursed him. His childish bids for attention were the talk of Hollywood. He turned up at dress affairs in sweatshirt and jeans; at a dinner party with Elia Kazan, Tony Perkins and Karl Malden, when the steaks arrived, Dean picked his up and threw it out the window. He spat at the portraits of Bogart, Cagney and Muni that adorned the walls of Warners' reception hall. At Chasens' his requests for service were accompanied by table-banging and silver-clanging.

He hid money in his mattress, slept on the floor at the homes of acquaintances, forgot rehearsals, and stayed out all night balling on the eve of studio calls. Toward the end, he was slow to learn his lines. He fluffed dialogue and fumed on the set. He was a confirmed pot-head. Writers who obtained interviews with him (few did) came away in consternation. The actor had babbled irrelevancies or sat still and mute, staring at his visitors without batting an eye.

On the eve of his death, he had attended a gay party at Malibu, which had ended in a screaming match with an ex-lover, a man who accused him of dating women just for the sake of publicity. On September 30, 1955, he was doing a reckless 85 miles an hour in his silver Porsche on Highway 41 at Chalome, near Paso Robles. He was speeding, en route to a sports car race at Salinas, when he smashed into another vehicle. He was mangled, DOA at Paso Robles Hospital.

At first, public grief was modest. Warners was grieved for financial reasons – *Rebel* and *Giant* had not been released and films starring recently deceased actors generally had bad track records. Then, without any studio hype, a legend grew. It was only several months after his death that the cult began to grow to vast proportions. The release of *Rebel* set off the greatest wave of posthumous worship in Hollywood history; it exceeded that for Valentino. Some fans committed suicide. Although Dean's career had been but a brief comet, many of his fans refused to accept his death. Thousands of letters poured in at the studio each day; most were from teenagers. Today, thirty years after his death, the fan mail for Jimmy still keeps arriving.

Kids across the country identified with the troubled youngster, the man-boy anti-hero played by Dean in *Rebel*. Warners found that it had a hot cold

CONTINUED

property on its hands. As the cult spread, mementos of the actor – plastic models of his head, bits of his wrecked car, parts of his motorcycle – were auctioned at top prices.

It is quite likely that, even if he'd not been killed, Dean would not have made another movie after *Giant*. He was coming apart at the seams, on a self-destructive course, well before he was totaled with his car.

His tombstone in Fairmount, Indiana, bears only his name and the stark dates: '1931–1955.' A brief epitaph might have been: 'Pretty much of a tramp.' And yet, today, if Richard Gere, or Matt Dillon – or any of the other members of the boring regiment of James Dean clonettes spewed out by Francis Ford Coppola in *The Outsiders* – were to suffer Dean's fate, would cults arise, fans commit suicide, would mash note arrive thirty years after their demise? Doubtful – Jimmy may have had crabs, but he also had durable charisma.

Anger 1984: 127–138)

▼ 8 REALISM

It must be possible to represent reality as the historical fiction it is.

Alexander Kluge

True realism consists in revealing the surprising things which habit keeps covered and prevents us from seeing.

Jean Cocteau

'Realism is not a style of literature,' wrote Georg Lukacs in *The Meaning of Contemporary Realism*, 'it is the basis of every literature.' For 'literature' one might substitute any 'art' and especially 'film'. The point is that all our attempts to make representations of our experiences, of our world, of ourselves even, must make reference to the criterion of reality. At a superficial level this may be about being lifelike or 'authentic'; many theories talk of 'verisimilitude', the state of being a faithful copy. Artists (including film-makers) have always hankered for more than this, for a realism that is more than merely recognisable.

Film is a medium with an unparalleled and instant access to 'verisimilitude', offering a literal take on the painter Paul Klee's claim that 'Art makes visible.' From the very early days of Lumière's *Demolition of a Wall* and *Exiting the Factory* the technology allowed an easy and instant naturalism, where what you see appears to be only what there is. Similarly when audiences of *Le Repas de bébé* (the baby's meal) thrilled not to the foreground action but to the moving leaves behind the baby's head, they were opening a debate about a new kind of realism (and ultimately about new definitions of reality). When Lukacs wrote of 'true great realism' he was writing for films as much as he was of literature:

> True great realism thus depicts man and society as complete entities, instead of showing merely one or the other of their aspects. Measured by this criterion, artistic trends determined by either exclusive introspection or exclusive extraversion equally impoverish and distort reality. Thus realism means three-dimensionality, an all-roundedness, that endows with independent life characters and human relationships.
>
> (Lukacs, *The Meaning of Contemporary Realism*)

Lukacs also said that 'the central aesthetic problem of realism is the adequate presentation of the complete human personality', in other words the representation of people inside and out. This is a challenge that makes particular demands on film as a medium and ultimately as a technology. Lukacs helps to clarify the extent of the problem, particularly for film, by stressing the difference between 'true realism' and (mere) 'naturalism'. For Lukacs, naturalism is a limited and limiting perspective, and Susan Haywood's definition implies much the same:

naturalism (*see also* **realism**) A term closely associated with realism. Naturalism first came about in the theatre of the late nineteenth century with the work of, among other dramatists and theatre directors, the Frenchman André Antoine. Antoine's **theory** was to get the actors to move away from the theatrical **gesturality** so prevalent at the time. To do this he created the principle of the fourth wall, which mean that the actors would not address or acknowledge the **audience**. They acted as if the audience was not there. In this regard, the proscenium arch of theatre is effectively abolished and the audience feels as if it is witnessing a slice-of-life realism; it is as if viewers are literally dropping in, unseen (a fly on the fourth wall!), on the goings-on of the people on stage. To sustain this effect the décor is realistic, the subject matter contemporary and dialogue delivered naturally – 'they speak just like us'. Actors enter the personae of their characters rather than represent them. They impersonate their characters and reveal their complexity from within. This form of naturalistic acting would later become labelled **method acting** (interestingly, the French talk of actors as 'encamping' their roles).

Antoine went on to direct films and took this principle of naturalism with him, adapting it to the cinema. He insisted on location shooting, the use of a multi-camera point of view (which he believed would parallel the effect of the fourth wall) and an **editing** style that would involve the **spectator** in the narrative (through identification with the mediating camera). He was, incidentally, the first to show female nudity in **narrative** cinema (L'*Arlésienne*, 1922).

Naturalism as an effect, then, places the spectator voyeuristically. We take up the position of the mediating camera. The characters seem so natural, their dialogue or verbal interchanges so real, the **setting** and **mise-en-scène** so totally realistic that an easy identification takes place. We are there alongside the characters. Take, for example, O*n the* W*aterfront* (Elia Kazan, 1954) and the use of the **diegetic** audience to place us as one of the protagonist's entourage (Marlon Brando as Terry Malloy). The reality of what we see before us, with which we identify, stitches us into the illusory nature of the representation so that it appears innocent, natural. In this way, naturalism has an ideological effect much like **naturalizing**. It purports to show reality but in fact has little to do with the representation of the contradictions which underlie social structures and political processes. It gives, therefore, a surface **image** of reality.

(Haywood 2000: 259)

All is delivered in the final line: 'a surface image of reality'. She effectively re-dubs this 'seamless realism' when reflecting on the various means film sometimes uses to 'cover its tracks': to make the thoroughly unnatural process of film-making as if it were an unobtrusive eavesdropping on reality. Clearly for Haywood (and others) this is significant chiefly because it has ideological implications: at worst it allows versions of reality to operate as if they were merely reflections of reality. Haywood compares this to Gramsci's concept of 'naturalisation', whereby the arguments of powerful groups are presented as if they are merely common-sense accounts of the way things are. In her entry on 'Realism' Haywood uses the phrase 'keeping reality safe' to indicate the degree to which realism functions as part of the hegemonic manufacturing of consent:

> **realism** (*see also* **documentary**, **naturalism**, **seamlessness**, **sociorealism**, **suture**) The term *realism* comes from a literary and art movement of the nineteenth century which went against the grand tradition of classical idealism and sought to portray 'life as it really was'. The focus was on ordinary life – indeed the lives of the socially deprived and the conditions they had to bear. As far as the film camera is concerned, it is not difficult to see why it is perceived as a 'natural' tool for realism, since it reproduces 'what is there' (that is, the physical environment). Film as cinema makes **absence** presence, it puts reality up on to the screen. It purports to give a direct and 'truthful' view of the 'real world' through the presentation it provides of the characters and their environment. Realism functions in film on both the **narrative** level and the figurative (that is, pictorial/photographic). In this regard, physical realism marries into psychological realism via the narrative structures. Generally speaking, realist films address social issues. However, because the narrative closure of these films tends to provide easy solutions, this form of realism on the whole serves only to naturalize social problems and divisions and not provide any deep insight into causes.
>
> There are, arguably, two types of realism with regard to film. First, seamless realism, whose **ideological** function is to disguise the illusion of realism. Second, aesthetically motivated realism, which attempts to use the camera in a non-manipulative fashion and considers the purpose of realism in its ability to convey a reading of reality, or several readings even. As far as the seamless type of realism is concerned, film technique – supported by narrative structures – erases the idea of illusion, creates the 'reality effect'. It hides its mythical and **naturalizing** function and does not question itself – obviously, because to do so would be to destroy the authenticity of its realism (see **myth**). Nothing in the camera-work, the use of **lighting**, **colour**, **sound** or **editing** draws attention to the illusionist nature of the reality effect. The whole purpose is to stitch the spectator into the illusion – keeping reality safe.
>
> Conversely the realist aesthetic, first strongly advocated by French film-makers in the 1930s and subsequently by André Bazin in the 1950s, is one that recognizes from the start that realist **discourses** not only suppress certain truths, they also produce others. In other words, realism produces realisms. And, although due caution must be exercised when making a realist film, this multiplicity of realisms means that a film cannot be fixed to mean what it shows – as occurs in seamless realism. The realist aesthetic recognizes

the reality-effect produced by cinematic **mediation** and strives, therefore, to use film technique in such a way that, although it does not draw attention to itself, it none the less provides the spectator with space to read the text for herself or himself. In other words, technique functions in this instance so as not to provide an encoded **preferred reading**. Rather, it seeks to offer as objectively as possible a form of realism. So this type of realism uses location shooting and natural lighting. Most of its cast is composed of non-professional actors. It employs long **shots** using **deep-focus** cinematography (to counter manipulation of the reading of the image), long takes (to prevent the controlling effects of editing practices) and the 90-degree angled shot that, because it is at eye level, stands as an objective shot.

(Haywood 2000: 311–313)

What Haywood is really identifying are tendencies within the discourse of realism, the conversation that all films must have with both themselves and their audiences about reality. Haywood uses the phrase 'Reality produces realisms' to emphasise that this is a broad church, that no 'denomination' of realism can ever claim to be the one, true way. It stretches from *cinema verité* and documentary realism on the one hand through to work which founds its realism on the exposing of its own manipulation of conventions.

Nicholas Abercrombie, writing specifically about television, suggests that the three key features of realist texts are:

1. Realism offers a 'window on the world'.
2. Realism tells stories which have rationally ordered connections between events and characters.
3. Realism conceals its construction process.

Abercrombie makes it very clear that 'the form conspires to convince us that we are not viewing something that has been constructed in a particular fashion'. Lest we forget he reminds us that 'realism is only a convention': this is always worth restating:

However powerful its effects, realism is only a *convention*. Television may appear to be a window on the world but it is not really transparent. What it offers is essentially a construction of the world, a version of reality. This is not a conspiracy to mislead the audience. It is simply that there is no way in which any description of reality can be the only, pure and correct one, just as people will give very different descriptions of what they see out of their kitchen window. As soon as television producers start to film, they are necessarily selecting and interpreting; they *must* do so in order to present a coherent programme of whatever kind. As a result, of course, all sorts of things can be excluded by realist conventions.

(Nicholas Abercrombie in Raynor *et al.* 2003)

Ultimately what we are being reminded of is that realism is a code or set of codes, but an especially important one given a medium that is essentially photographic. This

FILM STUDIES: THE ESSENTIAL RESOURCE

tension is further explored in the work of the critic most associated with the advocacy of cinema's 'vocation for realism', Andre Bazin. Bazin wrote extensively and provocatively about all aspects of cinema (collections of his essays in English bear the primal title *What is Cinema?*), but his central platform was that 'realism' is the cinema's natural mode of address. In his essay 'an aesthetic of reality: neorealism' for example, written in the 1940s, he describes Italian neo-realism as 'progress in expression, a triumphant evolution of the language of cinema, an extension of its stylistic'. However he, like Abercrombie, is clear about the means by which this 'faithfulness to everyday life' must be achieved:

But realism in art can only be achieved in one way-through artifice.

Every form of aesthetic must necessarily choose between what is worth preserving and what should be discarded, and what should not even be considered. But when this aesthetic aims in essence at creating the illusion of reality, as does the cinema, this choice sets up a fundamental contradiction which is at once unacceptable and necessary: necessary because art can only exist when such a choice is made. Without it, supposing total cinema was here and now technically possible, we would go back purely to reality. Unacceptable because it would be done definitely at the expense of that reality which the cinema proposes to restore integrally. That is why it would be absurd to resist every new technical development aiming to add to the realism of cinema, namely sound, color, and stereoscopy. Actually the 'art' of cinema lives off this contradiction. It gets the most out of the potential for abstraction and symbolism provided by the present limits of the screen, but this utilization of the residue of conventions abandoned by technique can work either to the advantage or to the detriment of realism. It can magnify or neutralize the effectiveness of the elements of reality that the camera captures. One might group, if not classify in order of importance, the various styles of cinematography in terms of the added measure of reality. We would define as 'realist,' then, all narrative means tending to bring an added measure of reality to the screen. Reality is not to be taken quantitatively. The same event, the same object, can be represented in various ways. Each representation discards or retains various of the qualities that permit us to recognize the object on the screen. Each introduces, for didactic or aesthetic reasons, abstractions that operate more or less corrosively and thus do not permit the original to subsist in its entirety. At the conclusion of this inevitable and necessary 'chemical' action, for the initial reality there has been substituted an illusion of reality composed of a complex of abstraction (black and white, plane surface), of conventions (the rules of montage, for example), and of authentic reality. It is a necessary illusion but it quickly induces a loss of awareness of the reality itself, which becomes identified in the mind of the spectator with its cinematographic representation.

(Bazin 1978: 26–27)

Although Bazin claims to be simply stating the fact that 'the general trend of cinema has been towards realism', there is palpably an agenda here, or at least a momentum. Bazin writes persuasively, implicitly challenging film-makers to engage in 'further conquest of reality'. A less passionate account is provided by Robert Stam. In his essay 'The Question of Realism', he explains that 'in relation to cinema, the issue of "realism" has always been present'. He then usefully places it at the very centre of Film Studies, whether as something to aspire to or as an object of hateful derision.

The very names of many aesthetic movements ring the changes on the theme of realism: the 'surrealism' of Buñuel and Dali, the 'poetic realism' of Carné/ Prévert, the 'neo-realism' of Rossellini and de Sica, the 'subjective realism' of Antonioni, the 'bourgeois realism' denounced by Marxist critics. Several broad tendencies coexist within the spectrum of definitions of cinematic realism. The most conventional definitions of realism make claims about verisimilitude, the putative adequation of a fiction to the brute facticity of the world. These definitions assume that realism is not only possible (and empirically verifiable) but also desirable. Other definitions stress the differential aspirations of an author or school to mold what is seen as a *relatively* more truthful representation, seen as a corrective to the falseness of antecedent cinematic styles or protocols of representation. This corrective can be stylistic – as in the French New Wave attack on the artificiality of the 'tradition of quality' – or social – Italian neo-realism aiming to show postwar Italy its true face – or both at once – Brazilian Cinema Novo revolutionizing both the social thematics and the cinematic procedures of antecedent Brazilian cinema. Still other definitions acknowledge a certain conventionality within realism, seeing realism as having to do with a text's degree of conformity to widely disseminated cultural models of 'believable stories' and 'coherent characters.' Plausibility also correlates with *generic* codes. The crusty conservative father who resists his show-crazed daughter's entrance into show-business, can 'realistically' be expected, in a backstage musical, to applaud her on-stage apotheosis at the end of the film.

Another psychoanalytically inclined definition of realism involves spectatorial belief, a realism of subjective response, rooted less in mimetic accuracy than in spectatorial credence. A purely formalist definition of realism, finally, emphasizes the conventional nature of all fictional codes, seeing realism simply as a constellation of stylistic devices, a set of conventions that at a given moment in the history of an art, manages, through the fine-tuning of illusionistic technique, to crystallize a strong *feeling* of authenticity. Realism, it is important to add, is both culturally relative – Salman Rushdie claims that Bollywood (Bombay) musicals make Hollywood musicals look like neo-realist documents (Rushdie, 1992) – and historically conditioned. Generations of filmgoers found black-and-white more 'realistic,' for example, even though 'reality' itself comes in color.

(Stam 2000: 224)

Abercrombie has argued that 'the concept of realism itself is very difficult to define' and Stam's attempt does nothing to challenge this. It is widely claimed, he says, that realism is about 'verisimilitude, the putative adequation of a fiction to the brute facticity of the world'. Realism is about the struggle to achieve the means of film adequate to the sheer plurality and complexity of reality, in the name of 'truth to life'. The film reader *Realism and the Cinema* edited by Christopher Williams offers many accounts of this struggle and the introduction that Williams writes to the book is extremely good at staking out the broad issues and options. Here he addresses the realist functions of film:

The first major realist function film has fulfilled consists of its ability to provide various kinds of documents, i.e. accounts of things outside itself. This function has a long and varied history, from its straightforward beginnings through the organised, 'public service' strand developed by Grierson and his followers, to a more modern variety of habits and styles summarised by Alan Rosenthal as 'working in looser and bolder forms'. In this field the ultimate dream is often of a film without any commentary, notionally without any language at all, so that the content may be left free to 'speak for itself'. But such films normally obey rules of structure, of tempo and sometimes of dramatic form; their aim is almost invariably presented as being to tell 'the truth', but it would, in fact, be more appropriate to say that they tell their truths within the framework of the particular set of languages available to them. It also seems clear that although their aim is to tell the truth or to say something about the truth, such films are invariably guided by a single basic concept about how to do either of these things – a concept which may be obvious or complicated. The concept sometimes requires events to be staged, since the things necessary to the realisation of the concept are not likely to occur in front of the camera of their own accord. The concept will also require a distinct process of selection out of the filmed material; the more demanding the concept, the more likely it is that material judged by the film-makers to be technically 'good' will in fact be left out of the finished film or severely adapted to fit the concept. Thus the editing process, though often thought to be difficult for films with documentary aspirations, is not usually seen as obstructive in itself; often, in fact, it is presented as an aid to the film-maker who wants to bring out the 'real truth' rather than 'mere appearances'. The process of filming itself, however, and the restraints it imposes, are often seen as an obstacle. Thus the BBC Television internal handbook on *Principles and Practice in Documentary Programmes*: 'the equipment is a constant obstruction between the producer and his subject, and a great deal of his skill is devoted to presenting his subject matter as if the equipment and the technical processes were not there.' This sense of the obstructiveness of equipment (camera, sound-recording, lighting, crew members) has led to large investments in ever smaller and more manageable equipment that can be handled by fewer and fewer people. This increased flexibility make a quantitative difference, but not a philosophical one; the intervention of technology is always crucially important in documentary, and some modern film-makers believe that its operations should be acknowledged as

part of the film itself, incorporated into the film's style. Interesting conflicts are sometimes generated between the characteristics of the material itself and the manner of filming it.

Some people would argue for a sub-category of the documentary film: the film that uses its material to present a specific socio-political argument or case. It seems to me that the difference between this kind of film and the apparently less 'militant', more orthodox type of documentary is only of degree and not of kind. The orthodox documentary makes a case too; but the very conventions it tends to use – objectivity, respect for the material, sense of 'real life', etc. – oblige it to some extent to appear to conceal its argument. The socio-political argument needs to be in a positive relationship with the film's basic production concept for the results to be interesting. This seems to be the rule for all documentaries whether they are overtly 'argumentative' or not.

The second area of form which is important in discussion of realism is the area of narrative. This is an area which has been quite scandalously neglected in film criticism, because traditionally a narrative was held to be merely the 'hook' on which the artist hung his more meaningful thoughts and patterns. More recently, since the development of semiotics, some attention has been paid to it, but usually from narrow, prejudged positions, so that although the huge majority of films are cast in narrative forms we still know very little about how these forms work. To summarise what is known, it is clear that films have borrowed or adapted aspects of a story-telling tradition that goes back at least to Homer. The stylistic history of this tradition in literature is usefully described in Erich Auerbach's book *Mimesis*. It is often suggested that narrative films have parameters deriving from the nineteenth-century realist or naturalist novel. While it is true that films and novels share some of the same institutions – plots, characters, problems, resolutions – the methods film uses to handle and develop those institutions resemble novelistic methods in only a passing and tangential manner. When the forms of film narrative come to be studied in the detail they deserve, it is probable that they will be more usually compared with the flexibility of the narrative tradition as a whole, rather than with any specific nineteenth-century form of it.

The difficult thing about film narratives is that they are both open and closed at the same time: closed in that every narrative organises its material so as to start at one point and finish at another; and however extensive the trials and tribulations in between, there is always a strong and structured relationship between the two points. The material that the narrative thus organises is of course shot through with conventions of all kinds, but it is at least arguable that the convention which holds all these events together is the most important convention of all. But in two senses the system is also open: first, because the spectator is aware of it as a system, as a piece of machinery (a large part of his/her pleasure in the film derives precisely from watching the unfolding of the mechanism of the narrative, through its subtle, or crude, or simultaneously subtle *and* crude patterns of repetition and variation), and second, because as with documentary there is a referent outside the film itself. This referent is not precisely 'the real world', nor is it the spectator's ideas about the real world, though it can partake of both. The pleasure of the film-text invites the spectator to think about what gives him/her pleasure, but perhaps more importantly it tries to give him/her pleasure at the same time. Hence the charge so often levelled at film, and at narrative film in particular, of being 'escapist' or narcotic. Traditional liberal high culture and marxist-influenced modernism agreed to recommend to the spectator that he/she should undertake hard and rigorous work to avoid the danger of succumbing to the swamp-like fascinations of the narrative, whose manipulations are seen as deceiving by entertainment. No real progress can be made with narrative while this simple politico-psychological model prevails. The pleasures that narrative methods provide need to be recognised, and indeed shifted towards the centre of discussion, rather than deplored or condescended to.

It is obviously important to give the concepts of manipulation and closure positive senses, since they are central to narrative film construction even in the case of the most apparently 'natural' and/or 'open' films. But the question remains of what, if any, the relationship between these concepts and the realist/anti-realist spectrum may be. It has been argued that there is a meaningful parallel between the constraints and tensions internal to the film itself and the constraints and tensions experienced by the spectator in viewing it. Here I think one has to be cautious; the idea is that there is some kind of psychic connection between the world of the film and the world of the spectator. While it is clear that spectators of all kinds get involved-in/excited-by/interested-in the manipulations of films, and that some films attempt to play with the forms of this kind of involvement in their own narrative patterns (e.g. suspense), nothing very serious is known about the general demands viewers make of the film medium or the specific responses they have to it. Yet the area is one that certainly asks to be explored.

It is also true that the narrative film shows the spectator a 'world' which on one level had to be taken as 'real' or at any rate real-in-its-own-terms. Yet this *is* only one level; it cannot be read as implying a total mimesis or illusionism. As Thomas Elsaesser has suggested, 'the only element which is mimetic in even the most realistic film is the physical movement of the characters'; understanding of the other important elements, such as the characters themselves, the sets or location, the lighting and/or colour, and, on a different but related level, the articulation of the narrative, has to be based on a sense that they are only partially and variably mimetic, and that before being mimetic they are self-referential, which is to say that they refer back to themselves, or to their likes. One film protagonist-character refers to another, sets and lighting in one film refer to sets and lighting in others, and so on.

(Williams 1980: 6–9)

The division that Williams highlights within the discourse is between documentary films and narrative films: between those films which attempt to frame what they find in the world and those which use stories as a means of referencing reality, of getting to the truth of it. This may be a useful division to pursue since it offers two starting points which are both at extremes and yet converging on the same vanishing point: reality itself. In short, both 'film as document' and ' film as narrative' are attempts to reveal and/or express certain truths about human beings and the world they live in. Williams is quite explicit in his determination to put aside 'the truth' in favour of 'they tell their truths within the frameworks of the particular set of languages available to them'. What remains of this chapter is an attempt to point the way to some of these 'sets of languages', using three more 'signposts' which will hopefully encourage you on to further explorations.

First, an extract from Trinh T. Minha-ha's contribution to Michael Renov's *Theorizing Documentary* in which the issues pertaining specifically to documentary realism are given more than an airing. He called his piece 'The Totalising Quest for Meaning' to underline the central issue. Minha-ha is keen to tease out the issues, the problems, the contradiction which come with the documentary as a mode of production and an attitude towards life. He is particularly interested in the tensions between what is intended and what is possible, which Bazin earlier called 'a fundamental contradiction which is at once unacceptable and necessary'.

Truth has to be made vivid, interesting; it has to be 'dramatized' if it is to convince the audience of the evidence, whose 'confidence' in it allows truth to take shape. *Documentary – the presentation of actual facts in a way that makes them credible and telling to people at the time* (William Stott).

The real? Or the repeated artificial resurrection of the real, an operation whose overpowering success in substituting the visual and verbal signs of the real for the real itself ultimately helps to challenge the real, thereby intensifying the uncertainties engendered by any clear-cut division between the two. In the scale of what is more and what is less real, subject matter is of primary importance ('It is very difficult if not impossible,' says a film festival administrator, 'to ask jurors of the documentary film category panel not to identify the quality of a film with the subject it treats.') The focus is undeniably on common experience, by which the 'social' is defined: an experience that features, as a famed documentary-maker (Pierre Perrault) put it (paternalistically), 'man, simple man, who has never expressed himself.'

The socially oriented filmmaker is thus the almighty voice-giver (here, in a vocalizing context that is all male), whose position of authority in the production of meaning continues to go unchallenged, skillfully masked as it is by its righteous mission. The relationship between mediator and medium or, the mediating activity, is either ignored – that is, assumed to be transparent, as value free and as insentient as an instrument of reproduction ought to be – or else, it is treated most conveniently: by humanizing the gathering of evidence so as to further the status quo. (Of course, like all human beings I am subjective, but nonetheless, you should have confidence in the evidence!) Good documentaries are those whose subject matter is 'correct' and with whose point of view the viewer agrees. What is involved may be a question of honesty (vis-à-vis the material), but it is often also a question of (ideological) adherence, hence of legitimization.

Films made about the common people are furthermore naturally promoted as films made for the same people, and only for them. In the desire to service the needs of the unexpressed, there is, commonly enough, the urge to define them and their needs. More often than not, for example, when filmmakers find themselves in debates in which a film is criticized for its simplistic and reductive treatment of a subject, resulting in a maintenance of the very status quo which it sets out to challenge, their tendency is to dismiss the criticism by claiming that the film is not made for 'sophisticated viewers like ourselves, but for a general audience,' thereby situating themselves above and apart from the *real* audience, those 'out there,' the undoubtedly simple-minded folks who need everything they see explained to them. Despite the shift of emphasis – from the world of the upwardly mobile and the very affluent that dominates the media to that of 'their poor' – what is maintained intact is the age-old opposition between the creative intelligent supplier and the mediocre unenlightened consumer. The pretext for perpetuating such a division is the belief that social relations are determinate, hence endowed with objectivity. By *'impossibility of the social'* I *understand ... the assertion of the ultimate impossibility of all 'objectivity' ... society presents itself, to a great degree, not as an objective, harmonic order, but as an ensemble of divergent forces which do not seem to obey any unified or unifying logic. How can this experience of the failure of objectivity be made compatible with the affirmation of an ultimate objectivity of the real*? (Ernesto Laclau).

The silent common people – those who 'have never expressed themselves' unless they are given the opportunity to voice their thoughts by the one who comes to redeem them – are constantly summoned to signify the real world. They are the fundamental referent of the social; hence, it suffices to point the camera at them, to show their (industrialized) poverty, or to contextualize and package their unfamiliar life-styles for the ever-buying and donating general audience 'back here,' in order to enter the sanctified realm of the morally right, or the social. In other words, when the so-called 'social' reigns, how these people (/we) come to visibility in the media, how meaning is given to their (/our) lives, how their(/our) truth is construed or how the truth is laid down for them(/us) and despite them(/us), how representation relates to or *is* ideology, how media hegemony continue its relentless course is simply not at issue.

> *There isn't any* cinema-vérité. *It's necessarily a lie, from the moment the director intervenes – or it isn't cinema at all.*

> (George Franju)

When the social is hypostatized and enshrined as an ideal of transparency, when it itself becomes commodified in a form of sheer administration (better service, better control), the interval between the real and the image(d) or between the real and the rational shrinks to the point of unreality. Thus, to address the question of production relations as raised earlier is endlessly to reopen the question: How is the real (or the social ideal of good representation) produced? Rather than catering to it, striving to capture and discover its truth as a concealed or lost object, it is therefore important also to keep on asking: How is truth being ruled?

(Minha-ha 1993: 96–97)

Minha-ha is very sceptical about many of the claims of documentary film-makers to have some kind of privileged handle on reality or 'the truth'. He is also particularly suspicious of those film-makers who treat the unadorned lives of 'silent common people' as if they contain some kind of visible profundity ('it suffices to point the camera at them'). He asks profound and yet simple questions which get to the heart of the matter: questions like 'How is the real ... produced?' and 'How is truth being ruled?' The fundamental arguments of the traditional documentary are gently unpacked and addressed via Alexander Kluge's three-camera model of documentary film (which functions also as a workable and useful model of all generic film).

For Kluge the three 'cameras', the three levels in which 'framing' takes place, are:

1. in the technical equipment;
2. in the film-maker's mind;
3. in the expectations of the audience generated by the conventions of the genre.

Kluge concludes that 'In and of itself the documentary is no more realistic than the feature film.' Minha-ha then goes on to talk about the way that 'progressive fiction films are attracted and constantly pay tribute to documentary techniques'. Minha-ha endorses these techniques, recasting documentary film-makers as 'composers' of films (see the similarities with Godard on page 394). He quotes Franju on this matter and uses Franju's comments as the start of a mini-manifesto for a new take on documentary:

You must re-create reality because reality runs away; reality denies reality. You must first interpret it, or re-create it. ... When I make a documentary, I try to give the realism an artificial aspect. ... I find that the aesthetic of a document comes from the artificial aspect of the document ... it has to be more beautiful than realism, and therefore it has to be composed ... to give it another sense (Franju). A documentary aware of its own artifice is one that remains sensitive to the flow between fact and fiction. It does not work to conceal or exclude what is normalized as 'nonfactual,' for it understands the mutual dependence of realism and 'artificiality' in the process of filmmaking. It recognizes the necessity of composing (on) life in living it or making it. Documentary reduced to a mere vehicle of facts may be used to advocate a cause, but it does not constitute one in itself; hence, the perpetuation of the bipartite system of division in the content-versus-form rationale. To compose is not always synonymous with ordering-so-as-to-persuade, and to give the filmed document another sense, another meaning, is not necessarily to distort it.

(Minha-ha 1993: 99)

You will find reference to 'progressive fiction films' attracted to 'documentary techniques' (though not on these terms) in Chapter 14 on British cinema. The Free Cinema Movement of the late 1950s and early 1960s emerged from a documentary tradition to produce some of the most beautiful examples of social realism ever made. Walter Lassally's cinematography in *A Taste of Honey*, for example, has documentary film as its starting point but goes so much further to capture 'the poetry of everyday life'. Social realism is that other, narrative, tradition that Williams identified, the attempts to tell the stories of contemporary reality, of contemporary culture. By the 1990s this culture was decidedly cosmopolitan and international, and yet at the same time decidedly regional, and one of the jobs of realism was to unite them. Social realism, by definition, addresses social divisions directly and in detail, and in doing so, in Hallam and Marshment's words, 'can reaffirm cultural solidarities and sub-cultural identities across regional/national boundaries'. Hallam and Marshment identify films such as *Boyz N the Hood* (US 1991), *Once Were Warriors* (NZ 1994) and *La Haine* (France 1995) as important examples of the 'hybridized forms of contemporary social realism'. The discussion of *Once Were Warriors*, for example, is very keen to site it both within a tradition of social realism (confronting what Stam called 'the brute facticity of the world') and beyond this within a symbolic, ideological and essentially narrative framework.

Once Were Warriors concerns the blighted lives of a family struggling to rear their children in a suburban ghetto of Auckland, and shares a number of similarities with the work of African-American filmmakers such as Singleton. The filmscript was developed by Maori playwright Riwia Brown from a controversial best-selling novel by Alan Duff, and directed by Lee Tamahori with a primarily Maori cast and crew. In its home country, the film broke all box office records, and has sold in more than fifty countries worldwide.

The first film to portray Maori life from the 'inside', the film tells the story of an imploding, dysfunctional family trying to cope with unemployment, alcoholism and male alienation. Jake loses his job and takes to drinking heavily, beating up his wife Beth and ignoring the plight of his younger son Boogie, due to appear in court on a minor charge. Boogie is sent to reform school, where a Maori social worker teaches him traditional cultural values. The older son Nig joins an urban gang that is similarly affiliated to Maori fighting culture. During a night of heavy drinking, thirteen-year-old Grace is raped by one of Jake's friends. Unable to cope with the humiliation and her father's constant violence, Grace hangs herself from a tree in the backyard. Beth arranges a traditional Maori funeral with her high caste relatives who sill live in the countryside. Jake, from a lower caste group, resents his wife's

REALISM

assertions of traditional identity and refuses to attend the funeral, embarking on yet another drinking spree. Beth discovers the truth of the rape in Grace's diary; in the bar, she confronts Jake and his friends with the truth and walks out, taking the children with her.

This 'slice of life' family drama has an expositional narrative structure that is in some ways typical of social realism. From Jake's losing his job and starting to drink heavily, which creates the initial disruption to family life, the rapid spiral into chaos is motivated by situation and events rather than deliberate actions undertaken by the characters. Where the film departs from an aesthetics of social realism is in its apparent degree of artifice, particularly the stylised use of costume and colour and its melodramatic closure. The film is given a rich sepia look to emphasise the skin tones of its protagonists and emphasises black, red and white, predominant colours in Maori art. All vestiges of green were removed from the urban scenes to emphasise the barren, smog-laden urban environment. Women in the film wear dresses printed with animal and snakeskin designs, the men in Nig's gang flaunt plaited leather jackets, leather trousers, dark sunglasses; their hair and faces are intricately patterned and decorated. This attention to visual style is enhanced by the large, muscle-bound bodies of the men and the beauty of the women, creating an image of a resilient, proud people amidst the poverty of the urban environment. The frequent fight scenes emphasise the physical stature of the men, who appear large and powerfully erotic but increasingly self-destructive as their violence destroys not only their immediate environment but also those they love.

Urban confinement is contrasted in this film with the natural beauty of the New Zealand countryside. The film opens with a shot of the hills and mountains, typically reminiscent of tourist brochures, only for the camera to pull back and reveal an advertising billboard beside a drab urban highway where Beth walks with her shopping. But there is vitality here; an urban market echoes with the sounds of rap music, children playing and the hustle and bustle of city life. The huge barn-like bars are full of people enjoying themselves, dancing and talking, until violent confrontation disturbs their pleasure. As the film progresses, these images of everyday life are increasingly fractured by the aggressive drunken behaviour of the men. In an attempt to bring the family together, Beth arranges a day out to the countryside; it is here that we learn of Jake's resentment of her upper caste (*ariki*) heritage. The film suggests that salvation for Beth and her family can only be found by returning to her family's roots in the *marae* – the ancestral place; Beth takes Grace to be buried here in a traditional ceremony that reunites the alienated sons Nig and Boogie with their cultural and spiritual roots. Jake, rejecting this heritage, is left alone in the city with Beth reminding him that he is still a slave – 'to your fists, the drink, yourself . . .'.

Women tend to be a background presence or to feature as victims in many contemporary urban dramas, their aspirations and hopes for a better life doomed to unfulfilled resolution. *Once Were Warriors* repeats this trope through the rape and suicide of Grace, but it is Beth's ability to overcome her fear of Jake's violence and take the lives of herself and her children into her own hands that shifts the film from its stylised gang rhetoric. Although the key to Beth's empowerment – Grace's death – is something of a cliché, through her strength and resilience to the graphically depicted beatings and constant bullying she refuses to endorse Jake's nihilism and self-hatred or find solutions to her problems in the white world. From the beginning of the film, where she walks with her shopping next to the billboard image of the mountains, Beth is associated with nature and the traditional spiritual values of Maori culture. This cluster of feminine associations contrasts with the barren urban values of an exhausted modernity and the aggressive machismo that defines homosocial masculinity. These oppositions are present early in the film, but become more apparent once Grace dies, shifting the focus of narrative attention away from Jake towards Beth; with this shift, the film becomes more melodramatic in structure so begins as a stylised social realist 'boys movie' becomes a celebration of female power, albeit couched in the rather conventional family melodrama.

(Hallam and Marshment 2000: 201–204)

Once Were Warriors is a film which features scenes of sickening, visceral violence but it is in the end the symbolic narrative framework that places this brute reality in a meaningful context, that reconciles our relationship. When Jake beats Beth mercilessly we are as an audience situated as passive, appalled and helpless observers, caught in a medium close-up while all other potential witnesses are leaving, but that is not our only position or perspective. The meanings of the film and its impacts are not dependent on it verisimilitude (its truth to life) but rather on its mythic power, its willingness to expose the cultural contexts in which this violence occurs, to see beyond the present moment. When Beth delivers the violence back to Jake as an understanding of how it has killed their daughter Grace, and made him 'a slave to your fists', the moment is pure melodrama. An artificial light streams through her hair as, tightly framed, she delivers the 'epilogue', which returns cataclysmically to the film's (up until this moment's) cryptic title. 'Our people once were warriors,' she hisses, 'But unlike you, Jake, they were people with mana, pride; people with spirit. If my spirit can survive living with you for eighteen years, then I can survive anything.' The director Lee Tamahori then offers us a visual equivalent with a perfectly structured long zoom out which features Jake screaming into the night 'You'll be back' and which ends with his collapse and the end credits. In this way a harsh social reality is confronted but also controlled, or at least interpreted. This has to some extent also corresponded with a new (visible) subjectivity in a recently rejuvenated documentary genre. The success, for example, of Michael Moore, and the controversy his films have caused merely because they have a particular view, centres on the desire of audiences and critics to see 'documentary' and 'narrative' as entirely different.

Certainly the 'Neo-realism' that characterised Italian cinema in the late 1940s was keener to place 'life as it is' as the primary focus (see also Chapter 15). Here the conscious confusion/blending of fact and fiction was an aesthetic decision as 'documentary' footage was purposefully cut into dramatic material. In Rosselini's *Rome, Open City* (1945), for example, the final months of the war in Italy are furtively filmed to create a compelling historical document onto which Rosselini grafts his narrative. The textures of this film were also to have a far-reaching impact on the visual definition of the 'realistic', despite being largely a result of the absence of a consistent supply of film stock. Certainly a grainy texture and handheld techniques became the stock in trade of film realism, as did the use of 'real' locations. Nearly twenty years later when Tony Richardson made his version of Alan Sillitoe's autobiographical novel *Saturday Night and Sunday Morning* he filmed Albert Finney at the very lathe at which Sillitoe worked at the Raleigh factory in Nottingham, while his former workmates created a 'realistic' background by going about their 'real' business. The 'real' business of Italian neo-realism was an Italy defeated and devastated by the Allied invasion of 1943 to 1944 and an audience with a need to both confront and understand this.

James Chapman has noted that 'like so many other critically privileged film movements Neo-realism was relatively short lived and represented a small corpus of key texts'. The implication here is that, as so often, a particular set of circumstances demanded from cinema a particular set of responses. This partly reinforces our understanding that cinema was becoming a more and more significant form of social communication, a debating chamber for society's problems. Chapman argues that the urgent need to first record the Italy destroyed by war (and fascism) was soon replaced by a more reflective and composed mood in which reconstruction could be contemplated and interpreted. It is almost as if the need to 'see' is overtaken by the need to 'understand': hence the development of and ultimately the demise (or some would say reconstitution in other forms) of neo-realism. In the inevitable period of post-war improvement the striving for a starker, bleaker realism finally lost step with the desire for what nowadays is called the 'feel-good factor'. Aesthetically too the preoccupation with means, with technique (albeit a paring down of this) ultimately led to the tensions Bazin earlier described as the 'necessary' and 'unacceptable' implications of a photographic medium. This is the story of an aesthetic that is technologically striving for a reality which its very existence will forever frustrate. The camera may never lie, but it always has a view. The story of contemporary realism is told between these oppositions which are made ever more complex in a postmodern reality defined more and more by the hyperreal 'magic' of digital technology.

Gill Branston addresses these issues head-on in her book *Cinema and Cultural Modernity* (2000), presenting realism as to all intents and purposes a dysfunctional metanarrative (see page 246). What use is realism if our sense even of reality itself has become insecure? One answer, at least, is to talk about realisms as we came earlier to talk about truths and talk of realities. Branston's useful account of the 'crisis' is thus headed 'Realisms' and her unwillingness to accept that the debate is over leaves plenty for us to consider.

REALISMS

Some sense of the real is always at stake in any politics, and certainly in the claims of 'a politics of representation'. Yet realist forms and connections are under pressure, from theoretical approaches announcing the end of any certainty about what texts, or the rest of the real, consist of. There have been several key changes, including:

- The development of digital forms (anything can be simulated on screen; nothing is necessarily 'true') which de-secure claims on the part of photography, films or documentaries to the status of evidence for political debate.
- An accompanying awareness that many of realism's 'codes' (hand-held unsteady camera, black and white film stock as 'historical') can be, and have been simulated and therefore cannot act as certain 'evidence' – the camera shake is no longer clear evidence of filming under difficult or uncertain conditions, for example.
- An excitement, in film study, at exploring other, lower status film forms and genres, such as fantasy, comedy, melodrama, which were lampooned for years, often in highly gendered terms, for being 'unrealistic' but which now look set to take over the whole agenda of attention.
- An increasing awareness of the ways that cinema does not only 'mean', just as it is not only a realist 'mirror'. Aesthetic and formal operations have to be understood, and may often run counter to a desire to declare the work of fictions to be realistic.
- The claims of realism to access 'truth'. This term is now more likely to be replaced by 'truths', moving targets rather than 'a thing' which will stay still while a fully realistic image is drawn. Truths are seen as re-presented and even constructed through *discourses* and *discursive regimes*, a term which replaces 'stereotypes' in many accounts. This last is part of a broad shift towards Foucauldian models of discourse rather than the less plurally conceived 'ideology' of earlier Marxist models. What is often lost, however, is a sense of the unequal distribution of discursive power: some discourses, such as that of consumer advertising, are emphatically more powerful than others.

However, attempts to theoretically 'undo' the supposed vice like grip of the 'classic realist text' (see Corner 1998a: 68–75) raised as many problems as they sought to address, and too easily sought to dismiss the longing for 'realistic images', especially of marginalized groups or experiences. John Corner argues a valuable distinction between these two:

- 'thematic realisms', which propose a relation between what a text is about and reality
- 'formal realisms', or the ways that texts achieve real-seemingness in their representation of the world, especially in the way they 'look'.

(Branston 2000: 164–165)

And so we return to the continuing and energising dichotomy (division): from 'seamless' and 'aesthetically motivated' realism through 'document' and 'narrative' to 'thematic' and 'formal' and beyond. In Susan Haywood's 'other words': 'realism produces realisms'. Despite theoretical and technical limitations, across multiplex and art-house cinemas, the discourse of realism (that great conversation with the real) goes on, and wherever and whenever the world is framed as film, struggles to embrace and elude its 'vocation for realism'.

▼   **9 THEMES OF TEXTUAL ANALYSIS**

Narrator: And of course, with the birth of the artist came the inevitable afterbirth – the critic.

Mel Brooks, *History of the World Part I*

In the arts, the critic is the only independent source of information. The rest is advertising.

Pauline Kael (b. 1919), U.S. film critic, *Newsweek* (New York, 24 December 1973)

This chapter returns us to the simplest and most pragmatic relationship of all, that between the individual reader and the individual film text in terms of the different ways films can be 'read'. These are sometimes divided into two sets, which are described as the 'micro' and 'macro' elements of a film. The micro elements are those that constitute each shot. This is typically a list which includes both technical codes (camera, lighting, editing, sound) and performance codes (costume, setting, acting, props). The macro elements on the other hand are those features that work across the film to negotiate with the audience modes of address and reception: in other words, which tell us on many levels what kind of a film we are watching and thus how we are supposed to respond. This list includes such elements as genre, narrative, realism, auteur, star, even theme.

A focus on either of these sets produces very different kinds of film reading, so it is as well to be clear from the start what each intends and produces. Macro readings tend to be more expansive, dealing with comparative issues; for example, how a film sits in relation to others in its genre. Micro readings are much more likely to be concerned with how key sequences of films are constructed, often on a shot-by-shot basis. For this reason a film course such as the popular WJEC Film Studies A level requires candidates to attempt both of these kinds of analysis. This is what is specifically asked:

FILM FORM

This unit requires a study of both 'macro' aspects of film form (**narrative** and **genre**) and 'micro' aspects (***mise-en-scène*, cinematography, editing** and **sound**).

Narrative includes study of the overall structure of the film, the way in

CONTINUED

which the elements of the story are organised. Within the study of a specific sequence, study will include consideration of how narrative information is communicated.

Genre will, for the purposes of this module, be studied primarily as an efficient means by which a narrative film communicates meaning, especially through exploitation of signifying features readily recognisable to an audience, such as iconography.

Mise-en-scène and **Cinematography** include setting, costume and make-up, figure expression and movement, lighting, framing and composition, off-screen space, photographic elements (e.g. camera position, colour, lens, depth of focus) and special effects.

Editing includes the organisation of time, both within a sequence and across sections of the narrative and the organisation of space, especially in creating coherence for the spectator. The principal conventions of continuity editing, such as shot/reverse shot and the 180-degree rule, will be studied. The uses of montage editing will also be considered.

Sound includes the variety of ways in which aural elements, speech, music and noise, are used in relation to visuals.

WJEC Film Studies Specification

For the 'macro' reading, what is required is an intelligent commentary which connects what you are seeing and efficiently describing with your broader knowledge of films and what they (can) do. Here film student Kaye Hall offers her reading of the opening of Oliver Stone's *Platoon*.

The film follows Chris Taylor, a middle-class college student who joins the army and is sent to Vietnam only to find out that he is not only fighting the Viet Cong but also some members of his own crew. The heat and exhaustion also prove to be obstacles he must overcome. The mode of address of *Platoon* is from Taylor's point of view as we see what is happening to him and hear how he feels by what he says in his letters to his grandmother. This is a useful if conventional narrative device made sharper by the unconventional audience: stereotypically these are not experiences to tell your grandmother.

The scene I am analysing starts with the words 'An Oliver Stone film' appearing on screen. This is useful, as it suggests the work of an auteur and thus a serious film. A quote from the Bible then appears: 'Rejoice O young man in thy youth' (Ecclesiastes), which also gives it weight, as it is about youth and death, which normally don't go together. Non-diegetic sound then appears, in the form of *Adagio for Strings* by Samuel Barber. This creates an atmosphere that is a further index of seriousness. As the titles start to come up on screen they are strangely appropriate, as they look almost like a jungle-type font which is reinforced by the colour green. The green may also be seen as the camouflage resembling what the soldiers wear which fits completely with this film. The titles are awkward in the sense that they lack style.

The 'story' starts with the soldiers being dropped somewhere so that something can happen to them, which is a classic narrative technique. The characters are delivered out of the mouth of the plane, which is whale-like in the 'Jonah in the Bible' sense. This is an ironic journey to danger instead of away from it. When the characters appear we can see that they are only young and they look confused.

Charlie Sheen is the identifiable star, which tells us immediately that he is more likely to drive the narrative than the others are. The camera tightly frames him, which establishes him more firmly. The cut away to a body bag is almost thematic montage, inserting death before we have really begun. The body bag is a version of war. We see the new soldiers entering and some other soldiers who have already served in the war leaving; this symbolises life. The new soldiers are coming in (birth) and the other soldiers are leaving (death). This is serious stuff.

We see the reactions of Sheen as he sees the other soldiers leaving; he is our representative. The soldiers entering represent innocence and the soldiers leaving represent experience; this shows us that the war makes you come of age, it is a definition of youth, a rite of passage. The film was marketed with the passage 'the first casualty of war is innocence', which fits perfectly with this scene, where our innocence is also exposed for the first time.

We are shown parallel action between the soldiers leaving and entering which uses continuity of form. This is reinforced by the man-to-man horrific comparison between Sheen and a soldier leaving. Although these men are around the same age the war has 'aged' the man leaving and he looks a great deal older and more experienced than Sheen. In addition, the difference in the way they are dressed forces us to make comparisons. Sheen wears a clean and correct uniform, whereas the soldier leaving wears a dirty uniform with the hat missing. This gives us an idea of the horrific living conditions that occur when one is fighting in a war.

The camera cuts to a classic aerial shot of the jungle, which is very theoretical. It could be a natural history document. The shot is anchored by its caption with specific authenticity. There is then a shot of light through the trees, an ironic shot of beauty. This can be metaphorical in a number of ways: an appropriate prefiguring of light and darkness; the depiction of the journey they are about to make to find the light at the end of the tunnel; a restatement of the theme of life and death. In a sense these three things are what the film is about. Throughout the film Charlie Sheen gets closer and closer to the end of the

CONTINUED

tunnel. To an extent this symbolises Oliver Stone and his journey through the war because clearly he made it out alive and saw the light again. The camera then cuts to a second shot of the jungle, this one more realistic. The soldiers cut through the trees literally and also symbolically. This is their symbolic journey through difficulty to knowledge and enlightenment. As in *Apocalypse Now* the search is for meaning. We are shown the two sergeants. We immediately know which one is going to be the 'good' sergeant (Willem Dafoe) and which one is going to be the 'bad' sergeant (Tom Berenger). Again the crude character functions mark out the direction of the narrative and its nature. This is always going to be an allegory; a story with symbolic implications, whatever else it becomes. This also tells us that there is going to be another war going on in the jungle apart from the one fighting the Viet Cong.

Of course there are references to the cinematic codes but the focus is on the ways in which the film negotiates its identity, its mode of address. A micro reading is more specifically interested in how a sequence is realised cinematically, in the specific ways in which specific codes deliver specific meanings (or at least potential meanings). Take Zareena Raqib's reading of *Natural Born Killers*.

It starts with one-colour images of animals which are working in the symbolic codes (the rattlesnake often reappears in the film: it represents wisdom). There are four or five black-and-white shots then it goes back to colour, with a shot of a train tinted in red. Trains also constantly reappear in this movie. Leonard Cohen is playing in the background. A television is being switched a few times, going through time: the 1950s, 1960s, Nixon's resignation, right up until the present day. TV and the media are the demons in this movie. The setting is neutral, an American café diner which could be anywhere (or nowhere). The couple, Mickey and Mallory, resemble two people in a film: with Mickey in his leather jacket and sunglasses and Mallory in her bikini top, they are typical 'boy' and 'girl'. From the start it is obvious that this pair are the actors and everyone else around them is acted upon.

It is established quite early on in the scene that the mode of address is somewhat surreal, the scene so over the top that it is not realistic in the ways we expect it to be. The screaming demon motif of the waitress appears and reappears which gives a sense of weirdness as well. The blousy waitress represents normal, averagely attractive people but Hollywood doesn't want people who are attractive on a normal level so she gets shot. The codes of this film are media-based: the lack of moral and ethical codes is the point of the film. The only important codes are technological and aesthetic.

The director deliberately keeps using the colour green; for example, the vinyl record playing says green on the label, the green pie that Mickey's eating. The diegetic sound adds to the special effects and the non-diegetic sound starts with Leonard Cohen on the soundtrack but then becomes a part of the film so that it is hard to distinguish the soundtrack. The cuts to green objects such as the green juke-box are associated with sickness, envy, jealousy and aggression. The film is about this sickness and reactions to it but it is also about the way meaning is manipulated by the media in quite simplistic ways.

It is hard to understand every change-over, every clever trick. It plays off texture, instinct, deconstruction of reality.

The film cuts to a black-and-white close-up shot of a deer crying (a sign of things to come). The camera angles used are oblique, coming in low on the two cowboys who enter the café. Camera throughout the scene is a metaphor for our response to violence; the obscure angles and constant menacing cutting disorientate the viewer.

Mickey has a yin-n-yang tattoo on his left arm – a sign of balance. Mickey's introduction is coming off the newspaper first, and then vertically he reacts to the man's attitude to his girlfriend Mallory, with a cross-cutting of his own psychedelic visions of hell, anger and demonology. The opposition of monochrome and colour is again in evidence.

When Mallory starts beating up the cowboy it shocks the audience. It grabs our attention because this little stick-thin girl demolishes this man and uses our surprise as a place to address issues of representation and meaning. This boy-girl thing is another simple construct.

Reality is the violence; it is made very clear that most of the action could have been cut out. The stunt shot in black and white where the camera follows the bullet and stops before it hits the fat lady with the butcher knife in her hand and just cuts to the splash of blood. The knife follows through the window and into a fleeing cowboy's back. The whole scene is drawn out so we must suffer it; we have to watch Mallory stamping on the man. It is not chopped out for reasons of conformity so that the viewer gets the full ferocity of the onslaught and their attack. It is clear it should not be taken seriously (e.g. the camera following Mallory's finger and Mickey's gun in his hand). Mallory cheats; really they should have shot the man. Mallory deliberately does an impression of a witch. She arbitrarily chooses the waitress and leaves the fat old cowboy. They always leave one person alive to tell their tale, that's their methodology of murder. It is dangerously ceremonial: dangerous because fascinating. . . .

The reason for leading off this chapter with these beautifully proficient but essentially 'non-professional' readings is to headline and prioritise the first of the chapter's themes: 'value the personal'. This means that you are at the centre of any textual analysis, even more significantly than the text, since even the text is chosen by you. In the end little benefit will be gained unless you have the honesty to 'say what you see'. Everything else builds on this and 'amplifies' it, but without foundations nothing can be built. Films attempt various kinds of communication and it is the job of criticism to try to understand and appreciate these attempts at communication. We might also occasionally warn against them, though bad films, like bad books, are best ignored.

This leads rapidly to theme two: 'know the game'. In 'Against Interpretation' the critic Susan Sontag speaks out against the idea 'that a work of art is primarily its content'. This is particularly dangerous with regard to film since content appears very readily and straightforwardly to be offered and available. What happens in a film (or appears to happen) can too easily overwhelm how it happens, how it is organised and how it looks. For Sontag this derives from and leads back to a criticism which looks to interpret content rather than respond to form, which seeks to explain rather than explore. At worst she concludes, 'The task of interpretation is virtually one of translation.'

It is not our job as readers to provide a symbolic key, an interpretive code, but rather to explore the codes which are specific to our medium. What textual analysis essentially provides is an informed commentary. Now while we are all too familiar these days with that DVD staple 'the director's commentary', commentaries are still more readily associated with sporting events, with enthusiastic radio and television outside broadcasts at football matches and horse-race meetings. Nor is this a fruitless association, for while we do appreciate the insights offered in these cases by post-match interviews with participants, the real deal is getting a version of the event from an engaged (and engaging) observer. This is undoubtedly what successful textual analysis delivers: a thoroughly engaged account of a sequence, or a work, or even 'the work'.

For Joseph McBride and Michael Wilmington in their assured study of the films of John Ford, the commentary covers a whole career, film by film. It presents Ford's 'authorship' (see Chapter 6) in a way that always makes us want to get involved, to visit or revisit the films. *The Man Who Shot Liberty Valance*, for example, may be, according to histories of the Western genre, an 'important' text, but McBride and Wilmington prove this merely through the energetic insistence of their commentary. At the same time they are explicitly constructing an 'auteur' analysis (see Chapter 6) in which Ford himself is the focus. In either case, film is a visual medium and the best commentaries generally begin by saying clearly what there is to see, be that the symbolic structure or the contents of a single, significant frame.

THE MAN WHO SHOT LIBERTY VALANCE

> It is practically the only question of the age, this question of primitivism and how it can be sustained in the face of sophistication.
>
> Jean Renoir

The Man Who Shot Liberty Valance opens on a shot of a iron horse passing through a tranquil Western landscape. We have seen this image in countless Westerns; like a folk song, it releases a flood of memories and associations. Yet the way Ford lets the camera linger a moment on the heavy trail of black smoke hovering in the wake of the train seems to question the convention. Decades earlier, Ford had uncritically celebrated the building of the transcontinental railway in *The Iron Horse*, but now the train, the traditional symbol of progress and the pioneering spirit, has become a polluting and corrupting force.

The opening and closing sections of *Liberty Valance* are set in the last days of the frontier period, the beginning of modern America. From this perspective, we study in a long flashback the events surrounding one of those epochal gunfights which carry all the romance and meaning of the Western myth for us today. *Liberty Valance* is told from the viewpoint of a transplanted Easterner, Ransom Stoddard, who had once 'taken Horace Greeley's advice literally'. Stoddard (James Stewart) became a prime mover in the early history of the territory as the legendary Man Who Shot Liberty Valance, and is now its United States senator. Yet by the end, his heroism has been revealed as sham, and the train carrying him and his wife back to the East in the final shot describes an arc exactly the inverse of the opening shot. Inside the train Mrs Stoddard gazes at the valley: 'Look at it. Once it was a wilderness. Now it's a garden. Aren't you proud?'

That is the basic question of the film. Hallie Stoddard's juxtaposition of the words 'wilderness' and 'garden' invokes the familiar vision of the Western migration defined in *Virgin Land*:

> They plowed the virgin land and put in crops, and the great Interior Valley was transformed into a garden: for the imagination, the Garden of the World ... When the new economic and technological forces, especially the power of steam working through river boats and locomotives, had done their work, the garden was no longer a garden. But the image of an agricultural paradise in the West, embodying group memories of an earlier, and simpler, and, it was believed, a happier state of society, long survived as a force in American thought and politics.

Stoddard has not only symbolically transformed the wilderness into a garden, through his showdown with the equally legendary Valance (Lee Marvin), but when the film opens he is on the verge of literally transforming it, as the author of an irrigation bill. He has destroyed the Old West to give birth to modern America. But the ruthless logic of the flashback will prove that he was not the prime mover, merely a catalyst for inevitable historical forces; the Old West destroyed itself to make way for him and the way of life he represents – law, book learning, progress.

Although Ford's sympathies clearly lie with the archaic simplicity of the wilderness – with John Wayne's Tom Doniphon, who shot Valance and let Stoddard take the credit – the film is not an indictment of Stoddard. Like Tom, Valance and Hallie, he is caught up in a process of destruction and change which he is all but powerless to control. In fact, Stoddard is almost a comic figure,

CONTINUED

and the casting of James Stewart (in a role Henry Fonda would have played had the film been made twenty years earlier) emphasizes the ambiguity. Stoddard's predicament as a false hero bears an uncanny likeness to the situation Edward G. Robinson faces in a 1935 Ford comedy, *The Whole Town's Talking*, when his resemblance to a famous killer brands him with the newspaper sobriquet of 'The Man Who Looks Like Mannion'. But because Stoddard *sought* his title, even if he has not really earned it, his situation is tragic.

(McBride and Wilmington 1974: 175–176)

At the other end of the scale is the almost frame-by-frame account Jurgen Müller gives of the opening of Kubrick's *A Clockwork Orange* in his introduction to Tassen's *Movies of the Seventies* companion. Entitled 'The Skeptical Eye' this is an introduction to key attitudes and themes in 1970s' cinema, which literally grows out of a painstaking account of Alex's arrival home. Müller reminds us both implicitly and explicitly of the artificial nature of film and of the degree to which all film operates as its own message.

'Municipal Flatblock 18a, Linear North. This was where I lived with my dada and mum,' says Alex (Malcolm McDowell), as he strolls home whistling between the houses of a suburban housing development somewhere in the middle of nowhere. The place is like a labyrinth. Lights burn in a few windows, weakly illuminating the protagonist's path. There's something strangely static about the camera that accompanies him through these streets in a single parallel tracking shot. The dramatic impression is not created by Hollywood's standard techniques – shot/reverse shot – but by a camera that glides like a ghost through dilapidated flowerbeds full of discarded junk.

In this dismal environment, the film's young hero is the only sign of life, and he's just enjoyed a good night out. Alex and his droogs have tol-chocked an old tramp and a writer, raped a devotchka, stolen a car, and forced a respectable number of fellow-drivers into the roadside ditch. Horrorshow.

Alex is in a splendid mood. Accompanying him homewards, we become highly aware of the camera's presence. We're waiting for a cut, but the camera does not blink, staring persistently at Alex as it slides along at his side. What we see here is more than a happily whistling hoodlum; we're seeing the fact that we see him.

Stanley Kubrick's A *Clockwork Orange* (1971, p. 62) is one of the key cult movies of the 70s, and certainly the most controversial. It might be described as the hinge that links the 60s with the 70s, for Kubrick's film may well be seen as a sceptical critique of the ideals formulated by the 60s student movement. Yet although the movie makes constant allusions to the progressive optimism of that decade, its purview includes the entire century and the inhuman ideologies that marked it out.

It's hard to think of another film that assigns us the role of voyeur so effectively. In a shocking way, A *Clockwork Orange* makes all of us share responsibility for the things it shows. Thus the eloquent off-screen narrator who tells us his story never doubts for a second that he has our sympathy – and our consent. Again and again, he addresses us as 'brothers.' Still, the risk remains that we might have to see things from another perspective; and once, indeed, we find ourselves in the role of the victim – with Alex insisting we take a *veddy* good look... In this respect, Kubrick plays with the viewer's expectations. The film insists on breaking the bounds of fiction and assigning a series of different roles to us, the spectators. It's as if the director wanted to demonstrate his awareness of the pleasure we take in voyeurism, while also demanding that we see the world through Alex's eyes.

But Kubrick takes possession of us to an even greater extent than this, using all cinematic means available to give an authentic representation of Alex's world. We don't just see through Alex's eyes; we hear through his ears; and the music that accompanies his atrocities 'allows' us to share his visceral pleasure in cruelty. As we watch a vicious brawl in a disused cinema, we hear Rossini's *La gazza ladra*; but this doesn't mean that Kubrick is trivializing violence.

On the contrary; the fighters' fun is simply being made plain to us. Kubrick is attempting to show – to make us *feel* – what violence looks like from the inside. Here, violence is presented as a creative principle. It signifies lust, intoxication, as described by Nietzsche in the 'The Birth of Tragedy.' The film sketches a theory of ecstasy as the true fulfillment experienced by any human being who escapes the limits of his individuality. One scene shows this with particular vividness: like a satyr of the ancient world, Alex embraces a stone phallus – life petrified into art – and reawakens it in a grotesque balletic dance.

As we accompanied Alex back to the flat, we got so close to him that we almost entered his Holy of Holies – home itself, with dadda and mum. In the entrance hall of his apartment block, the camera blinks; and now we're gliding along in front of a mural. Once again, the director has flouted our expectations. Naturally, we interpret this tracking shot as if we see what we're seeing through Alex's eyes, or as if we had just escorted him into the foyer; yet now, to our surprise, we see him enter the frame from the opposite direction. And while we wait for him to arrive, there's time to examine the heaps of garbage, the parched and trampled lawns. With the passage of time, this once impressive stairwell, with its murals and its potted plants, has adapted itself to the forbidding and inhospitable concrete jungle that surrounds it. The tenants' rage is directed at the 'beautifications' – and especially at the mural, which is now disfigured by paint smears and obscene graffiti. The building's inhabitants, waiting in vain for the broken-down elevator, can only have taken pleasure in this fresco for a very short period. For they've 'improved' it by adding enormous male sex organs, along with some helpful advice:

'Suck it and see,' says a boy bearing a narrow barrel, as he gazes down on his beholders from the painting on the wall.

Yet even without the obscenities, these heroic images of the working class don't really fit into their grim concrete environs. We see men and women of all ages united in their praise of skilled labor, agriculture and industry, an assurance of the happy future awaiting mankind. Here, careful planning and conscientious work are two sides of the same coin. Thinkers and doers, young and old, farmers, laborers and craftsmen, all striving together in the service of a better life, a new world forged by a vigorous humanity. At the center of the painting stands a man whose physique and headgear mark him out as a leader; brave and strong, he gazes heroically towards the future.

The fresco in the foyer of Alex's parents' apartment block seems very familiar – as if we had encountered it all over Europe in course of the 20th century. We know this kind of agitprop art; we've seen it in Berlin and Rome, in Bucharest and Moscow. It's as if Kubrick wished to comment in passing, on a century marked by totalitarian systems. But this director doesn't make it easy for the audience; for he's set us a trap by asking us to sympathize with this apparently peaceful world, now defiled by vandalism. But who in fact are the vandals? The kids who've desecrated the artwork with filthy graffiti? Or the state technocrats who think they know the fate of humanity, and who paint a rosy future to conceal the inhumanity of the present?

Alex and his droogs counter moralists of all colors with the growled refrain, 'If it moves, kiss it,' while attaching outsized phalli to the heroes of classical antiquity. The droogs are shamelessly, indeed proudly, evil, and they're clearly convinced that work is for jerks.

(Müller 2003: 4–5)

One of the significant functions of detailed textual analysis is to test out theories you may have about whole texts or sets of texts. It is in this spirit that Warren Buckland offers his 'A Close Encounter with Raiders of the Lost Ark: Notes on Narrative Aspects of the New Hollywood Blockbuster'. In a section aptly entitled 'Textual analysis with a vengeance', Buckland examines the degree to which accusations that Spielberg and others have imported a non-film aesthetic (from TV and comic books) are useful. Buckland shows that while the argument that 'each shot ... presents a content closed and unified' works in some circumstances, it is not true to say that the style is 'self-sufficient and autonomous'. Rather, Buckland suggests, it is 'subordinated to the film's themes and narrative' (he is explicitly discussing *Raiders of the Lost Ark*). When this text is actively read, its narrative does seem to support Spielberg's own theory that 'You need good storytelling to offset the amount of ... spectacle.' Again all the bases are being touched: personal engagement, effective use of critical and technical vocabularies, forthright argument supported by textual detail.

For directors of New Hollywood films, a variety of compositional norms exists for exploitation. These include: the selective quotation of Old Hollywood films, the visual rhetoric of comic books, the norms of television aesthetics, and the compositional norms of European art film and the avant garde. One aim of a historical poetics is to determine what norms dominate the composition of each particular film. In *Raiders of the Lost Ark*, one can find references to Old Hollywood films. Indeed, Omar Calibrese argues that 350 references to other films can be detected in *Raiders*. As I point out below, *Raiders* is structured according to the serial format of the B-movie adventure stories, and we can also detect the influence of comic books, particularly in the storyboarded action sequences. Finally, elements of a television aesthetics are present (and it is important to remember that Spielberg worked in television from 1969–72).

Jerzy Toeplitz has argued that 'characteristically the directors who have come to film from television, regard montage as a much more important part of their skills than did the filmmakers of the 1930s and 1940s. ... They seem closer to the tradition of the silent screen'. Richard Maltby has suggested why editing and montage are fundamental to TV aesthetics. He argues that, due to the small size of its screen and its lack of resolution, television has little use for complex, deep focus shots. Instead, it is dominated by close-ups (showing single objects in isolation), rapid cutting (since the close-up requires less time for its content to be exhausted), a highly mobile camera (for the same reason as rapid cut), and a shallow, lateral space, partly created by the use of telephoto lenses.

For many critics, the consequence of television's aesthetics is that it foregrounds or overemphasizes action and divorces style and technique from narrative. Mark Crispin Miller has graphically illustrated the result of Hollywood's adoption of television aesthetics (as found in TV adverts and music videos in particular): 'Each shot [in contemporary Hollywood films] presents a content closed, unified, like a fist, and makes the point right in your face: big gun, big car, nice ass, full moon, a chase (great shoes!), big crash (blood, glass), a lobby (doorman), sarcasm, drinks, a tonguey, pugilistic kiss (nice sheets!), and so on.' For Maltby, Miller and others, this aesthetic is created through an overemphasis on techniques such as saturated colours, strong backlighting, rapid editing or constant camera mobility, sound effects and special effects that directly assault the spectators' responses and nervous system. The result, according to these critics, is that style of the New Hollywood film becomes self-sufficient and autonomous, rather than being subordinated to a film's themes and narrative.

There are scenes in *Raiders* which would seem to support such argument. The fight which ensues when Jones returns to Marion's bar provides an example of an action sequence that is structured according to television and comic book

aesthetics. The sequence lasts two minutes forty-four seconds, and consists of ninety shots. This makes for an average shot length of (or a cut every) 1.8 seconds. Moreover, one-third of the shots are close-ups (including medium close-ups). Although they don't appear to have been shot with a telephoto lens, many of the close-ups have a very simple, graphic composition and shallow space, since the characters are filmed against simple backgrounds such as walls. Moreover, there is no extensive use of camera movement, since the frenetic effect of the scene is created by the rapid cutting and by movement within the image. The overall effect of these stylistic choices is indeed to foreground the action and assault the senses and nervous system of the spectator.

But this is not, as it were, the end of the story as regards sequences such as these or the film as a whole. To begin with, it is worth noting that Spielberg himself has emphasized the importance of narrative, not least in terms of its commercial appeal. 'You need good story-telling to offset the amount of … spectacle the audiences demand before they'll leave their television sets. And I think people will leave their television sets for a good story before anything else. Before fire and skyscrapers and floods, plane crashes, laser fire and spaceships, they want good stories.' In addition, Peter Biskind has argued that both Spielberg and Lucas initially set out to re-establish traditional – causal and linear – narrative values in the New Hollywood context in which they found themselves.

Biskind himself goes on to suggest that their attempts backfired, because they each tended to over-emphasize the plastic, formal and sensual qualities of sound and image. The 'attempt to restore traditional narration had an unintended effect – the creation of spectacle that annihilated story. The attempt to escape television by creating outsized spectacle backfired, and led to television's presentational aesthetic.' Whatever the merits of Biskind's argument, it is clear that Spielberg was – and is – committed to narrative. It is also clear that *Raiders* itself tells a story, a story which is structured according to the principles of the serial format that operated in B-movie adventure films in the 1930s and 1940s – a style or mode of storytelling suppressed or dismissed as marginal in most accounts of 'classical' Hollywood narrative.

(Buckland 1995: 169–171)

Narrative codes are also the focus in the next example which is taken from an unpublished undergraduate dissertation on 'Traditional Narrative and the Children's Film'. The author, Bree Wilkinson, is interested in the ideological implications of the domination of children's films of a certain kind of traditional linear narrative structure. She sets about this task by contrasting Disney's *The Lion King* (Hamlet with lions) and *Jumanji*, which she argues adopts a postmodernist approach (see pages 246–252) to narrative. Again the detailed analysis of text is the foundation of a broader critical argument. It is almost as if we are eavesdropping on the very thoughts of the 'reader' as she is watching the film and testing her conclusions.

Having established that the linear narrative is the preferred model of narrative in films for children, backed up by detailed reference to the Disney feature, Wilkinson strikes out alone. She suggests that, though they are few and far between, there are films which challenge this 'normality' (a Marxist might prefer 'hegemony'). The writing on *Jumanji* which follows is genuinely exploratory, as if *Jumanji* is being revealed and understood for the first time. In clarifying the non-linear nature of the narrative, Wilkinson unavoidably arrives at the ideological nature of all narratives (which are, after all, purposeful sequencings of material). It is the very randomness explicit in the title ('Jumanji' is a dice-led board game) that undermines the predictability and 'authority' of the traditional linear narrative.

They begin to play the game and explore the alternative paths through which a narrative can be constructed and by which it can deliver meaning. As they play they have to face the elements and fears thrown at them by the game, which are on closer inspection merely the manifestations of 'Blind Chance', an aggressively alternative worldview. These include a safari stampede, an infestation of African spiders and a monsoon: 'nature raw in tooth and claw'. The image of Africa that the game creates is that of an inhospitable African jungle which is full of dangerous elements. It has an objectivity that sits alongside its apparent symbolism as if as a challenge to the comfortable 'jungle' and wildlife of *The Lion King*. The film stays away from racist stereotype by not using an image of a black savage hunter. Instead the film opts for a big game hunter, decked out in pith helmet and cream fatigues, Van Pelt (Wilson 1996: 144).

Van Pelt represents another world order, a dominant ideological position that is implicitly challenged by the chaos which surrounds him. He clarifies the relationship between the film's special characters and the game and what it specifically unleashes. In contrast to stampeding zebra and elephant is the purposeful hunter intent on shooting Alan, which surely is a terrible image of what Barthes called 'anchorage', a meaning-fixing device. This is about the evil that men do, in the context of a nature that is allowed its own dispensations, and not one that is subjected to some Judaeo-Christian ideological project. Once the game is open it is not the game but the premise of the game that must be resolved: chance is as chance does. The myth of Africa is therefore only yet another ideological issue, another imposition on a fast receding reality.

This is where the film reinforces the relationship Alan had with his father, since Van Pelt and Alan's father are played by the same actor. Here the alternative and psychological reality is made apparent. Even though Alan was sucked into the board game, his relationship problems with his father continued in the game, through Van Pelt acting as a father figure. The fact that Van Pelt,

this father figure, is stalking this jungle is at once powerful and ironic, even paradoxical. Of course Alan is addressing his relationship with his father, but this is only the first level of what is a wider and deeper ideological discussion. If texts behave like parents we must still learn to think for ourselves. These constructed elements of the game ruin this pleasant American town because that is the ideological point: the town is a construct as well and fragile in the face of reality. The final repercussions of the game are presented in the form of an earthquake, as in every sense the ground is taken away not only from under their but also our feet. What is shaken is ideological bedrock. As the Parrish house is split down the middle (even we as an audience baulk at the destruction), Alan has the chance to finish the game. However, he finds himself appropriately in a predicament when Van Pelt catches him. Van Pelt instructs Alan to drop whatever he has in his hand, the die, so Alan does. As he does this, the camera follows the die that falls into the deep crack caused by the earthquake, revealing the number on the die; the number Alan needs to finish the game. This is yet another facet of the chance code: literally anything can happen including what we would wish to happen. As this occurs the game begins to suck everything back in that it had thrown at the four characters. A whirlwind of flying elephants, monkeys, spiders and Van Pelt plummet into the centre of the game. He is destroyed by his own logic; he has unwittingly helped Alan to find an answer. Of course the answer is that there is none, the die will roll and continue to do so. As this whirlwind comes to an end and Alan and Sarah are seen to be hugging, the narrative returns to 1969 where they continue to hug but are back in Alan's home as it was previously. There is no Peter and Judy, and Alan and Sarah are both children again, but with the knowledge of what has just happened. Has it all been a dream? It seems a blur between reality and fantasy. Alan and Sarah throw the game into the river and presumably this will be the end of the narrative and they will live happily ever after, if we haven't understood the story.

The narrative jumps forward again to 1995, where Alan and Sarah are happily married and live in Alan's house. History has been changed as Alan did not disappear, and he took over his father's business, another reference to the son's transcendence of the father. At a Christmas party the doorbell rings and Alan's new employee arrives with his wife and family. It turns out to be Peter and Judy's parents, accompanied by Peter and Judy who have no recollection about the part they played in Alan and Sarah's future. The future is changed again as Judy and Peter's parents suggest a skiing trip. Alan and Sarah oppose this, as they know that if Peter and Judy's parents go they will be killed in a car crash. This enables Alan and Sarah to play some part in Peter and Judy's future and in some weird sense return the favour that was never knowingly carried out, if it was carried out at all.

(Wilkinson 2004)

Although there is a real sense of engagement which inevitably persuades you that *Jumanji* is worth a second look (or even a first look), Wilkinson's writing is properly academic. Most significantly this means that it has the time and space to properly explore its themes without recourse to a specific audience (beyond an examiner). This is, in many ways, an ideal context in which to write about films but it is not typical of the way in which most film texts are addressed. As Susan Sontag pointed out earlier, film's special position as an art form is partly explained by the fact that films 'for such a long time were just movies, in other words, they were understood to be part of mass as opposed to high culture'.

As an increasingly important part of mass culture, films need to be addressed and evaluated at a number of levels. The first of these, the standard film review in a newspaper, magazine, on television, radio or even online, offers us the most popular definition of 'film criticism' and the role of the 'film critic'. Whereas most academic work on films deals with films long after their release, most film reviews are immediate, and time and space dictated. This kind of film criticism gives a film's potential audience a chance to be forewarned about its character and quality. Hundreds and thousands of these reviews appear each day and constitute an unavoidable and important film resource. These 'textual analyses' are essentially 'macro' readings which place the film in a context that is most often defined by genre, star, auteur and narrative. It is also a 'format' which observes and addresses the 'themes' of this chapter directly: offering personal, informed, professional and forthright opinions on the widest range of films from *Three Colours: Blue* to *Dude, Where's my Car?* It is not the easiest resource to use as a film student since, beyond the 'authority' of reputation and context, it is often difficult to deal with the sheer volume of material with discretion and discrimination. One way to sift this mountain of material is to recognise that different reviews and reviewers have different kinds of agenda. Put simply they derive from different kinds of relationship between the critic and the work. Three common versions are listed and exemplified below, which probably cover 90 per cent of all reviews. We have labelled them:

- The appreciation
- The demolition
- The evaluation

The 'appreciation' is a review in which the critic attempts to support the work of the film-maker(s), often by 'seeing' the film as it was intended (so far as this can be known). Some critics will champion the work of particular film-makers in order to encourage certain kinds of film-making. A good example is Roger Ebert's review of Fernando Meirelles' *City of God*. Here the writing carefully seeks a language to express Mirelles' vision, which Ebert devastatingly suggests 'feels like sight itself'. Ebert offers the film in 970 words, including a detailed rendering of the opening sequence, and always remains on the film's side of things. It concludes with a statement that is as true as a description of the review as it is of the film: *City of God*, Ebert writes 'simply looks, with a passionately knowing eye, at what it knows'.

City of God churns with furious energy as it plunges into the story of the slum gangs of Rio de Janeiro. Breathtaking and terrifying, urgently involved with its characters, it announces a new director of great gifts and passions: Fernando Meirelles. Remember the name. The film has been compared with Scorsese's *GoodFellas*, and it deserves the comparison. Scorsese's film began with a narrator who said that for as long as he could remember he wanted to be a gangster. The narrator of this film seems to have had no other choice.

The movie takes place in slums constructed by Rio to isolate the poor people from the city center. They have grown into places teeming with life, color, music and excitement – and also with danger, for the law is absent and violent gangs rule the streets. In the virtuoso sequence opening the picture, a gang is holding a picnic for its members when a chicken escapes. Among those chasing it is Rocket (Alexandre Rodrigues), the narrator. He suddenly finds himself between two armed lines: the gang on one side, the cops on the other.

As the camera whirls around him, the background changes and Rocket shrinks from a teenager into a small boy, playing soccer in a housing development outside Rio. To understand his story, he says, we have to go back to the beginning, when he and his friends formed the Tender Trio and began their lives of what some would call crime and others would call survival.

The technique of that shot – the whirling camera, the flashback, the change in colors from the dark brightness of the slum to the dusty sunny browns of the soccer field – alerts us to a movie that is visually alive and inventive as few films are.

Meirelles began as a director of TV commercials, which gave him a command of technique – and, he says, trained him to work quickly, to size up a shot and get it, and move on. Working with the cinematographer Cesar Charlone, he uses quick-cutting and a mobile, hand-held camera to tell his story with the haste and detail it deserves. Sometimes those devices can create a film that is merely busy, but *City of God* feels like sight itself, as we look here and then there, with danger or opportunity everywhere.

The gangs have money and guns because they sell drugs and commit robberies. But they are not very rich because their activities are limited to the City of God, where no one has much money. In an early crime, we see the stickup of a truck carrying cans of propane gas, which the crooks sell to homeowners. Later there is a raid on a bordello, where the customers are deprived of their wallets. (In a flashback, we see that raid a second time, and understand in a chilling moment why there were dead bodies at a site where there was not supposed to be any killing.)

As Rocket narrates the lore of the district he knows so well, we understand that poverty has undermined all social structures in the City of God, including the family. The gangs provide structure and status. Because the gang death rate is so high, even the leaders tend to be surprisingly young, and life has no value except when you are taking it. There is an astonishing sequence when a victorious gang leader is killed in a way he least expects, by the last person he would have expected, and we see that essentially he has been killed not by a person but by the culture of crime.

Yet the film is not all grim and violent. Rocket also captures some of the Dickensian flavor of the City of God, where a riot of life provides ready-made characters with nicknames, personas and trademarks. Some like Benny (Phelipe Haagensen) are so charismatic they almost seem to transcend the usual rules. Others, like Knockout Ned and Lil Ze, grow from kids into fearsome leaders, their words enforced by death. The movie is based on a novel by Paulo Lins, who grew up in the City of God, somehow escaped it, and spent eight years writing his book. A note at the end says it is partly based on the life of Wilson Rodriguez, a Brazilian photographer. We watch as Rocket obtains a (stolen) camera that he treasures and takes pictures from his privileged position as a kid on the streets. He gets a job as an assistant on a newspaper delivery truck, asks a photographer to develop his film, and is startled to see his portrait of an armed gang leader on the front page of the paper.

'This is my death sentence,' he thinks, but no: The gangs are delighted by the publicity and pose for him with their guns and girls. And during a vicious gang war, he is able to photograph the cops killing a gangster – a murder they plan to pass off as gang-related. That these events throb with immediate truth is indicated by the fact that Luiz Inacio Lula da Silva, the newly elected president of Brazil, actually reviewed and praised 'City of God' as a needful call for change.

In its actual level of violence, *City of God* is less extreme than Scorsese's *Gangs of New York*, but the two films have certain parallels. In both films, there are really two cities: the city of the employed and secure, who are served by law and municipal services, and the city of the castaways, whose alliances are born of opportunity and desperation. Those who live beneath rarely have their stories told.

City of God does not exploit or condescend, does not pump up its stories for contrived effect, does not contain silly and reassuring romantic sidebars, but simply looks, with a passionately knowing eye, at what it knows.

(Ebert, review of *City of God*)

In the appreciation, to some extent, the critic tends to disappear and the film is allowed to take over. However, as film criticism itself is part of the entertainment industry, there is bound to be a market for the clever put-down, and the bigger the star or film-maker the harder the fall: veteran *New York Times* critic Vincent Canby famously dismissed

Michael Cimino's *Heaven's Gate* as 'an unqualified disaster', comparing it to 'a forced four-hour walking tour of one's own living room'. The 'demolition' is a sometimes harrowing, systematic attack on something that cannot fight back, save perhaps at the box-office. To appreciate this distinctive mode of address, why not 'taste' Mark Kermode's review of *The Exorcist 3* from *Sight and Sound*, with the knowledge that Kermode considers William Friedkin's original, *The Exorcist*, to be one of the best films ever made.

As recurrent nightmares go, the production story of this imbecilic, ill-advised *Exorcist* cash-in is hellish indeed. Smelling a profit in the wake of a successful re-release of *The Exorcist*, franchise-holders Morgan Creek commissioned numerous drafts of a dopey script addressing Father Merrin's first encounter with the demon Pazuzu in Africa, an episode touched upon in William Peter Blatty's source novel which had already been plundered in the dismal 1977 sequel *Exorcist II The Heretic*.

From the outset the omens were bad. First, scheduled director John Frankenheimer fell terminally ill, delaying production and causing leading man Liam Neeson to drop out. Next, independent spirit Paul Schrader was signed on to direct a movie, but his version dismayed executives at Morgan Creek who deemed it too low on shocks to be salvageable. Thus, having started again with a new script, new cast and new director, *Exorcist The Beginning* finally reached our screens under the helmsmanship of action-hack Renny Harlin looking even more awful than this farcical backstory would suggest.

Harlin's hamfisted horror-show offers an hour and a half of tooth-grinding boredom followed by 20 minutes of all-singing, all-dancing, knees-up stupidity involving supernatural wrestling, CGI spiderwalking and the kind of drop-your-popcorn demonic dialogue ('Don't you want to stick your rotten cock up my juicy ass?') not heard since *Showgirls*. If only the *Exorcist*-spoof *Repossessed* (1990) had been half as funny.

According to Harlin, he approached *Exorcist The Beginning* with the intention of mirroring the tone of William Friedkin's original so that 'if you watch this film and then watch *The Exorcist*, the original naturally follows, as if it were a sequel'. This is, of course, nonsense. The only stylistic debt that this debacle owes to its predecessor is in the numerous clumsy 'quotes' (verbal and visual) which litter the screen: from the hammering of market metal-workers and the drooling of asylum inmates which mimic early shots from Friedkin's original through the cheesy facial appliances which fail to replicate the organic horror of Dick Smith's possession make-up to the final shot in which Stellan Skarsgård dons hat and bag to mimic the iconic image of Father Merrin arriving on Prospect Street.

(Kermode 2004: accessed at www.bfi.org.uk)

It may seem obvious to locate the 'evaluation' somewhere between 'appreciation' and 'demolition', but there is slightly more to it than that. The 'evaluation' offers a model which demands balance and appears on the surface to be both rational and scholarly. However, the expectation that all work has strengths and weaknesses creates its own problems. Partly this redefines the role of the reviewer, implying a kind of 'authority' or 'judgement' independent of the power or otherwise of the response. This crucial shift of emphasis radically alters the role of the critic. The temptation to which we too often succumb is the desire to assess, to award grades rather than experience, explore and respond. We forget that it is not our assessment of films that is important but rather our accounts of them.

The need to find the pros and cons of any film imposes its own limitations and has its own implications. A simple impact is on how much space/time is left to talk about the specific film under scrutiny. Peter Brunette's assessment of Ken Loach's *Sweet Sixteen* is by no means extreme or ineffective but it does feel the need to take Loach to task at either end of an often engaged and engaging reading of the film. Initially he is accusing Loach of building 'the same pre-formed moral into his films', which he claims leads to a 'clash with Loach's simultaneous all-out effort to present real life directly, in all its rawness and unpredictability'. However, these 'problems' are soon forgotten when Brunette begins to write about the film:

> As always in a Loach film, however, what redeems the grim scenario recounted above is the abundant laughs that the director always manages to find in his working-class heroes cleverly ripping off the system. (A quality that **Mike Leigh**'s '**All or Nothing**,' also in the competition here, needs desperately.) Liam and Pinball, both 15, are a delight as they brilliantly perpetrate one gutsy, outrageous scam after another, for example, when they invent a way to speed up their heroin deliveries by enlisting the aid of their pizza-delivering buddies. Or just little hilarious things like air-conducting an opera on the radio of a Mercedes they've just stolen, great little gags that pop up every few minutes. Incarnated convincingly by first-time actors, these spunky figures remind us of the glories of the supremely natural Italian neo-realism in the late 1940s, yet also a whole lot funnier. Martin Compston, who's a natural, is particularly charismatic in the role of Liam and has, I think, a fine career ahead of him.
>
> A further mark of the film's authenticity is the ostentatiously impenetrable Glaswegian dialect that these Scottish characters speak. Wisely, Loach has decided – as he has in some previous films – to provide English subtitles as well as French, since even native Englishmen I talked to said they couldn't understand the dialogue otherwise. It goes without saying, of course, that every inch of the grimy locations is truthful to the Nth degree.
>
> The only real problem with the film, in addition to the sense of a prescribed moral mentioned earlier (which is easily enough forgiven in the face of the

THEMES OF TEXTUAL ANALYSIS

film's inventiveness), is that Loach and screenwriter **Paul Laverty** revert to some shameless melodrama to wrap things up. It's not that it's badly done, or embarrassingly unconvincing. It's just that whereas the rest of the film has seemed so open-ended, at least on the level of event (there's one particularly wonderful surprise regarding a gangland killing), at the end genre elements take over and we suddenly know exactly where we're headed. While in many ways a victim of his surroundings, Liam has been portrayed as a bold, natural leader willing to do whatever he needs to do to fulfil his dream, and thus the reversion to the inevitability of Greek tragedy seems misguided. But this is a minor fault, ultimately, in a movie that reflects so deeply, and so powerfully, on the savagery and innocence of youth.

(Peter Brunette, review of *Sweet Sixteen*)

Whereas, armed with your critical tools you will 'reflect "so deeply, and so powerfully, on the savagery and innocence of" film and films'.

▼ 10 THEORETICAL PERSPECTIVES

Film theory has nothing to do with film.

Roger Ebert

You are looking for theory to use, not theory that will use you.

Peter Barry

The opening extract of this chapter first appeared (in a longer version) in the *Los Angeles Times Magazine* as the cover story for 13 July 2003. Its banner headline attracts attention because of the almost absurd tension between the two sets of items presented here in parallel.

LIGHTS, CAMERA, ACTION. MARXISM, SEMIOTICS, NARRATOLOGY

In the red corner we have the vocabulary of film practice and in LA that immediately means Hollywood, mainstream, conventional. In the blue corner we have the discourse of film theory: alternative, European, obscure. Well, that's what author David Weddle would have you believe. It's the treatment he gives in his article (see edited highlights below) to his discovery, as a film graduate and writer on film himself, of the changes that have been made to Film Studies courses since he graduated in the 1970s (man). This confrontation is necessitated by his daughter's experiences as a contemporary film student beset, in his terms, by film theory. As such this piece is a clear polemic (it wants to be controversial), a biased (not in itself a bad thing) and partly anecdotal account but it does air many of the arguments for and against the use of theoretical perspectives in Film Studies as a discipline. The piece's subheading is the quirky '*Film school isn't what it used to be, one father discovers!*' This also gives a feeling of the register of the piece which is in part satirical and comic.

'How did you do on your final exam?' I asked my daughter.

Her shoulders slumped. 'I got a C.'

Alexis was a film studies major completing her last undergraduate year at UC Santa Barbara. I had paid more than $73,000 for her college education, and the most she could muster on her film theory class final was a C?

'It's not my fault,' she protested. 'You should have seen the questions. I couldn't understand them, and nobody else in the class could either. All of the kids around me got Cs and Ds.'

She insisted that she had studied hard, then offered: 'Here, read the test yourself and tell me if it makes any sense.'

CONTINUED

I took it from her, confidently. After all, I had graduated 25 years ago from USC with a bachelor's degree in cinema. I'd written a biography of movie director Sam Peckinpah, articles for *Variety*, *Film Comment*, *Sight & Sound*, and written and produced episodic television.

On the exam, I found the following, from an essay by film theorist Kristin Thompson:

> Neoformalism posits that viewers are active that they perform operations. Contrary to psychoanalytic criticism, I assume that film viewing is composed mostly of nonconscious, preconscious, and conscious activities. Indeed, we may define the viewer as a hypothetical entity who responds actively to cues within the film on the basis of automatic perceptual processes and on the basis of experience. Since historical contexts make the protocols of these responses inter-subjective, we may analyze films without resorting to subjectivity. . . . According to Bordwell, 'The organism constructs a perceptual judgment on the basis of nonconscious inferences.'

Then came the question itself:

'What kind of pressure would Metz's description of "the imaginary signifier" or Baudry's account of the subject in the apparatus put on the ontology and epistemology of film implicit in the above two statements?'

I looked up at my daughter. She smiled triumphantly. 'Welcome to film theory,' she chirped.

Alexis then plopped down two thick study guides. One was for the theory class, the other for her course in advanced film analysis. 'Tell me where I went wrong,' she said.

The prose was denser than a Kevlar flak jacket, full of such words as 'diegetic,' 'heterogeneity,' 'narratology,' 'narrativity,' 'symptomology,' 'scopophilia,' 'signifier,' 'syntagmatic,' 'synecdoche,' 'temporality.' I picked out two of them 'fabula' and 'syuzhet' and asked Alexis if she knew what they meant. 'They're the Russian Formalist terms for "story" and "plot,"' she replied.

'Well then, why don't they use "story" and "plot?"'

'We're not allowed to. If we do, they take points off our paper. We have to use "fabula" and "syuzhet."'

Forget for a moment that if Alexis were to use these terms on a Hollywood set, she'd be laughed off the lot. Alexis wants a career in film. She chose UC Santa Barbara because we couldn't afford USC and her grades weren't lustrous enough for UCLA. Film programs at those schools have hard-core theoreticians on their faculty, as do many other universities. Yet no other undergraduate film program in the country emphasizes film theory as much as UCSB, and the influence of those theoreticians is growing. We knew that much before Alexis enrolled. In hindsight, we had no idea what that truly meant for students.

Is there a hidden method to these film theorists' apparent madness? Or is film theory, as movie critic Roger Ebert said as I interviewed him weeks later, 'a cruel hoax for students, essentially the academic equivalent of a New Age cult, in which a new language has been invented that only the adept can communicate in'?

At USC cinema school a quarter-century ago, one of the most popular teachers was Drew Casper, a young, untenured professor with an unbridled love for movies. Casper didn't lecture, he performed: jumping on a chair to sing a song from the musical he was teaching, covering his blackboard with frenetic scrawls as he unleashed a torrent of background material on the filmmaker's life, the studio that produced the movie, and the social forces that influenced it.

Casper, and most other film studies professors at USC, approached film from a humanist perspective. He taught students to focus on the characters in the movies, the people who made the films, and the stories the movies told and what they revealed about the human condition, our society and the moment in history they dramatized.

Yes, students read theoretical essays and books. But they were about the nuts and bolts of moviemaking. Aristotle's 'Poetics' laid out the basic principles of dramatic writing. Sergei Eisenstein explained the intricate mechanics of montage editing, which used quick cutting to provoke visceral emotions from audiences. And André Bazin described how directors Orson Welles and William Wyler used a 'long-take' method of filming scenes that was the opposite of montage, the camera and actors moving poetically around one another in intricately choreographed shots.

By the '70s, film theory was spreading to the United States, and moving beyond simple politics. A kind of metaphysical inquiry into the nature of cinema was underway. Discussions about movie characters, plots and the human beings who created them were on the way to being replaced by theories such as semiotics, structuralism, post-structuralism, Marxism, psychoanalytics and neoformalism.

When I share the criticisms of film theory with UCSB staff, they look truly wounded, then quickly mount a vigorous defense.

'Film theory is philosophy, and people have made the same criticisms of philosophy for years,' Branigan says. 'They say, "What relevance does philosophy have to the real world? It's merely idle thought, personal feeling, pointless speculation." If we listened to them, we would do away with teaching and studying the works of Plato, Aristotle, Descartes, Kant, Wittgenstein and Sartre. Do we really want to do that? I think not.'

CONTINUED

Anna Everett, an associate professor who specializes in new media, says, 'It's galling for me to hear those kinds of charges when we expect our students to be able to grapple with complex ideas in math and science and a lot of them won't go on to use them. Math and science are part of our everyday lives. So why is it then illegitimate for us to ask students to be just as rigorous with something that has a much greater impact on an everyday basis?'

'Art, film and video games really do help to shape their ideas and experiences and their relationships. I think the critics are unfair. It's a way of thinking that doesn't really take into account what the university is about. We're not a trade school. We're trying to develop minds, to create a better world.'

(Weddle 2003)

David Weddle is a writer/producer for the television series *Battlestar Galactica* and has written for such television shows as *Star Trek: Deep Space Nine* and *The Twilight Zone*. He has also written for the following publications: *Sight and Sound, Film Comment, Variety*, the *Washington Post, Rolling Stone*, the *San Francisco Chronicle, San Jose Mercury News* and *L.A. Weekly* and is the author of '*If They move ... kill 'em!' The Life and Times of Sam Peckinpah.*

Beyond the obvious cynicism Weddle raises some important questions as well as facilitating the debate about the place of film theory within Film Studies as an academic subject. Put most simply, he is asking for a justification of film theory in terms of its usefulness, both vocationally and educationally. Of course in the account he gives, which partly takes its character from its journalistic context, he seems very clear what kind of film theory is not useful. At his most extreme that kind of film theory is 'any' kind of film theory. In this respect he is endorsed by leading movie critic Roger Ebert whose words open this chapter. Ebert's claim leads him to sum up film theory as 'a cruel hoax for students'.

However, we must not let ourselves be so easily taken in by this disingenuous argument. Arguing against specific theories, discrediting their validity or questioning their usefulness, is very different to arguing against theory per se. The latter is clearly a dead-end since formulating the idea that all theory is pointless is in itself a useful theory for the individual concerned. We can afford Weddle a certain amount of artistic licence but we cannot ignore the positive similarities between the attitudes of Weddle and his apparent opponents. He talks about 'one of the most popular teachers', 'Drew Casper':

Casper, and most other film studies professors at USC, approached film from a humanist perspective. He taught students to focus on the characters in the movies, the people who made the films, and the stories the movies told and what they revealed about the human condition, our society and the moment in history they dramatized.

At the end of the day Weddle's issue is not with theories, with what he and this chapter call 'perspectives'. Weddle's inkling is for a humanist, rather than a structuralist perspective. They are not equal but they are equally valid, and this chapter will hope to provide an illustrated introduction to some others, which might be labelled 'postmodernist, feminist, Marxist, postcolonial and psychoanalytical'. Even the approach the chapter is taking constitutes a theoretical position which is pluralist or relativist depending on how we relate these points of view to one another. All of these perspectives have something to say about the different meanings film and films might contain and embody, while paying more or less attention to such matters as gender, ethnicity, social class, age.

In many ways the real point of a collection such as this one, which purports to be an 'essential' resource, is to inform and energise these debates, to identify this 'multiplicity of factors' or at least to suggest where to look. All of the chapter headings to some degree describe 'perspectives', ways of looking at film and cinema which privilege one aspect over others, be that institution, or genre, or even audience (which in itself has many formal 'theories'). We do this in the implicit belief that these are valuable and useful ways of looking at film, that 'theorising' is an unavoidable human activity with significant benefits. Put very simply, theories are attempts to look at something which is complex and difficult to understand, and try to make it comprehensible, though sometimes, as Slater points out, they also 'suggest that something which had always seemed perfectly simple and straight-forward is actually complex'. In the long run both of these are desirable outcomes, which help to justify the investment of time you will need to make. The quotation from Peter Barry's 'Approaching Theory' which introduces this chapter is an excellent place to start: 'we are looking, in ... theory, for something we can use, not something which will use us'.

This is a timely warning and a response to Ebert's 'nothing to do with film' gibe. Whatever your personal position, being encouraged to see a text from a number of different angles is rarely a fruitless activity. It is also true to say that if the central question of Film Studies is 'What does film (or a film) mean?' the first and most intelligent answer is 'it depends'. On what it depends is very much the concern of this and any other film book but also in this case especially of the Part 3 headed 'Contexts'. It may be argued that films only have meaning specifically (in context) when one or more of the following 'contexts' is activated: financial, institutional, social, cultural, personal, aesthetic, ideological.

The influential Marxist critic Walter Benjamin argued as early as 1936 that film was 'the most powerful agent' of processes that 'lead to a tremendous shattering of tradition'. Benjamin's argument suggested that 'the technique of reproduction' undermines the 'traditional value' of the film as a work of art discretely and uniquely produced. For Benjamin this makes film as a medium uniquely free since it escapes the control exerted through the traditional arts and empowers rather than enthralls its audience. As James Monaco succinctly put it: 'not only is art available on a regular basis to large numbers of people, but it also meets observers on their home grounds, thereby reversing the traditional relationship between the work of art and its audience'. Monaco goes on to point out that this ability to be plural and infinitely reproducible must 'directly contradict romantic traditions of art and therefore invigorate and purify'. For Benjamin this invigoration and purification was to be both aesthetic and social (in fact Benjamin made no distinction between the two):

Its [film's] social significance, particularly in its most positive form, is inconceivable

THEORETICAL PERSPECTIVES

without its destructive cathartic aspect, that is, the liquidation of the traditional value of the cultural heritage.

Monaco dubs this film's 'revolutionary' existence and contrasts it sharply with the fact that 'the content is most often conservative'. It is a clash that works through much of the theory cited here, the collision of a radical, often optimistic, agenda and a radical, yet pessimistic, critique. However, it is interesting that the closer the arguments get to mainstream Hollywood cinema the more significantly the revolutionary essence of the medium is neutered or subverted by 'the dominant myths of the culture'. Moreover the optimism in Benjamin that film 'in its most positive form' would 'liquidate' traditional values seems to have been at least deferred. Instead, in a multi-media age, culture has imploded rather than being gloriously swept aside. This has left an insecurity and angst which is sometimes labelled 'the postmodern condition'.

POSTMODERNISM AND FILM

One of the architects of postmodernism, the French intellectual Jean-Lyotard, wrote about the 'postmodern condition' that 'we live in a cultural Disneyland where everything is parody and nothing is better or worse'. This does much to remind us of the flavour of much postmodernist thought and usefully acts as an antidote to the playful energy of some of the work described as 'postmodernist'. Both Lyotard and Baudrillard offer a largely pessimistic description and critique of contemporary life. There is a lot of potential in this critique but no real feeling that this potential will be anything but squandered. Postmodernism is a philosophy formulated for a new and changing world, a world transformed by technology and its attendant costs.

Film is central to these arguments since it is an intrinsic part of the 'explosion' of mass communication and its technologies, which in turn has caused the 'implosion' of the old cultural values, and in fact has resulted in a new cultural dispensation. Popular culture has become 'the' culture and its concern with appearance, with the 'virtual' rather than the 'real' world, has become a dominant theme. In what Raymond Williams called 'a dramatized society' (one where re-enactment has become a vital mode of address or rhythm) everything is 'up for grabs', even personal identity. In such a world, the postmodernists argue, there can be no explanations and so all of the 'old' explanations, such as Marxism and Feminism (see later in this chapter) are considered obsolete. These were dismissed with the almost pejorative term 'metanarrative', or big story, and the age of the big story was officially declared 'over' and with it the age of ideology.

In its place, postmodernism describes a world with the potential to be individually negotiated, a world of signs infinitely reforming and reclustering. It is a world which first of all recognises that the primary negotiation is with reality which is all too often indistinguishable from that 'hyperreality' (to borrow Baudrillard's term) created by our responses to it: our films, our television, our computer technology. Baudrillard also borrowed the term 'bricolage' ('do-it-yourself') to characterise the challenge of piecing together our own and implicitly to make us aware of the character of others' 'concoctions'.

As the great popular art form of the twentieth century and the one that moves us most significantly, and discretely, into a confrontation with reality (and realism: see Chapter

8), film is at the centre of these arguments. As a character in Pedro Almodóvar's film *Pepi, Luci, Bom* has it: 'Cinema has nothing to do with life. In the cinema everything is false.' Some films address these issues explicitly: Peter Weir's *The Truman Show* opens with a stage light falling from the sky. Others are implicitly negotiating with us through their use, for example, of genre (hybridity is a key postmodernist issue since it highlights genre as an aspect of film's artifice). As a result, the arguments of postmodernism tend to enter Film Studies in two quite different ways.

The first way is relatively superficial in the sense that it provides a critical vocabulary for describing films made over the past twenty years or so (most frequently this is a blanket designation: quirky films of all kinds are often labelled 'postmodernist'). More usefully it identifies themes, such as confusion over time, a style that is based on the techniques of bricolage and formal structures like the conscious undermining of the classical Hollywood narrative in order to find connections between a broad paradigm of films which might otherwise seem unconnected. In doing this it offers a perspective in which the organising principles, rather than being based on genre or personnel, are cultural and historical. Dominic Strinati in his *Introduction to Theories of Popular Culture* provides such a context:

Postmodernist arguments clearly concern the visual, and the most obvious films in which to look for signs of postmodernism are those which emphasise style, spectacle, special effects and images, at the expense of content, character, substance, narrative and social comment. Examples of this include films like *Dick Tracy* (1990) or *9½ Weeks* (1986). But to look only at those films which deliberately avoid realism and sell themselves on their surface qualities can obscure some of the other things which are going on in contemporary cinema. The films directed and produced by Steven Spielberg and his associates, such as the *Indiana Jones* (1981, 1984 and 1989) and *Back to the Future* series (1985, 1989 and 1990), equally display elements of postmodernism since their major points of reference, and the sources they most frequently invoke, are earlier forms of popular culture such as cartoons, 'B' feature science-fiction films, and the Saturday morning, movie-house, adventure series people of Spielberg's generation would have viewed in their youth. It is likewise argued that these films appear to stress spectacle and action through their use of sophisticated techniques and relentless pursuit sequences, rather than the complexities and nuances of clever plotting and character development. Sometimes it is suggested that the narrative demands of classical realism are being increasingly ignored by postmodern cinema. Moreover the *Back To The Future* series and other films like *Brazil* (1985) and *Blue Velvet* (1986) are said to be postmodern because of the way they are based on confusions over time and space. Others like *Who Framed Roger Rabbit?* (1988) can be seen to be postmodern because of their deliberate use of distinct (cultural and technical) genres: the cartoon strip and the detective story. Yet others like *Body Heat* (1981) can be claimed to be postmodern because they are parasitic on the cinema's past, recycling

– in this example – the crime thriller of the 1940s. They thus engage in a kind of 'retro-nostalgia'. Related to this are films which recycle themselves in a number of sequels once the magic box office formula has been discovered, like the *Rocky* (1976, 1979, 1982, 1985 and 1990) or *Rambo* (1982, 1985 and 1988) films and the many other repeats which could be mentioned. This tendency is argued to be postmodern partly because it ignores the demands of artistic originality and novelty associated with modernism. None the less, it is argued to be postmodern mainly because it goes no further than recycling the recent past, making films which are merely imitations of other films rather than reflections of social reality.

A frequently cited example of the postmodern film is *Blade Runner* (1982) (Harvey: 1989, chapter 18; Instrell: 1992). Amongst the more noticeable characteristics of this film (which is about Los Angeles in the early part of the twenty-first century), we can note how its architectural look, or production design, clearly mixes styles from different periods. The buildings which house the major corporation have lighting characteristic of contemporary skyscrapers but the overall look of ancient temples, while the 'street talk' consists of words and phrases taken from a whole range of distinct languages. These architectural and linguistic confusions can be said to contribute to an elusive sense of time since we appear to be in the past, the present and the future at the same time. It is a science fiction film which is not obviously futuristic in its design. This effect is accentuated in two ways. First, the 'non-human humans' in the film are not mechanical robots but 'replicants', almost perfect simulations of human beings. Second, the genre of the film is not clear. It has been defined as a science fiction film, but it is also a detective film. Its story unfolds as a detective story, the hero has many of the character traits we associate with the 'tough-guy' policeman or private investigator, and his voice-over, which relates the investigation, draws upon the idioms and tone of *film noir*.

(Strinati 1995: 229–231)

Here 'postmodern' is largely a reflection of the social, cultural and economic context in which these films were created. They are being used, in Strinati's version, as evidence of the postmodern as applied to a theory, a movement. It is also, less profoundly, a collection of issues, of techniques, the current 'vibe': less a philosophical, critical position, more the latest style ('stylish' is often a key qualifier for the films in this category). As a body of work gains the label so the label is confirmed and consolidated. The point is to know where to go after you have identified the 'postmodern' features: what does this mean for your understanding of the films themselves? Strinati was writing in the 1990s, since when the label has gained even greater purchase on films as diverse as *Momento*, *The Truman Show*, and even the James Cameron blockbuster *Titanic*, where 'spectacle', 'virtual reality' and 'hybridity' were very much the order of the day.

The other way in which postmodernism has proved influential is as a factor in the outlooks and intentions of significant film-makers. If you look at the work of Quentin Tarantino, for example, there is a much more obviously postmodernist agenda where hybridity and film allusion are used in an entirely conscious bricolage to create a reality that stands outside of the conventions of film realism. Postmodernists talk of the 'hyperreal' being constructed out of used or borrowed signs: Baudrillard uses the term 'simulacrum (plural: simulacra)' to suggest that these signs are essentially fake, representations of representations. A film such as *Kill Bill* exemplifies this, not as analysis but as technique. What we see in both of these films is something we have seen before somewhere, presented in a new combination, as if we are witnessing a new deal of old cards. However, on closer inspection there is one further 'trick': these are not old cards but carefully (lovingly) made reproductions (simulacra). This is also the case with someone like Baz Luhrman, whose modern myth-making is based on the conscious use of anachronism (bringing together elements from different historical periods without resolving the tensions between them). In *William Shakespeare's Romeo and Juliet* there is more than merely an updating of Shakespeare's classic text, there is a confrontation with it. Here is cultural implosion in action as the energy and technology of contemporary popular culture is seen to encompass rather than reactivate an ailing high culture (Shakespeare is included on our terms rather than those of traditional high culture). This process is extended in *Moulin Rouge* so that the very fabric of the film exposes its layers as bohemian Paris of the 1890s rocks to a contemporary pop music soundtrack, which is both diegetic and non-diegetic.

Here postmodernism is a matter less of style than of purpose which informs technique. This is not merely to make 'postmodernism' a film movement but rather to register that a number of international film-makers are understanding 'contemporary' in similar ways. One of these is the innovative Spanish director Pedro Almodóvar, whose work has delighted and astonished audiences in the English-speaking world. The concluding chapter of Mark Allinson's book-length study of his films, *A Spanish Labyrinth*, is headed 'Postmodernism, Performance and Parody' and addresses clearly his postmodernist credentials:

> Ever since its invention, the cinema has sought to exploit its photographic advantage over earlier representational arts, and Hollywood made (a particular kind of) realism its conventional goal. Other cinemas, particularly European, stress auteurist values such as aesthetics or irony. Almodóvar's independence from the conventions and constraints of mainstream Hollywood films is matched by his manifest distance from the often abstract, hermetic or even solipsistic tendencies of much of European film. Thus, the originality of Almodóvar's cinema lies in its hybridity; it takes much from the world of Hollywood movies, but maintains a more intellectual, European scepticism, a distance marked by irony and self-reflexiveness The free mixing of popular elements of mass culture such as Hollywood movies, advertising and television with the more artistic 'high culture' of auteurist, poetic cinemas

has earned Almodóvar the label of postmodernist. Certainly, a number of characteristics of contemporary culture, often described as postmodern, can be usefully applied to Almodóvar's cinema. The breaking down of orthodox frontiers between mass and high culture, the opening up of media to new social groups, the tendency towards performance, simulation and parody, the absence of so-called 'grand narratives' and the weakening of historicity, are the double-edged swords of postmodernism. Some lament the contamination of high culture with commodified pop/trash/kitsch, while others celebrate postmodernism's plurality and accessibility. The reflection and exploitation of these features of postmodernism in Almodóvar's films is, on balance though, to their benefit.

Almodóvar owes his career in part to opportunities opened up by a distinctly modern attitude to the production of culture. Unlike his predecessors who all came from the middle classes and attended film school, he acquired his own camera and began making films – spoof adverts – while working for the Spanish telephone company. His bricolage mode of production gave an eclectic quality to his films: pop culture, advertising, narrative, intertextuality, music and kitsch decor were mixed with a substantial ironic and self-reflexive distance usually equated with 'high' culture. From the beginning, Almodóvar turned the difficulties of producing his first film into playful self-reflexivity. Protagonist Pepi has a project for a film (to be shot on video, that most domestic of media), the story of Luci and Bom. As Pepi explains in the film, representation is all, to be natural is not sufficient. Almodóvar's documentation of his contemporary reality (making films) is very different from the life-documentary style of Warhol. Where the American pop artist set the camera running and told the protagonists *not* to act, for Almodóvar, acting is all; the story of Luci and Bom must be *represented*. Pepi tells them, 'It's not just a matter of standing in front of the camera. Not only do you have to be yourselves but you have to represent your characters and representation is always artificial'. And Pepi's justification for her film is also perfect for Almodóvar in his first full-length feature: 'At the end of the day it's only a game. If it doesn't come out right, there's no problem.' The concept of acting or performance colours much of Almodóvar's work.

Michel Benamou (1977) describes performance as 'the unifying mode of the postmodern' and Steven Connor (1996) affirms its importance in 'a culture that is so saturated with and fascinated by techniques of representation and reproduction, that it has become difficult for us to be sure where action ends and performance begins'. Almodóvar's work testifies to the performativity of human behaviour. To perform means to act, display certain skills, or even to dissimulate or pretend. The films are intrinsically performative in that they involve action simulated for the camera lens. Even where the action can be regarded as authentic, not simulated (as in the case of inserted performances which are merely recorded by the camera), the mode is still one of performativity, as actors (people who *do* things) know they have an audience. Almodóvar's characters are constantly dissimulating, taking on roles, false identities and shamelessly lying. Indeed, the very first action in Almodóvar's very first film is dissimulation: Pepi pretends not to be able to hear the policeman.

In true postmodern style, Almodóvar also shows how life itself becomes performance, how life imitates art. In *Matador*, the final death scene – set to music and with careful colour co-ordination – is a choreographed performance, though the spectators are Diego and María alone. The ending of *Women on the Verge* – expressed in the song 'Teatro' – is that Ivan (and, by extension, all men) are performers. And in the first scene of *Flower*, the 'doubleness' of performance is explicitly acknowledged in the video recording of a simulated hospital scene. While it is clear that some kind of representation is taking place, it is not until after the scene that we are aware of the purpose behind it: the training of doctors to break the news of a family member's death and gently broach the subject of donating organs. The doctors perform their roles with clichés from film and television. The nurse Manuela simulates a grieving mother, her performance clearly identified as such; she is at pains to distance herself from her role when the audience mistake her character's attitudes for her own.

[....]

The representation of identities (motherhood, gender) and other human activities as performance or simulation, invites the charge – levelled at postmodernism and at Almodóvar as a postmodern filmmaker – of depth-lessness, of what Baudrillard (1981) called 'simulacra', the copy without the original. Jameson's (1991) study of postmodernism critiques pastiche – defined as 'parody without a vocation [...] amputated of the satiric impulse' – for its cannibalization of dead styles, empty of any critical or satirical commentary. The same charge is brought against Almodóvar by critics who signal his 'irresponsible' pillaging of cultural traditions merely for their aesthetic qualities (Sanchez-Biosca 1989). The prominence of glossy images and design in the films certainly corresponds to more general trends in contemporary culture and its marketing. But, as Yarza (1999) points out, Almodóvar's recycling of cultural traditions is not only aesthetically motivated; there is a clear critical distance operating between the old and the new. I would go further: parody is Almodóvar's general mode of address. (And it features in every chapter of this book, almost on every page.) National identity, power and gender relations, sexuality, history, politics, cultural tradi-tions, visual and musical choices are all mediated by a questioning, parodic distance. From the 'general erections' contest conflating the democratic process with the television gameshow format in his first film, to the almost

CONTINUED

nostalgic recuperation of the movie theatre newsreel format (the NoDo) in his twelfth, Almodóvar subjects cultural forms to variously light or savage parody.

(Allinson 2001: 209–216)

Pedro Almodóvar: The International Movie Database calls him 'The most internationally acclaimed Spanish filmmaker since *Luis Buñuel*'. Films such as *Women on the Verge of a Nervous Breakdown* (1988) and *All About My Mother* (1999) have delivered both commercial and critical acclaim as well as considerably raising the profile of Spanish cinema.

THE END OF IDEOLOGY?

Whatever follows postmodernism is at one level bound to be a reaction since it is part of the contemporaneity of postmodernism that it cancels out everything that has gone before it, most especially ideology. If the age of ideology is over, then each of the alternative perspectives that follow betray themselves as 'metanarratives', big stories that no longer hold true, because each provides a variation on a theme and that theme is ideology. The general premise of each is that films contain within them evidence of the attitudes and values of the society and culture that produced them. Moreover, they betray the power relationships inherent in those societies whether they are based on social class or gender or ethnicity. Ideology constitutes the various codes through which this information is communicated.

The French Marxist Louis Althusser defined ideology most usefully as 'a system of representation'; in other words, as a set of prompts or conventions as to how the world is to be shown and understood. Ideology works through its invisibility; it convinces us that what it shows is 'natural', 'neutral' and 'objectively true', untainted by opinion, perspective or bias. As a photographic medium, film perhaps offers an unprecedented context in which ideology can prosper. Certainly classical Hollywood realism is seen by some as an essentially ideological deceit whereby 'looks like life' becomes a front for ideological manipulation. When the world is being represented so directly it is easy to see how our guards will often be down.

The perspectives that follow tend to be responses to this proliferation of ideology in theory and in practice. In other words, they are trying to warn us and then remedy each negative implication. What De Fleur warned of television, that it depicted 'social values' not 'social reality', seems in film terms to have progressed. In a film industry dominated by 'realism' it is more like 'social values' masquerading as 'social reality'.

PSYCHOANALYSIS, FEMINISM AND FILM

As critic Barbara Creed points out, 'Psychoanalysis and the cinema were born at the end of the nineteenth century. They share a common historical, social and cultural background.' The fact that psychoanalytical criticism is juxtaposed here with feminism is an almost inevitable result of the fact that psychoanalysis as a discipline was founded on a problematic (one might say controversial) take on gender. Sigmund Freud, who is generally accepted as the founding father of psychoanalysis, may have offered a revolutionary perspective on human behaviour and motivation but it was a perspective that was male-oriented, male-led and in every sense phallocentric. Both Freud and his follower and co-worker Carl Jung were interested in systematically addressing those elements of human experience which had hitherto (if Shakespeare is to be believed) been the province of 'poets, madmen and fools': the realm of imagination and the subconscious. In plumbing the unconscious mind, their work took them into issues of identity, repression and deviance (all, in their own right, powerful themes within Western art and film). Film certainly embraced these issues in all of its new and exciting ways, both experimentally and conventionally in terms of a developing narrative cinema (where getting to the bottom of a character's psyche was a common issue). Film also freely embraced both critically and structurally Freud's perhaps most controversial theory, that of the Oedipal nature of child sexuality. Here Freud borrowed his imagery from an ancient Greek text: *Oedipus Rex* by the classical dramatist Sophocles. Sophocles tells the story of a man who flees an awful prophecy that he will kill his father and 'marry' his mother only to unerringly end up in the city ruled by his natural parents (who had their child sent away for much the same reason). Inevitably he kills a man (his father) in a dispute on the highway and then comforts that man's widow to the point at which they marry. When all is finally revealed he brutally blinds himself in horror and shame.

Perhaps surprisingly Freud found in this arcane tale parallels with our experiences of growing up. Everyone, he claimed, goes through (acts out) a version of the Oedipal dilemma, negotiating with our father and mother figures in order to become balanced adults. Barbara Creed explains the implications of this for film narratives and film criticism very clearly:

> Sexuality becomes crucial during the child's Oedipus complex. Initially, the child exists in a two-way, or dyadic, relationship with the mother. But eventually, the child must leave the maternal haven and enter the domain of law and language. As a result of the appearance of a third figure – the father – in the child's life, the child gives up its love-desire for the mother. The dyadic relationship becomes triadic. This is the moment of the Oedipal crisis. The boy represses his feelings for the mother because he fears the father will punish him, possibly even castrate him – that is, make him like his mother, whom he now realizes is not phallic. Prior to this moment the boy imagined the mother was just like himself. On the understanding that one day he will inherit a woman of his own, the boy represses his desire for the mother. This is what Freud describes as the moment of 'primal repression'; it ushers in the formation of the unconscious.

> The girl gives up her love for the mother, not because she fears castration (she has nothing to lose) but because she blames the mother for not giving her a

penis-phallus. She realizes that only those who possess the phallus have power. Henceforth, she transfers her love to her father, and later to the man she will marry. But, as with the boy, her repressed desire can, at any time, surface, bringing with it a problematic relationship with the mother. The individual who is unable to come to terms with his or her proper gender role (activity for boys, passivity for girls) may become an hysteric; that is, repressed desires will manifest themselves as bodily or mental symptoms such as paralysis or amnesia. Alfred Hitchcock's *Psycho* (USA, 1960) and *Marnie* (USA, 1964) present powerful examples of what might happen to the boy and girl respectively if they fail to resolve the Oedipus complex.

Freud's theories were discussed most systematically in relation to the cinema after the post-structuralist revolution in theory during the 1970s. In particular, writers applied the Oedipal trajectory to the narrative structures of classical film texts. They pointed to the fact that all narratives appeared to exhibit an Oedipal trajectory; that is, the (male) hero was given a crisis in which he had to assert himself over a man (often a father figure) in order to achieve recognition and win the woman. In this way, film is seen to represent the workings of patriarchal ideology.

This is the point at which psychoanalytical criticism bumps into feminism, since it is unlikely that ideas such as 'penis-envy' and 'woman as castrated man' are unproblematic. Writing at the end of the nineteenth century Freud is writing from a significantly patriarchal context. By the 1970s there was pressure to challenge what was (and remains) the socially regressive 'institution' which is mainstream Hollywood film. If, as someone claimed, Heavy Metal music is largely about 'elves and shagging [sex]', then it is probably fair to say that most mainstream cinema is about 'fighting and shagging': Jean-Luc Godard suggested that all you need for a film is 'a girl and a gun' with ill-concealed irony. The point is that female characters tend in this limited world to be active only on the 'shagging' side of the equation (save in the exceptions that prove the rule, which is why every book on mainstream cinema has an obligatory still from *Thelma and Louise*). It is as if the major female contribution to mainstream film over the past fifty years is a mixture of the decorative, the erotic and the descriptive (whereby information is communicated about male characters via their relationships with female characters). Content analysis of mainstream films would have to concede the following:

- The main protagonists of most films are male: named male stars outnumber named female stars five to one.
- This male dominance becomes more marked the further down the credits you go.
- The list of directors on the Internet Movie Database is over 95 per cent male.
- While a significant number of films made feature unattached male protagonists, practically none feature female 'loners'.
- Films for and about women are a sub-genre (popularly referred to as 'chickflicks'), while films for and about men are mainstream.

Enter Laura Mulvey who in 1975 published what Creed calls 'a daring essay': Mulvey herself later admitted that it was 'deliberately and provocatively polemical' (controversial). In *Visual Pleasure and Narrative Cinema* Mulvey set about giving a systematic psychoanalytical analysis of mainstream cinema which placed gender very much at the centre of its exploration of film form, mode of address and spectatorship. Mulvey basically argues that in a society organised along gender lines, film will necessarily model gender inequalities. Hence the spectacle described above where the male star gets to 'act' and the female star (if one exists) is acted upon. Mulvey thus presented a situation in which the film female existed merely (though often powerfully) as passive image to be perceived and then rewarded or punished (prized or despised). This in turn fixes the modes of address and reception such that the pleasure we derive from watching films is also ideologically conditioned. In coining the useful critical term 'male gaze' Mulvey was seeking to stress the remarkable degree to which most films channelled the audience's response (male and female) through the male protagonist and thus indirectly to the female image. In simple terms (and Mulvey's work is deeply technical and psychological), the ways in which women are 'seen' and shown in films are not only determined by the ways in which men 'see' women but also organised so as to be pleasurable to the male spectator. This 'pleasure' is also addressed, Mulvey argues, within the film narrative by the male protagonist whose job it is to neutralise the 'threat' created by gender differences by either punishing the female leads (keeping them in their place) or by celebrating them as images (Mulvey talks about 'fetishising their physical characteristics: hair, breasts, legs etcetera'). Mulvey thus sees mainstream cinema as both male, and, as a consequence, voyeuristic and a mouthpiece for patriarchy (male dominance). By focusing on the issue of 'pleasure', she is stressing how central what she perceives as misogyny (woman-hating) is to mainstream cinema. In her own practice as a film-maker she attempted to address this directly by creating a 'counter-cinema' which was in this specific sense 'anti-pleasure'.

Mulvey's original essay makes very stimulating reading and is widely available in collections of key film readings. Mulvey herself has made at least two significant 'reclarifications' of her original thesis which tend to soften the line a little. A useful, critical survey of the issues and of Mulvey's contribution to the debate is provided by Matthew Henry in his essay 'The Eyes of Laura Mulvey':

THE EYES OF LAURA MULVEY: SUBJECTS, OBJECTS AND CINEMATIC PLEASURES

Matthew Henry

The universalization of subjectivity as maleness is without a doubt, and justifiably, the primary target of feminist theory and criticism.

D.N. Rodowick, 1991

The question of how film plays both to and upon socially established systems of desire, fantasy, and fear received one of its most significant treatments in Laura Mulvey's 'Visual Pleasure and Narrative Cinema.' Originally published in 1975, this essay has become one of the most important and influential in contemporary film studies and feminist theory. Mulvey's objective in the essay is clear: she wishes to place questions of sexual difference at the center

of the debate surrounding the application of psychoanalysis to film studies. Mulvey is concerned with exploring, through psychoanalysis, the representation of woman as image in film and the concomitant 'masculinization' of the spectator position. Her objective here is also quite polemical, as noted by Mulvey herself in the introduction: 'Psychoanalytic theory is ... appropriated here as a political weapon, demonstrating the way in which the unconscious of patriarchal society has structured film form' (14).

Mulvey begins from the premise that mainstream Hollywood cinema both reflects and reveals the psychological obsessions of the society that produces it. In arguing this, she draws heavily upon both Freudian and Lacanian forms of psychoanalysis. According to Mulvey, mainstream Hollywood film 'coded the erotic into the language of the dominant patriarchal order' (16). Mulvey implies that this coding is, in essence, the establishment of the 'male gaze.' Narrowly construed, the male gaze refers to the act of looking upon women as objects, of adopting the role of spectator; but metaphorically, it refers to a way of thinking about and acting within society (Devereaux 337). 'Visual Pleasure and Narrative Cinema,' and much of Mulvey's early work, organizes around questions of spectatorial identification and its relationship to the male gaze. In exploring these questions, she targets and examines the codes and mechanisms through which classic Hollywood cinema has traditionally exhibited sexual difference as a function of its narrative and representational forms. Mulvey also seeks to explore what effects these codes and mechanisms might have on spectators as sexed individuals and what their role might be within the general ideological structure of patriarchal culture. However, her project is not one of simply identifying and condemning 'sexist' representations of women on the screen: she is less concerned with textual analyses than with 'the definition of structures of identification and the mechanisms of pleasure and unpleasure that accompany them' (Rodowick 5).

In a section of "Visual Pleasure' entitled 'Woman as Image, Man as Bearer of the Look,' Mulvey succinctly states her organizing principle: 'In a world ordered by sexual imbalance, pleasure in looking has been split between active/male and passive/female' (19). Drawing upon terms found in Freud's 'Instincts and Their Vicissitudes,' Mulvey establishes a binary relationship between subject (spectator/protagonist) and object (narrative film/image) in which the subject is associated with the active/male position and the object with the passive/female position. Such an analysis of sexual difference is revealing and quite in keeping with Mulvey's feminist critique of patriarchal structures: since sexual differences in film function to produce pleasure, and this pleasure is produced for someone, whom Mulvey identifies as the male, then this production sustains a situation in which relations of social imbalance are maintained, both in the filmic representation and in the 'real' world outside the film (Rodowick 6).

Mulvey argues that the subject and object positions cited above are the product of point-of-view mechanisms in Hollywood cinema. Point-of-view mechanisms – such as the shot/counter-shot and the lingering close-up – function to reconfirm and reproduce set positions, both within and without the film, by avoiding avenues of unpleasure and seeking avenues of pleasure. For Mulvey, there are a number of possibilities for pleasure in the cinema, but she focuses primarily on only two, which divide for her quite neatly along gender lines. The first is what Freud calls 'scopophilia,' or the pleasure of looking at another person as an object. Mulvey argues that this is an active practice, and she describes it in largely Freudian terms: 'the position of the spectator in the cinema is blatantly one of repression of their exhibitionism and projection of the repressed desire onto the [female] performer' (17). The second pleasure Mulvey defines is that of narcissism, which for her is essentially passive and developed through identification with the object/image on the screen. Thus it is that scopophilia is inscribed as male (active) and narcissism as female (passive). The spectator's gaze is then male in two senses: from without, in its direction at women as objects or erotic desire, and from within, in its identification with the male protagonist. For Mulvey, ultimately, 'the meaning of woman in the cinema is sexual difference' (21), and her lack of a penis invariably connotes the threat of male castration. According to Mulvey, there are two avenues of escape for the spectatorial male unconscious: the demystification of the woman through devaluation or punishment, or the complete disavowal of castration through the substitution of a phallic fetish object (21).

The only escape allowed for the female in Mulvey's schema is through an avant-garde form of film that breaks completely with the Hollywood traditions. In the introduction to *Visual and Other Pleasures*, Mulvey speaks to this in reminiscing upon her active involvement with the Women's Movement during the 1970s and the origins of 'Visual Pleasure and Narrative Cinema': she argues here for the need of film makers who could and would 'forge an alliance between the radical tradition of the avant-garde and the feminist politicisation of images and representation' (ix). This alternative was realized, and thus provided space for the female as subject, by Mulvey herself: she has, over the intervening years, co-directed a number of independently produced 'feminist' films.

The major critique lodged against Mulvey since the publication of 'Visual Pleasure and Narrative Cinema' is that she focuses only on the experience of a male spectator. While discussing at length the forms of male desire and identification, built on voyeuristic fantasies of the female body, Mulvey largely ignores speculating on the possibility of female desire, identification and spectatorship. According to the analysis provided in 'Visual Pleasure,' the filmic gaze, in terms of both gender representation and gender address, belongs exclusively to the male, to the patriarchy; this leaves the female spectator with little agency: she must either identify with the male as subject or with the female as object/image. If she does the former, the female spectator aligns herself with what Mulvey explicitly defines as voyeurism; if the latter, she aligns herself with narcissism and, implicitly, masochism.

Mulvey's rigidly gendered approach to cinematic pleasure has also been criticized for being taken as axiomatic by feminists and film theorists. Kaja Silverman, writing in 1984, emphasizes just how firmly the suppositions of a monolithic construction of sexual difference had taken hold less than a decade after the appearance of Mulvey's 'Visual Pleasure':

> It is by now axiomatic that the female subject is the object rather than the subject of the gaze in mainstream narrative cinema ... It is equally axiomatic that the female subject as she has been constructed by the Hollywood cinema is denied any active role in the discourse (131–32).

Since examples of such objectification were abundant, many feminists took Mulvey's observations as truisms regarding not only patriarchal Hollywood cinema but patriarchal American society itself. Thus the ingrained belief that spectatorial relationships were strictly binary oppositions.

Mulvey attempts to redress the perceived errors of 'Visual Pleasure' in the essay 'Afterthoughts on "Visual Pleasure and Narrative Cinema" Inspired by King Vidor's *Duel in the Sun*' (1981).

In this essay, Mulvey acknowledges the binary nature of her work in 'Visual Pleasure' and concedes that her exclusive focus on male spectatorship closed off avenues of inquiry pertaining to questions about 'the women in the audience' (29). Nevertheless, Mulvey's tack here is not to refute her earlier proposition – she says more than once that she 'stands by' what she has already said – but to refine it in light of her viewing *Duel in the Sun*, a film that purports to have a 'female hero.' In reading this film, Mulvey asserts

> ... the emotions of those women accepting 'masculinization' while watching action movies with a male hero are illuminated by the emotions of a heroine of a melodrama whose resistance to a 'correct' feminine position is the critical issue at stake (30).

While conceding that this dual context offers a 'sense of the difficulty of sexual difference in the cinema that is missing in the undifferentiated spectator of "Visual Pleasure,"' Mulvey maintains that the heroine of traditional cinema is unable to achieve a stable sexual identity and that her oscillation between masculine and feminine positions is 'echoed by the woman spectator's masculine point of view' (30). In short, the female spectator still has to adopt the male perspective, though this now derives from the 'grammar' of the film narrative and traditions which make trans-sex identification habitual and 'second nature' (32–33). This sentiment is also echoed in the more recent work of scholars sympathetic to Mulvey's early claims. Mary Devereaux, for example, distinguishes between sex, which she says is physical, and gender, which she sees as social, and concludes that 'the male gaze is not always male, but it is always male dominated' (339). This may be the case, but it then begs the question: is there a female gaze? And if so, what mechanisms structure it?

Though theories of the female gaze were offered shortly after the publication of Mulvey's 'Visual Pleasure' – Mary Ann Doane's influential essay on this topic appeared in 1982 – they remain rare and run into difficulties of conceptualization. One of the key problems is the basis of theories of desire and spectatorship in Freudian and Lacanian psychoanalysis. Recently, numerous critics have spoken to this problem. D.N. Rodowick, for example, calls the work of Freud into question by asking whether it can conceive of a position for femaleness outside the paradigm that universalizes subjectivity as male (19). Similarly, Jackie Byars critiques the work of Lacan for positing sexual identity as produced by language and, thereby, constructing woman as *not* man, as the Other (112). Byars also argues that feminist theorists mistakenly focused, a lá Mulvey, on an avant-garde film making for evidence of female power instead of on Hollywood film and network television, which had been dismissed as patriarchal (111). Byars asserts that female power exists within these forms, and to demonstrate this, she focuses on moments of the mutual gaze in two specific examples: the film *Coma* and the television show *Cagney and Lacey*.

I think Byars makes a cogent argument for a reassessment of traditional film and television, but her thesis still contains a significant problem, one inherent in Mulvey's work and one that has only recently been given serious attention: the assumption of a singular male and/or female spectatorial experience. This issue is clearly addressed by Deidre Pribram in the introduction to her book *Female Spectators: Looking at Film and Television*. Pribram states that while both Freudian and Lacanian psychoanalytic practices have succeeded in recognizing gender as a primary factor in subject formation and social division, they have failed to address the formation and operation of other variables, such as age, class, and race (2). D.N. Rodowick echoes Pribram's ideas: he declares that the phallocentric and patriarchal model of the ideological function of classic cinema is totalizing, hegemonic, and allows no room for 'historical variability.' The variabilities he notes are the same as those identified by Pribram with the addition of one other: sexual orientation. Rodowick thus critiques Mulvey's original binary schema as follows: 'neither a historical experience of race, class, nationality, nor deviant sexuality … will alter an experience of texts that only the sexed body can identify' (44). Though Mulvey does address the concept of the female spectator in 'Afterthoughts,' her argument remains flawed by its acceptance of *the* female experience, of the singular shared response. Implicit in her essay is the idea that the experience of a white,

middle-class, heterosexual, American woman represents the experience of all women. In similar fashion, Rodowick also criticizes early notions of the female spectator, such as those developed by Mary Ann Doane: What one gains by positing the singular specificity of 'feminine' experience is achieved only at the cost of glossing over the variegate possibilities of hetero- and homosexual identities and pleasures, not to mention the multiple dimensions of subjectivity defined by class, race, and nationality (45).

Obviously there is much concern in recent film theory with defining and redefining the female spectator in terms of variables such as age, race, and class. Mulvey is, as we have seen, guilty of the 'glossing over' that Rodowick speaks of, and she has thus been roundly criticized for it. But it seems to me that this last issue raised by Rodowick – the issue of sexual orientation or preference – is of great significance to the concept of spectatorship in general and in need of further exploration. This exploration would begin with a redefinition of the role of the male spectator. In 'Visual Pleasure,' Mulvey hints at the issue of male homoerotic pleasure but dismisses it, arguing that 'man is reluctant to gaze at his exhibitionist like' (20). This, of course, stands as a corollary to Mulvey's comments on female spectators: it too assumes that one man views for all men, and it blatantly disregards the issues of sexual preference raised by Rodowick. Moreover, Mulvey's insistence upon the heterosexual male gaze denies the possible functioning of man as erotic object. This, like Mulvey's insistence that the female spectator is forced to accept some uniform 'male' position, is unnecessarily limiting. It seems to me, then, that what is needed is a theory of spectatorship that will simultaneously examine both the male and the female experience, not one in the absence of the other; a theory that will add to its assessment of viewing pleasure and unpleasure, in terms both male and female, the influence of variable such as age, race, class, and – perhaps most importantly, since it has been so greatly lacking – sexual orientation.

WORKS CONSULTED

Byars, Jackie. 'Gazes/Voices/Power: Expanding Psychoanalysis for Feminist Film and Television Theory.' In Pribram 110–29.

Devereaux, Mary. 'Oppressive Texts, Resisting Readers and the Gendered Spectator: The New Aesthetics.' *Journal of Art and Art Criticism* 48.4 (1990): 337–47.

Doane, Mary Ann. 'Film and the Masquerade: Theorizing the Female Spectator.' *Screen* 23.3/4 (1982): 74–85.

Mulvey, Laura. 'Visual Pleasure and Narrative Cinema.' *Screen* 16.3 (1975): 6–18. Rpt. In *Visual and Other Pleasures*. Bloomington: Indiana UP, 1989. 14–27.

——. 'Afterthoughts on "Visual Pleasure and Narrative Cinema" Inspired by King Vidor's *Duel in the Sun.' Framework* 15/16/17 (1981). Rpt. in *Visual and Other Pleasures*. 29–38.

Pribram, E. Deidre. *Female Spectators: Looking at Film and Television*. London: Verso, 1988.

Putnam, Ann. 'The Bearer of the Gaze in Ridley Scott's *Thelma and Louise.' Western American Literature* 27.4 (1993): 291–302.

Rodowick, D.N. *The Difficulty of Difference: Psychoanalysis, Sexual Difference & Film Theory*. New York: Routledge, 1991.

Silverman, Kaja. 'Dis-embodying the Female Voice.' *Re-vision: Essays in Feminist Film Criticism*. Eds. Mary Ann Doane, et. al. Frederick, Maryland: University Publications of America, 1984. 131–49.

(Henry, *The Eyes of Laura Mulvey*, accessed at http://www.rlc.dcccd.edu/annex/ comm./english/mah8420/Eyes of Laura Mulvey)

Henry, while acknowledging the central position Mulvey has played in this debate, is also keen to show the ways in which she has been superseded, to underline the current sites of debate. His critique of Mulvey briefly states:

- She focuses only on the experience of a male spectator (ignoring 'the possibility of female desire, identification and spectatorship').
- She reduces the relationship between subject (spectator/protagonist[hero]) and object (Image/story) to the simple binary opposition of male/active and female/passive.
- She ignores examples of female power which exist within the mainstream structure.
- She ignores other variables such as age, social class, sexual orientation and ethnicity: 'implicit in her essay is the idea that the experience of a white, middle-class heterosexual American woman represents the experience of all women'.

POSTCOLONIALISM AND FILM

Some similar issues arise when the argument moves to the representation of other potentially disempowered groups within the context of American and European cinema. Some critics define these issues in terms of postcolonialism, which as the title suggests sees ethnicity as being defined essentially by historical relationships, by a colonial past. They see culture, with film as a key component, as a place where the old colonial 'differences' are still influential. This may mean, for example, that African cinema is categorised in specific ways as outside the mainstream ('authentic' and 'energetic' may be the words used) and as a result is treated as a special case, which at its worst leaves the films as cultural rather than expressive artefacts, anthropology rather than art. Here difference is not being addressed; it is being accepted, in a coded way, as a signifier of non-specific value (as if the very fact of a sub-Saharan cinema is in itself an event). The very fact that 'African Cinema' operates as a category on the same level as European national cinemas confirms an unbalanced perspective.

Even Bollywood is not immune to this 'essentialist' treatment, though there is an extra tension when the picture is muddied by massive commercial success, mass production and the spectre of popular culture. The marginalising of 'World Cinema', as postcolonialists would see it, is more conventionally dependent on its presumed, if primitive, artistic merit and cultural distance and 'colour'. The recent emergence of Bollywood film into the European and even American mainstream via both the greater general release of Hindi films and a series of 'cross-over' successes (e.g. *Bend It Like Beckham* and *Bride and Prejudice*) has asked significant questions about non-European (and American) film.

INFOBOX

ESSENTIALISM

Diana Fuss says that essentialism:

is most commonly understood as a belief in the real, true essence of things, the invariable and fixed properties which define the 'whatness' of a given entity. ... Importantly, essentialism is typically defined in opposition to difference. (Fuss 1989: xi–xii)

In a specifically postcolonial context, we find essentialism in the reduction of the indigenous people to an 'essential' idea of what it means to be African/Indian/Arabic, thus simplifying the task of colonisation.

Postcolonial theorists see these simplifications as evidence of the unresolved implications of colonisation and colonialism (the first the act, the second the justifying theory). The status of, for example, Asian and African cinemas has profound implications for the identities of those living in the multicultural and multiethnic societies of contemporary Europe.

In a Britain that still feels a need for a 'Black History' month, there is clearly some way to go. For Black and Asian film-makers working in Britain the following essay by Olivier Barlet on the questions postcolonial theory is asking of French cinema will probably be all too familiar. Barlet's piece is subtitled 'From Difference to Relationships' which describes perfectly the journey we are all trying to make.

POSTCOLONIALISM AND CINEMA: FROM DIFFERENCE TO RELATIONSHIPS

By Olivier Barlet

Postcolonialism in film theory still only rarely tackles the question of difference head on. And yet, it is thus that it could encourage Western critical discourse at last to focus on something other than reducing the Other to his/her difference, to accept questioning its own view of the Other. The question is essential in the French context.

There can be no ethnology possible 'other than that which studies the anthropophagous behaviour of the white man'.

Stanislas Adotevi, Négritudes et nécrologues, UGE 10/18 1972, p. 182.

The concept of difference marks the sphere of French critical thought to such an extent that it is, no doubt, useful to summarize the situation:

– The complex relation between France and Africa is evolving. The films made by filmmakers of African origin reflect and/or herald these evolutions and ruptures. New styles and new aesthetics are emerging. This is especially so amongst the filmmakers living in France, who, in general, are born after Independence, are often mixed-race, and who always articulate – once they have moved beyond the ideological schemas of their predecessors – a questioning of the concepts of authenticity and identity, in order to go beyond a simple African belonging, thereby challenging the communalistic, culturalist, or essentialist discourse, which places cultural values before the quality of the works themselves. These 'Afro-Europeans' – as they sometimes call themselves – urgently address both African social reality and the question of memory, but also examine the experience of Africans in the West, confronted as they are with the difficulty of living in a society which finds it hard to accept its multiculturalism.

– Faced with this difficulty related to the all-consuming universality of the dominant culture, anti-racism was lured into founding its combat on the defence of cultural differences, which became seen as absolute values. This ran the risk of limiting the Other to a place, a role, to mythical values. In order to break free from this, immigrants in France changed from demanding the 'right to difference' in the Eighties (with SOS-Racisme), to the 'right to indifference' the following decade. In the light of society's discriminations, then, they demanded the same rights as every 'Tom, Dick or Harry', to quite simply be left alone at a time when racist discourse became banalized (in a recent opinion poll, over 60% of French people declared themselves to be racist, which is not so much worrying because they are racist – we already knew that – but because they dare to admit it openly).

- This straight jacket of racist prejudice – be it provocative comments, or the choice of words and images, from the counter of the local bar to the most profound of media – poisons relations with Black people (and Arabs, but with their own specific projections). It plays on a constant contradiction. On the one hand, are the worrying, or even scary archetypes (fascinating for Judaeo-Christians, who are frustrated in their relation to the body by the repression of desire, conjugal norms, the social utility of behaviour): the animality of the Black, who is difficult to tame due to his/her proximity to nature (brutality, transgression of the sacred through anthropophagy, unbridled sexuality, etc). On the other hand, is the moral duty to 'civilize': paternalism towards this good savage, 'big-child', who, at heart, is crying out to be educated. The fundamental misunderstanding of French republican assimilationism thus consists of 'civilizing' whilst, at the same time, carefully keeping this Other subaltern, thereby reducing him/her to reductive stereotypes: naïve, primitive, contemplative, ingenuous, candid, inexperienced, and, thus, ultimately, intellectually limited. This contradiction is the basis of a relation to the Other which comprises projections in which difference serves as a foil for forging one's own identity, but which also offer an escape from the mundaneness of the daily routine.
- Film criticism is no exception, widely reiterating these prejudices. It replays the old tune introduced by the cubists with their 'art nègre' when, by appropriating it, they glorified it so as better to deny it, elevating it to the status of the work of art, and thereby confining it in their own aesthetic criteria: recognition and distancing, respect and being placed in a position of respect. At the end of the day, the quest for authenticity is still at the service of a fundamentally unauthentic relation, in which seduction is prioritized over understanding. 'To caricature the situation', Roland Louvel notes, 'the Africans can only produce beauty unintentionally, whereas Westerners reserve themselves the privilege of a disinterested aesthetic production'. Hence, by portraying the Other as exotic or folkloric, or, much more recently, accusing his/her creations of being old-fashioned or academic, we trap him/her in his/her difference, making sure that he/she stays there. A Republic which claims to be universalist, levelling and assimilationist, paradoxically considers part of its population – its former colonial subjects – as incapable of evolving and integrating the precepts of civilization. It would be interesting to draw a parallel with the mythical American *melting pot*...
- In the light of this, and anxious to escape the categories of authenticity, identity and a single origin, filmmakers of African origin often claim the undifferentiated status of 'filmmaker full stop', which, paradoxically, boils down to denying their specificity. Yet, the label 'African' remains their main selling point, in terms of distribution (paid, but often for want of being able to release their films on the movie circuit) in the specialized festivals, but

also for the financing of their films, as it gives access to funds to which the French filmmakers are not entitled (the Fonds Sud, Francophonie, Coopération, foundations, etc.). They thus play a tango that hedges the issue, between defending their African identity and their desire to be rid of it to avoid projections.

This desire to escape being trapped in one's difference is the source of new misunderstandings:

– the risk of non-differentiation, at a time when everybody is exploring his/her roots, his/her origins, in order to highlight the specificities which define his/her originality.
– the fantasy of a undifferentiated status, as if there were such a thing as a 'filmmaker full stop', devoid of cultural contingencies, and beyond the power relations of the post-colonial situation.

This desire is a reaction against restrictions and prejudices. In order to be free of them, the filmmakers tend to affirm that their specificity is precisely that they have none, defining it, rather, as in the process of becoming, a quest, a cultural going-between in constant mutation, a fluctuating hybridity between two cultures.

(Barlet, 'Postcolonialism and the cinema', accessed at http://www.africultures.com/anglais/articles_anglais/postcol_cine.htm)

Barlet takes a very positive view, claiming that 'postcolonial thought … re-poses the question of difference' and that those who once defined themselves (and were defined) as 'other' are 'shaking off the universalizing codes of Western thought centres'. He believes, in the French context, at least, that postcolonialist analysis has forced Western critical thought to address films, as he would put it, 'in the flesh'. This means moving the debate from the notional validity of the films to their aesthetic quality by addressing the 'colonial codes' that support this position. A telling phrase is 'stop taking the unfamiliar as difference' which is often the prompt for bogus criticism. Unfamiliarity is a feature of films from many sources but it can be used too easily to define an unhelpful 'otherness' in relation to ethnicity or cultural difference.

Postcolonialism asks significant questions which privilege ethnicity as an ideological issue, particularly with reference to issues of representation. This does not mean that we are only concerned with how non-whites are represented in contemporary films but how all ethnic groups are represented in relation to one another. It is also important to consider to what extent groups are represented: sometimes the most significant feature of the representation of a group is the fact that they are not represented at all. The key is 'activity': an open and active negotiation needs to take place between spectators, film-makers and critics. This active negotiation is beautifully demonstrated in the opening paragraphs of Fiona Villella's reading of the French film *Chocolat*.

Postcolonialism is a contemporary sensibility, which in general terms, foregrounds elements of difference, heterogeneity and pluralism. It involves a deconstruction of 'grand narratives' of history, modernisation and progress, and a recognition and celebration of difference and 'unspoken' narratives. It emphasizes the local, the specific and difference, and the idea that no one can speak unilaterally for another.

The contemporary French film, *Chocolat* (Claire Denis, 1988), can be seen to be somewhat informed, thematically and formally, by this broad contemporary sensibility.

Postcolonialism involves a process of reflecting, re-assembling and remembering the colonial and pre-colonial past. It provides a moment of liberation insofar as it enables the recognition of precolonial 'culture' and 'language', and a moment to reformulate identity and experience not based on Western Eurocentric discourses.

(Fiona Villella 1995, accessed at www.senseofcinema.com/contents/00/1/ chocolat.html)

MARXISM AND FILM

The 'paradigm of master and slave' is also central to the Marxist perspective, which sees social class as modern society's essential problematic. Marx saw human history as the story of class conflict which would ultimately be resolved in favour of the proletariat (working class) but only after a prolonged struggle with the bourgeoisie (the ruling class). In this 'final' struggle Marx suggested that the ruling class would fight with all they have (economic power, the law, education, culture) to maintain their position. Chief among their weapons would be their ability to control the intellectual means of production (the ways in which the world is discussed) and through the use of ideology to disguise the true nature of the struggle. Marx would, for example, identify arguments about 'human nature' and the inevitability of human suffering as key ways in which the poor were prevented from understanding their position.

Marx believed that social progress worked through the opposition of material forces and interests, and critics like Walter Benjamin saw this so-called 'dialectic' as the essence of Marxist film practice. Benjamin was quoted earlier in this chapter extolling the revolutionary nature of film as a medium, and so it has been in one place or another for most of its life. The work of two Marxist film-makers, Sergei Eisenstein and Jean-Luc Godard, will perhaps best identify the issues.

In Eisenstein's case what montage offers is 'a kind of collision and conflict, especially between a shot and its successor'. According to Mast and Cohen this was important to Eisenstein because 'he took it to be an expression, in the realm of images, of the Marxist's dialectical principle'. This is very clear in his strident manifesto *A Dialectical Approach to Film Form,* which includes the following:

A dynamic comprehension of things is also basic to the same degree, for a correct understanding of art and of all art forms. In the realm of art this dialectic principle of dynamics is embodied in CONFLICT as the *fundamental principle for the existence* of every art work and every art form.

For art is always conflict:
1. according to its social mission,
2. according to its nature,
3. according to its methodology.

EISENSTEIN AND THEMATIC MONTAGE:

Eisenstein's innovations focused on refining D. W. Griffith's cross-cutting techniques into what was labelled thematic montage. This kind of editing involves not only juxtaposing separate times and locales, but it also links together ideas.

Eisenstein believed that montage was the foundation of film art. Again, he argued that each shot in a sequence is incomplete – contributory rather than self-contained – and it's only as one shot flows into another that a deeper meaning can be revealed. Thus, Eisenstein constructed his films from many separate, jolting images instead of merely filming a flowing narrative. He defined his principle of montage as one of collision, conflict and contrast.

(http://www89.homepage.villanova.edu/elana/starr/pages/eisenstein_montage.htm)

For Godard the approach is even more fundamental towards what Brian Henderson calls 'a non-bourgeois camera style'. The technical explanation suggests a camera scanning an area of concern:

Godard has developed a new camera style in his later period. Its prime element is a long slow tracking shot that moves purely laterally – usually in one direction only (left to right or right to left), sometimes doubling back (left to right then right to left, right to left, then left to right) – over a scene that does not itself move in any relation to the camera's movements.

The implications of this are significant since what Godard is doing by allowing no movement of the subject in relation to the the camera is to deny the potential of the third dimension: in simple terms it emphasises the 'flatness' of the screen. This makes film much more like painting where a single perspective is an inevitable feature.

It is precisely cinema's capacity for depth which Godard excludes in *Weekend*. His moving camera, by adhering rigidly to the single-perspective, one-sided view of painting, eliminates the succession of aspects. The tracking shot's lateral motion *extends* this single perspective rather than alters it, very much as a mural does.

Kubrick reinforces this aspect of the tracking shot in the sequence of *A Clockwork Orange* which is analysed in Part 3 (pages 228–230). Here a defaced mural is subjected to a lateral tracking shot, whose very flatness is presented as an aspect of the hopelessness of Alex's situation.

In Godard's case the implications are more militantly Marxist, as 'non-bourgeois' becomes 'anti-bourgeois'. If cinema is to subject bourgeois society to the searing critique that Godard wants, it must first find ways to 'negotiate' the defences provided by ideology. This is the central purpose of Godard's camera technique, namely to leave the spectator, immunised against the ideological infections, in a position where she is able to examine what Henderson calls 'a single flat picture of the world'. Henderson is very clear about Godard's project and on the challenges that the bourgeois hegemony (the accepted version of reality which favours those in and with power) makes to Marxist film-makers:

What are the implications of these shifts from three dimensions to two, from depth to flatness? An ideological interpretation suggests itself – composition-in-depth projects a bourgeois world infinitely deep, rich, complex, ambiguous, mysterious. Godard's flat frames collapse this world into two-dimensional actuality; thus reversion to a cinema of one plane is a demystification, an assault on the bourgeois world-view and self-image. *Weekend*'s bourgeois figures scurry along without mystery toward mundane goals of money and pornographic fulfillment. There is no ambiguity and no moral complexity. That space in which the viewer could lose himself, make distinctions and alliances, comparisons and judgments, has been abrogated – the viewer is presented with a single flat picture of the world that he must examine, criticize, accept or reject. Thus the flatness of *Weekend* must not be analyzed only in itself but in regard to the previous modes of bourgeois self-presentment, particularly of composition-in-depth. The subject of *Weekend* is the historical bourgeoisie, the bourgeoisie in history; the film's flatness must not be seen statistically, as a single moment, but dialectically, as a *flattening*. Given this overall correlation, the specific correlations of the several senses of flatness fall into place. The succession of aspects not only multiplies viewpoints on the bourgeois world so that final judgment and any kind of certainty become impossible, it projects a bourgeois world infinitely inexhaustible and elaborable. Godard's tracking shot format insists on a single perspective and on the sufficiency of a single comprehensive survey for understanding of the transparent, easy-to-understand bourgeois world. Whereas in montage and composition-in-depth, complex form works on simple material, working it up as complex also, in Godard simple form works on simple material. The tracking shot and single-plane construction suggest an infinitely thin, absolutely flat bourgeois substance that cannot be elaborated but only surveyed. Finally, the single camera range represents not only a refusal to participate in bourgeois space, through forward camera movement, intercutting camera ranges, etc., it also has to do with the maintenance of critical perspective. Given that the film's subject is the historical bourgeoisie, Godard keeps his subject before him at all times. He refuses to pick and choose within the bourgeois world or to prefer any part of it to any other – even for a moment – because that involves partial eclipse of the whole. The nature of the bourgeois totality and the project of criticizing it require that it never be lost from view, or broken up into parts and aspects, but always be kept before the viewer as single and whole. Obviously the long-shot range is the range of the totality and the tracking shot the instrument of its critical survey. For this reason also Godard does not allow the close-up and medium-close ranges to be filled, for a face or figure huge in the foreground literally obstructs the whole and distracts attention from it in an emotional and intellectual sense also. Flatness in *Weekend*, in its various senses, is in fact the result of a formal totality that refuses to relinquish total perspective on the socio-historical totality that is its subject

(Henderson 1979: 846–847)

In a sense Marxist film criticism tries to do much the same job, namely to demystify the ways in which films are carriers of ideology. The French Marxist Louis Althusser suggested that film constitutes part of what he called 'the communications Ideological State Apparatus [ISA]', one of a series of ways in which we are controlled intellectually. Other ISAs include 'the family', 'the law' and 'education', and these function by promoting those ideas which protect the way things are. Much Marxist film criticism and film history addresses the ways in which mainstream Hollywood film functions symbolically to support the dominant ideology, which John Fiske has described as 'white, patriarchal capitalism'.

▼ 11 INDUSTRY

It was clear that, for the most part, film-makers and executives in Europe were preoccupied with the creative art of production rather then with the business of distribution and marketing.

David Puttnam

I think that films are made for one or maybe two people.

Jean-Luc Godard

Film Studies differs from art history or English literature in that we must consider film texts not only as works of art but also as product, as mass culture. This poses problems. The phrase 'mass culture' verges on the self-contradictory. 'Culture' with 'intellectual development' as part of its definition conjures up notions of art and enrichment, since when a person is cultured he or she is educated, refined, elegant. 'Mass', on the other hand, is a mass present in 'mass marketing' and 'mass production' and has connotations of uniformity, and therefore of dullness and dumbing down. Similarly paradoxical is the term 'artistic industry'. Art is borne of the human desire to create and express oneself, conflicting somewhat with industry and the desire to profit. Film, probably more so than popular music and television, is the most prevailing mass culture. Easily the biggest 'artistic industry' within that culture is Hollywood. Indeed, sometimes referred to as 'the dream factory', the Hollywood studio system of the 1930s and 1940s employed a production model inspired by the Ford Motor Company.

The 'big five' studios (Paramount, MGM, Fox, Warner and RKO) each had their own roster of writers, producers, directors and stars, all on long-term salaried contracts. Regimented division of labour meant that supposedly creative positions became repetitive and artists had little control over the final product. The real creative power lay in the hands of executive producers who would organise their workforce and oversee every stage of production. The final say was theirs and they would often drastically reshape a picture at the editing stage (Hitchcock fought against this by editing 'in camera', allowing little opportunity for alteration).

In addition to fixed staff, the studios owned their own stages, offices, accommodation, sets, development labs, construction yards and restaurants. Some, such as the aptly named Universal City, even had their own police force and zoo! This allowed them to regulate production and match strict yearly quotas of films. In fact, so like a production line was the system during the 1930s that top directors were expected to produce two and a half minutes of finished film for every day's shooting (Schatz 1998: 140).

It is debatable whether such factory-like conditions are conducive to the creation of art; indeed many would argue that the moment decisions are made on the basis of financial gain, the work loses its integrity and ceases to be art. Yet at its peak, between the years

1939 and 1940, the Hollywood studio system produced such classics as *Ninotchka, Mr Smith Goes to Washington, The Philadelphia Story, The Wizard of Oz, Gone With the Wind, Rebecca* and *Stagecoach. Citizen Kane* and *Casablanca* followed in 1941 and 1942 respectively. This period of cinema is widely labelled a 'Golden Age': a fondly recalled time following the end of the silent era when the system was such that it allowed producers to take a chance on magical and original movies which were produced with almost effortless regularity. It was a time before dwindling cinema audiences (partly a result of the rise of television) and the Hollywood Anti Trust Case of the late 1940s contributed to the dismantling of the studio system as it was, and it was replaced by the now more recognisable structure of agents and package deals.

The big companies like MGM and Paramount and Warner Bros. continued to survive, of course – indeed they flourished in the age of television and the New Hollywood. But things had changed since that halcyon era when Selznick and Hecht and Mayer were making movies. Gone was the cartel of movie factories that turned out a feature every week for a hundred million moviegoers. Gone were the studio bosses who answered to the New York office and oversaw hundreds, even thousands, of contract personnel working on the lot. Gone was the industrial infrastructure, the 'integrated' system whose major studio powers not only produced and distributed movies, but also ran their own theater chains. Something was 'over and done with' in the early 1950s, all right, but it wasn't the movies. It was the studio system of moviemaking and the near-absolute power that the studio wielded over the American movie industry. The Hollywood studio system emerged during the teens and took its distinctive shape in the 1920s. It reached maturity during the 1930s, peaked in the war years, but then went into a steady decline after the war, done in by various factors, from government antitrust suits and federal tax laws to new entertainment forms and massive changes in American life-styles. As the public shifted its viewing habits during the 1950s from 'going to the movies' to 'watching TV,' the studios siphoned off their theater holdings, fired their contract talent, and began leasing their facilities to independent film-makers and TV production companies. By the 1960s MGM and Warners and the others were no longer studios, really. They were primarily financing and distribution companies for pictures that were 'packaged' by agents or independent producers – or worse yet, by the stars and directors who once had been at the studios' beck and call.

• • •

The chief architects of a studio's style were its executives, which any number of Hollywood chroniclers observed at the time. Among the more astute chroniclers was Leo Rosten, who put it this way in *Hollywood: the Movie Colony*, an in-depth study published in 1940:

Each studio has a personality; each studio's product shows special emphases and values. And, in the final analysis, the sum total of a studio's personality, the aggregate pattern of its choices and its tastes, may be traced to its producers. For it is the producers who establish the preferences, the prejudices, and the predispositions of the organization and, therefore, of the movies which it turns out.

Rosten was not referring to the 'supervisors' and 'associate producers' who monitored individual productions, nor to the pioneering 'movie moguls' who controlled economic policy from New York. He was referring to studio production executives like Louis B. Mayer and Irving Thalberg at MGM, Jack Warner and Hal Wallis at Warner Bros., Darryl Zanuck at 20th Century-Fox, Harry Cohn at Columbia, and major independent producers like David Selznick and Sam Goldwyn. These men – and they were always men – translated an annual budget handed down by the New York office into a program of specific pictures. They coordinated the operations of the entire plant, conducted contract negotiations, developed stories and scripts, screened 'dailies' as pictures were being shot, and supervised editing until a picture was ready for shipment to New York for release. These were the men Frank Capra railed against in an open letter to *The New York Times* in April 1939, complaining that 'about six producers today pass on about 90 percent of the scripts and edit 90 percent of the pictures.' And these were the men that F. Scott Fitzgerald described on the opening page of *The Last Tycoon*, the Hollywood novel he was writing at the time of his death, in 1940. 'You can take Hollywood for granted like I did,' wrote Fitzgerald, 'or you can dismiss it with the contempt we reserve for what we don't understand. It can be understood too, but only dimly and in flashes. Not a half dozen men have been able to keep the whole equation of pictures in their heads.'

Fitzgerald was thinking of Irving Thalberg when he wrote that passage, and it would be difficult to find a more apt description of Thalberg's role at MGM. Nor could we find a clearer and more concise statement of our objective here: to calculate the whole equation of pictures, to get down on paper what Thalberg and Zanuck and Selznick and a very few others carried in their heads. After digging through several tons of archival materials from various studios and production companies, I have developed a strong conviction that these producers and studio executives have been the most misunderstood and undervalued figures in American film history. So in a sense this is an effort to reconsider their contributions to Hollywood filmmaking; but I don't want to overstate their case or misstate my own. Hollywood's division of labor extended well into the executive and management ranks, and isolating the producer or anyone else as artist or visionary gets us nowhere. We would do well, in fact, to recall French film critic André Bazin's admonition to the early auteurists, who were transforming film history into a cult of personality. 'The American cinema is a classical art,' wrote Bazin in 1957, 'so why not then admire in it what is most admirable – i.e., not only the talent of this or that filmmaker, but the genius of the system,'

(Schatz 1998: 4–7)

Even in the light of Schatz and Bazin's comments, you may still react cynically to the 'ars gratia artis' motto (art for art's sake) that frames Leo the lion as part of MGM's logo. But this is possibly more than merely an art versus entertainment debate. Perhaps it is not just a question of whether Hollywood enriches or titillates; fills with wonder of fills pockets, but a much bigger argument. In their seminal 'The Dialectic of Enlightenment' Adorno and Horkheimer of the Frankfurt School argue that 'Culture Industries' such as Hollywood have a much more sinister and worrying influence on society.

> Under monopoly all mass culture is identical, and the lines of its artificial framework begin to show through. The people at the top are no longer so interested in concealing monopoly: as its violence becomes more open, so its power grows. Movies and radio need no longer pretend to be art. The truth that they are just business is made into an ideology in order to justify the rubbish they deliberately produce...
>
> It is alleged that because millions participate in it, certain reproduction processes are necessary that inevitably require identical needs in innumerable places to be satisfied with identical goods... it is claimed that standards were based in the first place on consumers' needs, and for that reason were accepted with so little resistance. The result is the circle of manipulation and retroactive need in which the unity of the system grows ever stronger. No mention is made of the fact that the basis on which technology acquires power over society is the power of those whose economic hold over society is greatest.
>
> It has made the technology of the culture industry no more than the achievement of standardisation and mass production, sacrificing whatever involved a distinction between the logic of the work and that of the social system.
>
> ...The need which might resist central control has already been suppressed by the control of the individual consciousness. The step from the telephone to the radio has clearly distinguished the roles. The former still allowed the subscriber to play the role of subject, and was liberal. The latter is democratic: it turns all participants into listeners and authoritatively subjects them to broadcast programs which are all exactly the same. No machinery of rejoinder has been devised, and private broadcasters are denied any freedom. They are confined to the apocryphal field of the 'amateur,' and also have to accept organisation from above.
>
> But any trace of spontaneity from the public in official broadcasting is controlled and absorbed by talent scouts, studio competitions and official programs of every kind selected by professionals. Talented performers belong to the industry long before it displays them; otherwise they would not be so eager to fit in.
>
> (Adorno and Horkheimer 1979: 120)

Ardorno and Horkheimer's broader hypothesis is as follows:

■ Culture industries are intertwined with and dependent on bigger companies. Their conflicts of interests are stark and gargantuan.
■ Reproductive technology means that mass culture is homogeneous; all works are the same.
■ The culture industry is self-perpetuating; its products further an ideology that creates a (false) demand for still more of its products.
■ Only the few participate in the creation of culture: those most eager to conform.
■ Individuality is suppressed both through lack of public participation and the representation of only a narrow scope of difference.
■ The culture industry is ultimately a way of ensuring that the populous remain passive in order to maintain the structures of capitalism.

Whether or not you subscribe to all of these arguments, it is difficult to deny Hollywood's standing as the world's biggest culture industry and its considerable influence and power over much of the world. It has maintained this dominance since the 1930s – in the face of significant competition from other media forms and leisure activities – largely through its structures of distribution and exhibition and through the foregrounding of technological developments (sound, colour, widescreen, etc) as attraction. Here Graeme Turner discusses both:

TECHNOLOGY

The most recent attempt to use advances in technology to lure audiences into the cinema has been in the area of special effects, particularly computer-generated special effects. The box-office success of a number of films which employed spectacularly convincing special effects – *Jurassic Park*, *Terminator 2*, the *Alien* trilogy – encouraged a trend for movies which were marketed for their appeal as spectacle rather than as narrative. Disaster movies such as *Twister* and *Dante's Peak*, comedies such as *Men in Black* and *Mars Attacks*, sci-fi apocalypse action epics such as *Deep Impact* and *Armageddon*, and children's films like *Babe* and *Toy Story* were all marketed through trailers which promoted their spectacular visual effects rather than their content or storyline. Consequently, for a large part of the 1990s, the blockbuster and the special-effects movie has been almost synonymous; even the success of *Titanic* seems to have been tied, in large part, to director James Cameron's use of computer-generated images to create the illusion of the sinking liner. In such films, the creation of the illusion itself becomes the explicit object of audience attention and admiration. More importantly for the purposes of the industry, the inherently spectacular and visceral nature of the experience of watching such films insistently recommends the pleasures of the cinema over those of television, home video or other forms of entertainment. It is an expensive way to produce a film, however, and the audience's enthusiasm for the purely spectacular seems as likely to fade in this case as it did for the earlier gimmicks like Cinerama or 3D. As Peter Weir's *The*

Truman Show indicated in 1998, box-office success could still be generated by a strong narrative; alternatively, and as the failure of *Godzilla* indicated, whiz-bang special effects no longer guarantee an audience.

DISTRIBUTION AND EXHIBITION

Capitalizing on the insurance of a large home market, American companies used their new dominance to change the structure of the industry. Once, production of films, their distribution to cinemas, and the management of cinemas exhibiting them were separate enterprises. As the American domination grew, it became apparent that control over the industry could be guaranteed if a company could produce, distribute, and screen its own movies. This change in structure, called vertical integration began after the First World War. Throughout the 1920s Paramount, Loew's, Fox, and Goldwyn embarked on programmes of expansion, integration, and, most importantly, acquisition of first-run theatres in the major cities. Restrictive practices, such as Paramount's block booking, followed. Block booking enabled producers to extract agreement from exhibitors to take all their pictures in a total package, sight unseen, thus guaranteeing a screening for their product and making the exhibitor bear much of the risk for the film's success or failure. This practice was eventually outlawed in the US in 1948, and later in most other countries, but it exercised an important influence over the nature and conduct of the industry.

(Turner 1999: 25, 17)

In the 1980s, Reagan's US Department of Justice (perhaps sensing Hollywood's enormous contribution to the advancement of American values across the world) relaxed its anti-trust laws and the film industry moved back into vertical integration. However, on its return it was no longer a simple model of the structures of production and distribution merging with those of exhibition. Studios, distribution houses and theatre chains were now but a few components of huge conglomerates that also included television and cable networks, record companies, video manufacturing companies, video rental and retail outlets, theme parks, ISPs and publishing houses. The dirty secret was concealed behind the varying names of their many wings and subsidiaries.

Perhaps unsurprisingly, film is no longer a self-contained article; it exists outside of the multiplex as part of a wider symbiotic framework of strategic marketing campaigns, endless tie-ins and official merchandise. In the following, Meehan argues that in the age of globalisation and multinational expansion, films are a calculated business decision. Our analyses must therefore consider not only the art, but the economics behind the art.

Batman took the United States by storm in the spring and summer of 1989. Tee shirts, posters, keychains, jewelry, buttons, books, watches, magazines, trading cards, audiotaped books, videogames, records, cups, and numerous other items flooded malls across the United States with images of Batman, his new logo, and his old enemy the Joker. Presaged by a much pirated trailer, *Batman* the film drew unprecedented crowds to theatre chains, of which the two largest (United Artist Theater Circuits and American Multi-Cinema) distributed four to five million brochures for mail order Bat-materials. *Batman*'s premiere on the big screen was matched by appearances on the small screen. Film clips were packaged as advertisements and free promotional materials for the interview and movie review circuits on both broadcast and cable television; Prince's 'Batdance' video played in heavy rotation on MTV. Over radio, 'Batdance' and other cuts from Prince's Batman album got strong play on rock stations and 'crossed over' for similarly strong play on black radio stations. Subsequently, retail outlets filled with Bat costumes and Joker make-up kits for Halloween; Ertl Batmobiles and ToyBiz Batcaves and Batwings were being deployed for Christmas shoppers. In the speciality stores serving comics fandom, the *Advance Comics Special Batlist* offered 214 items ranging from $576 to $2 in price. And in grocery stores, special Bat-displays offered children a choice between Batman coloring books, Batman trace-and-color books, and Batman magic plates. It would seem that Batman and his paraphernalia transcend age, gender, and race. . . .

If the prevalence of Bat-paraphernalia in the stores and the ubiquity of the Bat-logo on the streets are indicators, then indeed *Batman* has struck a chord deep in the American psyche. Certainly the temptation to speculate on the larger significance of *Batman* is strong given the irony of this dark, yet ultimately hopeful, film being released at a time when the mythic Gotham of the *Dark Knight's Return* and the myths of the American Imperium both seem to crack under the strains of social injustice and personal irresponsibility.

This speculation, however tempting, is not quite fair to us or to the film. Such speculation requires an assumptive leap that reduces consciousness, culture, and media to reflections of each other. It assumes that the American psyche can be read off the film, which reflects American culture which deter-mines how we see the world and how the film is constructed. This old and much criticized error retains its emotional force, despite the articulation of more careful theories about media texts and intertexts, about reception and reinterpretation of those materials by active viewers . . . In this essay, however, I will argue that another dimension must be added to our analyses of media generally and of *Batman* specifically. Namely, economics must be considered if we are fully to understand the texts and intertexts of American mass culture. Most cultural production in the United States is done by private, for-profit corporations. These corporations comprise the entertainment/information sector of the American economy and encompass the industries of publishing, television, film, music, cable, and radio. Significantly, American capitalism organizes the creation of cultural artifacts as a process of mass production carried out by profit-oriented businesses operating in an industrial context. Profit, not culture, drives show business: no business means no show.

For much of the American culture, corporate imperatives operate as the primary constraints shaping the narratives and iconography of the text as well as the manufacture and licensing of the intertextual materials necessary for a 'mania' to sweep the country. This is not a claim that evil moguls force us to buy Bat-chains: such reductionism is as vulgar and untenable as the assumptive leap from a film to the national psyche. Rather, the claim here is that mass-produced culture is a business, governed by corporate drives for profit, market control, and transindustrial integration. While movies may (and do) flop, the decision to create a movie is a business decision about the potential profitability of a cinematic product. Further, as film studios have been either acquired by companies outside the industry or have themselves acquired companies in other entertainment/information industries, decisions about movies are increasingly focused on the potential profitability of a wide range of products. The film per se becomes only one component in a product line that extends beyond the theater, even beyond our contact with mass media, to penetrate the markets for toys, bedding, trinkets, cups and other minutiae comprising one's everyday life inside a commoditized, consumerized culture.

To understand *Batman*, then, requires that our analyses of the text and intertext, and of fandom and other audiences, be supplemented by an economic analysis of corporate structure, market structures, and interpenetrating industries. These conditions of production select, frame, and shape both *Batman* as a commercial text and the product line that constitutes its commercial intertext.

(Meehan: 47–65)

The period leading up to this conglomeration of media industries is commonly referred to as 'The New Hollywood'. This (perhaps over-sentimentalised) period, from between about 1967 and the end of the 1970s, is seen as a time of artistic freedom when a new breed of film-school educated directors, immersed in the history of cinema, injected an intelligence, energy and uniqueness into American mainstream film. The list of classics from this era begins with *Bonnie and Clyde* and includes *The Godfather, M*A*S*H, Chinatown, Mean Streets, One Flew Over the Cuckoo's Nest, Midnight Cowboy, The Graduate* and *Annie Hall*. This was before the high-spectacle, simple narratives of *Jaws* and *Star Wars* set the trend for the years to follow:

Barely distant over the Hollywood horizon was a monster. ... This monster was a supercharged, simpleminded creature, an Aesop's fable on crystal meth, a movie that any producer could pitch in thirty seconds and any audience could understand without even thinking. It was the big-screen equivalent of popcorn served in the lobby: tasty, devoid of nourishment, free of any resonance ... this is the monster that ate Hollywood.

(Fleming 1998: 14)

Thus the High Concept movie was born. And the continued success of Spielberg, Cameron, Columbus and Bruckheimer, coupled with the revelation that Hollwood studios now pitch their blockbusters at 15-year-olds (the biggest cinema-going market) proves that, three decades on, High Concept is yet to grow up.

Whereas *All That Jazz* was produced despite the lack of inherent marketing opportunities, *Grease*, with its target of young and old, could be defined by its marketing possibilities. The latter film's marketing hooks are numerous and strong. In addition, the dependence on *Grease* on marketing through stars, a pre-sold property, music, merchandising, and a single image has become increasingly significant as a marketing approach. This approach can be succinctly described in a 'pitch' or a one-line concept: 'John Travolta and Olivia Newton-John star as the '50s greaser and the 'good girl' in the screen adaptation of the hit stage musical *Grease*.' In contrast, the disparate themes and complexity of *All That Jazz* cannot be reduced readily to a concept or a single ad-line.

These differences might be articulated by describing *Grease* as a relatively high concept project, while *All That Jazz* would fall into the low concept category. This classification offers an entry point into an understanding of a significant focus for mainstream studio motion picture production. The term 'high concept' originated in the television and film industries, but it was soon adopted by the popular presses, who seized the term as an indictment of Hollywood's privileging those films which seemed most likely to reap huge dollars at the boxoffice

[...]

... Disney president Jeffrey Katzenberg ... attributes the term *high concept* to Michael Eisner. According to Katzenberg, Eisner used high concept while working as a creative executive at Paramount to describe a unique idea whose originality could be conveyed briefly. Similarly, Columbia Pictures Entertainment President Peter Guber defines high concept in narrative terms. Rather than stressing the uniqueness of the idea, Guber states that high concept can be understood as a narrative which is very straightforward, easily communicated, and easily comprehended.

[...]

... within the film and television industries, high concept most frequently is associated with narrative and, in particular, a form of narrative which is highly marketable. This marketability might be based upon stars, the match between a star and a premise, or a subject matter which is fashionable. In practice, the locus of this marketability and concept in the contemporary industry is the 'pitch.' In fact, in order to pitch a project succinctly the film must be high concept; consider Steven Spielberg's comment: 'If a person can tell me the idea in 25 words or less, it's going to make a pretty good movie. I like ideas, especially movie ideas, that you can hold in your hand,' Spielberg's opinion relates well to the vision of high concept expressed by other Hollywood representatives: a striking, easily reducible narrative which also offers a high degree of marketability.

[...]

Although narrative is still a focus, high concept suggests another set of meanings to the popular presses and analysts of Hollywood. These meanings are summarized aptly by Richard Schickel, who points out that with the term high concept, 'high' is actually a misnomer: 'What the phrase really means is that the concept is so low it can be summarized and sold on the basis of a single sentence.'

[...]

... critics describe high concept as relying heavily upon the replication and combination of previously successful narratives. In the extreme, critics describe high concept films as merely combinations of other films; the *Los Angeles Times*, for instance, presented a High Concept Match Game in which *RoboCop* was defined as *Terminator* meets *Dirty Harry* and *Harry and the Hendersons* as *Gentle Ben* meets *E.T.* To a lesser extent, this replication can involve 'revitalizing' past successes through a star or shift in emphasis. At the time of release for *Flashdance* (1983), Jon Peters remarked that he was certain of the boxoffice success of the film since *Flashdance* was, in essence, a *Rocky* (1976) for women.

[...]

Inherent in the media's usage of the term is the importance of not just summarizing, but also selling the film through the concept. In fact, Timothy Noah foregrounds this aspect in his definition of high concept: 'The "high concept" approach is favored by the seller – say, a producer trying to convince a studio to put up money for his movie – because it renders a proposal misunderstanding-proof. High concept proposals are by definition easily grasped by the studio executives on the run and, further down the road, by the movie audiences, who are given only a week or two from a film's opening to determine whether it will stay in theaters.' This 'shorthand' form of communication between industry and audience occurs through the marketing of the high concept, which is aided by the simplicity and directness of the concept … these films are designed to be sold [. . .]

At the most basic level, high concept can be considered as one result of the tension between the economics and aesthetics on which commercial studio filmmaking is based. All mainstream Hollywood filmmaking is economically oriented, through the minimization of production cost and maximization of potential boxoffice revenue. However, the connection between economics and high concept is particularly strong, since high concept appears to be the most market-driven type of film being produced. … Historically, as the forces forming the mode of production change across time, so does the product of film, privileging a certain 'look and sound' within filmmaking. This new 'look and sound' is evident in the style of the high concept picture. Second, the relation between economics and high concept exists at the level of marketing: the high concept film is designed to maximize marketability and, consequently, the economic potential at the boxoffice. This marketability is based upon such factors as stars, the match between a star and a project, a pre-sold premise (such as a remake or adaptation of a best-selling novel), and a concept which taps into a national trend or sentiment.

[. . .]

… this style is based upon two major components: a simplification of character and narrative, and a strong match between image and music sound-track throughout the film. In the high concept film, the narrative frequently is composed of stock situations firmly set within the bounds of genre and viewer expectation. In fact, with the high concept film, one can see the movement of the narrative from the single-sentence concept. So, for example, *'Top Gun* (1986) in race cars' aptly describes the narrative trajectory of *Days of Thunder* (1990): the concept encapsulizes the establishment, animation, intensification, and resolution of the plot structure, as well as the star, the style, and genre of the film.

[. . .]

Perhaps the most important component of this style is the relation of the image to the soundtrack, since frequently a major portion of these films is composed of extended montages which are, in effect, music video sequences. These musical sequences serve as modular set pieces which fragment the narrative. The soundtrack also accompanies a set of formal techniques which often hamper or actually halt the narrative progression: these techniques include extreme backlighting, a minimal (often almost black-and-white) color scheme, a predominance of reflected images and a tendency toward settings of high technology and industrial design.

[. . .]

> If high concept can be described as a style of filmmaking at a particular point in film history, there are causal mechanisms creating and demarcating this period. The larger structural changes within the industry – such as conglomeration, the development of new technologies, and the rise in marketing and merchandising – operate to privilege films which can be summarized and sold in a single sentence.
>
> (Wyatt 1994: 7–18)

THE BRITISH CINEMA INDUSTRY

You would be forgiven for thinking that sharing a language with Hollywood would enable the British cinema industry to share in some of its profits. The truth is that the British cinema industry has endured a troublesome history (Chapter 14) and shows that Britain's lack of efficient industrial organisation has not necessarily freed it up to produce more original and critically acclaimed works.

Part of the blame rests with a lack of sustained and sufficient investment, and a 'talent drain', where rising British actors and directors are tempted across the Atlantic by Hollywood's money and glamour. Yet these are both 'chicken-and-egg' arguments: Are financiers reluctant to invest because of Britain's poor commercial track record? And does the industry lack glamour and money in the first place because émigré talent fails to stay around long enough to foster the right atmosphere or generate the cash to keep it at home? Even on the rare occasion when films are furnished with sufficient investment and star billing, their success is far from guaranteed (e.g. *Charlotte Gray*, with Cate Blanchett and a £14 million budget was a colossal flop, responsible for a massive scaling down of its production company Film Four). Of course, British cinema has been privy to some astounding, albeit unpredictable success storys. *Trainspotting*, *Four Weddings and a Funeral* and *The Full Monty* are often held up as examples of British Cinema's potential in the 1990s. Yet it is difficult to see any magic formula common to all these films. The real problem, Micheal Chanan finds, is the way British films are (or are not) distributed.

> ... Alan Parker, says 'We have to stop defining success by how well British films perform in Milton Keynes'. (Why Milton Keynes? Because it's supposed to be in the middle of the country?) Parker's logic is that successful British films like *Notting Hill* make 85% of their revenues outside the UK, so we need to 'abandon forever the "little England" vision of a UK film industry comprised of small British film companies delivering parochial British films.' But there's something askew in this argument, on at least two counts.

Firstly, which are the films he meant to call parochial? He can't be speaking about Ken Loach, for whom he's declared his admiration, since Loach is much admired abroad. And not presumably about Mike Leigh, who is recognised abroad as one of the great originals of British Cinema. Nor of a film like *The Full Monty*, which broke all records in the USA where they don't even know where Sheffield is. And I presume he can't be talking about Michael Winterbottom's *In This World* which has just won the Golden Bear at the Berlin Film Festival, or Peter Mullan's *The Magdelene Sisters*, which won at Venice last year. So what exactly is he talking about?

Secondly, too many of these supposedly parochial films don't get anywhere near Milton Keynes, because they often don't get distributed at all. Since lottery funding began in 1995, production has increased but so has the number of films the distributors decline to release, thereby denying them any chance to succeed. More than one hundred films were made in the UK in 1999; 27 still had no distribution deal in place by July 2001. A year later, there were 83 new films, but only 24 of them secured a release. It's jumping the gun to suppose, like Evening Standard film critic Alexander Walker railing over the wastage of lottery funds, that they can't be any good. This is not a normal situation, it isn't found in other European countries, and it is not, as he suggests, because films are being made without securing a distribution deal first. If this were a sine qua non, then many proven films would not have been made.

This situation also runs counter to what might be expected when cinema audiences have been growing and the number of screens has increased. There are now more than 2,500 screens in the country, 2½ times the number in 1987 – and thereby, we are always told, the audience has more variety from which to choose. Except that it patently isn't true. The multiplexes are dominated by Hollywood, and they're swamped by the blockbusters. According to one estimate, out of 30–40 films on release in Britain at any one time, 90% of box-office goes to the top three, the next four take 9%, and the remaining 25 scramble for the last 1%. Parker must be aware of these figures, but for all his emphasis on the problem of distribution, he doesn't come clean about it. The real situation is this. On the one hand, lottery funding saved UK film production from finally disappearing altogether. On the other, all the major distributors in Britain, who control access to the multiplexes, are American, and obviously have their own quite un-British agenda. The two things don't join up.

[...]

... the problem is that the relation between budgets and markets is not transparent; films still have to pass through distributors in order to get exhibited. In 1996, the average UK film production budget was £3m, compared to £23.4m in the United States, but even low budgets like this are too much if you can't get more than half a dozen prints into circulation, and this is all that is possible without the multiplexes. Even if you believe the exhibitors' habitual claim that they'll show anything that makes them money, they don't have the choice – and therefore nor does the audience – because distribution is structured to exclude the 'small' firm. The distributor pays the print and advertising costs, and the less popular a film, the higher the proportion of the box office that stays with the exhibitor. The problem is circular. Without sufficient publicity, the film is unlikely to capture a big audience, distributors are reluctant to invest in sufficient publicity or even handle the film at all. And when they do, the release might be limited to eight or ten prints, compared to a Hollywood blockbuster with hundreds; which means they're unlikely to recoup their costs, because you can't do that if you don't get into the multiplexes; and if you haven't got decent exposure in the cinemas, you won't get a lot from selling on to television and video either.

This situation is doubtless exacerbated by using Lottery funds to make films without prior distribution agreements, but I repeat this is not the root of the problem. It isn't just the market, either, because this is a market which is distorted by an imbalance of interests. Production, distribution and exhibition are out of sync with each other, and the injection of public funds has had counter-intentional effects.

[…]

The same situations keep recurring. Independent producers go out of business because their films aren't reaching the screens. The results of legislation are the opposite of what was intended. An unexpected success temporarily boosts the industry, only for It to collapse back into depression. The evidence repeatedly points to the distributors' control over exhibition, the restricted screen space their methods allow for independent production, the limitation in the number and source of the films which the public is offered – contrary to the free market claim that the public gets to see what it wants to pay to see.

[…]

… the problem with the cinema and what we get the chance to see is exacerbated by growing concentration in the exhibition sector. In 1988, multiplex venues accounted for only 10% of the UK screens. Ten years later, over 50%, three-quarters of them owned by only five companies – and more than half by just three. The problem is much bigger than national cinema, because it isn't only British films which aren't being seen on British screens. It is also the films of other countries and cultures which are being denied us, at the same time that official policy talks up the ideas of multiculturalism and cultural diversity which are indeed the social realities of the postcolonial world. It is not clear what the Film Council proposes to do about this, but the signs are not too good. A report commissioned by the Council from professional consultants recommends a method of support similar to the French system, which reduces the risks for distributors in taking on low-earning films. The Council now speaks of this area of activity as 'specialised' films, a denomination which worries me, because it seems disparaging and at the same time an attempt to hive this cinema off and keep it away from the popular mainstream. When these are in fact the films we really need, because they're capable, with other perspectives on the world, of opening our eyes.

(Chanan 2003: 3–20)

If you want to see a film about a happy little elf, I'm sure there is plenty of seating in Theatre No 2.

Lemony Snicket's *A Series of Unfortunate Events*

Film audiences provide interesting avenues through which to study cinema. Clearly one particular element that needs to be taken into account when we consider any film is its success at the box-office. Of course this is not to be confused with its aesthetic value.

ALL TIME HIGHEST GROSSING MOVIES WORLDWIDE

The chart below contains figures for all 209 movies to make over $250 million globally. This table is updated each week.

Note: This chart is *not* adjusted for inflation.

	Released	Film Name	Total Box Office
1	1997	**Titanic**	$1,835,400,000
2	2003	**Lord of the Rings: The Return of the King**	$1,129,027,325
3	2001	**Harry Potter and the Sorcerer's Stone**	$974,557,891
4	1999	**Star Wars: Phantom Menace**	$925,600,000
5	2002	**Lord of the Rings: The Two Towers**	$924,291,552
6	1993	**Jurassic Park**	$920,100,000
7	2004	**Shrek 2**	$916,121,703
8	2005	**Harry Potter and the Goblet of Fire**	$892,213,036
9	2002	**Harry Potter and the Chamber of Secrets**	$878,987,880
10	2001	**Lord of the Rings: The Fellowship of the Ring**	$867,683,093
11	2003	**Finding Nemo**	$864,614,978
12	2005	**Star Wars: Revenge of the Sith**	$848,470,577
13	2002	**Spider-Man**	$821,700,000
14	1996	**Independence Day**	$816,969,255
15	1977	**Star Wars**	$797,900,000
16	1982	**ET: The Extra-Terrestrial**	$792,910,554
17	2004	**Harry Potter and the Prisoner of Azkaban**	$792,538,952
18	1997	**Lost World: Jurassic Park**	$786,686,679
19	2004	**Spider-Man 2**	$783,924,485
20	1994	**Lion King, The**	$767,900,000

(http://www.the-numbers.com/movies/records/worldwide.html)

Indeed some would argue that the two are inversely proportional. However, box-office figures provide, in the same way as do television ratings, immediate access to what is currently popular as well as a set of historical statistics which reveal interesting trends in popularity of individual films and genres.

On page 285 is a list of the highest grossing worldwide films of all time taken from The Numbers website (and see Chapter 4, pp. 91–93). You can find more information about box-office takings in the US and internationally by visiting this site. Information about British box-office takings may be found on the BFI website at: http://www.bfi.org.uk/filmtvinfo/stats/boxoffice.html

Of course, size, although important, is not the only issue that needs to be addressed in terms of audience study. In this chapter we also look at the significance of the context of consumption, specifically the rise of the multiplex cinema. We also explore the idea of the film fan whose interests often focus on specific stars or genres of film.

An important element of the film audience is the 'fan'. Fans represent those members of the audiences who have specific and dedicated interests in particular aspects of cinema. These interests may vary from adulation for a particular star through to an obsession with a particular genre of film. The word 'fan' can carry with it the connotation of an uncritical reading of such aspects of film on the one hand, but on the other a detailed and sympathetic knowledge of them. The stalker and the anorak are extremes of fandom. This term has been coined to describe the behaviour and attitudes of fans as well as their activities in the production of websites and fanzines, for example.

It is interesting to note that the connotations of the word film buff carry no such negative charge. The film buff is erudite and informed and worthy of respect. Henry Jenkins discusses many of these issues in his influential book *Textual Poachers (Television Fans and Participatory Callers)* (Routledge 1992). Jenkins is interested in the various ways in which fans make their own meanings from apparently superficial, ideological and manipulative texts. He sees this as a kind of subversion, a semantic guerrilla warfare. In fact he uses military language to sum up the 'war' between a controlling media and individual consumers, suggesting that we have 'tactics' to deal with their strategies. Jenkins is also keen to explore the supposedly gendered nature of fandom, as this female reader/reviewer implies:

> When most people think of a Star Trek fan, they imagine a young man with glasses and a polyester uniform stretched tight over his paunch. In this book Henry Jenkins explodes that myth. The typical television fan – of *Star Trek* or any other show – is female, educated, and often caught in a job that doesn't make full use of her abilities. In media fandom, she finds a social and intellectual world that is a rich complement to her mundane existence. Jenkins also discredits a more pervasive myth – that of the TV viewer as an addicted idiot passively receiving broadcasters' ideology of consumerism. In truth, fans appropriate material from TV shows, making new meaning. They write stories and folk-songs, and even make videos from re-edited programmes. Not all viewers are as active and creative as fans, but it's clear that we need to rethink basic ideas about the viewing process.

FILM STUDIES: THE ESSENTIAL RESOURCE

For readers like myself who are involved with modern interactive technologies such as The Well, Internet multimedia, and virtual reality, this book is an important reminder not to view more traditional media forms as 'passive'.

(Amy Bruckman)

ACTIVITY

> ➤ To what extent do you think fandom is gendered? For example, do you think specific genres and specific star/directors appeal more to one gender than another?

The following extract is a good example of qualitative research in which a survey was made of female horror fans across the UK. It makes for absorbing reading, particularly in terms of the gratifications and pleasures women find in horror movies:

4 SCREAMING FOR RELEASE: FEMININITY AND HORROR FILM FANDOM IN BRITAIN

Brigid Cherry

Horror fandom in the UK takes a variety of forms. A number of groups and societies exist which are dedicated to horror, although there is a much larger number of fan groups based around related genres such as science fiction and fantasy in which horror fans participate. It is impossible to consider horror fandom as having distinct boundaries and there is a great deal of overlap with other fan cultures. As Reeves *et al.* argue in their work on fans of *The X-Files* (1996: 32): 'horror/dark fantasy fan groups ... exist on the margins of sci-fi fandom.'

The results presented here derive from data supplied by female horror film fans from a number of such fan organizations, including the British Fantasy Society and various vampire groups, as well as the readerships of horror magazines and fanzines. As part of a research project on the female horror film audience,[1] an audience study of female horror fans was conducted during the 1990s, drawing participants from across the UK. Qualitative data were collected from a number of sources. A total of 109 participants responded to a questionnaire containing open-ended questions which was circulated to the female memberships of the British Fantasy Society and the Vampyre Society or who wrote in reply to a request for participants in horror magazines and fanzines (including *Shivers*, *The Dark Side* and *Samhain*). Additional written material in the form of letters and electronic mail messages on the participants' horror film tastes, viewing patterns and opinions was obtained from a further sixteen women. Fifteen further participants took part in focus groups held across the central belt of Scotland. These participants were recruited from local horror,

CONTINUED

science fiction and vampire societies, and people at a horror film festival and a science fiction convention running a programme strand on vampires, as well as by word of mouth contact. All participants were female.

There is every indication, however, that in general there is a low participation rate of women in traditionally organized fandom. Certainly this is true of literary science fiction fandoms (see Jenkins 1992: 48). As Jenkins has observed, female science fiction fans tend to congregate in specific areas of fandom dedicated to subjects of greater interest for women. One such horror fandom congregates around vampire films and fiction. Given the strong liking women have for vampire films (over 90 per cent of all female horror film viewers in this study liked all or most vampire films[2]), it might be expected that more women join these groups than others. The membership of the Vampyre Society confirms this with a 49 per cent female membership. This would seem to confirm, then, that, as with science fiction fandom, certain sections of horror fandom are more appealing or accommodating to female fans.

This situation of, on the one hand, women taking part in a specific area of horror fandom and, on the other, being diverted into other fandoms, may account (at least in part) for the seeming invisibility of female horror fans. A publicly professed liking for science fiction may be accompanied by a private taste for horror, to be seen to like science fiction being thought more acceptable. Several respondents stated that they had not made public their taste for horror. A 22-year-old stated that: 'People seem to find an interest in horror more disturbing in a woman, and I consider this most unfair.' Many of the respondents specified a liking for science fiction in addition to horror and several pointed out that they discovered their taste for horror through reading or viewing science fiction. It should be acknowledged, then, that many fans are nomadic (ibid.: 36), focusing their attention on a series of different fan objects including science fiction, fantasy and other related genres. Accordingly, there are large areas of overlap in the membership of fan cultures. Higher levels of active involvement in related fandoms, and in vampire fandom in particular, may be attributable to nomadic behaviour and to the social acceptability of science fiction, but many women have also experienced a lack of welcome in horror fandom. They are largely ignored by the mass market and fan-based horror publishing industry and, in addition, often derided by male fans. The female horror film fan, then, is doubly marginalized within horror fan culture.

MODELS OF FAN BEHAVIOUR

Since participation in horror fandom is thus not widespread among female horror film viewers, it is necessary to construct an alternative fan profile. Although the women who took part in this study viewed horror films frequently and habitually, as nomadic subjects, horror tended to form part of a group of genres which they watched and which may change over time. Many were isolated viewers with low rates of participation in fan culture, others were members of literary or multi-media fan organizations.

Despite the alienating environment and nomadic fan practices, many of the respondents did define themselves as fans in order to indicate a particular interest in a cultural product. Eighty-four per cent of participants were happy to describe themselves as horror fans. Only 12 per cent rejected this label, while 4 per cent were unsure about whether they were fans; this may indicate either an ambivalent attitude towards fans generally or doubt about whether they fit the typical horror fan profile.

There were two main differences in fan behaviour or consumption between those who would call themselves fans and those who would not. Those who considered themselves to be fans were significantly more likely to like slasher films than those who did not think of themselves as fans,[3] but there were few other differences between fans and non-fans in their preferences for horror film types. There was little indication, then, in the tastes of the respondents as to whether or not they classed themselves as fans. A liking for slasher films may be an indication of horror film viewers classing themselves as fans, but there may be another root cause for both these factors. Certainly, there was a strong correlation between the age at which the respondents first started watching horror films and whether they considered themselves to be fans.[4] Those who were under 12 years old when they first watched horror films were far more likely to consider themselves to be fans than to reject the label. The converse was true for those who started watching horror films at 16–18 years old. This indicates that the formation at an early age, certainly pre-teens, of an habitual liking for being scared is an indicator of classing oneself as a fan in later life. This could be related to adolescent gender socialization, in that female viewers who begin watching horror films in their teens may be discouraged by peer group pressure from admitting a liking for horror, as it is seen as unfeminine.

There are other possible reasons for not wanting to consider oneself a fan. Fans in general are depicted as other (Tulloch and Jenkins 1995), and terms such as 'nerd', 'geek' or 'anorak'[5] are often applied to fans. Some respondents did not wish to be too closely associated with such nerdish behaviour or labelled, as female fans often are, as kooky and associated with groupies, given that label's attendant implications about sexual behaviour. In addition, viewers of horror films are often equated with dangerous or insane criminals (rapists, mass or serial murderers) whose psychopathic behaviour is blamed on horror film viewing. Moral panics have led to the perception of horror films (and their viewers) as being a danger to society. This comes partly from the climate of censorship in the UK and the idea that 'video nasties' in particular have the potential to 'deprave and corrupt'. Such social pressures, in addition to the fact that it is considered unfeminine for women to like horror films, make it likely that many women would not willingly admit to a taste for horror. Those respondents who developed a liking for horror later in life may be more sensitive to these factors. A 32-year-old indicated that such sensitivity may fade with time: 'I used to watch them alone … because I didn't want people to know I watched them; now I watch as many as possible and don't care who knows.'

It is thus no surprise to find that female viewers do not wish to be labelled as fans, since this renders them abject on a number of counts – as fans they are geeks or nerds, as horror fans they are depraved, and as female horror fans they are unfeminine. It is solely for such reasons that some respondents did not consider themselves as fans – a 21-year-old, for example, stated her self-image precluded such character traits. A 33-year-old, who had not publicly admitted to being a fan (although she did readily admit to partici-pating actively in science fiction, fantasy and horror fandom by attending conventions), nevertheless considered her 'nerdish' behaviour to be like that of a fan:

> I don't know about being a horror fan, I'm very much in the closet so to speak. There's a big stigma attached to it. It's basically the spotty anorak type – I think I probably am a female version of that actually; you know, school swot and all that.

Such depictions are, according to Tulloch and Jenkins (1995: 15), exaggerated caricatures which allow ordinary viewers to reassure themselves that their own media consumption is on the normal side of 'the thinly drawn yet sharply policed boundaries between normal and abnormal audience behaviour'. As indicated by the above example, some respondents in this survey were quite keen to be seen to be on the 'right' side of that boundary, even to the extent that they thought of themselves as 'in the closet'. Certainly, the majority of female horror fans surveyed were keen to emphasize wide-ranging interests outside of horror, and many insisted that their behaviour and/or appearance was unlike that of a fan. This may partly account for female horror fans being invisible within large areas of fandom: many deliberately isolate themselves by not going to conventions and by not participating in fan consumption. The 27-year-old organizer of a horror film festival stated that female fans frequently asked her if it was okay for women to attend the festival since they had never dared to go to one before. A 20-year-old reported negative reactions from male fans:

> I think females who like horror are looked on as strange. I've had a lot of people come up to me and tell me I'm a bit strange because I'm female and I wear a leather jacket and I do vampire role playing and I run the

science fiction society. They go 'oh, they're guy things' and I always think what does that make me, just because I like something different, am I supposed to be a man or something?

Other responses indicated different reasons why women might not wish to get involved in male-dominated fandoms. These ranged from not finding attractive the men involved (a 19-year-old student said: 'I had a look at the guys, I went: "oh no"') to not having the depth of knowledge required to participate in fandom. A 22-year-old said:

> I don't read horror books, I'm not interested in magazines or anything, I only watch films. I can't even remember what most of the things I've watched are called. 'Oh is that the one in the London Underground: a boy and a girl and the girl had really great boots on and really cool hair and then she got caught by this monster . . .?' But I hadn't a clue what it was called. That's what I think of fans, like fans of football knowing every score for the last ten years. I don't know anything. Basically I just watch the films and I don't know who the actors are or whatever. I'm just not interested in all that in-depth knowledge in anything really.

The acquisition of trivial knowledge is considered a masculine attribute. A 20-year-old said: 'I guess men get more attracted to knowing, they enjoy knowing all the directors and then telling you he's made this film and did that.' The quote above also suggests that some female viewers might be interested in a different set of trivial details: here, fashions and hairstyles.

The respondents also differed from the accepted profile of the typical horror film fan in terms of age. The typical fan is often thought of as an adolescent who quickly 'grows out' of his (for it is most frequently assumed to be male) liking for horror. However, the respondents' liking for horror did not fit the pattern of a passing adolescent fan interest. Many started watching or reading horror (or related genres) before their teens and their liking for the genre had persisted into adulthood. Those who considered themselves to be fans also dated their fan status from childhood. For these women, it is a life-long interest.

Given that neither the fans nor the non-fans among the respondents fitted the pattern of typical horror fans, different patterns of fan behaviour have to be considered in ascertaining the reasons behind the fan/non-fan split. In this respect it is interesting to note that Stuart Hall's 'preferred reading strategies' (1980) have been related by Reeves *et al.* (1996) to three levels of spectatorship identified in science fiction fans: casual viewers, devoted viewers and avid fans. It thus might appear likely that those who described themselves as fans in this study corresponded to avid fans, while the non-fans were more like devoted viewers. However, since horror film viewing patterns and fan behaviour did not seem to differ significantly between the two former groups, this division too may not be apt in this case. Several of the respondents who did not classify themselves as horror fans were members of fan groups and might, therefore, have considered themselves to be fans of other genres such as fantasy or science fiction. It is more useful, then, to examine other patterns of fan behaviour.

Lewis (1992) identifies four types of female fans: avid, intense, follower and hater. The avid fan is categorized by extreme behaviour, a high level of textual competence and is heavily involved in media interactions. There were a number of such fans in this study. They were very knowledgeable about horror and had seen large numbers of horror films which they were able to discuss in detail. These respondents could discuss films at length and could provide details on the making of films. A 35-year-old, for example, demonstrated a high level of textual competency when discussing the work of Clive Barker. She could name the novels from which Barker adapted his films as well as the characters in them, and also demonstrated a detailed knowledge of the special effects team that worked on his films. She also related the films to other works in the horror genre. However, such avid fans constituted the smallest group among the respondents and avid fan behaviour was something many respondents criticized as being a negative feature which they associated with masculine fan behaviour. The rejection of male-dominated fandom led some respondents to less formal fan groups, as with the small group of women who formed their own women-only club, Women in Favour of Movies with Mindless Violence.

The behaviour of many respondents matched that of intense fans, identified by a distanced perspective and linked to life goals. Many respondents were themselves involved in the writing of horror fiction or other material, often for fanzines or on the Internet, and hoped one day to be published professionally. Such writing is often strongly linked to horror film viewing. A 38-year-old said of her horror film viewing: 'I like to examine the way things are done – and make note of the things I think best not to do.' A 29-year-old stated that:

> As a writer I need to keep abreast of changes in the genre. A friend once asked why I wrote horror/fantasy fiction as opposed to writing about 'real life'; my answer was that I have to live 'real life', why should I have to write and read about it too?

It may be, however, that female horror film fans and followers are seeking goals or pleasures in their participation in fandom which have thus far been accorded little recognition. One area of horror fandom in which female fans participate in large numbers is that centred around vampire films and fiction. The high participation rates in vampire fandom reflect the strong liking for vampire films, but there are other reasons for the high levels of participation by female fans, and these will be explored later in this chapter. In particular there are links to patterns of fan consumption described by Stacy (1994), especially commodity purchase and fashion.

FAN CONSUMPTION: MAGAZINE AND FANZINE READERSHIP

For horror fans, one of the largest areas of fan commodity purchase is magazine and fanzine publishing. There is a large number of professional titles on sale in the UK, a number of American imports, and a substantial number of fanzines. Despite the fact that many respondents in the study wrote horror fiction and others wrote reviews of horror, very few women were frequent readers of the mass-market horror publications. Of the UK magazines, only 13 per cent of all respondents read all or most issues of one leading title, *The Dark Side*, and 12 per cent all or most issues of another, *Shivers*. Sixty per cent never read *The Dark Side* and 57 per cent never read *Shivers*. Regular consumption of imported American magazines was even lower (most probably due to their limited availability, usually in specialist SF/comic shops not frequently visited by women). Nine per cent read all or most issues of the effects and make-up oriented *Fangoria*, while only 2 per cent regularly read the science fiction and horror title *Cinefantastique*.

If regular readership of horror publications was clearly low, many women did read the magazines on an irregular basis: 25 per cent read *Cinefantastique* occasionally, 34 per cent *Fangoria*, 20 per cent *Shivers* and 26 per cent *The Dark Side*. This appears to be because the respondents were choosy about which issue they bought, purchasing a magazine only when it had something of particular interest to them in it. A 35-year-old reported: 'I tend to buy issues related to specific films or topics such as design/special effects I'm interested in.' This suggests that the respondents may have been interested in special effects not in their own right but in association with particular films.

Of those respondents who read horror magazines only infrequently, they were just as likely to read an American import as a British title. This may have been because they were interested in specific films, which are covered earlier in the American publications than in UK ones due to earlier release in the US. The respondents were also particularly interested in Hammer films and this explains the popularity of the short-lived UK magazine *Hammer Horror*, which reflected their tastes and interests more than other titles.

Regular consumption of any particular horror magazine by the respondents was, by and large, absent, with 33 per cent of respondents never reading any horror magazines at all, and a further one-third reading one or more titles only irregularly. Of the one-third who did read one or more horror magazines regularly, less than half of these read more than one title regularly.

Fanzine readership was similarly low. Rather than women being unrecognised consumers of horror magazines, it would seem that they often do not read these publications at all, and, indeed, the editor of the UK fanzine *Samhain* has confirmed that women rarely subscribe.

While the low female readership of magazines and fanzines may be due to the fact that the respondents did not like these publications, or bought them only selectively, it might also be that such magazines are simply unavailable, especially outside of the major metropolitan centres. Some respondents indicated that they were not aware of some or all of the titles. A few had never heard of the magazines, others found that they were just not available in the area in which they lived. Access to horror magazines, then, is restricted and this was undoubtedly compounded by women's low rates of participation in horror fandom or association with other fans: knowledge of these titles is unlikely to be handed down by word of mouth to the isolated viewer. Often the magazines are available only in specialist shops which women tend not to frequent in large numbers; where they *are* available in high street stores, they are unlikely to be with traditional women's titles and, therefore, may be overlooked by this group of viewers. There is also a possibility that they are deliberately overlooked, either because it is not thought socially acceptable for women to read them, or because they are aimed at a young male readership with an attendant emphasis on gore, sex and trivial facts. In fact several respondents found many of the titles distasteful. A 46-year-old did not like most professional horror magazines 'as they seem to lay an emphasis on gore, which I'm not fond of.' A 42-year-old thought they were 'appalling', adding: 'I do not read most because they aim for the lowest common denominator and I find them rubbish.' The emphasis on gore as the reason for disliking most horror magazines reflected the tastes of the participants and, in particular, the dislike of gory, special effects-driven horror films. Some respondents also perceived an obsession with trivia in the magazines, repeating one of the main objections to male-dominated fandom. A 20-year-old stated: 'I did once see a *Hammer Horror* magazine and although I was tempted – I flicked through it – I thought it seemed quite sad to enthuse about horror in a fanatical way.'

Many more respondents took exception to the objectification of the female body that some titles reproduce. The contents of some horror magazines were seen as near-pornographic and as perpetuating negative female stereotypes or representations of violence against women. For example, a 25-year-old said:

> I look through things like *Fangoria* to see what's coming up but most fanzines spend too much time on 'tits and arse'. They seem to have concluded that all horror fans are sex starved adolescent males who will drool over any naked female body, so cram the issues with glossy photos of scantily clad women.

This is not restricted to the American titles. The UK title *The Dark Side* comes in for particular criticism in this area. A 23-year-old stated:

> I used to read *The Dark Side* but got disillusioned with the continual coverage of sado-porn videos in which I have no interest. I understand that the editor also edits a magazine devoted to the porn video industry and I think he may get a little confused as to which films should be discussed in which magazine!

Many of the respondents found this approach offensive. A 19-year-old felt 'its attitude and coverage of certain subject matter deeply sexist.' The 42-year-old quoted above, who had children, disliked seeing 'naked babes' in the magazines and found the photos 'frankly embarrassing'. This attitude was not related solely to feminist arguments about pornography. Some respondents felt that the coverage of horror in such magazines was not representative of their definitions of the genre. The 19-year-old again: 'One reason that I stopped buying *The Dark Side* was that it concentrated on the worst examples of sexism in the horror genre when the vast majority of horror films are not like this at all.' Although *The Dark Side* did come in for most criticism over its representations of women, it was, paradoxically, the most widely read magazine among this group of viewers – as reported above. This may indicate that some women are prepared to overlook sexist or pornographic content in their desire to find out more about particular films or subjects (as they may indeed do in certain horror films).

Reasons given for reading horror magazines were varied, but the patterns do seem to conform to those of fan consumption existing elsewhere, particularly among women. Notable reasons given were the coverage which magazines give to favourite horror films, stars or characters. A 19-year-old read *Hammer Horror* magazine because:

> I ... really like the actors in those films. I think the magazine has good pictures, is very informative and has lots of little 'interesting bits'. ... I also hope (although he didn't do much work with Hammer) to get more info about Vincent Price!

Such respondents were searching for pictures of their favourite stars – this particular respondent was looking for 'coverage of vampire films, pictures of good films, stories on horror actors like Vincent Price, Peter Cushing'. For one 18-year-old this involved cutting out the pictures. Another, a 26-year-old, collected *Hammer Horror* magazines: 'I have a habit of buying them for a few months without looking at them. Then when I get some time to myself I read the lot from cover to cover.' This is similar to forms of fan behaviour commonly associated with fan adoration of actors and popular music stars, particularly among teenage girls.

From this evidence, the low rate of horror magazine and fanzine purchase and consumption by female fans seems to be attributable to the fact that they are predominantly written, edited and published by men for men. Like female science fiction fans, who are ghettoized into 'feminine' forms of fanzine publishing (Tulloch and Jenkins 1995: 12), female horror fans are excluded from male-dominated horror fan commodity purchase and production.

VAMPIRE FANDOM

Fan cultures surrounding the vampire film, by contrast, have high rates of participation by female fans. There is nothing to suggest that vampire fandom is dominated by women, but female fans do seem to play a more active role in this area than in other sectors of horror fandom. Women such as this 23-year-old fan do seem to be more comfortable with participating in vampire fandom; as she put it: 'I started a fanzine ... to give me an opportunity to explore my interest [in vampires] and share my ideas more widely.' Aside from a strong interest in vampire films and fiction, a more equal female-to-male ratio in the vampire societies (than in, say, the British Fantasy Society) may be one of the main reasons why women are active participants in this area of fan culture. They are encouraged and supported by fellow female members and not subject to the negative remarks made by male fans in male-dominated fan groups.

Female participation in vampire fandom illustrates the attraction of vampire films for many fans. The wearing of vampire costumes – often consisting of period, usually Victorian, dress – is popular (and there is also a concomitant interest in the Gothic and historical costume drama). Dressing up and fashion are the principal forms of commodity purchase associated with vampire fan culture. Fans often make their own period costume and purchase garments such as opera cloaks and Victorian or Elizabethan corsets. In keeping with the Goth subculture, to which many vampire fans also belong,[6] they dress in predominantly black clothing, wear their hair long, black or vibrantly dyed and crimped, and wear white or very pale makeup with black or blood red lipstick, heavily black-lined eyes and black nail polish. Typical clothing is remodelled on Victorian, Georgian and other historical fashions (frock coats, poet's shirts, cloaks and capes, fans, ornate walking sticks and top hats) as well as punk and fetish clothing, velvet, lace, leather and PVC being predominant materials. Styles borrow heavily from funerary, religious, pagan or vampiric imagery, including crucifixes, coffins, skulls and bats. The 23-year-old quoted above is typical:

> My enjoyment of horror films used to be evident in that I adopted a Gothic style based primarily on my envy of those beautiful vamps in horror films and their exotic glamour. I began to feel ridiculous like this

as I got older and grew out of it, but my interest in horror is as strong as ever.

For many of these women, their liking for horror and vampires was a reason for them being attracted to the Goth movement. A 21-year-old respondent stated that:

> When I was 14 I started getting interested in Gothic music. So that's what happens when your parents buy you horror stories. The Gothic scene watches horror movies so you get even more attracted to it. You have all this music and then you read ghost stories together and it goes on and on.

This dual attraction to vampires and to the Goth subculture seems to be strongly linked to an expression of femininity and the female masquerade. The vampire look adopted by some vampire fans appears to be an aberrant form of the feminine masquerade (Rivière 1929). Vampire costumes conform to (historical) extremes of femininity, particularly according to Victorian standards, and are predominantly black which, although symbolic of mourning or death, is also associated with a fetishistic (and dangerous) sexuality. This impression is reinforced by the wearing of underwear as outerwear (corsets over dresses, sheer or lacy fabrics exposing underwear or the body) and the use of fetishistic materials. Basing their appearance on images of predatory female vampires, these fans adopt extremes of femininity in opposition to contemporary social norms. Long, sharpened finger nails, exaggerated lips, eyebrows plucked into extreme arches, excessive amounts of jewellery, Victorian styles of dress and the wearing of corsets all mark this look as aberrant. The wearing of vampire fangs and abnormally coloured contact lenses also renders the wearer as a figure of monstrosity or danger, emphasising the lack of conformity to current ideas of femininity. This parallels a reversal of the Gothic role of victim which Gallafent (1988) has called the anti-masquerade.

The vampire masquerade forms, in many instances, an outward sign of the respondent's identity. Although the masquerade takes place largely within fandom, several stated that they had worn vampire-style or Goth clothing on an everyday basis at some point in their lives. This was not uneventful for some: one 21-year-old, for example, complained about people calling her 'Morticia' in the street. For a few, this appropriation of vampire imagery spread to other areas of their lives, influencing how they decorated their homes or named their pets. A 23-year-old reported:

> Horror films influence my taste in clothes, objects and literature and give my imagination scope to roam. The clothes that vampires [wear] have influenced my dress sense, as the sets have influenced my taste in décor. I have named my black cat Louis (after the vampire of course), he has small sharp white teeth and I love him.

CONTINUED

It would appear that, for many vampire fans, participating in fan culture allows them to dress up and to act out a fantasy. As Baert (1994) states, this contains the potential for destroying the dominant codes of gender. The 'bad girl' look of the vampire masquerade, like the punk street fashions discussed by Evans and Thornton (1989: 42), mangles sexual codes, confounds given meanings, valorizes 'bad taste', advocates an unpretty look of menace and threat and subverts the mask of femininity. The Goth vampire costume thus works as subversive anti-fashion, but for the respondents it is a glamorous image which embodies femininity, albeit a differently articulated one. Such clothing may, as Baert suggests, offer the woman a partial means to 'play her way out of ... the impasse of femininity' (ibid.: 143). The adoption of the vampire masquerade seems related to a desire for a more extreme form of femininity (or, at least, style of dress) than that currently fashionable in contemporary society; a yearning 'for bygone days of opulence and elegance' that reveals 'hidden passions and [a] sensual nature', as one maker of vampire costumes put it. A 28-year-old explained that: 'It was a hobby before I went to college as I used to make elaborate ball gowns for my dolls when I was 11, which progressed to making all my own clothes.' Thus, a traditional feminine childhood interest had been subverted by an attraction to horror but, nevertheless, can still be coded as feminine. For female vampire fans, the pleasure in dressing up could be seen as an extension of the young girl's desire to dress up in adult or fairy tale costumes. However, here it has developed into an aberrant form of dress (dark and vampiric, often highly sexualised or fetishistic) which lasts into adulthood and frequently spills over into everyday life; as one 26-year-old commented: 'Prance around in pink dresses all day? Huh. I don't think so.'

The adoption of the vampire masquerade is a way of coding allegiance to a subculture (the Goth movement of vampire fandom), but such behaviour might also be read as subversive. Adoption of the vampire masquerade may provide the female horror fan with a 'liminal moment outside the time and space of the dominant order' (Mulvey 1987: 16). It may even allow entry into the language of politics for, as Cosgrove (1989) says, the adoption of subcultural fashions can be 'an inarticulate rejection of the straight world and its organisation'.

These fan activities, then, can be related to rituals of resistance against social norms of femininity, as well as to other forms of feminine consumption such as the romance, historical novel and Gothic fiction. This offers further evidence that female horror film spectatorship, although complex and possibly contradictory, might be feminine in nature, yet aberrant. The adoption of the vampire masquerade and the acting out of vampire fantasies in real life are important forms of appropriation of horror film texts and a source of pleasure. This can also be seen as a form of cultural resistance against accepted ideals of femininity, but, again, does not break away entirely from patterns of feminine behaviour. This is linked to the relationship between style, fashion and beauty and female spectatorship. In particular, it can be seen as a form of commodification which links a film or star with a specific product (Doane 1989). As a form of consumerism this is connected to extra-cinematic identification as described by Stacey (1994: 138–70). Transformation of the self occurs not just as a viewing fantasy but to various extents in real life, including an extension of dressing up into the realms of play-acting through the adoption of a vampire persona.

FAN PRACTICES

In conclusion, then, it should be noted that female horror fans follow patterns of practice similar to other types of fans, particularly in the areas proposed by Stacey for female fans of classic cinema. There are some notable differences, however, between male and female horror fan practice, most notably in the consumption of horror merchandise such as magazines and fanzines. In this respect, the respondents in this study who were active fans practised a form of behaviour similar to other groups of female genre fans, specifically, female science fiction fans – for example, in the area of fan fiction. Although these respondents – like many other fans – can be described as nomads, the findings here suggest that female horror fans seek out space where feminine fan practices can be exercised without attracting negative comments from male fans in particular and society in general. In addition, many respondents go through a process of incorporating the vampire appearance, mannerisms and behaviour into everyday life 'as if they were aspects of the fan's private sectarian world' (Eco 1987: 198).

A significant proportion of the respondents did not participate at all in horror fandom. They hid their liking for horror, watched horror films alone on television or video, did not mix with other fans or followers, and were not able to talk about it with friends or family, who did not understand the liking for horror. This was not necessarily through choice. Some simply did not know any other women who like horror. One 28-year-old lamented that: 'If I'm the only female horror buff out there, I'd like to know.' The following quote from a 34-year-old demonstrates why many women might view alone:

> One reason I watch some horror on video is that I have no female friends who like this and it can be awkward going to the cinema on your own at night, when this is on the programming. Therefore, for purely practical reasons, video makes things easily accessible.

Some did reject certain forms of fandom, but most found some area in which they could indulge their interest. It may be that a broad-based, literary-oriented and long-established fan organization is more acceptable to some

women, while others find fandoms organized around sub-genres which are popular with women more accommodating to female fans. Within horror fandom, an 'us and them' mentality operates along similar lines to the general population's view of fans as other (Jenkins 1992), in this case working along gender lines.

Obviously, much of what has been said about extra-cinematic identification in this chapter will not apply to the respondents who did not participate in fandom to any great extent. Nevertheless, it would be wrong to ignore this group entirely. It may be that such female horror film viewers are representative of a 'silent majority' whose primary form of fan consumption is to view horror films in the privacy of their own homes, either alone or with a trusted viewing partner, often a close friend or husband or other family member. It may be that, for these fans, the main source of pleasure from such fan consumption is an enrichment of their fantasy lives, but that it may be a guilty pleasure, like romance reading or soap opera viewing. Some fan practices may then act as a form of reassurance that there are others out there with similar interests and that the fan is not abnormal in her tastes, as the following 32-year-old indicated:

> I … read the magazines just to see why others make/write/like horror.
> I like to hear about how an idea got started, why it was done instead of another idea. I like to know about the people behind the horror … somehow, it makes me feel not quite so weird.

Female horror film viewing may have been rendered invisible in the same way that soap opera and romantic fiction has at times been devalued and denigrated. This study has revealed that female horror fans and followers have found areas of support among fellow fans and developed ways of expressing resistance against social norms. The areas of fan practice and commodity purchase explored here need to be reviewed in the context of popular pleasures and feminine subjectivity within cinema studies.

NOTES

1 Undertaken as research for the author's PhD thesis (Cherry 1999a).
2 See Cherry 1999b for an account of the female viewers' horror film tastes.
3 The chi-square value indicates a probability about 95 per cent confidence that there is a relationship between liking slasher films and thinking of oneself as a fan ($\chi^2 = 5.86$, p = 0.00).
4 The chi-square value indicates a probability above 95 per cent confidence that there is a relationship between age at which horror films are first viewed and thinking of oneself as a fan ($\chi^2 = 32.78$, p = 0.00).
5 The term 'anorak' – first applied to trainspotters (after the item of clothing which they wore as protection against the elements while standing on train

platforms) – is now widely used to refer dismissively to other groups of fans and hobbyists.

6   Although the interest in vampires is strong, it should be pointed out that not all vampire fans would consider themselves to be Goths, or indeed do all Goths have a liking for vampires. Indeed, there is evidence that this leads to frequent splits and heated debates in both camps. One member of the Vampyre Society participating in this research expressed her dislike of the fact that many active members of the society were Goths and that it had been said to her that one had to be a Goth in order to have a strong liking for vampires and be in the society. From the evidence of this research, this is obviously not the case, and some respondents are unaware of the Goth subculture. Conversely, discussion of vampires in Goth circles is frequently met with disapproval.

7   In reference to the character from the American comic strip, TV comedy and films of *The Addams Family*.

REFERENCES

Baert, R. (1994) 'Skirting the issue', *Screen* 35, 4: 354–60.

Cherry, B. (1999a) *The Female Horror Film Audience: Viewing Pleasures and Fan Practices*, PhD thesis (unpublished) University of Stirling.

Cherry, B. (1999b) 'Refusing to refuse to look: female viewers of the horror film', in M. Stokes and R. Maltby (eds) *Identifying Hollywood Audiences: Cultural Identity and the Movies*, London: British Film Institute.

Cosgrove, S. (1989) 'The zoot suit and style warfare', in A. McRobbie (ed.) *Zoot Suits and Second-hand Dresses: An Anthology of Fashion and Music*, London: Macmillan.

Doane, M.A. (1989) 'The economy of desire: the commodity form in/of the cinema', *Quarterly Review of Film and Video* 11: 23–33.

Eco, U. (1987) *Travels in Hyperreality*, London: Picador.

Evans, C. and Thornton, M. (1989) *Women and Fashion: A New Look*, London: Quartet.

Gallafent, E. (1988) 'Black satin: fantasy, murder and the couple in *Gaslight* and *Rebecca*', *Screen* 29, 3: 82–105.

Hall, S. (1980) 'Encoding/decoding', in S. Hall, D. Hobson, A. Lowe and P. Willis (eds) *Culture, Media, Language*, London: Hutchinson.

Jenkins, H. (1992) *Textual Poachers: Television Fans and Participatory Culture*, London: Routledge.

Lewis, L.A. (1992) 'Something more than love: fan stories on film', in Lewis (ed.) *The Adoring Audience: Fan Culture and Popular Media*, London: Routledge.

Mulvey, L. (1987) 'Changes: thoughts on myth, narrative and historical experience', *History Workshop Journal* 23: 3–19.

Reeves, J.L., Hague, A. and Cartwright, M. (1996) 'Rewriting popularity: the

cult files', in D. Lavery, M. Rodgers and M. Epstein (eds) *Deny All Knowledge*:
Reading The X-Files, London: Faber & Faber.

Rivière, J. (1929) 'Womanliness as a masquerade', reprinted in V. Burgin,
J. Donald and C. Kaplan (eds) (1986) *Formations of Fantasy*, London:
Methuen.

Stacey, J. (1994) *Star Gazing: Hollywood Cinema and Female Spectatorship*, London:
Routledge.

(Cherry 2002: 42–57)

As you may have noted in Chapter 5 on genre, a frequent objective of the film producer
is to produce a film that will appeal to a wide audience. This is particularly true of
Hollywood where vast sums are invested in films in the expectation of high box-office
rewards. Of course there is no guarantee of success and it is not unusual to find that the
success of a film is based upon factors that may seem outside the control of both the
producers and the publicity machine employed to market it. When reading the following
extract, consider how films 'find their audience' in these unexpected ways.

SPECIFYING THE AUDIENCE

Contrary to popular wisdom, audiences are not gulled into attending films
by distorting or misleading advertising campaigns. A phrase often used by
producers refers to a film 'finding its audience' and this is a more accurate
description of what actually happens. A film needs to specify its audience,
not only in its text but also in its advertising campaign; in the series of
interviews and promotional performances that may surround it; in the
selection of exhibition venues (if there is a choice); even in the choice of the
distribution company (again, if there is a choice). It is up to the producers
and distributors to agree on the ways in which they wish to specify the
audiences (or represent the film), and in many cases bad judgements are
made. The Australian film, *The Chant of Jimmie Blacksmith*, was a sympathetic
and thoughtful study of the plight of a half-caste in rural Australia, as well as
a narrative around a true incident involving the mass murder of white settlers
by three Aborigines. In the advertising campaign, emphasis was placed on
the latter aspect – the logo featured an axe dripping blood – and links were
thus constructed with horror films rather than with social-problem films.
Already potentially marginal because of it racial subject, it did not 'find its
audience' in Australia. Alternatively, the surprise success of *The Gods Must Be
Crazy* in some countries seems to be related to its unassuming pattern of
release (that is, the number, type, and location of cinemas screening it): it
was allowed to 'sleep' for a while almost without promotion, until it built up
'good word of mouth'.

No amount of advertising will continue to pull people into a film they do not enjoy and cannot speak well of to their friends. The history of Hollywood is full of films which cost fortunes, which were expensively promoted, and which lost millions at the box-office. (*Waterworld* is a recent example.) *Heaven's Gate* is now a film which many have heard of simply because it was such a box-office disaster; few have ever seen it. Film producers experience great difficulty in predicting how audiences will react to each new production – and in convincing their backers to support any prediction they might eventually make. All they can do is try to specify as carefully as possible just whom this film is going to be for, and then try to ensure – through the release patterns and promotional campaigns – that this audience is reached.

Speaking of classical Hollywood cinema, John Ellis (1982) has said that there were two main ways in which its narrative image could be deployed to specify audiences: through the genre and through the stars. Although the audiences 'specified' are much more specific today, this is still largely the case. Audiences choose movies through their representations in the press and on television, and through conversations and other social contacts. These representations are understood in terms of genre, or stars where they are not already enclosed by genre. There is, perhaps, a third set of determinants: the broad cultural context in which the audience and the film are situated. The notion of genre was dealt with in the preceding chapter, so I will concentrate on the latter two categories here.

As suggested in the opening chapter, the context in which any film is released is constituted by a limitless number of components. There are the promotional and 'tied-in' productions – music videos, advertisements, hit songs, merchandise such as T-shirts, interviews, magazine stories, reviews, fan magazine items, and many more. In addition we might find that particular genres or particular stars have themselves cultural or subcultural status that is important. Attendance at a film can become a statement of membership of a subculture; certainly the cult around *The Rocky Horror Picture Show* supports this. Seeing rock music films often has the same significance; U2's audience will confirm their membership of the group by seeing *Rattle 'n' Hum*. The act of attendance itself becomes a signifier of commitment to the ritual of the fan.

Some films become newsworthy or topical at the time of release, often accidentally. Alan Parker's *Angel Heart* acquired useful pre-publicity on the basis of an explicit sex scene involving Lisa Bonet, the 18-year-old star of the wholesome American TV family sitcom *The Cosby Show*. (The example reveals how interwoven and comprehensive our cultural networks are.) As a result of the controversy, the film was at least initially constructed as 'explicit' (a small genre in itself) and had a recognizable name even before release. Brandon

CONTINUED

303

AUDIENCE

Lee's death while filming helped turn *The Crow* into a cult film. In another case, the coincidence of the release of *The China Syndrome* at the same time as the nuclear accident at Three Mile Island certainly had an effect on the fortunes of the film as well as on the residents of the contaminated area. In some cases, the context when the film is released is markedly different to that when it was made. A case in point is Susan Seidelman's casting of Madonna in *Desperately Seeking Susan*. In the period between casting and release, from being a virtual unknown Madonna became an international star. On the one hand, this had the effect of specifying a large, possibly inappropriate audience – Madonna fans. On the other hand, it became very hard for this clever and interesting film not to be seen as an opportunistic star vehicle by some of its critics, or to be ignored by potential audiences who had a less than high regard for Madonna as a pop singer and, especially, as a politically regressive signifier of female sexuality. For what could be seen as a feminist film, this was a critical rather than a commercial problem. In a final example, Madonna's own *Truth or Dare* directly capitalized on her personal notoriety by claiming to document her on and off stage behaviour while on tour.

The cultural context can be a factor, then, in determining whether or not the film and its audience 'find' each other. However, overwhelmingly, most choices are determined by issues that are essentially generic or essentially to do with the role of the stars.

(Turner 1999: 116–120)

One aspect of audience study which is easily overlooked is the issues that relate to the context of consumption. Films are consumed in a variety of different contexts from first-run blockbusters at West End cinemas through to movies broadcast on terrestrial television watched on portable TVs in people's bedrooms. You may like to consider how these different contexts for consuming films might change the way in which audiences may read them.

ACTIVITY

➤ Make a list of your personal preferences for watching a film. Explain which particular 'contexts of consumption' you most prefer and consider whether different types of films are better in some contexts rather than others.

One thing you may note is that the nature of film consumption has changed over the years, often in response to technological developments. The advent of the DVD, for example, has made video technology seem somehow clumsy and inflexible. Similarly, the development of satellite and digital technologies is likely to make the distribution of film on celluloid obsolete within the foreseeable future.

FILM STUDIES: THE ESSENTIAL RESOURCE

One especially important change that has influenced the way in which films are consumed at the cinema is the arrival of the multiplex cinema in the early 1990s. As the following extract indicates, the multiplex was foreshadowed in the 1960s when the Odeon in Nottingham became the first cinema to be redesigned to accommodate two screens.

As Mark Jancovich and Lucy Faire explain in the following article, the development of the multiplex and the blockbuster film are intimately intertwined. The multi-screen nature of the multiplex allows a blockbuster to open simultaneously on several different screens, enabling distributors to significantly increase box-office takings by maximising capacity in cinemas for heavily hyped movies.

As you will see in what follows, audiences' responses to the multiplex have not been wholly uncritical.

The term 'blockbuster' can be a misleading one. Historically, there have been several different types of blockbusters and each type has been connected to a different type of exhibition. For example, after World War II, the blockbuster referred to prestigious event movies that were associated largely with big, metropolitan picture palaces (Schatz 1993). It is therefore significant that, when the Nottingham Odeon was redesigned in the 1960s, it not only became the first twin-screen cinema in Britain, but the upstairs cinema, Odeon 1, was clearly designed with these films in mind. It was to 'show the 70 mm, wide-screen films' while downstairs, in Odeon 2, 'continuous performances in ordinary 35 mm' were to be shown. As this suggests, the shows in Odeon 1 would be 'on a bookable basis' due to the use of separate performances, a supposed '"first" for Nottingham' (*Guardian Journal*, 30 June, 1965: 4).

More recently, however, the term 'blockbuster' has come to be associated with the multiplex, and the two are intimately related. The multiplex has not only transformed the meaning of the blockbuster but was itself a response to developments in the blockbuster. On the one hand, the blockbuster no longer refers solely to the prestigious event movie but has come to mean little more than films that are successful at the box office. On the other hand, as Gomery has noted, the success of multiplex cinemas is specifically based on their ability to use their multiple screens to reap maximum profits from blockbusters. For example, he describes Cineplex, a 'Canadian enterprise [that] significantly altered the standards by which North America judged "going to the movies"' (Gomery 1992: 105), who would 'open a popular, well-advertised film on three or four of its screens, and then slowly cut back the number of auditoria as the popularity of the film waned,' or, if they found themselves with a major hit on their hands, 'they would move it into a half-dozen of their largest auditoria ... and not miss a single possible customer' (ibid.: 107). However, while associations between the multiplex and the blockbuster proved finally profitable, and also stimulated renewed interest in cinemagoing as an activity, both remain high contested objects.

CONTINUED

Complaints about the blockbuster are not simply about the films themselves but rather the specific modes of consumption with which they are associated. While different cinemas are contrasted on account of the films that they show, films can also change meaning if shown in different cinemas. For example, in the 1990s, the then director of the Broadway Cinema, Nottingham's regional art film theater, claimed: 'There's certainly no way that we're in competition with the city centre mainstream cinemas ... I just can't conceive of us showing *Jurassic Park* [1993] for instance.' Here a blockbuster stands for the difference between the art cinema and the mainstream, but the director then qualifies this remark: 'not unless we are doing a season on special effects films or we got Steven Spielberg over to do an introduction to it' (*Nottingham Evening Post* (NEP), July 20, 1993). It is not the film itself that is the problem but specific contexts of consumption. *Jurassic Park* might be shown at the Broadway, but only in an educational or intellectual context.

In other words, cinemas are associated with, and come to represent, modes of consumption that are hierarchically ranked and valued. For example, in its strategy for exhibition, the East Midlands Region Media Agencies Partnership (EMRMAP) draws on a specific metaphorical distinction: 'Like the restaurant sector, specialist cinemas offer a different menu and a different ambience compared to the 'fast food' multiplexes' (EMRMAP 2001: 23). Nor is such a distinction peculiar to EMRMAP: it draws on a series of discourses and associations that surround the multiplex more generally.

The problems associated with the multiplex are not simply about the films shown. It is often criticized for its relationship to, and effects upon, the city more generally. It is frequently linked with the growth of other out of town developments such as the shopping mall, and is subject to very similar debates (Gomery 1992; Hanson 2000; Jones 2001: Paul 1994; Hubbard forthcoming). According to Miller and his collaborators, the 'often contested meanings of these shopping places' can be divided into two main concerns (Miller *et al.* 1998: ix). On the one hand, these shopping malls are seen as a solution to the problems of the inner city – 'the now widespread fear of public space' (ibid.: xi) – fears that are often expressed in 'highly racialised terms ... sometimes mediated through notions of dirt and pollution' (ibid.: x). On the other hand, there are also 'fears about the increasingly "artificial" nature of contemporary shopping' (ibid.: xi). As a result, Miller and his colleagues not only discuss concerns about the absence of 'natural' light in Brent Cross Shopping Centre but also the middle-class preference shopping area that was perceived as authentic and communal (ibid.: 123). Through these activities and identifications, consumers sought to distinguish themselves from the 'ordinary' consumer through a rejection of the supposed commercialism and homogeneity of mass consumption. However, this desire for diversity is not necessarily an appreciation of others; it can be a way of differentiating oneself from the masses.

These concerns were also related to other features of the shopping center and the multiplexes where blockbusters are shown. The success of these developments was precisely that they were geared to customers who not only had access to autos, but had also largely deserted consumption in the town center due to the problems of parking there. However, the auto has increasingly been seen as symbolic of the destruction of the city (Jancovich *et al.* forthcoming). Its demands tear up neighborhoods and pollute the environment, but it also creates social exclusion. As auto ownership has increased, public transport has not only been cut back but has become increasingly associated with the poorest sections of the population. Out-of-town multiplex developments are, in part, seen as safe exactly because only certain sections of the population have the transport necessary to gain access to them.

Furthermore, as leisure and consumption have increasingly moved out to these developments, town centers have declined still further, and these developments have therefore become important symbolically. Unlike in America, where they were produced out of the processes of urban sprawl, most of the British shopping centers and multiplexes have been built on 'redundant industrial land' (Gray 1996: 129), and therefore symbolize the transformation of the city from a place of production to one of consumption (Hannigan 1998; Harvey 1991). They represent the literal replacement of industrial factories with cathedrals of consumption that has created a 'tale of two cities': a landscape of increased luxury and prosperity for some and extreme poverty for others (Hannigan 1998: 53).

This chapter will therefore examine the contested meanings of the blockbuster by focusing on the meanings of the multiplex as a place. In the process, it will demonstrate the ways in which both films, and the places where they are 'ordinarily' consumed, figure within debates over the nature of modernization. The meanings of both the blockbuster and the multiplex are usually organized around a series of related concerns about Americanization, mass consumption, and youth culture, in which these terms can acquire both position and negative meanings. Drawing on these ideas, the next section will analyze the ways in which the local press have reported on Nottingham's multiplex to examine the public debates over this building. The following section will then discuss the findings of a range of interviews that were conducted as part of a larger project on film consumption within Nottingham.

SELLING THE MULTIPLEX

Nottingham's multiplex, the Showcase, was opened on Thursday June 16, 1988, with eleven screens, which was more than any other cinema in the country at the time. Bowden Wilson of Leicester, the company that had acquired the site, were planning to build a garden center, a DIY store, an auto accessory store,

307

AUDIENCE

and either a public house or a restaurant (NEP, February 13, 1987). However, the area became a center of leisure and entertainment rather than retail, and the multiplex was soon joined by the Megabowl and Isis Nightclub.

As with earlier periods of cinema-building, the promotional and publicity materials all stressed the new cinema's modernity and comfort. An advert in the NEP claimed that the Showcase would be 'very upmarket' (February 4, 1987), while the press claimed that it combined 'Comfort ... Convenience ... Luxury' with 'the healthful comfort of perfectly controlled air-conditioning' (advert in NEP, June 17, 1988). Also like earlier cinemas, it was 'yet another "first"' and demonstrated that Nottingham was fully up-to-date (NEP, June 17, 1988). Not only was it 'Britain's newest and largest cinema' (ibid.), but it would also be part of 'one of the most exciting leisure areas in Europe' (NEP, October 1, 1987).

The cinema's claims to being modern and innovative were also consolidated through its presentation as an 'an all-American operation.' According to the 'American' manager, American National Amusements, the company that owned the Showcase, was 'bringing American standards of quality to Britain in an industry which has a great future' (NEP, May 13, 1988). The NEP added to these positive associations with America: 'the 11-screen cinema is nothing like anyone remembers; nothing like anyone in this country has ever known.' The 'splendid American venture on the ring road' may have represented an 'American invasion of the city,' but this was definitely presented as a 'good thing' (NEP, October 15, 1987).

These reports worked to construct an imaginary America that was consumed through the practice of cinemagoing (Webster 1988; Morley and Robins 1995), particularly the watching of blockbuster movies. For the NEP, an interview with the manager claimed that the '"all-American" outlook on life' was encapsulated in the words 'movies,' 'corporate images,' 'concession stands,' 'multiplex concepts,' and 'quality customer service' (NEP, October 15, 1987). The cinema was also associated with America through its 'glamour.' Its 'glittering celebrity opening' (Nottingham Trader, June 22, 1988) had 'a grand reception in grand American style' that gave the guests a 'taste of Hollywood' (NEP, June 17, 1988).

However, the company was also worried that some Nottingham residents would not appreciate the associations with America and tried to counteract potential problems. They stressed not only that the cinema's American style was synonymous with quality, but that the company would not simply impose itself upon Nottingham:

> Our theatres, with more comfort, more space and more attention to detail, are recognised as the finest in the United States – and that's the standard we're bringing to Nottingham ... The addition of this kind of enterprise serves as a magnet for and contributes to the development

of a myriad of other business enterprises, with the resulting additional employment and revenue to the community. We aim to play a significant role in not only the civic but also the economic affairs of the communities in which we operate.

(NEP, October 14, 1987)

It was also stated: 'We're not saying British cinemas aren't run well, but we just like to run our business in a certain way' (NEP, June 14, 1988).

As a place where blockbuster movies might be watched, the cinema additionally marked its distinction from more traditional cinemas in other ways. For example, it was stressed that there was parking for 850 automobiles and that everyone would find a space. It was also designed in ways that, as can be seen from the comments above, were clearly supposed to signify spectacle, comfort, and luxury, although as we shall see, others have read the multiplex as bland and functional. The 'product' was also different: there were no adverts, no smoking, no double features, no interval, and no ice-cream lady (NEP, May 23, 1988). However, there was a massive concession stand that dominated the central foyer and which one had to pass to gain access to the auditoria. Food was therefore central in the construction of the Showcase's image, and the selection of foods associates the cinema with America and the mass-produced abundance that it represents (Lyons, n.d.). The cinema management also emphasized that for the first time Nottingham audiences could see films at the same time as the West End of London. The Showcase, it was implied, gave one direct access to Hollywood cinema and, as a result, Nottingham was no longer marginal to London.

Nonetheless, there were several features that question Nottingham's claim to being at the cutting edge of cinema. First, while the Showcase was the first cinema in the UK with eleven screens, it was certainly not the first multiplex. The Point in Milton Keynes, which was opened in 1985, predated the Showcase by three years, and by the end of 1988 there were fourteen multiplexes in Britain. Nor did the Showcase ensure that Nottingham had more choice in venues or screens: there had been more screens in the 1930s and 1940s.

Indeed, while the Showcase's management made claims to the cinema's newness and modernity, it also associated the cinema with this earlier era. The advertising played heavily on the nostalgic glamor of the Hollywood past, even though it sought to assert the Showcase's superiority over that past in certain respects. In short, it tried to negotiate a relationship between the past and future. In a similar way, Lynn Spigel has claimed that her students were able to maintain both a nostalgic desire for the past and a sense of the present as progress from that past, and that they did so in part by imagining the future as an idealized time in which they could reconcile the pleasures associated with both past and present. As she claims: 'Nostalgia in this regard

CONTINUED

is not the opposite of progress, but rather its handmaiden. Like the idea of progress, nostalgia works to simplify history into a time-line of events that lead somewhere better' (Spigel 1995: 29).

The management even enlisted the veteran local film critic Emrys Bryson to endorse the cinema by dedicating an auditorium to him. In response, Bryson is quoted as saying:

> I was worried at first about the effect the Showcase would have, but in fact it cleared out a lot of dead wood and it put the other cinemas on their mettle ... I think that the multiplexes have actually done a great deal for the cinema industry.

> (NEP, 25 June, 1998)

While he acknowledged certain anxieties about the multiplex, he ultimately condoned it as embodying both the best of the past and the best of the present.

THE MEANINGS OF THE MULTIPLEX

These perceptions of the Showcase were shared by a great many of our respondents. Many saw it as the best of the Nottingham cinemas (Dalbir, aged 14, student), and associated it with America in ways that were wholly positive (Tony, 67, retired teacher). For these respondents, the Showcase was a distinctive and spectacular building. It was 'overwhelming' (ibid.) in a positive sense, providing sensorial abundance even to the point of dizzying overload. This abundance was not limited to the spectacle of the building or its food, but also to the range of blockbuster films on offer. It was particularly popular with the groups of Asian youth and with the youth of Southwell, a nearby town, for whom it represented something that was clearly divorced from what they regarded as the provincial location of their everyday lives (cf. Interviews with Tarnjit, 16; Dalbir, 14; Subaigh, 11; Suroop, 10; Harprit, 18; Harjot, 10; Bikrumjit, 14; and GCSE English Class, 14–15, Minister School, Southwell). Parents often claimed that their young children loved the place and frequently pleaded to be taken there (Donna, 30 clerical officer; Whitegate Mothers and Toddlers Group). However, while some parents were clearly ambivalent about their children's attachment to the place, its success as a cinema is also closely tied to its function as a 'safe environment' for young people. The area was largely cut off from the surrounding city, and its security system meant that youth were not only protected but monitored (GCSE English Class). Safety was an issue for disabled respondents too, who stressed that the Showcase was distinguished by its provision of level access (Joe, 36, volunteer).

However, many adults saw the cinema as an unappealing and alienating space, and those adults who were positive about it were often associated with it through a teenage intermediary. Some elderly respondents, for example, took their grandchildren there, and time spent with their grandchildren colored their feelings about the cinema more generally. Another respondent often went with her son. The Showcase was also seen as a place where the family could do something together, although this situation does not necessarily imply that they occupied the same auditorium. Several respondents said that one of the advantages of the multiplex was precisely that one could go out together as a family, but watch different movies (Donna, 30, clerical officer).

For these respondents, the cinema was not only visually impressive but also welcoming and with friendly staff (John, 55, lecturer; Charlotte, 16, occupation unknown). For others, however, the cinema was a deeply unpleasant and even repellent place whose audience is a mindless mass simply duped by marketing (Stefan, 25, unemployed teacher). For these respondents, the Showcase was not a spectacular and visually impressive building but a characterless and even 'placeless' place. However, it was not simply the building that was being discussed here. Thus while some described the showcase as 'soulless,' 'clinical,' and 'like an airport' (anonymous female, 30, occupation unknown; Lynnette, 26, clerical assistant; Helen, 40, project worker), these descriptions also suggested that it is 'impersonal' (Catherine, 25, student). These terms therefore had two implicit meanings: on the one hand they suggested that the place lacked identity, but on the other that it was associated with functionality and rationality – with technology, materialism, and commerce. Furthermore, while Miller and his colleagues found that the supposed 'artificiality' of Brent Cross Shopping Centre was frequently framed in terms of the absence of 'natural' light, from its first opening, concerns about the Showcase were framed in terms of its 'atmosphere.'

The air-conditioning units that had been used to sell the place were criticized almost immediately, and customers complained that the cinema was too cold. This was more than simply a complaint about the temperature; it was metaphorically linked to a generalized criticism of the cinema as an emotionally cold place – clinical and impersonal – and to other associations with the atmosphere. Most obviously, many respondents claimed that the cinema had 'no atmosphere,' by which they meant again that it lacked personality and character and was emotionally cold and empty (Bakersfield and Sneinton Women's Co-Op Guild). However, other respondents complained that the cinema 'smells funny' (Dorothy, 61, occupation unknown), or that they experienced a feeling of revulsion at the smell of popcorn which, it was claimed, permeates the cinema (Vic, 59, part-time teacher; Christine, 60, retired secretary; Judith, 60, administrative assistant).

At this reference to popcorn makes clear, this visceral intolerance to the air of the cinema was actually related to broader cultural meanings. One respondent condemned the cinema as 'popcorn city' (anonymous female, 41, nurse), and

CONTINUED

311

AUDIENCE

so associated it with low and debased cultural forms and activities. Popcorn has become a symbol for negative evaluations of the Showcase as an American place and, by implication, as a place of popular amusements and 'unashamed indulgence in trash' (Barker and Brooks 1998: 195). This is made clear by the frequent references to the cinema as 'vulgar' and 'brash' (Jackie, 49, part-time student advisor; John, 75, retired), and to the claims that the cinema was part of a process of Americanization (Stefan, 25, unemployed teacher; Neil, 55, welfare worker), a process which, a Duncan Webster has pointed out, is used to displace anxieties about modernity through a deflection of it effects onto an alien invading other (Webster 1988). Thus, America comes to signify the negative features of materialism and mass production in a way that not only lets Britain off the hook but is 'mediated through notions of dirt and pollution,' even if this process is seen in terms of nation rather than race.

Thus, people complained about the corporate image of National Amusements (anon female, 40, careers advisor), and claimed that they resented being 'herded' or 'treated like a number' (Helen, 40, project worker; Marc, 25, student). Here the suggestion is that the cinema turns its customers into mere product to be processed – cattle – and it draws on the distinction between the rationalized mass and the authentic community. As a result, many claimed that there is no place to interact with one another or talk about the film afterwards (Brian, 46, probation officer). It is also for this reason that while those who identified with the Showcase used the term 'overwhelming' positively, those who disliked the place also referred to it as 'overwhelming' (Catherine, 25, student). For these people, it was too big, too overpowering, and hence inhuman. These people complained about the crowds, but also the range of choice which, it was claimed, produced a passive and undiscriminating customer who had no idea of what they were going to see before they arrived at the cinema (Stefan, 25, unemployed teacher; Gray, 1996: 131).

This concern with the undifferentiated mass also shaded over into concerns about the effect of the multiplex upon the city center. For example, the planning officer, Dick Blenkinsop, claimed that he was afraid that the public's choice would be reduced, rather than increased, by the presence of the multiplex, if its presence forced the city center cinemas to close (NEP, February 12, 1987). However, the NEP displayed considerable optimism in their claim that there would be plenty of customers for the city center cinemas, and that the Odeon was 'meeting the challenge not with moans and groans about competition but with typical enthusiasm and verve.' The presence of the multiplex was therefore read as 'healthy competition' in which the 'customer invariably wins' (NEP, June 17, 1988). However, the NEP also believed that Nottingham was a unique case; that the city was such a vibrant center of leisure and culture that it could easily sustain another large cinema: 'No other city outside London offers so much and no other city buzzes with people and activity during the leisure hours in the way that Nottingham does' (ibid.).

While this might sound a lot like boosterism, which it no doubt was, it also seems to have been partly correct. Ironically, it was not the Showcase that killed off the Odeon and the Cannon/ABC. In the late 1990s, there were growing concerns about the impact of out-of-town leisure and retail developments. As a result, while the Odeon and ABC had seen 'the arrival in 1989 of National Amusements' edge-of-town Showcase complex,' it was the Cornerhouse, a large leisure complex built as part of the new concern with city center development, that was the 'straw [that broke] the camel's back' (NEP, Weekend, January 27, 2001).

However, no other city in the East Midlands region fared in this way. Nottingham has long established itself as the center of consumption, leisure, and culture within the area, and it has therefore been able to sustain a more diverse film culture than other towns. In Derby, for example, the presence of a multiplex resulted in the removal of all cinemas from the town center with the exception of a small regional film theater, the Metro, while Leicester has two multiplexes, an art house cinema, and two cinemas that specialize in Asian films, one of which is in the town center. Neither was able to sustain a cinema like the Odeon or the Cannon/ABC. Nonetheless, whatever the prevailing tendencies elsewhere, the Showcase only added to the number of screens in Nottingham, although many respondents saw the choice provided by the multiplex as no 'real' choice, but only a homogeneous and standardized fare. For these respondents, a more meaningful degree of choice was provided by the supposedly 'non-commercial' cinemas.

CONCLUSION

Cultural distinction ranks not only films, but also the places within which they are consumed. As a result, the multiplex itself has been consumed differently by different social groups, due to the ways in which it has been associated with specific types of cultural consumption. Most obviously, the multiplex frequently figures as a place of mass and undifferentiated consumption as opposed to the art cinema, which figures as a place of diversity and distinction (Jancovich *et al.* forthcoming). Ironically, while both the multiplex and the blockbuster are associated with mass consumption, they are also supposed, as we have already seen, to cater only for specific audiences. Here it is often youth that figures as the key concern and one of the repeated assumptions is that these cinemas and the blockbusting films that they show are aimed at a juvenile audience. However, even here quite incompatible notions of 'the juvenile audience' are in operation. On the one hand this audience is associated with the teenager, and on the other it is associated with young children. It is therefore important that we distinguish between different types of multiplex blockbusters: the Disney film aimed at children; the action movie aimed at teenagers; the Spielberg or Lucas feature aimed at a variety

313

AUDIENCE

of audiences. In other words, while those opposed to the multiplex see it as a place of undifferentiated consumption, the audiences that identify with the place can be seen as far more diverse and differentiated, and may even be fractured and opposed to one another. For example, teenage audiences are often keen to distinguish themselves from the audiences for 'children's films,' while even teenage audiences are not homogeneous but are often deeply combative (Jancovich 2000 and 2002). In other words, it is not that the multiplex audience so often characterized as the blockbuster's audience is an undifferentiated mass, but rather that this is how others have perceived it. As Raymond Williams put it: 'There are in fact no masses; there are only ways of seeing people as masses' (Williams 1961: 289).

(Jancovich and Faire 2003: 190–9)

Clearly, one real issue for any film student is the accessibility of films they might want to see. This is a particular issue when it comes to the theatrical screening of films. The ability of audiences to see the films they want in cinemas is determined by the nature of the system of film distribution. This system has evolved very much in the interests of the major Hollywood studies. These studios operate under the economic imperative to ensure that they see a decent return on the capital sums they have invested in producing their films. Access to the box-office is therefore of paramount importance to them.

As you will have just read, one strategy for doing this is the evolution of the multiplex, which while on the surface seems to increase choice, in the opinion of many cinema-goers it actually reduces it. One reason for this is the inability of independent production companies to have their films exhibited unless they sell the rights to the Hollywood majors. The relationship between producers, distributors and exhibitors has an important impact on what audiences can get to see.

In the following article, business professors Hoskins, McFadyen and Finn explore how this system of film distribution works and the effect the Hollywood majors have upon determining what is screened at your local cinema.

Feature films are produced by the seven major Hollywood studios and by hundreds of independents with various types of working arrangement with the majors. What distinguishes the majors and the independents is not just their size. Each major possesses a distribution network in the US and around the world that ensures that its products reach exhibitors and are made available to final consumers everywhere. In this chapter we will explore how the US majors operate their distribution system in order to show why distribution is such a critical factor in their global success.

Feature film producers around the world are in the same situation as US independents – they possess no distribution network to ensure that their product reaches consumers. Such independents sometimes sell completed films outright to the majors (the so-called 'negative pick-ups', because it is the negative of the completed film that is being acquired). Alternatively, the majors may take on distribution of such films on a contract basis. Or, smaller – sometimes national – distributors, or even the producers themselves, may carry out the distribution function.

The average filmgoer knows very little about distribution and the distribution function. In the feature film business, producers rely on distributors to reach exhibitors and final consumers while exhibitors in turn rely on distributors for a steady supply of product attractive to audiences. While one could imagine the hundreds of film producers dealing directly with the thousands of exhibitors around the world, the negotiation and shipping costs would be exorbitant. A major distributor can minimize the transaction costs, ensuring profitability of the system as a whole. As a consequence of organizing and operating this system the distributors are able to capture the lion's share of the profit created. The Americans were the first to recognize the importance of distribution in generating revenues and controlling markets. The early Hollywood dominance of the film industry was not based on favourable production conditions but rather on an early emphasis on distribution and exhibition strategy.

It sometimes seems that US dominance of national cinema markets is a state of nature. But such is not the case. Before the First World War the French and Italians were in a stronger position in export markets. The large US domestic market initially deflected the attention of US firms from export markets:

> In the meantime, foreign producing companies, especially the giant Pathé Freres, had already expanded into the international market and had invaded the USA. The great demand created by the nickelodeon boom could only be met by adding imports to the domestic release schedules. (Thompson, 1985: 2)

But the early success of Pathé was itself built on an effective distribution strategy. 'By encouraging local entrepreneurs to open theatres the firm created a demand for Pathé films. Pathé would then open a film exchange in the area, saturate the market and keep other film companies out' (Thompson, 1985: 5). To build a dominant market position American firms had to counter this strong European competition, both at home and abroad. Domestically they attempted to limit imports and to adopt restrictive trading practices; abroad they opened subsidiaries to control distribution of their own product. As Thompson (1985: x) argues:

> long term American dominance [of foreign markets] came about not only because American firms were able to export more film during the [First

World] war itself, but because they instituted new distribution procedures abroad; rather than selling primarily through agents in London,
they opened their own offices in a variety of countries ... by eroding
the European film industry's base of support abroad (i.e. their export
markets), American competition permanently weakened the strong pre-
war European producing countries.

In the US itself, initially, patent control of projection equipment was used
to limit competition and risk. Later, market control was exerted through the
ownership of large numbers of theatres.

During the "Golden Age' of the Hollywood studios, in the 1930s, the industry
was a mature oligopoly (a small number of large interdependent firms, each
controlling a significant share of the market). Each of the majors (at that time
Warner Bros., Loews/MGM, Paramount, RKO, and Twentieth Century-Fox) was
vertically integrated – controlling all aspects of production, distribution and
exhibition. Vertical integration reduced studio risk because in-house product
was always guaranteed a minimum market in the studio-owned up-scale
theatres; also, non-integrated competitors could be excluded from theatres.

Majors have continued to dominate despite government moves to eliminate
vertical integration (with the Paramount Decree of 1949 requiring studios to
divest themselves of their theatre assets) and to limit anti-competitive practices
such as blind bidding and block booking. Of course, since the Second World War,
the industry they dominate has been greatly reduced in size. For instance, US
box office receipts in nominal terms (i.e. without adjustment for price change)
fell over 43 per cent from $1,692 million in 1946 to $955 million in 1961 (US
Dept. of Commerce). The introduction of television and the growth in consumer
incomes since the war have been related to this relative decline, but these very
forces have opened up new distribution possibilities for the studios.

Prior to 1945 the studios operated on a Fordist basis (i.e. employing industrial mass production methods) and reduced product risk by controlling the
market with their strong distribution position. Wyatt (1994: 68) argues: 'The
lowered demand for motion pictures, added to the Paramount Case, aided
the dissolution of the mature studio system and the movement toward
"the package-unit system" of production.' In that system, 'Rather than an
individual company containing the source of the labour and materials, the
entire industry became the pool for these' (Staiger, 1985: 330). Rather than
having a studio like one of Henry Ford's factories, producers maintain a very
lean operation, bringing together teams of specialists as needed to perform
the various required production functions.

The implications for distribution of these changes in the Hollywood production
system, described in more detail in Chapter 10, are usually overlooked. Wyatt
(1994: 68–9) points out:

With projects existing on a film-by-film basis, the economic 'cushion' of the studio could no longer offset the downfall created by a risky commercial project. Accordingly, films with the greatest inherent chance of returning their investment became more significant in this era. ... After the move to the package-unit system, the studios were no longer vertically integrated; in fact, the studios became primarily distributors of film after this time.

In the early 1960s Universal, Paramount, and Warner were absorbed into large conglomerates while MGM, Columbia and Twentieth Century-Fox remained unaffiliated. Conglomerate control provided the financial depth of resources to be able to shoulder the increasing financial risks associated with a new film making strategy. Wyatt (1994) describes how the majors moved to the 'High Concept film' – characterized by the Hollywood 'look', the 'hook' or star-studded market identifier, and the 'book' or associated products that could be successfully marketed by other divisions of the conglomerate. Although Hollywood blockbusters may appear on the surface to represent big gambles, they really reflect financial conservatism – the pressure to combine financially proven components to enhance the chances of producing a movie with appeal for large audiences. Such films are also appealing to foreign audiences, and the growth in international markets has stimulated their production.

It would be a mistake to think of the Hollywood majors as monolithic constants in the feature film landscape. Not only have there been important ownership changes over the years, with two firms recently falling into foreign hands, but also there has been attrition and large swings in the market shares of particular films. The changes in the market share are shown in Table 1. As well as the majors there are hundreds of US independent film and television production companies with productions to be distributed and exhibited.

Table 1 Changing shares of the movie market (% of total)

Company	1939	1949	1956	1964	1972	1980	1986	1990	1995
Columbia (Sony)	7	8	9	15	9	14	9	5	13
Fox	17	21	18	8	9	16	8	14	8
MGM	22	22	17	17	6	7	4	3	6
United Artists	7	4	10	16	9				
Paramount	14	14	13	17	22	16	22	15	10
Universal	7	7	10	12	5	20	9	14	13
Warner Bros.	14	11	15	6	18	14	12	13	16
RKO	9	9	4						
Disney/Buena Vista	1	1	1	9	5	4	10	16	19
Others	4	3	3	1	16	9	25	20	15

Source: J. W. Finler, *The Hollywood Story* (London: Mandarin, 1992), p. 52; Standard and Poor's Industry Surveys, *Leisure Time*, 1 (18 Apr. 1996), p. L27.

Sometimes the US independents sell all rights to completed films to one of the majors in what is termed a 'negative pick-up'; sometimes they negotiate a distribution deal with one of the majors or some smaller distributor; sometimes they distribute on their own. Non-US producers have similar options, but in their case the smaller distributor might be one based in their home country. A theatrical film passes from the producer to one of these distributors and is then rented to exhibitors in each country.

Until the 1950s all exhibition took place in theatres. Subsequent technological advance, however, has created new exhibition windows – video, pay-per-view television, network television, and basic cable – in each market. The distribution in these other windows is, however, patterned on the feature film model, with the Hollywood majors playing a dominant role. The basis economic rationale behind this is the desire by the distributor of the feature film to capitalize as much as possible on the marketing and promotional activities undertaken for the feature film.

The distributor–exhibitor relationship is one of mutual dependence: the distributors need exhibitors to provide venues so that films can be seen by audiences, while exhibitors need distributors to provide them with a steady stream of good films to maintain the viability of their theatres. Donahue (1987: 99–142) provides a detailed analysis of this relationship. This mutual dependence is an important motivation for vertical integration in the feature film industry. Ever since the Paramount decree forced the majors to divest themselves of their theatre holdings there has been conflict between distributors and exhibitors. Also, conflict between independent producers and the majors has occurred. Prindle (1993: 17) notes:

> Independents accuse the majors of being too lacking in vision to recognize the merit in their films (and therefore refusing to distribute them) or having distributed them, of marketing them incompetently so that they do not make money; or having distributed and marketed them well so that they generate a great deal of revenue, of cheating them out of their just share of the profits.

These same concerns are often voiced by non-US producers, seemingly little aware that the distribution power of the Hollywood majors affects all production companies without distribution capability regardless of nationality.

Two trade practices, used by distributors to lessen their risks are block booking and blind bidding. Block booking occurs when exhibitors are required to take a group of films, including a number of films they would not normally choose to exhibit, in order to secure rights to some other film that is believed to have high market potential. Blind bidding occurs when exhibitors are required to bid on forthcoming films before they are available for viewing. Despite being outlawed in over twenty US states these practices continue because they provide a method of market control for distributors and security of supply for exhibitors.

THE IMPORTANCE OF FILM DISTRIBUTORS AS PROVIDERS OF INFORMATION

A feature film is a product that consumers must pay for before they know how much enjoyment they will receive. Attending large numbers of other films provides little guidance in choosing a new movie. Seeing the film once to become informed and then returning to the theatre is no solution to this problem, since the enjoyment of the second viewing would be much reduced. In other words, search activity and experience, which are valuable to consumers for many other products, are of little guidance to consumers in choosing which movie to attend. This causes a fundamental difficulty for the feature film business because, if product quality cannot be communicated, then producers have an incentive to produce shoddy products and consumers have an incentive to buy little since they are never aware of truly enjoyable offerings.

There are two general ways of getting around this problem. One is the use of reputation as a proxy for quality. Another is for consumers to rely on alternative sources of information about a product such as research, consumer reports, advice from friends, and advertising. In the case of features the main pieces of information required by consumers (aside from exhibition venue information) are: first, the target audience of the film and second, the quality of the film. Film reviews and advice from friends (word of mouth) can help on both scores, but the distributor who deals with trailers, promotion, and the advertising campaign plays a critical role.

London Economics (1992· 11- 13) provides an insightful analysis of the distributor's role. When the Hollywood majors first became dominant the studio name alone was used as a method of quality certification. Later the branding switched to the creative personnel – the star system. 'Stars established the value of motion pictures as a marketable commodity. In economic terms, stars by virtue of their unique appeal and drawing power stabilized rental prices and guaranteed companies operated at a profit' (Klaprat, 1985: 131). Sequels work on the reputation dimension in another way – consumers satisfied with earlier episodes will use the reputation of these episodes as a guide to attending the sequel. Advertising budgets of releases by the majors now average well over $10 million, but with good reason. Advertising can not only convey the target audience of the film but also, by its very existence, provide consumers with a proxy measure of quality. A big advertising campaign means that knowledgeable people in the business believe the advertised movie to be a quality product; consumers can take this into account in deciding on which films to attend. . . .

Just as information provided by the distributor influences consumer decision-making, it should be no surprise to find that it is also very important in influencing production decisions in the independent film sector. The backing of a distributor is an important element in obtaining financing for an independent film for two reasons: it shows that those expert in such matters are supportive and it also gives assurance that the film will be distributed. But how do distributors decide which films they should be involved with? If they are profit-oriented businesses they will want to be distributing the films that will attract big audiences. Therefore the same factors that influence the decisions of audiences to attend the showing of a movie (discussed above) will be the factors that will influence the distributor's decision.

London Economics (1992: 13) caricatures these self-reinforcing tendencies:

> consumers watch films which are well promoted and feature big names: distributors and financiers direct their finance and efforts to well promoted films with big names ... success breeds success in this industry ... films are cut to fit the cloth they have, but the cloth they have matches the size of the cut they are expected to make.

Distributors are responsible for advertising, promotion and branding. They decide on the release pattern which also conveys quality signals to consumers (a wide release is a big gamble on a marginal film); similarly for the type of theatre booked (prestige locations in major markets are a vote of confidence). Through all of these tools the distributor builds awareness and 'want-to-see' for the film. In addition the distributor must ensure that the film is available in suitable venues. But it is this control over the flow of information to both sources of finance and consumers that gives the distributor such a central role in independent film-making.

DISTRIBUTION: HOW DOES IT WORK?

With marketing and distribution budgets of $50 million for some recent Hollywood blockbusters, it is obvious that distribution costs play an important role in the overall financial success of a film. But what is behind these big figures? Let us take a look at how a typical distribution deal is set up and then examine the implications of such a setup for the independent film producer.

Goldberg (1991: 169–70) provides an excellent description of the typical 90:10 percentage deal. Consumers pay the exhibitor in order to view the film. The total of all ticket sales for the film is termed its 'box office gross'. Exhibitors, in order to obtain the right to exhibit the film, must agree to give the distributor a share of the box office gross. In the 1990s most films, especially those from the majors, have been sold on the basis of a 90:10 sharing of the box-office gross. The distributors take 90 per cent of the box-office gross, the exhibitors retaining 10 per cent. This is not as unfavourable to the exhibitors as it appears on the surface, since the exhibitors first deduct the house expenses, called the 'nut', from the gross before calculating the distributor's share. Goldberg provides the following example:

Box-office gross for one week	$10,000
House expenses	−3,000
Net gross	7,000
Exhibitor's share (10%)	700
Distributor's share (90%)	6,300

The 90 : 10 deal generally specifies floors or minimum percentages each week. For example, a contract may specify that the distributor will receive 90% of the net gross after house expenses are deducted or 70% of the box office gross before house expenses, whichever is higher. If you apply this to the example described above, the distributor would receive $7,000 or 70% of the theatre gross, instead of $6,300 or 90% of the net gross after the nut is deducted. The floors are generally specified for the entire run. For example, a contract for an exclusive run might require 90 : 10 over house expenses of $3,000, with minimum terms as follows: Week 1, 70%; Week 2, 70%; Week 3, 60%; Week 4, 60%; Week 5, 50%; Week 6, 50%; Week 7, 40%; Week 8, 40%. In other words, for each week of the engagement, the theatre will owe the distributor 90% of the net gross after deduction of the house expenses or 70, 60, 50, or 40% of the box-office gross – whichever is higher.

The exact terms agreed upon depend on the quality of the film and the relationship between the distributor and the exhibitor. The Hollywood majors with their continuing stream of desirable product and their strong market position do not have to enter into weak agreements or allow adjustments. Their position is that if exhibitors want access to their films they must honour the standard contract.

Looking at distributor–exhibitor relations in this way may lead the reader to sympathize with the plight of the exhibitor, forced to subsist on a small fraction of the gross revenues his/her theatre generates because of a necessarily unfavourable bargain with powerful distributors. But exhibitors have some flexibility in calculating the expenses taken off the top, and they keep all of the concession revenues (which can be very substantial). And, in any event, the less distributors and exhibitors retain of gross revenues the more left for creators. But is this really true? How does box office revenue translate into money in the pockets of producers?

The Economist (10 May 1986) provides a nice example. Assuming the exhibitor's house expenses (the nut) to be 10 per cent of box office gross, if a standard 90 : 10 split agreement is in place the distributor will collect 81 cents in the dollar as rentals. But this 81 cents is not passed on to the producer. Thirty per cent of rentals goes to the distributor as a distribution fee (say 24 cents on the dollar). Advertising and promotion of the film will account for somewhere in the neighbourhood of 25 per cent of rentals (another 20 cents), leaving only 37 cents. If prints, taxes, and transportation account for 5 cents and recoupment of negative cost 30 cents, there are only 2 cents in the dollar left for profit. Even this two cents may have to be split with the studio if they have provided up-front financing of some kind. If leading actors possess sufficient star appeal to have negotiated 'points' or participation in the original gross rentals of 81 cents, then the producer will end up in the hole.

Before proceeding we should note one important caveat. It is true that independent producers have difficulty generating profits on projects. But there is no shortage of producers. Why? Many producers produce not for profit but for fees. Their remuneration comes from the (at times quite generous) producer's fees built into the project budget. Even if the project recoups nothing for the investors and the public agencies putting money into it, the producer may pocket all that he/she ever expected to from the project – their production fee. The incentive implications of this for an independent production industry reliant on public funding are clear. Financial discipline, imposed by the market, forces Hollywood creators to tailor their films to the desires of the moviegoing public; independent producers able to draw on public funds are much better placed to pursue artistic and creative agendas unrelated to what moviegoers wish to see.

The key to survival is skilful foreign distribution. The Hollywood majors offer the safest approach, but it is a high-cost solution. They have a strong distribution infrastructure worldwide and are able to include independently produced product in their block-booking packages. But the majors charge hefty distribution fees (30–40 per cent of rentals) and incur large promotion and marketing costs. Also, cross-collateralizing projects may mean that big gains for a project in some countries may be offset against losses in other countries. Alternatively, the producer can negotiate market by market, often with a local distributor who will charge a lower distribution fee. Cross-collateralization is avoided, but the lower fee reflects a lower level of market-place clout, and perhaps even exclusion from the best play-dates and venues. A third possibility is to split off the various types of rights (cinema, pay-TV, basic cable, and video) and make separate deals for each.

The processes of subdividing the rights bundle by technology and dealing with independent distributors in each geographic market share a fundamental shortcoming. Since the owners of the rights for each technology or for each market do not possess world rights, they adopt a limited (i.e. limited to their technology or their geographical area) perspective in their promotional activities. Only the majors can spend big with the hope of generating revenue all along the value chain as a result of their efforts.

(Hoskins *et al.* 1997: 51–59)

▼ 13 HOLLYWOOD

Everybody wants to be Hollywood. The fame, the vanity, the glitz, the stories.

Miss Kittin
(Madam Hollywood 2001)

Hollywood is a place where they'll pay you a thousand dollars for a kiss and fifty cents for your soul.

Marilyn Monroe

The name 'Hollywood' and the idea of cinema are synonymous in the popular imagination. Hollywood is cinema, a film factory where dreams are made. Indeed, Martin Scorsese has described cinema as the great indigenous American art form. It is therefore worth looking at the origins of this important cultural influence that dominates not only American culture but is exported worldwide to have a globalised influence. The website 'Digital History' is worth a visit to find out about the development of the Hollywood film industry.

Hollywood dominates the production of film across the globe and provides an interesting example of globalisation. It also represents American cultural imperialism in that it exports the ideological values of the USA. Many national cinemas have sought to defend themselves against the domination of world markets by Hollywood.

So why is Hollywood so dominant and powerful in world cinema? As indicated above indicate, part of the importance and impact of Hollywood lies in its sheer scale. No one makes films bigger than Hollywood. No other country has a film industry that can afford the huge budgets which are lavished on Hollywood films. The seductive nature of the glamour of Hollywood can easily blind us to the fact that it is ultimately a production line. Just like a production line turning out automobiles, a vast amount of capital is invested in fixed assets in the form of studios, plant and equipment. Such an investment has to make a return, so that money invested in new film ventures has to have a good chance of making a high profit. In the extract that follows, Richard Maltby offers us an insight into the economics of Hollywood and identifies some of the processes by which the studios seeks to ensure that they make a profit on their investment in new films.

HOLLYWOOD AFTER DIVORCE

In economic terms, it is perhaps necessary to think of the industry as being in two distinct parts. The $2 billion invested in the industry's real estate in 1939 was a largely fixed sum, quite separate from the $187 million spent on production in that year. The smaller figure can be thought of as the cost of the raw material required to make movies. The sale of the processed goods had to turn a sufficient profit not just to recoup its own costs, but to produce a worthwhile return on the $2 billion fixed capital investments. The stability of its fixed investments enabled the major companies to raise capital from Wall Street backers. Generating the resources for production by itself was, however, a different matter. This capital needed to be generated out of current resources; a movie had to pay for itself. The obvious economic facts of the industry complicated this simple equation, however. A movie had to be completed, and have all its costs paid for, before it could begin to earn money for anyone, and the money it earned reached the producer last. During the Classical period, a theater owner might keep between half and three quarters of the box-office receipts to cover overheads and profit. The remainder would go to the distributor as rental for the movie. The distributor would again keep at least half the rental to cover costs and profit, leaving as little as 15 percent of the box-office receipts to be passed back to the producer to cover the costs of production. Of the average 1930s seat price of 25 cents, a mere three or four cents would go to the producer, to pay off the costs of producing an item which might well have cost three quarters of a million dollars to produce.

Although the dollar sums involved have increased exponentially since then, with individual movies in the early 1990s occasionally budgeted at over $50 million, the split of the box-office dollar remains about the same. The size of the audience for the most successful movies has also, surprisingly, changed relatively little. In 1941, sixteen million people in the United States saw *Sergeant York*, the most successful movie of that year. In 1988, *Who Framed Roger Rabbit* drew an American audience of nineteen million, although it took nearly twenty times as much money at the box-office. The great difference between the two periods has been that since 1970, attendance and profit have been concentrated on a relatively small number of **blockbuster** movies. In the studio period, far many more movies made profits, but on a relatively modest scale. The studio system allowed the production industry to spread the economic risks of production across several movies, with the intention of maintaining a constant level of income to finance its flow of product, with the income from one production financing the next. Distributors and exhibitors also needed a steady supply of product to keep audiences coming to the theater, and exhibitors worked hard to establish a sense of stability and continuity in supplying a standardized entertainment package to their audience. The exhibitor's concern was to promote the habit of moviegoing, and it was the maintenance of that habit, rather than the profitability of any individual movie, that was economically most important to the industry. Under these circumstances, it made little economic sense for any of the parties in production, distribution, or exhibition to buy or sell each movie as an individual item.

After divorcement, the logic of movie production changed, encouraging companies to concentrate on more lavish and spectacular features that would play for longer runs at higher ticket prices, and earn bigger grosses. The commercial success of CinemaScope pictures in the early 1950s confirmed the belief that big-budget movies were more profitable than smaller productions, particularly as far as distributors were concerned. Inevitably, this strategy led to profits being concentrated in fewer movies, as what became known as the 'blockbuster phenomenon' developed. Before 1960, only 20 movies had grossed over $10 million in the domestic market; by 1970, more than 80 had. For the successful, the profits were enormous, far greater than those made under the old studio system. In 1965, *The Sound of Music*, which was made for $8 million, earned $72 million in the US and Canada alone. Three quarters of the movies released, however, failed to recoup their costs at the box-office.

Attempts to repeat the phenomenon of *The Sound of Music* led to a number of very costly mistakes and a cycle of overproduction that nearly bankrupted several of the major companies. In the early 1960s Hollywood's feature film output had dropped to about 130 a year; in 1969, it rose to 225, and the major companies registered corporate losses of $200 million. Between 1969 and 1971 the industry was plunged into a financial crisis that suggested that it had lost the ability to predict what its audience wanted to see, but in fact had more to do with the industry simply spending too much money on production to make profits. By 1975, the level of production had fallen back to around 120 movies a year, but the successes of such movies as *The Godfather* (1972), *The Poseidon Adventure* (1972), and *Jaws* (1975) confirmed the blockbuster principle by which the industry's profits were concentrated into a handful of enormously successful movies in each production season. In 1977, for instance, the top six movies in the North American market earned one third of the total rental received by distributors. To an even greater extent than was the case in the studio system, figures such as these appear to make the movie business an immensely risky one. For production executives it is. In the 1980s, Twentieth Century-Fox and Columbia each had five different studio heads.

In the late 1960s many of the majors merged with, or were taken over by, large corporations with diverse interests. This was only the first stage of a gradual reorientation in which film production and distribution companies have become components in multimedia conglomerates geared to the marketing of a product across a number of interlocking media. The blockbuster evolved into the **event movie**: *Star Wars*, for example, became the highest-grossing movie of

CONTINUED

all time in 1977, taking in over $500 million at the box-office, but the income from sales of ancillary goods – toys, games, books, clothing, bubblegum – far exceeded its box-office takings, as well as extending the life of the product and thus guaranteeing the success of its sequels. In the early 1980s, world-wide sales of *Star Wars* goods were estimated to be worth $1.5 billion a year, while *Batman* (1989) made $1 billion from merchandising, four times its box-office earnings. *Jurassic Park* (1993) went so far as to advertise its own merchandising within the movie· at one point, the camera tracks past the Jurassic Park gift shop, showing a line of T-shirts, lunch boxes, and other souvenirs identical to the ones available for purchase in the lobby of the theater.

As well as stimulating this cross-marketing, the event movie is a product designed to maximize audience attendance by drawing in not only the regular 14- to- 25-year-old audience, but also that section of the audience who attend the cinema two or three times a year, often as a family, at Christmas and summer holidays. This sales strategy requires a different form of distribution. A Classical Hollywood movie was released in a slow manner, playing to each tier of the exhibition sector in sequence, so that it might take as long as two years to work through a complete exhibition cycle from first-run to the lowest neighborhood theater. Big-budget event movies have to offset their costs much faster than that, and their use of television advertising has also encouraged saturation-booking, in which a movie is simultaneously released to theaters all over the United States. When this strategy was first used for *Jaws* in 1975, the movie opened in 464 theaters. By 1990, it was not uncommon for a movie to be saturation-booked in 2,000 theaters, a practice that of course necessitated 2,000 prints of the movie to be struck, perhaps ten times more than might have been made of a movie released in 1940. From the mid–1980s, the growth of additional markets in video sales and pay-TV added a new life to both old and new movies. The earnings from these additional 'profit centers' affected the structure of production in two ways. They forced companies to diversify into other businesses, from publishing to bottling Coca-Cola, since the profits from 'supergrossers' like *Close Encounters of the Third Kind* (1977) or *E.T.* (1982) were larger than could sensibly be invested in servicing the limited demand for movies. They also affected the nature of the movie product: how well a movie could service ancillary markets became an increasingly important question as budgets escalated during the 1980s. Sequels, which were even more effectively 'pre-sold' than adaptations of successful stage plays or novels, accounted for 10 percent of Hollywood's output.

Although divorcement had forced the majors to cut their direct ties with theatrical exhibition, they continued to be heavily involved in these other ways of circulating their product, through video, cable television, and associated merchandising of an expanding range of 'software,' from books-of-the-film and soundtrack CDs to toys and computer games. In the early

1980s, saturation-booking notwithstanding, the economic logic that emerged from this diversification downplayed the importance of cinema exhibition as a whole. Rather, a conglomerate such as Warner Communications Inc. (WCI) saw its goal as being to 'bring movies conveniently and economically into the home,' so that it can 'reach the enormous market that rarely, if ever, attends movie theaters.' Along with Gulf and Western (Paramount), Disney and MCA (Universal), WCI dominated production and distribution during the 1980s. All four companies were diversified operations with interests in related businesses in publishing and music, but they shed most of their operations that were less connected to software distribution. A second tier of companies, with fluctuating shares of the market, were similarly connected to ancillary markets: MGM/UA, Columbia (owned for most of the decade by Coco-Cola), and Twentieth Century-Fox. Although the ownership, management, and profitability of these seven companies changed quite frequently during the decade, their common underlying strategy of diversification combined with multimedia distribution of software was firmly established. On a tier down the production hierarchy were the mini-majors, companies such as Orion, Cannon, and Dino De Laurentis, financing movies by pre-selling their distribution rights before production began. These companies flourished in the mid–1980s, then overexpanded through diversification and an excess of product. Cannon collapsed in 1986, De Laurentis in 1988, and Orion in 1992. Servicing the low-budget sectors of the market were the descendants of Poverty Row companies, including American International Pictures, Crown International, and New Line.

In the latter half of the decade, encouraged by the Reagan administration's relaxed attitude to business regulation, several of the majors returned to theatrical exhibition, buying up some of the larger national theater chains. Although first-run theatrical release continues to be the vital evidence of product quality that will attract the interest of later 'distribution windows,' the distributors' return to ownership in the exhibition sector was not an attempt to recreate the vertical integration of Classical Hollywood. Rather, they were simply securing an additional element in a new strategy of what Wall Street analyst Harold Vogel has called 'entertainment industry consolidation.' By the end of the decade, theatrical release accounted for only 30 percent of the studios' total receipts, while ancillary markets made up the other 70 percent. *Batman*, released in 1989, earned $250 million in the first five months of its theatrical release. When Warners released it on video, it earned another $400 million. Expanding exponentially in the late 1980s, the second-run video market also provided a financial cushion for movies that failed at the theatrical box-office: the science fiction adventure *Willow*, produced by George Lucas in 1988, cost $55 million and grossed only $28 million in American theaters. But it earned an additional $18 million in video sales, and $15 million in television sales. Combined with its foreign earnings of $42 million

in theaters and $22 million in video and television sales, its earnings from ancillary markets ensured its profitability. Such profits fueled the continuing increase in production costs and budgets. During the second half of the 1980s, and allowing for inflation, the average Hollywood budget rose by 40 percent. In 1990, a major movie might be budgeted at $25 million, with additional marketing and distribution costs of $20 million. With overheads and interest charges, the studio that financed it would have to recoup more than $50 million to break even. Such budgets reflected the doubling of the total world market between 1984 and 1989, an expansion primarily brought about by the development of video as an additional system of release. But these extravagant budgets were also part of a cyclical economic pattern that has affected the film industry since the early 1960s, in which a number of spectacular successes push production costs to new heights until overproduction results in a sharp downturn in profits. Because its effect is concentrated on so few products, what is in effect a stabilization of the market appears to be the catastrophic failure or one or two movies: *Cleopatra* in 1963 and *Heaven's Gate* in 1980 are perhaps the two most notable examples.

Although the economic changes following the Paramount decision had substantial effects on the kinds of movie produced in Hollywood as well as the circumstances of their production, the system's consistencies are to be found in more than just the familiar names of the companies. Re-establishing something not unlike the previous oligopoly, the industry has stabilized its production and distribution system in alliance with the producers of associated 'software' and the 'hardware' manufacturers such as Sony, which bought Columbia in 1989 in order to be able to market a software library alongside its own new equipment. The same year also saw the creation of the world's largest media conglomerate, Time Warner Inc., through a merger of Warner Communications with Time Inc., which owned Home Box Office, the largest pay cable television service in the United States. The *Wall Street Journal* predicted that the end of the century would see the industry dominated by a few giant concerns, each 'controlling a vast empire of media and entertainment properties that amounts to a global distribution system for advertising and promotion dollars.' Nevertheless, the identity of that future industry is likely to remain 'Hollywood.' As one executive observed in 1983, 'When television started in the 1950s, there was a strong view that that was the end of Hollywood. When cable came, we thought that would kill our sales to the networks. None of these things happened. Every time the market expands the combination is greater than before. After all, it should be immaterial to Hollywood how people see its product so long as they pay.'

Maltby 1995: 73–78)

As you will have read in the extract above, an important weapon in the Hollywood armoury to ensure profit is the 'event' movie. This film 'happening' enables larger profits to be made by additional marketing ploys such as the release of ancillary goods (e.g. games and clothing) to add to, and often surpass, takings at the box-office. In the extract that follows, Geoff King considers the Hollywood blockbuster or 'event' movie, so called because the release of this large-scale film becomes an event in itself.

Spectacle, spectacular imagery; sheer scale, lavishness and (hopefully) quality of big-screen audio-visual sensation: however the blockbuster is defined, qualities such as these have often been close to the center of its appeal, from the early Italian historical epics of the 1910s to today's digital special-effects extravaganzas. Overt, large-scale spectacle is not a major feature of all films that enjoy blockbuster-scale success at the box office. But it is often a major ingredient at the high-budget end of the spectrum and in production and/or distribution-led definitions of the blockbuster. The spectacular variety of blockbuster, on which this chapter focuses, is usually meant to constitute an 'event,' something that stands out from the cinematic routine. It is sold this way even if the formation of the 'event' itself becomes routinized, as is the case in contemporary Hollywood, where the heavily preplanned and presold prospective blockbuster is a central feature around which each year's slate of production revolves, rather than something that departs from the norm. A substantial part of the appeal of many blockbusters lies precisely in the scale of spectacular audio-visual experience that is offered, in contrast to the smaller-scale resources of rival films or media. The definition of the blockbuster in terms of spectacle (as with other attributes such as length and budget) tends to be relative rather than absolute.

Two aspects of the spectacular movie blockbuster are considered in this chapter. The first part looks more closely at the production of spectacular qualities, primarily in terms of visual strategies. Two alternative modes of spectacle are outlined, in relation to shifting contexts of production and consumption: one based on the visual scope of the big-screen experience offered by the cinematic blockbuster, the other related to the impact of visual strategies drawn in recent decades from small-screen media such as advertising and music video. The second part of the chapter focuses on the issue of narrative. If spectacle is so central to a particular kind of blockbuster experience, what is the role of narrative structure. Many have been quick to announce the death, or at least the fading, of narrative in the spectacular context of recent Hollywood blockbuster production, a judgment that, as I and others have argued, is precipitate. To what extent, though, does the spectacular blockbuster adhere to the conventions of 'classical' narrative structure. Has it utilized other types of narrative organization; if so, to what extent, and what challenge might this post more generally to our understanding of the classic Hollywood style?

SPECTACLE: FROM LARGE-SCREEN VISTA TO (LARGE *AND* SMALL-SCREEN) MONTAGE-IMPACT

An epic scale of spectacular representation unavailable in rival media products is one of the promises that has long been made by the would-be blockbuster. From the early 1910s, Italian epics such as *The Fall of Troy* (*La caduta di Troia*, 1910) and *Quo Vadis?* (1913) attracted crowds by offering a scale of events and production value that dwarfed and stood out from more routine cinematic fare (Bowser 1990). The American film industry's response included D. W. Griffith's *Judith of Bethula* (1913), *The Birth of a Nation* (1915), and *Intolerance* (1916) and the traditional biblical-historical epic in the studio era most commonly associated with the films of Cecil B. DeMille. Ingredients these early blockbusters have in common include expense, length, a focus on 'weighty,' 'important,' or epic-mythical subject matter and – of more central relevance here – a largeness in the *staging* of the spectacular on-screen events. Great vistas are offered, along with more intimate moments, often involving the reconstruction of epic events on a grand scale: the Civil War battlefield in *The Birth of a Nation*, massive teeming edifices of Babylon in *Intolerance*, the exodus from Egypt in *The Ten Commandments* (1956); the proverbial 'cast of thousands,' and large outlays on the building of massive sets and/or travel to exotic locations.

An emphasis on spectacular epic production of this kind gained particular prominence in Hollywood in the 1950s and 1960s, decades in which the industry struggled to regain equilibrium in the face of the combined threats of the divorcement exhibition from production and distribution, the decline in cinemagoing that resulted from broader social change such as migration to the suburbs, and the rival attraction of television and other leisure pursuits. As a more or less habitual pattern of visiting the cinema declined, the spectacular blockbuster was envisaged as potential saving of Hollywood. Its quality as extra-larger-than-life special event was seen as a way to attract back to the cinema viewers whose more routine attendance could not be guaranteed. Hence, the advent of widescreen formats, among others, institutionalised in the form of 20th Century-Fox's CinemaScope process. Visually, the emphasis was put, again, on sheer scale of imagery: the width of the screen and the vast panoramas it could encompass.

The particular forms of spectacular blockbuster adopted in the 1950s and 1960s ran into difficulties, especially in the later decade, and especially the Roman-historical epic (in the shape of *Cleopatra*, 1963) and the epic musical after what proved to be the deceptive triumph of *The Sound of Music* (1965). The foregrounding of the large-scale, big-screen vista has remained an important ingredient in more recent blockbusters, however, including the successful revisiting of the Roman epic in *Gladiator* (2000). Blockbusters continue to base much of their appeal on the promise of providing a variety of spectacle that befits the nature of the specifically *cinematic* context of exhibition. From *Star*

Wars (1977) to *Titanic* (1997), *Pearl Harbor* (2001) and the heavily pretrailed *Lord of the Rings* trilogy (2001, 2002, 2003), epic or fantastic events are designed to play strongly to the audio-visual qualities of the theatrical experience. There appears to be a paradox, however, in the economic basis of contemporary Hollywood's blockbuster production. The large vistas of spectacular attraction are designed to work at their best on the big screen. But the bulk of revenues are currently earned through viewings on the *small* screen, via videotape/disc or broadcast television of one variety or another.

The big-screen vista remains important in Hollywood today. But it has been supplemented, in the creation of overt visual spectacle, by the use of techniques more suited to the creation of spectacular impact within the confines of the small-screen image. At the risk of oversimplification, two varieties of spectacle might be suggested. One has its roots in the creation of impact on the big screen. The other draws on techniques associated in part with small-screen spectacle. In the former case, as in much of the tradition of spectacular blockbuster production, the emphasis is put on the presentation before the viewer of large vistas, at the level of what appears to be the *pro-filmic* reality. For the purpose of this argument, I include here elements of special effects that are not strictly pro-filmic, but that are designed to create that impression (matte paintings or models, for example, or digitally composited images, meant to blend more or less seamlessly with more substantially 'real' sets, locations and action). Images such as extreme long shots of the construction of Goshen, the exodus from Egypt, or the parting of the Red Sea in *The Ten Commandments*, or of the ship in *Titanic*, are offered as forms of large-scale spectacle the viewer is invited to sit back and admire on the big screen in a relatively leisurely fashion. This is a form I have described elsewhere as offering a 'contemplative' brand of spectacle (King 2000). Time is permitted for a certain amount of scrutiny of the image: admiration of texture or detail produced by lavish expenditure on sets, locations, props and extras, or of the latest illusions available with the use of state-of-the-art special effects. The viewer might as a result be taken more effectively 'into' the diegetic world on screen – if the overall effect is a 'convincing' representation and helps in the process of 'suspending disbelief.' Alternatively, or at the same time, the viewer might admire the spectacle *as* impressive construct, testament to the illusionary powers of high-cost, resource-heavy spectacular cinema (for more discussion of this in relation to special effects, see LaValley 1985; Landon 1992; Barker and Brooks 1998; Darley 2000; King 2000). The latter effect, based on the selling of the spectacular capabilities of the medium itself, has always been a significant component of the attraction of large-scale blockbuster production.

What happens, though, when spectacle of this variety is reduced to the spatial limits of the small screen? Widescreen spectacle is particularly

vulnerable, either being shown in pan/scan versions, in which only parts of the image are visible and original compositions are subjected to reframing, or 'letterbox' screenings that maintain more of the integrity of the frame but reduce still further the scale of the image. The large-scale spectacular qualities of blockbusters such as *The Ten Commandments* and *Titanic* are not entirely destroyed in this process but they are substantially reduced in impact. Other forms of spectacle, however, suffer relatively less in the move from big screen to small – specifically, those based on technique such as rapid editing or rapid and/or unstable movement of the camera. Constant change of image-content is needed to maintain heightened levels of visual stimulus on the small screen (Ellis 1989), a strategy Hollywood appears to have learned from formats such as advertising and music video.[1] Hyperbolically rapid editing and camera movement have become important sources of heightened spectacular impact in contemporary Hollywood, either replacing or (probably more often) being used in conjunction with images of grander visual scale. This is especially the case in action-oriented blockbuster production, with its basic currency of explosive destruction. The impact of the contemporary action film is often constructed through patterns of rapid montage-effect editing combined with 'unstable' camera movement designed to create an impression of subjective immersion in the action, an 'impact aesthetic' often increased by the practice of propelling debris and other objects out toward the viewer (for detailed analysis of examples, see King 2000). Particularly notable, given its generic allegiance to the large-vista Roman–biblical tradition, is the use of such techniques as the dominant aesthetic in the action-fighting scenes of *Gladiator* (for more detail, see King 2002a).

A typical strategy today is to combine moments of broader, more expansive spectacle with those of tightly framed explosive-montage-impact effects. The central action sequence in *Pearl Harbor*, for example, offer larger shots, the spectacle of a large number of American ships in various stages of destruction during and after the initial Japanese attack, and closer and more rapidly cut detail – making claims to a more 'subjective' location – including the obligatory outward-moving fireball/debris effects and a bomb's-eye-view perspective. What this offers in the realm of heightened spectacle is, in fact, in keeping with a central aspect of the classical Hollywood *decoupage* more generally: a combination of relatively 'objective,' distanced and closer, quasi-subjective perspectives. The difference, however, is that the more subjective-seeming position is constructed as a variety of spectacular impact (as opposed, for instance, to a less frenzied, more quotidian point-of-view shot).

The appeal of a more 'contemplative' end of the spectacular spectrum might be understood in the context of a long tradition of larger-than-life spectacular representation. This includes pre-cinematic forms such as the magic lantern show and the diorama as well as earlier forms of spectacle, both secular and religious in origin. The pleasures offered might include a sense of being taken beyond the scale of everyday life to something suggesting a grandeur, an awe, or a sense of the sublime, even if a format such as blockbuster cinema might offer a rather debased and commercialized version of such an experience. Richard Dyer's attempt to analyze some of the characteristics of the pleasurable/entertaining dimension of the more spectacular varieties of Hollywood cinema (specifically, in his case studies, the musical) offers a useful vocabulary in which to understand some of these pleasures. Of most direct relevance are the qualities of 'abundance' and 'intensity' identified by Dyer (1992) that can be contrasted with the scarcity and banality that characterizes much of the typical reality of everyday life. The pleasure of experiencing greater-than-life intensity also applies to the high-impact variety of spectacle, a form that offers an intense engagement for the viewer. This is a quality actively discussed as a source of enjoyment by some enthusiasts of the action genre (Barker and Brooks 1998) and also offered by other media targeted at a similar audience, such as action-adventure videogames (King 2002b). The prominence of this format in contemporary Hollywood can be explained by more than just its suitability for translation to the small screen, which may or may not be a consciously exploited causal factor. A more indirect route can also be suggested, given the tendency of Hollywood to embrace style used in other popular media consumed by its key target audience of younger viewers, including music video, and the employment of directors (such as Michael Bay, director of *Armageddon* [1998] and *Pearl Harbor*) with backgrounds in music video and/or advertising, two of the key training ground for recent generations of filmmakers.

Whatever the precise causal factors behind – and audience appeals of – the two, a combination of large-scale and more impact-centered spectacle makes sense in the contemporary industrial context. Video and television screenings are the principal sources of revenue, in the longer term. But their potential remains dependent to a large extent – especially at the prestigious, high-budget blockbuster end of the market – on success in the theatrical realm. It is success at the box office, in most cases, that determines the likely scale of revenue to be earned in subsequent forms such as video sales/rentals and sale to pay- and free-to-air television broadcast. Spectacular dimensions that play especially well on the big screen remain important. They help to create the 'event movie' impact, in terms of wider media coverage as well as promotion and box office returns, that translates into subsequent success on the small screen for a franchise or a one-off blockbuster.

NARRATIVE STILL MATTERS

What, though, of narrative in the spectacular blockbuster? It is common parlance in both journalistic criticism and some academic writing to assume or to assert that the emphasis on visual spectacle is at the expense of

333

HOLLYWOOD

narrative. 'Impressive effects, shame the same effort wasn't put into the plot,' is a standard response. The plot of the typical Hollywood spectacular blockbuster may not be terribly challenging or complex; a basic mistake that is often made, however, is to confuse this – a perfectly valid qualitative judgment, but one that could be applied to many other Hollywood films, with the idea that narrative is in some way *absent* or *displaced* by spectacle. It is surprising how often this slippage seems to occur, as if prominent narrative dimensions somehow become invisible once the focus turns to the production of spectacular impact. Different aspects of this argument can be related to the two different versions of spectacle considered above, each of which has been cited as an impediment to narrative. In what follows, I begin by sketching briefly some of these claims and suggesting why they are often mistaken. Having established that narrative remains important, and usually quite central, to the contemporary blockbuster, this section concludes by examining some of the specific qualities of the kind of narrative structure found in the context of spectacular production. My principal focus here will be on the recent spectacular Hollywood blockbuster, rather than earlier examples, as it is here that arguments about the decline of narrative have been concentrated.

Contemporary blockbusters of the large-scale spectacular variety are often lumped together with spin-off forms such as movie-based theme-park rides or videogames. The fact that films are sometimes converted into such formats is used by some commentators as a basis on which to imply that the films themselves exhibit the far less narrative-based qualities of rides or games (see, for example, Bukatman (1998)). Narrative is said to be subordinated to the provision of a spectacular 'thrill-ride.' The logic of this kind of argument is flawed, however, other than as a species of rhetoric, a way to 'bash' Hollywood rather than to engage in serious analysis. Even if constructed with one eye on their potential for conversion to ride or videogame, it does not follow in principal that the films should be lacking in narrative dimensions, so different are the requirements of cinema from those of ride or game. Another major strain in these arguments focuses on the prominence of special-effects sequences in the spectacular blockbuster. Narrative dynamics are said to be 'bracketed' in many cases by major effects sequences (Pierson 1999), powerful illusions/spectacles that threaten to 'overwhelm traditional concerns with character and story' (Darley 2000: 103). The style of visual spectacle and impact that draws on techniques used in advertising and music video, including rapid and emphatic montage-editing, has also been identified as a threat to narrative, most notably in Justin Wyatt's much cited book on 'high concept' in Hollywood (Wyatt 1994).

The fact remains, however, that spectacular Hollywood blockbusters, of both varieties, continue to invest strongly in narrative dynamics, and at more than one level. They tell carefully organized, more or less linear cause/effect stories organized around central characters. They also manifest what a structuralist analysis would term 'underlying' narrative structural patterns, on which I have written at length elsewhere (King 2000). Take, for example, *Terminator 2: Judgment Day* (1991), a quintessential example of the recent Hollywood spectacular blockbuster production, and a blockbuster in all contemporary senses of the term (expensive, large-scale, spectacular, and a substantial box-office hit). *Terminator 2* is one of the films regularly cited by commentators such as Pierson and Darley. As such, it is a useful example to revisit in a little more detail, with attention to exactly how it is structured in terms of the relationship between spectacle and narrative.

Terminator 2 is, clearly, a film *driven by* the dimension of spectacle more than that of narrative, which is one reason why it is a good test case. It is safe to assume, I think that the reason for making the film was to capitalize on the success of *The Terminator* (1984), a modestly budgeted film, in the typical contemporary Hollywood manner of producing a 'bigger,' 'better,' more spectacular and special-effects-oriented sequel. The distinctive spectacular attraction of *Terminator 2*, the morphing transformation scenes involving the new-generation shape-shifting T–1000 terminator, was also driven by specific developments in special effects technologies – principally the adaptation and the extension of 3-D computer generation techniques used to create the water pseudopod in director James Cameron's earlier film *The Abyss* (1989). The principle *raison d'être* of *Terminator 2* is the production of special-effects-based spectacle, along with the more conventional action-movie recipe of chase, combat and destruction. *The Terminator* left plenty of undeveloped *narrative* potential – an ending in which the central character Sarah Connor (Linda Hamilton) drives off ready to bear a son who will lead the human resistance in a post-apocalyptic future – but it seems reasonable to conclude that fulfilling this potential was not the major factor in the decision to fashion a sequel. Even if some of the narrative dimensions of the film might be interpreted as responses to socio-cultural issues or anxieties, it is difficult to make any very direct argument to support the claim that these are an identifiable *causal factor* in the appearance of the film.

If *Terminator 2* owes its existence primarily to its potential to create a particular form of spectacular blockbuster attraction, a product of the particular Hollywood regime in place at the time (and very much with us today), it does not follow that, as a result, it is lacking in narrative dynamics, or even that narrative is in a particularly secondary position in the actual structure of the film. The distinction between these two propositions is important, but one that tends to be overlooked in many accounts. *Terminator 2* has strong and carefully orchestrated narrative dimensions. Like most other spectacular blockbusters, it offers a combination of spectacular and narrative appeals, a quality clearly marked from the outset. In its opening moments, *Terminator 2* supplies both large-scale spectacle (images of apocalypse and post-apocalyptic warfare between human and machine) the narrative exposition (a voice-over from Sarah Connor that establishes the narrative context). Outbursts of spectacle and special effects are narratively situated; they serve narrative purposes. The opening vision of apocalypse – repeated later, when located in Sarah's dreams – hangs over the film as its basic, narratively located fulcrum of suspense (will it really occur, or be averted?). Celebrated sequences such as the transformation in which the figure of the T–1000 emerges seamlessly from a checkerboard floor, or when it passes through the metal bars in a hospital hallway, gain their *full* impact also through their location at narratively heightened moments of tension: the ability of the T–1000 to perform such manoeuvres directly places the sympathetic characters in danger.

Such sequences are designed to show off the effects. If they are experienced *as* effects, something less than total engrossment in the ongoing events of the diegetic universe must be entailed: the viewer 'sits back,' as it were, distanced to some extent from the on-screen world, aware of the nature of the image as construct. To interpret this as a spectacular/special-effects *interruption* or bracketing of narrative, however, is to assume a rather one-dimensional model of the experience of film viewing – as if, for example, the *normal* experience of spectatorship was anything close to *total* and undivided engrossment or 'suspension of disbelief.' The example of special-effects-led spectacle might be used, more helpfully, to illustrate the complex and multidimensional modalities in which any particular film, type of film, or individual sequence is likely to be consumed.[2] If high-definition computer-generated special effects can be experienced simultaneously as 'highly realistic and convincing' and as 'amazing *illusions* of the highly realistic and convincing,' the same kind of oscillations might be available more widely – between that which draws the viewer acceptingly 'into' the fictional world on screen, and that which marks its more distanced status as pleasurable illusion (the pleasure resulting partly from awareness of its status *as* illusion).

If the major spectacular sequences of *Terminator* 2 are themselves narratively situated, the film also exhibits many other features usually associated with the 'classical Hollywood' style of narration (as defined by Bordwell 1985). It has a primarily linear, forward-moving structure, across the different narrative threads, based on cause-and-effect relationships between one event and another. It is organized around the qualities and experiences of a distinctive small group of characters who undergo significant development. This would not need to be stated, so obvious does it seem, were it not for some of the sweeping claims made about such films. It does not take any great feats of academic ingenuity, either, to suggest a number of not very deeply 'underlying' narrative dynamics of a structural variety, often entailing the establishment and imaginary reconciliation of thematic oppositions. Obvious examples include the theme of 'humanity vs. technology' and issues of gender roles and parenting. Plenty has been written about these (for example, Telotte 1995; Tasker 1993), but such dimensions often seem to be lost from sight during discussion of spectacle or special effects. A full and adequate understanding of spectacular blockbusters such as *Terminator 2* requires simultaneous attention to the various dimensions that make up the experience offered to the viewer. The same can be said of films that use the montage-based form of spectacular impact, whether in the form of hyperkinetically edited action sequences or the surface-style oriented music-video aesthetic examined by Wyatt. They still exhibit most if not all of the qualities usually associated, loosely, with 'classical Hollywood' narrative and are structured around various thematic oppositions (for more on this in detail, see King 2000 and 2002a).

The continued importance of narrative structure in Hollywood blockbuster-style production has been acknowledged by some recent commentators, in an attempt to redress the balance against assumptions that narrative has been undermined (especially Buckland 1998; Cowie 1998; Thompson 1999). But does narrative have any distinctive characteristics in this context, when combined with an emphasis on the production of spectacular impact? Does it depart in any way from the 'classical' version? Spectacular blockbusters of recent decades have sometime been associated with the more episodic structure of B-movie serials produced in Hollywood in the 1930s and 1940s, a structure in which less emphasis is placed on overarching narrative dynamics. Some of the landmark spectacular blockbusters of the 1970s and 1980s are designed very much with the serial template in mind, obvious examples being *Star Wars* (1977) and *Raiders of the Lost Ark* (1981). As Warren Buckland suggests, the latter can be broken down into a series of six distinct episodes, but these are tied together quite strongly through their position in the development of a feature-length narrative that reaches resolution in the final episode: 'The point to make here is that this pattern transcends individual episodes, and is dependent for its very existence on the presence of a feature-length story' (1998: 172). The dynamic is very different from that which results from the shorter serial format, in which a substantial gap occurs between one episode and another.

One quality often associated with recent spectacular blockbuster production is pace. For Thomas Schatz, the distinguishing characteristic of a film such as *Star Wars* is not an absence of narrative drive but a hell-bent and careening form of narrative that emphasizes 'plot over character' (1993: 23). This account seems to contradict the claim that the production of spectacular or impact aesthetics has an interruptive or bracketing effect in relation to narrative. The accusation is of lack of narrative depth, rather than of narrative itself (and, whatever the distinctive characteristics of the film, it is hardly the case that character is other than a central component in the armature that drives *Star*

Wars or other titles in the franchise). The generation of spectacular impact within what might be described as an incessant, forward-driving narrative-spectacle context is characteristic of many recent Hollywood blockbusters and less-than-blockbuster-scale action films. Exactly *how* major sequences of spectacle or special effects occur within this kind of framework is variable, however, on more than one ground. Large-scale computer-generated effects remain expensive, which is one reason why they are unlikely to overwhelm narrative at present, even if filmmakers were prepared to dispose of the narrative dimension in any substantial manner (which itself seems highly unlikely). *Terminator* 2 is a prominent example in this respect, the trademark transformational effects being absent from large stretches of the film.

The rapid succession with which moments of spectacular impact come in some films – a strong example is *Armageddon* – might be seen as a point of distinction from earlier spectacular blockbusters, which tend to be more 'stately' in their mode of presentation, moving (in some cases, lumbering) more slowly between larger scale spectacular set-pieces and sequences of greater intimacy. In this sense, it might be said that narrative momentum is 'bracketed' a good deal less in the contemporary Hollywood spectacular blockbuster than in some other examples. An alternative might be suggested, in these two different forms of spectacular, between degrees of narrative momentum (forward-moving drive) and narrative depth (complications, ramifications, nuances, etc.), but these are only relative. The trouble with any sweeping judgments, either way, is that narrative/spectacle dynamics vary within as well as between different industrial-historical contexts. Some contemporary spectacular blockbusters are clearly designed to hark back to the 'grander' earlier style, prominent examples including *Titanic*, *Gladiator*, and *Pearl Harbor*. The duration and pacing of these films, in particular, is very different from that of the *Star Wars/Raiders of the Lost Ark/Armageddon* variety. Lengthy scenes of slow-paced, character-based narrative development account for large segments of the running time. For viewers attracted by the promise of spectacle, it might be these sequences that are experienced as the interruptive dimension. The same might be said of *The Ten Commandments*, in which extra-large-scale spectacle is witnessed only on occasion and accounts for a small fraction of the running time (compared, say, to the large-scale scenes of conflict in *The Birth of a Nation*, which are held for more extensive periods). The typical rhythm of the film during its set-pieces is to move quite swiftly from the enormous vista to a more conventionally studio-bound scale of more localized detail at which the principals interact.

Differences can also be identified between films in the same blockbuster franchise. *Jurassic Park* 3 (2001), for example, has a structure rather different from that of either of its two predecessors. Less time is spent dwelling on the broader ramification of the creation of the dinosaurs (a substantial component of the first film, especially) and there is no new twist of a corporate-conspiratorial nature (as there is in the second in the series). There are no human enemies this time. The film, as a result, is some thirty minutes shorter than the first two instalments. Emphasis is put on a forward-driving rescue–survive–escape scenario that delivers a tight succession of spectacular engagements with dinosaurs. This might seem to confirm the suggestion by Timothy Corrigan (1991) that the prevalence of sequels has been a major factor in what he describes as the attenuation of narrative in Hollywood since the mid–1970s in favor of the spectacle provided by the display of cinematic technology. In the sequel, the series film, and the remake, Corrigan argues, 'figures of technological or stylistic extravagance … detach themselves from the path of character psychology and plot incident' (1991: 170). The main *point* of the blockbuster sequel, in this case as in *Terminator* 2, might be to provide the opportunity to display the latest advances in special-effects capabilities (as well as simply providing 'more of the same,' as a 'thrill ride'). But plenty of narrative structure is still in evidence, even in the relatively stripped-down second-sequel format used by *Jurassic Park* 3. The experience of the special-effects-led spectacle is closely linked to character (including differences in the attitudes and reactions of different characters to the dinosaurs); it also drives the basic 'jeopardy' narrative. The narrative structure of events embodies a typical Hollywood moral economy: the fact, for example, that the cavalier young assistant to the dinosaur expert will redeem himself and appear to die in the process (rescuing a young boy from the clutches of a pterodactyl) after being castigated for stealing a pair of eggs from the nest of a velociraptor. Judgments such as that of Corrigan tend to flatten the picture, overstating certain tendencies to the detriment of close understanding of precisely how such films are structured. Broad historical-industrial factors are clearly important in shaping the spectacle/narrative dynamics of blockbusters, but accounts in these terms usually need to be supplemented by more local and specific analysis. Differences of genre, for example – which might include the favoring of different genres on different occasions – seem to play as important a part as shifts from one era to another in accounting for some of the specific qualities found in examples such as *Gladiator* and *Star Wars* or *Jurassic Park* 3.

If some contemporary Hollywood blockbuster are relatively episodic, they are far from alone, historically speaking. As Elizabeth Cowie suggests, episodic structure – in which narrative events are sometimes displaced by set-pieces and not always given clear causal explanation – is found in plenty of products from the 'classical' period (for examples see Cowie 1998: 185). This is the case from the levels of 'prestige' and spectacular blockbuster production to the B-movie tradition on which one trend in more recent blockbuster filmmaking has drawn. Hollywood production in the studio era, in general, was often not as 'classical' as is sometimes implied (most notably in David Bordwell's

influential account). Once reasonably coherent narrative became established as a primary basis of organization (by the 1910s) it was constantly subject to combination with all sorts of other appeals, ranging from the presence of larger-than-role star performers to the vicissitudes of melodramatic coincidence and the pleasures of large-scale spectacular attraction (see, for example, Altman 1992; Maltby 1995). This may sometimes be foregrounded to an extra degree in the spectacular blockbuster, but the differences, generally, are relative and of degree rather than absolute. Narrative has never since played less than a substantial role, either, in combination with other dimensions, whether in the most hell-bent or the most heavy-handed and lumbering varieties of spectacular blockbuster production. The experience of spectacle in the blockbuster is usually organized and given resonance by narrative dimensions, in an assortment of different combinations and style, each of which merits careful analysis in its own right: a weighing up of the balance between narrative and spectacle, their interactions, the specific qualities of each, and the industrial and historical contexts in which a particular format is encouraged.

NOTES

1 These devices also have cinematic precedents, of course, most notably the montage style adopted by Sergei Eisenstein.
2 For more on the subject of varying 'modalities of response,' in reference to special effects sequences and to Hollywood films more generally, see Barker with Austin (2000: 55, 79, 81).

REFERENCES

Altman, Rick (1992) 'Dickens, Griffith, and Film theory Today,' in Jane Gaines (ed.), *Classical Hollywood Narrative: The Paradigm Wars*, Durham, NC: Duke University Press: 9–47.

Barker, Martin, with Austin, Thomas (2000) *From Antz to Titanic: Reinventing Film Analysis*, London: Pluto Press.

Barker, Martin, and Brooks, Kate (1998) *Knowing Audiences: Judge Dredd, Its Friends, Fans and Foes*, Luton: University of Luton Press.

Bordwell, David (1985) 'The Classical Hollywood Style, 1917–60,' in Bordwell, David, Staiger, Janet, and Thompson, Kristin, *The Classical Hollywood Cinema: Film Style and Mode of Production to 1960*, London: Routledge & Kegan Paul: 1–84.

Bowser, Eileen (1990) *The Transformation of Cinema 1907–1915*, Berkeley: University of California Press.

Buckland, Warren (1998) 'A Close Encounter with *Raiders of the Lost Ark*: Notes on Narrative Aspects of the New Hollywood Blockbuster,' in Steve Neale and Murray Smith (eds), *Contemporary Hollywood Cinema*, London: Routledge: 166–77.

Bukatman, Scott (1998) 'Zooming Out: The End of Offscreen Space,' in Jon Lewis (ed.), *The New American Cinema*, Durham, NC: Duke University Press: 248–72.

Corrigan, Timothy (1991) *A Cinema Without Walls: Movies and Culture After Vietnam*, London: Routledge.

Cowie, Elizabeth (1998) 'Storytelling: Classical Hollywood Cinema and Classical Narrative,' in Steve Neale and Murray Smith (eds), *Contemporary Hollywood Cinema*, London: Routledge: 178–90.

Darley, Andrew (2000) *Digital Visual Culture: Surface Play and Spectacle in New Media Genres*, London: Routledge.

Dyer, Richard (1992) *Only Entertainment*, London: British Film Institute.

Ellis, John (1989) *Visible Fictions: Cinema, Television, Video* (rev. edn), London: Routledge.

King, Geoff (2000) *Spectacular Narratives: Hollywood in the Age of the Blockbuster*, London and New York: I. B. Tauris.

—— (2002a) *New Hollywood Cinema: An Introduction*, London: I. B. Tauris.

—— (2002b) 'Die Hard/Try Harder: Narrative, Spectacle and Beyond, From Hollywood to Videogame,' in Geoff King and Tanya Krzywinska (eds), *ScreenPlay: Cinema/Videogames/Interfaces*, London: Wallflower Press.

Landon, Brooks (1992) *The Aesthetics of Ambivalence*, Westport, CT: Greenwood Press.

LaValley, Albert J. (1985) 'Tradition or Trickery?: The Role of Special Effects in the Science Fiction Film,' in George E. Slusser and Eric S. Rabkin (eds), *Shadows of the Magic Lamp: Fantasy and Science Fiction Film*, Carbondale: Southern Illinois University Press: 141–58.

Maltby, Richard (1995) *Hollywood Cinema: An Introduction*, Oxford: Blackwell.

Pierson, Michele (1999) 'CGI Effects in Hollywood Science-Fiction Cinema 1989–95: The Wonder Years,' *Screen*, 40, 2: 158–76.

Schatz, Thomas (1993) 'The New Hollywood,' in Jim Collins, Hilary Radner and Ava Preacher Collins (eds), *Film Theory Goes to the Movies*, New York and London: Routledge, 8–36 [reprinted in this volume].

Tasker, Yvonne (1993) *Spectacular Bodies: Gender, Genre and the Action Cinema*, London: Routledge.

Telotte, J. P. (1995) *Replication: A Robotic History of the Science Fiction Film*, Urbana: University of Illinois Press.

Thompson, Kristin (1999) *Storytelling in the New Hollywood*, Cambridge, MA: Harvard University Press.

Wyatt, Justin (1994) *High Concept: Movies and Marketing in Hollywood*, Austin: University of Texas Press.

(King 2003: 114–127)

Of course, Hollywood's dominance as an economic and cultural force has grown stronger as the world offers up more of its global markets. Hollywood is in the position of being able to make films which can recoup their initial costs from box-office and ancillary takings in the United States and then increase profits further by exporting movies globally often more cheaply than the distribution costs to the home market. In this way it is possible for the Hollywood industry to swamp the markets of other countries, including the UK and Europe, which makes it difficult to produce profitable home-grown films. However, there is increasing resistance to the dominance of Hollywood, since many countries have sought to protect their native film industries.

The news article that follows from the BBC on 20 October 2005 describes one such attempt by Unesco (The United Nations Educational, Scientific and Cultural Organization) to help countries protect their home-grown film industries:

COUNTRIES TURN BACKS ON HOLLYWOOD

UNESCO MEMBER STATES HAVE FORMALLY VOTED TO SUPPORT THEIR OWN FILM AND MUSIC INDUSTRIES AGAINST GLOBALISATION

The United Nations cultural body voted in favour of a cultural diversity convention, backed by France, Canada and the UK.

The US had said the 'deeply flawed' convention could be used to block the export of Hollywood films and other cultural exports.

The vote follows French moves to protect its film and music industries.

STRICT QUOTAS

France already awards large subsidies to its own film, music, theatre and opera industries to support its cultural heritage.

It also imposes strict quotas on the level of non-French material broadcast on radio and television.

The new convention on cultural diversity aims to recognise the distinctive nature of cultural goods and services.

It enables countries to take measures to protect what it describes as 'cultural expressions' that may be under threat.

The majority of Unesco's 191 member states voted for the convention.

Britain's representative to Unesco, Timothy Craddock, said the wording was 'clear, carefully balanced, consistent with the principles of international law and fundamental human rights'.

But it was opposed by the US, which said the convention was unclear and open to wilful misinterpretation.

French culture minister Renaud Donnedieu de Vabres said nations had a right to set artistic quotas because 85% of the world's spending on cinema tickets went to Hollywood.

The US suggested 28 amendments to the convention, which were almost unanimously rejected by Unesco delegates.

It was feared that Thursday's vote could isolate the US, which rejoined Unesco in 2003 after a 19-year absence.

The convention will need to be ratified by 30 member states in order to take effect.

(http://news.bbc.co.uk/1/hi/entertainment/arts/4360496.stm)

Thank God for British films, they don't care what shape you are.

Kate Winslet

I love British cinema like a doctor loves his dying patient.

Ben Kingsley

It now seems almost customary to open an account of our nation's cinema with François Truffaut's famous estimation that the phrase 'British cinema' is a contradiction in terms. Perhaps we should look to a far less frequently cited (yet equally deprecatory) scene from Italian director Federico Fellini's *La Dolce Vita* (1960) for the international attitude to our national output. Glamorous American movie star Sylvia Rank (Anita Ekberg) touches down in Rome for a press conference and is showered with questions from adoring European journalists. The stylishly dressed assembly offer both trivial and philosophical inquiry, met with well-rehearsed and quotable aphorisms. A short bald man, with an absurdly pompous, wispy moustache, asks in stuffy English RP: 'When do you intend to come to Britain to make a film Miss Rank?' This is greeted with heavy guffaws from all in the room except Miss Rank, who doesn't even dignify the suggestion with a response.

ACTIVITY

> ➤ Are there any British films that you feel are worthy of critical acclaim?

What is it about British cinema that the Europeans (and probably the rest of the world) find so ridiculous and uninspiring? Assuming that these critical directors Truffaut and Fellini don't reside in fragile, transparent dwellings, we might consider what it is they have that us Brits do not. Both are associated with a stylistic virtuosity; their films progressive, skilfully and playfully self-reflexive. Neither is afraid of self-expression, and thus their films resist the generic and are often intensely personal affairs. Much of their work poses and attempts to answer often impossible and insurmountable questions on the human condition, the meaning of life, the nature of love and so on. Ultimately their films exhibit a concrete and expert understanding of the medium; Truffaut and Fellini are artists, auteurs, cinematic poets. And 'poetry', in this debate, is an interesting word.

In literature the term 'poetry' may be employed as a value judgement, an indication of how hard language is working. One can only write verse in the hope that it becomes 'poetry'. In film studies then, the word 'cinema' functions in similar fashion: film-makers can only achieve 'cinema' if their work has the necessary depth, intensity or effect, qualities which Truffaut, with his infamous dig, finds lacking in our home-grown efforts.

In 2002 *Sight and Sound* gathered prominent critics for its ten-yearly 'greatest film' poll. As in previous polls there was a paltry showing from the home nations. In the following article, Nick James examines this discrepancy and begins to explain why Britain produces films but does not create *cinema*.

Why should anyone care if British films, as opposed to, say, German or Iranian films, do badly in all-time best-film polls? After all, we've tried to make these polls as outward-looking as we can. And yet our electorate's inevitable Anglophone weighting renders the spotty showing of British movies an interesting agony. Other parts of Europe still hold their own against the Hollywood hegemony, it seems, but little 'properly' British work is highly regarded by critics (I say properly to discount Kubrick's films, which, though made in the UK, were always Hollywood-studio financed).

Reasons for this poor rating are easy to find. You can start with François Truffaut's prejudice that British cinema is an incompatibility of terms, or you can blame the stiff competition for British talent from better career-building options such as Hollywood, the theatre or British television. These are plausible, if specially pleaded, contingencies.

Or you could argue that Britain's critical favourites Powell and Pressburger made too many great films that split their vote. But when you add up the Critics' Poll scores for A *Matter of Life and Death* (3), A *Canterbury Tale* (3) and *Black Narcissus* (4) – the three P&P movies that more than one contributor voted for – you get a total of ten, which would place a P&P composite at equal eighteenth alongside Welles' *Touch of Evil*, with still less than a quarter of the vote for Welles' *Citizen Kane*. And if you take the Powell and Pressburgers out, you'll find only the highest-placed British film, Carol Reed's *The Third Man* (6), and two of David Lean's, *Lawrence of Arabia* (5) and *Brief Encounter* (3), among the films with more than two votes. The fact is that all the votes for all the British films with more than one vote add up to just 32, leaving them way short of *Kane* and demonstrating that Welles alone gets more votes than all the British films put together.

How about that for a goad to nationalists: one American director is worth more than all the British movies ever made! Coincidentally, only ten 'properly' British films garner more than one vote, creating another *Sight & Sound* list. It runs: 1 *The Third Man*; 2 *Lawrence of Arabia*; 3 *Black Narcissus*; =4 *Brief Encounter*, A *Canterbury Tale*, A *Matter of Life and Death*; =7 *The Lady Vanishes* (Hitchcock); *Orlando* (Sally Potter), *Performance* (Nic Roeg), *Topsy-Turvy* (Mike Leigh). Compare this to the top ten of the *bfi*'s 100 British Films as voted for by the great and the good of the British film industry in 1999: 1 *The Third Man*; 2 *Brief Encounter*; 3 *Lawrence of Arabia*; 4 *The 39 Steps* (Hitchcock); 5 *Great Expectations* (Lean); 6 *Kind Hearts and Coronets* (Robert Hamer); 7 *Kes* (Ken Loach); 8 *Don't Look Now* (Roeg); 9 *The Red Shoes* (Powell and Pressburger); 10 *Trainspotting* (Danny Boyle).

What's most striking about both these lists is the poor showing for British realism. Ever since the documentary-film movement of John Grierson came to dominate British film thinking in the 1930s, it has been widely assumed that realism is what the British do best – it's what news pundits tend to expect from British cinema and what television drama commissioners have routinely promoted. With the standout exceptions of *Brief Encounter* and *Kes*, these polls suggest otherwise. They reflect the general shift in cinema tastes towards spectacle and away from the reflection of ordinary life. Even Mike Leigh's most successful film here is his paean to High Victorian fantasists Gilbert and Sullivan.

What comfort then, if any, can British film-makers draw from this poor rating? Both British top tens do at least recognise the value of more recent films than those featured in the main top tens. *Orlando*, *Topsy-Turvy* and *Trainspotting* were made in recent times of relative financial difficulty and their flights of fancy are all well realised within tightish budgets. The alternative to such restrictions remains, of course, Hollywood, where the likes of Chaplin, Hitchcock and Ridley Scott achieved their best work. They too fall naturally into the camp of fantasists and dreamers, for all Scott's recent protestations over *Black Hawk Down* that real-life stories can't be bettered.

It's not that the British film industry hasn't been trying to replicate the success of its putative 'best' films. *The Third Man* and *Lawrence of Arabia* are war-based tales of subterfuge and derring-do. A string of such subjects has been tried since the Oscar success of *The English Patient* (1996), but the scale of imagination in the Reed and the Lean far outstrips the palely imitative likes of *Enigma* and *Charlotte Gray*. And these war films are still rooted in a class-ridden vision of Britain that remains an obstacle to making a truly universal cinema.

All the comfort the British may be left with, then, is that the world's second-favourite director, Alfred Hitchcock, learned his trade in his homeland. But had Hitchcocks's *Vertigo* been shot similarly but set in Liverpool (with a fatal trip to a clifftop chapel) and starred, say, Alec Guinness as Scottie and Vivien Leigh as Madeleine, would it still be regarded as the second-greatest film ever made? Somehow, for all Hitchcock's imaginative talent, all of the above – and maybe something to do with scale and quality of light – make me doubt it.

(James 2002: 38)

We can place James' reasons for Britain's failure to win consistent critical acclaim into two categories. First, industrial:

- *The talent drain.* British actors and directors – indeed all the important members of a crew – are drawn to the glamour and substantially bigger financial rewards of Hollywood production, leaving an arguably impoverished workforce with which to pool from.

- *Scale of production.* Be it geographical limitations, or the more likely financial restrictions of film production on home soil, British films are inferior in scope and size when compared to their Hollywood counterparts.

Yet these two factors apply, to more or less the same degree, in every non-American film-producing nation with the exception of India, while many of these nations – France, Italy, Germany, Japan – have a far healthier presence in the critical canon than Britain. The second set of, this time unique, obstacles to a respectable and artistic British *cinema,* we might label 'socio-cultural':

- *Class.* Britain, famously, is a nation obsessed with class. This obsession is reflected in its cinema. James notes that even the attempts to replicate the critical successes of *The Third Man* and *Lawrence of Arabia* are 'class ridden'. At one level this fascination with our own unique and peculiar class system alienates the international spectator. However, British film's limited focus also leaves our domestic audience cold, as they hunger for films that tackle other, arguably bigger issues.
- *Realism.* The realist tradition of film-making has dominated British cinema. James sees this as the most significant determinant in our poor scoring in the *Sight and Sound* poll.

Inspired by the pioneering documentary works of Grieson in the 1930s and the subsequent short-lived Free Cinema Movement in the 1950s, the British 'New Wave' set the trend for a realist approach to film-making. Until this point, cinema had left the British working classes relatively untouched. When they did feature, representations were stylised and stereotypical, limited to chirpy cockneys and selfless 'salt-of-the-earth' servicemen. But by the 1950s, the working classes were finally gaining proper access to universities and this meant that the south saw an influx of 'angry young men' from the north of England, with left-wing views and very different backgrounds. There was no doubt that Britain, a country rapidly declining in power (it was publicly humiliated in the 1956 Suez crisis), was in for a cultural landslide. The first novels of 'angry young' writers such as John Braine, Alan Sillitoe and Stan Barstow were published, and playwrights John Osborne and Arnold Wesker were also enjoying successful productions. As the BBFC had notably liberalised its absurdly restrictive policies, the time was right for fresh new directors Karel Reisz, John Schlesinger, Tony Richardson and others, to adapt these exciting new works, which – with their location shooting, available lighting, deliberate use of black-and-white stock, unknown actors and everyday subjects – were much cheaper to produce than the industry's big budget war films, already declining in popularity.

A common criticism against the British New Wave films such as *Saturday Night and Sunday Morning* (1960), *A Taste Honey* (1961) and *A Kind of Loving* (1962) is that the, mainly middle-class, Oxbridge-educated directors were not qualified to capture and present the grimy factories and tenements of the north on film. They are accused of being unfeeling and patronising towards their subject; fascinated by poverty merely because it is alien to them. John Hill examines this viewpoint in *Sex Class and Realism*:

It has been a common enough criticism of the 'new wave' films that, although about the working class, they nonetheless represent an outsider's view. Roy Armes, for example, argues that they follow the pattern set by Grierson: 'the university-educated bourgeois making "sympathetic" films about proletarian life but not analysing the ambiguities of their own privileged position.' Durgnat is even more scathing: 'the Free Cinema radicals are uninterested in the masses except as images for their own discontent.' The importance of the point, however, is less the actual social background of the film-makers, none of whom ever lay claim to be just 'one of the lads', than the way this 'outsider's view' is inscribed in the films themselves, the way the 'poetry', the 'marks of the enunciation' themselves articulate a clear distance between observer and observed. In the Free Cinema documentaries of Lindsay Anderson, for example, this is the result of the use of associative editing (a self-consciously 'artistic' patterning of images, in part influenced by Jennings) and, above all, of sound. As Bill Nichols suggests, *Every Day Except Christmas* (1957) is typical of a 'classical expository cinema' in which the primary principle of ordering derives from a direct address commentary. It is in this voice-over commentary, delivered by an invisible narrator, that final authority resides, guaranteeing the coherence of the organisation of images and maintaining a privileged interpretation of their meaning (bolstered, in turn, by the class authority of the narrator's accent). What is absent is the voices of the workers themselves, or their interpretation of events, either reduced to inconsequential chatter or overlaid with a musical soundtrack (significantly classical rather than 'popular', 'high art' rather than 'low').

O *Dreamland* (1953) does not employ a narrator, yet is similarly 'authoritarian' in its use of soundtrack (the laughter of models, the song 'I Believe') to impose a privileged interpretation of events and create meanings (usually ironic) not contained in the images themselves. What, once again, is absent is the attitude or point-of-view of the characters themselves, strictly subordinated to the authorial point-of-view announced by the film's aesthetic organisation.

With the shift to feature film-making there is, however, a concern to 'fill in' the interiority which is absent from the documentaries. The films are conventionally organised around one dramatically central character, occasionally bestowed with interior monologue (*Saturday Night and Sunday Morning*, *Loneliness of the Long Distance Runner*) or 'subjective' flashbacks (*Loneliness of the Long Distance Runner*, *This Sporting Life*). Point-of-view shots, in turn, are occasionally employed in a way which amplifies this first person modality. While, as Stephen Heath suggests, the conventional point-of-view shot is, strictly speaking, 'objective' – 'what is "subjective" in the point-of-view shot is its spatial positioning (its place), not the image' – in some of the 'new wave' films it is the content of the image which is also 'subjective'. When Colin and Mike turn down the volume of the television set in *Loneliness of the Long Distance Runner*, the image of the television spokesman is quite noticeably speeded up as he continues to mouth off in silent agitation. The image does not merely show 'objectively' what would be seen from the boys' point-of-view, but also their 'subjective' perception of the speaker's irrelevance and inanity. It was, indeed, this confusion of 'objective' and 'subjective' modes of narration in the film which made it impossible for Dilys Powell to decide whether she was a witness to what 'the central figure sees . . . or fact'.

This use of point-of-view shots is less pronounced in other films, but is still, in part, in evidence. The shots of Arthur's fellow workers at the beginning of *Saturday Night and Sunday Morning* and the point-of-view shots of Vic in the coffee bar in *A Kind of Loving* may more closely conform to the conventional 'objective' viewpoint; yet by means of editing, composition and the postures of the characters there is a suggestion of something more: that these are indeed as Arthur and Vic 'see' (or, indeed, imagine) them, rather than as they would appear, strictly 'objectively'.

It has often been noted how such British films (especially *Loneliness of the Long Distance Runner*) were indebted to the French *nouvelle vague* (which provided the shorthand title by which the British films became known). Part of the influence, here, was undoubtedly in the adoption of these 'subjective' techniques. As Terry Lovell indicates, 'the subjective and objective worlds are fused' in the French *nouvelle vague*. 'Cartesian epistemology, egocentric and individualistic, is . . . reduced to absurdity. Egotisation of the world reaches the point of solipsism, where the ego submerges the world, and is in turn submerged in it.' In the British 'new wave', however, such 'egotisation of the world' can only go so far. The subjective mode never becomes dominant but is always held in check by the 'objective' point-of-view and the authority of the inscribed authorial voice. Thus despite the dramatic prominence of the main character there are always scenes which exclude him or her (e.g. the scenes between Jack and Brenda in *Saturday Night and Sunday Morning*, between Ingrid and her mother in *A Kind of Loving*). Even apparently 'subjective' flashbacks contain shots of events which it would be impossible for the character concerned to have witnessed (e.g. the graveyard scene in *This Sporting Life*, the beating up of Stacey in *Loneliness*).

Such a superiority over the characters' own subjectivity is, of course, characteristic of the conventional film's employment of an omniscient camera, but, as Paul Willemen suggests, there is a distinction between such films and those which employ a first person narration: 'wherever conjunctions, overlaps, frictions, dislocations etc. occur in relation to the first person narration, the presence of another "person" is signified by a concrete mark'. In this respect, the look of the camera is not merely anonymous but also 'authored', the look from the 'outside' is rendered 'visible'.

This is more generally true of the 'poetic' transformation of the subject-matter of the films, the foregrounding of the 'artistry' rather than the 'reality'. The shots of Vic running home in A Kind of Loving and the shots of Jo by the canal in A Taste of Honey reveal not so much an interest in their characters (their 'subjectivity') as their subordination to aesthetics, their visually pleasing positioning as 'figures in a landscape'. As Andrew Higson suggests, it is in the aerial viewpoints of the city, characteristic of practically all these films, that this 'enunciative look' becomes most transparent: 'That Long Shot Of Our Town From That Hill involves an external point of view ... an identification with a position outside and above the city ... the scope of the vision, the (near) perfection of the vantage-point is stressed: spectator and cameraman are masters of the world below'.

But what then are the implications of this inscription of an 'outsider's' authorial view? It has become something of a commonplace of recent cultural criticism to argue that the introduction into art of 'new contents', such as working-class life, does not in itself guarantee radicalism: what is important is the treatment of such subject-matter. Walter Benjamin, for example, has pinpointed how the potentially disturbing image of photography can be rendered 'safe' by an assimilation into aestheticism:

> Let us follow the ... development of photography. What do we see? It has become more and more subtle, more and more modern, and the result is that it is now incapable of photographing a tenement or a rubbish-heap without transfiguring it ... In front of these, photography can only say 'How beautiful' ... It has succeeded in turning abject poverty itself, by handling it in a modish, technically perfect way, into an object of enjoyment ... it has turned the struggle against misery into an object of consumption.

By codifying its images of cities and factories in terms of 'art' so the British 'new wave' runs a similar risk of transforming them into objects of 'comfortable contemplation'. 'Richardson has used the place and its objects as he uses people', commented Isabel Quigly on A Taste of Honey, 'moodily, lovingly, bringing beauty out of squalor'.

But, what is also apparent is that it is only from the 'outside' that such 'squalor' can assume its fascination. Robin Wood suggests what might be at stake here: 'The proletariat ... remains ... a conveniently available object for projection: the bourgeois obsession with cleanliness, which psychoanalysis shows to be closely associated, as outward symptom, with sexual repression, and bourgeois sexual repression itself, find their inverse reflections in the myths of working-class squalor and sexuality.' What is, indeed, striking about the 'new wave' films is how readily their treatment of 'kitchen sink' subjects ('working-class squalor') became attached to an opening up of the cinema's treatment of sex. Pascall and Jeavons' history of 'sex in the movies', for example, explains the 'breakthrough' of the 'new realism' in precisely such terms. Riding on the back of the 'social commitment' to observe 'ordinary people', then, emerges a kind of sexual fascination with 'otherness', the 'exotic' sexualities of those it now has a licence to reveal, just as the Victorian 'social explorers', described by Mick Eaton, reported back 'the licentiousness of their objects of study'. 'Audiences could identify with the people and places on screen', observes Nina Hibbin in her discussion of *Saturday Night and Sunday Morning*. Yet the look which the films encourage is not so straightforward. 'Outside and above', marking a separation between spectator and subject, the pleasures delivered may well rely less on recognition than the very sensation of class difference.

(Hill 1986: 132–136)

Whether or not this opinion is shared by critics or the public, the 'social-realist' approach of the New Wave has colonised the British cinematic landscape ever since. Proof of the style's longevity may be seen in recent popular successes (*The Full Monty, Billy Elliot*) and critical in the work of Ken Loach and Mike Leigh. These successes are infrequent however, and still relatively small when compared to American cinema. Many, like James above, pin responsibility for Britain's general commercial and critical insignificance on this very predictable style. This predictability is apparent in Coveney's (1996: 5) all-too-familiar summing up of Mike Leigh's output:

A grungey domestic scenario, with pop up toasters and cups of tea, fake-fur coats and rugs, pink bobble carpet slippers, bad haircuts, domestic arguments on leatherette sofas, and adolescent anxieties. Welcome to the slump, the outer London *anomie*, the china animals, the flying geese on brown wallpaper, the smoky pub, the cold light of dawn and cheerless laundrette.

The minor success of Leigh's *Secrets and Lies* in the 1997 Oscar nominations was heralded by some as the beginnings of a rebirth in British cinema. It inevitably proved to be another false dawn (scriptwriter Colin Welland famously, *wrongly*, proclaimed that 'the British are coming' in his acceptance speech at the 1982 Oscars ceremony), and Britain quietly continued the production of sincere and well-meaning social realist movies that would fail to impact upon the world stage. Paul Marris (2001: 47) feels the game was up for this 'exhausted tradition' well before *Secrets and Lies'* release, while a *Brassed-Off* Alex Collins offers some praise to *Trainspotting* for effort, but is still frustrated by its lack of adventure, resigned to the fact that even this supposed beacon of originality and progression is still tethered to social realism.

GRIM REALITIES

The show begins. Whoopie Goldberg, our host for the evening, enters to rapturous applause. Moving to stage right, Whoppie begins her opening monologue. In a broad Yorkshire accent, she proceeds to tell the assembled Hollywood luminaries of her grindingly depressing childhood in the North of England. Brought up on a deprived council estate, Whoppie's only means of venting her anger at an uncaring world was to kill her brother's kestrel.

This could well be the scene, come this year's Oscar night. With writer/director Mike Leigh's film, Secrets and Lies, nominated in several of the high-profile categories, the media on both sides of the Atlantic have been sent into a frenzy of excitement over great British 'social realism'.

The success of Secrets and Lies, coupled with the recent announcement of a lottery cash bonanza for film-makers, has led writers and broadcasters, once again, to herald a renaissance for British cinema. As a student film-maker on the verge of leaving education in search of a career in the industry, I find it impossible to share such enthusiasm.

To my mind, critical fawning over a film such as Secrets and Lies does more to hinder than to advance the development of a vibrant national cinema. Far too long, British film-making has been in a state of creative stagnation. Too many of our film-makers toil under the mistaken belief that the only artistically valid approach to dealing with social and political themes is the production of 'Grim Oop North' realism. The release of every Secrets and Lies, every Carla's Song, every Brassed Off, serves only to tighten the chains which bind the British film to the kitchen sink.

Social realist films are an anachronism. While they may have once succeeded in revealing the shocking deprivation experienced by many of Britain's working class (though that is questionable), they certainly do not challenge our perceptions any more. That a film directed by Mike Leigh has been nominated for the Best Film Oscar is evidence that this genre is now part of the status quo.

So why is it that the bulk of British films are so restricted in their subject matter and aesthetics? It is largely thanks to the proclamations of documentary supremo, John Grierson. In the 1930s, he sought to distance the 'artful' business of documentary film production from the 'trivial' concerns of fiction. Documentary was, Grierson decided, grounded in 'actuality', able to deal candidly with serious social issues, and thus, of a greater artistic significance than fiction could ever hope to be.

Grierson's words, it seems, have rung loud in the ears of British film-makers from the '30s to the present. Fearful of being seen to plumb the cultural depths of expressionist approaches to fiction, our film-makers have continually restricted themselves to a realist approach derived primarily from the traditional documentary. Even when British cinema experienced its 'New Wave' in the 1950s, the films which emerged stuck unerringly to an agenda of social realism.

The newly available lottery grants could, and should, be seized upon as an opportunity to provide the financial support necessary for a break with this past. Given the current critical enthusiasm for films such as Secrets and Lies, however, I feel that this money will only be used to groom yet another generation of Griersonian realists.

If British cinema is ever to be creatively revitalised, funding agencies must seek out film-makers with the courage to reject the cultural elitism which deems gritty realism the only path worth treading. Last year, Trainspotting made a brave stab at that by employing some wonderfully expressionistic devices. But, for my money, the film did not go far enough – it was still social realism at heart. If the next generation of British film-makers can take up this challenge and, instead of producing yet another Secrets and Lies, begin where Trainspotting left off, perhaps we can at last begin to foster a truly new British Cinema.

(Collins 1997)

Brown (1997: 189) observes that 'British cinema has marked class boundaries. The notion that realist films could embrace characters of the upper-middle class and beyond has rarely been considered. Realistic characters in British films wear cloth caps, not top hats.' Yet social-realism is not the only film style to occupy an enlarged position within our national cinema; the 'upper-middle class and beyond' provide an equally healthy subject for cinematic investigation, albeit with a markedly different approach. In 'Representing the National Past' Andrew Higson analyses a particular type of British film and labels it 'Heritage'.

Heritage films operate at very much the culturally respectable, quality end of the market, and are key players in the new British art Cinema, which straddles the traditional art-house circuit and the mainstream commercial cinemas in Britain. These are the sort of films that are invited to festivals and that win prizes. They are discussed in terms of an authorship that, at least in the case of the literary adaptations, is doubly coded – in terms of both film director and author of the source novel. Their audience is primarily middle-class and significantly older than the mainstream film audience, and they appeal to a film culture closely allied to English literary culture and to the canons of good taste (see Higson 2003: 101–6). The hand-to-mouth production base of these films, along with the terms of their reception and circulation, indicate that they function within a *cultural* mode of production, as distinct from Hollywood's *industrial* mode of production (Elsaesser 1989: 3; see Higson 2003, chaps 3 and 4, for an account of the commercial context of these films): their significance

is accounted for culturally rather than financially, even though several of them (including *Chariots of Fire*, *A Passage to India* and *A Room with a View*) were in the end considerable box-office successes relative to their budgets.

We must also recognise that this cycle of films, as with so many recent British films, depends on television in a variety of ways. Several were partially funded by television companies: *A Room with a View* and *Maurice* by Channel Four, and *A Handful of Dust* by London Weekend Television, for instance. Hugh Hudson and Charles Sturridge, the directors, respectively, of *Chariots of Fire* and *A Handful of Dust*, came from the television industry. All of the films arguably owe as much to the tradition of the BBC classic serial and the quality literary adaptation on television as they do to the filmed costume drama or to art-house cinema (on the classic serial, see Kerr). Thus, in addition to the films already mentioned, the cycle of heritage adaptations should also perhaps include prestige television serials of the 1980s, such as *Brideshead Revisited* (1981) and *The Jewel in the Crown* (1983), the former directed by Sturridge. Indeed, Channel Four's policy – and its influence on the policies of other television companies – of co-funding filmed dramas for a theatrical as well as a televisual release, rather than funding serialised drama on video, temporarily replaced the television classic serial in the mid–1980s, while employing many of its aesthetic conventions for the films that emerged.

John Corner and Sylvia Harvey argue that the radical economic and social reconstructions of Britain in the 1980s required the Thatcher government to find novel ways of managing the conflict between old and new, tradition and modernity. They identify the key concepts in this process as 'heritage', with its connotations of continuity with the past and the preservation of values and tradition, and 'enterprise', with its connotations of change and innovation. The terms are vitally interconnected: 'What has come to be called "the heritage industry" is itself a major component of economic redevelopment, an "enterprise", both in terms of large-scale civic programmes and the proliferation of private commercial activity around "the past" in one commodified form or another' (Corner & Harvey 1991c: 46). One of the more obvious manifestations of official concern with the values and properties of the past can be found in the National Heritage Acts of 1980 and 1983. As Patrick Wright shows, these acts reworked concepts of public access and use in terms of commodification, exhibition, and display, encouraging the forthright marketing of the past within a thoroughly market-orientated heritage industry (Wright 1985: 42ff; see also Hewison 1987, and Higson 2003: 48–53). The heritage industry has thus developed as a vital part of contemporary tourism and related service industries such as the leisure industry, which of course embraces cinema.

The heritage film and its reconstruction of the past thus represents just one aspect of the heritage industry as a whole. Of course, the heritage impulse, 'one of the most powerful imaginative constructs of our time' (Samuel 1989a: xii), is not confined to Thatcherite Britain, but is a characteristic feature of postmodern culture. The heritage industry may transform the past into a series of commodities for the leisure and entertainment market, but in most cases the commodity on offer is an image, a spectacle, something to be gazed at. History, the past, becomes, in Fredric Jameson's phrase, 'a vast collection of images' designed to delight the modern-day tourist-historian (Jameson 1984: 66; see also Urry 1990: chaps 5 and 6). In this version of history, a critical perspective is displaced by decoration and display, a fascination with surfaces, 'an obsessive accumulation of comfortably archival detail' (Wright 1985: 252), in which a fascination with style displaces the material dimensions of historical context. The past is reproduced as flat, depthless pastiche, where the reference point is not the past itself, but other images, other texts. The past as referent is effaced, and all that remains is a self-referential intertextuality (Jameson 1984: 60ff). Yet, at the same time, the sense of pastness and historicity are important, for as Andreas Huyssen suggests, the search for tradition is a vital feature of the contemporary response to the felt failure of modernism.

The heritage films, too, work as pastiches, each period of the national past reduced through a process of reiteration to an effortlessly reproducible, and attractively consumable, connotative style. The films turn away from modernity toward a traditional conservative pastoral Englishness; they turn away, too, from the hi-tech, special effects dominated aesthetics of mainstream popular cinema. Where Hollywood in the late 1970s and 1980s specialised in the production of futuristic epics, the heritage film prefers the intimacy of the period piece, although their visual splendour lends them an extravagant, epic scale. The postmodernism of these films is actually an anti-modernism that clothes itself in all the trappings of classical art – but the more culturally respectable classicism of literature, painting, music, and so on, not the classicism of Hollywood (indeed, the image of American-ness against which Britishness/Englishness is contrasted in *Chariots of Fire* is explicitly technological and machinelike).

The image of the past in the heritage films has become so naturalised that, paradoxically, it stands removed from history: the evocation of pastness is accomplished by a look, a style, the loving recreation of period details – not by any critical historical perspective. The self-conscious visual perfectionism of these films and their fetishisation of period details create a fascinating but self-enclosed world. They render history as spectacle, as *separate* from the viewer in the present, as something over and done with, complete, achieved. Hence the sense of timelessness rather than historicity in relation to a national past which is 'purged of political tension' and so available for appreciation as visual display (Wright 1985: 69). As Cairns Craig suggests, this is 'film as conspicuous consumption' (10) – or rather, because it is only

images being consumed, it is a *fantasy* of conspicuous consumption, a fantasy of Englishness, a fantasy of the national past.

Yet at the same time, the version of the national past offered is above all a modern past, an imaginary object invented from the point of view of a present that is too distasteful to be confronted head-on. Thus Raphael Samuel shows how Christine Edzard's *Little Dorrit* produces a Dickens for the 1980s, despite, or perhaps precisely because of, the care taken to reproduce period details (Samuel 1994). Samuel contrasts the 1980s Dickens, which seeks to conserve the heritage of Victorian values, with the grotesque realism, the 'dark Dickens' of the 1940s, when the Victorian period was being re-viewed as problematic and repressive. Thus Edzard's film cleans up the city's slums and workshops, its inhabitants and their authentically period costumes: 'The artefacts so lovingly assembled turn the London of [Edzard's] film from a prison-house – Dickens' guiding metaphor – into a showcase of period delights' (Samuel 1994: 423). The film effaces the gothic aspects of the novel in favour of a conservationist urban pastoral in which 'London is ... a playground, and poverty – provided it is safely period – picturesque' (Samuel 1989b: 284).

In a move typical of the heritage industry (see Wright), these key films in the *national* cinema of the 1980s are fascinated by the private property, the culture and values of a *particular* class. By reproducing these trappings outside of a materialist historical context, they transform the heritage of the upper classes into the national heritage: private interest becomes naturalised as public interest. Except, of course, these are still films for a relatively privileged audience, and the heritage is still refined and exclusive, rather than properly public in the sense of massively popular. The national past and national identity emerge in these films not only as aristocratic, but also as male-centred, while the nation itself is reduced to the soft pastoral landscape of southern England untainted by the modernity of urbanisation or industrialisation (or, in the case of *Little Dorrit* or *The Fool*, a tasteful urban pastoral). In each instance, the *quality* of the films lends the representation of the past a certain cultural validity and respectability.

These films share a particularly strong group style, not least because of the degree to which they work as pastiches. The central intertextual focus of the cycle, and of the broader historical genre which informs these films (see Higson 1995, chap. 4), is, as noted above, undoubtedly the adaptation of literary and theatrical properties. In the case of adaptations of canonical texts, the 'original' is as much on display as the past it seeks to reproduce. The literary source material, of course, functions as an important selling point, playing on the familiarity and prestige of the particular novel or play, but also invoking the pleasures of other such quality literary adaptations and the status of a national intellectual tradition. The genre can also invent new texts for the canon by treating otherwise marginal texts or properties to the same modes of representation and marketing.

The genre involves much more than simply the adaptation of literary or dramatic text and plunders the national heritage in other ways, too. Almost all of these films contain a recurrent image of an imposing country house seen in extreme long shot and set in a picturesque, verdant landscape. This image encapsulates much that is typical of the films as a whole, and indicates that the notion of heritage property needs to be extended to cover in addition the types of ancient architectural and landscape properties conserved by the National Trust and English Heritage, and the costumes, furnishings, *objets d'art* and aristocratic character-types that traditionally fill those properties. These properties (the term, with its theatrical connotations, seems more than appropriate) constitute the iconography of the genre. In what is both a bid for historical realism (and visual pleasure) and a function of the nostalgic mode (seeking an imaginary historical plenitude), the past is delivered as a museum of sounds and images, an iconographic display. This iconography bring with it a particular moral formation and set of values, which the films effortlessly dramatise at 'significant' historical moments.

The intertextuality of the heritage cycle is also particularly noticeable in the casting of the films. The same actors play similar role and class-types in several different films, bringing a powerful sense of all the other heritage films, costume dramas, and literary adaptations to each new film. In fact, these films draw on two groups of actors: on the one hand, established actors who specialise in character parts (Denholm Elliot [A *Room With a View, Maurice*], Judi Dench [A *Room With a View, A Handful of Dust*], Maggie Smith [A *Room With a View*], Simon Callow [A *Room With a View, Maurice*]) and who bring with them all the qualities and connotations of the British theatre tradition; on the other hand, various younger actors virtually groomed for their parts in the heritage films (Helena Bonham Carter [A *Room With a View, Maurice, Where Angels Fear to Tread*], Nigel Havers [*Chariots of Fire, A Passage to India*], Rupert Graves [A *Room With a View, Maurice, A Handful of Dust, Where Angels Fear to Tread*], James Wilby [*Maurice, A Handful of Dust*] Hugh Grant [*Maurice*]).

Set against the intertextual, generic qualities of these films are the discourses of authorship and authenticity, which stress originality and uniqueness rather than similarity and repetition. These discourses work in various ways: the literary adaptations strive to reproduce the tone that distinguishes the book, to respect the 'original' text and the 'original' authorship. The period films, which, of course, include the literary adaptations, seek to reproduce the surface qualities that define the pastness of the particular period. Yet, at the same time, there is a foregrounding of filmic authorship, too, the attempt to make a unique and original film. Each strategy is a means of stressing authorship, originality, authenticity – but the authenticities are not all of the same category, each potentially pulling in a different direction, while the generic qualities *deny* the sense of originality altogether. Paradoxically, the preoccupation with authorship, the display of good taste and a self-consciously

aesthetic sensibility, are themselves generic qualities that bind the films together. Literary authorship, the process of writing itself, is foregrounded in the recurrent narrative episode of a character writing or reading a letter or a book, either aloud or in voiceover, thus celebrating the purity of the word. Literary adaptations also, of course, foreground the authenticity of the 'original' by their effort to reproduce dialogue from the novel for characters in the film, or to transpose the narrative voice of the novel to the speech of those characters. There is also a studied reference to and reproduction of other art objects and art forms – classical paintings, statues, architecture, and music all add weight to the tasteful production values of these films.

Narratively, the films move slowly and episodically rather than in a tightly causal manner; they demonstrate a greater concern for character, place, atmosphere and milieu than for dramatic, goal-directed action. There is also a preference for long takes and deep focus, and for long and medium shots, rather than for close-ups and rapid cutting. The camera is characteristically fluid, but camera movement is dictated less by a desire to follow the movement of characters than by a desire to offer the spectator a more aesthetic angle on the period setting and the objects that fill it. Self-conscious crane shots and high-angle shots divorced from character point of view, for instance, are used to display ostentatiously the seductive mise-en-scène of the films. This is particularly clear in the Merchant-Ivory films. In A *Room with a View*, there is a typical interior shot of Lucy playing the piano at the Pensione Bertolini: Lucy, the ostensible focus of *narrative* interest, sits in the background, while artifacts and furnishings fill and frame the foreground; the camera gracefully, but without narrative motivation, tracks slowly around one splendid item of furniture to reveal it in all its glory. In the same film, the shots of Florence are always offered direct to the spectator unmediated by any shots of characters within the diegesis looking at the view. Such shots, in fact, *follow* the views, rather than preceding and thus motivating them. Insert shots of Cambridge function similarly in *Maurice*, having only a minimal function as establishing shots. In this way, the heritage culture becomes the object of a public gaze, while the private gaze of the dramatis personae is reserved for romance: they almost never admire the quality of their surroundings. Heritage culture appears petrified, frozen in moments that virtually fall out of the narrative, existing only as adornments for the staging of a love story. Thus, historical narrative is transformed into spectacle; heritage becomes excess, not functional, not something to be used, but something to be admired.

All in all, the camera style is pictorialist, with all the connotations the term brings of art photography, aesthetic refinement and set-piece images (Higson 1995: 48ff). Though narrative meaning and narrational clarity are rarely sacrificed, these shots, angles and camera movements frequently exceed narrative motivation. The effect is the creation of heritage space, rather than narrative space: that is, a space for the display of heritage properties rather than for the enactment of dramas. In many respects, therefore, this is not a narrative cinema, a cinema of storytelling, but something more akin to that mode of early filmmaking that Tom Gunning calls the cinema of attractions. In this case, the heritage films display their self-conscious artistry, their landscapes, their properties, their actors and their performance qualities, their clothes, and their often archaic dialogue. The gaze, therefore, is organised around props and settings – the look of the observer at the tableau image – as much as it is around character point of view.

(Higson 2006: 110–118)

The Heritage movie may thus be identified as a film (or television programme) ...

■ adapted from a literary source (often E.M. Forster);
■ set in the past and featuring the British upper-middle and upper classes;
■ featuring a cast pooled from a particular group of actors, often with theatrical backgrounds, including Helena Bonham-Carter, Anthony Hopkins, Judi Dench, Nigel Havers;

with ...

■ a nostalgic view of Britain the thriving empire;
■ a recurring image of a country house;
■ associations of quality, usually garnered through other art forms: literature through the narrative, theatre through casting, and classical art through the *mise-en-scène*;
■ shared pleasures and a symbiotic relationship with the Heritage tourist industry;
■ a superficiality or surface nature, where constructions of 'the past' are primarily visual;
■ a prioritisation of *mise-en-scène* over narrative, through slow, mannered and meticulously composed cinematography, fashioning a 'museum aesthetic' or 'sensuousness' (Dyer 1995: 205).

Many voices in this discourse see the Heritage text as 'women's film' and there are a number of points to support this notion. Many of the films contain repression-sexual-liberation narratives, where prim-and-proper female protagonists eventually reject 'the done thing' for wilder, untamed and unconventional love. Lingering shots of attractive, sometimes naked, young men seem to function purely as spectacle, ensuring Mulvey's notion of the male gaze (see Chapter 10, pp. 255–261) is transformed into a female or homoerotic one. Finally, and we are on slightly dubious ground here, the satisfaction gained from the elaborate detail of period costumes and furniture is traditionally seen as a female pleasure.

If the Heritage movie is a 'women's film', then the third and final prominent trend in British cinema examined here might be considered 'men's', or more specifically, 'lads'' film. In 'From Underworld to Underclass' Claire Monk explains how widening drug use and the rise in 'new lad culture' has changed the face of the British gangster movie.

When *Face* (Antonia Bird, 1997) – an East End tale of robbery gone wrong, shot during the last months of Conservative government, and released in the changed political climate of Autumn 1997 – was praised as possibly 'the best British thriller since *The Long Good Friday*' (Quentin Curtis, *Daily Telegraph*, 26 September 1997), the comparison revealed more than its author might have intended. The blend of imperialism and aspirational entrepreneurialism embodied by *The Long Good Friday*'s yacht-owning gang boss, Harold Shand, had uncannily prefigured the values that would dominate the 1980s. *Face*, by contrast, was one of a crop of late-1990s British films – from the comedies *Brassed Off* (Mark Herman, 1996) and *The Full Monty* (Peter Cattaneo, 1997) to Danny Boyle's heroin drama *Trainspotting* (1996) – whose subtext was the economic and social damage that Thatcherism and longer-term industrial decline had wrought on the once-working classes. In the eighteen years separating the two films, *everything* – socially, culturally and politically – had changed. The fact that, in the face of such transformations, *Face*'s makers and critics were able to enhance its cultural value and commercial appeal by claiming similarities not just with *The Long Good Friday* but with a still older London gangster 'classic' – Mike Hodges' 1971 *Get Carter* – exposed a little-trumpeted trait of the film culture of 'Cool Britannia': its uncritical, backward-looking self-referentiality and unacknowledged nostalgia. Above all, it spoke of the endurance of the gangland film as the preferred model for what a British crime film 'should' be.

But, as *The Long Good Friday* had suggested, the traditional London gangster, with his attachment to obsolete social, sexual and racial hierarchies and open nostalgia for the vanished days of empire, was already an anachronism by 1979, let alone 1997. So too, I will argue, was the genre prototype provided for British cinema by the gangland films of the 1960s and 1970s. In particular, the real-life organisational and technological models of both crime and 'legit-imate' business, as well as gender relations, public morality and the wider social formation, had been transformed almost beyond recognition since the 1960s heyday of the Richardsons and the Krays.

Although *Face* represented a genuine attempt to 'modernise' the London gangland film – by rejecting and feminising the gangster subculture's tradi-tionally reactionary politics and offering a critique of 1980s and 1990s social changes from the Left – the difficulties it faced in doing so from within the genre are revealing. My analysis will argue that the 1990s British films that responded best to the social realities shaping 1990s crime were those that departed from traditional genre models. It will also seek to illustrate why the gangland film's continuing appeal (for parts of the male audience in particular) may lie precisely in its celebration of regressive ideologies and obsolete models of criminal, gender and social organisation.

GENDER POLITICS AND THE GANGSTER

As the celebrations of the gangster's explosive, anti-rational male aggression in films such as *Get Carter* and *Villain* (Michael Tuchner, 1971) testify, the 'classic' British villain has been centrally defined by his contempt for women as well as his reactionary politics. The villain's reputation for misogyny is, of course, far older than these films and is firmly rooted in biographical fact (Pearson, 1995: 31–32, 37). Indeed, it is possible to go further and read this vehement opposition to the 'feminine' spheres of home life and 'respectable' society as the primary organising logic explaining the peculiar character of the underworld as an inherently homosocial subculture, in which male rituals, hierarchies and rivalries often seem to take precedence over gangland's ostensible business of illegal money-making. The gang or 'firm' itself is likewise a homosocial space; in both cases, the intrusion of women – or, conversely, in *Performance* (Nicolas Roeg and Donald Cammell, 1970), the entry of the gangster into a zone of sexual and gender ambiguity – is always a threat.

In the 1970s British gangland films, this masculinist dynamic and the corresponding subordination/exclusion of women had been accepted traits of the genre. However, the shifting perceptions of gender power and actual shifts in gender relations that had taken place in Britain since 1979 (not least due to the rule of a powerful woman Prime Minister) made this genre blueprint less feasible in the 1990s. It seems significant that Margaret Thatcher's final year in power brought two British films – Peter Greenaway's *The Cook, the Thief, His Wife and Her Lover* and Peter Medak's *The Krays*, released in the UK in October 1989 and April 1990, respectively – which deployed the London gangland milieu in ways that were not only read by some as allegories of Thatcherism (Desjardins, 1993; Walsh, 1993) but also rendered transparent, dissected and critiqued ganglord's misogyny and subjugation of women. However, as their timing (and allegorical slant) indicate, these films represented a closing comment on the Thatcherite 1980s rather than the beginnings of its aftermath and the art-cinema characteristics of both films increase their distance from the crime genre. After *The Krays*, the masculinist gangster vanished from British cinema until 1993, when he returned in Danny Cannon's *Young Americans* as a Krays-era veteran who steps in at the last minute to gun down the film's London-based American drug-lord villain. By 1997, he had metamorphosed into a sensitive character open to female influence in *Face*; and a deflationary self-parody in J.K. Amalou's ultraviolent, and less successful, thriller *Hard Men* (1997).

GENDER, WORK, AND CRIME: SOCIAL CHANGE AND THE 1990S BRITISH CINEMA

During the Thatcher and Major years, changes relating to gender, the organisation and technologies of work, and attitudes to crime had implications for how crime would be represented by the 1990s British cinema. In the 1990s women made increasingly confident inroads into the workforce, especially in the white-collar and service industries. Although the desirability of women as employees was in many cases due to their 'flexibility' in tolerating work that was part-time, insecure and ill-paid, the impression grew of a society in which women were in the ascendancy in the workplace and beyond. By contrast, masculinity – particularly young, skill-less, goal-less working-class masculinity – was increasingly defined as a problem.

As the 1990s progressed, male unemployment and social exclusion, and broader problems of masculinity, became the subtexts or themes of an increasing number of British films. Some of the most commercially successful of these – *Brassed Off* and *The Full Monty* – transformed this material into feel-good comedy. But the predicament of the jobless underclass male was also a taken-as-read ingredient in a number of more pessimistic social dramas and crime thrillers beginning with Mike Leigh's *Naked* (1993). British cinema's youth-orientated crime dramas – *Shopping* (Paul Anderson, 1994), *Twin Town* (Kevin Allen, 1997) – and gang thrillers – *Face* – took a less-than-complex stance on the underclass male. For Antonia Bird, *Face* was simply about 'the choices that you have if you come from a working-class background in inner-city London and you're bright. ... There's no work, so either you go into crime or you give in' (quoted in McCabe 1997: 11).

The working woman who is more clued-up than her male counterparts was a recurrent figure in these films. In *Face*, the mother and girlfriend of lapsed Communist armed robber, Ray, committed activists who have kept the political faith, function as critics of the futility and unprofitability of his lifestyle. By contrast, in *Twin Town*, the working female (like much else in the film) is cynically caricatured: the teenage sister of the two young car-nicking protagonists sees herself as several cuts above them because she *works*, but it is no shock when her job as a massage-parlour receptionist proves to be less respectable than she claims.

A second change taking place in the 1980s and 1990s workplace was the restructuring and 'downsizing' of organisations, producing structures that were ostensibly less hierarchical than the traditional firm. In eliminating unskilled workers and middle-management, this trend was one of the root causes of 1990s male unemployment and disempowerment. The death of the old business structures had profound implications for the conceptual viability of the gangland model as a blueprint for a contemporary crime cinema. The organised crime 'family' or 'firm' has always modelled itself on 'legitimate' business, and the structures of the Richardson and Kray gangs had a clear (if parodic) relationship to the authoritarian/paternalistic management hierarchies of their 1960s heyday. Lines of command were dictatorial and rigid, but the 'workers' felt secure and cared for, breeding loyalty and a sense of belonging.

This model was a standard genre ingredient in the British gangland films of the 1960s and 1970s; but the transformations of the 1980s and 1990s severed its roots in social reality. It is no coincidence that at this moment of male insecurity and loss, the old-school London gangster, and the films that had paid him homage, were reappropriated as comforting nostalgia. The one *new* 1990s British film to exploit this mood directly was the transatlantic policier *Young Americans*. Although it was aggressively targeted at the US market and a young UK multiplex audience, its themes and narrative resolution – in which an ageing London gangster emerges as the eleventh-hour hero – yearned for an idealised, parochial 1960s gangland in which codes of of behaviour were honoured and crime was, above all, a British affair. Its implication was that the old-school gangster was a figure from the past who was nevertheless sorely missed, and needed, in the present. For the most part, however, this wistful nostalgia for 'olde gangland' was a media rather than cinematic phenomenon. Images of the 1960s Michael Caine and profiles of the septuagenarian ex-gangster 'Mad' Frankie Fraser became typical fare in men's monthly magazines such as *Loaded* and GQ; and the gangland films of more optimistic eras, from *Get Carter* to *The Long Good Friday*, were canonised as genre classics by the taste-makers of 'lad' culture.

The social factor that had the most visible impact on 1990s British cinema's treatment of crime was the increased complexity of public attitudes to crime. There was not merely a lack of consensus in public opinion regarding certain areas of activity defined by the law as 'criminal' – most obviously on questions around the distribution and use of illegal drugs – but also an increasingly evident gulf between the law and the actual behaviour of the public. In many working-class communities where the closure of local industries had brought multi-generational unemployment, theft and drug-dealing became normalised as strategies for survival. Among the clubbers who discovered Ecstasy from the late 1980s onwards and the broader, cross-class section of society who followed them, the blanket illegality of a diverse spectrum of recreational substances fostered a certain contempt for the law, and brought millions of people into direct or indirect contact with the criminal black market. In 1990s Britain, the boundaries between underworld and underclass, petty and organised crime and criminality and mainstream society came to seem increasingly blurred.

This blurring of moral boundaries, coupled with a degree of cynical disillusion with the law, was reflected in a considerable number of 1990s British films in which crime was portrayed as a matter-of-fact aspect of life. Certain figures recur across these films: slow, ineffectual police (*Shopping*; *Face*); the viciously bent cop who controls his local organised crime scene with a ruthlessness unmatched by the nominal career criminals; and the equally ruthless all-powerful criminal top-dog, who functions on a corporate scale, abides by no

codes of honour, and seeks to dominate or eliminate the small fry by any means possible. In *Twin Town* and *Face*, these last two figures are effectively one and the same. They represent an equal threat to the former film's teenage car thieves and the latter's professional armed robbers. In both cases, the activities of the (relatively powerless) lawbreakers are presented as legitimated by the power abuses and/or organised corruption of the law.

In the context of this disillusioned relativism, the fact that few 'crime films' of the traditional kind (i.e. primarily concerned with the subculture or organised/career crime or the battle between law and disorder) were made in Britain in the 1990s is both revealing and deceptive. Crime in society had, in effect, entered the mainstream. In keeping with this, much of the 'criminal' activity taking place in 1990s British cinema could be found dispersed into genre or genre mixes in which the law-breaking nature of the activity was not always the central issue at stake. Crime in the 1990s was also characterised by its multifaceted links with youth and style subcultures: indeed, in the sense that certain types of crime in 1990s Britain were predominantly the province of juveniles, crime *was* a youth subculture. In this regard, it is highly significant that the portrayal of crime as 'normal' in a succession of 1990s British films was closely associated with the emergence of young film-makers who aspired to compete with Hollywood on its own terms by making commercial films that would play to the tastes of an under–25 (and, implicitly, largely male) audience.

(Monk 1999: 172–176)

The problem with this, and many other views about British cinema, is that it is an Anglocentric account; the three styles detailed so far are *English* rather than British traditions. Although Wales has delivered the occasional landmark (*Twin Town*, *Charles*) history proves it is an erratic, sometimes trifling, often dormant cinema. Scotland however, especially in recent years, has proved it has a comparatively healthy, vibrant film industry. The country enjoys a fairly unique position, in that it is a national cinema *within* another national cinema; it is Scottish and yet at the same time British. This, coupled with its historically turbulent relationship with the English and the fact that it is too small to be self-sufficient (only 10 per cent of the box-office for Scottish films is Scottish money), means the nation has its own peculiar set of film-making traditions – Tartanry, Kailyard, Clydeside – which, although unavoidably related to the conventions of English cinema, are at the same time oppositional and different. A University of Glasgow media website summarises these traditions below:

Tartanry was based upon the romantic image of Scotland, or as critics would describe it the 'shortbread tin' image of Scotland. This romantic image was based largely on the novels of Sir Walter Scott. These novels were set around the time of the Jacobite rebellion in 1745. This is when Charles Edward Stuart, or Bonnie Prince Charlie, a descendant of King James the VI landed in Scotland and led a rebellion to overthrow King George the III. The rebellion was eventually crushed at the battle of Culloden, when the Jacobite army, mostly made up of Highland clansmen, was defeated by government forces from the lowlands of Scotland led by the Duke of Cumberland. In the wake of the rebellion the government banned many symbols of Highland identity such as the wearing of the kilt and the playing of bagpipes.

In an attempt to preserve some of Scotland's Highland culture Sir Walter Scott wrote about the rebellion in his novels, which presented the Highlander as a kind of noble savage. It was eventually through Scott's efforts that the ban on Tartan and other symbols of Highland culture was lifted.

The picture which Scott painted of Highland life, however, was not entirely accurate. What he was attempting to do was capture a way of life which had already largely disappeared. One example of Scott's poetic licence was his invention of the idea of clan tartans. Scott came up with this idea when he persuaded King George to travel to Edinburgh and find out what Scottish culture was really like. Scott decided that in order for the King to tell the different clans apart each clan would wear a different tartan. Historically no such thing as a clan tartan existed, different tartans being associated with the different areas which produced them.

In creating certain myths about Scottish history many people believed that what Scott was doing was presenting a sanitised version of history which placed any idea of Scottish independence or political struggle firmly in the past. Since Scott largely invented many images which we now associate with the Scotland of the past these images have little or nothing to do with how modern Scots see themselves. Nevertheless these images still provide the basis for how other cultures see Scotland. In many cases Scots themselves have used these images to present Scotland, one famous example being Sir Harry Lauder.

What the Scotch Reels critics argued was that such representations, which formed the basis for a great deal of early films about Scotland and which can still be seen in films such as *Rob Roy* (1995) and *Braveheart* (1994), are not true representations of Scottish history or of where Scotland currently stands. By romanticising history the discourse of Tartanry effectively negates any chance of understanding Scotland as existing in a political present.

'**Kailyard**' is a Scots word which literally means 'cabbage patch'. It was used to describe a genre of Scottish literature produced by writers such as J. M.

CONTINUES

Barrie (author of Peter Pan) and Ian McLaren. In the kailyard novel Scotland is seen as a parochial country made up entirely of small towns. The people who live in these communities have little interest in what goes on in the rest of the world. The central characters of such novels are often church ministers or other prominent members of a small local community such as the 'dominie' (school teacher) or doctor, and they describe to the reader a community which is based upon local intrigue and homespun wisdom.

Like the discourse of Tartanry Kailyard fiction makes no attempt to engage with the realities of modern life. In film such a discourse is present in Hollywood films such as *The Little Minister* (1934), *Bonnie Scotland* (1935), and *Wee Willie Winkie* (1937). It is also present in British films such as *Whisky Galore!* (1949), *Laxdale Hall* (1953), *The Maggie* (1954) and *Rockets Galore* (1958).

These films are based upon the sudden intrusion of modern life into a small rural Scottish community. Such intrusion often takes the form of city dwellers or people from the mainland (in the case of island communities) there to represent big business or the government. These characters are often foiled in their plans by the canny locals, or change their plans after falling in love with both the local community and a particular member of that community. The Scotch Reels critics argued that such representations are fantasies where economically and politically powerless villagers are able to defeat the force of government and big business thanks to their native cunning and charm. Again such representations have little to do with the realities of modern Scottish life.

The third discourse which the critics identified was the discourse of '**Clydesideism**'. This kind of film did deal with the realities of modern life, generally being set in and around Glasgow at the height of the shipbuilding industry in the 1940s and 1950s. This genre defined Scotland as being a world dominated by working class male labour. While these representations were more positive, in that they attempted to deal with contemporary urban issues, the political aspects of such films were usually obscured by melodramatic subplots of family conflict. Films such as *Red Ensign* (1934), *Shipyard Sally* (1939), *The Shipbuilders* (1943) and *Floodtide* (1949) are all notable representations of the place of industrial labour in Scotland.

While many people have subsequently criticised the Scotch Reels analysis of representations of Scotland it still provides a very important starting point for debates around the issue.

There are also a number of other interesting topics which you may wish to consider. These include:

■ The ways in which women are represented in Scottish films.
■ The ways in which men are represented in Scottish films.

FILM STUDIES: THE ESSENTIAL RESOURCE

- The way in which childhood is represented in Scottish films.
- The ways in which economic difference is represented in Scottish films.

(University of Glasgow database, available at www.hatii.arts.gla.ac.uk/ MultimediaStudentProjects/00–01/9704793m/mncourse/project/html/issue. htm.)

ACTIVITY

➤ Using the Internet Movie Database construct a list of twenty Scottish films. Using synopses, reviews, stills and promotional posters only, see if you are able to categorise them as Tartanry, Kailyard and Clydeside.

▼ 15 NATIONAL CINEMAS (OR WORLD CINEMA EXPLODED)

It's great that national cinemas are making films as specific to their cultures as Americans do. Even if this means limiting the box office.

Gonzalo Melendez

A comparative perspective is essential even in the study of national cinemas, for only by establishing what one country's cinema has in common with others, as well as how it differs, can its unique characteristics be identified.

James Chapman

One may legitimately ask why we need the term 'world cinema'. Without a qualifier, doesn't 'cinema' alone adequately encompass the film cultures of every nationality? The fact is that cinema itself is a partly loaded term and 'World Cinema' is something of a misnomer. Like the 'world' in 'world music' above a dusty record shop shelf, 'world', in this instance, signifies something less than *everything* of this earth. It is partly a compensation, the institution of which admits implicitly that something is wrong. It is something different and special, something apart from the predictable mass culture, something 'other' but also by implication something neglected, sidelined and undervalued. Problematically, in a world where American movies are so dominant that they account for over 70 per cent of films seen, world cinema's 'otherness' is merely 'other-than-Hollywood'. This is hardly an appropriate place from which to lead a recognition and celebration of diverse and vibrant national film culture.

INFOBOX

One way of dealing with the issue is seen in the World Cinema section of the WJEC GCE A Level specification which attempts to make sense of this sprawling 'otherness' by carving it up into national and historical movements.

- German and Soviet Cinemas of the 1920s
- Neo-realism in Italy and Beyond
- Cinematic New Waves (General, French or East Asian)
- Japanese Cinema 1950–1970
- Surrealist and Fantasy Cinema (see Chapter 16)

These mainly geographical labels are not simply a way of organising the growing, increasingly unfathomable canon of 'world cinema'. These labels encourage the student to think about the nations in which the films were produced.

> ➤ Before we start looking specifically at what is on offer, take a few minutes to consider what world cinema means to you. Try to think in terms of:
>   - Experience
>   - Expectation
>   - Films
>   - Genres
>   - Directors

Many of the chapters in this book are simply a way of approaching a body of films with a basic common thread: 'Auteur', films with the same director; 'Star', films with a common cast member; 'Genre', films with shared iconography, themes, narrative or function. This is one such chapter; the 'National' approach allows us to concentrate on films from the same country, considering both their production context (finance, facilities) and structures of distribution, in addition to the way these films display and create a sense of national identity.

This is not an unproblematic approach. The Left has always been uncomfortable with ideas of national identity; in branding a nation with specific labels we may begin to fuel nationalism:

> The word [nation] is meaningless: all 'nations' are mongrel, a mixture of so many immigrations and mixings of peoples over time. ... Nations are artificial constructs, their boundaries drawn in the blood of past wars. And one should not confuse culture and nationality: there is not one country on earth which is not home to more than one different but usually coexisting culture. Cultural heritage is not the same thing as national identity.

(Grayling 2002, p. 78)

You should be aware of this and resist cementing stereotypes with broad generalisations in your work. It is better to acknowledge the stereotype rather than stumble into crass statements such as 'The Irish are all big drinkers.'

Couple these ideas with the fact that, as globalisation quickly shrinks our planet, films, in terms of finance, cast, crew, location and setting, have become multinational affairs. 'National cinema' is an increasingly irrelevant, seemingly indefinable term.

> The concept of national cinema has been appropriated in a variety of ways, for a variety of reasons: there is not a single universally accepted discourse of national cinema. In general terms, one can summarise these various mobilisations of the concept as follows. First, there is the possibility of defining national cinema in economic terms, establishing a conceptual correspondence between the terms 'national cinema' and 'the domestic

film industry', and therefore being concerned with such questions as: where are these films made, and by whom? Who owns and controls the industrial infrastructures, the production companies, the distributors and the exhibition circuits? Second, there is the possibility of a text-based approach to national cinema. Here the key questions become: what are these films about? Do they share a common style or world view? What sort of projections of the national character do they offer? To what extent are they engaged in 'exploring, questioning and constructing a notion of nationhood in the films themselves and in the consciousness of the viewer'?[1] Third, there is the possibility of an exhibition-led or consumption-based approach to national cinema. Here the major concern has always been to do with the question of which films audiences are watching, and particularly the number of foreign, and usually American films which have high-profile distribution within a particular nation state – a concern which is generally formulated in terms of an anxiety about cultural imperialism. Fourth, there is what may be called a criticism-led approach to national cinema, which tends to reduce national cinema to the terms of a quality art cinema, a culturally worthy cinema steeped in the high-cultural and/or modernist heritage of a particular nation state, rather than one which appeals to the desires and fantasies of the popular audiences.

In other words, very often the concept of national cinema is used prescriptively rather than descriptively, citing what *ought* to be the national cinema, rather than describing the actual cinematic experience of popular audiences. As Geoffrey Nowell-Smith has noted, it has always been something of a struggle to enable 'the recognition of popular forms as a legitimate part of national cultural life'.[2]

If these are some of the ways in which the term national cinema has been used, what are the processes by which, or what are the conditions under which, a particular mode of film practice, or a specific range of textual practices, or a particular set of industrial practices comes to be named a national cinema? Indeed, what is involved in calling forth the idea of a national anything, cultural or otherwise. In other words, what is involved in positing the idea of nationhood or national identity?

To identify a national cinema is first of all to specify a coherence and a unity; it is to proclaim a unique identity and a stable set of meanings. The process of identification is thus invariably a hegemonising, mythologizing process, involving both the production and assignation of a particular set of meanings, and the attempt to contain, or prevent the potential proliferation of other meanings. At the same time, the concept of a national cinema has almost invariably been mobilised as a strategy of cultural (and economic) resistance; a means of asserting national autonomy in the face of (usually) Hollywood's international domination.

The process of nationalist myth-making is not simply an insidious (or celebratory) work of ideological production, but is also at the same time a means of setting one body of images and values against another, which will very often threaten to overwhelm the first. The search for a unique and stable identity, the assertion of national specificity does then have some meaning, some usefulness. It is not just an ideological sleight of hand, although it must always also be recognised as that. Histories of national cinema can only therefore really be understood as histories of crisis and conflict, of resistance and negotiation. But also, in another way, they are histories of a business seeking a secure footing in the market-place, enabling the maximisation of an industry's profits while at the same time bolstering a nation's cultural standing. At this level, the politics of national cinema can be reduced to a marketing strategy, an attempt to market the diverse as, in fact, offering a coherent and singular experience. As Thomas Elsaesser has suggested, 'internationally, national cinemas used to have a generic function: a French, Italian or a Swedish film sets different horizons of expectation for the general audience – a prerequisite for marketing purposes',[3] and it is this attempt to establish a generic narrative image, a particular horizon of expectation, which is at stake.

There are perhaps two central methods, conceptually, of establishing or identifying the imaginary coherence, the specificity, of a national cinema. First, there is the method of comparing and contrasting one cinema to another, thereby establishing varying degrees of otherness. Second, there is what might be termed a more inward-looking process, exploring the cinema of a nation in relation to other already existing economies and cultures of that nation state.

1 Susan Barrowclough, 'Introduction: the dilemmas of a national cinema', in Barrowclough, ed, *Jean-Pierre Lefebvre: The Quebec Connection*, BFI Dossier no 13, 1981, p 3.
2 Popular Culture, *New Formations*, no 2, Summer 1987, p 80.
3 'Chronicle of a death retold: hyper, retro or counter-cinema', *Monthly Film Bulletin*, vol 54, no 541, June 1987, p 167.

(Higson 1989: 36–38)

The conceptualisation of national cinema in such a broad sense will forever be an abstract process. In examining nationality we are examining difference; each individual nation presents its unique set of complications and implications. In their introduction to 'Contemporary Spanish Cinema' Jordan and Morgan-Tamosunas investigate what we actually mean by 'Spanish Cinema'.

Knowledge of a nation's socio-political history is essential to our understanding of its films' messages and values. Some films are overtly and obviously political in their message, others more subtly so, as in the case of the allegory. Even films without an implicit politic are indicative of the attitudes, lifestyles and ideologies of the nation in which they are born. We should also consider the very direct influence national politics can have on film output. Movies are shaped by censorship, film policy and propaganda, they are commissioned by a government to further and propagate a doctrine or cause. As a form of public communication film opens itself up to the political and psychological mood of its time. As such it reflects both wittingly and unwittingly its aesthetic and by implication its roots: geographically, culturally and politically.

GERMAN AND SOVIET CINEMA OF THE 1920S

Situated between the wars, 'Weimar cinema' (1918–1933) gives us a fascinating insight into the national consciousness of a defeated Germany. A wounded nation, weakened by spiralling inflation and facing suspicion and abandonment by the rest of the world, Germany in the aftermath of the First World War lacked a concrete identity and endured persistent social unrest. Yet this was a period of intellectualism and great creativity in which the Bauhaus and expressionist movements flourished. The resulting modernist nightmares of Weimar cinema embodied the country's sense of fear, and – with their tales of destruction and plague – foresaw the true horrors to come. 'Remarkable for the way it emerged from a catastrophe, more remarkable for the way it vanished into a still greater catastrophe, the world of Weimar represents *modernism* in its most vivid manifestion' (Marcus Bullock).

EXPRESSIONIST FILM – EVERYONE'S FAVOURITE NIGHTMARE?

The German cinema of the early 1920s, sandwiched by film historians between the pioneering effort of American directors Griffith, de Mille and Chaplin in the 1910–19 era and the Soviet cinema of the late 1920s (Eisenstein, Pudovkin and Vertov), is invariably associated with 'Expressionism'. Not least to advertise the turn from plebeian amusement to high modernism, this label, borrowed from the German pre-First World War avant-garde movement in literature and the fine arts became the generic term for the cinema of the period as a whole.

From the perspective of the 1990s, this is a contentious, but passably benign view. It somewhat too readily assumes the 'baton relay' or 'roving spotlight' narrative of 1920s cinema history, and it takes as representative a rather small sample of films, favouring often carefully crafted export productions at the expense of a wide array of domestically targeted films: detective films and comedies, (male and female) star 'vehicles', operetta subjects, social and erotic melodramas, epics and costume films enjoyed by popular audiences. Expressionist cinema, on the other hand, was an *auteur* cinema: self-conscious, sophisticated, state-of-the-art film making that was initially calculated to promote a company – Decla – its producer Erich Pommer, and his team of directors, screenwriters, cameramen, set designers and male acting stars. Nowhere near as well known today are other leading figures not associated with Expressionist films, such as Joe May, Richard Oswald, Max Mack, Ludwig Berger, Reinhold Schünzel, Richard Eichberg. They were prolific directors, often more successful and sometimes no less accomplished than the famous names. Given this preference of high-art films over popular mainstream cinema as an index of Germany's national cinema, it is the more surprising how many films that subsequently became part of the canon carry titillatingly sensationalist titles: besides *The Cabinet of Dr Caligari*, there is *Dr Mabuse The Gambler*, *Destiny/Der Müde Tod*, *The Golem*, *The Street*, *Backstairs*, *Waxworks*, *Warning Shadows*, *Metropolis*, *Nosferatu The Vampire*, *The Hands of Orlac*, *Pandora's Box*, *Joyless Street* and *Secrets of a Soul*.

Either popular taste was taking its toll after all, or another story was being told as well. One of these stories is the canonical one: establishing film as art and signifying the unexpected flowering of creative talent in a defeated nation, Expressionist film came to connote that sudden, brief *frisson* of a

CONTINUED

never-to-be-forgotten glimpse into the abyss – of unconscious urges, of the German soul, of Germany's fatal destiny. The nightmare visions and psycho-horrors have not only led to conjectures about the society giving birth to these monsters on the screen. Testifying to the troubled political reality of post-First-World-War German society or already foreshadowing the ideological turmoil to come, both rang true, depending on whether one thought of the lost war of 1918 or of the rise of Nazism at the end of the decade.

Trying to decide why these films seem so morbid, traumatised and full of foreboding has kept a lively but also often murky debate smouldering, thanks largely to two well-known books, Siegfried Kracaurer's *From Caligari to Hitler* (1947) and Lotte Eisner's *The Haunted Screen* (1969) (the latter published originally in French: *L'Écran démoniaque*, Paris: Le Terrain Vague, 1952). Rarely before or since has a body of films exerted such a pull towards verbal paraphrase, in which epithets like 'dark' and 'demonic', 'twisted', 'haunted' and 'tormented' leap onto the page. A narrative of fear and trembling, instinct and drive, Eros and Thanatos have fed the notion that the German cinema is 'psychological' and 'inward', prompting other historians, in the wake of Kracauer and Eisner, to speculate about the national character responsible for these aberrant fantasies or eccentric fictions. As a case study of a 'movement', a period, a national cinema or the relation between cinema and society, German Expressionist film is still a favourite in textbooks, film style surveys, in books about the sociology of cinema, and in general film histories.

The general cultural memory, on the other hand, has retained neither the directors nor the convoluted story lines of the films. It is the often eponymous heroes, or rather villains, that have caught the imagination: the mad doctor and magician Dr Caligari; the underworld mastermind Dr Mabuse; the cruel tyrant Ivan the Terrible or the series killer Jack the Ripper from *Waxworks*; lean weary Death from *Destiny/Der Müde Tod*; the legendary Golem; Attila and Hagen from *The Nibelungen*; the student of Prague and his murderous double; the vengeful scientist Rotwang and the robot Maria from *Metropolis*; Orlac of the severed hands; the vampire Nosferatu, the German Dracula; Haghi the super-spy; the leering Mephisto of *Faust*; the insinuatingly smooth Tartuff and the creepily pitiable child murderer in M. These figures are often indissociable from the (male) actors who incarnated them: Conrad Veidt, Emil Jannings, Rudolf Klein-Rogge, Max Schreck, Werner Krauss and Peter Lorre. Their roles and the films' titles come, however, from *Grand Guignol* or the fairground (a frequent setting as Kracauer noted) and the villains resemble the bogeymen of children's fairy tales and folk legend, precisely the regions of the popular imagination and entertainment that Expressionist films are said to have helped the cinema leave behind.

The irony almost suggests that the film makers and writers involved may have had their tongues firmly in their cheeks. This would be the other story: the present chapter equally firmly keeps in mind the possibility that these art films may have functioned on a double register – straight-faced and put-ons, performative 'expression', not only of Expressionism, but of neo-romantic decadence and *Jugendstil* as well as of Bauhaus modernism and constructivist futurism. If some of the films do look back to the traumas of trench warfare in the muddy fields of Flanders, others (or the same in another register) also look forward to the time of style warfare in the high streets of Berlin. Technological bonfires of eclectic tastes and daring fashions, they certainly ignited and delighted an international public that was otherwise deeply suspicious of everything German.

What in the films is identified with 'Expressionism' is the unusual lighting, the stylisation of the sets and the acting, the 'Gothic'-story material and fairy-tale motifs, angular exteriors, claustrophobic interiors, and above all, that excess of soul ascribed to things 'typically German'. The political–ideological readings challenge the inherent formalism of such a label and prefer the term 'Weimar cinema', in order to distinguish the period style 'Expressionism' from the broader analysis of a mentality and political conjuncture, identified with the still fascinating phenomenon 'Weimar culture', lasting from 1918 to 1933.

(Elsaesser 2000: 18–21)

Further east there was a national cinema even more entwined and aligned with its country's politics. Under state control, the Soviet cinema of the 1920s synchronised its propagandist intentions with that of its government. Films of this era denounced everything that was pre-revolutionary Russian in a bid to forge an entirely new cinema. One of the ways they attempted this was through style. Whereas German cinema of the time is associated with expressionism, Soviet cinema is noted for formalism and the 'montage' approach to film-making, where the meanings of shots arise not from their content, but from the way they are arranged and juxtaposed.

The application of the method of the montage of attractions (the comparison of facts) to cinema is even more acceptable than it is to theatre. I should call cinema 'the art of comparisons' because it shows not facts but conventional (photographic) representations (in contrast to 'real action' in theatre, at least when theatre is employing the techniques we approve of). For the exposition of even the simplest phenomena cinema needs comparison (by means of consecutive, separate presentation) between the elements which constitute it: montage (in the technical, cinematic sense of the word) is fundamental to cinema, deeply grounded in the conventions of cinema and the corresponding characteristics of perception.

Whereas in theatre an effect is achieved primarily through the physiological perception of an actually occurring fact (e.g. a murder),[1] in cinema it is made

up of the juxtaposition and accumulation, in the audience's psyche, of associations that the film's purpose requires, associations that are aroused by the separate elements of the stated (in practical terms, in 'montage fragments') fact, associations that produce, albeit tangentially, a similar (and often stronger) effect only when taken as a whole. Let us take that same murder as an example: a throat is gripped, eyes bulge, a knife is brandished, the victim closes his eyes, blood is spattered on a wall, the victim falls to the floor, a hand wipes off the knife – each fragment is chosen to 'provoke' associations.

An analogous process occurs in the montage of attractions: it is not in fact phenomena that are compared but chains of associations that are linked to a particular phenomenon in the mind of a particular audience.[2] (It is quite clear that for a worker and a former cavalry officer the chain of association set off by seeing a meeting broken up and the corresponding emotional effect in contrast to the material which frames this incident, will be somewhat different.) I managed to test quite definitively the correctness of this position with one example where, because what I should call this law had not been observed, the comic effect of such a well-tried device as the alogism fell flat. I have in mind the place in *The Extraordinary Adventures of Mr West in the Land of the Bolsheviks*[3] where an enormous lorry is pulling a tiny sledge carrying Mr West's briefcase. This construction can be found in different variants in any clown's act – from a tiny top hat to enormous boots. The appearance of such a combination in the ring is enough. But, when the whole combination was shown on the screen in one shot all at once (even though it occurred as the lorry was leaving the gates so that there was a short pause – as long as the rope joining the lorry to the sledge), the effect was very weak. Whereas a real lorry is immediately perceived in all its immensity and compared to a real briefcase in all its insignificance and [for comic effect] it is enough to see them side by side, cinema requires that a 'representation' of the lorry be provided first for long enough to inculcate the appropriate associations – and then we are shown the incongruous light load. As a parallel to this I recall the construction of an analogous moment in a Chaplin film where much footage is spent on the endlessly complicated opening of the locks on a huge safe[3] and it is only later (and apparently from a different angle) that we are shown the brooms, rags and buckets that are hidden inside it. The Americans use this technique brilliantly for characterisation – I remember the way Griffith 'introduced' the 'Musketeer', the gang-leader in *Intolerance*: he showed us a wall of his room completely covered with naked women and then showed the man himself. How much more powerful and more cinematic this is, we submit, than the introduction of the workhouse supervisor in *Oliver Twist* in a scene where he pushes two cripples around: i.e. he is shown through his deeds (a purely theatrical method of sketching character through action) and not through provoking the necessary associations.

From what I have said it is clear that the centre of gravity of cinema effects, in contrast to those of theatre, lies not in directly *physiological* effects, although a purely *physical* infectiousness can sometimes be attained (in a chase, with the montage of two sequences with movements running against the shot). It seems that there has been absolutely no study or evaluation of the purely physiological effect of montage irregularity and rhythm and, if it has been evaluated, this has only been for its role in narrative illustration (the tempo of the plot corresponding with the material being narrated). 'We ask you not to confuse' the montage of attractions and its method of comparison with the usual montage parallelism used in the exposition of a theme such as the narrative principle in *Cine-Pravda* where the audience has first to guess what is going on and then become 'intellectually' involved with the theme.

The montage of attractions is closer to the simple contrasting comparisons (though these are somewhat compromised by *The Palace and the Fortress* where the device is naively revealed) that often produce a definitely powerful emotional effect (chained legs in the ravelin and a ballerina's feet). But we must point out that in *The Palace and the Fortress* [from which this example comes] any dependence on comparison in the construction of the shots for this sequence was completely ignored: their construction does not assist association but disrupts it and it enters our consciousness through literary rather than visual means. For example, Nechayev, seen from the waist up and with his back to the camera, hammers on a barred door and the prison warder, seen in long shot somewhere in a corner by a window, holds a canary in a cage. The chained legs are shown horizontally whereas the ballerina's points are shot about four times larger and vertically, etc.

The method of the montage of attractions is the comparison of subjects for thematic effect. I shall refer to the original version of the montage resolution in the finale of my film *The Strike*: the mass shooting where I employed the associational comparison with a slaughterhouse. I did this, on the one hand, to avoid overacting among the extras from the labour exchange 'in the business of dying' but mainly to excise from such a serious scene the falseness that the screen will not tolerate but that is unavoidable in even the most brilliant death scene and, on the other hand, to extract the maximum effect of bloody horror. The shooting is shown only in 'establishing' long and medium shots of 1,800 workers falling over a precipice, the crowd fleeing, gunfire, etc., and all the close-ups are provided by a demonstration of the real horrors of the slaughterhouse where cattle are slaughtered and skinned. One version of the montage was composed roughly as follows:

1. The head of a bull. The butcher's knife takes aim and moves upwards beyond the frame.
2. Close-up. The hand holding the knife strikes downwards below the frame.

3. Long shot: 1,500 people roll down a slope. (Profile shot.)
4. Fifty people get up off the ground, their arms outstretched.
5. The face of a soldier taking aim.
6. Medium shot. Gunfire.
7. The bull's body (the head is outside the frame) jerks and rolls over.
8. Close-up. The bull's legs convulse. A hoof beats in a pool of blood.
9. Close-up. The bolts of the rifles.
10. The bull's head is tied with rope to a bench.
11. A thousand people rush past.
12. A line of soldiers emerges from behind a clump of bushes.
13. Close-up. The bull's head as it dies beneath unseen blows (the eyes glaze over).
14. Gunfire, in longer shot, seen from behind the soldiers' backs.
15. Medium shot. The bull's legs are bound together according to Jewish custom (the method of slaughtering cattle lying down).
16. Closer shot. People falling over a precipice.
17. The bull's throat is cut. Blood gushes out.
18. Medium close-up. People rise into the frame with their arms outstretched.
19. The butcher advances towards the (panning) camera holding the blood-stained rope.
20. The crowd rushes to a fence, breaks it down but is met by an ambush (two or three shots).
21. Arms fall into the frame.
22. The head of the bull is severed from the trunk.
23. Gunfire.
24. The crowd rolls down the precipice into the water.
25. Gunfire.
26. Close-up. Teeth are knocked out by the shooting.
27. The soldiers' feet move away.
28. Blood flows into the water, colouring it.
29. Close-up. Blood gushes from the bull's throat.
30. Hands pour blood from a basin into a bucket.
31. Dissolve from a platform with buckets of blood on it . . . in motion towards a processing plant.
32. The dead bull's tongue is pulled through the slit throat (one of the devices used in a slaughterhouse, probably so that the teeth will not do any damage during the convulsions).
33. The solder's feet move away. (Longer shot.)
34. The head is skinned.
35. One thousand eight hundred dead bodies at the foot of the precipice.
36. Two dead skinned bulls' heads.
37. A human hand in a pool of blood.

FILM STUDIES: THE ESSENTIAL RESOURCE

38.   Close-up. Filling the whole screen. The dead bull's eye.
Final title.

[1] A direct animal audience action through a motor imitative act towards a live character like oneself, as distinct from a pale shadow on a screen. These methods of theatrical effect have been tested in my production of *Can You Hear Me Moscow?*

[2] In time (in sequence) clearly: here it plays not merely the role of an unfortunate technical condition but of a condition that is necessary for the thorough inculcation of the associations.

[3] And a large number of bank premises are shown first.

(Eisenstein 1988: 41–44)

NEO-REALISM IN ITALY AND BEYOND

One of the problems of a chapter such as this is that it attempts to glean the essence of specific national cinemas (or at least movements) in only one or two short extracts. It is an impossible and ultimately reductive undertaking, given the individual artists working outside any definable scene or movement and the many varied regional and subcultures within a nation's boundaries. The articles here should therefore be seen as merely perspectives, some of the numerous ways of approaching national cinemas. In reality, they are merely an index of a further-reaching, far more complicated and conflicting discourse. That said, Bert Cardullo's outline of Kinder and Houston's essay on neo-realism, in his 'What Is Neorealism?', is an extremely neat summary of the movement. As he writes himself, 'There is nothing earthshaking here, but it's nice to see all this information gathered in one essay.'

1. The neo-realists tried to make films that documented the external reality of their immediate local environment by exploring its society, politics, and economic activities. These filmmakers, dealing with current problems, were committed and involved; their movement had a moral basis. They followed in the documentary tradition of England and of Russian expressionist films by making social and moral commentaries in an effort to bring about social change. They developed a theory and a number of techniques to define their conception of realism and the film medium. The neo-realists focused on what is normal in experience rather than on what is exceptional. Their task was to draw significant implications out of ordinary events that usually pass unnoticed. By focusing on the normal, neo-realistic films frequently celebrate the values of the common man who is exploited by corrupt institutions.
2. Like the Soviet cinema of the 1920s and the British documentary of the 1930s and the 1940s, neo-realism abandoned the traditional well-made plot, which was seen as an artificial contrivance distorting normal life. Thus

CONTINUED

these films do not offer simple neat solutions to the problems they raise. They almost never end happily, for that would falsify reality and minimize the need for prompt social action.

4. Striving for authenticity led the neo-realistic filmmakers to shoot on location, rather than in studio sound stages, and to use ordinary people rather than professional actors for many of the roles. Partly because of the use of nonprofessional actors and partly for economic reasons, the films were shot without sound and the dialogue was synchronized back in the studio, a process that gave the director much greater freedom in capturing what was happening spontaneously in front of the camera.

4. Neo-realism departed from the practices of Soviet cinema and the British documentary in tending to use real time rather than relying heavily on montage. If they were going to record daily events as they happened, then these filmmakers had to rely on long takes that captured the pace of normal life.

5. The movement's conception of realism was confined to external conditions and common experience and was unconcerned with exploring the psychological reality of the individual.

Kinder and Houston go into more detail than Ted Perry on Fascism's ironic role in contributing a great deal to the development of neorealism:

> Like the German Nazis and the Russian Communists, the Italian Fascists realized the power of cinema as a medium of propaganda, and when they came to power, they took over the film industry. Although this meant that those who opposed Fascism could not make films and that foreign films were censored, the Fascists helped establish the essential requirements for a flourishing film industry. In 1935 they founded the Centro Sperimentale in Rome, a film school headed by Luigi Chiarini, which taught all aspects of film production. Many important neo-realist directors attended this school, including Rossellini, Antonioni, Zampa, Germi, and De Santis; it also produced cameramen, editors, and technicians. Chiarini was allowed to publish *Bianco e Nero*, the film journal that later became the official voice of neo-realism. In 1937 the Fascists opened Cinecittà, the largest and best-equipped movie studio in all Europe. Once Mussolini fell from power, the stage was set for a strong left-wing cinema.

(Cardullo 1991: 10–11)

CINEMATIC NEW WAVES: FRANCE

Whenever and wherever it happens, a cinematic 'new wave' is the label we give to a group of emerging directors whose films indicate a marked departure from existing traditions of film-making. Sometimes they are formally organised movements with manifestos and meetings, more often they are organic and accidental, labelled 'new' by critics after the films are released. The first and most famous is the French New Wave or *Nouvelle Vague*. The seeds of this movement began in the late 1940s when a group of young cineastes attending screenings of classics at the Cinemathèque Française became critics for their self-published film journal *Cahiers du Cinéma*. Their polemical, often poetic writings pioneered a way of evaluating and discussing films that provided the foundation for much of the academic film criticism to follow. Placing more emphasis on the role and significance of the director, writers such as Truffaut and Bazin deified the likes of Hitchcock, Hawkes and Ford, and were some of the first to consider the gangster and Western output of 1930s and 1940s Hollywood as 'art'. They showed far less enthusiasm for their native cinema of staid literary adaptations with well-known stars and elaborate studio sets. The *Nouvelle Vague* was an attack on this kind of film-making (what Truffaut called 'The Tradition of Quality' or *Cinéma du Papa*).

The rise of television in the 1950s inevitably affected the French box-office and by the end of the decade its film industry was in ruins. This created a window for Cahiers' budding directors who, with their new lightweight Camiflex cameras, were able to produce extremely cheap films on the Parisian streets.

Some recurring characteristics of the *Nouvelle Vague* are as follows:

- Fresh, different, young
- Shot on location (Paris)
- Loosely adapted from 'pulp' American thriller fiction – what the French call *Un Roman de Gare* (train station literature)
- Improvised, innovative, self-conscious cinematography
- References to Hollywood
- Low budgets.

Without placing these films in context it is hard to understand their classic status.

ACTIVITY

> 'New Wave' has become a very flexible title which can and has been used to address a wide range of so-called 'fresh/different/young' film movements in many different places. Using the internet as a primary resource, see what you can find out about cinematic new waves, particular those in Britain and the United States. What do 'new waves' have in common?

The French New Wave pioneered a new language of film which has been so imitated and is now so recognisable, that the originals no longer seem fresh. In this very personal recollection of a young cinephile, David Thomson attempts to capture the immense power that films such as *A Bout de Souffle* and *Vivre sa Vie* would once have had.

AS JEAN-LUC GODARD'S GROUNDBREAKING FIRST FEATURE 'BREATHLESS', WITH ITS JUMP CUTS AND JAZZY YOUNG CAST, IS RE-RELEASED, DAVID THOMSON RECALLS BEING ALIVE IN THE AGE OF GODARD

In the late 50s there seemed ample reason for being in love with movies. On American screens alone, between 1955 and 1959, you could see *The Searchers*, *Attack*, *The Killing*, *Beyond a Reasonable Doubt*, *Run of the Arrow*, *Sweet Smell of Success*, *Vertigo*, *Touch of Evil*, *Bitter Victory*, *Funny Face*, *Man of the West*, *North by Northwest*, *Rio Bravo*, *Anatomy of a Murder* and *Some Like It Hot*. There's 15 pictures for your top 10. Look further afield and you could add *Wild Strawberries*, *Nazarin*, *Bob le flambeur*, *A Man Escaped*, *Lola Montès*, *Le amiche*, *Yang Kwei Fei*, *Floating Weeds*, *Ashes and Diamonds*, *The World of Apu*, *The Nights of Cabiria*, *French Cancan*, *Hiroshima mon amour*, *Eyes without a Face*, *Letter from Siberia* and one you seldom hear mentioned, today, Alexandre Astruc's *Une Vie*.

Of course, with hindsight, you might look back on those lists and see that by 1960 Ford, Lang, Hitchcock, Hawks, Anthony Mann, Preminger, Wilder, Buñuel, Renoir and Ozu were all close to 55, or way beyond it. No one remarked on it then but there was something about those late–50s films that contained a sigh, a way of saying old rules and genre can go only so far. Even then Hitchcock's *Vertigo* felt like a master's sudden onset of horror at his own control. Hawks' *Rio Bravo* wasn't a Western (as *Red River* had been); it was a riff on some cool dudes in 1958 messing about kidding a Western. *Touch of Evil* had a sardonic note of confession or self-annihilation as Welles betrayed himself with a 'cane'. Preminger's *Anatomy of a Murder* and Lang's *Beyond a Reasonable Doubt* asked who can feel suspense in a courtroom drama, when you can't trust the law? And Hitchcock's *North by Northwest* and Wilder's *Some Like It Hot* were the beginnings of camp, as if someone had at last seen that you could no longer take movie scenarios seriously. You played with them the way be-bop jazz had reworked the chord progression of 'standards'. Neither film quite knew it, but there was something like madness or the implosion of genres at hand. After all, people were still striving to make movies in the old way. Yet television had taken that audience. Movies were at the brink of mannerism.

If you were smart enough, I suppose, that warning was there to be heard. Even had I heard it, though, I was stubborn enough to ignore such a diagnosis. 1959, after all, was the year in which I decided not to read history at Brasenose College, Oxford. Instead, I would try something called the London School of Film Technique, then situated at Electric Avenue in Brixton. My teachers shook their heads over me. My parents were clinging fearfully to the wilting mast of a vessel called 'let him decide'. What no one knew, especially not me, was the luck coming my way. For in the summer of 1959 Jean-Luc Godard shot A *bout de souffle*.

It wasn't only that corrosive sketch, or even the rush of Godard's early films. By 1961, in fact, as *Tirez sur le pianiste* and A *bout de souffle* opened only a few months apart, I found Truffaut warmer, funnier and more seductive. To this day Jacques Demy's *Lola* and Jacques Rivette's *Paris nous appartient* mean more to me as first films by *nouvelle vague* directors. But by 1962 or 1963, and above all with *Vivre sa vie*, it was clear Godard was the most helplessly and ruefully cinematic of them all. We were alive in the age of Godard – for however long he could keep it up.

So within a year or so A *bout de souffle* and its absolute modernity fell into place: its gnawing awareness of the nature of film, tinged already with a kind of contempt or dismay; the slightness of the story, or incident, and the bravura novelty of its telling, which led to the simultaneous beauty and severity – like an eloquent man willing himself to be blunt and aggressive; the handheld camera and the jump cuts, the lightweight shooting on the lam, the spill of natural light, all so suited to catching the impulsive words and gestures of such jazzy, show-off kids as Jean Seberg and Jean-Paul Belmondo, owning the camera yet so unimpressed, or defiantly insolent, about being in a film. There was, above all, the escape, the artful, cool dodging of any feeling of monumental embrace. This was filming done in a day and a night, so if you didn't like your first try, throw it away and try again. Already film was becoming as wipeable as videotape. Film was no longer the final achievement – it was the attempt.

For a 19-year-old at film school (then the only one in the UK) making an idiot of himself both loading cameras with that sticky, grey, elongated sperm, the emulsion, or sounding off about Anthony Mann in the new film-criticism classes we had (to teachers who knew nothing of Mann), the air of the attempt was precious. And the moment of A *bout de souffle* (as well as its stinging momentariness) meant so much to so many aspirations.

I had become a member of the National Film Theatre to see its first Ingmar Bergman season (I'll guess that was 1958) and that meant reading *Sight and Sound* in a moment when it was uncertain about the American films I'd come to love. One editor, Gavin Lambert, had gone to work for Nicholas Ray. In his wake the new editor, Penelope Houston (who would become a good friend), was not a hero-worshipper of the great auteurs. There's no need to open up old wounds, but several of those films of the late 50s I mentioned earlier (and I think that 'we', whoever we are, agree to their quality now) were given short shrift in *Sight and Sound* or not reviewed at all. Mann's *Man of the West* got a

three-line notice on a back page. But Godard had written about it in *Cahiers du cinéma* for February 1959 and he had known it was a great film: 'an admirable lesson in cinema – in modern cinema'.

There were a few people in London then who read, or tried to read, the yellow *Cahiers*, and the *nouvelle vague* meant all the more to us because we had begun to follow Godard, Truffaut and Rivette as writers and valiant defenders of the American films we thought neglected. This wasn't easy. My French was halting, and Godard's language was often abstract, high-flown and crammed with references I couldn't follow. As I look back now on his review of *Man of the West*, I remember the tingle of excitement I felt when he said: 'One could talk about the delightful farm nestling amid the greenery which George Eliot could have loved.'

I relished that association (because I got it) and I wondered whether this guy had really read all of Eliot, the way he knew all of Murnau. Yet his point was wrong: the farmhouse isn't 'delightful', it's sad, sunken, grey and chill: it's the forgotten, faded place of youth, just as Lassoo, the allegedly boom city, will turn into a ghost town; and its mood is part of a carefully controlled colour scheme that eliminates sunlight as much as possible, or keeps it thin, pale and autumnal. That was part of something Godard didn't feel in his review: the way *Man of the West* was about the close of an era and a genre, with Gary Cooper hardly strong enough to be Coop any longer and the itinerant 'singer' so resigned she might as well take up schoolteaching.

Such magazine writing meant a great deal then because hardly a reliable book existed on the art of film or any useful placing of those who had tried to make pictures. What reminds me of another reason why 1959 was a lucky year to be trying – that was when Richard Roud took over the programming of the National Film Theatre. Far more than the London School of Film Technique could offer, he provided a university for film history. He had only one theatre to play with but he filled it with seminal events: a sweeping French survey; most of Renoir and Lang; then Hawks; the Japanese; Joseph Losey and Nick Ray, and so on. With a friend, Kieran Hickey, I had discovered the need for basic lists – all the films made by Edgar G. Ulmer, or Samuel Fuller, or Robert Siodmak, or Mitchell Leisen. Such fundamental materials didn't exist, and we went into the BFI library, the night it stayed open late, to compile them. John Gillett helped us find the American trade journals we needed to plough through and Richard Roud took some of our lists and added them to his programme notes. We discovered that Ray's *The Lusty Men* had always been 20 minutes short in Britain. Others worried over Profumo and Christine Keeler – but we had found our scandal.

We had become a little French, I don't doubt it. Trying to translate *Cahiers* went along with Roud's marked French sympathies and the unequivocal victory of

French opinions, if only because of the liveliness of the films their holders had gone on to make. As the critical controversy between *Sight and Sound* and *Movie* (derived from *Oxford Opinion*, and dependent on Ian Cameron, V. F. Perkins, Mark Shivas and Paul Mayersberg) developed, the decision was already settled. The French attitude was borne out on and off screen. In those early 60s, it was entirely proper to note the novelistic integrity of Antonioni's trilogy (*L'avventura*, *La notte*, *L'eclisse*); you could see Losey's breakthrough in England (with *The Servant*); there was the darkening in Bergman's view and fresh vitality in Buñuel. There were movies as disparate and raw as *What Ever Happened to Baby Jane?*, *The Miracle Worker*, *Lolita*, *The Trial*, *El Cid*, *Kiss Me, Stupid*, *Repulsion*, *Mickey One*, *Lilith*, *Blow-Up*, *Point Blank*, *Chimes at Midnight* and even *Bonnie and Clyde* (where America seemed to have breathed deep and filled west Texas with a kind of pretty, misty Frenchness). But Godard was so central that nearly all those other films could be taken as proofs of his criticism, illustrations of his theories and gestures towards his brazen attempt.

For me the moment of full recognition with Godard came with his fourth film *Vivre sa vie*. That had as much to do with chance as the film itself. I still think it's his first great film in which the very set limits (the chapters, a mere 85 minutes, black and white, the palpable economy) do nothing to prevent the lyrical flowering of a movie that absorbs every attitude to life, from the most bleak to the most romantic. Here was evidence, too, that Anna Karina was not simply the designated girlfriend (a very common figure in student cinema) but more and more the subject of, or the reason for, the film. Indeed there were emerging in Godard already an obsession with the medium, a poetic regard for women (or one woman) that never hid his misogyny, cynicism, and an urge to make no more films. *Vivre sa vie* had intense passages of film and being (Nana at the movies; Nana dancing at the billiards hall), and that inner foreboding that being might slip into nothingness.

Godard was a passionate film-maker, crazy for scenes that held the screen. But at the same time he was something of a snob, an intellectual and a puritan, ready to put film behind him. As such he was as alert as anyone to that late–50s notion that film (or the movies) had run out of narrative conviction or audience credulity. Thus no Godard film was a straight story, but a scenario fragmented by his doubting gaze and a basis for critical commentary or cross-examination. *A bout de souffle* was a messy little love affair, with violence. Edgar G. Ulmer in 1945 would have shot it in six days, filled with crazed commitment. In 1955 Nick Ray would have made it a wounded study of the end of love. Godard shot it in a few weeks with every sort of distance, dysfunction and interruption he could think of. It was as if he needed the raw material of a film about which he could lecture and theorise.

'As a critic,' he told *Cahiers* in December 1963 when a group that included Bertrand Tavernier interviewed him, 'I think of myself as a film-maker. Today

I still think of myself as a critic, and in a sense I am, more than ever before. Instead of writing criticism, I make a film, but the critical dimension is subsumed. I think of myself as an essayist, producing essays in novel form or novels in essay form: only instead of writing, I film them. Were the cinema to disappear, I would simply accept the inevitable and turn to television; were television to disappear, I would revert to pencil and paper. For there is a clear continuity between all forms of expression. It's all me.'

From that it's not too difficult to foresee the modern Godard and especially the grave but still inspired overseer of *Histoire(s) de cinéma* – the eternal assembler/editor of cross-reference in the culture of moving imagery, the threnodist for lost realities. And surely it helps us grasp the mind behind *Pierrot le fou*, say, attempting to make a tragic novel or a notebook of the elements of sun-drenched *noir* and finding so many ways to visualise and animate written text. From the outset Godard loved to film signs and words. They were for him at least as reliable as faces and the components of discourse that would exist after movies just as they had helped bring imagery into being.

I mentioned luck where *Vivre sa vie* was concerned. I saw that film at the London Film Festival in October 1962 – or during what is often referred to as the Cuban missile crisis. You could wonder then whether you'd ever see another film, or the end of this one. That apprehension sharpened Nana's crucial decisions. But it stressed something else: that too many of us moviegoers preferred to live in the dark, without much thought of the daylight world. Also, because Godard was so advanced in seeing that the people in film had become as real or no more ghostly than those in alleged life, he had identified the fragility in our cultural system.

The films that followed *Vivre sa vie* are one of the greatest runs of work anyone has had in film – to be compared to von Sternberg at Paramount with Dietrich, Antonioni in the early 60s and Hawks as the 30s slipped into the 40s: *Les Carabiniers*, *Le Mépris*, *Bande à part*, *Une Femme mariée*, *Alphaville*, *Pierrot le fou*, *Masculin féminin*. *Made in U.S.A.* never worked for me. But *2 ou 3 Choses que je sais d'elle* is another masterwork. That's also 13 films in eight years. Has anyone except Fassbinder come close to that sort of fecundity? Which is a way of asking whether anyone has ever survived such a pace?

We all take our chances with history. Some were young and tender as Eisenstein did his best. Some were yearning to be moved or reached in the drab late 80s. I count myself as fortunate to have entered into my own attempt at the moment of Godard – it's like having seen Law and Best together for Manchester United, or Peter Osgood when he might have settled everything.

For me Godard taught so many things: to be parsimonious with beauty – the thing can become as easy and as fatuous as David Lean's spectacle; the essential role of montage or collage in a modern art (and the prior given

– that of explosion or disruption); the idea that film cannot be trusted any longer to mere film-makers – that it required ethnology (Godard's training), political scientists, painters, novelists, dancers, scholars and even critics; that the computer which now poses such a threat to the validity of light itself had much earlier invaded and organised the elements of story. ('There is a little harbour, like in a novel by Conrad. A sailing ship, like in the novels of Stevenson. An old brothel, like in the novels of Faulkner and so on.) And the possibility that the medium is already dead, and we are all necrologists.

Godard now is overlooked. He will be 70 this December, old enough for lifetime-achievement awards such as are showered on far lesser survivors. Yet there are those who sometimes forget him altogether when asked to list the great living directors. His reputation has suffered over the years – the personal meanness, the disdain for women, the way Truffaut trounced him in their letters. But he was always chilly. He kept dark glasses on when he gazed at Anna Karina in their best days. Some say he was never the same after she left him (they say the same about von Sternberg and Dietrich), as if the woman took away the man's last faith in story. But *Pierrot le fou* makes it plain that that ending was always guaranteed by his suspicions, his solitariness, his insistence on entropy. Still, I'd love to read a biography of those years – if they left room for life.

In the 60s and 70s, often in Godard's name and nearly always in admiration of him, film culture spread, all over the world, even in England and America. I cannot see how anyone can regard him now as other than one of the most important of directors and the crucial visionary for an age in which film has yielded to video and worse. The dozen or so films he began with are as good as ever, as fresh as wounds. He was as far ahead as Welles – and perhaps he was as bored because of it.

For myself, I can only repeat a motto – watch out – by which I mean that Godard's attention to the scene and our way of seeing it altered my way of life. I hope he's right that making films and writing about them can be connected, and part of the same conversation.

(Thomson 1994: 29–31)

CINEMATIC NEW WAVES: EAST ASIA

Like the *Nouvelle Vague*, the so-called Chinese New Wave rejected the staid traditions of film-making that preceded it. Divided into 'Fifth' and 'Sixth Generations', and arguably encompassing mainland as well as Taiwanese and latterly Hong Kong industries, the Chinese New Wave as a cohesive movement is somewhat harder to define. In fact, in terms of a cinematic style, the only thing that characterises all of these movies is their originality and individuality compared to the predictable social-realist melodramas they supplanted.

The 'Fifth Generation' refers to the films of directors first to graduate from the newly reopened Beijing Film Academy in the early 1980s: Chen Kaige, Zhang Yimou, Tian Wu Ziniu, Zhou Xiaowen and Hu Mei. Narratives of the 'Fifth Generation' often critiqued the entrenched traditions they saw to be holding their country back. Their movies embraced the Western attitudes and styles that the Cultural Revolution's propaganda had shunned and, while generally varying in aesthetic, they are united by their artistic inventiveness, intellectualism and self-reflexivity.

Although lauded on the international art house and festival circuit, films such as *Farewell My Concubine, Raise the Red Lantern* and *Woman Sesame Oil Maker* made less of an impact at the native box-office. When the baton was grasped by the Sixth Generation following the Tiananmen Square massacre, they found a weakened industry unwilling to take chances on unproven maverick directors such as themselves. Thus the films of Wang Xiaoshuai, Jia Zhangke, Zhang Yuan and others, are necessarily low-budget affairs, shot quickly in a contemporary setting with a *cinema-verité*, documentary aesthetic. Gritty, dynamic and urgent, Sixth Generation films are sometimes censored for revealing modern China's forbidden urban underclass of drug dealers, users, homosexuals and prostitutes.

Now again a part of Chinese sovereignty, Hong Kong cinema presumably sits beneath the umbrella 'Chinese cinema'. Yet this is a problematic, and one suspects purely academic relabelling. The far eastern outpost of Western ideology, Hong Kong enjoyed considerably more freedom than China, and was thus able to develop a thriving film industry, which for many years has been one of the most successful in the world. This has largely remained since the repatriation. Its own New Wave (usually referring to the late 1970s to early 1990s) is less of a definable movement than the *Nouvelle Vague,* and the films of Tsui Hark, Allen Fong, Ann Hui, Patrick Tam and Yim Ho are really only linked by the new life they breathed into very differing older traditions of social realism, the ghost story and martial arts. It is actually difficult to sense a unified opposition to any particular cinema or ideology. If anything, Hong Kong New Wave films exhibited slicker production techniques and quickly became the mainstream. A subsequent 'Second Wave' with directors including Wong Kar-wai and Stanley Kwan is arguably more distinguishable than its predecessor. With its documentary-style cinematography and focus on contemporary issues, Hong Kong's New Wave is somewhat similar to China's and proves that, to some extent, the two national cinemas *are* blurring along with their political boundaries.

Chungking Express / Chongqing Senlin (1994), looks and plays like a revitalised Godard movie. When Hong Kong's own new wave broke in 1979, its aesthetics were overtaken by a kind of moral compunction based on a search for identity and nationality: crime thrillers and social dramas about rejected youth made up the bulk of the first new wave films. Technically, the directors of the new wave (Ann Hui, Tsui Hark, Yim Ho, *et al.*) were certainly aware of style, but style was largely subordinated to function, seen as an effective means to a conventional narrative end. Only one director in this first period, Patrick Tam, adopted the kind of aesthetics that one would normally associate with avant-gardist experimentation in structure and narrative. Wong Kar-wai served a kind of apprenticeship with Patrick Tam, writing the script for Tam's *Final Victory*, while Tam was supervising editor on Wong's *Days of Being Wild* and *Ashes of Time*.

The sensual slow motion shots which open *Chungking Express*, showing a cop in plain clothes chasing a drug suspect in Hong Kong's lovely hub of Asian multiculturalism – the Chungking Mansion building – signal a slow recognition that the Hong Kong new wave is coming full circle. *Chungking Express* is an expression of the convergence of Hong Kong's postmodern aesthetics and a curiously old-fashioned, but not outmoded, romanticism. Wong's work to date sums up the circuitous development of the Hong Kong new wave. However, the film doesn't look back as much as it attempts to push forward. Indeed, at times Wong even seems to be shoving a new genre at his audience – a postmodern romance, a new wave editing style, on-location realism and narrative dissonance. It may well be a slight work, but it is by no means an impersonal one. Half the fun lies in working out the interlocking motifs between the film and Wong's previous *Days of Being Wild*.

The film is made up of two separate, unrelated but somehow interlocking stories, both featuring cops. The cop in the first story is Taiwanese He Zhiwu (played by the new star Takeshi Kaneshiro, of mixed Taiwanese–Japanese parentage) who collides with an unnamed mysterious woman wearing a blonde wig (played by Lin Ching-hsia) while chasing a suspect in Chungking Mansion. She is a drug dealer left high and dry when would-be couriers run off with her goods. He is reeling from a broken affair with a girl named May. Both meet by chance in a bar and end up spending the night together, but not in bed. Their affair remains desultory, unconsummated, unresolved. The story ends nonchalantly, with the woman killing the foreigner who has betrayed her in the drug deal and walking off minus her wig. This theme of a man abandoned by a former lover who has a chance meeting with another woman who then becomes his surrogate lover for a short while, is re-played (with variations) in the second episode. There a cop (played by Tony Leung Chiu-wai) has an affair with an air stewardess. Their usual meeting place is a streetside takeaway restaurant where a girl (unnamed until the end when we learn that she is called May) works behind the counter. The airline stewardess

walks out of the cop's life, putting the key to the cop's apartment in an envelope and leaving it at the restaurant. Leung doesn't bother to open the envelope. Instead he forms a budding but uncertain relationship with May (played by pop star Faye Wong), who serves him in the restaurant. May steals into the cop's apartment by opening the letter to the jilted cop and using the key. She lies in his bed and generally makes her presence felt. In short, she becomes a surrogate replacement for Leung's departed lover. She even quits her job to become an air hostess, realising her dream to go to California. Back in Hong Kong, she goes to the restaurant only to discover that Leung has bought the place. The identities of the characters have shifted and it is not clear whether their affair will take off.

As in *Days of Being Wild*, plot is secondary to character as Wong develops motifs from his previous film. There is the same preoccupation with time, dates and memory: because May loves to eat pineapples, He Zhiwu is eccentrically obsessed with buying cans of pineapples that have a use-by date on 1 May, his birthday, believing that this will bring May back to him. The motif of the uniformed cop pursuing a relationship with an emotionally unstable woman is given a lighter treatment while conforming to the themes of loneliness and unrequited love. Above all, Wong is consistent in adopting a free-flowing, transitional approach to narrative construction that is further strengthened by a literary quality in the dialogue (spoken in voice-over monologues) with each character given their own space to tell their stories. Although the stories here may not be as affecting, the accent on style conveys a feeling of sharp-edged excitement and a sense of high-octane elation recalling the impact of the French new wave in Europe. However, despite the pyrotechnics of his style, Wong's approach is highly impressionistic, largely because his narratives give way to the characters' intensity. Whether it is they who determine the style and outlook of the narrative, or whether Wong manipulates the different planes of narrative style and character in order to play them off against each other, it is not always clear. In so far as he is a poet who relies on words but knows that they must be translated into a visual medium, Wong clearly favours an abstract reading of his films.

(Teo 1997: 196–197)

JAPANESE CINEMA

Since the Second World War, film technology has progressed at a faster rate in Japan than probably any other country. Yet its native cinema has moved in its own direction at its own rate apart from general international trends. While most countries were quick to take up sound on film in the late 1920s, the Japanese resisted the conversion until several years later, preferring to maintain their *benshi* tradition, where a narrator would accompany the film explaining scenes and performing voices of the characters. The *benshi* was as much an attraction as the moving image itself and experiences would vary depending on a performer's interpretation (an interesting idea in relation to the differing points of view of *Rashomon*). The *benshi* has long since gone, yet many Japanese films still function as part of a wider cultural movement, making sense through their relation to the extremely specific genres that exist across various art forms and run throughout their history.

CONTENT

The content of the Japanese film is not radically different from that of films in other countries. The average period-film finds a ready equivalent in the American Western; the home drama is much at home in France; *Stella Dallas* and René Clément's *Gervaise* alike are *haha-mono*. The main difference, perhaps, is in the attitude of the Japanese film-maker and his audience, the singular way in which both tend to think of the film product.

The non-Japanese film-maker thinks of his film as an entity, standing by itself. To be sure, if he is making a Western he realizes that he is working in a genre, but otherwise he does not usually tend to see his film as belonging to a given category. The Japanese film-maker, on the other hand, is conscious not only that he is working in a given genre but also that within this genre he is specializing in a rigidly defined type, or *mono*, which, in turn, is often even further subdivided.

The Japanese tend to classify to such an extent that they have a category for everything, Japanese or not. Any film with a self-sacrificing heroine is a *kachusha-mono*, named after the heroine of Tolstoy's *Resurrection*; the type of film in which Marilyn Monroe appears is a *monro-mono*; Harold Lloyd has given his name to both a comedy genre and also to rimmed spectacles which are still called *roido*.

The largest genre division, as has earlier been indicated, is that between the *jidai-geki*, or period-film, and the *gendai-geki*, or film about contemporary life. The period-film is distinguished by both period and content. The former is usually the Tokugawa era; the latter is always feudalistic and was developed from the popular arts of the period, the *kodan*, the *naniwa-bushi*, and – to a much lesser extent – the Kabuki.

Both the *kodan* and the *naniwa-bushi* are recited stories, complicated in plot and endless in number, most of which Japanese know from earliest childhood. When the *kodan* tales appear on film, the audience comes to the theater already knowing the basic story. A certain prior knowledge is assumed by the film-maker and there is no attempt made to provide full exposition since it is familiarity more than novelty which entrances the Japanese audience. Still, the *kodan* stories on film often concern themselves with underdeveloped phases of a well-known character's life, the movie often becoming a series of

such tidbits, the better-known connecting sections left out, to the complete bafflement of anyone not familiar with the character.

The favorite stories are, naturally, those most often filmed. These usually center around a beloved feudal hero: Musashi Miyamoto, Mataemon Araki, Chuji Kunisada, Jirocho of Shimizu, the Soga brothers, or Komon Mito. Year in and year out these characters appear on the Japanese screen. Though there may be new interpretations and new minor characters, the story is basically always the same because the audience will have it no other way. The hardiest of the perennials is the Kabuki play, *The Loyal Forty-seven Ronin*, of which one or even two film versions are made every year.

All of these period-stories share a majority of elements, one such being a respect for the *giri-ninjo* conflict: the battle between obligation and human feelings, the contention between duty and inclination. There are various ways of treating this conflict. Sometimes duty means doing bad, personal belief and emotion symbolizing the course of action which would benefit society. Sometimes duty means doing good; human feelings and inclination would demand a bad action. At other times the 'social' evil of refusing to do one's duty is outweighed by the humanity and the righteousness of the opposing course of action. Sometime the audience does not know whether an action has been performed for the sake of duty or for the sake of human feelings; or it knows which action is for duty but does not know which action has been performed. In any event, the action in either direction is usually compelled by forces outside the characters involved, because the governing philosophy is that an individual's ability to influence his future is almost non-existent. Hence, the course of action is usually compelled by fate.

(Anderson and Richie 1982: 315–316)

At its most radical the avant-garde asks us to rethink fundamentally our preconceptions about cinema.

Murray Smith

All of us were supporters of a certain concept of revolution.

Luis Buñuel

Art cinema: A term usually applied to films where the director has clearly exercised a high degree of control over the film-making process and thus the films may be viewed as a form of personal expression.

Avant-garde cinema: The practice of innovative and inventive use of the cinematic form outside the codes and conventions of mainstream film-making (that is, classical Hollywood narrative). It is essentially non-narrative in structure and often intellectual in content.

Murray Smith's survey of international and avant-garde alternatives to mainstream cinema begins as follows:

The types of cinema that I will be discussing are extremely varied and it might be argued that the only thing that unites them all is their status as 'other' to orthodox film-making. Another index of this heterogeneity is the cluster of distinct, if overlapping terms denoting the filmic practices to be discussed: art, avant-garde, experimental, independent and underground, to name the most widespread.

(Murray Smith 'Modernism and the Avant-gardes' in John Hill and Pamela Church Gibson (eds), *The Oxford Guide to Film Studies*)

Smith offers an approach 'to frame the discussion more generally in terms of modes of film practice'. Smith sees the essential difference between art cinema and avant-garde cinema as economic with the former 'still a commercial cinema which depends for its existence on profits, rather than the more ethereal rewards of status and prestige'. At the same time he acknowledges the 'many practical and aesthetic crossovers', citing, for example, the British film-makers Peter Greenaway and Derek Jarman. In simple terms 'alternative takes' may be alternative in a number of ways: differently financed, differently staffed, differently made, differently distributed, differently structured.

To return to the definition at the start of this chapter, 'It is essentially non-narrative in structure.' For Murray Smith also, 'narrative and realism have often been prime targets,

because of their perceived dominance in commercial film-making'. Given that one of the premises of mainstream cinema is inarguably that film is a narrative medium, this will be our focus here. Exploring approaches that challenge and sometimes contradict the premises of mainstream cinema is always partly about learning to listen to the character of these 'alternative takes'.

Alternative cinema is a cinema of theories and theorists; its 'otherness' is never a matter of 'accident' since the mainstream is simply unignorable. It is peopled by those who have walked away from the mainstream (as did Jean-Luc Godard somewhere between *Weekend* and *One Plus One*), those who have barely ever made the effort to engage with it (e.g. Jarman and Greenaway) and those who are simply interested in imagining a radically different 'counter-cinema' (in the case of theorists-turned-film-makers Peter Wollen and Laura Mulvey). Either way this is a debate about what film is, can be and should be, that 'fundamental rethinking of our preconceptions about cinema', that Smith hopes for. As such, it is not surprising that it has, in James Chapman's slightly jaundiced terms, 'been furthered by film theorists who ... have been obsessed with exposing the ideological and aesthetic conservatism of classical Hollywood cinema'. In other words Hollywood is attacked because it is unadventurous both in terms of content/themes (promoting traditional values) and form (working within established patterns and genres).

Jean-Luc Godard, one important film-maker who was 'championed' by critics, was prepared to rise to the challenge and his Dziga-Vertov group pursued a 'philosophical' direction, where 'films' became 'essays'. Godard had reached this point via what Murray Smith describes as 'an unparalleled playfulness' in his early films, most notably in *Breathless*. Here, as James Monaco observes,

> Ignoring the established conventions of narrative ... Godard operated on a number of levels simultaneously. *Breathless* was at one and the same time a Gangster story and an essay about Gangster films.

Here, at the very beginning, was the germ of the essay form, what Monaco calls setting up 'a direct communication with the viewer'. It is this consistency that marks Godard out as a film artist with the experimental material from the late 1960s and early 1970s every much a part of his 'project' as either the stylish genre films of the *Nouvelle Vague* or the 'series of reprises' he has been working through since 1980. As he himself pointed out, 'Cinema is close to a religion. It is somewhat an act of faith.'

ON FILM TECHNIQUE AND VIDEO

JEAN-LUC GODARD: 'I've always been interested in technique, not in art for technique's sake. In the last installments of "History of Cinema", I keep saying – or often have it said – that cinema is neither an art nor a technique, but a mystery. That's what differentiates it from painting, literature or music, all arts when undertaken by artists. Cinema is close to a religion. It is somewhat an act of faith, it is immediately perceivable, through photography, or a certain relationship between man and the world – is the world the work of man or vice-versa? I don't know. The two go together. . . . One could say television has "un-taught" us to see. Television manufactures a few memories, but cinema – as it should have been – creates memory, i.e. the possibility of memory.

'Video has its own specificity. It can be used for its uniqueness, but, in my opinion, rarely is. One of its main interests is that you can work at it at home, if you can afford it or have a production company that allows you to do so. You can therefore work a bit more, perhaps, like a painter or a musician, and realize that the image is not only space but also time.

'On video, I love doing superimpositions, real superimpositions, almost as in music, where movements mix – sometimes slowly, sometimes brutally – then something happens. You can have two images at the same time, much like you can have two ideas at the same time, and you can commute between the two, which, to me, seems very close to childhood. Cinema has reached adulthood and you can reflect more. In cinema, you write the novel. But you have to have a philosophical idea in order to write a good novel.'

(Godard interviewed by Henri Béhar at the 1995 Montreal Film Festival available at www.filmscouts.com/scripts/interview.cfm?File =2800)

The elements which jar with accounts of the mainstream are the need for a philosophical idea, the idea of mystery and the idea of the film-maker being more 'like a painter or musician'. This final point was made explicitly in his 1980 film *Every Man for Himself* (aka *Slow motion*) which is credited as 'un film composé par Jean-Luc Godard'. As the standard histories of Godard's work dub this film his return to commercial film (even Godard himself called it his 'second first film'), it is pleasing to register the degree to which it nevertheless belongs to an aesthetic avant-garde, a decidedly alternative take. Lars Penning's review merely confirms this:

EVERY MAN FOR HIMSELF (AKA SLOW MOTION)

Sauve qui peut (la vie)

1980 – FRANCE/SWITZERLAND/FRG/AUSTRIA – 88 MIN. – DRAMA

DIRECTOR JEAN-LUC GODARD (*1930)

SCREENPLAY JEAN-CLAUDE CARRIÈRE, ANNE-MARIE MIÉVILLE, JEAN-LUC GODARD DIRECTOR OF PHOTOGRAPHY WILLIAM LUBTCHANSKY, RENATO BERTA, JEAN-BERNARD MENOUD EDITING ANNE-MARIE MIÉVILLE, JEAN-LUC GODARD MUSIC GABRIEL YARED PRODUCTION ALAIN SARDE, JEAN-LUC GODARD for SONIMAGE, SARA FILMS, MK2 PRODUCTIONS, TÉLÉVISION SUISSE-ROMANDE, ZDF, ORF.

CONTINUED

STARRING ISABELLE HUPPERT (Isabelle Rivière), JACQUES DUTRONC (Paul Godard), NATHALIE BAYE (Denise Rimbaud), ROLAND AMSTUTZ (Second Customer), ANNA BALDACCINI (Isabelle's Sister), FRED PERSONNE (First Customer), NICOLE JACQUET (Woman), DORE DE ROSA (Elevator Boy), MONIQUE BARSCHA (Opera Singer), CÉCILE TANNER (Paul's Daughter).

'IF I HAD THE STRENGTH, I'D DO NOTHING.'

Jean-Luc Godard called *Every Man For Himself* his 'second first film,' for it marked his return to 'commercial' filmmaking, using 35-mm equipment and star actors. In the 60s, he had turned his back on the mainstream cinema with films such as *Weekend* (*Week-End*, 1967) and *One Plus One/Sympathy for the Devil* (1968). For years thereafter, he made Marxist-Maoist film tracts in collaboration with Jean-Pierre Gorin and the 'Groupe Dziga Vertov.' Sometime in the mid–70s, Godard then began to experiment with video, his last commercially distributed film being the 1972 piece *Everything's Fine* (*Tout va bien/Crepa padrone, tutto va bene*), a political drama starring Yves Montand and Jane Fonda. *Every Man For Himself* thus signified a new beginning. But although the film opens with a scrawled image of the figure 'zero,' Godard is – of course – not really starting from scratch: the movie, in fact, is a compendium of his ideas and techniques after 20 years of practice in the cinematic medium.

For one thing, *Every Man For Himself* comes across as an experimental collage of images (people, cities, landscapes) and sounds – which sometimes fit the image, yet often appear totally unrelated. Occasionally, indeed, there's no sound there at all, so that the viewer has to imagine what he ought to be hearing. The images too, have an occasional tendency to 'drift away:' in the middle of a dialog, the camera may suddenly turn its attention to other people who apparently have nothing to do with the matter at hand. Music plays an important role: in one scene, an accordionist competes with the composition on the soundtrack; and throughout, the protagonists are constantly enquiring about the music that accompanies their scenes – which only they seem to hear. (The opening credits contain the announcement: 'Un film composé par Jean-Luc Godard.')

On top of all this, we have off-screen literary monologs, a homage to Marguerite Duras and her film *The Truck* (*Le Camion*, 1977), and various experiments with the depiction of motion. Certain sequences are slowed down or broken up into their component single frames. These passages are a direct result of Godard's work with the medium of video. He claimed it had allowed him to discover that girls move quite differently from boys, and that they also have a much larger repertoire of gestures and facial expressions. As such differences are imperceptible at the standard film speed of 24 images per second, he concluded that conventional male-dominated film technology had failed to do justice to the phenomena.

On the other hand, this film also marks Godard's return to non-linear narration. We are told the story of three people, who each represent a different 'velocity,' One 'chapter' is devoted to each of them. Denise Rimbaud (Nathalie Baye) works in television but risks breaking out and making a fresh start: she ditches both her job and her boyfriend TV director and producer Paul Godard (Jacques Dutronc), and moves out to the country, where she takes up farming and plans to write a novel. For Godard, Denise embodies 'the Left, and what's left of it:' she travels everywhere by bicycle, but the faster she pedals, 'the more slowly she progresses.' Paul Godard would also like to change, but he doesn't have the nerve; his chapter is entitled 'Fear.' When Denise leaves him, Paul suffers a crisis. He meets up with his ex-wife and his 12-year-old daughter, but their relationship now consists solely of money and presents. Naturally, the bespectacled cigar-smoker Paul is in part Jean-Luc Godard himself. A quote from Duras functions as his motto: 'I make movies to fill up my time. If I had the strength, I'd do nothing.'

Isabelle Rivière (Isabelle Huppert) is a prostitute. She spends a night with Paul, and eventually moves in to the apartment abandoned by Denise. Isabelle is 'a person of medium velocity' who goes about her business calmly and coolly. The exchange of sex for money is a subject that has always interested Godard, and prostitution has always been his favored metaphor for commercial filmmaking. It's no wonder, then, that Isabelle's relationships to her clients are *staged* affairs, which in turn raise questions about the relationship of sound to image. A client who has just arranged the images of an orgy to his satisfaction concludes by creating the 'sound track:' 'Ay! Oh! Aaah!'

In *Every Man For Himself*, human relationships are characterized exclusively by violence or indifference. In the final chapter ('Music'), Paul is run over by a car; yet he can't believe he's really going to die, for his life hasn't yet passed before his eyes as it does in the movies. Paul's ex-wife and his daughter simply leave him lying where he is. As they walk away, they pass an orchestra stationed by the side of the road. At last, we know where that music's been coming from...

(Penning 2003 670–673)

Despite the 'return to commercial film-making', Godard is far from making a conventional or generic film. There is still a feeling that he is identifying key film components and then taking them away or combining them with other elements in new ways. What gets produced by this process is what the *New York Times* called 'a single, seamless endeavour, a stunning, original work ...'. This is 'work' in the artistic sense and the review goes on to reinforce the aesthetic and cultural implications of this, concluding 'I trust it will outlive us all'. Here the ability of Godard to command critical attention (and get his films widely screened) stems not from his 'otherness' but rather from his status as an artist in the old-fashioned sense. His films are laying bare the mechanisms through which they themselves attempt to communicate: even time itself is subject to this examination. The three central characters, Penning informs us, 'each represent a different "velocity"'; hardly a pitch for a High Concept movie.

Godard acted as an inspiration to many film-makers in many places. He demonstrated a commitment to experiment with a purpose. He also maintained a political stance that is embodied in his work. His experiments with technique are essential to his project which is to arrive at an honesty of expression, perhaps a project that mainstream cinema could not allow or afford.

In a much more modest way the work of British director Derek Jarman took a similar course. Across work as diverse as a life of St Sebastian with entirely Latin dialogue to an adaptation of Shakespeare's *The Tempest* via his punk masterpiece *Jubilee*, Jarman also offered his own take on film and through film the wider reality. His too was a cinema of personal sensibilities and political commitment. He too was a relentless experimenter both formally and thematically. Jarman was a painter by training and the ways of working that Godard implies in the earlier interview, 'like a painter', are fully employed. In films such as *Caravaggio* and *The Last of England*, Jarman emphasised a painterly technique which employed composition and lighting as its principal tools in a way quite contrary to the mainstream. Like Godard, Jarman was inclined to 'negotiate' with the 35mm format to incorporate other film 'formats'. In Jarman's case, the format of choice was super–8, and the problematic was the synthesis of the film-maker's life and his work, which by the early 1980s was reaching a wider audience. Tony Peake's biography of Jarman includes the following account of an interview with the film-maker in 1985, which sums up Jarman's alternative take very well:

> The fourth important strand threading through the early eighties was a re-examination and consequent regeneration and ramification, of Jarman's work in super–8. In a 1985 interview, he is quoted as saying:
>
>> The feature films were an attempt to make a rapprochement between [the world of super–8] and the more formal world of film-making ... when *The Tempest* was finished, I thought perhaps I would be able to carry on making bigger films and somehow keep my subject matter ... [but] it turned out to be quite impossible if I wasn't to just do what most people do, which is adapt a script and say, this will be commercial. I could have easily done that at that point ... But somehow it was too late. I was already middle-aged and I knew what I really wanted to do, and it became a sort of crisis of middle-age, like 'Okay, so if I sell out and do the sort of films that they want, what sort of life am I going to have for the next 20 years?' ... There was no home to go to. There was no consistent funding in this country for the smaller feature film. The Gay element made it even more difficult ... I went back to doing super–8s ... and last year I finally had the courage of my convictions to say right, that sort of film-making, my own peculiar sort of film-making, is really my film-making.
>
> He had found that 'narrative is the first trap of commercial cinema', scripts the first form of censorship – 'because when a script lands on the desk of a

commissioning editor, from that moment they're mucking about with it'. The script, with all the inherent limitations it places on spontaneity, becomes joint property and therefore wrests control from the film-maker; in this case, a film-maker with clear ideas about the sort of free-floating films he wanted to make. If one thinks of narrative as a straight line drawn through a script, Jarman's abhorrence of it calls to mind the boy who used to stare so intently at the flowers, absorbing their every texture; the adult who preferred poetry to the novel. He once said, 'in my films it's important to look into the corners'. His obsession with texture, shape and light was why, in his work, each design element, each object, is so charged with significance; and why his interest lay with the objects rather than in the demands of story. His was cinema as an extension of our ability to study our surroundings; cinema as a way of reminding us, even teaching us, how better to see. 'I don't make films,' he would explain, 'I make moving pictures.'

(Peake 1999: 325–326)

There is the strong sense here of linear narrative as an ideological issue (see Bree Wilkinson on children's films on pp. 232–235), 'the first trap of commercial cinema'. Script is also cited by Jarman as 'the first form of censorship', a kind of emblem of the hierarchical authority implicit in industrial-scale film-making. A script, you see, implies an order, a control, real parameters. Jarman recognised at an early stage that maintaining 'honest discourse' was 'quite impossible if I wasn't to just do what most people do', and so he argued consistently for a freer form of film-making unfettered by the needs of 'story'. Peake's point about Jarman's cinema 'as a way of reminding us, even teaching us, how better to see' is simply the flip-side of Godard's claim that 'Television has "untaught" us'. There are other similarities between the methods of these two otherwise very different film-makers. In an interview with Colin McCabe, Godard actress (and former wife) Anna Karina revealed that 'free-floating films' were also Godard's style: 'Godard doesn't really direct anybody you know. He's like holding you, inventing everything. It's like a ballad. It's like something you…it just works.'

Even Karina's descriptions years on seem necessarily vague, like an act of faith. She also confirmed, 'we never had a script'. Godard himself expressed it in this way: 'What I am doing is making the spectator share the arbitrary nature of my choices'. This description covers hardly anything in the mainstream, where script is the control track of time and budget and most of the avant-garde, right as far as the point at which film becomes visual installation.

Two film-makers (and academics) who pushed this all the way were Laura Mulvey and Peter Wollen, both of whom have important contributions to make to this resource in their 'day jobs' as critics and academics. Their film-making was an attempt to put their theoretical insights into practice principally in two films: *Pentheselia* and *Riddles of the Sphinx*. Explicitly, this meant addressing head-on the issues which Mulvey raised in her seminal essay 'Visual Pleasure and Narrative Cinema' (see pp. 256–263) in which she

identified mainstream narrative cinema as a place where 'pleasure' was largely generated patriarchally through what she termed 'the male gaze' . For Mulvey, mainstream cinema sees the world from a male perspective and thus women are diminished within it by either being idealised or demonised and in each principally as a source of male pleasure. The films that Mulvey made with Wollen aim explicitly to undermine this pleasure, producing what critic James Chapman calls 'the polar opposite of the classical Hollywood style: narrative intransitivity instead of transitivity, estrangement instead of identification, unpleasure instead of pleasure'. Chapman is however by no means ambivalent about the fruits of this collaboration, calling *Riddles of the Sphinx* 'arguably the most incomprehensible film ever made'.

The Mulvey–Wollen hypothesis: for the record

The principles of 'counter-cinema' as described by Chapman may merit further explanation in the sense that they highlight important 'issues' in the analysis and understanding of the differences between mainstream and 'alternative' cinemas. Interestingly these tendencies were identified by Wollen when attempting to define precisely the distance Godard had put between himself and the Hollywood mainstream:

Hollywood	Godard
Narrative transitivity	Narrative intransitivity
Identification	Estrangement
Transparency	Foregrounding
Single diegesis	Multiple diegesis
Closure	Aperture
Pleasure	Unpleasure
Fiction	Reality

To clarify:

- **Narrative intransitivity** is the tendency of the narrative to be complex and non-linear from a desire to break the simple spell of narrative sequence where one thing follows the next.
- **Estrangement** is the process through which the spectator is dissuaded from identifying with characters and events in order to maintain a critical distance (for example, by directly addressing the audience so that the unreality of film is acknowledged).
- **Foregrounding** also describes this effect whereas **transparency** reinforces the degree to which we are all susceptible to the lure of film as 'a window on the world' (see Chapter 8, p. 206).
- **Diegesis** is, of course, the world created by the story which may be 'homogeneous' (single), where we gain access to a coherent and self-sustained world, one in which time and space have a consistent order and logic to them or

- 'heterogeneous', where the worlds we see on the screen are not coherent and integrated.
- **Aperture** suggests that the film is 'open' in the sense of not being self-contained whereas dominant cinema seeks a **closure** where the film world exists on the screen and ends with the closing of the curtain.
- **Unpleasure** is an attempt to deprioritise 'fantasy' and 'escape' as the principal experiences of film and to concentrate instead on 'provocation', 'disruption' and 'irritation'.
- **Reality** is juxtaposed to **fiction** here to emphasise the different 'projects': on the one hand acting out scripted stories and on the other a process that Picasso described more generally as 'a lie that makes us realise Truth'. Godard himself was very suspicious of fiction as a form of ideological (political) manipulation.

All of these 'tendencies' are manifest in our final 'alternative take' and the only genuine artistic movement to use film as a significant part of its expression: surrealism. The surrealists were an untidy collection of like-minded writers and artists interested in exploring the ideas about the subconscious and the irrational uncovered by the psychoanalyst Sigmund Freud and his circle. Luis Buñuel described their project as simply 'a certain concept of revolution' in which established thinking in all spheres was to be overturned. However, despite the anarchism of much of their propaganda and artistic practice, they were, as Murray Smith points out, 'a formal movement, with a dominant leader (André Breton) and a more elaborate theory'. This formality was evident in their commitment to a series of manifestos which became objects of faith, demanding rules which meant that even as the movement was forming it was wracked by a series of departures and expulsions. The movement's most significant film-maker, Buñuel, was himself called to a 'trial' for agreeing to publish the screenplay of his and Salvador Dali's masterpiece *Un Chien Andalou* in *La Revue de Cinéma* (commercial success was in complete contradiction of their stated aim to 'explode the social order'). Thus though surrealism as a formal artistic movement was relatively short-lived, its influence on the visual imagination and film in particular has been profound and extensive. It produced one great film-maker in Buñuel (who later wrote, 'No matter what the cost, I wanted to stay a surrealist'), at least one film masterpiece and offered a completely new vocabulary for both film and film criticism which remains extremely influential.

Here was an international artistic movement which had film-making at its heart. The two collaborations between Buñuel and the eccentric Spanish painter Salvador Dali gave the movement its focus. It is easy to over-intellectualise surrealism: at its heart was a strenuous and militant simplicity, a categorical and systematic assault on the rational, the organised and the conventional. It was a movement of gestures and slogans and provocations: as Artaud best put it, 'We must make reason shit!' This is what the surrealists relentlessly pursued: Buñuel stresses the moral nature of the movement. Buñuel's account resembles some kind of conversion and as such connects with Godard's 'cinema as religion'.

What fascinated me most, however, in all our discussions at the Cyrano, was the moral aspect of the movement. For the first time in my life I'd come into contact with a coherent moral system that, as far as I could tell, had no flaws. It was an aggressive morality based on the complete rejection of all existing values.

(Buñuel 1983: 107)

Buñuel was encouraged, or perhaps inspired, by the surrealist group to use film as a weapon, for as Buñuel said, 'The simplest surrealist gesture consists in going out into the street, gun in hand, and taking potshots at the crowd.' In fact Buñuel's own account of the movement in his autobiography is far more revealing of its character than any academic account or even of Breton's numerous 'manifestos'.

All of us were supporters of a certain concept of revolution, and although the surrealists did not consider themselves to be terrorists, they were constantly fighting a society they despised. Their principal weapon wasn't guns, of course; it was scandal. Scandal was a potent agent of revelation, capable of exposing such social crimes as the exploitation of one man by another, colonialist imperialism, religious tyranny – in sum, all the secret and odious underpinnings of a system that had to be destroyed. The real purpose of surrealism was not to create a new literary, artistic or even philosophical movement, but to explode the social order, to transform life itself.

(Buñuel 1983: 107)

Buñuel recalls meeting Breton years later and finding him despairing because 'It's no longer possible to scandalise anybody!' Buñuel was not so easily deflected: 'As for me there was no going back after *Un Chien Andalou*: making a commercial film was out of the question.' What did happen in film was a seismic shift in the ways film understood itself: new themes, new focus, a whole new visual vocabulary. The implications and repercussions of that were long lasting and will serve to further bind together this chapter's diverse parts. When Buñuel found himself in Paris in that hectic May of 1968, the very place and month that spawned Godard's *Weekend*, he was amazed to find 'old surrealist slogans painted everywhere, slogans such as "All power to the imagination!" and "It is forbidden to forbid".'

More extraordinary perhaps is that Buñuel was in Paris seeking locations for his film *The Milky Way* at the tender age of 68 and would make his final masterpiece *That Obscure Object of Desire* at 77. This was a career, as we have implied, of 'alternative takes' that continually challenge and innovate. His method is instructive of much that might be genuinely dubbed 'counter-cinema' again with the desire to maintain an 'honest discourse' paramount. The surrealists had celebrated 'automatic writing' (literally writing down disconnected thoughts) as 'a true photography of thought', arguing that moments of revelation are most often accidental. This was built into Buñuel's method and partly explains the speed of his film-making: he rarely took more than six weeks to make a feature film. The story of the inexplicable 'sack' which Fernando Rey's character carries on a date in *That Obscure Object of Desire* is typical:

As inexplicable as the accidents that set it off, our imagination is a crucial privilege. I've tried my whole life simply to accept the images that present themselves to me without trying to analyze them. I remember when we were shooting *That Obscure Object of Desire* in Seville and I suddenly found myself telling Fernando Rey, at the end of a scene, to pick up a big sack filled with tools lying on a bench, sling it over his shoulder, and walk away. The action was completely irrational, yet it seemed absolutely right to me. Still, I was worried about it, so I shot two versions of the scene: one with the sack, one without. But during the rushes the following day, the whole crew agreed that the scene was much better with the sack. Why? I can't explain it, and I don't enjoy rummaging around in the clichés of psychoanalysis.

(Buñuel 1983: 175)

Un chien andalou remains one of the most visually startling films ever made, and Buñuel's account of the collaboration with Dali is compelling in its straightforwardness:

A few months later, I made *Un chien andalou,* which came from an encounter between two dreams. When I arrived to spend a few days at Dali's house in Figueras, I told him about a dream I'd had in which a long, tapering cloud sliced the moon in half, like a razor blade slicing through an eye. Dali immediately told me that he'd seen a hand crawling with ants in a dream he'd had the previous night. 'And what if we started right there and made a film?' he wondered aloud. Despite my hesitation, we soon found ourselves hard at work, and in less than a week we had a script. Our only rule was very simple. No idea or image that might lend itself to a rational explanation of any kind would be accepted. We had to open all doors to the irrational and keep only those images that surprised us, without trying to explain why.

(Buñuel 1983: 103–104)

Miraculously, 'the filming took two weeks' and 'most of the time no one quite knew what he was doing'. Buñuel was so nervous at the opening of the film that he put stones in his pockets 'to throw at the audience in case of disaster'. At the 'prolonged applause' he dropped his 'projectiles' discreetly on to the floor behind the screen. Buñuel was behind the screen playing a selection of his own records as a makeshift, impromptu, 'soundtrack' which again gives something of the experimental yet also touchingly personal flavour of the production. As Buñuel admits above, he certainly understood that *Un chien andalou* was 'an original and provocative movie that no ordinary production company would touch'. It is a credit to the film that this has remained true in every successive decade. The published shooting script still feels as if it has come from nowhere: it has a visual sense and certainty that is both unnerving and yet strangely reassuring. This is not a script in any real sense (another theme of this chapter!): it is a record of images rather than ideas, and as such is very much outside the Western preoccupation with 'the word'.

ONCE UPON TIME ...

A balcony. Night. A man is sharpening a razor by the balcony.

The man looks through a window at the sky and sees ...

A light cloud passing across the face of the full moon.

Then the head of a young woman with wide-open eyes. The blade of the razor moves towards one of her eyes.

The light cloud now moves across the face of the moon. The razor-blade slices the eye of the young woman, dividing it.

EIGHT YEARS LATER

A deserted road. It is raining.

A man, dressed in a dark-grey suit and riding a bicycle, appears. The man's head, back and waist are decked in white frills. A rectangular box with black-and-white diagonal stripes hangs from a thong on his chest. The man's feet pedal automatically and he is not holding the handlebars: his hands are resting on his knees. Medium shot of him seen from behind, then shot of him superimposed on shot of the street, down which he is cycling with his back to camera. He cycles towards camera until the striped box fills the screen.

A room on the third floor of a building overlooking the street. A young woman in a brightly-coloured dress is sitting in the centre of the room; she is absorbed in reading a book. She gives a start, listens for something and throws the book onto a nearby couch. The book remains opened on a reproduction of Vermeer's 'The Lace-Maker'. The young woman is now convinced that something interesting is taking place; she gets up, half-turns and walks quickly over to the window. The cyclist has just stopped, below in the street. Out of sheer inertia, without trying to keep his balance, he topples over into the muddy gutter.

The young woman, looking resentful and outraged, dashes out of the room and down the stairs.

Close-up of the cyclist lying on the ground, expressionless, in exactly the same position as when he fell.

The young woman runs out of the house towards him and throws herself on him to kiss him passionately on the lips, the eyes and the nose.

It is now raining so hard that the rain blots out what is happening on screen.

Dissolve to the box: its diagonal stripes are superimposed on the diagonal lines of falling rain. Hands holding a little key open the box and pull out a tie wrapped in striped tissue paper.

The rain, the box, the tissue paper, and the tie make up a pattern of diagonal stripes of varying sizes.

The same room.

The young woman is standing by the bed, looking at the various items worn by the cyclist – frilly cuffs, box, starched collar and plain black tie. All these things are laid out on the bed as though they were being worn by someone lying on the bed. The young woman finally decides to reach out and she picks up the collar, removes the plain tie from it, and puts in its place the striped tie which she has just taken out of the box. She then puts the collar back where it was and sits down by the bed like someone at a vigil. The blanket and pillow on the bed are slightly rumpled as though a body really was lying there. The young woman seems to be aware of someone standing behind her and she turns to see who it is. Without showing any surprise, she sees that it is the same man, no longer wearing any of the items that are laid out on the bed. He is looking at something in his right palm with great concentration and some distress.

The young woman goes over to him and also looks at what he has in his hand.

Close-up of the hand full of ants crawling out of a black hole in the palm. None of the ants fall off.

Dissolve to the hairs on the armpit of a young woman who is lying on a beach in the sunshine. Dissolve to the undulating spines of a sea-urchin. Dissolve to the head of a girl seen directly from above. This shot is taken as though through the iris of an eye: the iris opens to reveal a group of people standing around the girl and trying to push their way through a police barrier.

In the middle of the circle, the young girl is using a stick to try and pick up a severed hand with painted fingernails which is lying on the ground. A policeman goes up to her and begins rebuking her. He leans down, picks up the hand, wraps it up carefully and puts it inside the striped box which had been hanging around the cyclist's neck. He hands the box over to the girl; she thanks him and he salutes.

As the policeman gives her the box, she seems to be completely carried away by a strange emotion and is oblivious of everything that is going on around her. It is as though she were listening to some distant religious music, perhaps music she heard when she was a child.

The crowd's curiosity has died down. People are moving off in all directions.

The couple has been looking at the scene from behind the window on the third floor all this time. We can see them through the window, from which we too have been watching the end of the scene. When the policeman gives the box

CONTINUED

to the young girl, the two people in the room also seem overwhelmed with the same emotion. They nod as though in rhythm to that distant music which only the young girl can hear.

The man looks at the young woman and makes a gesture as though to say, 'You see? Didn't I tell you?'

She looks down at the street again, where the young girl, all alone now, stands as if rooted to the spot, incapable of moving, as cars drive past her at great speed. Suddenly one of the cars runs her over and leaves her lying in the street, horribly mangled.

The man, with the determination of someone who feels sure of his rights, goes over to the young woman and, after staring at her lustfully with rolling eyes, grabs her breasts through her dress. Close-up of the man's hands fondling the breasts which appear through the dress. The man's face has a terrible look, almost of mortal anguish, and a stream of blood-flecked saliva begins to run out of the corner of his mouth onto the naked breasts. The breasts disappear to become a pair of thighs which the man kneads. His expression has changed. His eyes now shine with cruelty and lust. His mouth, which was wide open, now puckers up like an anus. The young woman moves back towards the centre of the room, followed by the man, still in the same state.

She suddenly breaks his hold on her and escapes from his grasp. The man's mouth tightens with anger. The young woman realizes that a really disagreeable and violent scene is about to take place. She inches away until she reaches a corner of the room where she crouches behind a little table.

(Buñuel and Dali 1994: 3–5)

Of course the very strength of the film, its visual power and vigour, has left it entirely open to that which Dali and Buñuel struggled to avoid, namely interpretation (see also Sontag in Chapter 1, p. 10). Despite the numerous warnings, there have been many attempts to rationalise the irrational! *Un chien andalou* asks us plainly and boldly to deal with what we see without the luxury of leaning on the connectedness of images or other extraneous material. From the first frames it asks us to be unflinching about this as if looking for meaning is equivalent to looking away. Godard's dictum is very useful here: he said 'the eye must listen before it looks'. Less formally, an A level film student once suggested that a better critical guide to *Un chien andalou* might be TV game show host Roy Walker, whose 'catchphrase' was simply 'Say what you see.' This is what critic Gwynne Edwards attempts in his book-length study *The Discreet Art of Luis Buñuel*, which is accurately described on its cover as 'A reading of his films'.

Un Chien andalou begins with one of the most disturbing sequences in the history of the cinema. A title on the screen suggests the commencement of a fairy tale: *Once Upon a Time*. The mood is enhanced by a shot of a man looking out through the window at the moon in an almost cloudless sky and by the face in close-up of a young, wide-eyed girl. Then, in a series of alternating shots the fairy-tale mood, and any complacency the spectator might have had, are ruthlessly destroyed. A thin cloud moves towards the moon. A razor moves towards an eye. The cloud slices the moon. The razor slits the eye. Buñuel, taking the part of the man who wields the razor in the film, compels us to pay attention to it, shatters our comfortable illusions, and destroys our accustomed way of looking at things, making us look anew. In its illogicality, its dissolves and its shifting focus, the sequence has too the character of dream and of the unconscious that is to distinguish the film as a whole. The images also have particular Freudian connotations and point to the consistency of the film's symbolism in this respect. Razor and eye are the male and female sexual organs and, inasmuch as the man uses the razor on the woman, the incident anticipates the film's sexual violence. But it has too, beneath the surface, a very conscious artistry that is equally characteristic of Buñuel.

The prologue becomes another subtitle: *Eight Years Later*. The film's protagonist, a young man, is seen cycling along a Paris street. He wears a dark grey suit and on his head and around his shoulders and waist there are white, frilly trimmings. He carries around his neck a box with diagonal stripes and he rides the bicycle in a listless, mechanical manner. Both dress and movement indicate sexual immaturity and emotional paralysis, even castration, while the box symbolizes female sexuality. The suit points too to his bourgeois respectability. He is the first of the many bourgeois cripples that people Buñuel's films.

The young man has his bourgeois counterpart in a young woman who is seen seated at a table in a room, reading a book. She becomes suddenly agitated, goes to the window in time to see the young man fall from his bicycle into the mud, rushes downstairs to his assistance and begins kissing him passionately (in Freudian terms falling indicates sexual anxiety while ascending or descending stairs is synonymous with sexual desire). The young woman, clearly, feels the sexual drive that the young man lacks. She trembles inexplicably before she sees him, as though in response to some deep and powerful impulse. Her rejection of the book in response to her instinctive feelings represents an over-throwing of the inhibiting influences – tradition and culture – that have shaped her upbringing, and of which the young man, lying inert in the gutter as she kisses him, is already the crippled victim. In their first encounter Buñuel has given expression to one of the film's most important themes: the power and the frustration of love.

CONTINUED

> A new sequence begins with a close-up of hands removing a striped tie from the box that the young man carried around his neck. The diagonal stripes link the tie, the paper in which it is wrapped, the box in which it is carried, the rain falling in the street, and the shirt of the man with the razor. The diagonal stripes are a recurring motif which strongly underlines sexual aggression (especially in connection with phallic metaphors like the tie) and also make a connection between apparently disjointed episodes in a way which endows them too with the obsessive character of dream.
>
> (Edwards 1991: 44–45)

Others would argue that 'symbolism' is that which Buñuel and Dali's technique set out to prevent or deny. The consistency of the film's symbolism which Edwards argues perhaps suggests a level of intention that would alarm Buñuel. On the other hand it may be that the subconscious can only be revealed unwittingly, and Buñuel's unwitting testimony arrives through what he tries to 'suppress'. Other critics have taken the hint and concentrated on form and technique rather than meaning as such. Haim Finkelstein is much more interested in the implicit and explicit assault the film makes on the conventions of traditional narrative cinema. He also provides a reminder of the mood of the film and of the movement that produced it: 'We exalted passion, mystification, black humour, the insult and the call of the abyss.'

> Dalí and Buñuel emphasize in their script the young woman's lack of surprise as she turns around and sees the absent cyclist – whose frills, box and collar she has just arranged on the bed – standing in another corner of the room (Buñuel, 86). Later, pulling hard at the door in which the cyclist's hand has been caught, the woman turns away to look at the room which proves to be the same room she had escaped from not a moment ago (Buñuel, 89). These are just a few instances of the film's overall design of subverting the conventions of traditional narrative cinema; of utilizing the conventions of montage against the grain of traditional filmic continuity. Titles indicating time, that appear to establish narrative continuity by suggesting links between the different sequences (eight years later; about three in the morning; sixteen years before), betray the spectator's expectations, thus disrupting the illusion of a coherent narrative form. Those disruptions and betrayals are characterized by the unassuming way, the deadpan manner, in which they come about. This subversive attitude is further enhanced by the parody directed at familiar film conventions associated with the silent movie melodrama. This point has been fully treated by J. H. Matthews (86). The script conveys a full measure of the passionate gestures and exaggerated expressions characterizing film melodrama: the young woman kisses the cyclist 'passionately on the lips";

the man 'now looking like the villain in a melodrama' stares at the woman 'lustfully with rolling eyes' (Buñuel, 86–88). Buñuel, as his writings reveal, is fully aware of the inadvertent comic potential inherent in the melodramatic style of acting. The tango which in the original screening accompanied the stylized chase across the room is a further indication of their parodistic intention. The parodying of silent film conventions is spelled out in the script even in the small detail concerning the bell made out of two hands shaking a cocktail shaker which, according to the script, replaces the silent film convention of showing the actual electric bell ringing (Buñuel, 89). Parody is not limited, however, to the conventions of film; the ludicrous procession of 'burdens,' cork, melon, two priests, pianos and carcasses of donkeys is a malicious caricature of a religious procession. The humorous deflation of seriousness in the film is indicative of a wholly irreverent mood which permeated the making of the film from its early script stages. 'The title of my present book is *The Andalusian Dog*, which made Dalí and me piss with laughter when we thought of it,' wrote Buñuel to a friend around the time he and Dalí were working on the script (Aranda, 59). Much of this mood was passed to the film together with the title.

(Finkelstein 1986: 132–133)

Given the many interpretations there have been of the title (translated as *The Andalusian Dog*), it is reassuring to learn that when they thought of it, it made them 'piss with laughter': critic beware! This helps to rehumanise the movement and the process, and returns us to another theme of the chapter: a cinema which allows and sometimes demands a personal response and vision. When asked to provide a foreword to a recent collection of 'New Readings' of his father's work, Juan Luis Buñuel performed a similar role:

FOREWORD: A DESPERATE CALL FOR MURDER

Juan Luis Buñuel

'A desperate call for murder'. That was the meaning of L'*Âge d'or*. And now, as time goes, by people's vision of Luis Buñuel has been softened by this new mythological, museum-bound figure. Before, when one of his films came out, crowds would destroy the theatre, some liberal politicians would ensure his works and others wanted to expel him from the country he was living in. That's what his films and writings were all about. To provoke, to shock, to destroy a society which he found corrupt and idiotic, to ridicule a religion which had oppressed millions of people, and continues to do so. 'The search for Truth is wonderful. Beware of the person who then claims to have found that Truth.'

Some towns in Spain are governed by rightist politicians who name streets after him. Don't they know what he thought of them? How he and his comrades fought against them during the Civil War, against their mentality? He has become these politicians' hero. It brings the tourists in … He told me once, as he looked up at the new 'Luis Buñuel' street sign: 'They name a street after me now; a few years ago they would have put me up against a wall.'

Now many of his books and belongings are on display in museums. He was never over-fond of museums. His last scenario was about a group of youthful terrorists who wanted to place an atom bomb in the Louvre Museum in Paris. Finally they didn't do it. They came to the conclusion that humanity didn't need any help to destroy itself. They were *dépassés* and disillusioned with today's society.

Buñuel must not be remembered as a politically correct individual. He was kind and good … but he was also violent and vengeful … against a bourgeois morality and social system that has always suppressed real freedom and love for Humanity.

(Buñuel 2004: xi)

One defining characteristic of the alternative which emerges is the desire to visually re-educate the audience numbed by a diet of eye candy. As Buñuel writes:

Movies have a hypnotic power, too. Just watch people leaving a movie theatre; they're usually silent, their heads droop, they have that absentminded look on their faces, unlike audiences at plays, bullfights, and sports events, where they show much more energy and animation. This kind of cinematographic hypnosis is no doubt due to the darkness of the theatre and to the rapidly changing scenes, lights, and camera movements, which weaken the spectator's critical intelligence and exercise over him a kind of fascination. Sometimes, watching a movie is a bit like being raped.

There is also a desire to include the personal as a category in an honest way as a means of cleansing the 'vocabulary' of film, of a 'return to zero', as if even the idea of making a film contains a kind of ideological corruption. Of course by definition 'personal vision' is a key element in the work of all the great mainstream Hollywood auteurs, but here it is not so much an organising principle as it is a device for undermining the conventions of narrative fiction. In some ways all of the film-makers presented here are fighting for the potential of film as a medium in the face of its universal exploitation. One way is to put aside the term 'film' as a devalued term. Godard preferred 'essay'; Jarman was also clear: 'I don't make films,' he said, 'I make moving pictures.'

▼ REFERENCES

PUBLICATIONS

Adorno, T. and Horkheimer, M. *The Dialectic of Enlightenment*, Allan Lane.

Allinson, M. (2001) *A Spanish Labyrinth: The Films of Pedro Almodovar*, I B Tauris.

Anderson, J.I. and Richie, D. (1982) *The Japanese Film: Art and Industry*, Princeton University Press.

Anger, K. (1984) *Hollywood Babylon II*, E.P. Dutton.

Barthes, R. (1982) 'Introduction to the structural analysis of narratives', in S. Sontag (ed.) *A Barthes Reader*, Hill & Wang.

Bazin, A. (1991) 'An aesthetic of reality: neorealism', *What is Cinema* 2.

Bordwell, D. and Thompson, K. (1990) *Film Art: An Introduction*, McGraw Hill.

Branigan, E. (1992) *Narrative, Comprehension and Film*, Routledge.

Branston, G. (2000) *Cinema and Cultural Modernity*, Oxford University Press.

Bresson, R. (1985) 'Notes on sound', trans. J. Griffin, in E. Weis and J. Belton (eds) *Film Sound: Theory and Practice*, Columbia University Press.

Brown, G. (1997) 'Paradise Found and Lost: The Course of British Realism', in R. Murphy (ed.) *The British Cinema Book*, BFI.

Buckland, W. 'Note on narrative aspects of the new Hollywood blockbuster', in S. Neale and M. Smith (eds) *Contemporary Hollywood Cinema*, Routledge.

Buñuel, J.L. Foreword to *New Readings*, ed. P. Evans and I. Santasella.

Buñuel, J.L. (2003) *My Last Breath*, Vintage.

Buñuel, J.L. and Dali, S. *Un chien andalou*, original shooting script, Faber.

Burke, F. (1991) *From Postwar to Postmodernism*, University Press of America.

Callow, S. (1999) 'Millennium Masterworks: *Citizen Kane*', *The Sunday Times*.

Cardullo, B. *What is Neorealism? A Critical English-language Biography of Italian Cinematic Neorealism*.

Chanan, M. (2003) 'The chronic crisis of British cinema', Inaugural lecture as Professor of Cultural Studies, April.

Cherry, B. (2002) 'Screaming for release', in Chibnall and Petley (eds) *British Horror Reader*, Routledge.

Coe, J. (1995) *What a Carve Up!*, Penguin.

Collins, A. (1997) 'Grim realities', *Guardian*, 11 March.

Coveney, M. (1996) *The World According to Mike Leigh*, HarperCollins.

Crittenden, R. (1981) *Manual of Film Editing*, Thames & Hudson.

de Vany, A. (2004) *Hollywood Economics: How Extreme Uncertainty Shapes the Film Industry*, Routledge.

Dyer, R. (1979) *Stars*, Bfi.

Dyer, R. (1995) *Entertainment and Utopia*, Routledge.

Edwards, G. (1991) *The Discreet Art of Luis Bunuel*, Marion Boyers.

Eisenstein, S. (1988) 'The montage of film attractions', in R. Taylor (ed. and trans.) *Selected Works. Volume 1 Writings 1922–34*, Bfi/Indiana University Press.

Ellis, J. (1992) 'Stars as cinematic phenomenon', in G. Mast, M. Cohen and L. Brandy (eds) *Film Theory and Criticism*, Oxford University Press.

Elsaesser, T. (2000) *Weimar Cinema and After*, Routledge.

Finkelstein, H. (1986) 'Dali and un chien andalou: the nature of a collaboration', in R. Kuernzi (ed.) *Dada and Surrealist Film*, MIT Press.

Fuss, D. (1989) *Essentially Speaking*, Routledge.

Grayling, A.C. (2002) *The Meaning of Things*, Phoenix.

Hallam, J. and Marshment, M. (2000) *Realism and Popular Cinema*, Inside Popular Film.

Haywood, S. (2000) *Key Terms in Cinema Studies*, Routledge.

Henderson, B. (1979) 'Towards a non-bourgeois camera style', in M. Mast and M. Cohen (eds) *Film Theory: A Reader*, Oxford University Press.

Higson, A. (1989) 'The concept of national cinema', *Screen* 30:4, 36–38.

Higson, A. (1993) 'Re-presenting the national past: nostalgia and pastiche in the Heritage film', in L. Friedman (ed.) *British Cinema and Thatcherism*, University College of London Press.

Hill, J. (1986) *Sex, Class and Realism*, Bfi.

Hoskins, C., McFadyen, S. and Finn, A. (1997) *Global Television and Film: An Introduction to the Economics of the Business*, Oxford University Press.

James, N. (2002) 'Nul Britannia', *Sight and Sound* 12:10.

Jancovich, M. and Faire, L. (2003) 'The best place to see a film', in J. Stringer (ed.) *Movie Blockbusters*, Routledge.

Jordan, B. and Morgan-Tamosunas, R. (1998) *Contemporary Spanish Cinema*, Manchester University Press.

Kael, P. (1963) 'Trash, art and the movies', in P. Kael (ed.) *I Lost it at the Movies*, Little, Brown.

Kawin, B. (1987) *How Movies Work*, Macmillan.

Kermode, J. (2004) 'Exorcist – the beginning', review, *Sight and Sound* December.

King, G. 'Narrative and the spectacular Hollywood blockbuster', in J. Stringer (ed.) *Movie Blockbusters*, Routledge.

Kolker, R. (2001) *Film Form and Culture*, McGraw Hill Education.

McBride, J. and Wilmington, M. (1974) *The Films of John Ford*, Secker & Warburg.

MacDonald, P. (1995) 'Star studies', in M. Janovick and H. Hollows (eds) *Approaches to Popular Film*, Manchester University Press.

Maltby, R. (1995) *Hollywood Cinema*, Blackwell.

Mamet, D. (1991) *On Directing Film*, Penguin.

Meehan, E. (1991) '"Holy commodity fetish Batman!": the political economy of a commercial intertext', in R. E. Pearson and W. Uricchio (eds) *The Many Lives of the Batman: Critical Approaches to a Superhero and his Media*, New York: Routledge.

Minha-ha, Trinh T. (1993) 'The totalising quest for meaning', in M. Renov (ed.) *Theorizing Documentary*, Routledge.

Modleski, T. (2000) 'The terror of pleasure', in K. Gelder (ed.) *The Horror Reader*, Routledge.

Monaco, J. (2000) *How to Read a Film* (3rd edn), Oxford University Press.

Monk, C. (1999) 'From underworld to underclass', in S. Chibnall, *British Crime Cinema*, Routledge.

Muller, J. (2003) 'The sceptical eye', an introduction to *Movies of the Seventies*, Taschen.

Murphy, R. (1989) *Realism and Tinsel*, Routledge.

Neale, S. (1999) *Genre and Hollywood*, Routledge.

Peake, T. (1999) *Derek Jarman*, Little, Brown.

Penning, L. (2003) 'Review of Godard's *Every Man for Himself*', in J. Muller (ed.) *Movies of the Seventies*, Taschen.

Perkins, V. (1993) *Film as Film*, Da Capo Press.

Phillips, P. (2003) 'The Auteur Theory' in J. Nelmes (ed.) *An Introduction to Film Studies*, 3rd edition.

Raynor, P., Wall, P. and Kruger, S. (2003) *Media Studies: The Essential Introduction*, Routledge.

Roberts, G. and Wallis, H. (2002) *Key Film Texts*, Arnold.

Ryall, T. (2001) 'The notion of genre', *Screen* 11:2, 23–6.

Sammon, P.M. (1996) *Film Noir: The Making of* Blade Runner, HarperCollins.

Schatz, T. (1998) *The Genius of the System*, Faber.

Schrader, P. (1986) 'Notes on film noir', in B.K. Grant (ed.) *The Film Genre Reader*, University of Texas Press.

Sergi, G. (1998) 'A cry in the dark', in S. Neale and M. Smith (eds) *Contemporary Hollywood Cinema*, Routledge.

Sontag, S. (2001) *Against Interpretation*, Picador.

Stam, R. (2000) 'The question of realism', in R. Stam and Miller (eds) *Film Theory: An Anthology*, Blackwell.

Strinati, D. (1995) *Introduction to Theories of Popular Culture*, Routledge.

Swallow, J. (2003) *Dark Eye: The Films of David Fincher*, Reynolds & Hearn.

Tasker, Y. (1993) *Spectacular Bodies*, Routledge.

Teo, S. (1997) *Hong Kong Cinema: The Extra Dimensions*, Bfi.

Thomson, D. (1994) 'That breathless moment', *Sight and Sound* 7, 29–31.

Turner, G. (1999) *Film as Social Practice* (3rd edn), Routledge.

Uhl, J. (1999) *Fight Club*, Screenpress Books.

Walker, J. (ed.) (2000) *Halliwell's Film and Video Guide 2001*, HarperCollins.

Walker, M. (1992) 'Film noir introduction', in *The Movie Book of Film Noir*, Studio Vista.

Weddle, D. (2003) 'Lights, camera, action: Marxism, semiotics, narratology', *Los Angeles Magazine*, 13 July.

Wenders, W. (1998) 'Why do you make films?', in *The Logic of Images*, Faber.

Wharton, D. and Grant, J. (2005) *Teaching Analysis of Film Language*, Bfi.

Wilkinson, B. (2004) 'Losing the plot: *The Lion King, Jumanji* and the ideological implications of the linear mythic narrative in mainstream children's films', dissertation submitted in partial fulfillment of degree of B.A. (Hons) in Communications and Public Relations, University of Lincoln.

Williams, C. (1980) *Realism in the Cinema*, Routledge.

Williams, R. (1983) 'British film history: new perspectives', in J. Curran and V. Porter (eds) *British Cinema History*.

Wollen, P. (1997) *Signs and Meaning in the Cinema*, Bfi.
Wollen, P. (1998) 'Why do some films survive and others disappear?', *Sight and Sound* 3:5.
Wyatt, J. (1994) *High Concept*, University of Texas Press.

▼ INDEX

Guns in the Afternoon 103–4

Haine, La 215
Haliwell's Film and Video Guide 79
Hall, Conrad 17
Hall, Kaye 222
Hall, Stuart 291
Hallam, J. and Marshment, M. 215–17
Halloween 158, 159
Hammer films 293
Hammer Horror (magazine) 293, 295
Hammett, Dashiell 137–40, 148, 173
Handful of Dust, A 354, 357
handheld shots 19–20
Hanks, Tom 196, 197, 199
Hard Men 361
'hard-boiled' private eye character 137–40
Harder They Fall, The 106
Harlin, Renny 238, 239
Harry Potter films 285
Harvey, Sylvia 354
Hathaway, Henry 146
Havers, Nigel 357
Hawks, Howard 163, 167, 168, 169–70
Haywood, Susan 203–4, 205–6, 220
Hayworth, Rita 186
Healey, Les 55
Heath, Stephen 158, 187, 348
Heaven's Gate 237, 303, 328
Hellinger, Mark 146
Helliwell, Arthur 71
Hemingway, Ernest 148
Henderson, Brian 267, 268–9
Henry, Matthew 255–61
heritage films 353–9
heritage industry 354–5
Hibbin, Nina 351
High Concept movie 278–81, 317
High Noon 102
Higson, Andrew 350, 353–9, 369–71
Hill, G. 191
Hill, John: *Sex Class and Realism* 347–51
Hindi films 262
Hirsch, E.D. 114–15, 116
Hirsch, Foster 135
historical films 121
Hitchcock, Alfred 29–30, 84, 162, 174, 270, 346, 382
Hoffman, Dustin 189, 197
Hollywood 31, 249, 260, 270–81, 314, 316, 323–43, 353; attempts by countries to protect home-grown film industries 342–3; and blockbuster *see* blockbusters; budgets 328; differences between alternative cinema and 400–1;

distribution and major studios 314–22; dominance ad influence of 273, 274, 323, 342; economics of 323–8; feature film output 325; New 277–8; studio system 270–2, 324
Home Box Office 328
Hong Kong cinema 388, 389–90
horror films 107, 121; female fans of 287–302; magazine and fanzine readership 293–6; perception of as dangerous to society 289–90; and postmodernism 156–9; and vampire fandom 292–3, 296–9
Hoskins, C. *et al* 314–22
Houston, Penelope 383
Howard, Ron 198
Hughes, David 69–70
Huston, John 172
Hutchings, Peter: 'Genre Theory and Criticism' 100
Huyssen, Andreas 355
hybridity 247, 249
hyperreal 249

iconography: and genre 98, 102, 104–8
iconology 104, 105, 106
Ideological State Apparatus (ISA) 269
ideology 252
image, star 181, 182
IMDB 91, 94
impersonation 189
In This World 282
Independence Day 285
independents 314, 315, 317–18, 320, 322
Indiana Jones 247
intertexuality: and stars 182–4
Intolerance 330, 376
Iron Horse, The 227
Italian cinema 380; and neo-realism 218

Jackson, Peter 53
James, Nick 345–6, 347
Jameson, Fredric 184, 251, 355; *Marxism and Form* 134
Jancovich, Mark 305–14
Japanese cinema 390–2
Jarman, Derek 298–9, 393, 410
Jaws 19, 325
Jenkins, Henry: *Textual Poachers* 286, 288
Jones, Vinnie 98
Jordan, B. and Morgan-Tamosunas, R. 371–2
Judith of Bethula 330
Jumanji 232–5
Jung, Carl 253
Jungle Book, The 92

A2 Film Studies: The Essential Introduction
Sarah Casey Benyahia, Freddie Gaffney and John White

Building on the groundwork laid by the AS Film Studies syllabus, *A2 Film Studies: The Essential Introduction* introduces students to the diversity of cinematic styles and to different film cultures as well as positioning film within wider political, cultural and artistic debates. The book is designed to support students through the transition from a focus on textual analysis to the consideration of the wider contexts that inform any study of film.

Individual chapters cover the following key areas:

- The Small Scale Research Project
- Practical Application of Learning
- Studies in World Cinema
- The Film Text and Spectator
- Producers and Audiences – Issues and Debates
- Messages and Values – Critical Approaches

Specially designed to be user-friendly, *A2 Film Studies: The Essential Introduction* includes:

- Activities
- Sample exam questions
- Further reading
- Glossary of key terms and resources
- Case studies

A2 Film Studies: The Essential Introduction is a great way for film students to continue their studies at A Level.

ISBN10: 0-415-39957-2 (hbk)
ISBN10: 0-415-39956-4 (pbk)

ISBN13: 978-0-415-39957-9 (hbk)
ISBN13: 978-0-415-39956-2 (pbk)

Related titles from Routledge

AS Film Studies: The Essential Introduction
Sarah Casey Benyahia, Freddie Gaffney, John White

AS Film Studies: The Essential Introduction will give students the confidence to tackle every part of the AS Level Film Studies course. The authors, who have wide-ranging experience as teachers, examiners and authors, introduce students step by step, to the skills involved in the study of film. Individual chapters address the following key areas:

- Film Form
- Narrative
- Genre
- Practical Application of Learning
- Hollywood and British Cinema
- Films as products
- Audiences as fans and consumers
- Stars
- New technologies and the film industry
- British and Irish Cinema

Specifically designed to be user friendly, *AS Film Studies: The Essential Introduction* includes:

- Activities
- Example exam questions
- Suggestions for further reading
- A glossary of key terms and resources
- Case studies

ISBN13: 978-0-415-39310-2 (hbk)
ISBN13: 978-0-415-39311-9 (pbk)

ISBN13: 978-0-415-39310-2 (hbk)
ISBN13: 978-0-415-39311-9 (pbk)

Available at all good bookshops
For ordering and further information please visit:
www.routledge.com